THE OXFORD HANDBOOK OF
DIVERSITY IN ORGANIZATIONS

THE OXFORD HANDBOOK OF

DIVERSITY IN ORGANIZATIONS

Edited by
REGINE BENDL, INGE BLEIJENBERGH,
ELINA HENTTONEN,
and
ALBERT J. MILLS

OXFORD
UNIVERSITY PRESS

OXFORD
UNIVERSITY PRESS

Great Clarendon Street, Oxford, OX2 6DP,
United Kingdom

Oxford University Press is a department of the University of Oxford.
It furthers the University's objective of excellence in research, scholarship,
and education by publishing worldwide. Oxford is a registered trade mark of
Oxford University Press in the UK and in certain other countries

© Oxford University Press 2015

The moral rights of the authors have been asserted

First Edition published in 2015

Impression: 1

All rights reserved. No part of this publication may be reproduced, stored in
a retrieval system, or transmitted, in any form or by any means, without the
prior permission in writing of Oxford University Press, or as expressly permitted
by law, by licence or under terms agreed with the appropriate reprographics
rights organization. Enquiries concerning reproduction outside the scope of the
above should be sent to the Rights Department, Oxford University Press, at the
address above

You must not circulate this work in any other form
and you must impose this same condition on any acquirer

Published in the United States of America by Oxford University Press
198 Madison Avenue, New York, NY 10016, United States of America

British Library Cataloguing in Publication Data
Data available

Library of Congress Control Number: 2015945521

ISBN 978-0-19-967980-5

Printed and bound by
CPI Group (UK) Ltd, Croydon, CR0 4YY

Links to third party websites are provided by Oxford in good faith and
for information only. Oxford disclaims any responsibility for the materials
contained in any third party website referenced in this work.

"For my husband, Anne Pier, who shows me that diverse backgrounds can be a continuous source of dialogue and inspiration" – Inge Bleijenbergh

"To my daughters Sanni, Sonja and the Little one - may you experience life in all its diversity" – Elina Henttonen

"In memory of my uncle Dave and for my Aunt Marion (Findlay), who together instilled in me the values of care and consideration for humanity in all its diversity" – Albie (Albert J. Mills)

Contents

List of Illustrations — xi
List of Contributors — xiii

Introduction: Mapping the Field of Diversity in Organizations — 1
REGINE BENDL, INGE BLEIJENBERGH, ELINA HENTTONEN, AND ALBERT J. MILLS

PART I PLURALISMS OF THEORIZING, ORGANIZING, AND MANAGING DIVERSITY

1. The Politics of Equality and Diversity: History, Society, and Biography — 15
   GERALDINE HEALY

2. Duelling Dualisms: A History of Diversity Management — 39
   JUDITH K. PRINGLE AND GLENDA STRACHAN

3. Theories of Difference, Diversity, and Intersectionality: What Do They Bring to Diversity Management? — 62
   JEFF HEARN AND JONNA LOUVRIER

4. Rethinking Diversity in Organizations and Society — 83
   DAVID KNIGHTS AND VEDRAN OMANOVIĆ

5. Reflections on Diversity and Inclusion Practices at the Organizational, Group, and Individual Levels — 109
   RUTH SESSLER BERNSTEIN, MARCY CRARY, DIANA BILIMORIA, AND DONNA MARIA BLANCERO

6. Reframing Diversity Management — 127
   ALEX FARIA

PART II EPISTEMOLOGICAL PLURALITY

7. Advancing Postcolonial Approaches in Critical Diversity Studies 153
   GAVIN JACK

8. A Postcolonial Deconstruction of Diversity Management and Multiculturalism 175
   ANNA-LIISA KAASILA-PAKANEN

9. Queer Perspectives Fuelling Diversity Management Discourse: Theoretical and Empirical-Based Reflections 195
   REGINE BENDL AND ROSWITHA HOFMANN

10. Ambiguous Diversities: Practices and Perceptions of Diversity Management 218
    ANNETTE RISBERG AND SINE NØRHOLM JUST

11. Individuals, Teams, and Organizational Benefits of Managing Diversity: An Evidence-Based Perspective 235
    EDDY S. NG AND JACQUELINE STEPHENSON

12. Organizational Benefits through Diversity Management: Theoretical Perspectives on the Business Case 255
    KELLY DYE AND GOLNAZ GOLNARAGHI

PART III DIVERSITY OF EMPIRICAL METHODS

13. Explaining Diversity Management Outcomes: What Can Be Learned from Quantitative Survey Research? 281
    SANDRA GROENEVELD

14. Challenges and Opportunities: Contextual Approaches to Diversity Research and Practice 298
    JANET PORTER AND ROSALIE HILDE

15. In Search of the 'Real': The Subversive Potential of Ethnography in the Field of Diversity Management 317
    PAUL MUTSAERS AND MARJA-LIISA TRUX

16. Collecting Narratives and Writing Stories of Diversity: Reflecting on Power and Identity in Our Professional Practice 337
    PATRIZIA ZANONI AND KOEN VAN LAER

PART IV DIVERSITY OF CONTEXTS AND PRACTICES

17. Rethinking Higher Education Diversity Studies through a Diversity Management Frame 357
    MARY ANN DANOWITZ

18. Global Diversity Management: Breaking the Local Impasse 370
    MUSTAFA BILGEHAN ÖZTÜRK, AHU TATLI, AND MUSTAFA F. ÖZBILGIN

19. Entrepreneurship and Diversity 388
    DEIRDRE TEDMANSON AND CAROLINE ESSERS

20. Practices of Organizing and Managing Diversity in Emerging Countries: Comparisons between India, Pakistan, and South Africa 408
    ANITA BOSCH, STELLA M. NKOMO, NASIMA M. H. CARRIM, RANA HAQ, JAWAD SYED, AND FAIZA ALI

PART V INTERSECTIONS OF DIVERSITY

21. Intersectionality at the Intersection: Paradigms, Methods, and Application—A Review 435
    DANIELLE MERCER, MARIANA INES PALUDI, JEAN HELMS MILLS, AND ALBERT J. MILLS

22. The Intersectionalities of Age, Ethnicity, and Class in Organizations 454
    EDELTRAUD HANAPPI-EGGER AND RENATE ORTLIEB

23. People with Disabilities: Identity, Stigmatization, Accommodation, and Intersection with Gender and Ageing in Effects on Employment Outcomes 469
    DAVID C. BALDRIDGE, JOY E. BEATTY, ALISON M. KONRAD, AND MARK E. MOORE

24. Of Race and Religion: Understanding the Roots of Anti-Muslim Prejudice in the United States 499
    ALI MIR, SAADIA TOOR, AND RAZA MIR

25. Intersectionality, Social Identity Theory, and Explorations of Hybridity: A Critical Review of Diverse Approaches to Diversity 518
    GLEN POWELL, LAKNATH JAYASINGHE, AND LUCY TAKSA

PART VI WHERE TO GO FROM HERE?

26. Examining Diversity in Organizations from Critical Perspectives: The Validity of the Research Process 539
    INGE BLEIJENBERGH AND SANDRA L. FIELDEN

27. Future Challenges for Practices of Diversity Management in Organizations 553
    YVONNE BENSCHOP, CHARLOTTE HOLGERSSON, MARIEKE VAN DEN BRINK, AND ANNA WAHL

28. From Here to There and Back Again: Transnational Perspectives on Diversity in Organizations 575
    BANU ÖZKAZANÇ-PAN AND MARTA B. CALÁS

Index 603

List of Illustrations

Figures

9.1	The heterosexual matrix: the normative entanglement of 'sex-gender-sexuality'	197
14.1	Immigrant workplace experience in Canada	310
17.1	Diversity management elements	364

Tables

2.1	Dualistic map of workplace diversity	40
2.2	Dichotomizing equal opportunity and managing diversity	43
2.3	Dualistic tensions to dialectic transformations	55
5.1	Summary of practices at the organizational, group and individual levels that cumulatively engender a diversity dividend	121
7.1	Overview of critiques of diversity management	157
9.1	Diversity management and queer approaches	201
9.2	Sex, gender and sexual orientation in the CoCs	207
12.1	2013 Canada's best diversity employers	268
12.2	For-profit and non-profit companies selected for study	270
27.1	The 3D-model: dimensions for the design of diversity practices	555
27.2	Recommended combinations of the 3D-model for diversity training, mentoring programmes, and diversity networks aiming at transformative change	567

List of Contributors

Faiza Ali is Senior Lecturer in Business Management at Liverpool John Moores University, UK. Her research interests include gender and diversity in organizations, international human resources management, and cross-cultural management issues. In particular, she is interested in exploring gender equality issues in the workplace in Muslim majority countries.

David C. Baldridge is Associate Professor of Management and Director of Off-campus MBA programs at Oregon State University, US. His research interests include diversity in organizations, workplace experiences of people with disabilities, accommodations, and career success.

Joy E. Beatty is Associate Professor of Organizational Behavior at the University of Michigan-Dearborn. Her diversity-related research has appeared in *Academy of Management Review, Employee Responsibilities and Rights Journal, Organizational Dynamics*, and *Women in Management Review*. Her research interests include disability, chronic illness, and invisible stigma in the context of work.

Regine Bendl is Associate Professor, Vienna University of Economics and Business (WU Vienna, Austria). Her research focuses on managing and organizing diversity in organizations, intersectionality, subtexts, and queer perspectives in organizational theories. Among her many publications are articles for *Gender Work and Organization, Journal of Management and Organization, British Journal of Management, Gender in Management—An International Journal, European Journal of International Management*, and *Equality, Diversity and Inclusion—An International Journal*. The recipient of numerous awards, she is editor of *Equality, Diversity and Inclusion—an International Journal* and of *Diversitas—Zeitschrift für Managing Diversity and Diversity Studies*, Associate Editor of *Gender, Work and Organization*, and President of the Austrian Society for Diversity.

Yvonne Benschop is Professor of Organizational Behavior at the Institute for Management Research, and affiliated with the Institute for Gender Studies at the Radboud University of Nijmegen, the Netherlands. Her current research projects include gender practices in networking, the role of power and resistance in organizational change towards gender equality, and gender and precarious academic careers in Europe. Co-editor in chief of *Organization*, she is also associate editor for *Gender, Work and Organization* and serves on the editorial boards of several other journals. Among her publications in English are articles in *Journal of Management Studies,*

Organization Studies, International Journal of Human Resource Management, Journal of Organizational Change Management, Sex Roles and *Gender, Work and Organization*.

Ruth Sessler Bernstein is a Professor at the University of Washington Tacoma, Interdisciplinary Arts and Sciences faculty. She was formerly Visiting Professor at in the area of management and nonprofit studies at the School of Business, Pacific Lutheran University. She earned her PhD from Case Western Reserve University. Her publication and research interests focus primarily on diversity, intercultural interactions, and inclusion within multicultural communities such as voluntary organizations and non-profit boards and, secondly, on non-profit governance. Her research has been presented at AOM, ARNOVA, and NASPA.

Diana Bilimoria is KeyBank Professor and Chair and Professor of Organizational Behavior at the Weatherhead School of Management, Case Western Reserve University, Cleveland, Ohio, US. She has published several books including *Women in STEM Careers* (2014), *Gender Equity in Science and Engineering* (2011) and *Women on Corporate Boards of Directors* (2009). She has also published extensively in leading journals, and has contributed to several edited volumes. She served as the chair of the Gender and Diversity in Organizations Division of the Academy of Management, and was the editor of the *Journal of Management Education*. She has received awards for her scholarship, teaching, and professional service.

Donna Maria Blancero is an Associate Professor of Management at Bentley University. She received her PhD from Cornell University's ILR School. Her research focuses on Latinos in the workplace, including issues of careers, psychological contracts, fairness, and work–family balance. She currently teaches courses in managing diversity and organizational behaviour. Her journal articles have appeared in the *Journal of Organizational Behavior, Cross Cultural Management, Industrial Relations, The Business Journal of Hispanic Research*, and *Human Resource Management*. She is the co-editor of *Hispanics at Work: A Collection of Research, Theory and Application* (2010).

Inge Bleijenbergh is an Assistant Professor in Research Methods at the Nijmegen School of Management at the Radboud University in Nijmegen, the Netherlands. She specializes in participatory research strategies in the field of gender and diversity in organizations. She has published in several international peer reviewed journals, and is Associate Editor of *Gender, Work and Organization*.

Anita Bosch is an Associate Professor in Human Resource Management at the University of Johannesburg, South Africa. She is the lead researcher of the Women in the Workplace research programme at the Department of Industrial Psychology and People Management, and is the editor for Africa of *Equality, Diversity and Inclusion—An International Journal*. Anita is also the editor for the annual *Women's Report of the South African Board for People Practices*, an evidence-based publication aimed at people professionals. She has published research on human resource management, identity and workplace diversity in several journals.

Marieke van den Brink is Associate Professor at the Institute for Management Research at the Radboud University Nijmegen, the Netherlands. Her main research interests are gender and diversity in organizations, organizational learning, and talent management. She is currently researching a large-scale case study on diversity, organizational learning, and change, and undertaking comparative research on gender and precarious workers in European universities. Her work has been published in *Journal of Management Studies, Organization Studies, Organization, Human Relations, Gender, Work and Organization and Social Science and Medicine*.

Marta B. Calás is Professor of Organization Studies and International Management in the Department of Management at the Isenberg School of Management, University of Massachusetts, Amherst, US. Her publications have explored the epistemological roots, the gendered features, and the transnational conditions of contemporary issues in management and organizations. She is a recipient of the SAGE Award for her academic leadership and the impact of her body of work in the area of gender and diversity. In 1994 Professor Calás co-founded the journal *Organization*, serving in an editor-in-chief position for more than fifteen years.

Nasima M. H. Carrim is a Senior Lecturer in the Department of Human Resource Management at the University of Pretoria, South Africa. Her main academic interests include gender in management, identity, culture, religion, and minorities in the workplace. Her PhD research focused on the identity work of Indian women managers during their upward mobility in corporate South Africa. She is currently researching the challenges Indian males experience in reaching senior and top managerial positions.

Marcy Crary is an Associate Professor of Management at Bentley College. She has a PhD in organizational behaviour from Case Western University in Cleveland, Ohio. Her current teaching, writing, and research interests include diversity dynamics and change in organizational systems, intimacy at work, transitions in the 'third phase' of life, and the emotional underworld of knowledge integration/creation. She has published in *Academy of Management Learning and Education, Human Relations, Organizational Dynamics*, and *Journal of Management of Education*.

Mary Ann Danowitz is a Professor of Higher Education Administration and Head of the Department of Leadership, Policy and Adult and Higher Education at North Carolina State University, US. Her research interests include gender, diversity, and equality in the areas of leadership, governance, management, organization change, and careers, particularly regarding the higher education sector in the United States and Europe. Her two most recent books are *Women, Universities and Change* (edited, 2007) and *Diversity in Organizations: Concepts and Practices* (edited, 2012)

Kelly Dye has been teaching and training in the field of business management since 1998, in various capacities, including one-day seminars, customized training, and master's level management courses. She is a Professor at the F. C. Manning School of Business at Acadia University, Nova Scotia, Canada, and currently teaches organizational behavior, gender and diversity in organizations, and change management. Key areas of her research include gendered organizations, alleviating poverty through microfinance, and the employment and economic outcomes of rural girls. Kelly Dye's work has been published internationally in various books, encyclopaedias, and journals.

Caroline Essers is Associate Professor of Entrepreneurship at VU University Amsterdam and an Assistant Professor Strategic Human Resource Management at the Radboud University Nijmegen, Faculty of Management. Caroline's research focuses at the social dynamics of entrepreneurship, such as the identity constructions of (female migrant) entrepreneurs and their networking. She uses diverse perspectives in her research on entrepreneurship, such as postcolonial feminist theory and social constructivist approaches like the narrative/life-story approach. Her work has been published in *Organization Studies, Organization, Human Relations, Gender, Work and Organization, British Journal of Management, Entrepreneurship and Regional Development*, and the *European Journal of HRM*. She is also an Associate Editor for *Gender, Work and Organization*.

Alex Faria is a Professor of Management at Brazilian School of Public and Business Administration at the Fundação Getulio Vargas (EBAPE/FGV). He is ex-Chair of the Critical Management Studies Division of the Academy of Management, and his research interests have a main focus on (de)colonial, historical, cultural, and international issues in different subfields within management and organization studies.

Sandra L. Fielden is a Senior Lecturer in Organizational Psychology in the Manchester Business School at the University of Manchester, UK. She is well known globally for her work as Editor of the Emerald journal *Gender in Management: An International Journal*, and was awarded Editor of the Year 2002, 2005 and for Outstanding Service in 2010. She has published five books and numerous chapters in the area of women's entrepreneurship and her current research interests include gender and ethnic entrepreneurship, gender in management, coaching and mentoring, sexual harassment, and evaluation studies.

Golnaz Golnaraghi, a diversity advocate, is passionate about gender and visible minority issues. After a fifteen-year marketing career with high-performing multinationals, in 2006 Golnaz pursued her passion to teach. Currently a Business Professor at Sheridan College, Toronto, Canada, her research interests include diversity, identity, discourse, and management education. She regularly presents at international conferences and in 2013 gave her first TEDx Talk titled *From Silence to Voice: Embracing My Hybrid Identity*, exploring her personal immigrant experiences as a Muslim-Canadian woman. In 2012, she was a recipient of the National Institute for Staff and Organizational Design Excellence Awards.

Sandra Groeneveld is a Professor of Public Sector Management at the Institute of Public Administration, Leiden University, Campus The Hague. She studies the structure and management of public organizations, with a special focus on diversity-related issues.

She also teaches courses for bachelor's, master's and PhD students on research methodology. Her expertise covers quantitative research methods, especially survey research.

Edeltraud Hanappi-Egger holds a PhD in Computer Science and is Full Professor for Gender and Diversity in Organizations. She is Head of the Department Management at the Vienna University of Economics and Business (WU). She was guest researcher at several international research institutions. Edeltraud Hanappi-Egger has published more than 300 articles, books, and book chapters on gender and diversity, organization studies, and diversity management.

Rana Haq is Assistant Professor at the School of Commerce and Administration in the Faculty of Management at Laurentian University in Sudbury, Ontario, Canada. She teaches organizational behaviour and human resources management, both on campus and online. Her research is primarily in the area of employment equity and managing diversity in the workplace, focusing particularly on Canada and India. Her work has been published in contributed books and in journals including the *International Journal of Human Resource Management, Gender in Management: An International Journal, European Journal of Industrial Relations, Journal of International Migration and Integration,* and *Entrepreneurial Practice Review*.

Geraldine Healy is Professor of Employment Relations at Queen Mary University of London, and her research interests lie in the interconnecting fields of employment relations, inequalities, and career. She has served on the editorial board of four journals, is the author of articles in leading journals and is joint author of *Gender and Union Leadership* (2013, with Gill Kirton), *Ethnicity and Gender at Work* (2008, with Harriet Bradley), *Diversity, Ethnicity, Migration and Work: International Perspectives* (2011, with Franklin Oikelome), co-editor of *Equalities, Inequalites and Diversity* (2010) and *The Future of Worker Representation* (2004). She has undertaken a number of research projects (with funding from the ESRC, EOC, Leverhulme) and is currently (2014) undertaking a project for the TUC titled *The Challenges of Organising Atypical Workers*.

Jeff Hearn is Professor of Management and Organization, Hanken School of Economics, Finland; Guest Research Professor in the Faculty of Humanities and Social Sciences, based in Gender Studies, Örebro University, Sweden; Professor of Sociology, University of Huddersfield, UK; and a UK Fellow of the Academy of the Social Sciences. He has published in a wide range of journals and his latest books are: *Rethinking Transnational Men* (edited with Marina Blagojević and Katherine Harrison, 2013) and *Men of the World: Genders, Globalizations, Transnational Times* (2015). He is managing co-editor of *Routledge Advances in Feminist Studies and Intersectionality* book series, co-editor of *NORMA: International Journal of Masculinity Studies*, and associate editor of *Gender, Work and Organization*. His research focuses on gender, sexuality, violence, organizations, and transnational processes.

Elina Henttonen works as an independent research and entrepreneur at Valtaamo Ltd, studying and developing work life from the perspectives of diversity and meaningful work. Previously she worked as a postdoctoral researcher and lecturer in the Department of Management, Aalto University, Finland, and published her work in refereed journals and scientific books.

Rosalie Hilde is a faculty member of Thompson Rivers University and College of New Caledonia in British Columbia Canada. She earned her Doctorate of Business Administration (D.B.A.) degree at Athabasca University, Alberta Canada and in that summer won the best dissertation award of the Academy of Management (AoM) Critical Management Studies (CMS) Division business conference. Her research interests include identity work, immigrants' work experiences, qualitative research methodology, and organizational behaviour. She is elected as Divisional Treasurer (2014–17) and had served as a representative-at-large and webmaster for the AoM CMS division between 2010 and 2013.

Roswitha Hofmann is a researcher, lecturer (WU Vienna and University of Applied Sciences Wr. Neustadt/Austria), author, and scientific consultant. With a doctorate in sociology, she was formerly Assistant Professor at the WU Vienna. Her main working areas are: gender- und diversity research with focus on gender identity, sexual orientations/identities and age; diversities and diversity management under queer theoretical perspectives; sustainable organizational development and technical developments from a feminist point of view.

Charlotte Holgersson is researcher and teacher at the Department of Industrial Economics and Management, KTH Royal Institute of Technology, Sweden. Her research is located in the intersection between organization and management studies and gender studies. She is interested in the empirical and theoretical exploration of gender ordering in organizations, in particular issues of management, change, and sexuality. One of her main empirical concerns over the years has been the perpetuation of men's dominance on top positions in organizations but she is also interested in processes of change. Several of her research projects focus on gender equality and diversity practices in organizations. She has recently published articles in *Gender, Work and Organization* and in *Gender in Management*.

Gavin Jack is Professor of Management at Monash University, Australia. He has research interests in international and cross-cultural management studies, and gender and diversity in organizations. He is Past Chair of the Critical Management Studies Division of the *Academy of Management*, and currently an Associate Editor of the journal *Organization*. His work has appeared in journals including the *Academy of Management Review, Sociology, British Journal of Management, Management International Review, Organization* and *Journal of Management Inquiry.*

Laknath Jayasinghe is Lecturer in Media Marketing at Macquarie University, Australia. He is a consumer researcher interested in brand and advertising consumption, consumer identity value, family identity, and masculinity and sexuality. He holds a PhD in marketing from Melbourne Business School and has written about issues of diversity and masculine identity practice in consumer culture contexts.

Anna-Liisa Kaasila-Pakanen is a doctoral candidate at the Oulu Business School, University of Oulu, Finland. Her research interests include cultural diversity at the workplace, postcolonialism, socio-cultural aspects of entrepreneurship and subjectivity construction of entrepreneurs.

David Knights is Professor of Organization Studies at Lancaster University and the Open University in the UK. His research interests can be divided into several areas each of which have various degrees of overlap—organization studies, management control, power, identity and resistance; gender and diversity studies; financial services consumption, education and regulation; information communication technology; organizational change and innovation; theory, knowledge, epistemology and methodology. He jointly created and continues to edit *Gender, Work and Organization* and is on the boards of several other journals.

Alison M. Konrad is Professor of Organizational Behaviour and holder of the Corus Entertainment Chair in Women in Management at the Ivey Business School, Western University. Her research interests include gender and diversity in organizations, workplace experiences of people with disabilities, work–life interface accommodations, and diversity management practices.

Jonna Louvrier is a postdoctoral fellow at the Clayman Institute for Gender Research at Stanford University. She obtained her PhD at Hanken School of Economics in Helsinki Finland. Her research interests include comparative studies on equality, gender equality, and diversity management.

Danielle Mercer is a PhD Management Candidate and a Research Assistant at Saint Mary's University in Halifax, NS, Canada. She completed both her Bachelor of Commerce (B.Comm) and Masters of Business Administration (MBA) degrees at Memorial University of Newfoundland. In 2013, she was awarded the SSHRC Joseph Armand-Bombardier CGS Scholarship for her doctoral dissertation work on leadership and gender. Her specific interests relate to gender equality, leadership, and worker well-being.

Jean Helms Mills is a Professor of Management at the Sobey School of Business, Saint Mary's University, Canada. She is an Associate Editor of *Gender, Work and Organization* and serves on the editorial boards of several other journals. Her books include *Making Sense of Organizational Change* (2003), *Understanding Organizational Change* (2009) and the forthcoming *Routledge Companion to Critical Management Studies*.

Albert J. Mills is Professor of Management and Director of the PhD Program in the Sobey School of Business at Saint Mary's University, in Halifax, Nova Scotia, Canada. He is the author of nearly forty books and edited collections that focus largely on the gendering of organization over time.

Ali Mir is a Professor of Management at William Paterson University. He has published on a range of topics including the changing nature of work in late capitalism, the international division of labour, knowledge transfer, postcolonialsm, secularism, radical poetry, and Indian cinema.

Raza Mir is a Professor of Management in the College of Business at William Paterson University. His research mainly focuses on the transfer of knowledge across national boundaries in multinational corporations, and issues relating to power and resistance in organizations. He currently serves as the Chair of the Critical Management Studies Division of the Academy of Management.

Mark E. Moore is an Associate Professor in the Department of Kinesiology at East Carolina University. His research interests include issues on disability, diversity, and marketing.

Paul Mutsaers is an anthropologist and postdoctoral research fellow at Tilburg University (the Netherlands) and as a researcher for the Police Academy of the Netherlands. His research can be described as a public anthropology of policing that is explicitly concerned with the policing of migrants in the Netherlands. He works as a co-editor for the online platform Anthropoliteia and has published in journals such as the *British Journal of Criminology, Critique of Anthropology* and *Anthropology of Work Review*. He is also a member of the Border Criminologies research group in Oxford.

Eddy S. Ng is F.C. Manning Chair in Economics and Business and Associate Professor of Management at Dalhousie University. His research focuses on managing diversity for organizational competitiveness, the changing nature of work and organizations, and managing the millennial workforce. His work has been funded by the Social Sciences and Humanities Council of Canada and Canadian Studies grants. He has served as Chair of the Diversity and Inclusion Theme Committee (D&ITC) of the Academy of Management, as well as the Gender and Diversity in Organizations (GDO) Division of the Administrative Sciences Association of Canada. He is presently an Associate Editor of Personnel Review.

Stella M. Nkomo is a Professor in the Department of Human Resource Management at the University of Pretoria, South Africa. Her internationally recognized research on race and gender and diversity in organizations has been published in several journals and edited volumes. She is an Associate Editor for the *British Journal of Management*. Professor Nkomo is the co-author of *Our Separate Ways: Black and White Women and the Struggle for Professional Identity* (2001) and *Courageous Conversations: A Collection of Interviews and Reflections on Responsible Leadership by South African Captains of Industry* (2011).

Sine Nørholm Just Sine is an Associate Professor at the Department of Business and Politics, Copenhagen Business School. Sine works at the interdisciplinary nexus of the social sciences and the humanities, studying rhetorical processes of meaning formation. She is particularly interested in conceptualizing and studying diversity management from a critical angle. This work ties up with broader theoretical and empirical interests in the relationship between performativity and rhetorical agency.

Vedran Omanovic is Senior Lecturer and Researcher at the University of Gothenburg and his research interests are focused on organizational change, transformation, and the notion of diversity in organizations. More specifically, Vedran seeks to understand how the ideas of different organizational phenomena are socially produced and why they are produced in particular ways. Vedran is also interested in understanding the ideas of different organizational phenomena through the lenses of alternative theoretical and methodological approaches. His recent publications have appeared in *Scandinavian Journal of Management* (2013) and *The Handbook of Gender Work and Organization* (2011).

Renate Ortlieb is Full Professor of Human Resource Management at the University of Graz, Austria. Her research interests are in human resource strategies, especially with a focus on migrant employees, gender and power relations in organizations, employee absenteeism, and empirical research methods. Her publications have appeared in the *Journal of the Royal Statistical Society—Applied Statistics, Management Revue, Schmalenbach Business Review, International Journal of Human Resource Management, Equality, Diversity and Inclusion, Feminist Economics,* and *Group and Organization Management*.

Mustafa F. Özbilgin is Professor of Organisational Behaviour at Brunel Business School, London. He also holds two international positions: Co-Chaire Management et Diversité at Université Paris Dauphine and Professor of Management at Koç University in Istanbul. His research focuses on equality, diversity and inclusion at work from comparative and relational perspectives. Editor-in-chief of the *European Management Review*, he has authored and edited twelve books and large number of papers in journals, including for the *Academy of Management Review, British Journal of Management, Journal of Vocational Behavior, International Journal of Human Resource Management, Human Relations, Gender, Work and Organization,* and *Social Science and Medicine*.

Banu Özkazanç-Pan received her PhD in Organization Studies from the University of Massachusetts, Amherst. Her research and writing has focused on issues of identity formation under globalization, international entrepreneurs, and critical perspectives in international management. Currently she is the Graduate Program Director for the Organizations and Social Change track of the newly launched doctoral degree in Business Administration as well as the professional development workshop co-chair for the Critical Management Studies Division of the Academy of Management. She has published in the *Academy of Management Review, Equality, Diversity and Inclusion, Scandinavian Journal of Management,* and *Qualitative Research in Organizations and Management* among others and contributed to six book chapters.

Mustafa Bilgehan Öztürk is Senior Lecturer in Management at Middlesex University Business School, UK. His research focus involves the field of equality, diversity, and inclusion with a range of interests including gender, gender identity, and sexual orientation. His previous research has appeared in journals such as the *British Journal of Management, Human Relations,* and *International Journal of Human Resource*

Management, and in edited volumes published by Cambridge University Press, Edward Elgar, and Routledge.

Mariana Ines Paludi is a PhD candidate at the Sobey School of Business, Saint Mary's University, Canada and a Teaching and Research Assistant at Universidad Nacional de General Sarmiento, Argentina. Her areas of research include critical management, gender, culture, Latin America, postcolonialism. She teaches undergraduate courses in organizational behaviour both in Canada and Argentina.

Janet Porter is Professor, Logistics at the Humber Institute of Technology and Learning (Ontario, Canada). Her work focuses on organization, with particular attention paid to gender, class, and resistance.

Glen Powell is a PhD candidate at Macquarie University in Sydney. His research is on leadership development, identity, social inclusion, and diverse forms of capital. Before commencing doctoral studies he was a community organizer with a non-partisan coalition of unions, community and faith groups, working to build and mobilize grassroots power for diverse communities.

Judith K. Pringle is Professor of Organisation Studies, coordinator of the Gender and Diversity Research Group at Auckland University of Technology, and also adjunct professor at the Centre for Work and Wellbeing, Griffith University. Her research focuses on: workplace diversity, women's experiences in organizations, bicultural research, intersections of social identities (gender/ethnicity/sexuality/age), and reframing career theory. She was co-editor of the Sage *Handbook for Workplace Diversity* (2006) and has published numerous book chapters, and in scholarly journals such as *Gender, Work and Organization*, *British Journal of Management*, *Equality, Diversity and Inclusion*, *International Journal of Human Resource Management*, *Journal of World Business*, and *Career Development International*.

Annette Risberg is an Associate Professor at the Department of Intercultural Communication and Management, Copenhagen Business School, and earned her PhD at Lund University. Annette is interested in the behavioural and human aspects of organizations and has studied that in the context of diversity in organizations as well as merger and acquisition integration. She is particularly interested in practices of diversity work in organizations and to study this from a critical perspective.

Jacqueline H. Stephenson is an adjunct post-doctoral Research Associate with the University of Leicester, UK. Her research interests include diversity, discrimination, equality and fairness in employment.

Glenda Strachan is Professor, Department of Employment Relations and Human Resources, Griffith Business School, Griffith University, Australia. Her research focuses on women and work, especially gender equity within organizations, in both contemporary and historical settings. Her Australian Research Council grants have focused on equal employment opportunity policies and practices and gender equity in university employment. She is co-editor of *Managing Diversity in Australia: Theory and Practice* (2010) and the author of numerous book chapters and articles in scholarly journals such as the *British Journal of Industrial Relations, Women in Management Review, Equality, Diversity and Inclusion*, and *Continuity and Change*.

Jawad Syed is Professor of Organisational Behaviour and Diversity Management at the Business School, University of Huddersfield, United Kingdom. His main academic interests include gender, race and diversity in organizations, international HRM and organizational knowledge. He has co-edited *Managing Cultural Diversity in Asia: A Research Companion* (2010), and *Managing Gender Diversity in Asia: A Research Companion* (2010). He has also edited a text book titled *Human Resource Management in a Global Context: A Critical Approach* (2012).

Lucy Taksa is Professor of Management and Associate Dean (Research) in the Faculty of Business and Economics at Macquarie University, Australia. She has published on management and labour history; gendered workplace cultures in transport and finance; migrant employment, diversity management, and identity. She is currently working on an Australian Research Council funded project: 'Affinities in Multicultural Australia' and an industry funded project considering the socioeconomic and identity impacts of living with lymphoedema. She is a member of the Australian Research Council College of Experts, Associate Editor for the *European Management Review*, and the *Economic and Labour Relations Review* Area Editor for Gender.

Ahu Tatli is a Senior Lecturer at Queen Mary University of London, UK. Her research explores intersectionality of disadvantage and privilege at work; inequality and discrimination in recruitment and employment; diversity management, agency and change in organizations. She has widely published in edited collections, practitioner and policy outlets and international peer-reviewed journals such as *Academy of Management Review, British Journal of Management, Canadian Journal of Administrative Sciences, European Journal of Industrial Relations, Entrepreneurship and Regional Development, International Business Review, Human Relations* and *International Journal of Management Reviews*.

Deirdre Tedmanson is a Senior Lecturer and Program Director for Social Sciences in the School of Psychology, Social Work and Social Policy at the University of South Australia, an Associate Researcher with the Hawke Research Institute, and a Research Scholar with the Centre for Aboriginal Economic Policy Research at the Australian National University. Deirdre has published widely on a range of subjects including Indigenous community and enterprise development, women's empowerment, and participatory action research. A major focus of Deirdre's research is working in collaborative partnerships with people and organizations from the Anangu Pitjantjatjara Yankunytjatjara Lands of central Australia.

Saadia Toor is Associate Professor of Sociology at the College of Staten Island, City University of New York. She is the author of *The State of Islam: Culture and Cold War*

Politics in Pakistan. Her research focuses on issues, which lie at the intersection of political economy, race, gender/sexuality, and nationalism.

Marja-Liisa Trux , born 1965, received her PhD from Helsinki School of Economics. Her interdisciplinary career combines psyhology, cultural anthropology and organization studies. She has worked with Keijo Räsänen at Aalto University as a member of the practice theoretically oriented team of researcher-teachers. Her field experience includes work with immigrant cleaners and high-tech professionals. She is currently investigating work beyond wage labour, as an independent scholar.

Koen Van Laer works as a Lecturer at the Faculty of Business Economics at Hasselt University, Belgium, where he is a member of SEIN, a research team whose research focuses on identity, diversity, and inequality. His main research interests are ethnicity, religion, and sexual orientation at work, the way 'difference' is managed and constructed in organizations, and the way it influences workplace experiences and careers. His work has appeared in books as well as in international organizations studies journals.

Anna Wahl is Professor (Chair) Gender, Organisation and Management at the Royal Institute of Technology (KTH), Stockholm. Previously she was Guest Professor at Tema Genus, Linköping University (2012–14) and Department of Business Administration, Karlstad University (2004–05). Her current research interests are the gendering of management in different contexts, work for change, and the impact of gender equality in organizations. Her recent publications include book and journal articles, including in *NORA—Nordic Journal of Feminist and Gender Research*.

Patrizia Zanoni is Professor of Organization Studies at Hasselt University, Belgium. Drawing from various bodies of critical theory, she investigates the discursive construction of socio-demographic identities in workplaces, the role such identities play in capital–labour relations, and organizational practices reducing inequality at work. Her research has been published in various international organization studies journals and in international educational journals. Since 2009 she has been leading SEIN—Identity, Diversity & Inequality Research, a team researching diversity in the work sphere. She is one of the co-founders of EqualDiv@Work, a transnational academic network of researchers investigating topics related to diversity in organizations and work settings.

INTRODUCTION
Mapping the Field of Diversity in Organizations

REGINE BENDL, INGE BLEIJENBERGH, ELINA HENTTONEN, AND ALBERT J. MILLS

WHAT is diversity and what does it have to do with organizations? This is a question we aim to answer in this *Handbook of Diversity in Organizations*.

However, the answer is not going to be straightforward. In recent years diversity and its management have become popular topics of discussion in all kinds of organizations. Diversity management practices have spread around the globe focusing on the organizing and management of inclusion and exclusion of different genders, sexualities, ethnicities, ages, classes and (dis)abilities, and many other identity categories. Different organizations in different cultural contexts still make very different interpretations of diversity and its meaning, and practice diversity and its management in various different ways. Some diversity management practices, although typically intended for achieving inclusion, have also the potential to reproduce exclusion as well. Therefore, practicing diversity management and dealing with diversity in organizations is never without controversy.

Furthermore, and as we have learned as scholars of diversity and editors of this book, it is not always easy to study diversity in organizations. There are a variety of theoretical, epistemological, methodological, and empirical perspectives to the phenomenon. They all have differing agendas and ideas about why diversity is worth pursuing, how we could best achieve inclusion, and in what contexts the management focus of diversity (re)produces exclusion by (re)stereotyping or by establishing new norms and again othering processes. The question becomes even more complex when we add the multiple organizational, institutional, and cultural contexts where diversity emerges.

There is nevertheless no need to get anxious about the complexity ahead of us. In the heart of diversity of any kind is a celebration of pluralism, which embraces different views and stands to the world. We believe that our duty as editors of this collection is to embrace these different views and stands within diversity research and suggest fruitful points of departure for developing our scholarship.

We aim to present what are the shared foundations of organizing, managing, and studying diversities, but instead of trying to find one common lexicon for talking about diversity in organizations we have made our duty in this book to embrace the diversity in the diversity scholarship. We include a plurality of *theoretical perspectives* on organizing and managing diversity in organizations ranging from positivist to constructivist and critical approaches, including intersectional, postcolonial, and queer perspectives. *Methodologically*, we highlight a broad range of empirical methods and approaches from surveys to ethnography in studying diversity in organizations. With regard to *contexts*, we look at diversity from the global diversity management phenomenon to 'local' perspectives.

At the core of the book are multidisciplinary, intersectional, and critical analyses of diversity, its organizing and management in organizations. The twenty-eight chapters of this book, organized in six parts, address these issues from multiple theoretical and methodological standpoints, and open up fresh perspectives to the diversity debate.

Editing a book on diversity has also made us very aware not only of the themes and approaches represented in the book, but also of the social positioning of the contributors of the chapters. The editorial team took their initiative for the book from the Standing Working Group of Gender and Diversity in the European Group of Organization Studies (EGOS), but we have consciously aimed at broadening the scope of the book beyond the EGOS community. We have also continuously discussed how the selection of authors, themes, and chapters will satisfy our effort to represent the field of diversity studies in all its diversity.

At the end of the process we are extremely happy to host an excellent team of contributing authors, from very diverse backgrounds and in diverse phases of their careers. Our geographically diverse team of contributors even made one of the reviewers of the book proposal to comment that we do not have a convincing number of US-based authors in the book. From the diversity perspective this was a very illuminating comment, especially given that US-based authors actually were the second most represented geographical group in the book after the European authors who represent seven countries of the European Union, and thus, different European cultures.

As editors we have also considered our own position as diversity scholars. As four white, western, middle-class academics we may not be the best representation of cultural and social diversity. However, within this condition we have a little gender diversity (three women and one man), rather more geographical diversity—from Finland to Austria and from the Netherlands all the way to Canada (or the other way around, if you prefer)—and also professional diversity when it comes to our professional age and experiences. Does this matter? It always matters when it comes to diversity. While we use our intellect our thoughts and directions are shaped by our embodied experiences, our own varied sets of relationships and the context and time in which the book is being developed. Cognizant of these challenges, we have tried to move beyond our own boundaries and mentalities in the choices of authors we approached and in the associated topics we suggested. As an extra layer we tried to ensure that the diverse experiences of the authors were taken into account so that we were not engaging in an unintended process of marginalization and privileging. Nonetheless, we were not completely successful in pulling together our ideal foci and authors. Some scholars were just too busy to take on yet another project, no matter how worthy. Others were kind enough to say yes when their workload made their commitment quite unattainable. In the end, despite our various limitations and challenges, we feel that we have brought together some of the very best scholars in the field of diversity. We hope readers will agree with us.

As editors and contributors we found the process challenging in other ways. Each new chapter that we received and reviewed for the book invariably made us think. Therefore, before presenting the standard description of each chapter we provide reflections based on the texts grouped in the six parts.

Part I: Pluralisms of Theorizing, Organizing, and Managing Diversity

It may not be a great surprise for diversity scholars but plurality and multiplicity represent the basis for theorizing diversity and its organizing and managing in organizations. In this context the saying 'That context matters' is not just a mere saying, context defines how scholars of the field approach and address diversity in organizations. The authors involved in this part of the book may have in common some starting points or parts of theoretical frameworks for their perspectives on diversity in organizations (e.g. inclusion, equality, anti-discrimination, intersectionality, or gender theories) and they may refer to the same sources but what diversity issues they consider, how they address and analyse phenomenons of diversity not only depends on their disciplinary approach but also on their geographical location. In this sense, there is no 'grand theory' for Diversity Studies, no common theoretical framework to address diversity in organizations and also no one historical background to refer to. The selection of theoretical frameworks generates the outcome of how diversity is perceived, managed, and organized fuelled by local contexts and the choice of level of analysis (international, national, local, micro, meso, macro). In other words, theoretical perspectives on diversity in organizations are based on the phenomenon that they claim to explore: diversity which may also produce incommensurable perspectives.

In this sense, Geraldine Healy argues that to explore the politics of equality and diversity demands an interrelated approach bringing together three perspectives: history, society, and biography. In Chapter 1, 'The Politics of Equality and Diversity: History, Society, and Biography', she opens up a framework which serves to link these three perspectives with colonial history, voluntarism and regulation, and diversity careers. All in all, the text shows that the historical and international nature of diversity is crucial in understanding the complexity of the politics of diversity at all levels.

Next, in Chapter 2, 'Duelling Dualisms: A History of Diversity Management', Judith K. Pringle and Glenda Strachan present a history of diversity management through the use of dichotomies that cross-cut the field. They trace the shift from the normative reasoning to the business case, put diversity management in context, refer to the change from 'gender' to other demographic diversity dimension, and argue that diversity research in organizations needs multiple methodologies. Altogether they observe a need to move beyond dualities and see a 'fractured future' of diverse diversities.

In their Chapter 3, 'Theories of Difference, Diversity, and Intersectionality', Jeff Hearn and Jonna Louvrier link diversity, diversity management, and intersectionality. In their discussion of the three different concepts they examine the relationship of diversity and diversity management to various theorizations of intersectionality, specifically the relevance of theories of intersectionality for understanding diversity. They come to the conclusion that the weakness of the term 'diversity' may function as an ideological signifier and that the concept of intersectionality not only complicates but also demystifies the ideological power of diversity and diversity management. Finally, Hearn and Louvrier also remind us of the contexts in which not only social categories of 'difference' but also research accounts are constructed.

David Knights and Vedran Omanovic examine a range of analytical frameworks, epistemologies, and methodologies surrounding discourses of diversity in Chapter 4, 'Rethinking Diversity in Organizations and Society'. Based on the results of an extant literature review introducing four different philosophical traditions as structural criteria (positivism, interpretation, critical-discursive, and critical-dialectic), the authors suggest that more radical and embodied approaches to diversity are needed to focus more directly on the marginalized actors who are often identified as the subjects of diversity. For the authors posthumanist feminism can provide such perspectives in diversity research.

In 'Reflections on Diversity and Inclusion Practices at the Organizational, Group, and Individual Level' the focus shifts from the societal and theoretical conceptual level of diversity management to the level organization. Ruth Sessler Bernstein, Marcy Crary, Diana Bilimoria, and Donna Maria Blancero provide reflections on the practices that are being employed by organizations to diversify the workplace and maximize the potential for a diversity dividend by practices of inclusion. In detail they present specific diversity and inclusion practices which impact group cohesiveness and outcomes.

In 'Reframing Diversity Management', the last chapter of this part, Alex Faria examines the concept of diversity management from a decolonial perspective. He unveils the colonial side of diversity management in order to open a space for decolonial possibilities which have been negated so far for reframing diversity management. The basic argument is that diversity management is a controversial concept due to its attachment to Eurocentric narratives of modernity/coloniality, which have been transformed into 'universal' knowledge by mechanisms of knowledge management inaugurated when European conquerors discovered and conquered America over five centuries ago.

Part II: Epistemological Plurality

Examining diversity in organizations from a plurality of epistemological perspectives may turn self-evident assumptions upside down and conceptualize diversity in organizations outside existing frameworks, like our chapters from postcolonial and queer theory perspective do. Other chapters aim to create clarity within existing frameworks of diversity management for example by reviewing empirical and theoretical discussions about the business case. A third position is embracing ambiguity in diversity management rather than solving it, so allowing space for a context specific diversity practices.

In Chapter 7, 'Advancing Postcolonial Approaches in Critical Diversity Studies', Gavin Jack argues for the need to underpin critical research on diversity in organizations by a postcolonial perspective. He argues that postcolonial theory is a potentially powerful tool to support critical research, which is at present underdeployed. First he recommends critical diversity scholars to engage with psychoanalytic and discursive variants of postcolonial theory (Hook 2012), in order to generate understandings of the psychological dimensions of (post)colonial subjectivities and the persistence of racism in organizations. Second, he recommends critical diversity scholars to consider the merits of 'Southern Theory' (Connell 2007) in order to move beyond the noted Eurocentric limits of existing gender and diversity research.

Anna-Liisa Kaasila-Pakanen picks up the challenge to adopt a postcolonial perspective, using it to critically review the notion of multiculturalism that underlies the current paradigm for diversity in Chapter 8, 'A Postcolonial Deconstruction of Diversity Management and Multiculturalism'. She shows how a multiculturalist discourse can serve as an instrument of control deeply connected to broader institutionalized power structures. Diversity research and practice based on multiculturalist discourse presents diversity through simplistic and fixed categorizations of identity and culture, which reinforces rather than addresses inequalities. Kaasila-Pakanen introduces the concept of Third Space as an alternative approach for theorizing cultural diversity.

In Chapter 9, 'Queer Perspectives Fuelling Diversity Management Discourse: Theoretical and Empirically Based Reflections', Regine Bendl and Roswitha Hofmann argue that diversity management theories and strategies often neglect issues of 'sexual orientation' or 'sexuality', and so unwittingly reinforce patterns of exclusion in organizations. In their chapter, they highlight the transformative potential of queer theory for supporting theory and practice of diversity management. Bendl and Hofmann present queer-theoretical concepts and discuss how limited these have been used in research on diversity management. On the basis of an investigation of Codes of Conduct from twenty multinational corporations, they exemplify the reproduction of hetero- and cis-normative patterns as well as opportunities for change. They conclude with recommendations for diversity management research and practice from a queer perspective.

Annette Risberg and Sine Nørholm Just approach diversity in organizations from the highly original perspective of ambiguity in Chapter 10, 'Ambiguous Diversities: Practices and Perceptions of Diversity Management'. They begin from the assumption that ambiguity is an unavoidable and constitutive condition of organizational practices in general and of diversity practices in particular. They suggest embracing the ambiguity of diversity management to facilitate the cultural change that is needed if specific diversity initiatives are to succeed. They explore three ambiguous forms that potentially enhance, but also hinder diversity in organizations: strategic ambiguity, contradiction, and ambivalence. They conclude that the value of ambiguity for diversity management cannot be assigned a priori; it must be studied in and through managerial practices and employee perceptions.

In 'Individuals, Teams, and Organizational Benefits of Managing Diversity: An Evidence-Based Perspective' (Chapter 11), Eddy Ng and Jacqueline Stephenson take a neopositivist epistemological perspective, adopting an evidence-based approach to integrate knowledge about the benefits of diversity at the individual, team, and organization levels. Ng and Stephenson suggest the positive effects of diversity on performance at all levels, but only under the appropriate conditions. Equal employment opportunity and affirmative action programmes appear helpful for increasing the employment of women and minorities. At the team level, an understanding of group level processes and dynamics is key to minimizing communication barriers, cohesion, and intragroup conflicts arising out of diversity. At the organizational level, firm strategy and leadership are crucial for firms to capitalize on the benefits of employee diversity.

In Chapter 12, Kelly Dye and Golnaz Golnaraghi also focus on the benefits of diversity in organizations, but from a theoretical rather than an empirical perspective in their text on 'Organizational Benefits through Diversity Management: Theoretical Perspectives on the Business Case'. They explore how the business case for diversity is situated within the broader discourse of diversity management. Dye and Golnaraghi argue the business case is related to the aim to attract and retain top talent, to address diverse customer groups, to reduce costs, and enhance innovation and creativity. Despite the business case being the most dominant discourse for underpinning diversity in organizations, awareness about the impact of demographic, historical, social, institutional, and geopolitical contexts on our understandings of diversity in organizations is dangerously absent from the business case discourse.

PART III: DIVERSITY OF EMPIRICAL METHODS

In diversity research we find a broad range of empirical methods from survey research to ethnography. The four chapters in this third part of the book illustrate these different methodological approaches to studying diversity. What is noteworthy is that each methodological standpoint crafts unique questions and conceptualizations of diversity, and offers unique potential in understanding both the field we study as well as our own research practice. This methodological plurality is vital for increasing our understanding of the complexity of diversity and its management. In Chapter 13, 'Explaining Diversity

Management Outcomes: What Can Be Learned from Quantitative Survey Research?', Sandra Groeneveld provides an overview of the quantitative survey research in the field of diversity management. She further discusses the contribution of survey research to our knowledge of diversity management and its outcomes, as well as its advantages and disadvantages in understanding diversity management phenomena. As a conclusion she outlines a future research agenda for survey research on diversity management which focuses on questions about when and why diversity management would lead to favourable outcomes. Following this, in Chapter 14, 'Challenges and Opportunities: Contextual Approaches to Diversity Research and Practice', Janet Porter and Rosalie Hilde showcase textual analysis methodologies that provide situational and contextual interpretations of diversity and production of differences in organizations. They specifically focus on two approaches of textual analysis: Helms Mills' (2010) critical sensemaking and Laclau and Mouffe's (1985) discourse theory. These approaches tackle both linguistic and non-linguistic dynamics of discrimination in the workplace by analysing how power differences are subtly produced among and between social groups. This awareness of power differences is then vital in challenging the status quo and creating strategies for change. Next, Paul Mutsaers and Marja-Liisa Trux introduce us to the subversive potential of ethnography in the field of diversity management in Chapter 15, 'In Search of the "Real": The Subversive Potential of Ethnography in the Field of Diversity Management'. They compare two ethnographic case studies which include several years of participant observation in two different organizational and national contexts in Finland and in the Netherlands. They argue that in their academic quarrels many diversity scholars tend to lose touch with reality in the workplace. Mutsaers and Trux counterweight mainstream diversity rhetorics with what really happen *in situ* and what it means to people, in this case the addressees of diversity management initiatives, and how they interpret and strategically deploy diversity discourses in their daily life. Finally, in Chapter 16, 'Collecting Narratives and Writing Stories of Diversity: Reflecting on Power and Identity in Our Professional Practice', Patrizia Zanoni and Koen Van Laer draw from their personal accounts as researchers of diversity in order to discuss the praxis of doing qualitative diversity research. Reflecting on their histories and experiences as diversity scholars they focus on the socialization to certain research norms and practices defining the status of 'good academic', identity dynamics, and dilemmas confronting researchers of diversity, and the challenges in translating research findings into writing. By highlighting the complex politics of reflexivity in diversity research the chapter concludes the section by challenging us to think and rethink our research practice.

Part IV: Diversity of Contexts and Practices

This section of the book highlights studies of diversity and their outcomes in various different national, cultural, and organizational contexts. The chapters deal with how to address the context and its specific practices, and how to develop these practices towards more equal and inclusive direction. What we learn is that understanding contextual dynamics is crucial not only in providing justified interpretations of people's lives but also for developing useful practical tools for increasing equality and inclusion. Chapter 17, 'Rethinking Higher Education Diversity Studies through a Diversity Management Frame', addresses diversity in the context of higher education. Mary Ann Danowitz proposes a definition of diversity management for higher education institutions, and further uses this definition as a framework for analysing literature on the diversity management in higher education. She argues that higher education diversity initiatives should be incorporated more fully into organizational and managerial practices. Furthermore, diversity initiatives need to be implemented with consideration of contextual factors, including the national context and the connection between public institutions and educational policies. In Chapter 18, 'Global Diversity Management: Breaking the Local Impasse', Mustafa Bilgehan Öztürk, Ahu Tatli, and Mustafa Özbilgin address the problematic of implementing global diversity management standards locally. They take the United Kingdom as the local context for their analysis, and report findings from a study that focused on the use of equality and diversity toolkits. Their empirical evidence emphasizes the importance of specific, local contexts and context-sensitive tools when local diversity officers of global companies progress their change agendas. More broadly, they argue for the business case for diversity management, as the effectiveness of diversity management hinges on securing the buy-in of businesses in this business-friendly, voluntaristic diversity management context. Next, Deirdre Tedmanson and Caroline Essers introduce us to contexts of entrepreneurial activity that challenge the Western, masculine notions of entrepreurship in Chapter 19, 'Entrepreneurship and Diversity'. They first explore aspects of Indigenous entrepreneurship in Australia, and then experiences of female Turkish entrepreneurs both in the United Kingdom and in the Netherlands. These diverse entrepreneurs from diverse contexts do entrepreneuring against the grain by inventing and applying particular identity strategies. The chapter questions the ethnocentrically biased and gendered foundations of entrepreneurial practices, and reveals some of the diverse experiences of these entrepreneurial 'others'. The final chapter in this section, Chapter 20 by Anita Bosch, Stella Nkomo, Nasima MH Carrim, Rana Haq, Jawad Syed, and Faiza Ali, describes and discusses practices of organizing and managing diversity in three emerging countries: India, Pakistan, and South Africa. In their chapter 'Practices of Organizing and Managing Diversity in Emerging Countries: Comparisons Between India, Pakistan, and South Africa' they compare the countries in terms of organizational diversity practices in relation to each country's definitions of diversity and equality, as well as major legislative frameworks that protect the rights of diverse groups. This illustrates how organizations within each country are responding macro-level legislative practices, whilst dealing with country-specific realities. In addition to parallels in equality challenges in these three countries all three of them also struggle with their uniquely nuanced sources of diversity, and search for strategies towards achieving equality and inclusion.

Part V: Intersections of Diversity

In line with the exponential growth of interest in the concept of intersectionality we received a considerable number of chapters focused upon intersections of diversity. Danielle Mercer, Mariana Paludi, Jean Helms Mills, and Albert J. Mills argue in Chapter 21, 'Intersectionality at the Intersection: Paradigms, Methods, and Application: A Review', that the notion of intersectionality is an increasingly popular term in use in diversity studies, which is a potentially good thing, but that many of those studies utilize the term as if it has *universal* meaning. However, they found no unified definition of intersectionality and also very little sense of how such a perspective should be applied. Indeed, it was not clear if intersectionality is a theoretical framework, a perspective, a theory, a heuristic, or a method. Few studies involve applications of the term, which is a major limitation if the term is to ultimately prove useful. The authors problematize the notion of intersectionality and the challenges of utilizing an intersectional lens if the attendant underlying ontological, methodological, and epistemological issues involved are not taken into account.

Focusing more specifically on practice, other chapters in this section reinforce these insights and reveal the challenges and the promise of studying age-ethnicity-class and of studying disabilities. In Chapter 22, 'The Intersectionalities of Age, Ethnicity, and Class in Organizations', Edeltraud Hanappi-Egger and Renate Ortlieb remind us that although 'the social categories of age and ethnicity are well studied by diversity scholars, literature on the combined effects of these dimensions for individuals and organizations' is still scarce, and especially in relation to class. Further, they point out that the very complexities of each 'category' are such that it makes it difficult to study them individually let alone in interaction with other categories of difference. To deal with that issue they propose a method of study that initially identifies social groups based on age, ethnicity, or class but here they warn against over-simplification and assumptions of homogeneity across the identified group. They then propose that each identified group is, in turn, examined in dyadic relationship to one other 'category' (e.g. age-class; class-ethnicity; age-ethnicity). In the process, they state, research should closely examine 'the mechanisms by which organizational practices (re-)inforce or mitigate inequalities associated with the intersections of age, ethnicity and class'.

In Chapter 23, 'People with Disabilities: Identity, Stigmatization, Accommodation, and Intersection with Gender and Ageing in Effects on Employment Outcomes', David Baldridge, Joy Beatty, Alison M. Konrad, and Mark E. Moore, in their focus on 'disabilities' and (to a lessor extent) gender, look beyond structural solutions (which they regard as important) to the link between discriminatory practices and sociological and social-psychological dynamics. In the former case they draw on the concept of stigma and stigmatization to examine how certain identity markers (i.e., disabled) become seen as socially deficient. In the latter case they argue that in the process of stigmatization at work it is not enough to focus on workplace practices but to visit the various contributions of employers, organizational leaders, and team members in the creation of such practices and the stigmatization of selected groups.

Context—especially historical context—is also to the forefront of Chapter 24 by Ali Mir, Saadia Toor, and Raza Mir, 'Of Race and Religion: Understanding Anti-Muslim Prejudice in the United States'. Focusing particularly on the intersections of race and religion, the authors contend that the dynamic spaces between history and practice need to be explored to understand the various ways that discriminatory images of 'the Other' are created. As a timely exemplar they draw on current construction of 'the Muslim' in the United States to reveal the importance of understanding the complex interplay of historic and contemporary relations in making sense of how certain 'differences' become co-joined or intersected.

In the final chapter in this section, 'Intersectionality, Social Identity Theory, and Explorations of Hybridity: A Critical Review of Diverse Approaches to Diversity', Glen Powell, Laknath Jayasinghe, and Lucy Taksa return us to the issue of the theorization of intersectionality—proposing a fusion of social identity theory (SIT) and intersectionality, arguing that these are two of the leading approaches to the issues of identity work that are rarely considered together. Through a focus on the different disciplinary origins, epistemology, ontology, political, and ideological orientations, the authors reveal important debates around the multiplicity and complexity of identity work and diversity, in order to serve as a gateway to further dialogue.

PART VI: WHERE TO GO FROM HERE?

The former parts of this book give insights into the variety of theoretical-conceptual, methodological, empirical, intersectional, and contextual perspectives of existing diversity research in organizations. That wide range will not be limited in the projections of the authors of this part. On the contrary, based on the knowledge created and bundled in the former parts, future research on diversity in organization will, they argue, be even more complex and, thus, maybe also more complicated. The chapters in this section represent relevant examples and provide further insights in the complexity of future diversity research.

In Chapter 26, 'Examining Diversity in Organizations from Critical Perspectives: The Validity of the Research Process', Inge Bleijenbergh and Sandra Fielden explore the meaning of validity in research from critical perspective by discussing how methodological decisions in different phases of the research process influence knowledge creation. The authors offer perspectives which help to reveal organizational norms, in particular hierarchical organized dichotomies, in order to make organizations more inclusive.

On a more conceptual level, Yvonne Benschop, Charlotte Holgersson, Marieke van den Brink, and Anna Wahl discuss 'Future Challenges for Practices of Diversity Management in Organizations' in Chapter 27. In order to highlight the transformative potential of diversity management practices, which in the context of this text refers to changing inequalities, the authors present a model which provides dimensions for the design of diversity practices. In particular, the authors focus on transformative potential of diversity training, networks, mentoring, and coaching.

Finally, Banu Özkazanç-Pan and Marta Calás focus on the transnational perspective of the research field diversity in organizations. In Chapter 28, 'From Here to There and Back Again: Transnational Perspectives on Diversity in Organizations', the two authors highlight the incommensurability of diversity literature and the transformation of the subject diversity in organizations as it travelled beyond the original US-centred literature. By articulating four modes of diffusion (internationalizing diversity, provincializing diversity, the simultaneity of diversity, and the formation of mobile subjectivities) the authors open up the space for a post-identitiarian transnational understanding of diversity in organizations which shows the complexity of field.

To sum up: we as editors, together with our contributors, went through an intensive interdisciplinary cooperative and successful process of knowledge creation, production, and sharing in the field of diversity in organizations. Therefore, we are spirited to consider this *Handbook* as source for scholarly inspection, inspiration, and encouragement to further engage in and broaden the research on diversity in organizations. From a reader's perspective, we will be rewarded for our editorial undertaking if the included texts stimulate further intersectional equality-, inclusion-, and queering-oriented research representing the different diversity dimensions, critical texts on the boundaries of organizing and managing diversity and new methodological and methodical perspectives highlighting the relational, contextual, and transformative as well as transnational perspectives of organizing and managing diversity in organizations—all based on epistemological approaches which give voice to diversity and multiplicity and highlight constant processes of othering and exclusion. Inherent in such diversity-oriented research across levels and areas there may be not only interdisciplinary and multidisciplinary as well as incommensurable perspectives but also the transgression of disciplinary boundaries and cross-disciplinarity. As such, this book may be a step towards creating and developing a future research space for diversity in organizations which goes beyond the traditional boundaries of the disciplines, is freed from mainstream disciplinary constraints, and supports research on transnational post-identitarian perspectives which shape local diversity and influence diversity and its organizing and management in organizations.

PART I

PLURALISMS OF THEORIZING, ORGANIZING, AND MANAGING DIVERSITY

CHAPTER 1

THE POLITICS OF EQUALITY AND DIVERSITY

History, Society, and Biography

GERALDINE HEALY

Introduction

This chapter discusses the underpinning politics guiding the processes and subjective experiences of equality and diversity and its management in the workplace, and the wider macro struggles for equality and social justice. Uncovering the politics of diversity is no easy task because of the complex interconnections, contradictions, and multilayers inherent in the nature of inequalities and diversity. The chapter offers a number of ideas through which the analysis of the politics of diversity, and ultimately fairness, might be approached.

The politics of diversity is informed by multidisciplinary perspectives, including philosophical, sociological, economic, legal, historical, geographical, and, of course, the work in employment relations and management studies, in which field this volume sits. Moreover, history is a central aspect, as is the interrelationship between different levels of analysis from macro and meso to the experience of the self. Thinking from a historically informed, multi-level approach owes much to sociological ideas where, drawing on Layder (2005), the layering of social domains are seen as interconnected through social relations of power and also stretched out over time and space (p. 274).

The politics of organizations (and of diversity) is imbued with ideological processes (Edwards and Wacjman 2006). Such multiple ideological processes will be central to our understanding of the politics of diversity and we do not in any way assume that an emancipatory approach will characterize all diversity strategies and studies. Given the multiple ideological processes that come into play, the diversity term has been used in numerous ways, and any discussion of the management of diversity has to recognize value differences ranging from managerial instrumentalism to forms of resistance and liberatory ideals. Moreover, the use of the diversity terms may be primarily descriptive according to available statistics, defensive or even self-congratulatory in the light of the same statistics. Thus the diversity project is always and inevitably political even when it strives towards an unobtainable objectivity. The differences in the management of diversity types were well spelt out by Kirton (2008) who argued that, despite its emancipatory potential, the diversity concept had been appropriated by managerialists and the managerial language that infuses it.

In contrast to the managerialist approach, Iris Marion Young's work provides insightful philosophical underpinning to the term of diversity, although Young's preference is to explore 'the politics of difference' (1990). For her, a politics of difference argues, on the one hand, that equality as the participation and inclusion of all groups sometimes requires different treatment for oppressed or disadvantaged groups. Thus she argues that, to promote social justice, social policy should sometimes accord special treatment to groups (Young 1990: 158). Young is arguing for emancipation through a politics of difference, a form of democratic cultural pluralism (Young 1990: 163). In this reading of diversity, the 'good society' does not eliminate or transcend group difference, but ensures that there is equality among socially and culturally differentiated groups, who mutually respect one another and affirm one another in their differences. Much of this chapter is about the politics of the struggle for the 'good society'.

The politics of diversity are rooted in debates over forms of exclusion, inclusion, and discrimination at different levels in a society. The debates tend to focus on those aspects of diversity that are the subject of regulation, for example, ethnic origin, religion, sex, ability, sexuality, and age (among others), but, whilst not always foregrounded in contemporary studies of diversity, exclusion based on class has been common from time immemorial. The resulting inequalities and injustices shaped societies and the distribution of resources and wealth. From early history to the present day, a myriad of examples of exclusion may be found over centuries and across national boundaries, through multiple eras of slavery, exclusion, and subjugation based on the female sex, the outlawing of homosexuality, exclusion (legal and cultural) of different religions, and with always the certainty of the subjugation of the economically disadvantaged.

It is important therefore to ground the politics in the reality of societal effects of inequalities in contemporary everyday life. One important and influential source is *The Spirit Level: Why Equality is Better for Everyone* (Pickett and Wilkinson 2010). The book highlights the 'pernicious effects that inequality has on societies: eroding trust, increasing anxiety and illness, (and) encouraging excessive consumption'. It shows that, for each of eleven different health and social problems: physical health, mental health, drug abuse, education, imprisonment, obesity, social mobility, trust and community life, violence, teenage pregnancies, and child well-being, outcomes are significantly worse in more unequal rich countries. Despite this knowledge, what is particularly concerning is that the gap between the rich and the poor is growing in most developed countries. Neoliberal countries such as the United Kingdom and the United States are notable due to their relatively high levels of income inequality despite their overall wealth (Pickett and Wilkinson 2010). It is all the more concerning that the real value of incomes in recent years is static or declining. The effect of neoliberal policies begun in the 1980s and sustained through social democratic and conservative governments has led to an intensification of work and heightening of insecurity. Privatization and subcontracting have led to growing work intensification and insecurity and declining incomes through contractual change, casualization, and a reduction of employment protection. At the same time, near monopolies of large contractors have placed accountability to shareholders above considerations of fair wages and social justice. Such neoliberal policies have weakened the trade unions through a more hostile organizing environment, management strategies of union avoidance, and restructuring leading to decline in union membership (Heery and Simms, 2010; Kirton and Healy 2013b).

Alongside these trends, despite decades of employment protection, it is noteworthy, for example, that women's access to power, whether it is in politics or as heads of large private or public organizations remains significantly less than men's (World Economic Forum 2014). In no country in the world are women equal to men, the gap between men and women's pay remains wide, and women are more likely to be in poverty than men (World Economic Forum 2014). Moreover, women and girls continue to be subject to harassment in organizations. The more cut-throat economic context makes it harder and harder for people with disabilities to get work and simultaneously get support from the state and other bodies. At the same time, an ethnic penalty impacts negatively on groups of black and minority ethnic (BME) groups regardless of human capital, so that they too are underrepresented in positions with access to power, are more likely to be unemployed and earning lower incomes (Heath and Cheung 2006), and be excluded from networks of power. The intersection of these different strands is important, as women and BME groups, for example, are heterogeneous: their experiences will differ by their race, ethnicity, sex, sexuality, religion, ability, age, which tend to be covered by legislative protection. Discrimination on the grounds of social class is one of the most important markers of inequality yet is not outlawed in the same way as other strands of inequality. Moreover, other intersections, often rooted in particular contexts, come into play in understanding inequalities, for example, the significance of overseas qualifications (see Oikelome and Healy 2007, 2012; Healy and Oikelome 2011). Thus, intersectionality is an important factor in the politics of diversity, alongside the asymmetrical nature of power.

The background of power gaps shapes the politics of diversity, inequalities, inclusions, and exclusions, and provides compelling evidence for an emancipatory approach to the politics of diversity. In light of this, the chapter is organized around four interconnected themes with the first theme of *history, society, and biography* interrelating horizontally and vertically with the remaining three themes: *colonial history, voluntarism and regulation*, and *diversity careers*.

History, Society, and Biography

The interrelationship of history, society, and biography, with the different strands of inequality and their intersectionalities, affect and reflect the multi-levels of the politics of diversity. This theme takes as its starting point the idea that history demands a sociological imagination which enables us to 'grasp history and biography and the relations between the two within society'. Wright Mills's classic work on the sociological imagination, first published in 1959, is very much in the tradition of a public sociology. For him, 'no social study that does not come back to the problems of biography, of history and their intersections within a society has completed its intellectual journey' (ibid). Thus, the sociological imagination lends itself well to understanding the politics of diversity, and to separating out the individualism so strong in contemporary debates about fairness and diversity from the underpinning collectivism inherent in systemic structures of inequality. Mills sought to analytically separate the *'personal troubles of the milieu'* from the *'public issues of social structure'*; in this way his work speaks to the individualism that characterizes much diversity management (DM) thinking. His concerns were not diversity but inequalities, and he had its own biographical agenda (Brewer 2004: 5). Once Mills's book was distanced from the immediate biographical agenda that occasioned it, Brewer maintained that *The Sociological Imagination* could be approached for the undoubted quality of its argument, and that its popularity has been fundamental to Mills's capacity to transcend his time and place (Brewer 2004: 332). As was common with the academics of his day, the female pronoun was conspicuous by its absence. Nevertheless, Mills's work is insightful in the context of contemporary neoliberal policies and speaks to us with a refreshing relevance. He argued that rather than 'an indifference to the publics', he was seeking to get away from the dominant neoliberal approach of the US at that time, which, if anything, has intensified and globalized since 1959. He was also mounting a powerful critique of the way that the sociology of the late fifties had become dominated by abstracted empiricism and formalized grand theories.

Mills's work has been influential with writers concerned with inequality and injustice. Patricia Hill Collins (2000) sees the task and promise of the sociological imagination to grasp the relations between history and biography in society resembling the holistic epistemology required by black feminism, using one's point of view to engage the sociological imagination and empower the individual (2000: 308). For Collins, developing a black women's standpoint to engage a collective black feminist imagination can empower the group. Cooper also finds Mills's (1959) sociological imagination conceptual framework valuable in his critical examination of the connection between the personal biographies of black athletes at predominantly white institutions and the historical public issues facing black people in the US in order to discuss the athletes' experiences with racial discrimination/social isolation, academic neglect, economic deprivation, and limited leadership opportunities (Cooper 2012: 261). Moreover, intersectional challenges have been raised by black feminists to build an emancipatory consciousness of the domination of feminism by white (often middle-class) feminists and the neglect of the interests of their black sisters (Crenshaw 1991; Hooks 2000; Collins 2004).

Thus, inherent in the sociological imagination is an emancipatory intent. Moreover, this approach recognizes that the experiences of women, black people, lesbians and gays are rooted in historical patriarchal, raced, and homophobic structures that are reproduced through generations and acted out in individual biographies. Thus, individuals' choices are inevitably constrained. Nevertheless, the public issues flowing from societal structures characterize the collective work that is undertaken by emancipatory campaigners. Women's rights campaigners, for example, opposing women's unequal place in society, have worked through political parties, non-governmental organizations (NGOs), legislation, and policy development. Numerous international agencies are working to promote women's equality; for example, the World Bank has highlighted empowering women as smart economics and vital to ending poverty and boosting shared prosperity, and made this one of its Millennium Development Goals (World Bank 2014). Thus gender equality has become part of the wider agenda for international development.

Class is often a neglected theme in the diversity literature and almost totally ignored in diversity practice. Yet as Acker (2006a) argues, 'class' is still a necessary category of analysis (p. 39). Indeed, as she goes on to explain, 'As economic inequality and severe poverty deepen, as middle class families face increasing stress over time and money,[1] while redistribution to the corporate rich increases its pace in US and most other countries, any idea that class and capitalism are no longer relevant concepts must be seen as a delusion' (p. 40). Thus, for Acker, an historical-materialist analysis is still useful for feminism, and the starting place must be the material conditions of life and the relations involved in the production of those conditions in particular historical moments. Importantly, Acker includes class in her analysis of inequality regimes (Acker 2006a, 2006b) that permeate diversity practices. For her, thinking about 'the social' or society as human practice rather than as abstract structures, is necessary for developing the idea that class is gendered and racialized, as she argues that race and gender seem to disappear in structural class analysis. An intersectional sensibility reminds us that equality and diversity are concerned with multiple forms of disadvantage and that these play out in different ways (Healy, Bradley, and Forson 2011). While intersectional studies have been more likely to focus on gender and ethnicity (McGuire 2000; Kamenou 2008; Healy, Bradley, and Forson 2011; Özbilgin et al. 2011) other strands are important, including migration and place of qualification (Healy and Oikelome 2011) and sexuality (Wright 2013), and underline the complexity of intersectionality.

The complexity of intersectionality uncovers the connections and contradictions that are at the heart of the interrelationship of personal biographies, history, and society. Intersectional troubles form part of equality professionals' challenges in their working

---

[1] The US term 'middle class' is used to relate to 'hard-working Americans' and seems to be a euphemism for the UK use of working class.

lives, but the structures to support the resolution of such troubles are frequently missing at the meso or macro level. Nevertheless, recognition of the relationship between biography, history, and society was evident in the social justice orientation of equal opportunities officers studied by Cockburn (1991) in the 1980s. Kirton, Greene, and Dean (2007) studied diversity professionals in 2006 when the discursive turn to managing diversity was firmly embedded. 'Diversity professionals' were defined as people tasked with a role in developing and implementing diversity initiatives. Kirton et al. (2007) found Meyerson and Scully's concept of 'tempered radicals' useful in illuminating the experiences and biographies of people occupying and utilizing a position of ambivalence within organizations. Furthermore, they argue that, from this perspective, it is possible to avoid assuming that diversity professionals are not progressive, simply because they temper their radicalism (ibid 1993). The tempered radicals concept softens the binary divide of 'insiders' and 'outsiders' (Lorbiecki and Jack 2000) and of radicals and liberals (Jewson and Mason 1986), and enables the uncovering of tensions that people in these positions in organizations accept (both explicitly and implicitly) (Kirton, Greene, and Dean 2007). Kirton and colleagues argue that understanding how and why diversity professionals undertake their work may offer, by extension, some insight into the appropriateness, effectiveness, limitations, and constraints of diversity policies within organizations (ibid 1992).

The costs and contestations inherent in the intersections of biography, history, and society are evident in the work of diversity actors. Kirton and Greene (2009) demonstrate that the costs experienced by the equality specialist of the 1980s (Cockburn 1991; Lawrence 2000) were also experienced by the diversity professional of the twenty-first century. The organizational politics within the wider context of structural mechanisms play out in the focus and rhetoric of diversity, so that their study finds that there now seems to be less of a place in diversity work for people whose *primary* affiliation lies with pursuing a progressive agenda in the interests of disadvantaged groups. Importantly, they reason that the emphasis on the business case for DM can be explained partly by reference to the changed political climate in which diversity policymaking takes place (2009: 173). Thus, at the meso level, the politics and history are instilled in the strategy, actions, and discourse of key equality actors and the macroeconomic context.

The centrality of the contemporary nature of capitalism shapes much of the 'choices' made by actors on the diversity stage, but their agency is, to an extent, the outcome of the dialectical relationship between self and circumstance. At the macro level, the relationship between the state and equality and diversity initiatives is complex. Max Weber recognized the state, both national and local, as the focus of contestation, where different groups lobbied to get their interests represented (Weber 1978). This is not to say that the state was neutral, nor that interests were equally represented, more that equality and diversity outcomes represent the interplay of different interest groups and uneven power relations. For example, in the US, feminist activists, especially lawyers, developed a very powerful lobbying presence during the 1960s, and, as a result, the US took the lead in anti-sexist legislation (Gelb and Palley 1982). In Australia, a group of feminist activists were able to make their way into the state bureaucracy to become involved in policymaking from the inside, earning the name of 'femocrats', while such moves were slower to develop in Europe and the UK,[2] where feminism took a more grassroots form. Feminists in Britain had been campaigning for similar laws in Britain to the American Equal Pay Act of 1963 and the Equal Employment Opportunities Act of 1972 (interestingly, these acts covered both sex and race discrimination). However, it is taken to be the influence of the European Union (EU) that led the UK government to pass the Equal Pay Act 1970 and the Sex Discrimination Act 1975 (and other progressive legislation), which were later consolidated with later provisions into the Equality Act 2010. Improvements in these Acts were driven by the 1997 Labour Government signature to the EU social chapter.

Thus, it was only in a small window of recent UK history, and partly due to the increased number of women, resulting from positive action strategies, within the UK Parliament, that the 1997–2010 Labour Government took a more proactive lead in positively espousing the notion of diversity and championing the causes of women, ethnic minorities, disabled people, older people, and victims of other kinds of discrimination (religious minorities, gays, and lesbians) (Bradley and Healy 2008: 63). As the European superstate evolved, feminists were also able to gain important positions as advisers and commissioners within the EU bureaucracy, leading to the development of stronger policies on gender equality. Scandinavian states, which prided themselves on their egalitarian nature and place in the World Economic Forum Gender Gap Index, played an important role here. Borchorst and Siim (1987) took a more critical line on this; they argued that, in Scandinavian countries, a kind of benevolent state paternalism had developed, which freed women from dependency on men, but could trap them into dependency on the state.[3] Nevertheless, while these achievements are important, they are not unproblematic: Scandinavian women also suffer from contradictions in that equality of women's participation in the Scandinavian labour market conceals their relatively low representation in the hierarchies of organizations, including academia (Seierstad and Healy 2012).

Thus, with respect to laws prohibiting discrimination on the grounds of race and ethnicity, key actors were important, but societal events were also crucial in bringing about political change. The development of the race relations legislation in the UK, for example, was, from its inception, bound up with fear and often hysteria over immigration and, crucially, the problems of order, rather than social justice concerns. The early race relations laws were a direct result of the Nottingham and Notting Hill disturbances (or 'race riots' or 'uprisings') in 1958, which abruptly brought to the fore the issue of relations between white and black communities. This, and other agitations around the impact of postwar immigration, led to what Brown (1992) describes as 'the twin-plank policy of keeping out further migrants but giving fair treatment to those already in Britain'. Although in reality 'giving fair treatment' was partial, contingent, and questionable and has left an unhappy legacy, evident in the riots in Britain in 2013 and in

---

[2] With the exception of Finland—see Tyska 1988 (and likely the former East Germany).
[3] The above paragraph was mainly drawn from Bradley and Healy (2008: 61–2).

Ferguson, Missouri, in 2014 (see the section 'Colonial History is Fundamental to our Understanding of the Politics of Diversity'). In the intervening years, the debate about immigration has ebbed and flowed, but in the second decade of the twenty-first century immigration is central in the contemporary political debates, with strange allies of liberals and business owners combining in their support for and recognition of migrants' contribution.

Healy and Oikelome (2011) bring together the interrelationship of 'personal troubles' and 'public issues' in order to explore the experience of migrant workers, both highly qualified and low paid, and show how the history and the politics of migration ensure that migrant workers find themselves in particular, usually adverse, locations of the labour market. Moreover, the intersection of the subjective and objective conditions of migration and DM ensured the frequent reproduction of disadvantage, regardless of 'sophisticated policies' designed to challenge such disadvantage. Thus, studies show that even where migrant workers have security and legislative protection, they may still experience disadvantage in multiple ways (Healy and Oikelome 2011). Conversely, many migrant workers do not have economic security. Alberti, Holgate, and Tapia (2013) assert that migrant workers are vulnerable to considerable exploitation and abuse, where their jobs are precarious and they do not benefit from union protection. Moreover, the (albeit limited) benefits of equality and diversity measures, such as adherence to legislation or human resource management (HRM) good practice, are non-existent in the organizations within which many migrants work (Alberti, Holgate, and Tapia 2013).

The recent economic crises have brought the stalled progress on diversity and fairness into sharp relief. It is the case that it is those who are most vulnerable, disadvantaged, and oppressed who have experienced economic crises more sharply than those who are more privileged. Women, black, lower socioeconomic groups, those in casualized work, and migrants are most affected by the economic restructuring that is taking place globally. Moreover, public sector workers are also at the sharp end; again disproportionately it is women and BME workers, some of whom may have been attracted to the public sector by its espoused principles of fairness, who are affected by cut-backs. The focus on the individual and the market in contemporary DM fails to take account of the public issues of social structure. This therefore precludes an understanding of the reality and context of DM. While proclamations of commitment to diversity are widespread in the UK, there has been a subtle shift away from enabling public structures through legislation and a previous philosophy (however weak) of emancipation that has supported and justified relatively progressive equality initiatives.

It is to historical influences that we now turn. In line with Edwards and Wajcman (2006), we consider that historical continuities, as well as breaks, are central features of the capitalist system and are part of the politics of diversity. History shows that there are dominant continuities which affect the nature of diversity in organizations and whose influence may ebb and flow or may show a particular trajectory at moments in time. To understand the politics of diversity, therefore, it is important to understand the interrelationship of different histories, including colonial history, the second theme.

Colonial History is Fundamental to our Understanding of the Politics of Diversity

History and colonial history demonstrate the importance of the politics of diversity in research. Histories provide explanations and understandings of acceptance/rejection of the status quo and how it is reinforced and challenged over time. The history of empire and slavery continues to influence contemporary thinking and collective memories in former empire-building countries.[4] In Britain, the empire connections and contradictions from history are manifested in both shame and pride. Gilroy (2004: 100) argues that Britain's ambivalence about its empire is especially evident in its reactions to the fragments of brutal colonial history that emerge occasionally to unsettle the remembrance of the imperial project by undermining its moral legitimacy and damaging the national self-esteem.

In many ways, the British national self-esteem was built on class, exclusion, and race. Said's influential exposure of damaging colonial dichotomies (1978) and his later study of cultural imperialism (1993) revealed the deep and entrenched nature of colonial superiority and established hierarchies in history, politics, and culture. Moreover, it is difficult to read Said without being reminded of the importance of de Beauvoir's *Second Sex*, where she recognized that oppression by hierarchy happened in other categories of identity, such as race, class, and religion, but she claimed that it was nowhere more true than with gender, in which men stereotyped women and used it as an excuse to organize society into a patriarchy where women were always the 'other' (de Beauvoir 1949). While contemporary writers on intersectionality may question de Beauvoir's hierarchy of oppression, the negative discourses revealed by her insights are used to justify not only Western colonialism and gender oppression, but also what emerged as a Western *moral obligation* 'designed to civilize, improve and *help* those peoples who were "lagging behind" in the March of History and Civilisation' (Prasad 1993b: 12; italics in the original, cited in Prasad 2006).

Thus the consequence in, for example, the British imperialist context, is that, as Healy and Oikelome (2011) argued, the British national self-esteem was based on notions of British superiority which rendered other nations, particularly those conquered in the

---

[4] The chapter discusses how the long shadow of colonial history plays out in the current approaches to the management of diversity. Yet, it is also the case that a country's *pre-colonial* history may be relevant; however, this is often ignored and sadly is outside the remit of this chapter. Jones, Pringle, and Shepherd (2000) use the example of pre-colonial groups in New Zealand to remind us that the colonization of US discourse in the study of the management of diversity may too be imbued with US colonialism in its ethnocentrism and neglect of pre-colonial models of diversity. They assert that the politics of disregarded groups is embedded in the domination of the US approach to diversity. Their study of Maori and Pakeha women managers in New Zealand exposes the limitations of the US model of diversity (Jones, Pringle, and Shepherd 2000).

imperial project, inferior. *Ipso facto*, according to this logic not only was Britain superior, but therefore Britons were superior (and we would add here, the British male). Discussion of empire and slavery is important because many of the contemporary problems and difficulties facing settlers to Britain from former British colonies (and elsewhere) lie in the still potent legacies of white British supremacy. Such notions were not only the prerogative of those in positions of power; rather they were carefully constructed beliefs that formed part of the dominant ideologies that pervaded society. Healy and Oikelome contend that British people's own class subjugation was concealed by their belief in the propaganda that the British were a people of innate superiority regardless of class, a belief that belies the very real subjugation of the British working class. Thus, a hierarchy of subjugation emerged, characterized by the empire's divide and rule philosophy (Healy and Oikelome 2011: 41), with the most impoverished seeking solace in the shining light of the British Empire, a light in which its citizens basked. When the 'light' of empire faded, belief in supremacy, although diluted with the break-up and loss of empire, was nevertheless handed down through the generations, sometimes in diluted form, sometimes in unabridged supremacist versions (Healy and Oikelome 2011: 41). In the postcolonial era, we see, in different ways, how the resulting embedded racism plays out in contemporary Britain. We turn again to Gilroy who well made the connection between past history and contemporary racism:

> Once the history of the Empire became a source of discomfort, shame and perplexity, its complexities and ambiguities were readily set aside. Rather than work through those feelings, that unsettling history was diminished, denied and if possible actively forgotten. The resulting silence feeds an additional catastrophe: (that is) the error of imagining that postcolonial people are only unwanted alien intruders without any substantive, historical, political or cultural connections to the collective life of their fellow subjects. (2004: 98)

The human cost of colonization, particularly in the form of slavery, is immense but little attempt has been made to compensate the victims to this day. It is unsurprising, therefore, that the legacy of colonization is part of an ongoing dispute between Barbados and other Caribbean islands and the UK with respect to reparations (Beckles 2013). Beckles is concerned with building the moral case for reparations [5]—as a just and necessary response to historical crimes. The Caribbean Commission produced a ten-point plan which ranged from a 'full formal apology' by European governments to more concrete forms of reparation, including assistance for public health, education, and cultural development. Caribbean countries' demands ranged from the apology to aid equivalent to Britain's original compensation to West Indian slaveholders (just under £200 billion in today's money). So while diversity laws seek to combat the contemporary

---

[5] Professor Sir Hilary Beckles is Principal and Pro-Vice Chancellor of the University of the West Indies, Cave Hill Campus, Barbados. He is a distinguished university administrator, economic historian, and specialist in higher education and development thinking and practice; and an internationally reputed historian.

discrimination faced by the Caribbean migrants and their descendants in the UK, the legacies of colonization and imperialism are key causal factors leading to the impeded development of countries in the Caribbean and the migration of their citizens.

Prasad (2006) makes a powerful case for linking postcolonial theory and workplace diversity. Drawing on Said, he sees the discourse of Orientalism as constructing an elaborate architecture of hierarchical dichotomies by means of which the Occident (the West) was conceptually manoeuvred into a position of ontological superiority over the Orient (the non-West), resulting in a hierarchical system of colonist binaries' (p. 124). Prasad goes on to argue that promoting genuine workplace diversity involves efforts aimed at destabilizing and subverting the hierarchical system of binaries discursively produced in the course of Western (neo)colonial domination (p. 138). However, he asserts that, since power and identity of the white privileged groups (and in important ways, the identity of white groups *in general*) are deeply implicated in this system of binaries, workplace diversity efforts frequently face strong opposition from such groups (ibid).

To an extent, the postcolonial lessons for understanding the politics of diversity in the global north lie in the complexity and hierarchy of the migration process for migrants and their descendants, and in exploring the intersectional experiences of migrants' own lives in their homes, their workplaces, and organizations. Colonial history and its postcolonial understandings become particularly important in the context of migration and its link to the politics of diversity. It is evident that colonial history is played out in different geographical spaces. These spaces are crucial contexts through which the politics of diversity is enacted and embodied and experienced. Moreover, spaces are not fixed contexts in that, in different ways, the migrant lives both 'here and there' spatially and emotionally.

Thus migration, past or present, is a central aspect of the politics of diversity—shifting populations enable recipient countries to build their infrastructures, develop, and grow. Yet migrants are seen in the conservative press and in political discourse as a collective entity that create problems for so-called settled communities. Even citizens with long years of settlement find their ability to achieve acceptance as citizens (*de facto* rather than *de jure*) is often contingent on the colour of their skin. New migration hierarchies emerge. The negative perception of the Irish migrant in the US (Roediger 1999) and UK (Delaney 2007) in the 1850s was well charted and persisted in the UK through to the 1960s and 1970s, inflamed again by the struggles for a united Ireland in the 1970s. But in the twenty-first century, despite unevenness in public perception, the Irish migrants are more likely to be highly educated than their mid-twentieth-century relatives, and tend to be viewed more positively than their predecessors. Such transformation has, not on the whole, happened to the descendants of slaves in the US nor to the Caribbean migrant in the UK. Moreover, the EU enlargement has led to increased migration across Europe. In the UK, building the historical and contemporary exclusionary outlook of the press and many politicians, some migrants (e.g. Romanians in 2014) have been demonized in the public discourse, to the point where they may even conceal their national identities in work and social settings (evidenced by 2014 work in progress by Doldor and Atewologun[6]).

While it is true to say that there has been some significant progress in the US (Bell 2007) and the UK (CRE 2007), the gap between the minority and majority access to privilege remains wide. As the former UK Commission on Racial Equality stated in its valedictory publication, 'a lot done, a lot more to do' (CRE 2007). The queue-jumping of acceptance by the majority controllers of power resources in the equality stakes tends to ensure that, in certain contexts, visible ethnicity remains a negative marker of difference regardless of period of settlement or formal citizenship, ensuring equality of treatment and outcome remains a struggle. Despite the evident changes in the US, reform has been partial and patchy, and black Americans continue to be disadvantaged compared to their white counterparts. Moreover, the residential segregation and its associated poverty are extreme and results in political disaffection. The 2014 uprisings/riots in Ferguson, Missouri, was a sharp reminder of the fragility of race relations in the US. This case well illustrates the interrelationship of history, society, and biography. Younge (2014) reported in August 2014, that Ferguson, a mostly black town, was under curfew following the shooting of an unarmed 18-year-old black teenager, Michael Brown, by the police as he walked down the street. Following the shooting and the resulting riots, Ferguson, whose entire political power structure is white, including its highly militarized police force, was effectively under occupation. At the end of the first day of curfew, hundreds of police in riot gear swept through the streets, using tear gas, smoke canisters, and rubber bullets against an increasingly agitated crowd. Distrust of the highly decentralized police led to the governor deploying the National Guard. Younge concludes his piece with the recognition that nobody wants more [killings of] Michael Browns but that those two things—the violence of the state and the violence of the street—are connected and reminds us of a quote from Martin Luther King, 'A riot is the language of the unheard.' In the multiple newspaper articles around the time of the Ferguson riots (and indeed previous riots in the US and the UK), a question is inevitable, and asked bluntly by Stafford (2014), why is it nearly always black men that the police shoot? Stafford commented that, in Ferguson and in so many other cases, we see the deaths of unarmed black men as 'accidents'; he went on, 'until the day we all recognize them as casualties of something much bigger, we will continue to see black men dead on the news'. As this book goes to press in November 2014, riots again took place, following the lack of indictment of the officer responsible for the shooting.

In the UK, the police are also distrusted by the black community with respect to the police stop and search policy. The figures are stark: if you are a black person, you are at least six times as likely to be stopped and searched by the police in England and Wales as a white person. If you are Asian, you are around twice as likely to be stopped and searched as a white person (Equality and Human Rights Commission 2014). There is little doubt that the UK and London police have invested considerably in equality and

---

[6] Academics in the Centre for Research in Equality, Queen Mary University of London.

diversity training and policies, but the stop and search figures have remained stubbornly high. In addition, there are long-standing disputes about shooting 'accidents' in the black community. It is now likely that the police will introduce a positive action programme to ensure that the London Metropolitan Police is numerically representative of its population.

Paradoxically, there have also been examples where the police refrained from dealing with offenders from colonial backgrounds, apparently for fear of disrupting community relations. The case of child abuse in the UK town of Rotherham demonstrated the patriarchal disregard of teenage girls in danger and again demonstrated the intersection of class and sex in the politics of diversity. In Rotherham, sexual and often violent abuse of some 1400 female children was reported to the police over the period 1997 to 2013 but was not acted upon. A report led by Professor Alexis Jay, commissioned by Rotherham Council, detailed cases where children as young as 11 had been raped by a number of different men, abducted, beaten, and trafficked to other towns and cities in the north of England to continue the abuse. Jay found 'children who had been doused in petrol and threatened with being set alight, threatened with guns, made to witness brutally violent rapes and threatened they would be next if they told anyone'. Police failed to act on the crimes and treated the victims with contempt, deeming them to be 'undesirables' not worthy of protection (Peachey 2014). The girls were from poor families or in local authority 'care'. These examples demonstrate that the well-meaning investment in diversity initiatives by the police are so often superseded by the multilayered politics of diversity, and those politics may be rooted in a contradictory understanding of the colonial legacy but also of class.

Against this background, however well-meaning DM approaches are, they may remain a drop in the ocean. Moreover, the depolitcization of diversity in an era of individualism has also led to its sanitizing, so that the harsh realities of inequalities, racial prejudice, and patriarchal practices are avoided in the bread-and-butter diversity discourses of the business case, training, and policy development.

Voluntarism and Regulation

Scholars in the field of employment have long debated the relationship between voluntarism and regulation (Kahn Freund 1972), with a traditional preference for the autonomy of employers and unions to organize their own affairs rather than the state regulating on their behalf, and the state creating a 'rough equilibrium between the social forces of capital and organized labour' (Deakin 1986: 231). Voluntarism extended from the collective sphere to the individual level of labour relations (Deakin 1986: 232) and Deakin argues that women and the low paid ultimately paid the price for voluntarism (Deakin 1986: 242). Thus, voluntarism became increasingly associated with individualism and the neoliberal agenda. Increasingly, the role of law through regulation was seen as an important means to create a fairer workplace, although legal regulation continues to be contested in both the UK and the US, two of the most lightly regulated advanced economies.

Nevertheless, regulation has been important for those whom the laws, policies, and procedures governing equalities and diversity are ostensibly designed to protect. Equality and diversity is not done for them, they too are critical agents for change as, in order to achieve equality and fairness—in other words, legislative compliance—the aggrieved need to challenge current practice. Such challenges are often through collectivist strategies. Thus, despite the dominant discourse of the relentless march of individualism, collectivism continues to play an important part in challenging inequalities (Healy, Bradley, and Mukherjee 2004; Lucio and Perrett 2009; Perrett and Lucio 2009; Milkman 2011; Alberti, Holgate, and Tapia 2013). The collectivist role is also about ensuring compliance with equality and diversity legislation.

Nevertheless, a political analysis points to the denigration of rules (characterized as 'red tape' in the UK) that further weaken the fragile edifice of legal protection. Moreover, there is a clear tendency to move away from the regulative underpinning, which provides the resources for inequalities to be challenged, with a shift in discourse and practice to voluntarism (and volunteers), localism, and deregulation.

The rise of individualism (and voluntarism) has been a dominant media and academic discourse, yet Bradley and Healy (2008) argue that much is at stake politically in asserting or denying the rise of individualism and fall of collectivism. The debates, whether rooted in industrial relations, industrial sociology, or economics, have been characterized by a neglect of the link between collectivist values and the diversity project in the ideal type of the individualistic nature of diversity in organizations. More nuanced approaches recognize the continuing importance of collectivism, including the role of unions (see for example: Healy et al., 2004; Kirton and Greene 2006; Bradley and Healy 2008; Greene and Kirton 2009; Özbilgin and Tatli 2011; Jonsen, Tatli, Özbilgin, and Bell, 2013; Kirton and Healy 2013b). The false binary drawn between equal opportunities and DM enhances the belief in individualism (DM and the business case) as opposed to collectivism (equal opportunities). Bradley and Healy (2008) showed that the equal opportunities approach of the 1980s always used the business case in its rhetoric, and that the collective *and* the individual were both part of an equal opportunities approach. Thus, the stark differences espoused between equal opportunities and DM were never entirely convincing. Nevertheless, there has been an important discursive shift with the language of DM which, as Bradley and Healy (2008: 39) argued, built a sanitizing process into the discourse and often the practice of DM. As Oswick and Noon state with respect to the equal opportunities versus the diversity binary, 'Only by breaking free of the oppositional discursive patterns can the debate move on to anti-discrimination solutions that attempt to blend together equality, diversity and inclusion' (Oswick and Noon 2014: 23).

Multiple ideological processes come into play in the multi-level relational structures shaping the politics of diversity (for example, Healy 1993; Greene and Kirton 2009; Healy and Oikelome 2011; Kirton and Healy 2013a). Diversity stakeholders are key actors; Greene and Kirton (2009) highlighted the key role of, and differences between, stakeholders in a range of UK organizations in both public and private sectors. Özbilgin and Tatli's (2011) study also reveals that the emphasis and discourse of DM differs according to the different politics and positioning of institutions. Greene and colleagues' (2005) comparative study of UK and Danish trade union responses to DM enabled a demonstration of the importance of context in understanding the same kind of institutions, with Danish unions demonstrating enthusiasm for DM and UK unions, scepticism. Thus, Greene and colleagues are pointing to the motivations for compliance within the discourse of DM; however, in the case of the UK unions, such adherence to the language of diversity does not alter the political lens through which unions assess the problems of inequality. In this way, diversity and unions' politics are operating at different levels of analysis and are simultaneously contradictory and complementary, in order to achieve the required ends.

Following on from the implications of the voluntarist and collective confrontations in Ferguson, Missouri, and in London, the need for radical change is obvious, but will it follow a voluntarist or regulatory approach? A key aspect of regulation is affirmative action, the introduction of which remains contentious whether it is introduced in a more or a less developed country. The case against affirmative action or positive discrimination may, on the surface, be seen as compelling particularly when it is assumed that affirmative action may prevent the 'best person' from being appointed. Noon (2010) confronts the four main objections to positive discrimination and provides counter-arguments with respect to: (1) the failure to select the 'best' candidate; (2) the undermining of meritocracy; (3) the negative impact on the beneficiaries; and (4) the injustice of reverse discrimination. In doing so, he concludes that positive discrimination provides the necessary structural conditions in order for radical, transformative change towards equality to take place.

Yet, while geographies are very different, we see both similarities and differences with respect to the adoption and implementation of affirmative action. In the US, political interventions sought to ensure that the enforcement of affirmative action was curtailed (see Kelly and Dobbin 1998). In the UK, there has been strong resistance to introducing affirmative action. Indeed, existing law on equality was weakened during the 2010–15 Coalition Government, when the pressure to deregulate intensified and the equality agenda further diluted.[7] Yet Dickens warns that 'state intervention is critical to an equality agenda, because the market tends to produce discrimination, not equality' (2006: 305).

---

[7] Conley (2011) revealed the dilution of the public sector duty in the UK. The approach is not to remove the institutional equality but to weaken the mechanisms for enforcement. While legislation remains in place, the means of implementing that legislation is weakened (e.g. the enforcement arm, EHRC). Moreover, the individual seeking redress under the law following unfair treatment is deterred by the new costs of taking a case to the Employment Tribunal—there has been a fall of 79 per cent in one year since new fees were introduced in 2013 (Jones 2014). Thus, the aim of reducing the number of appellants to a tribunal has been achieved but at what cost when genuine claimants are priced out of the social justice market?

Despite the resistance to affirmative action in the most developed countries, affirmative action is a key tool used globally to rectify past wrongdoings in developing countries, and there are often common issues within regions and between regions, and Africa is no exception. Efforts to combat exclusion have taken place in Nigeria, South Africa, and Namibia, all divided societies, using affirmative action programmes aimed at bridging the profound inequalities between different segments of their population (Mustapha 2007). Kauzya (2001) states that one of the most pervasive problematic issues in Africa concerns the ethnic diversity of most of the continent's countries and the problems related to such diversity. In Western countries, the politics of diversity through legislation and policy tends to be played out more strongly in the public sector, and this is also the case in African countries.

There is much to learn from studies in the global south while still recognizing a country's unique context, the chapter therefore uses illustrations from one African country, Nigeria. This focus is mainly because most readers of this volume will already have an understanding of diversity in the US, UK, and other Western countries, including Scandinavia, whereas they are less likely to have engaged with the literature on diversity in developing countries: in this case, Nigeria, which is the most populous and ethnically diverse country in Africa (exceptions include: Healy and Oikelome 2007; Adeleye, Atewologun, and Matanmi 2014)

Healy and Oikelome's *Diversity, Ethnicity, Migration and Work* brought Nigeria to the attention of Western diversity scholars by bringing north (UK and US) and south (Nigeria) together, and it is from this work that this section draws (2011: 67–89). The authors stated that Nigeria's approach to ethnic diversity has been the consequence of divisions between ethnic groups and the subsequent uneven distribution of political, social, and economic resources. The Civil War (1967–70) in Nigeria had at its heart economic, ethnic, cultural, and religious tensions, while its roots were in the colonial settlement. Thus, the colonial legacy is crucial in unpacking contemporary politics of diversity in Nigeria. To understand the complexity of ethnicity in Nigeria, some understanding of the size and importance of the country is essential. Nigeria is a country of some 120 million people, divided into over 200 ethnic groups, who practise several religions and whose histories and cultures at times varied.[8] In order to create a representative bureaucracy, the 1979 constitution (section 14(3)) introduced a system of quotas.

---

[8] Colonial rule and the operations of the postcolonial state (from 1960) at times accentuated the differences (Afigbo 1988). Afigbo (1988) demonstrated that the operations of the colonial state created a dangerous myth of duality between north and south, as a result of which the postcolonial leadership worked towards 'balancing' the interests of the two halves of Nigeria—and of the three dominant groups (Hausa, Yoruba, and Igbo). The Hausa-Fulani in the north, the Yoruba in the south-west, and the Igbo in the south-east are each numerically and politically dominant in the three regions that governed the country in the early period of independence. All other ethnic groups are perceived as minority groups. Socioeconomic inequalities between, on the one hand, the Yoruba and Igbo, and, on the other, the northern-based Hausa-Fulani are very sharp. Poverty is concentrated in three north-western states and the north lags behind the south on indicators such as literacy, access to health facilities, electricity, and water.

The scope and intent of the 'federal character' provision have generated heated debate. Its advocates see it as the only safeguard against nepotism (Balogun 1987). Its critics regard it as a smokescreen for ethnic favouritism, and argue that it erodes the stability and quality of the service (Gboyega 1988; Oluwo 2001). A fuller assessment of the Federal Character may be found in Mustapha (2007). While recognizing that the affirmative action programme is inherently political, divisive, and does not tackle the wider issues of education, health, and infrastructural disadvantage, Mustapha concludes that affirmative action, properly done, can become a motor for wider social change by having self-perpetuating positive effects on employment and economic growth, even when the initial policy prop has been relaxed (Krislor 1974, Boston 1999 in Mustapha 2007).

Thus, politics imbue the Nigerian example, and the colonial legacy underpins the use of affirmative action to remedy past injustices. Changing geography, we see clearly in the Scandinavian example that it is in politics and in the boards of companies where women are more strongly represented—the reason of course is that forms of affirmative action have been instituted. While imperfect, and contested internationally, affirmative action is one means that needs to be extended but not abandoned.

The Politics of Diversity Influences Careers in the Academy

The fourth theme is perhaps a little indulgent; it discusses the society of which most of the readers of this book are part, the academy. Returning to the sociological imagination, and the sociological academy of 1959, Mills was a key actor in writing his own biography in relation to the sociological work of others. Thus, his critical approach was not only from a sociological stance, but also from a personal assault against the domination of the work of sociologists (for example, Parsons). For Mills, the personal was the political and those who practised, in his view, objective empiricism and clumsy grand theory were to be admonished. This he did liberally and often personally (Brewer 2004). In return, the sociological establishment, on the publication of *The Sociological Imagination*, spared him no mercy in their reviews, and the book was condemned on intellectual grounds.

For contemporary scholars of equality and diversity, this story is noteworthy. While most scholars do not enter the internecine warfare practised by Mills, they are still faced with the personal prejudices encased in the biographies of their reviewers that shape the society of their academic field. Thus, when feminist and/or anti-racist work is sent to unsympathetic or even hostile reviewers, it may be disproportionately criticized in comparison to work that is deemed more important and relevant because it is in line with the reviewers' conceptual and political stance. The more scholars stray from the dominant mainstreams, the harder they may find it to get published, particularly if they are not part of influential networks. A number of studies in different disciplines show that women are systematically cited less than men (although there has been improvement in the last two decades) (Jagsi et al. 2006, 2008; Maliniak, Powers, and Walter 2013; Jenkins, 2014) and the numbers of female editors-in-chiefs of journals remains low (Jagsi et al. 2008; Amrein et al. 2011). Moreover, in almost all academic fields, men cite their own research papers more often than women do. Despite increased representation of women in academia, the gender gap in self-citation has widened over the last fifty years (King et al. 2015). These studies are especially meaningful because citation counts count. They are increasingly important, and contested, as a key measure of the quality of research and impact. Or, as Smith and Lee (2014) contend with respect to the neglect of queer theory in political science, 'We should not underestimate the professional injustices that follow from intellectual injustices.' Thus, the politics of diversity is at the heart of the academy.

Mir, Mir, and Wong (2006) raise another issue. They argue that internationalization of the workforces means that studies in workplace diversity will have to deal with what they argue are new issues, that is, outsourcing, migration, international legal constraints, refugees, and the unravelling of the dominant discourses of globalization (p. 169), issues which tend to be critically discussed in the field of employment relations. Mir, Mir, and Wong's (2006) arguments are important and seek to widen the field of workplace and diversity and DM. Such 'new' issues have traditionally been part of the employment relations field, which underlines the importance of interdisciplinarity. In some ways, Mir, Mir, and Wong's (2006) assumption that workplace diversity is a 'discipline' is to limit horizons; rather, workplace diversity is a field of study and, as such, reflects the interdisciplinary field of employment relations.[9]

The debates in sociology resonate with the debates that academics are having in the field of equalities and diversity. Burawoy (2005), in his call for a shift to a public sociology, stated that 'The original passion for social justice, economic equality, human rights, sustainable environment, political freedom or simply a better world, that drew so many of us to sociology, is [now] channelled into the pursuit of academic credentials. Thus the politics of diversity enter not only the organization but the academy. This of course begs the question if the route taken by the equality specialist is mirroring that of their academic specialists. The equality specialist of the 1970s driven by principles of social justice has been succeeded by the diversity specialist schooled in 'the business case' (Greene and Kirton 2009). Moreover, for the contemporary diversity specialists, their routes through the organization may consider DM only one stopping place in their corporate careers' journeys (Greene and Kirton 2009). Thus, the more 'neutral' politics of the contemporary diversity manager may well have rejected the collectivist project in place of the career project of the self.

While, in academia, the increasing intensification of the struggles to build academic credentials ensure that 'publish or be damned' is the institutional pressure, yet the

---

[9] Industrial relations has always seen itself as a field of study (Edwards 2005) and, as such, has the potential to draw widely on studies from different disciplines. This does not prevent a particular type of work or method dominating, but it does at least open a field for the critical and thoughtful scholar.

politics of diversity begs the questions: What do diversity scholars do with the knowledge that they painstakingly uncover in the field of equality and diversity? How do they seek to influence? While scholars may intellectually engage with the politics of injustice in the diversity field, do they seek to engage with the politics of injustice in the public sphere? Or are academics instead silenced by the regulative and credentialist environment in which they now work?

There are, of course, striking examples of activist academics. A number work with trade unions or NGOs, seeing the data that they uncover as potential power resources that can be mobilized and used to provide reports, presentations, discussions, and to organize and build networks. At the same time, academics write for academic journals, and it is against these publications that they will be measured in their academic careers. Academics read, critique, and cite each other's work, and round and round it goes, with work often remaining within the rarefied world of academia. The promise of emancipation through involved research may be lost unless there is also public engagement with such findings.

Conclusion

These four interrelated themes of *history, society, and biography, colonial history, voluntarism and regulation,* and *diversity careers* provide partial insight into the wide and complex field of the politics of diversity. The chapter has shown that the politics of equality and diversity are rooted in history, society, and biography, and their connections and contradictions. How do we interpret this in the twenty-first century when European empires have long disappeared? Despite the shift from empire to Commonwealth and now the EU, and from European empires to American and soon perhaps Chinese, and the rise of emerging economies such as the BRIC (Brazil, Russia, India, and China) countries and the forecasted rise of the MINT (Mexico, Indonesia, Nigeria, and Turkey) countries, the long shadows of empire are still evident in the material and cultural effects that continue to play out, particularly through the processes of contemporary patterns of migration and of racism. Thus, the historical and international nature of diversity is crucial in understanding the complexity of the politics of diversity at all levels.

It is hard to disentangle the influence of colonialism from the contradictions inherent in the contemporary nature of place and globalization. Mir, Mir, and Wong (2006) capture the contradictions in the globalization/place discussion: first they argue that national or regional identity is not an effective category to analyse global diversity; second that globalization is not as easy to represent than monolithic categories, as one person's experience of the liberation associated with global consumption must necessarily be contrasted with another subject's experience of imperialism; and finally that the category of economic class never ceases to be fundamental in the analysis of the relations of production that bind human beings into economic and cultural networks (p. 168).

Thus Mir, Mir, and Wong (2006) bring together well the interrelationship of history, society, and biography, the connections and contradictions.

The chapter has warned of the dangers of reinforcing and deepening inequalities, which are evident in the ideological promotion of the discourse of individualism and voluntarism associated with aspects of instrumentality which work to deny the existence of collectivism. The importance of collectivism in challenging inequalities is important, whether formally constructed through collective bargaining, through (mainly left leaning) political parties or through issue-based interest organizations (including targeted groups) or collective challenges (including spontaneous uprisings). Moreover, collectivist values reflect Young's (1990) argument for social policy to sometimes accord special treatment for oppressed or disadvantaged groups.

By engaging with the politics of diversity and arguing for the interrelationship of biography and history within society, the relevance of context, and the importance of emancipatory principles to guide our research, and seeking to understand the politics that shape our own milieu as academics concerned with fairness, the chapter has sought to widen the parameters within which diversity is often written and discussed. Notwithstanding the rather dismal forces that often combine to ensure that we live in an unfair and individualistic world, the complex nature of the politics of diversity, while demonstrating hostile forces, importantly still enables progressive voices, through key actors and institutions, to be heard. Moreover, the rich research that emanates from equality and diversity scholars has the potential to shape public issues and debates and thereby the politics of diversity.

REFERENCES

Acker, J. (2006a). *Class Questions: Feminist Answers*. Lanham, MD: Rowman & Littlefield Publishers Inc.

Acker, J. (2006b). Inequality regimes: gender, class, and race in organizations. *Gender Society*, 20(4): 441–64.

Adeleye, I., Atewologun, D., and Matanmi, O. (2014). Equality, diversity and inclusion in Nigeria: historical context and emerging issues. In A. Klarsfeld, L. A. Booysen, E. Ng, I. Roper, and A. Tatli. (eds.), *International Handbook on Diversity Management at Work: Country Perspectives on Diversity and Equal Treatment*. Cheltenham: Edward Elgar, 195–216.

Afigbo, A. E. (1988). Federal character: its meaning and history. In P. P. Ekeh and E. E. Osaghae (eds.), *Federal Character and Federalism in Nigeria*. Ibadan: Heinemann.

Alberti, G., Holgate, J., and Tapia, M. (2013). Organising migrants as workers or as migrant workers? Intersectionality, trade unions and precarious work. *The International Journal of Human Resource Management*, 24(22): 4132–48.

Amrein, K., Langmann, A., Fahrleitner-Pammer, A., Pieber, T. R., and Zollner-Schwetz, I. (2011). Women underrepresented on editorial boards of 60 major medical journals. *Gender Medicine*, 8(6): 378–87.

Balogun, M. J. (1987). *Public Administration in Nigeria: a Developmental Approach*. London and Basingstoke: Macmillan.

Beckles, H. (2013). *Britain's Black Debt: Reparations for Caribbean Slavery and Native Genocide*. University of West Indies Press.
Bell, M. P. (2007). *Diversity in Organizations*. Mason: Thompson South-Western.
Borchorst, A. and Siim, B. (1987). Women and the advanced welfare state: a new kind of patriarchal power? In A. S. Sassoon (ed.), *Women and the State*. London, Hutchinson, 128–151.
Bradley, H. and Healy, G. (2008). *Ethnicity and Gender at Work: Inequalities, Careers and Employment Relations*. London and New York: Palgrave Macmillan.
Brewer, J. D. (2004). Imagining *The Sociological Imagination*: the biographical context of a sociological classic. *The British Journal of Sociology*, 55(3), 317–33.
Brown, C. (1992). Racial disadvantage in the employment market. In P. Braham, A. Rattansi, and Skellington R. (eds.), *Racism and Antiracism: Inequalities, Opportunities and Policies*. London: Sage/Open University, 46–63.
Burawoy, M. (2005). 2004 American Sociological Association presidential address: for public sociology*. *The British Journal of Sociology*, 56(2): 259–94.
Cockburn, C. (1991). *In the Way of Women: Men's Resistance to Sex Equality in Organizations*. Basingstoke: Macmillan.
Collins, P. H. (2000). *Black Feminist Thought*. New York: Routledge.
Collins, P. H. (2004). Learning from the outsider within: the sociological significance of black feminist thought. In S. Harding (ed.), *The Feminist Standpoint Theory Reader: Intellectual and Political Controversies*. New York and London: Routledge.
Conley, H. (2011). The road to equality: Legislating for change? In T. Wright and H. Conley (eds.), *Handbook of Discrimination at Work*. Hants: Gower Publishing.
Cooper, J. N. (2012). Personal troubles and public issues: a sociological imagination of Black athletes' experiences at predominantly White institutions in the United States. *Sociology Mind*, 2(03): 261.
CRE (Commission for Racial Equality). (2007). *A Lot Done, A Lot to Do: Our Vision for an Integrated Britain*. London: Commission for Racial Equality.
Crenshaw, K. (1991). Mapping the margins: intersectionality, identity politics and violence against women of color. *Stanford Law Review*, 43(6): 1241–99.
De Beauvoir, S. (1949). *The Second Sex* (tr. H. M. Parshley). Penguin.
Deakin, S. (1986). Labour law and the developing employment relationship in the UK. *Cambridge Journal of Economics*, 10(3): 225–46.
Delaney, E. (2007). *The Irish in Post-War Britain*. Oxford: Oxford University Press.
Denny, L. Lisa Denney 19 December 2011 <http://www.opendemocracy.net/5050/lisa-denney/nigeria-women-on-outskirts-of-politics>, accessed 7 May 2014.
Dickens, L. (2006). Re-regulation for gender equality: from 'either/or' to 'both'. *Industrial Relations Journal*, 37(4): 299–309.
Edwards, P. (2005). The challenging but promising future of industrial relations: developing theory and method in context-sensitive research. *Industrial Relations Journal*, 36(4): 264–82.
Edwards, P. and Wajcman, J. (2005). *The Politics of Working Life*. Oxford: Oxford University Press.
Equality and Human Rights Commission. (2014). Review of Stop and Search. Retrieved 5 September 2014, from <http://www.equalityhumanrights.com/about-us/our-work/key-projects/race-britain/stop-and-think>.
Gboyega, A. (1988). The public service and federal character. In P. P. Ekeh and E. E. Osaghae (eds.), *Federal Character and Federalism in Nigeria*. Ibadan: Heinemann.
Gelb, J. and Palley, M. L. (1982). *Women and Public Policies*. Princeton: Princeton University Press.

Gilroy, P. (2004). *After Empire: Melancholia or Convivial Culture.* London and New York: Routledge.

Greene, A.-M. and Kirton, G. (2009). *Diversity Management in the UK: Organizational and Stakeholder Experiences.* London: Routledge.

Greene, A.-M., Kirton, G. and Wrench, J. (2005). Trade union perspectives on diversity management: a comparison of the UK and Denmark. *European Journal of Industrial Relations* 11(2): 179–96.

Healy, G. (1993). Business and discrimination. In R. Stacey (ed.), *Strategic Thinking and the Management of Change: International Perspectives of Organisational Dynamics.* London: Kogan Page, 169–89.

Healy, G. and Oikelome, F. (2007). A global link between national diversity policies? The case of the migration of Nigerian physicians to the UK and USA. *The International Journal of Human Resource Management,* 18(11): 1917–33.

Healy, G. and Oikelome, F. (2011). *Diversity, Ethnicity, Migration and Work: An International Perspective.* Basingstoke: Palgrave Macmillan.

Healy, G., Bradley, H., and Forson, C. (2011). Intersectional sensibilities in analysing inequality regimes in public sector organizations. *Gender, Work and Organization,* 18(5): 467–87.

Healy, G., Bradley, H., and Mukherjee, N. (2004). Individualism and collectivism revisited: a study of black and minority ethnic women. *Industrial Relations Journal,* 35(5): 451–66.

Heath, A. and Cheung, S. Y. (2006). *Ethnic Penalties in the Labour Market: Employers and Discriminationdwp.gov.uk.* London: Department for Work and Pensions.

Heery, E. and Simms, M. (2010). Employer responses to union organising: patterns and effects. *Human Resource Management Journal,* 20(1): 3–22.

Hooks, B. (2000). *Feminist Theory: From Margin to Center.* Cambridge: South End Press Classics.

Jagsi, R., Tarbell, N. J., Henault, L. E., Chang, Y., and Hylek, E. M. (2008). The representation of women on the editorial boards of major medical journals: a 35-year perspective. *Archives of Internal Medicine,* 168(5): 544–8.

Jagsi, R., Guancial, E. A., Worobey, C. C., Henault, L. E., Chang, Y., Starr, R., et al. (2006). The 'gender gap' in authorship of academic medical literature: a 35-year perspective. *New England Journal of Medicine,* 355(3): 281–7.

Jenkins, F. (2014). Epistemic credibility and women in philosophy. *Australian Feminist Studies,* 29(80): 161–70.

Jewson, N. and Mason, D. (1986). The theory and practice of equal opportunities policies: liberal and radical approaches. *The Sociological Review,* 34(2): 307–34.

Jones, C. (2014). Dramatic Fall in Employment Tribunal Figures (Vol. 2014): Institute for Employment Affairs.

Jones, D., Pringle, J., and Shepherd, D. (2000). 'Managing diversity' meets Aotearoa/New Zealand. *Personnel Review,* 29(3): 364–80.

Jonsen, K., Tatli, A., Özbilgin, M. F., and Bell, M. P. (2013). The tragedy of the uncommons: reframing workforce diversity. *Human Relations,* 66(2): 271–94.

Kahn Freund, O. (1972). *Labour and the Law.* London: Hamlyn Trust.

Kamenou, N. (2008). Reconsidering work–life balance debates: challenging limited understandings of the 'life' component in the context of ethnic minority women's experiences. *British Journal of Management,* 19(s1): S99–109.

Kelly, E. and Dobbin, F. (1998). How affirmative action became diversity management: employer response to antidiscrimination law, 1961 to 1996. *American Behavioral Scientist,* 41(7): 960–84.

King, M. M., Correll, S. J., Jacquet, J., Bergstrom, C. T., and West, J. D. (2015). Men set their own cites high: Gender and self-citation across fields and over time. Accepted for presentation at the American Sociology Association, Chicago, IL.

Kirton, G. (2008). Managing multi-culturally in organizations in a diverse society. In S. Clegg and C. Cooper (eds.), *Handbook of Macro Organizational Behaviour*. London: Sage, 309–22.

Kirton, G. and Greene, A.-M. (2006). The discourse of diversity in unionised contexts: views from trade union equality officers. *Personnel Review*, 35(4): 431–48.

Kirton, G. and Greene, A.-M. (2009). The costs and opportunities of doing diversity work in mainstream organisations. *Human Resource Management Journal*, 19(2): 159–75.

Kirton, G. and Healy, G. (2013a). Commitment and collective identity of long-term union participation: the case of women union leaders in the UK and USA. *Work, Employment & Society*, 27(2): 195–212.

Kirton, G. and Healy, G. (2013b). *Gender and Leadership in Unions*. New York and Abingdon: Routledge.

Kirton, G., Greene, A.-M., and Dean, D. (2007). British diversity professionals as change agents: radicals, tempered radicals or liberal reformers? *The International Journal of Human Resource Management*, 18(11): 1979–94.

Lawrence, E. (2000). Equal opportunities officers and managing equality changes. *Personnel Review*, 29(3): 381–401.

Layder, D. (2005). *Understanding Social Theory*. Sage.

Lorbiecki, A. and Jack, G. (2000). Critical turns in the evolution of diversity management. *British Journal of Management*, 11 (Special Issue): S17–S31.

Lucio, M. M. and Perrett, R. (2009). The diversity and politics of trade unions' responses to minority ethnic and migrant workers: the context of the UK. *Economic and Industrial Democracy*, 30(3): 324–47.

McGuire, G. M. (2000). Gender, race, ethnicity, and networks: the factors affecting the status of employees' network members. *Work and Occupations*, 27(4): 500–23 (524).

Maliniak, D., Powers, R., and Walter, B. F. (2013). The gender citation gap in international relations. *International Organization*, 67(04): 889–922.

Milkman, R. (2011). Immigrant workers, precarious work, and the US labor movement. *Globalizations*, 8(3): 361–72.

Mills, C. W. (1970). *The Sociological Imagination*. Harmondsworth: Penguin Books Ltd.

Mir, R., Mir, A., and Wong, D. J. (2006). Diversity: the cultural logic of global capital? In A. M. Konrad, P. Prasad, and J. Pringle (eds.), *Handbook of Workplace Diversity*. London: Sage Publications Ltd.

Mustapha, A. R. (2007). *Institutionalising Ethnic Representation: How Effective is the Federal Character Commission in Nigeria?* Oxford: Centre for Research on Inequality, Human Security and Ethnicity.

Newman, C. (2013). Nigeria: women on the outskirts of politics. <http://www.telegraph.co.uk/women/womens-life/9790633/Will-Goves-posh-white-blokes-history-curriculum-ignore-women.html> accessed 11 January 2014.

Noon, M. (2010). The shackled runner: time to rethink positive discrimination? *Work, Employment & Society*, 24(4): 728–39.

Oikelome, F. and Healy, G. (2007). Second-class doctors? The impact of a professional career structure on the employment conditions of overseas- and UK-qualified doctors. *Human Resource Management Journal*, 17(2): 134–54.

Oikelome, F. and Healy, G. (2012). Gender, migration and place of qualification of doctors in the UK: perceptions of inequality, morale and career aspiration. *Journal of Ethnic and Migration Studies*, 39(4): 557–77.

Oluwo, B. (2001). Pride and performance in African public services: analysis of institutional breakdown and rebuilding efforts in Nigeria and Uganda. *International Review of Administrative Sciences*, 67(1), 117–34.

Oswick, C. and Noon, M. (2014). Discourses of diversity, equality and inclusion: trenchant formulations or transient fashions? *British Journal of Management*, 25(1): 23–39.

Özbilgin, M. and Tatli, A. (2011). Mapping out the field of equality and diversity: rise of individualism and voluntarism. *Human Relations*, 64(9): 1229–53.

Özbilgin, M. F., Beauregard, T. A., Tatli, A., and Bell, M. P. (2011). Work–life, diversity and intersectionality: a critical review and research agenda. *International Journal of Management Reviews*, 13(2): 177–98.

Peachey, P. (2014). Rotherham child abuse report: 1,400 children subjected to 'appalling' sexual exploitation over 16 years. *The Independent*, 26 August.

Perrett, R. and Lucio, M. M. (2009). Trade unions and relations with black and minority-ethnic community groups in the United Kingdom: the development of new alliances? *Journal of Ethnic and Migration Studies*, 35: 1295–1314.

Pickett, K. and Wilkinson, R. (2010). *The Spirit Level: Why Equality Is Better for Everyone*. London: Penguin.

Prasad, A. (2006). The jewel in the crown: postcolonial theory and workplace diversity. In A. M. Konrad, P. Prasad and J. Pringle, *Handbook of Workplace Diversity*. London, Sage Publications, 121–44.

Roediger, D. R. (1999). *The Wages of Whiteness: Race and the Making of the American Working Class*. London and New York: Verso.

Said, E. W. (1978). *Orientalism: Western Conceptions of the Orient*. London: Routledge and Kegan Paul Ltd.

Said, E. W. (1993). *Culture and Imperialism*. Random House LLC.

Seierstad, C. and Healy, G. (2012). Women's equality in the Scandinavian academy: a distant dream? *Work, Employment & Society*, 26(2): 296–313.

Smith, N. J. and Lee, D. (2014). What's queer about political science? *The British Journal of Politics & International Relations*, n/a-n/a.

Stafford, Z. (2014). I'm black, my brother's white... and he's a cop who shot a black man on duty. *The Guardian*, 25 August.

Weber, M. (ed.) (1978). *Economy and Society*. Berkeley, CA: University of California Press.

World Bank. (2014). Millennium Development Goals: Goal 3, Promote Gender Equality and Empower Women by 2015. Retrieved 2 September 2014 from <http://www.worldbank.org/mdgs/gender.html>.

World Economic Forum. (2014). *The Global Gender Gap Report*. Geneva: World Economic Forum.

Wright, T. (2013). Uncovering sexuality and gender: an intersectional examination of women's experience in UK construction. *Construction Management and Economics*, 31(8): 832–44.

Young, I. M. (1990). *Justice and the Politics of Difference*. Princeton, NJ: Princeton University Press.

Younge, G. (2014). In Ferguson the violence of the state created the violence of the street. *The Guardian*, 18 August.

CHAPTER 2

DUELLING DUALISMS
A History of Diversity Management

JUDITH K. PRINGLE AND GLENDA STRACHAN

INTRODUCTION

THIS history of workplace diversity is one of many versions of history that could be written (Mandelbaum 1967; Carr 1987). We use dualisms as a heuristic to tease out tensions between apparent contradictory positions. Submerged in our discussion is the chronological emergence of workplace diversity. It burst onto the equality scene from the United States and, in the 1990s, quickly spread its influence into public and private sector organizations. Into the 2000s, criticism was gathering against the dominance of the US diversity discourse that did not mesh well with different country and legislative environments such as Denmark (Risberg and Søderberg 2008), Australia (Strachan, Burgess, and Sullivan 2004), and New Zealand (Jones, Pringle, and Shepherd 2000), which has led to the contemporary 'country contexts' perspective on workplace diversity (Klarsfeld 2010; Klarsfeld et al. 2014). As the managing diversity (MD) discourse was gathering strength, a thread of critique began questioning the displacement of social justice concerns in MD (Liff 1997; Dickens 1999). These scholars criticized the 'depoliticised and ahistoric conception of difference' (Tatli 2011: 246) on which diversity management (DM) was founded. This critique has intensified into the development of a critical diversity studies (Zanoni et al. 2010).

The chronological development of workplace diversity has been riddled with dichotomies which confine scholars to isolated camps. Binary oppositional constructs lead to an emphasis on differences, with such divisions being counterproductive (Özbilgin and Tatli 2008). We use an organizing structure represented by five bipolar dimensions. In Table 2.1, the left-hand descriptor appeared historically prior to the right-hand marker.

Table 2.1 Dualistic map of workplace diversity

Social justice/moral case	Economic/business case
Practitioner initiatives	Academic research
US diversity discourse	Country context discourses
Gender issues	'Other' diversity dimensions
Quantitative focus	Qualitative focus

While some of these categories have coexisted, others have competed for attention. In the following discussion, we take each of these dimensions in turn, moving from left to right.

Social Justice and the Business Case

Historically, labour markets have been characterized by inequality in ways we would now describe as discrimination. Characteristics irrelevant to the job influenced judgements of performance, for example, the employee's sex, age, ethnicity, religion, caste, disability, sexuality, and family status. Inequality has been experienced in different ways across countries and has changed over time (Jain, Sloane, and Horwitz 2003; Kennedy-Dubourdieu 2006). For example, unequal (less) pay for women compared with men was a widespread phenomenon justified by a sex-based division of labour, where men were the bread-winners of the family, and women were care-givers.

In the nineteenth century, women and minority groups based their struggles for equality on arguments of social justice and the moral case (Cassell 1996), namely, on the ethical and right thing to do. These arguments were central to the second-wave feminist fight for equal opportunity (EO) within the labour force. However, it was the post-Second World War international declarations which set the scene for changes that shifted employment regulations from ones sanctioning inequality (discrimination) to ones supporting equality. The Declaration of Human Rights 1948 included the right to just and favourable conditions of work without any discrimination, equal pay for equal work, and just and favourable remuneration, ensuring that the worker and their family have an existence worthy of human dignity. From that time, United Nations (UN) and International Labour Organization (ILO) conventions contained detailed recommendations, notably the UN International Convention on the Elimination of All Forms of Racial Discrimination 1965 and the UN Convention on the Elimination of All Forms of Discrimination against Women 1979. These principles of equality in employment are emphasized in the UN Global Compact's Ten Principles: Principle 6 states that 'businesses should uphold the elimination of discrimination in respect of employment and occupation'. It defines discrimination in employment and occupations as 'treating people differently or less favourably because of characteristics that are not related to their merit or the inherent requirements of the job', and recognizes indirect discrimination, which 'often exists informally in attitudes and practices, which if unchallenged can perpetuate in organizations' (UN 2014).

Legislation in a number of countries (Klarsfeld 2010; Klarsfeld et al. 2014) covers specific groups in the labour market who have been discriminated against systematically and historically, such as women and specific ethnic and caste groups. The most common form of legislation prohibits discrimination on specified grounds such as sex and age, and offers an individual complaint-based mechanism for redress. The macro human rights framework (implemented through legislation) exists in conjunction with grassroots activism working for change. By its nature, this approach produces ad hoc, not systematic, outcomes.

We describe in detail the complex transition from EO to MD, because the bridging links are crucial to the debates within diversity studies, particularly from British Commonwealth countries with similar legal jurisdictions. We then describe the rise of MD within the US context, a somewhat different historical and socio-political context, with its more litigious environment and the Civil Rights movement, which played a pivotal role in mobilizing equality arguments (Lillevik, Combs, and Wyrick 2010). As MD was beginning to be discussed in the United Kingdom, Sonia Liff (1997: 11) asked provocatively, 'Has EO had its day? Or is MD a way of repackaging equal opportunity, strengthening it or undermining it?'

Equal Opportunity

The cornerstone of EO was equality and the elimination of discrimination based on social group membership (Liff and Wajcman 1996), the goal being that the representation of diverse social groups should reflect their proportion in the population (Jewson and Mason 1986). By the time that MD burst onto the scene in the United States, EO was theoretically developed with contrasting models that had evolved from industrial relations, anti-discrimination arguments, and legal challenges, together with social psychological theories of stereotyping and prejudice.

EO debates circled around two dichotomies: sameness and difference (Bacchi 1990; Liff and Wajcman 1996) and the process–outcomes dilemma (Jewson and Mason 1986). Discussions wrestled with the difficulty of arguing for sameness and difference between the sexes based on a single principle, for they 'are at the same time interdependent and exclusive' (Nentwich 2006: 502). Logically, women cannot argue to be treated the same (as men) in the workplace and request special conditions, to cover pregnancy, for example. Critics revealed the implicit standard of maleness in the sameness argument (Acker 1990, 2006; Liff and Wajcman 1996). MacKinnon's (1987) insight that arguments need to be based on equivalent value, rather than equality, has been largely ignored in workplace applications.

Jewson and Mason (1986) developed probably the best-known EO theories: the liberal and the radical approaches. The liberal approach was based on the principle of fair procedures, emphasizing the means rather than the ends. Liberals conceive of talent and ability as individual attributes and believe that the removal of barriers for the expression of individual talent will enable people to fulfil their potential. Discrimination is a blemish on the operation of a capitalist labour market. Consequently, liberal EO policies aimed to remove unfair distortions to the operation of the labour market by institutional fair procedures. Intervention in the liberal approach was concerned with applying the rules and processes consistently across all people. It led to the bureaucratization of decision-making, with detailed policy and procedures fuelling critic's cries of unnecessary red tape. Outcomes were signalled through the proportion of social identity groups employed: an indication that EO was present. Justice was seen to be done, and was documented.

In contrast, the 'radical' approach was based on the principle of a fair distribution of rewards. Using positive discrimination, differential measures could be applied to different groups, principally through the use of quotas, as seen in some US states, South Africa, and India (Jain, Sloane, and Horwitz 2003). Radical EO sought to intervene directly in workplace practices, and it was 'more concerned with the outcome of the contest rather than with the rules of the game' (Jewson and Mason 1986: 315).

The empirical case studies carried out by Jewson and Mason (1986) showed that while EO concepts were distinct, practice was confused and conflated. The mixed practices arose from intellectual confusion, misunderstandings, and deceptions generated from power struggles among employee and management groups within workplaces. Further empirical work usefully reconstructed these two approaches into the 'short' and 'long' agenda (Cockburn 1991), most organizations opting for short-term returns rather than longer-term workplace changes. This expediency was replicated in later accounts of how MD was being implemented (Thomas and Ely 1996).

With the rise of poststructuralism as an epistemological base, a third perspective emerged, a 'discourse approach' (Jones 2004; Nentwich 2006). Jones and Nentwich argued that 'sameness' and 'difference' was a false dichotomy given the interdependence of the concepts. However, the rejection of identity categories by poststructuralist scholars led to abstract arguments and the links to legislation and policy interventions becoming lost (Liff and Wajcman 1996). In many ways, EO theory had become too nuanced for organizational implementation, with practice becoming fragmented and opportunistic.

The Rise of MD

In the United States, the 'MD' discourse arose from an amalgam of social movements, disparate anti-discrimination legislation, and public policy initiatives (Prasad, Pringle, and Konrad 2006). It is commonly connected to a report funded by US Department of Labor, *Workforce 2000* from independent researchers in the Hudson Institute (Johnston and Packer 1987). The report considered global economic and labour trends, possible future US economic cycles, demographic shifts, and their impact on work, and made six considered recommendations. Subsequent summaries of their findings have emphasized the population demographic trends and implications for the future labour force. As Litvin

(2006: 81) noted in her critique: 'It would be difficult to overstate the influence of the demographic predictions attributed to *Workforce 2000*.' The finding that attracted people's attention was that white males would constitute a small minority (15 per cent) of new entrants to the workforce by 2000. Ironically, attracting less attention was the fact that women (from all ethnicities) would constitute 64 per cent of all new entrants. Alongside this frequently stated statistic of white men, came a realization that the influx of women and minority ethnic groups would constitute a major shift in the available workforce demographic (Johnston and Packer 1987). An MD discourse was quickly taken up, especially by corporations, partly in response to the backlash against US affirmative action (AA) legislation.

Commonly overlooked in the diversity literature is the significance of the US political context of the time. The conservative president Ronald Reagan (1981–89) implemented 'Reaganomics', a version of a neoliberal ideology that took hold in the United Kingdom (through Margaret Thatcher's government) and New Zealand (Kelsey 1995). Neoliberalism is characterized by the rise of the individual as the social unit (Ryan, Ravenswood, and Pringle 2014). Governments sympathetic to neoliberalism deregulated the economy, reduced the tax rate, and reduced government spending. The ideology extended US cultural tenets, but was resisted more in countries with a stronger social welfare structure, such as the United Kingdom and Australia. The rise of a neoliberal ideology grew from the same political roots as liberal EO, and radical approaches were eschewed.

The rise of the DM discourse saw a significant development in the history of workplace equality. It provided an acceptable economic argument for employers, diminishing the value of social or moral arguments. The existing and widely used business jargon such as 'added value', 'competitive advantage', and 'business benefits' provided a conduit to neutralize the more emotive persuasive language associated with EO (Jewson and Mason 1986), transforming the argument for recruiting and managing a more diverse labour force to an ostensibly rational business discourse based on the individual. Cassell (1996: 58) summarized this in Table 2.2.

Table 2.2 Dichotomizing equal opportunity and managing diversity

Equal opportunity	Managing diversity
Externally initiated	Internally initiated
Legally driven	Business-needs driven
Quantitative focus	Qualitative focus
Problem focused	Opportunity focused
Assumes assimilation	Assumes pluralism
Reactive	Proactive
Race, gender, and disability	All differences
Group-based	Individual-based*

* Added by authors.

The shift from EO to MD 'meant a shift from the ethical and legal case to business case arguments' (Tatli 2011: 242). The new argumentation diluted contentious power differences through legitimizing business language.

MD and the Business Case

While there was no agreement on what aspects of workplace diversity counted, diversity was viewed as more inclusive than the named social identity groups targeted by EO initiatives. Diversity consists of visible and non-visible differences, which can include factors such as sex, age, background, race, disability, personality, and work style. An early definition of diversity reflects this broad sweep:

> Diversity includes everyone; it is not something that is defined by race or gender. It extends to age, personal and corporate background, education, function, and personality. It includes lifestyle, sexual preference, geographic origin, tenure with the organization... and management or nonmanagement. (Thomas 1991: 12)

In a stroke, the historical disadvantages carried by some social groups were erased, as 'managing diversity is a comprehensive managerial process for developing an environment that works for all employees' (Thomas 1991: 10), including 'white males' (Thomas 1991: 28). This view is founded on the premise that harnessing these differences will create a productive environment in which everybody feels valued (Kandola and Fullerton 1994). The identified goal was 'to manage diversity in such a way as to get from a diverse work force the same productivity we once got from a homogenous work force': diversity could even 'perhaps' deliver a bonus in performance (Thomas 1990: 112).

The spread of MD ideas was swift and 'by the late 1980s, equal employment opportunity/affirmative action (EEO/AA) specialists were recasting EEO/AA measures as part of DM and touting the competitive advantages offered by these practices' (Kelly and Dobbin 1998: 972). Lorbiecki and Jack (2000: 20–2) describe four overlapping phases in the transmission of these ideas: first, demographic; second, political 'when its inclusive philosophy was seen as an attractive' alternative to '"affirmative action" policies'; and third, economic, 'which warned firms... that if they did not pay immediate attention to managing diversity their organization's performance or image would be put at risk'. In the fourth phase, the literature turned more critical, as efforts to implement diversity programmes met a variety of problems.

The business case for diversity is based on a view of economics which prioritizes the immediate cost factors in an organization ahead of equity or social justice agendas, as the economic business case explicitly 'links investments in organizational diversity initiatives to productivity and diversification' (Litvin 2006: 75). EO and AA recognize historic and ongoing systemic discrimination in a particular society. In contrast, DM is concerned with demographic representation and downplays the existence of systemic discrimination.

An overlooked implication of the business case is that it is persuasive only within a given economic climate. Donaldson (1993) explored effects of the 1990 British recession on EO developments, and concluded that positive initiatives for female staff were cut when cost-cutting became the key business imperative. This means that organizational policies are especially volatile during periods of economic change. By taking morality out of the debate, the rights of marginalized workers are subordinated to economic initiatives. This approach compromises the legitimacy of diversity programmes and the confidence that employees from diverse social groups have in the protection of their rights.

The shift from EO to MD and beyond continues in the scholarship. New terms are coined and their meanings debated. Equality and diversity researchers have added the concept of inclusion, which signifies a shift from the removal of obstacles to full participation, to a perceived sense of organizational belonging. When employees perceive that they are included, they believe they are connected to co-workers, have access to information, and the ability to participate in and influence decision-making (Roberson 2006). Subsequently, in contemporary writings, diversity is often referred to as EDI, equality, diversity, and inclusion (Özbilgin 2009).

PRACTITIONERS' ACTIVITIES VERSUS ACADEMIC RESEARCH

In the early days of MD, practitioners and academics-cum-consultants had a strong impact, with claims based more on advocacy than academic research (Thomas 1990; Copeland 1998). In the United States, the Civil Rights Act of 1964 prohibited discrimination on the basis of race and, by 1967, sex; but ambiguity in compliance led to government organizations and businesses hiring EO and AA specialists to design activities that would 'shield them from litigation' (Kelly and Dobbin 1998: 960). With the 1980s backlash against AA, the changed political environment threatened EO/AA consultants' professional lives: they needed to create a new way of 'thinking and acting about their professional services, namely, managing diversity' (Litvin 2006: 82). Reagan's federal cuts emphasized efficiencies and the 'goal of increasing profits by expanding diversity in the workforce and the customer base' (Kelly and Dobbin 1998: 961–2), building on a business case for AA. By the 1970s, only 20 per cent of organizations had EEO/AA rules (Kelly and Dobbin 1998: 964), but by 1997, 75 per cent of Fortune 500 companies in the United States had DM programmes (Konrad 2003: 5).

What was the MD practice in organizations? Irrespective of the rhetoric there was convergence between EO and MD initiatives. Some scholars asserted that the move to MD did not mark a break with existing equality practices in organizations (Kelly and Dobbin 1998: 978–9), while others (Wilson and Iles 1999: 31) painted MD as 'the new paradigm'. Common practices included commitment in mission statements, action plans, career development for minority group members, diversity education, and training of 'difference' (often lasting less than a day) (Kelly and Dobbin 1998). MD was outcome-driven; it had to be easily translatable into practice and the promise of financial dividends was an important motivator for companies.

While the emphasis of MD is at the individual level, initiatives and training seminars were, ironically, implemented at the group level (Strachan, French, and Burgess 2010a; Tatli 2011). Contemporary ways of MD at work have largely merged with human resources (HR) activities, including sourcing diverse labour through recruiting, selecting, inducting; interacting at work with colleagues and clients at work-related social events; organizing work such as full- and part-time casual, flexible hours, telecommuting; and developing careers through promotion, mentoring, coaching, and networking (O'Leary 2010). Efforts to gather supportive evidence for greater financial returns from a higher performing diversity workforce have been mixed and weak (Tatli 2011).

The emphasis on practice led to a lack of theory in workplace diversity. Academic-consultants initially filled the gap with what could be labelled applied management. Taylor Cox was an early mover with his *Academy of Management Executive* work (Cox and Blake 1991) becoming a classic piece providing practitioners and academics with a six-point rationale for the merits of managing cultural diversity: costs arising from higher absenteeism and turnover from employees from 'minority' identity groups, HR acquisition, marketing alignment between employees and potential customers, creativity from more diverse views, and problem-solving from heterogeneity between group members. Each of these arguments attracted the search for confirmatory research. Cox (1993) developed the field further by bringing together relevant concepts of stereotyping, inter-group conflict, and institutional bias into a model that linked these factors to the individual, group, and the organization as a whole.

Academics also filled the theory void by applying existing theory from social psychology, such as social identity theory (Elmes and Connelley 1997) and concepts of stigmatization and social prejudice (Nkomo and Cox 1996). In another much cited *Harvard Business Review* article, academics Thomas and Ely (1996) argued for a longer-term organizational change perspective, to try to dislodge the implicit assimilation discourse of MD.

The implementation of the business case sought to leverage employee differences to enhance business. Arguably, most attention focused on the rhetoric of good public relations (Tremaine and Sayers 1994), with competitions in most Western countries for being 'the best diversity employer'. For many organizations, the by-line on recruitment advertising reflected the shift from 'we are EO employers' to 'making the most of a diverse workforce' (EEO Trust 1992, cited in Jones, Pringle, and Shepherd 2000: 267). A recent development has been companies signing up to a public intention document. France was an early initiator (Klarsfeld 2010) with the development of *The Diversity Index* in 2004, and was followed by Germany, Austria, and other European countries with in the Europe Union developing the European Union (EU) Charter of Fundamental Rights in 2009 (Danowitz and Claes 2012).

A strand of academic research has connected theory and practice by using research subjects, such as diversity or equality practitioners (Özbilgin and Tatli 2008, 2011), and

HR managers responsible for policy and implementation (Zanoni and Janssens 2003). Collaboration between academics and practitioners has led to a range of diagnostic equality and diversity toolkits (Özbilgin and Tatli 2008; Risberg, Beaugard and Sander 2012). Educational impacts have been curriculum development and the writing of textbooks (e.g. Bell 2008) often using descriptive case studies resulting from company–academic collaborations. A critical base has come through the employment relations route (Kirton and Greene 2005; Strachan, French, and Burgess 2010b), often combined with a feminist critique (Gatrell and Swan 2008; Danowitz and Claes 2012). Academics are advocating for reflexive action on the part of practitioners and actionable knowledge as the outcome of academic research (Özbilgin and Tatli 2011). There is no doubt that linking practitioners and academics will build stronger diversity studies.

Transition from 'the' Diversity Discourse to Many Country Contexts

MD was initially seen as an US affair, with an emphasis on other countries learning lessons from the US experience (Kamenou and Syed 2012). MD is often taken as a universal discourse equally applicable in any country, yet employment is mediated by the unique national culture and legislation. While MD is voluntary and can be implemented in a myriad of ways, it must be practised in conjunction with relevant national legislation, such as anti-discrimination and industrial relations law. In the early diversity literature these links to country-specific legislation (Klarsfeld 2010) were ignored.

The geographic spread of the MD discourse often appeared under the wings of multinational corporation policy, and a discourse of global DM has developed (Özbilgin and Tatli 2008; Mor Barak 2014) with links to international human resource management (HRM) and international business. The tendency to universalize DM through standardized policies from head office was not necessarily well received. Head office HR managers' dictates for all employees to treat each other with 'candor' and 'respect' (Jones, Pringle, and Shepherd 2000: 375) did not translate easily to the New Zealand branch, for example, where it was received with scepticism and derision. It was resisted because it unwittingly imposed a number of US cultural assumptions along with the 'diversity' message. Similarly, many EO practitioners in New Zealand government organizations saw a US-based 'diversity' model as responding to a specifically US history of AA programmes (Jones, Pringle, and Shepherd 2000).

The relationship between global perspectives and implementation in local economies and non-US cultures is a dualism that produces uneasy tensions that are not yet resolved. Context has come to be viewed as more than a backdrop, rather, 'a complex array of power relations, discursive practices and forms of knowledge that need to be analysed' (Ahonen et al. 2014: 264). As examples, a brief description of two English-speaking countries is included. The resistance to the global diversity discourse in New

Zealand was due to special features in the domestic socio-political landscape that differed from the United States. In Australia, the diversity discourse was mapped onto already strong equity legislation in large organizations. Although New Zealand and Australia broadly share the same culture as well as being close geographic neighbours, their equality–diversity discourses have diverged. A closer examination of the country-specific factors helps to provide some understanding of how the importance of country context has fragmented a dominant diversity discourse into many hues (Klarsfeld 2010, 2014).

The New Zealand Context

Debates around biculturalism have emerged as a major factor in the MD discourse in Aotearoa New Zealand (Ryan, Ravenswood, and Pringle 2014). While indigenous Maori constitute 15 per cent of the population, their political place far outweighs their numeric status. Issues of equality and diversity are framed by the ideal of biculturalism, an equal partnership between indigenous Maori and Pakeha (white Anglo colonizers) emanating from the signing of the Treaty of Waitangi in 1840. This cultural mix changed in the late twentieth century, with significant immigration, particularly from Asia, the United Kingdom, and latterly from Eastern Europe and South Africa. The growing presence of multiple ethnicities from non-Anglo roots creates a drive to identify New Zealand as a multicultural nation; however, this denigrates the place of Maori that is enshrined in the bicultural treaty. Like most countries, contradictions exist in the EO legislation that directs the equity actions of the public sector, with Maori designated as just another target group (along with women, ethnic groups, and people with disabilities) alongside the bicultural discourse.

In the 1980s, New Zealand had one of few left-leaning governments in the world to wholeheartedly embrace neoliberal approaches and policies (Ryan, Ravenswood, and Pringle 2014). Consequently, the shift from 'soft socialism' and collective responsibility to 'almost unfettered liberalism' (Humphries and Grice 1995: 23) has shaped policy-level debates on how 'fairness' and 'equity' in employment outcomes can be achieved. New Zealand's approach has been through lenient regulation, with legislation 'light' on references to equality (Ryan, Ravenswood, and Pringle 2014). Only the public sector has legislation (State Sector Act 1988) which mandates EO programmes and the annual reporting of initiatives.

A study of ninety public and private sector organizations was undertaken as the term MD was being introduced (Pringle and Scowcroft 1996). It showed a high level of awareness of MD (81 per cent), understood as the need to value differences between individuals and to manage that difference. Clear positive and negative differences were identified for the effects of ethnicity and gender. Two-thirds of organizations had written policy (mainly about EEO), but a quarter or less had any kind of practices. Initiatives were modest and fragmented, with two-thirds having no initiatives relating to MD. The most striking findings were the low priority given to gender and ethnic issues, ranked nine and ten out of a list of ten HRM priorities. The authors concluded that 'there is a danger that "managing diversity" may become imported rhetoric without local roots' (Pringle and Scowcroft 1996: 40).

Fifteen years later, Houkamau and Boxall (2011) conducted a telephone survey of 500 employees, and their perceptions of EEO and diversity in New Zealand organizations. Diversity was defined as 'how people are different (in terms of gender, ethnicity, age, sexuality and physical ability). DM is like EEO and includes all things that employers do to hire develop and retain workers from diverse groups' (Houkamau and Boxall 2011: 446). As could be expected from the differential legislative environment across sectors, there was wider use of formal diversity policies in the public sector. The strongest finding across two-thirds of the sample was the high level of no and don't know responses. The most common diversity initiatives were support for family-friendly practices, people with disabilities, and practices relating to bullying or sexual harassment (part of employer's workplace responsibilities since 1991). There was a resounding silence on issues of ethnicity, biculturalism, or assistance for new immigrants. The public sector, with binding although weak legislation, had a stronger response than the private sector, reinforcing UK findings (Özbilgin and Tatli 2008) that legislation is pivotal to advance a social equity agenda. Even imperfect MD measures resulted in employees being 'more committed to their organisation, and more satisfied in their jobs and more trusting of their employer' (Houkamau and Boxall 2011: 440), leading the authors to promote an 'employee case' for diversity.

Taken together, these studies demonstrate a lack of progress around knowledge of and presence of diversity initiatives over almost two decades. The absence of HR functions and specialists in smaller-sized organizations tends to create an environment of unmanaged diversity (Jones 2004) that depends on informal personal relationships. Overall, New Zealand empirical studies have found that rhetoric is stronger than implementation.

The Australian Context

Historically, Australia has a legacy of inequality in employment where the Indigenous peoples, certain non-English speaking migrant groups, especially Asian and Pacific Island workers, and women were barred from certain types of employment, and in many cases paid less than white Anglo males. The forces moving Australia towards the goal of equality in employment came largely in the 1960s and 1970s with the influx of women into the labour market, the rise of women's and community groups, plus national obligations as Australia signed up to numerous international conventions supporting equality. By the 1980s, the ideal of equality in employment was enshrined in legislation and industrial decisions. In the twenty-first century, Australia has an extensive array of anti-discrimination legislation which prohibits discrimination in employment on a range of grounds (Strachan, French, and Burgess 2014).

In the 1980s, the federal government recognized that anti-discrimination legislation was insufficient to deliver employment equity and introduced another type of legislation unique to Australia. The focus of the legislation was women. Beginning with the Affirmative Action (Equal Opportunity for Women) Act 1986, continuing through the Equal Opportunity in the Workplace Act 1999, to the Workplace Gender Equality Act 2012, the broad approach has been to promote and improve gender equality (including remuneration) in employment and in the workplace; to support employers to remove barriers to the full and equal participation of women, and notably, to improve the productivity and competitiveness of Australian business through the advancement of gender equality in employment and in the workplace (WGEA Act 2012, section 2A). Organizations with more than 100 employees have to produce regular reports on gender equality, with a focus on organizational performance outcomes. In the public sector, similar legislation covered four groups recognized as suffering past and ongoing disadvantage and discrimination at work. The Commonwealth (Federal) public service goes further, mandating that plans must be in place 'to eliminate employment-related disadvantage' on the basis of membership in one of the four target groups: being an Aboriginal or Torres Strait Islander, gender, race or ethnicity, and physical or mental disability (Public Service and Merit Protection Commission 2001).

The legislation preserves an individual rather than collectivist focus, emphasizing the merit principle as 'competitive individualism is central to the process of appointment and promotion' (Thornton 1990: 246). The Acts have always excluded the use of quotas. The legislation is thus characterized as using a liberal approach with its focus on processes to achieve equality rather than outcomes (Thornton 1990). Studies about organizational policies using the reports submitted and case studies have shown that there is a wide variety in organizational policies and practice, ranging from little engagement to extensive policies (Burgess, Henderson, and Strachan 2010; Strachan, French, and Burgess 2010a). The focus of most of these policies is on flexibility at work and policies related to combining work and family commitments, which serve to maintain women's attachment to work but do less to progress their careers (French and Strachan 2007, 2009). There are gaps in this equity management system as the system does not cover employees in small firms nor those on temporary labour contracts who constitute 24 per cent of the labour force (ABS 2013; Strachan, French, and Burgess 2014: 23).

In the 1990s, the names of organizational programmes began to include the word diversity. In the Australian Public Service, for instance, these programmes are titled 'workplace diversity': 'Workplace diversity involves recognising the value of individual differences and managing them in the workplace.' However, 'the concept of workplace diversity includes the principle of equal employment opportunity (EEO). EEO policies address continued disadvantage experienced by particular groups of people in the workplace, including women, Indigenous Australians, people with disabilities and those who suffer disadvantage on the basis of race or ethnicity. These policies remain an important foundation for workplace diversity policy'. (Public Service and Merit Protection Commission 2001). It is difficult to see the differences between organizational programmes, based on whether they have equity or diversity in their titles. All programmes are underpinned by Australia's equity, anti-discrimination, and industrial relations legislation, so implicitly must include both social justice and business cases.

Within Australia, EO and diversity are imbued with gender issues, while in neighbouring New Zealand the diversity discourse is more about ethnicity and the place(s) of the Indigenous people. It is also significant that diversity in Australia is not an oppositional EO versus diversity discourse. While combining EO and diversity creates tension between these competing approaches (Tatli 2011), it also provides a place to consider power—the cornerstone of an emerging critical diversity studies.

Gender versus the 'Other' Diversity Dimensions

The roots of workplace diversity lay buried deep in the Civil Rights movements of the United States, but '[i]n most countries the gender equality debate prepared the groundwork' for diversity considerations (Özbilgin and Tatli 2008: 30). Questioning by women in the Civil Rights movement led to the rise of the second-wave feminist movement, firstly in the United States and quickly spreading to other Western countries. 'Sisterhood is powerful' became the rallying cry; but the solidarity of the women's cause became quickly undone. The demands and efforts by feminists for a change in social roles and for women's equality (in relation to men) was critiqued by black feminists, firstly in the United States and then elsewhere, and these voices were joined by indigenous women (Pihama and Johnston 1994) and women of colour (Mohanty 1988). 'Other' social identities clamoured for attention, with feminist theory becoming multiple: categorized and described in the now classic chapter by Calas and Smircich (1996) as Liberal feminism, Radical feminism, Socialist feminism, Psychoanalytic feminist, Poststructural feminist, and Transnational feminism. This fragmentation resulted from class analysis and critiques from the major identity groups of women: lesbian, African American, Hispanic and indigenous, women with disabilities. Transnationalism arose when globalization became coupled with critiques from women outside the first-world order (Calas and Smircich 1996).

A gender mainstream discourse (Danowitz and Claes 2012) has dominated in Europe, guided by EU directives. Gender is the normative benchmark for policy and action which has been extended to diversity identities. It has been implemented most strongly by public sector organizations, but has been modified by private sector organizations as the 'mainstreaming of diversity' (Danowitz and Claes 2012). The legal, cultural, and social context of each EU country shapes the ways in which companies approach DM (Danowitz and Claes 2012). Recognition of, and attention to, the needs of people with disabilities has seen recent advances in the United Kingdom and in EU, with other countries, such as Australia and New Zealand, following the trend.

In addition, a separatist approach has developed in New Zealand as contemporary Maori claims against historical injustice have resulted in Tribunal judgements which have provided substantial payments and the reclamation Maori *mana* (status/

dignity) in their struggle to actualize the bicultural partnership (Smith and Reid 2000). Reparations and reallocation of land stewardship have given Maori (some) control and have led to separate Maori education options (from kindergarten to postgraduate studies), and government support for independent Maori health providers.

One result of MD coming from the United States was its association with demographic markers (Konrad, Prasad, and Pringle 2006) which overlooked heterogeneity within social identity groups (Konrad 2003) and left the diversity discourse open to critiques of essentialism. As an example, the Gay Rights movement has given growing legitimacy to diverse (LGBTI: lesbian, gay, bisexual, transgender/sexual, intersex) sexual identities. In many Western countries, the legality of same-sex relations first appeared through anti-discrimination legislation that was then extended into human rights legislation and, in a growing number of countries, marriage equality (Ryan, Ravenswood, and Pringle 2014). The recognition of non-heterosexual identities is a result of long and hard-fought grassroots campaigns, often with a local flavour. For example, in New Zealand, the public sector union have adopted the acronym GLITTFAB, which signifies 'gay, lesbian, intersex, transgender, *takatapui* (Maori), *fa'afafine* (Samoan), and bisexual identities' (Jones et al. 2012), in an attempt to break through the tyranny of the sex dichotomy.

There has been a strong tendency for diversity studies to focus on separate demographic markers and to omit intersectional analyses (Healy 2009). Intersectionality is the view that different identity axes interact and produce interrelated systems of oppression, inequality, and injustice (Louvrier 2013), and has become an area of scholarship in its own right. While intersectionality first arose within critical race studies, it expanded within women's studies (special issue *European Journal of Women's Studies* 2006) and feminist sociology, and is spreading rapidly to other disciplines (special issue *Gender in Management* 2014). This has clear implications for diversity studies, which has emphasized social identity markers such as gender and race. Joan Acker (1990) has worked over decades to bring intersectional analyses to workplaces through her concept of an inequality regime (Acker 2006) which spotlights gender, race, and class inequality. Her scholarship primarily focuses within organizations (the meso level) and other scholars have called for this type of analysis to be expanded into the macro and micro layers of the relations model (Syed and Özbilgin 2009).While this research is in the realm of future developments, there is a constructive movement towards a place of Gender + (Verloo 2013): gender plus other identities.

Quantitative versus Qualitative Methodological Approaches

In the development of diversity studies, the discipline within which scholars were trained influenced their methodologies. As early academic research on DM came from

United States, it tended to emerge from a positivist paradigm, where hypotheses were developed and diverse identities were conceptualized as additional independent variables of interest (Milliken and Martins 1996). There was also positivist research investigating which organizational interventions were more effective, a stand-out example being careful empirical work studying the links between specific policy that was identity-conscious or identity-blind and measurable organizational outcomes (Konrad and Linnehan 1995; French 2001), such as the proportion of women at various management levels.

The acceptance of the quantitative focus in business studies research more broadly gave some legitimacy for research in areas that may not have been easily accepted. For example, Ragins, Cornwall, and Miller (2003) led research into the perception and attitudes of gay and lesbian employees, using time-honoured regression analysis; they found that the same or opposite sex of their supervisor had a significant effect on perceived discrimination. While quantitative analyses produce results that may clearly define group effects, the influences of the external environment and within group experience by individuals is more difficult to study and theorize.

Another major impact on (critical) diversity studies came from sociology scholars who significantly theorized identity as socially constructed. The notion of 'doing gender' (Butler 1999) has gained great traction in contemporary gendering of organizations studies (Calas, Smircich, and Holvino 2014), assisted by poststructural theory and queer theory. This scholarship was accompanied by the rise of qualitative research methodologies, such as ethnomethodology (West and Zimmerman 1987).

Qualitative enquiry began in the 1970s with the interpretive and critical paradigms (Grant and Giddings 2002; Denzin and Lincoln 2005) central to developments. Sensitivity to cross-group research owes much to feminist research methodology (Olesen 2005)—giving participants space for their own voices; using open-ended questions; paying attention to decreasing power differences between the researcher and the researched (Pringle, Wolfgramm, and Henry 2010). Reflexivity on the researcher's role and influence is especially salient when researching across different groups (Kamenou and Syed 2012).

It was not until research from Europe and the United Kingdom on DM (e.g. Zanoni and Janssens 2003) was published that the scholarly community gained deeper understandings of the experiences and reflections from individual managers and EO/diversity officers charged with organizational change. Links between meso-level organizational strategy and policy with the micro politics of everyday experiences are made possible by methodologies such as narrative enquiry and critical discourse analysis (Zanoni and Janssens 2003; Jones and Stablein 2006). Qualitative methodologies include 'epistemological and ethical criticisms of traditional social science' and business research (Denzin and Lincoln 2005: x), making it possible for research to be undertaken that is linked to an explicit social justice agenda. Hereupon, there appears recognizable synergy with diversity studies. The emergence of qualitative methodologies that connect research to political implications for social change provide the potential for diversity research to be executed within both the social justice and business agendas.

Another difficulty in diversity research has been that of gaining access to businesses (Louvrier 2013) willing to reveal their practices around inequality. Partly as a response, research has sprung up analysing secondary data sources such as annual EO reports (French and Strachan 2007, 2009) and corporate websites (Singh and Point 2006). Intention statements provide more easily accessible data for researchers. When data sources, such as corporation's codes of conduct (CoCs), are combined with clear theoretical positioning, such as queer theory, then insightful arguments can be made (Bendl, Fleischmann, and Hofmann 2009).

Academic scholarship on workplace diversity has been criticized for being atheoretical (Pringle 2009). Diversity research has been extended by using theoretical perspectives from other, usually sociological-based, disciplines. For example, researchers have applied queer theory (Bendl, Fleischmann, and Hofmann 2009) and Bourdieu's theory of social practice to diversity studies (Özbilgin and Tatli 2011; Tatli 2011). A sign of the mature development of a field, rather being practice-focused, is to provide clearer exposition of the theoretical bases of the research.

Future Transformations: From Dualisms to Diverse yet Inclusive Diversity Studies

As MD emerged, critique swiftly followed from EO scholars concerned at the narrow economic rationale accompanied by a severing of the link between morality, justice, and employee identity group membership. Although Cassell and Biswas identified a 'more critical approach to managing diversity' in 2000 (p. 271) it has been a long process, including mutterings of discontent beyond the United States (Jones, Pringle, and Shepherd 2000), combined with exhortations to place power analysis at the centre of diversity studies (Prasad, Pringle, and Konrad 2006). Arguments around the place of corporate social responsibility (CSR) has also put new pressures on diversity discourse, subsuming it into a broader discourse of socially responsible DM (Syed and Kramar 2009).

Underpinning all these attempts is the relatively recent acknowledgement (historically) that discrimination, disadvantage, and inequality within labour markets and organizations should be 'corrected' in some way, through the equality of opportunity, or recognition of workplace diversity. It is not surprising that the resultant legislation, policies, and practices are complex and, at times, contested. Academic literature has tried to tease out the variety of meanings and make sense of these complex issues and complicated responses, as well as assess whether they have succeeded in reaching their goals. This chapter is no different. We have tried to make certain issues clearer through using the concept of dualisms in order to foreground specific issues.

Dichotomous thinking has dogged EO and diversity studies. Although we list the dualisms in Table 2.1 and Table 2.2 as oppositional, we argue in this chapter that they are more fruitfully conceptualized as complementary. Combining the dualistic poles is

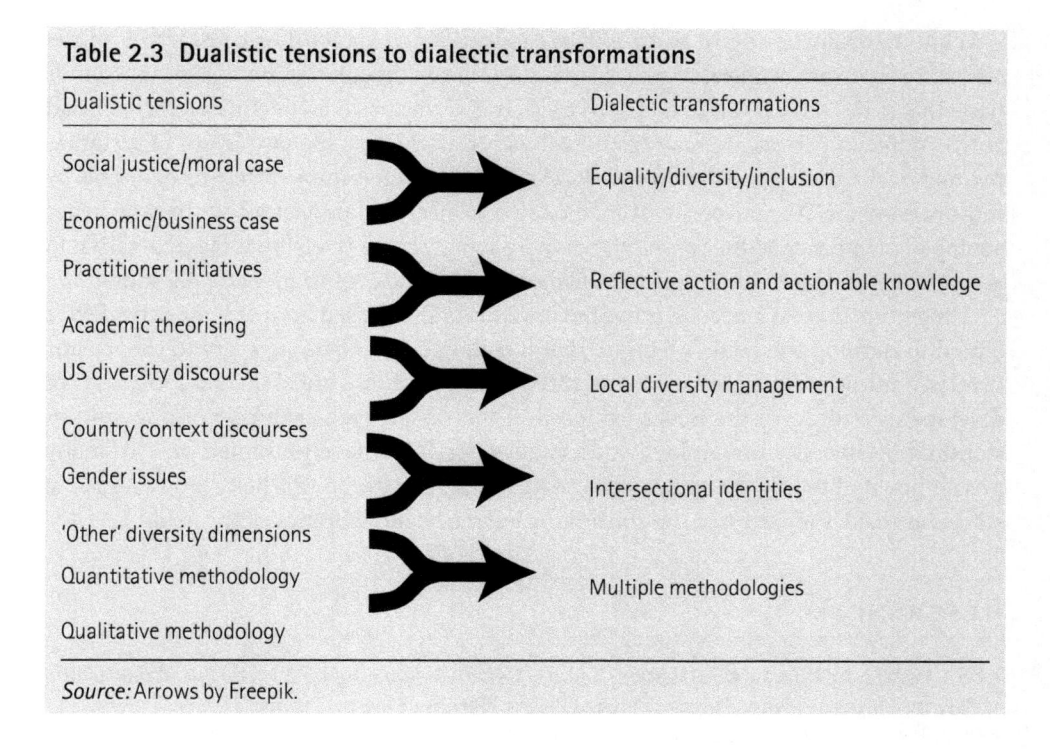

Table 2.3 Dualistic tensions to dialectic transformations

Dualistic tensions	Dialectic transformations
Social justice/moral case	Equality/diversity/inclusion
Economic/business case	
Practitioner initiatives	Reflective action and actionable knowledge
Academic theorising	
US diversity discourse	Local diversity management
Country context discourses	
Gender issues	Intersectional identities
'Other' diversity dimensions	
Quantitative methodology	Multiple methodologies
Qualitative methodology	

Source: Arrows by Freepik.

indicated somewhat optimistically in Table 2.3 as 'dialectic transformations', for we look forward to building on contributions made from each of the strands. Diversity research can build beyond a dichotomous emphasis of either social justice or the business case to scholarship and practice that considers equality/diversity/inclusion. The perception of inclusion is an outcome for individuals within an organization and society.

Subsequent to the proliferation and dominance of the US diversity discourse, researchers in other countries have brought attention to the crucial influences from socio-political and historical contexts. International research has continued to demonstrate how the influences in each country determine the power positioning of specific diversity groups and subsequent organizational initiatives. Each country context provides a dynamic geopolitical space influenced by global shifts which impact differently in each nation, thus creating a glocal DM. Diversity studies is an applied research area with a need for reciprocity between practitioners and academics. Practitioners will reflect on their practice and build understanding in conjunction with the academic development of theory by scholars who have a view to organizational application.

Demographic identities have expanded beyond the early concentration on gender and race as we recognize that more groups have suffered discrimination and truncated opportunities. This evolution of understanding has led to a stronger emphasis on intra-group variations. Concomitantly, the rise of the intersectionality research paradigm has brought a recognition that we all have and enact multiple identities, bringing an understanding of complexities that will grow in future.

While the distinction between quantitative and qualitative approaches to research is imprecise and somewhat artificial, these approaches indicate different epistemological assumptions that some scholars refer to as positivist versus postpositivist methodologies (Prasad 2005). While imperfect, we have continued with Cassell's terminology (1996) of quantitative and qualitative approaches to signal a distinction which is immediately recognizable by most researchers. As non-positivist methodologies grow and proliferate, we may be better equipped to understand the complexity of more sophisticated diversity studies that take into account intersecting identities, glocal influences, theory, and organizational applications.

Altogether, there is a need to move beyond the dualities used here as a heuristic device aimed to develop the field. We argue that it is illogical to envisage a 'grand theory' for diversity studies; rather, we see a 'fractured future' (Denzin and Lincoln 2005: 1115) of diverse diversities. All the issues explored in this chapter are examples of how understanding of diversity in employment has developed. We have presented one (of many possibilities) of telling the story of the changes and debates in this field. However these stories are told, they attest to the continuing currency and vibrancy of the field.

References

ABS (Australian Bureau of Statistics) (2013). *Employee Earnings, Benefits and Trade Union Membership, Australia, August 2013*. Catalogue Number 6310.0, Canberra.
Acker, J. (1990). Hierarchies, jobs, bodies: a theory of gendered organizations. *Gender & Society*, 4: 139–58.
Acker, J. (2006). Inequality regimes: gender, class, and race in organizations. *Gender & Society*, 20: 441–64.
Ahonen, P., Tienari, J., Meriläinen, S., and Pullen A. (2014). Hidden contexts and invisible power relations: a Foucaldian reading of diversity research. *Human Relations*, 67: 263–86.
Bacchi, C. (1990). *Same Difference: Feminism and Sexual Difference*. Sydney: Allen & Unwin.
Bell, M. (2008). *Diversity in Organizations*, 2nd edn. Mason, OH: South-Western Cengage Learning.
Bendl, R., Fleischmann, A., and Hofmann, R. (2009). Queer theory and diversity management: reading codes of conduct form a queer perceptive. *Journal of Management and Organization*, 15: 625–38.
Burgess, J., Henderson, L., and Strachan, G. (2010). Women in male-dominated industries: organisations do it differently. In G. Strachan, E. French, and J. Burgess (eds.), *Managing Diversity in Australia: Theory and Practice*. Sydney: McGraw Hill, 107–19.
Butler, J. (1999). *Gender Trouble*. New York: Routledge.
Calas, M. and Smircich, L. (1996). From 'the woman's' point of view: feminist approaches to organization studies. In S. Clegg, C. Hardy, and W. Nord (eds.), *Handbook of Organization Studies*. London: Sage, 218–58.
Calas, M., Smircich, L., and Holvino, E. (2014). Theorizing gender-and-organizations: Changing times...theories? In S. Kumra, R. Simpson, and R. Burke (eds.), *The Oxford Handbook of Gender in Organizations*. Oxford: Oxford University Press, 17–53.
Carr, E. H. (1987). *What is History?* 2nd edn. London: Penguin.
Cassell, C. (1996). A fatal attraction? Strategic HRM and the business case for women's progression at work'. *Personnel Review*, 25: 51–66.

Cassell, C. and Biswas, R. (2000). Managing diversity in the new millennium. *Personnel Review*, 29: 271.

Cockburn, C. (1991). *In the Way of Women: Men's Resistance to Sex Equality in Organisations*. London: Macmillan.

Copeland, L. (1998). Valuing diversity part 1: making the most of cultural differences in the workplace'. *Personnel*, 65: 52–60.

Cox, T. (1993). *Cultural Diversity in Organization: Theory, Research and Practice*. San Francisco, CA: Berrett-Koehler.

Cox, T. and Blake, S. (1991). Managing cultural diversity: implications for organizational competitiveness. *Academy of Management Executive*, 5: 45–56.

Danowitz, M. A. and Claes, M. (2012). Diversity in Europe: its development and contours. In M. A. Danowitz, E. Hanappi-Egger, and H. Mensi-Klarbach (eds.), *Diversity in Organizations: Concepts and Practices*. Basingstoke: Palgrave Macmillan, 33–63.

Denzin, N. K. and Lincoln, Y. S. (2005). Preface. In .K. Denzin and Y. S. Lincoln (eds.), *The Sage Handbook of Qualitative Research*, 3rd edn. London: Sage, ix–xix.

Dickens, L. (1999). Beyond the business case: a three-pronged approach to equality action. *Human Resource Management Journal*, 9: 9–19.

Donaldson, L. (1993). The recession: a barrier to equal opportunities? *Equal Opportunities Review*, 50: 11–36.

Elmes, M. and Connelley, D. (1997). Dreams of diversity and the realities of intergroup relations in organizations. In P. Pushkala, A. J. Mills, M. Elmes, and A. Prasad (eds.), *Managing the Organizational Melting Pot: Dilemmas of Workplace Diversity*. Thousand Oaks, CA: Sage, 148–67.

French, E. (2001). Approaches to equity management and their relationship to women in management. *British Journal of Management*, 12(4): 267–85.

French, E. and Strachan, G. (2007). Equal employment opportunity and women in the finance and insurance industry. *Asia Pacific Journal of Human Resources*, 45: 314–32.

French, E. and Strachan, G. (2009). Evaluating equal employment opportunity and its impact on the increased participation of men and women in the transport industry in Australia. *Transportation Research Part A: Policy and Practice*, 43: 78–89.

Gatrell, C. and Swan, E. (2008). *Gender and Diversity in Management: A Concise Introduction*. London: Sage.

Grant, B. M. and Giddings, L. S. (2002). Making sense of methodologies: a paradigm framework for the novice researcher. *Contemporary Nursing*, 13: 10–28.

Healy, G. (2009). Reflections on researching inequalities and intersectionality. In M. Özbilgin (ed.), *Equality, Diversity and Inclusion at Work*. Cheltenham: Edward Elgar, 88–100.

Houkamau, C. and Boxall, P. (2011). The incidence and impacts of diversity management: a survey of New Zealand employees. *Asia Pacific Journal of Human Resources*, 49: 440–60.

Humphries, M. and Grice, S. (1995). Equal employment opportunity and the management of diversity: a global discourse of assimilation? *Journal of Organizational Change*, 8: 17–32.

Jain, H., Sloane, P., and Horwitz, F. (eds.) (2003). *Employment Equity and Affirmative Action: An International Comparison*. Armonk, NY: M. E. Sharpe.

Jewson, N. and Mason, D. (1986). The theory and practice of equal opportunities policies: liberal and radical approaches. *The Sociological Review*, 34: 307–34.

Johnston, W. B. and Packer, A. H. (1987). *Workforce 2000: Work and Workers for a 21st Century*. Indianapolis, IN: Hudson Institute.

Jones, D. (2004). Screwing diversity out of the workers? Reading diversity. *Journal of Organizational Change*, 17: 281–91.

Jones, D. and Stablein, R. (2006). Diversity as resistance and recuperation: critical theory, post-structuralist perspective and workplace diversity. In A. Konrad, P. Prasad, and J. K. Pringle (eds.), *Handbook of Workplace Diversity*. London: Sage, 145–66.

Jones, D., Pringle, J. K., and Shepherd, D. (2000). 'Managing diversity' meets Aotearoa/New Zealand. *Personnel Review*, 29: 364–80.

Jones, D., Windelov, K. Daniel, A., Drew, M., and Randall, J. (2012). Out at work: sexual orientation and gender minorities in the New Zealand workplace. Proceedings of *HRINZ research forum*, Auckland.

Kamenou, N. and Syed, J. (2012). Diversity management. In J. Syed and R. Kramar (eds.), *Human Resource Management in a Global Context: A Critical Approach*. Basingstoke: Palgrave Macmillan, 75–97.

Kandola, R. and Fullerton, J. (1994). *Managing the Mosaic: Diversity in Action*. London: Institute for Personnel and Development.

Kelly, E. and Dobbin, F. (1998). How affirmative action became diversity management: employer response to antidiscrimination law 1961 to 1996. *American Behavorial Scientist*, 41: 960–84.

Kelsey, J. (1995). *The New Zealand Experiment: A World Model for Structural Adjustment?* Auckland: Auckland University Press.

Kennedy-Dubourdieu, E. (ed.) (2006). *Race and Inequality: World Perspectives on Affirmative Action*. Aldershot: Ashgate.

Kirton, G. and Greene, A.-M. (2005). *The Dynamics of Managing Diversity: A Critical Approach*, 2nd edn. Oxford: Elsevier.

Klarsfeld, A. (2010). *International Handbook on Diversity Management at Work: Country Perspectives on Diversity and Equal Treatment*. Cheltenham: Edward Elgar.

Klarsfeld, A., Booysen, L. A., Ng, E., Roper, I., and Tatli, A. (eds.) (2014). *International Handbook on Diversity Management at Work: Country Perspectives on Diversity and Equal Treatment*, vol. 2. Cheltenham: Edward Elgar.

Konrad, A. (2003). Defining the domain of workplace diversity scholarship. *Group Management and Organization*, 28: 4–17.

Konrad, A. and Linnehan, F. (1995). Formalized HRM structures: coordinating equal opportunities or concealing organizational practices. *Academy of Management Journal*, 38: 787–820.

Konrad, A., Prasad, P., and Pringle, J. K. (eds.) (2006). *The Handbook of Workplace Diversity*. London: Sage.

Liff, S. (1997). Two routes to managing diversity: individual differences or social group characteristics. *Employee Relations*, 19: 11–26.

Liff, S. and Wajcman, J. (1996). Sameness and 'difference' revisited: which way forward for equal opportunities initiatives? *Journal of Management Studies*, 33: 79–94.

Lillevik, W., Combs, G. M., and Wyrick, C. (2010). Managing diversity in the USA: the evolution of the inclusion in the workplace. In A. Klarsfeld (ed.), *International Handbook of Diversity Management at Work: Country Perspectives on Diversity and Equal Treatment*. Cheltenham: Edward Elgar.

Litvin, D. (2006). Diversity: making space for a better case. In A. Konrad, P. Prasad, and J. K. Pringle (eds.), *Handbook of Workplace Diversity*. London: Sage, 187–209.

Lorbiecki, A. and Jack, G. (2000). Critical turns in the evolution of diversity management. *British Journal of Management*, 11 (Special Issue): S17–S31.

Louvrier, J. (2013). *Diversity, Difference and Diversity Management: A Contextual and Interview Study of Managers and Ethnic Minority Employees in Finland and France.* No. 259 Helsinki: Hanken School of Economics.

MacKinnon, C. (1987). *Feminism Unmodified: Discourses on Life and Law.* Cambridge, MA: Harvard University Press.

Mandelbaum, M. (1967). *The Problem of Historical Knowledge: An Answer to Relativism.* Revised edn. New York: Harper Torchbooks.

Milliken, F. and Martins L. (1996). Searching for common threads: understanding the multiple effects of diversity in organizational groups. *Academy of Management Review,* 21: 402–33.

Mohanty, C. (1988). Under Western eyes: feminist scholarship and colonial discourses. *Feminist Review,* Autumn: 61–88.

Mor Barak, M. E. (2014). *Managing Diversity: Towards a Globally Inclusive Workplace,* 3rd edn. Thousand Oaks, CA: Sage.

Nentwich, J. C. (2006). Changing gender: the discursive construction of equal opportunities. *Gender, Work and Organization,* 13: 499–521.

Nkomo, S. and Cox, T. (1996). Diverse identities in organizations. In S. Clegg, C. Hardy, and W. Nord (eds.), *Handbook of Organization Studies.* London: Sage, 338–56.

O'Leary, J. (2010). Making managing diversity visible: a phenomenographic approach. University of Queensland, Brisbane, PhD thesis.

Olesen, V. (2005). Early millennial feminist qualitative research: challenges and contours. In N. Denzin and Y. Lincoln (eds.), *The Sage Handbook of Qualitative Research,* 3rd edn. London: Sage, 235–78.

Özbilgin, M. (2009). *Equality, Diversity and Inclusion at Work.* Cheltenham: Edward Elgar.

Özbilgin, M. and Tatli, A. (2008). *Global Diversity Management: An Evidence Based Approach.* London: Palgrave Macmillan.

Özbilgin, M. and Tatli, A., (2011). Mapping out the field of equality and diversity: rise of individualism and voluntarism. *Human Relations,* 64: 1229–53.

Pihama, L. and Johnston, P. M. G. (1994). The marginalisation of Maori women. *Hecate,* 20: 83–97.

Prasad, P. (2005). *Crafting Qualitative Research: Working in the Postpositivist Traditions.* Armonk, NY: M. E. Sharpe Inc.

Prasad, P., Pringle, J. K., and Konrad, A. (2006). Examining the contours of workplace diversity: concepts, contexts and challenges. In A. Konrad, P. Prasad, and J. K. Pringle (eds.), *Handbook of Workplace Diversity.* London: Sage, 1–22.

Pringle, J. K. (2009). Positioning workplace diversity: critical aspects for theory. In M. Özbilgin (ed.), *Equality, Diversity and Inclusion at Work.* Cheltenham: Edward Elgar, 75–87.

Pringle, J. K. and Scowcroft, J. (1996). Managing diversity: meaning and practice in New Zealand organisations. *Asia Pacific Journal of Human Resources,* 34: 28–43.

Pringle, J. K., Wolfgramm, R., and Henry, E. (2010). Extending cross-ethnic research partnerships: researching with respect. In S. Katila, S. Meriläinen, and J. Tienari (eds.), *Making Inclusion Work: Experiences from Academics Across the World.* Cheltenham: Edward Elgar, 214–43.

Public Service and Merit Protection Commission (2001). Archive: Guidelines on workplace diversity. <http://www.apsc.gov.au/publications-and-media/archive/publications-archive/workplace-diversity-guidelines> (accessed 23 September 2014).

Ragins, B., Cornwall, J., and Miller, J. (2003). Heterosexism in the workplace: do race and gender matter? *Group and Organization Management,* 28: 45–74.

Risberg, A. and Søderberg, A.-M. (2008). Translating a management concept: diversity management in Denmark. *Gender in Management: An International Journal*, 23: 426–41.

Risberg, A., Beaugard, A., and Sander, G. (2012). Organizational implementation: Diversity practices and tools. In M. A. Danowitz, E. Hanappi-Egger, and H. Mensi-Klarbach (eds.), *Diversity in Organizations: Concepts and Practices*. Basingstoke: Palgrave Macmillan, 185–237.

Roberson, Q. (2006). Disentangling the meaning of diversity and inclusion in organizations. *Group and Organization Management*, 31: 212–36.

Ryan, I., Ravenswood, K., and Pringle, J. K. (2014). Equality and diversity in Aotearoa (New Zealand). In A. Klarsfeld, L. A. Booysen, E. Ng, I. Roper, and A.Tatli (eds.), *International Handbook on Diversity Management at Work: Country Perspectives on Diversity and Equal Treatment*, 2nd edn. Cheltenham: Edward Elgar, 175–94.

Singh, V. and Point, S. (2006). Representation of gender and diversity in diversity statements on European company websites. *Journal of Business Ethics*, 68: 363–79.

Smith, L. T. and Reid, P. (2000). Maori research development, Kaupapa Maori principles and practices: Literature review, <http://www.kaupapamaori.com/assets/Maori_research.pdf> (accessed 11 November 2014).

Strachan, G., Burgess, J., and Sullivan, A. (2004). Affirmative action or managing diversity: what is the future of equal opportunity policies in organizations? *Women in Management Review*, 19: 196–204.

Strachan, G., French, E., and Burgess, J. (2010a). Equity and diversity within organisations: putting policy into practice. In G. Strachan, E. French, and J. Burgess (eds.), *Managing Diversity in Australia: Theory and Practice*. Sydney: McGraw Hill, 57–74.

Strachan, G., French, E., and Burgess, J. (2010b). *Managing Diversity in Australia: Theory and Practice*. Sydney: McGraw Hill.

Strachan, G., French, E., and Burgess, J. (2014). Equal access to the opportunities available? Equity and diversity laws and policies in Australia. In A. Klarsfeld, L. Booysen, E. Ng, I. Roper, and A. Tatli (eds.), *International Handbook on Equality and Diversity Management at Work: Country Perspectives on Diversity and Equal Treatment*, 2nd edn. Cheltenham: Edward Elgar, 13–34.

Syed, J. and Kramar, R. (2009). Socially responsible diversity management. *Journal of Management & Organisation*, 15: 639–51.

Syed, J. and Özbilgin, M. (2009). A relational framework for international transfer of diversity management practices. *International Journal of Human Resource Management*, 20: 2435–53.

Tatli, A. (2011). A multi-layered exploration of the diversity management field: diversity discourses, practices and practitioners in the UK. *British Journal of Management*, 22: 238–53.

Thomas, D. and Ely, R. (1996). Making differences matter: a new paradigm for managing diversity. *Harvard Business Review*, 74: 79–90.

Thomas, R. R. (1990). From affirmative action to affirming diversity. *Harvard Business Review*, March–April: 107–17.

Thomas, R. R. (1991). *Beyond Race and Gender: Unleashing the Power of Your Total Workforce by Managing Diversity*. New York: AMACOM.

Thornton, M. (1990). *The Liberal Promise: Anti-Discrimination Legislation in Australia*. Sydney: Oxford University Press.

Tremaine, M. and Sayers, J. (1994). *The Vision and the Reality: Equal Employment Opportunities in the New Zealand Workplace*. Palmerston North: Dunmore Press.

West, C. and Zimmerman, D. (1987). Doing gender. *Gender & Society*, 1: 125–51.

Wilson, E. and Iles, P. (1999). Managing diversity: an employment and service delivery challenge. *International Journal of Public Sector Management*, 12: 27–48.

UN (United Nations) (2014). The ten principles. <http://www.unglobalcompact.org/About TheGC/TheTenPrinciples/index.html> (accessed 19 August 2014).

Verloo, M. (2013). Intersectionality: from theory to policy and practice, presentation at *Interrogating intersectionality: What's missing and what's next?* 29 June–1 July, Simmons College, Boston, MA.

Zanoni, P. and Janssens, M. (2003). Deconstructing difference: the rhetoric of human resource managers' diversity discourses. *Organization Studies*, 25: 55–74.

Zanoni, P., Janssens, M., Benschop, Y., and Nkomo, S. (2010). Unpacking diversity, grasping inequality: rethinking difference through critical perspectives. *Organization*, 17: 9–29.

CHAPTER 3

THEORIES OF DIFFERENCE, DIVERSITY, AND INTERSECTIONALITY

What Do They Bring to Diversity Management?

JEFF HEARN AND JONNA LOUVRIER

Introduction

Diversity, diversity management (DM), and intersectionality are clearly interconnected: they intersect. The question is how. This chapter overviews these concepts and related researches, and seeks to contribute to understandings of interdisciplinary, relational, and intersectional approaches to diversity in organizations. It examines the relationship of diversity and DM to various theorizations of intersectionality, specifically the relevance of theories of intersectionality for understanding diversity.

The notion of 'diversity' is now widely in use in organizational, management, and analytical discourses, sometimes critically, often less so. Initially, academic interest in diversity and DM was somewhat limited and atheoretical (Prasad and Mills 1997), but nowadays diversity attracts numerous scholars studying the phenomenon from various theoretical perspectives. There is an annual conference devoted to equality, diversity and inclusion, a dedicated journal with the same name, and many academic titles on diversity have been published in recent years. Diversity is the focus of other institutional developments, for example, the Gender and Diversity Division at the Academy of Management, the Standing Working Group on Gender and Diversity at the European Group for Organizational Studies (EGOS), and the Strategic Interest Group on Gender, Race and Diversity in Organisations at the European Academy of Management (EURAM). Diversity has also entered academic institutions, as diversity chairs have been created in business schools and universities (see, for example, Bendl, Hanappi-Egger, and Hofmann 2010). At the same time, the concept of intersectionality

(Davis 1981; Crenshaw 1989, 1991; Collins 1990; Meekosha and Pettman 1991; McCall 2005; Meekosha 2006) has been much far less developed in studies of organizations, perhaps because it, in some ways, challenges any simple approach to, or prescription of, promoting 'diversity'.

The chapter is organized in three main parts. First, the broad arenas of difference, diversity, and DM are introduced, as they have become established in organization and management studies. Second, it considers the increasing complexity that can be engaged with through the notion of intersectionality. The third section considers how a broad view of different kinds of intersectionalities widens further understandings of diversity/ies and DM in organizations and management. These various formulations include external intersectionalities (formation, location, and form of organizations), internal intersectionalities (internal structuring and processes of organizations), and diversity and DM seen within intersectional contexts.

DIFFERENCE, DIVERSITY, AND DIVERSITY MANAGEMENT

Difference

DM has been said to be all about differences, identities (Nkomo and Stewart 2006), and categories (Anthias 2013). Indeed, different assumptions on difference and different forms of social categorization often shape the way not only diversity and DM, but also intersectionality, are understood. So, is difference something that 'we' have, prior to the interaction with 'our' environment? And who exactly is this 'we'? Where does our identity, or identities, come from? How do differences rest upon, or how are they invoked or formed by, immediate social and broader societal categories, beyond the organizational boundaries?

There are numerous answers to these questions. In a classic 1987 article, Barrett (1987: 30) discusses:

> [T]hree particular uses of the idea of difference. These are: (I) a sense of difference effectively to register diversity of situation and experience between women; (II) difference as an understanding of the positional rather than absolute character of meaning, particularly as developed in Derridean terms; and (III) modern psychoanalytic accounts of sexual difference. These three uses of the concept of difference seem to me to be quite distinct, although I should acknowledge here that the third category is difficult to place in relation to the other two, and involves significant contradictions and disagreements.

However, in general terms it is possible, as an initial statement and cutting across these three usages, to distinguish between and contrast two main and broad approaches: essentialist and constructionist. The essentialist perspective sees differences as inner characteristics of individuals. Differences and identities are rather stable and fixed, and stem from biology, from socialization into a group, or from more fixed structural categorization and positioning. The identity of a person may consist of several dimensions of difference, but these are, or tend to be, coherent. The individual is expected to be (relatively) unified and consistent in his or her differences. As differences here are seen as internal to the person, differences precede action. Therefore, the difference of a person can be used as a prediction of his or her behaviour, or at least as an explanation of it (Burr 1995). For instance, being a woman is often related to an expectation of being caring (or related to being a woman in some other way), and the act of taking care of an elderly person is seen as stemming from the gender identity of a woman, rather than a process where the gender identity is formed and performed (Butler 1990).

From a constructionist position, differences look quite different. Differences are not seen as internal to the individual but as constructed in interaction with others and the wider social environment. Difference is produced, rather than existing by itself. The production of difference takes place in the social context, where discourses shape the way that people are categorized as different and/or similar. There, where the essentialist approach sees differences as somehow neutral matters of fact, the constructionist approach sees differences as intimately related to the power relationships existing in society. Differences are not innocent, but reflect and perpetuate, or, on the contrary, resist and challenge, the given social order. From this latter perspective, an individual does not have a unified identity; instead, each individual has plural and fragmented identities, and may change identity from one situation to another (Weedon 1987, 1996). There are numerous ways in which individuals can identify; however, not all positions are available to everyone. Discourses of class, gender, or ethnicity may tend to limit identities to specific groups or dimensions. A constructionist approach does not deny that there may exist real differences between people. A Finn may speak better Finnish than a non-Finn, or vice versa. But the meaning of language skills, and the way that the language skill positions people, is not pre-given and obvious. Other differences could rather be focused on, and other patterns of similarity and difference could be put forward.

How do essentialist and constructionist approaches affect how DM is to be understood? If one follows essentialist assumptions, differences exist prior to the organization, and are at base unrelated to it. From a constructionist perspective, differences are (also) constructed in the organization, for instance, in the organizing of the work. These starting points give quite different bases for DM. Where an essentialist approach to DM manages fixed, stable, and pre-existing differences, a constructionist approach acknowledges that DM is also a site where differences are produced.

Having said this, there are many different versions of constructionism. According to some constructionist approaches, such as those using positioning theory (Davies and Harré 1990), individuals are free to choose the discourses that best suit them, and can be regarded more as strategic users of discourses (on different approaches to constructionism, see Burr 1995). Other approaches, such as poststructuralist approaches, hold that discourses define the ways in which individuals can come to understand themselves, and also delimit the range of positions that are available at a given moment or context (Weedon 1987, 1996). Individuals are never totally free from discourses, but always produced by them. Researchers can position themselves in an intermediate position in-between these two positions, emphasizing discursive agency or discursive determination (Alvesson and Kärreman 2000; Bergström and Knights 2006), and see that individuals understand themselves in ways that stem from interactions between their agency and existing structures and discourses. Such a tension between the free choice of individuals and the force of structures has a long history within the social sciences, as seen in the agency-structure debate (Weber 1968; Giddens 1984; Archer 1996).

Diversity and Diversity Management

The term 'diversity' has been part of organizational and management literature for more than twenty years. Defining the field of diversity is, however, still not easy (Nkomo and Stewart 2006). Indeed, the field is characterized by ambiguities, contradictions, and unclarities (Cox 1994). These stem, on the one hand, from the term 'diversity' itself, which lacks a binary opposition, and, as with any concept, is ascribed meanings only in context. On the other hand, even though diversity research has become more theoretically rigorous, fuzziness remain around uses of such terms as discourses, rhetorics, and practices in relation to DM.

Different overviews of DM have brought a richness and variety to the field. Nkomo and Stewart (2006) suggest a broad categorization into dominant or mainstream, and critical, perspectives. The difference between these two relies on the way social identities are understood—as essential properties of individuals or as socially constructed—and in the belief versus scepticism of whether DM will lead to significant changes in organizations. Bairoh (2007) suggests a broad threefold categorization of literatures into practitioner/consultant, mainstream, and critical. Her inclusion of consultant literature is a strength, as practitioner-focused diversity material is abundant, and indeed has been described as an industry (Prasad and Mills 1997). Practitioner literature, which could be said to vary in terms of its criticality, is also important in forming diversity practices in organizational and management contexts.

One of the more comprehensive categorizations has been that of Prasad, Pringle, and Konrad (2006), building on Burrell and Morgan's (1979) paradigms, and distinguishing positivist and non-positivist work. Within these two groups, they further distinguish work with a low versus high power awareness. In non-positivist work, a distinction is further made between research that considers identities as fixed versus fluid. This is a useful and detailed classification which, in contrast to Nkomo and Stewart's (2006) and Bairoh's (2007) classifications, sheds light on the great variety within both dominant and critical streams. Thus, it is clear that DM, like diversity, is indeed diverse. So how do these debates connect or not with those on intersectionality?

Intersectionality/ies: Some Genealogies

From even this brief introductory overview, the notions of *diversity* and *DM*, as used in organization and management studies, can be seen as having clear connections with that of *intersectionality*, even if all three concepts have rather different histories, located within different traditions, as we discuss further in this section. The term 'intersectionality', and to some extent the broader range of kindred concepts noted below in this section, have become very widely used in recent years (Davis 2008), and there are now several excellent broad reviews of the state of knowledge on intersectionality (for example, *European Journal of Women's Studies* 2006; Lutz et al. 2011; Cho, Crenshaw, and McCall 2013). However, we stress here that the broad notion of intersectionality, or more precisely intersectional social relations, is not new. This is despite the fact that, in various countries, regions, and epistemic communities, it has sometimes been asserted as some kind of 'new' concept or perspective, as when the concept is rediscovered or picked up to address some particular societal configuration or problematic, such as (im)migration or the recognition of multiple and complex identities.

Approaches to intersectionality range from those based in *one* dominant social division, such as class, with other divisions 'added on'; to more double or triple power framings of intersectionality (for example, class–gender–race); to more multiple models (including age, disability, sexuality), to multifactor models, to engagement with intra-categorical and inter-categorical boundary constructions; to anti-categorical approaches (McCall 2005).

Intersectional perspectives, and the complex social phenomena to which they refer, go under many different names and labels, including interrelations of oppressions, multiple oppressions, multiple social divisions, mutual constitution, multiple differences, hybridities, simultaneity, multiple oppressions, multiculturalisms, multiplicities, postcolonialities, multiple intersecting social inequalities (Walby 2007), and indeed 'diversity', amongst many more. Some researchers use the concept of intersectionality explicitly (Crenshaw 1989, 1991: Lutz et al. 2011); others discuss intersections under other conceptual categorizations, such as differential consciousness (Sandoval 2000), and inappropriate/d otherness (Minh-ha 1986/7; Haraway 1992). This partly reflects different disciplinary traditions, partly different societal contexts of those knowledges, and partly, it might seem, lack of awareness or evasion of other earlier societal contexts or traditions of knowledge.

Intersectionality can be understood, albeit very differently, within the full range of epistemologies. It can also be seen as methodology, ontology, and as combinations of methodology, ontology, and epistemology, including problematizing the separation of those framings. Intersectionality can be directed mainly at the level of identity, or, more generally, towards meso and macro structures and processes, whether organizational, societal, or transnational, or indeed may problematize those very distinctions.

Of special interest is in what times, places, and situations do intersectionalities, and indeed which intersectionalities, *appear* most evident. Historically, intersectionality can be said to have always been there, whether seen or not. 'Friends, Romans and countrymen' can easily be analysed intersectionally. In one sense, the concept of intersectionality can be understood as a reworking of some very persistent themes of modernist social theory and specifically modernist sociology, such as the place of individuals and groups in complex multidimensional societies. Indeed, such sociological theorizing and empirical work has fed directly into intersectional thinking. The traditions of the 'founding fathers' of sociology—Marx, Weber, and Durkheim—prioritized: class, class fractions and factions; multiple power relations; and industrialization and interdependence of divisions of labour under organic solidarity, respectively. These different traditions all feed into intersectional thinking. Most clearly, intersectional thinking is pervasive in the action sociology of Weber, and his writing on the intersections of class, status, party.

Intersectionality was, at least implicitly, spoken of in black feminism and the anti-slavery movement of the nineteenth century, in terms of the intersections of race and gender and class—and probably long before then too. In 1851 Sojourner Truth (Isabella Baumfree) (1797–1883) delivered the famous 'Ain't I a Woman?' speech at the Women's Convention, Akron, Ohio (<http://www.fordham.edu/halsall/mod/sojtruth-woman.asp>), which can be understood as an impassioned plea for intersectional thought and politics:

> Well, children, where there is so much racket there must be something out of kilter. I think that 'twixt the negroes of the South and the women at the North, all talking about rights, the white men will be in a fix pretty soon. But what's all this here talking about? That man over there says that women need to be helped into carriages, and lifted over ditches, and to have the best place everywhere. Nobody ever helps me into carriages, or over mud-puddles, or gives me any best place! And ain't I a woman? Look at me! Look at my arm! I have ploughed and planted, and gathered into barns, and no man could head me! And ain't I a woman? I could work as much and eat as much as a man—when I could get it—and bear the lash as well! And ain't I a woman? I have borne thirteen children, and seen most all sold off to slavery, and when I cried out with my mother's grief, none but Jesus heard me! And ain't I a woman?

Moreover, the concept of intersectionality has a rich feminist and anti-racist history (see, for example, Crenshaw 1989, 1991; Brah and Phoenix 2004; McCall 2005), and is sometimes seen as one of the major contributions of feminist thought. In the elaborations that followed so-called second-wave feminism of the 1960s (Rowbotham, Segal, and Wainwright 1979), it was reaffirmed, though often under different names, especially in calling attention to the intersections of gender, 'race' (or ethnicity), and class... the 'big three' of class–gender–'race'. Intersectional thinking is central to debates and analyses in the politics and political movements of race, racism and anti-racism, anti-imperialism, (neo-)Marxist feminism, (neo-)Marxist anti-racism, migration, and coalition politics (Carastathis 2013). The Combahee River Collective, a black feminist lesbian collective active from 1974 to 1980 in Boston, Massachusetts, is perhaps best known for developing the collective statement, on interlocking oppressions, racism and identity:

> As women, particularly [...] privileged white women, began to acquire class power without divesting of their internalized sexism, divisions between women intensified. When women of color critiqued the racism within the society as a whole and called attention to the ways that racism had shaped and informed feminist theory and practice, many white women simply turned their backs on the vision of sisterhood, closing their minds and hearts. And that was equally true when it came to the issue of classism among women. (hooks 2000: 16–17)

In 1981 Angela Davis published *Women, Race and Class* (also see Anthias and Yuval-Davis 1983); in 1984 bell hooks wrote on black women and black men as potential allies in *Feminist Theory: From Margin to Center*; and in the same year Mary O'Brien drew attention to the dangers of commatization (O'Brien 1984), critiquing lists of oppressions, separated by commas. And in 1989 Fiona Williams brought such ideas to the centre of critical debate on United Kingdom social policy, adding age, disability, and sexuality to make the 'big six'. More recently, more elaborate multidimensional analytical schemes have been developed:

> One of the most comprehensive attempts to include additional axes of social divisions is that of Helma Lutz—although in her formulation they are not axes but rather 'basic dualisms'; this is problematic and she herself considers it a 'challenge to consider the spaces in-between' (Lutz, 2002: 13). Her list includes the following 14 'lines of difference': gender; sexuality; 'race'/skin-colour; ethnicity; nation/state; class; culture; ability; age; sedentariness/origin; wealth; North–South; religion; stage of social development. Lutz, however, sees this list as 'by no means complete; other categories have to be added or re-defined' (Lutz 2002: 13). Indeed, the list is potentially boundless. (Yuval-Davis 2006: 202)

Such a list at times is framed slightly differently, for example, in terms of 'able-bodiedness' rather than 'ability', and 'property ownership' rather than 'wealth' (also see Lutz 2001, 2014). Recently, there have also been extensions of intersectional thinking into broader environmental issues, such as animal studies (Twine 2010) and climate change (Kaijser and Kronsell 2014). These approaches have further implications for widening debate on diversity, DM, and organizational analysis.

Probably the most cited scholar on intersectionality is the black feminist law professor, Kimberlé Williams Crenshaw. She codified the concept, arguing that you cannot understand black women's oppression and discrimination by considering only gender or only race/racialization: the two are intertwined, including when making legal claims. Accordingly, she developed the metaphor of crossroads, that is, intersections of roads:

> [A]n analogy to traffic in an intersection, coming and going in all four directions. Discrimination, like traffic through an intersection, may flow in one direction, and

it may flow in another. If an accident happens in an intersection, it can be caused by cars traveling from any number of directions and, sometimes, from all of them.

Similarly, if a Black woman is harmed because she is in an intersection, her injury could result from sex discrimination or race discrimination [...] But it is not always easy to reconstruct an accident: Sometimes the skid marks and the injuries simply indicate that they occurred simultaneously, frustrating efforts to determine which driver caused the harm. (Crenshaw 1989: 149)

Many other black feminists, for example, Patricia Hill Collins and Audre Lorde, have developed this field further. Debates on intersectionality can also be related to other debates around gender, class, and race. For example, the 1980s were a period of revision of the concept of patriarchy, and identification of multiple arenas, sites, structures, and historical forms of patriarchy that may operate in uneven development or contradiction. Walby (1986, 1990) specified these patriarchal structures: capitalist work, the family, the state, violence, sexuality, and culture; while Hearn (1987, 1992) specified reproduction of labour power, procreation, regeneration/degeneration, violence, sexuality, ideology. More recently, the concept of transnational patriarchies (transpatriarchies) (Hearn 2009) has been used.

A related set of theories around men and masculinities developed from the late 1970s, alongside feminist auto-critiques of the concept of patriarchy. While much intersectionalities debate has been directed towards recognition of differences, yet commonalities, among women, and their intersections, questions of difference and intersection, apply equally to men (Kimmel and Messner 1989/2009; Hearn and Collinson 2006). Masculinities operate as intersections of gender and other social divisions (Connell 1995): hegemonic masculinity as intersections of gender, class, ethnicity, and sexuality, legitimating patriarchy; subordinated masculinity as intersections of gender and sexuality, for example, gay masculinities; marginalized masculinity as intersections of class, ethnicity, and racialization, for example, black masculinities. Notions of plural, multiple, or composite masculinities, such as black straight masculinity or white gay masculinities (Hearn and Collinson 1994; Aboim 2010), are widely used. Jørgen Elm Larsen and Ann-Dorte Christensen (2008: 56) argue '(t)he concept of intersectionality complements the concept of hegemonic masculinities, in that it stresses the interaction between gender, class and other differentiating categories, and at the same time articulates different power structures and their reciprocating construction'.

Other inspirations for considering intersectionality have come from critical and feminist disability movements and studies, notably the work of Helen Meekosha (2006) and Ingunn Moser (2004) on interferences, and from studies on gender, sexuality, and other intersections in and around work organizations (Hearn and Parkin 1993). On the latter point, it is very difficult to study gender and sexuality in and around organizations without being aware of organizational position, hierarchy, work/labour, status, class, occupation, profession, and management. These inevitably intersect with gender and sexuality and much more.

Intersectionality also figures increasingly as a focus in policy development and policy studies (Verloo 2013). This is not least through the work of the United Nations (UN) and the

European Union (EU), including the EU Anti-Discrimination Directives, even if they only name six grounds for legal action on illegal discrimination—gender, ethnicity, disability, age, religion/belief, sexual orientation—but not class, which is excluded on the grounds it is not 'justicable' inequality (Walby, Armstrong, and Strid 2012). Intersectionality is open to many uses and abuses (Lewis 2013; Pringle 2006; also see Lewis 2015).

Broader geographical, geopolitical, transnational, and translocal understandings of intersectionality can also be developed. At a global and glocal level, the development and impact of postcolonialism in theory and practice has been a great stimulus to intersectional thinking, as, for example, in the work of Grewal and Kaplan (2002), *Scattered Hegemonies*, McClintock (2003), *Imperial Leather*, and Chandra Talpade Mohanty (2003), *Feminism without Borders* (see Lewis 2013). Patil (2013) has recently brought together debates on transnational feminism. Having said all this, there are certainly some neglected intersectionalities to be acknowledged, or at least some social arenas where intersectionality theory might be developed more fully. These include studies of ageing; disability and lived embodiment; virtuality; and transnationality (Hearn 2011). Such neglected intersectionalities are also a way of challenging the gender hegemony of men.

Intersections of Categories and Differences

It is clear that the term, intersectionality, has been used in many different ways—between relatively fixed social categories, in the making of such categories, in their mutual constitution, in transcending categories. In this respect, McCall's (2005) clarification is especially useful, distinguishing approaches that are:

- inter-categorical: adopting existing analytical, relatively fixed categories, with the focus on relations between them;
- intra-categorical: using more provisional categories; acknowledges stable, even durable, relationships that social categories represent at given point in time; also maintains critical stance towards categories; focus on particular social groups at neglected points of intersection—'people whose identity crosses the boundaries of traditionally constructed groups';
- anti-categorical: categories not basic; deconstruction of categories.

In broad terms this framework moves from more modernist inter-categorical conceptions of intersectionality to more ambiguous intra-categorical conceptions, to postmodernist/poststructuralist anti-categorical conceptions thereof.[1] These distinctions by

---

[1] Anthias (2013) has recently set out another framework for understanding social categories, and thus, by implication, difference, in terms of different levels of abstraction: as social ontologies, in terms of conceptions on how different realms of world are being organized; as providing criteria based on which people can be categorized; and as concrete relations. She locates intersectionality at the level of concrete relations, seen as embedded in both intersecting categorizations (and thus differences) that are distinct between themselves, as well as wider societal processes.

McCall mirror, to some extent, earlier discussions of more essentialist and more constructionist approaches to difference. The relationship between different differences, both substantive and conceptual, is thus a further aspect that differentiates more essentialist and more constructionist approaches to difference. More essentialist approaches to differences tend to highlight differences between groups and treat groups as relatively internally homogeneous. Constructionist approaches tend to focus more on variations within groups: not all women are alike, not all ethnic minorities are alike.

There are always several dimensions of difference that interact simultaneously and position people in different ways (Holvino 2010). A person may, for instance, be a woman, but she may also be white, educated, and heterosexual. These could be dimensions of difference that are of relevance in a certain professional context, while in the domestic context other dimensions could be more relevant. A DM programme based on an underlying assumption that differences are discrete and groups are internally homogeneous is likely to develop very differently from one taking an intersectional approach. DM has been criticized for treating differences as add-on categories, where individuals have difficulty fitting into specific groups, or can belong to all of the groups at the same time (Litvin 1997). An intersectional approach to DM might suggest building on the simultaneity of difference(s), seeking to avoid constructing generalizations about groups such as women or ethnic minorities (Holvino 2010). While non-intersectional programmes might treat women as a homogeneous group and promote gender equality by taking only gender into account in staffing, an intersectional diversity programme would highlight not only gender but also intersections with age, ethnicity, and other differences and divisions.

Essentialist and constructionist approaches to difference also give different importance to context in relation to the meanings of difference. The role of language can be seen as one aspect of context, but is also an important question of its own. As the essentialist view sees differences exist within the individual, the related assumption is that we do not need language in order for the difference to exist. Differences pre-exist language, and language is only seen as a medium we use to express the differences. The constructionist perspective radically differs from this point. According to the constructionist view, differences are produced through language. Language provides individuals with a way to structure their reality, and as there are a variety of languages available, reality can be structured in many different ways. In this way, simple distinctions between essentialist and constructionist approaches to difference can be problematized, with both existing and framed within languages.

Moreover, as different languages have different repertoires of words, different languages allow for different constructions of reality. Not all languages have, for instance, exactly corresponding words for 'diversity'. What in English is called 'diversity' is in French called '*diversité*', in Finnish it is expressed by the term '*monimuotoisuus*' (having many forms), and in Swedish by '*mångfald*' (multilayeredness). Even though the definitions of these terms in the different languages to some extent overlap, some differences can also be noted. While in English and French diversity is composed of many units and it is the variety of the units together that creates diversity, in Finnish and Swedish the terms also allow one to presuppose an ensemble having many sides or characteristics. Thus, in Finnish and Swedish it is possible to fragment a specific unit into many diverse parts on the basis of several criteria. However, it is not only the existence or non-existence of a particular word that shapes the way reality is perceived in a given language. Languages cannot be detached from their cultural contexts, and words within different languages have different social and historical backgrounds.

An example of a deconstructive linguistic approach is Walgenbach and colleagues' (2007) concept of *interdependence*. According to this, social categories are seen as dependent on and determined by other categorizations that are themselves interdependent. In this vein, Lorey (2008: 5) summarizes how:

> Hornscheidt investigates how people are organized into different categories through forms of naming, and thus how categories impose a hierarchical order [Hornscheidt 2007: 77]. In this perspective, categorizations are conceptualized not just as linguistic constructions with materializing effects that extend as far as structural discrimination. Categories are at the same time a 'structuring factor of knowledge' [Hornscheidt 2007: 73].

Thus not only intersectionality is a contested approach and concept, but the very coordinates that generally underpin the concept are also subject to deconstruction (cf. McCall 2005).

The Implications of Intersectionality for Diversity and Diversity Management

What are the implications of these broad theorizations of intersectionality for organizations and management? In this third main section we address two main implications: external intersectionalizing of organizations and management, and their internal intersectionalizing; and the placing of studies of diversity and DM in an intersectional context.

External and Internal Intersectionalizing of Organizations and Management

In many cases, these questions of diversity and intersectionality are illuminated by attention to historical and transnational issues, both contextualizing and embedded in practice. There is a need to bring together, in analysis, the internal intersectionalizing of organizations and the external intersectionalizing of organizations through transnationalizations. This is even the case, indeed perhaps even more so, when matters of diversity, intersectionality, and transnationalizations remain unnamed and unmarked. A move beyond national, societal cultural contexts has been prompted by global(ized) and transnational researches over recent years, and the intersectional effects of globalization. Transnationalizations constitute *external intersectionalizations* of organizations, as in such transnational issues as: environmental questions, 'Third World' development, war and armed conflict, finance capitalism, and information and communication technologies. Obvious candidates for intersectional gendered analysis are multinational enterprises (MNEs), and their organization and management within transnationalizations (Hearn and Louvrier 2011).

Intersectional transnationalizations form the business environment of MNEs, reconstructing their internal structures and processes. Concentrations of capital are increasing, with gendered and intersectional forms and effects. At the same time, MNEs are themselves vulnerable to huge risks, ranging from terrorism to financial crises and computer hacking and viruses. MNEs operate at the intersections of global, national, regional, and local traditions, and strategic international management, and are thus subject to contradictory intersectional gendered pressures. There is immense scope for far greater attention to such issues in the intersectional gendering of transnational business-to-business activity, alliances, supply chains, financial dependencies, and other inter-corporate relations—formal or informal, and often involving those at high levels.

These transnational processes can be translated into various forms of intersectional variation (Hearn, Metcalfe, and Piekkari 2012). At the *institutional* level, MNE headquarters may find it difficult to align less regulated forms of employment in developing regions, such as Eastern Europe, Asia, and Latin America, with their internally standardized practices. A second form of variation is *functional*, for example, in how MNEs have used changes in trade and financial agreements to move their production and services around the globe. Much production, such as electronics, toys, and sports goods, and business services, such as call centres, has become part of 'global assembly lines'. MNEs manage hidden production relationships in less developed countries through subcontracting networks employing low-paid female workers. Yet, in such blue-collar work contexts the business case for diversity is rarely made. Intersectional gendered production networks are evolving as a result of major changes in international political economy, themselves intersectionally gendered. In responding to and shaping these conditions, MNEs have used different strategies, in effect intersectional gendered strategies, in strategic management. In addition, there are intersections in *local cultural and religious* patterns with global restructuring. Recruitment and appointment processes can sometimes be contradictory processes, with local units sometimes resisting expatriate recruitment or standardization in methods, whatever corporate policies may say. Research here can be assisted by attention to transnational cultural change and various forms of deterritorialization and hybridity (Ong 1999; Hearn 2004, 2015).

DM is one means of managing external intersectionalizing within the internal intersectionalizing of corporations. In terms of internal intersections, corporations and many other organizations are themselves contexts of, and arenas and sites for, gendered intersectional relations—hence the need for the specific recognition of the intersectional gendered corporation (Hearn and Louvrier 2011). Most organizations can be seen as doubly intersectionally gendered: first, public domains and the organizations within them are dominantly valued, intersectionally gendered, over the private domains; and, second, within organizations their structures and processes are themselves intersectionally gendered, perhaps most obviously in certain men's usual domination through management and other mechanisms, including DM. In the case of MNEs and large business corporations, organizations can be seen as triply gendered, with the global and transnational dimension adding further intersectional gendered dominations, across space, place, cultures, interorganizational power relations, and virtual technologies.

Diversity and Diversity Management within Intersectional Contexts

As the concept of DM has become a global trend and has 'travelled' or has been 'translated' from the United States to other parts of the Western world (Boxenbaum 2006; Calás, Holgersson, and Smircich 2009), the importance of diverse contexts for understanding DM has been underlined (Prasad, Pringle, and Konrad 2006; Pringle 2009). In recent years much progress has been made in the area, for instance, in the form of an edited sixteen-country book on DM, diversity, and equality work (Klarsfeld 2010).

Empirical studies acknowledging the importance of national context have examined several different aspects of context. However, most studies have tended to treat context as a neutral given fact, focused on one or a few of the following aspects: national demographics (Glastra et al. 2000; Jones, Pringle, and Shepherd 2000; Risberg and Søderberg 2008; Omanovic 2009; Bendl, Hanappi-Egger, and Hofmann 2010); the institutional context of legislation and policies related to equality and anti-discrimination (Klarsfeld 2009; Bender, Klarsfeld, and Laufer 2010); labour market structures related to minority groups (de los Reyes 2000; Glastra et al. 2000; Omanovic 2009; Cornet and Zanoni 2010), minority groups' histories (Jones, Pringle, and Shepherd 2000; Booysen and Nkomo 2010); or public policies at the time diversity is recognized in specific national contexts (Glastra et al. 2000; Omanovic 2009). Less attention has been paid to how different aspects of diverse national contexts intersect with and give meaning to diversity and DM.

Both similarities and differences can be found between different contexts. National context intersects with the formulation of diversity: in particular, which differences are given voice, and which are silenced. In some contexts, such as in Sweden and the Netherlands (de los Reyes 2000; Glastra et al. 2000), diversity is mostly attached to ethnicity and immigrant status; in others, age is specifically focused on, such as in Austria (along with ethnicity) (Bendl, Hanappi-Egger, and Hofmann 2010), or gender, such as in Italy (Murgia and Poggio 2010). Diversity initiatives have been implemented locally, with differences in the extent to which diversity has attracted organizational and public authorities' attention in different countries (see contributions in Klarsfeld 2010).

Differences between diversity dimensions, approaches to diversity, and implementation of initiatives are also dependent on differences between organizations (Janssens and Zanoni 2005), units within organizations (Kamp and Hagedorn-Rasmussen 2004), and different parts of a given country (Cornet and Zanoni 2010).

When DM is adapted to new national contexts it is constructed in ways to correspond to the existing practices of naming and non-naming. It can be seen as an empty category, filled by, and used for, the purposes of corporate management. Indeed, DM is related to different dimensions of difference in different countries. Management ideology crosses national borders. DM can be seen as formulated in the crossing forces of international management ideology, reinforced and spread by large international companies, and national conceptions of 'us' and 'them'. It can thus be a way of managing internal intersectionality.

Not problematizing national context, and focusing on one aspect of context at a time, thus ignoring the intersectionality of context, significantly delimits the way in which diversity and DM are regarded in research. Kalonaityte (2006) has shown, by studying diversity in Sweden within the context of postcoloniality, how discourses on diversity illuminate the construction of Swedishness and non-Swedishness. Diversity studies should indeed bring context into the analysis and be open to how discourses of diversity construct knowledge about more than difference. Studying the meanings of diversity, difference, and DM in Finland and France, Louvrier (2013) treated the socio-historical contexts of Finland and France as discursive constructions, and examined how knowledge about context was key to the construction of diversity and DM. She showed that meanings of DM are constructed in discursive fields relating diversity to understandings of society, organization, the individual, and the contextual nature of differences. The complexities of the meanings of these are again difficult to understand without a thorough understanding of the specificities of context.

Overall, discursive approaches to categorization, difference, diversity, and intersectionality have highlighted the important assumptions that DM practices build upon, but may have also increased uncertainty, perhaps even confusion, within the field: Namely, what is the relationship between DM and discourse? Is DM a discourse? Or is diversity best seen as rhetoric, metaphor, or theory (Kersten 2000; Kirby and Harter 2003; Zanoni and Janssens 2003)? Does there exist a discourse of DM, or several such discourses (Sinclair 2006; Tomlinson and Schwabenland 2010)? Is there a managerial discourse of diversity, contrasting to some other type of discourse of diversity? Or is diversity a model (Barmes and Ashtiany 2003) or a platform for debating identity (Holvino and Kamp 2009)? All these approaches are viable, and all have contributed to critical analysis of the functioning of diversity in different contexts. Interestingly, the findings are often very similar in terms of how diversity is understood, regardless of the defining of diversity as discourse, metaphor, or something else.

The field of critical diversity research would, however, benefit from more rigorous usage of terms and consistent usage within specific studies. The most common diversity discourses discussed in the literature are the business discourse and the equality discourse (see also Chapter 12, this volume). These discourses have long been seen as separate oppositional discourses, identified through their different underlying arguments for diversity. Recently, the separation of these two discourses has, however, been questioned, and it has been suggested that they may indeed intertwine (Tomlinson and Schwabenland 2010). Diversity discourse should be looked at more broadly, not just through arguments for or against diversity. Discursive studies should be open to identifying the many knowledges diversity discourse produces, which certainly go well beyond the business versus equality arguments for diversity.

Concluding Remarks

In addressing DM, the weakness of the term 'diversity' is that in some senses it can mean almost anything to anyone; it can indeed function as an empty, often an ideological, signifier. The concept of intersectionality is also open to many interpretations, ranging from categorical to anti-categorical. Arguably, intersectionality complicates and to an extent demystifies the ideological power of diversity and DM.

While stressing the importance and contribution of thinking on intersectionalities, we do not seek to ignore or downplay *single* dimensions of difference. This is especially so, as across different geographical spaces signifiers of difference have different meanings, understandings, and legitimacies (Metcalfe 2010). A related challenge in research on diversity and intersectionality is to maintain a focus on difference without neglecting structured asymmetrical structural power relations (Hearn and Parkin 1993, 2001; Hearn and Collinson 2006; Holvino 2010). In discussions of such matters of power, men and masculinities are generally left unspoken; they are, in that sense, an 'absent presence', even despite (perhaps because of) their dominance, especially at the highest levels, and within management policy, practice, and discourse. In many organizations, particular groups of men are the most powerful actors. The (transnational) capitalist class is in practice very much a male (transnational) capitalist class (see Hearn, Blagojević, and Harrison 2013).

Finally, it is important to note that intersectionality is a very dynamic field, both empirically and theoretically, somewhat in contrast to more static conceptualizations of diversity and DM. Indeed, even broader understandings of intersectionality can be developed to locate intersections and diversity/ies, for example, multiple varieties and forms of intersections themselves. One example is presented as the policy position of the Routledge Advances in Feminist Studies and Intersectionality book series (<http://www.routledge.com/books/series/raifsai/>), as 'committed to the development of new feminist and profeminist perspectives on changing gender relations, with special attention to:

- Intersections between gender and power differentials based on age, class, dis/abilities, ethnicity, nationality, racialization, sexuality, violence, and other social divisions.
- Intersections of societal dimensions and processes of continuity and change: culture, economy, generativity, polity, sexuality, science and technology.
- Embodiment: Intersections of discourse and materiality, and of sex and gender.

- Transdisciplinarity: intersections of humanities, social sciences, medical, technical and natural sciences.
- Intersections of different branches of feminist theorizing, including: historical materialist feminisms, postcolonial and anti-racist feminisms, radical feminisms, sexual difference feminisms, queerfeminisms, cyberfeminisms, posthuman feminisms, critical studies on men and masculinities.
- A critical analysis of the travelling of ideas, theories and concepts.
- A politics of location, reflexivity and transnational contextualizing that reflects... diversity and transnational power relations.'

Each of these different developments and elaborations of intersectionality, as well as the intersections between them, has further and broader implications still for how diversity and DM are to be understood in theory and practice as multifaceted phenomena. Seen thus, diversity and DM are themselves open to multiple, diverse, intersectional, and often transnational understandings, rather than being a specific and separately identifiable field, with a single purpose or function.

Acknowledgements

We are grateful to the editors for their constructive comments on earlier drafts of this chapter.

References

Aboim, S. (2010). *Plural Masculinities*. Farnham: Ashgate.
Alvesson, M. and Kärreman, D. (2000). Varieties of discourse: on the study of organizations through discourse analysis. *Human Relations*, 53(9): 1125–49.
Anthias, F. (2013). Intersectional what? Social divisions, intersectionality and levels of analysis. *Ethnicities*, 13(1): 3–19.
Anthias, F. and Yuval-Davis, N. (1983). Contextualizing feminism: gender, ethnic and class divisions. *Feminist Review*, 15: 62–75.
Archer, M. (1996). *Culture and Agency: The Place of Culture in Social Theory*. Cambridge: Cambridge University Press.
Bairoh, S. (2007). *Current Debates on Classifying Diversity Management: Review and Proposal*, Working Papers 534, Swedish School of Economics and Business Administration, Helsinki.
Barmes, L. and Ashtiany, S. (2003). The diversity approach to achieving equality: potential and pitfalls. *The Industrial Law Journal*, 32(4): 274–96.
Barrett, M. (1987). The concept of 'difference'. *Feminist Review*, 26: 29–41.
Bender, A.-F., Klarsfeld, A., and Laufer, J. (2010). Equality and diversity in the French context. In A. Klarsfeld (ed.), *International Handbook on Diversity Management at Work: Country Perspectives on Diversity and Equal Treatment*. Cheltenham: Edward Elgar, 83–108.

Bendl, R., Hanappi-Egger, E., and Hofmann, R. (2010). Austrian perspectives on diversity management and equal treatment: regulations, debates, practices and trends. In A. Klarsfeld (ed.), *International Handbook on Diversity Management at Work: Country Perspectives on Diversity and Equal Treatment*. Cheltenham: Edward Elgar, 27–44.

Bergström, O. and Knights, D. (2006). Organizational discourse and subjectivity: subjectification during processes of recruitment. *Human Relations*, 59(3): 351–77.

Booysen, L. A. E. and Nkomo, S. M. (2010). Employment equity and diversity management in South Africa. In A. Klarsfeld (ed.), *International Handbook on Diversity Management at Work: Country Perspectives on Diversity and Equal Treatment*. Cheltenham: Edward Elgar, 218–43.

Boxenbaum, E. (2006). Lost in translation: the making of Danish diversity management. *The American Behavioral Scientist*, 49(7): 939–48.

Brah, A. and Phoenix, A. (2004). Ain't I a woman? revisiting intersectionality, *Journal of International Women Studies*, 5(3): 75–86.

Burr, V. (1995). *An Introduction to Social Constructionism*. London: Routledge.

Burrell, G. and Morgan, G. (1979). *Sociological Paradigms and Organisational Analysis: Elements of the Sociology of Corporate Life*. London: Heinemann.

Butler, J. (1990). *Gender Trouble: Feminism and the Subversion of Identity*. New York: Routledge.

Calás, M. B., Holgersson, C., and Smircich, L. (2009). 'Diversity management'? Translation? Travel? Editorial, *Scandinavian Journal of Management*, 25: 349–51.

Carastathis, A. (2013). Identity categories as potential coalitions. *Signs*, 38(4): 941–65.

Cho, S., Crenshaw, K. W., and McCall, L. (2013). Toward a field of intersectionality studies: theory, applications, and praxis. *Signs*, 38(4): 785–810.

Collins, P. H. (1990). *Black Feminist Thought: Knowledge, Consciousness, and the Politics of Empowerment*. Boston, MA: Unwin Hyman.

Connell, R. (1995). *Masculinities*. Cambridge: Polity.

Cornet, A. and Zanoni, P. (2010). Diversity Management in Belgium. In A. Klarsfeld (ed.), *International Handbook on Diversity Management at Work: Country Perspectives on Diversity and Equal Treatment*. Cheltenham: Edward Elgar, 45–67.

Cox, T. (1994). A comment on the language of diversity. *Organization*, 1(1): 51–8.

Crenshaw, K. (1989). Demarginalizing the intersection of race and sex: a black feminist critique of antidiscrimination doctrine, feminist theory and antiracist politics. *University of Chicago Legal Forum*, 4: 139–67.

Crenshaw, K. (1991). Mapping the margins: intersectionality, identity politics, and violence against women of color. *Stanford Law Review*, 43(6): 1241–99.

Davies, B. and Harré, R. (1990). Positioning: the discursive production of selves. *Journal for the Theory of Social Behaviour*, 20(1): 43–63.

Davis, A. Y. (1981). *Women, Race and Class*. New York: Random House.

Davis, K. (2008). Intersectionality as buzzword: a sociology of science perspective on what makes a feminist theory successful. *Feminist Theory*, 9(1): 67–85.

De los Reyes, P. (2000). Diversity at work: paradoxes, possibilities and problems in the Swedish discourse on diversity. *Economic and Industrial Democracy*, 21(2): 253–66.

European Journal of Women's Studies (2006). Special issue on intersectionality 13(3).

Giddens, A. (1984). *The Constitution of Society: Outline of the Theory of Structuration*. Cambridge: Polity.

Glastra, F., Meerman, M, Schedler, P., and de Vries, S. (2000). Broadening the scope of diversity management: strategic implications in the case of the Netherlands. *Industrial Relations,* 55(4): 698–724.

Grewal, I. and Kaplan, C. (2002). *Scattered Hegemonies: Postmodernity and Transnational Feminist Practices.* Minneapolis, MN: University of Minnesota Press.

Haraway, D. (1992). The promises of monsters: a regenerative politics for inappropriate/d others. In L. Grossberg, C. Nelson, and P. Treichler (eds.), *Cultural Studies.* London: Routledge, 295–338.

Hearn, J. (1987). *The Gender of Oppression: Men, Masculinity and the Critique of Marxism.* Brighton: Wheatsheaf; New York: St. Martin's Press.

Hearn, J. (1992). *Men in the Public Eye: The Construction and Deconstruction of Public Men and Public Patriarchies.* London/New York: Routledge.

Hearn, J. (2004). Tracking 'the transnational': studying transnational organizations and managements, and the management of cohesion. *Culture and Organization,* 10(4): 273–90.

Hearn, J. (2009). Patriarchies, transpatriarchies and intersectionalities. In E. Oleksy (ed.), *Intimate Citizenships: Gender, Sexualities, Politics.* London: Routledge, 177–92.

Hearn, J. (2011). Neglected intersectionalities in studying men: age/ing, virtuality, transnationality. In H. Lutz, M. T. Herrera Vivar, and L. Supik (eds.), *Framing Intersectionality: Debates on a Multi-Faceted Concept in Gender Studies.* Farnham: Ashgate, 89–104.

Hearn, J. (2013). Contextualizing men, masculinities, leadership and management: gender/intersectionalities, local/transnational, embodied/virtual, theory/practice. In R. Simpson, R. Burke, and S. Kumra (eds.), *The Handbook of Gender in Organizations.* Oxford: Oxford University Press, 417–37.

Hearn, J. (2015). *Men of the World: Genders, Globalizations, Transnational Times.* London: Sage.

Hearn, J. and Collinson, D. L. (1994). Theorizing unities and differences between men and between masculinities. In H. Brod and M. Kaufman (eds.), *Theorizing Masculinities.* Newbury Park, CA: Sage, 97–118.

Hearn, J. and Collinson, D.L. (2006). Men, masculinities and workplace diversity/diversion: power, intersections and contradictions. In A. Konrad, P. Prasad, and J. Pringle (eds.), *Handbook of Workplace Diversity.* London: Sage, 299–322.

Hearn, J. and Louvrier, J. (2011). The gendered intersectional corporation and diversity management. In S. Gröschl (ed.), *Diversity in the Workplace: Multi-Disciplinary and International Perspectives.* Aldershot: Gower, 133–46.

Hearn, J. and Parkin, W. (1993). Organizations, multiple oppressions and postmodernism. In J. Hassard and M. Parker (eds.), *Postmodernism and Organizations.* London: Sage, 148–62.

Hearn, J. and Parkin, W. (2001), *Gender, Sexuality and Violence in Organizations.* London: Sage.

Hearn, J., Blagojević, M., and Harrison, K. (eds.) (2013). *Rethinking Transnational Men.* New York: Routledge.

Hearn, J., Metcalfe, B. D., and Piekkari, R. (2012). Gender, intersectionality and international human resource management. In G. Ståhl, I. Björkman, and S. Morris (eds.), *Handbook of Research on International Human Resource Management.* Cheltenham: Edward Elgar, 509–31.

Holvino, E. (2010). Intersections: the simultaneity of race, gender and class in organization studies. *Gender, Work and Organization,* 17(3): 248–77.

Holvino, E. and Kamp, A. (2009). Diversity management: are we moving in the right direction? Reflections from both sides of the North Atlantic. *Scandinavian Journal of Management,* 25: 395–403.

hooks, b. (2000). *Feminism is for Everybody: Passionate Politics.* Cambridge, MA: South End.

Hornscheidt, A. (2007). Sprachliche Kategorisierung als Grundlage und Problem des Redens über Interdependenzen: Aspekte sprachlicher Normalisierung und Privilegierung. In K. Walgenbach, G. Dietze, A. Hornscheidt, and K. Palm (eds.), *Gender als interdependente Kategorie: Neue Perspektiven auf Intersektionalität, Diversität und Heterogenität*. Opladen: Verlag Barbara Budrich, 65–106.

Janssens, M. and Zanoni, P. (2005). Many diversities for many services: theorizing diversity (management) in service companies. *Human Relations*, 58(3): 311–40.

Jones, D., Pringle, J., and Shepherd, D. (2000). 'Managing diversity' meets Aotearoa/New Zealand. *Personnel Review*, 29(3): 364–80.

Kaijser, A. and Kronsell, A. (2014). Climate change through the lens of intersectionality. *Environmental Politics*, 23(3): 417–33.

Kalonaityte, V. (2006). Diversity that wasn't there: theorizing diversity management and organizational identity. EURODIV Paper 35.2006. <http://www.susdiv.org/uploadfiles/ED2006-035.pdf>. Accessed 21 December 2013.

Kamp, A. and Hagedorn-Rasmussen, P. (2004). Diversity management in a Danish context: towards a multicultural or segregated working life?. *Economic and Industrial Democracy*, 25(4): 525–54.

Kersten, A. (2000). Diversity management: dialogue, dialectics and diversion. *Journal of Organizational Change Management*, 13(3): 235–48.

Kimmel, M. and Messner, M. (eds.) (1989/2009). *Men's Lives*. Thousand Oaks, CA: Sage.

Kirby, E. L. and Harter, L. M. (2003). Speaking the language of the bottom-line: the metaphor of 'managing diversity'. *The Journal of Business Communication*, 40(1): 28–49.

Klarsfeld, A. (2009). The diffusion of diversity management: the case of France. *Scandinavian Journal of Management*, 25: 363–73.

Klarsfeld, A. (2010). *International Handbook on Diversity Management at Work: Country Perspectives on Diversity and Equal Treatment*. Cheltenham: Edward Elgar.

Larsen, J. E. and Christensen, A.-D. (2008). Gender, class, and family: men and gender equality in a Danish context. *Social Politics*, 15: 1–26.

Lewis, G. (2013). Unsafe travel: experiencing intersectionality and feminist displacements. *Signs*, 38(4): 869–92.

Lewis, H. (2015). The uses and abuses of intersectionality. *New Statesman*, May. <http://www.newstatesman.com/helen-lewis/2014/02/uses-and-abuses-intersectionality>.

Litvin, D. R. (1997). The discourse of diversity: from biology to management. *Organization*, 4(2): 187–209.

Lorey, I. (2008). Critique and category: on the restriction of political practice through recent theorems of intersectionality, interdependence and critical whiteness studies, tr. M. O'Neill. European Institute for Progressive Cultural Policies. <http://eipcp.net/transversal/0806/lorey/en>.

Louvrier, J. (2013). *Diversity, Difference and Diversity Management: A Contextual and Interview Study of Managers and Ethnic Minority Employees in Finland and France*. Published PhD thesis. Economics and Society 259, Helsinki: Hanken School of Economics.

Lutz, H. (2001). Differenz als Rechenaufgabe? Über die Relevanz der Kategorien Race, Class und Gender. In H. Lutz and N. Wenning (eds.), *Unterschiedlich verschieden. Differenz in der Erziehungswissenschaft*. Opladen: Leske und Budrich, 215–30.

Lutz, H. (2002). Intersectional analysis: a way out of multiple dilemmas?. paper presented at the International Sociological Association conference, Brisbane, July.

Lutz, H. (2014). *Intersectionality's (Brilliant) Career: How to Understand the Attraction of the Concept?* Frankfurt: Working Paper Series, Institute of Sociology, Goethe University, Frankfurt.

Lutz, H., Herrera Vivar, M. T., and Supik, L. (eds.) (2011). *Framing Intersectionality: Debates on a Multi-Faceted Concept in Gender Studies*. Farnham: Ashgate.

McCall, L. (2005). The complexity of intersectionality. *Signs: Journal of Women in Culture and Society*, 30: 1771–800.

McClintock, A. (2003). *Imperial Leather: Race, Gender and Sexuality in the Colonial Contest*. New York: Routledge.

Meekosha, H. (2006). What the hell are you? An intercategorical analysis of race, ethnicity, gender and disability in the Australian body politic. *Scandinavian Journal of Disability Research*, 8: 161–76.

Meekosha, H. and Pettman, J. (1991). Beyond category politics. *Hecate*, 17: 75–92.

Metcalfe, B. D. (2010). Reflections on difference: women, Islamic feminism and development in the Middle East. In J. Sawad and M. Ozgilbin (eds.), *Diversity Management in Asia*. Cheltenham: Edward Elgar, 141–60.

Minh-ha, T. T. (1986/7). She, the inappropriated other. *Discourse*, 8, Fall–Winter: 1–9.

Mohanty, C. T. (2003). *Feminism without Borders: Decolonizing Theory, Practicing Solidarity*. Durham, NC: Duke University Press.

Moser, I. (2004). On becoming disabled and articulating alternatives: the multiple modes of ordering disability and their interferences. *Cultural Studies*, 19(6): 667–700.

Murgia, A., and Poggio, B. (2010). The development of diversity management in the Italian context: a slow process. In A. Klarsfeld (ed.), *International Handbook on Diversity Management at Work: Country Perspectives on Diversity and Equal Treatment*. Cheltenham: Edward Elgar, 160–78.

Nkomo, S. M. and Stewart, M. M. (2006). Diverse identities in organizations. In S. R. Clegg, C. Hardy, T. B. Lawrence, and W. R. Nord (eds.), *The Sage Handbook of Organization Studies*, 2nd edn. London: Sage, 520–40.

O'Brien, M. (1984). The commatisation of women: patriarchal fetishism in the sociology of education. *Interchange*, 15(2): 43–60.

Omanovic, V. (2009). Diversity and its management as a dialectical process: encountering Sweden and the U.S. *Scandinavian Journal of Management*, 25: 352–62.

Ong, A. (1999). *Flexible Citizenship: The Cultural Logics of Transnationalism*. Durham, NC: Duke University Press.

Patil, V. (2013). From patriarchy to intersectionality: a transnational feminist assessment of how far we've really come. *Signs*, 38(4): 847–67.

Prasad, P. and Mills, A. J. (1997). From showcase to shadow: understanding the dilemmas of managing workplace diversity. In P. Prasad, A. J. Mills, M. Elms, and A. Prasad (eds.), *Managing the Organizational Melting Pot: Dilemmas of Workplace Diversity*. Thousand Oaks, CA: Sage, 3–27.

Prasad, P., Pringle, J. K., and Konrad, A. M. (2006). Examining the contours of workplace diversity: concepts, contexts and challenges. In A. M. Konrad, P. Prasad, and J. K. Pringle (eds.), *Handbook of Workplace Diversity*. London: Sage, 1–22.

Pringle, J. (2009). Positioning workplace diversity: critical aspects for theory. In M. F. Özbilgin (ed.), *Equality, Diversity and Inclusion at Work: A Research Companion*. Cheltenham: Edward Elgar, 75–87.

Pringle, K. (2006). The uses and abuses of intersectionality: making visible dominant power relations operating in the Swedish child welfare system—gender and ethnicity. Paper at the ESF Vadstena Conference on Intersectionality.

Risberg, A. and Søderberg, A.-M. (2008). Translating a management concept: diversity management in Denmark. *Gender in Management*, 23(6): 426–41.

Rowbotham, S., Segal, L., and Wainwright, H. (1979). *Beyond the Fragments: Feminism and the Making of Socialism.* London: Islington Community Press.

Sandoval, C. (2000). *Methodology of the Oppressed.* Minneapolis, MN: University of Minnesota Press.

Sinclair, A. (2006). Critical diversity management practice in Australia: romanced or co-opted?. in A. M. Konrad, P. Prasad, and J. K. Pringle (eds.), *Handbook of Workplace Diversity*, London: Sage, 511–30.

Tomlinson, F. and Schwabenland, C. (2010). Reconciling competing discourses of diversity? The UK non-profit sector between social justice and the business case. *Organization*, 17(1): 101–21.

Twine, R. (2010). Intersectional disgust? Animals and (eco)feminism. *Feminism & Psychology*, 20(3): 397–406.

Verloo, M. (2013). Intersectional and cross-movement politics and policies: reflections on current practices and debates. *Signs*, 38(4): 893–915.

Walby, S. (1986). *Patriarchy at Work.* Cambridge: Polity.

Walby, S. (1990). *Theorizing Patriarchy.* Oxford: Blackwell.

Walby, S. (2007). Complexity theory, systems theory, and multiple intersecting social inequalities. *Philosophy of the Social Sciences*, 37(4): 449–70.

Walby, S., Armstrong, J., and Strid, S. (2012). Intersectionality: multiple inequalities in social theory. *Sociology*, 46(2): 224–40.

Walgenbach, K., Dietze, G., Hornscheidt, A., and Palm, K. (2007). *Gender als interdependente Kategorie: Neue Perspektiven auf Intersektionalität, Diversität und Heterogenität.* Opladen: Verlag Barbara Budrich.

Weber, M. (1968). *Economy and Society: An Outline of Interpretive Sociology.* New York: Bedminster Press.

Weedon, C. (1987). *Feminist Practice and Poststructuralist Theory.* Oxford: Basil Blackwell.

Weedon, C. (1996). *Feminist Practice and Poststructuralist Theory: A Revised and Extended Second Edition.* Oxford: Blackwell.

Williams, F. (1989). *Social Policy.* Cambridge: Polity.

Yuval-Davis, N. (2006). Intersectionality and feminist politics. *European Journal of Women's Studies*, 13(3): 193–209.

Zanoni, P. and Janssens, M. (2003). Deconstructing difference: the rhetoric of human resource managers' diversity discourses. *Organization Studies*, 25(1): 55–74.

CHAPTER 4

RETHINKING DIVERSITY IN ORGANIZATIONS AND SOCIETY

DAVID KNIGHTS AND VEDRAN OMANOVIĆ

INTRODUCTION

DIVERSITY is a term that has assumed pre-eminence over recent decades as a way of representing populations that diverge through a wide variety of age-related, cultural, ethnic, racial, national, linguistic, religious, physical, and mental strengths or weaknesses, gender and sexual identifications or positionings. The genesis of 'diversity' as a topic in organizational studies has been traced to theory and practice in the United States that recognized its appeal when contrasted with the negative focus of anti-discrimination or affirmative action (AA) legislation (Nkomo and Cox 1996; Kelly and Dobbin 1998; Omanović 2009). The US Civil Rights movement of the 1960s had led to equal employment opportunity (EEO) and AA programmes that, although forerunners, were readily displaced by workplace diversity policies (e.g. Thomas 1990; Ashkanasy, Härtel, and Daus 2002). While such AA programmes met with some success in addressing social injustices resulting from the systematic advantaging or disadvantaging of people based on their group identities (Powell 1993), they were limited by the coverage of the legislation, which tended to concentrate primarily on issues of sexual and racial inequalities. Furthermore, certain political fashions of the day, such as the assimilation of immigrants in the United States (Janiewski 1995; Kurowski 2002) determined priorities. For a considerable time, overt racial discrimination and exclusion from the political process experienced by African Americans was given less attention (Janiewski 1995). Indeed, it could be argued that diversity in the workplace was marginalized by politicians and scholars because of the political priority of focusing on assimilation, ethnocentrism, and nativism (Kurowski 2002).

A report related to diversity in the workplace by Johnston and Packer (1987) entitled 'Workforce 2000: Work and Workers for the 21st Century' used demographic statistics to predict a significant increase in the employment of women and minorities and in the median age of people in the workforce. This report stimulated researchers, as well as practitioners, to begin examining the changing workplace demographics (e.g. Fine 1996; Litvin 2000, 2006). Diversity in the workplace thus became a major social and political issue as well as a topic for research, especially within management and organization studies. This early discourse on diversity was clearly grounded in humanistic (but also business-related) concerns to *value cultural differences*, while the AA approach concentrates on assimilating racial minorities and women into the business world (see, for instance, Powell 1993; Lynch 1997; Omanović 2006). As Powell (1993) states, organizations that value cultural diversity attempt to reach qualitative changes by improving interpersonal relationships and by minimizing latent racism and sexism. However, many advocates also began to promote exclusively a business-related agenda and the term *diversity management* (DM) or managing diversity began to assume significance (e.g. Thomas 1990, 1991; Taylor 1995; Robinson and Dechant 1997). Governments, management practitioners, academics, and the media found that managing diversity provided a useful rhetoric for making the case for equal employment opportunity in the workplace. Through its appeal to the 'business case' for diversity (see also Chapter 12, this volume), it attracted practitioners who had disliked the legislative constraints on their practices, and it appealed to a growing political backlash against AA and quotas as ways of addressing discrimination. At last, here was a positive and possibly productive way of subscribing to the liberal agenda for improving equity for diverse populations. Soon DM and its linking of the issue to business efficiency, competitive advantage, and commercial success became established practice, such that it began to eclipse all other approaches to diversity (Noon 2007, 2010). As a result, 'the motivation for social justice has been lost in mainstream writings on diversity in organizations, as well as in some critical work' (Ahonen et al. 2014: 264).

In this chapter, our concern is to examine a range of analytical frameworks, epistemologies, and methodologies surrounding discourses of diversity for purposes of proposing an alternative that would seek to avoid reproducing the very conditions that make it possible to discriminate against the disadvantaged. We believe that the dominant perspectives and methodologies of positivism and interpretivism have led research along channels where diversity becomes a problem to manage rather than a resource for stimulating political, social, and ethical changes reflective of the tradition of social justice (Rhodes 2012). Even critical approaches have tended to reproduce linear, binary, and disembodied representations of diversity that fail adequately to challenge the mainstream DM theories and practices. In this climate, social justice arguments within diversity discourses have lost favour in preference to a managerialist preoccupation with making diversity 'pay' in terms of a 'business case'; in short, limiting diversity practices to their potential to generate commercial benefits. As a way of seeking to stimulate developments that might reverse this trend and restore interests in social justice, we have conducted a literature survey of the various methodological and analytical frameworks deployed in diversity in organizations research in order to search for alternatives that do not reduce ideas about and interests in diversity to an object to be managed primarily as a resource for enhancing efficiency and/or profitability. In searching for alternatives we have consulted some of the posthumanist feminist literature (Grosz 1994; Ziarek 2001; Diprose 2002) that promotes and celebrates *difference* as opposed to focusing primarily on managing diversity.

In conducting our search of the literature, we found that it could broadly be classified in relation to the epistemological and methodological frameworks that were adopted. So, for example, although not always explicitly declared or reflected upon, we found that there were three major frameworks through which most studies could be identified. The most dominant framework was that of *positivism*, where there is a belief in the natural scientific model of causal analysis of independent and dependent variables and where social research is only slightly lower down the evolutionary chain of discovery and achievement (Popper 1947). These researchers see no discontinuity between nature and human life, whereas the second most dominant framework of *interpretivism* specifically works from the hermeneutic assumption that human life is a continual and unending process of seeking, interpreting, and often imposing meaning on the world (Douglas 1970). Because the subject and the 'object' (i.e. humans) of research in the social sphere both construct and are constructed by (and through) interpretations, meaning cannot simply be short-circuited through quantifying factors, categories, or variables as if these representations were self-evident. Diversity in organizations is studied mostly through one or other of these two research traditions, although there is a tendency for the positivist framework to be more dominant than interpretivism. A third framework through which diversity in organizations is researched is the *critical tradition(s)*, where not only is the natural science model rejected but also the tendency for interpretivist research to remain descriptive and apolitical. Critical research avoids imposing meaning so as to construct variables that can be subjected to causal analysis but, unlike some of the interpretivism, it refuses to remain politically neutral. Consequently, its moral focus to reverse discriminatory practices on the grounds of social justice generally renders critical research unsympathetic to the concentration on the business case within DM. As will be seen in the next section, there are several variants of each of these frameworks.

Through identifying alternative theories and methods in studying diversity in organizations, we hope to be able to facilitate a reconstruction of social and institutional arrangements. Instead of treating individuals or groups as 'objects' to be managed, we seek to recognize and celebrate the differences that constitute their diversity. We recognize how some theorists who seek to stress and celebrate difference deny focusing on group identity, let alone identities based on a category such as ethnicity or race (e.g. Roberson and Park 2007; McKay 2008). This is because they fear giving an essential status to something individuals might share in common at the expense of identifying their differences. We eschew such extremes and therefore seek to advance embodied understandings of difference and diversity that avoid undermining any kind of generalization on the basis of gender, ethnicity, or other base for discrimination (Bordo 1990; Nussbaum 1992; Hekman 1999). For a recognition and even celebration of difference need not displace all sense of commonality between people, as it is possible both to share certain aspects of life (e.g. gendered identity and practice) at one and the same time as exhibiting differences with respect to a range of dimensions (e.g. age, class, history, race, sexuality). Of course, it is also possible to share aspects of one or more of the latter dimensions, such as race, while perhaps giving lesser emphasis to gender. Furthermore, as intersectional theory argues (Crenshaw 1991; Styhre and Eriksson-Zetterquist 2008; Bagilhole 2009), where, in combination, two or more of these dimensions intersect, the potential discriminatory impact can be greater than the sum of its parts, and where several dimensions intersect, it can be exponential. In the section on posthumanist feminism, we go beyond the tendency of intersectional theorists to be largely preoccupied with identities. The argument is that, although recognizing the multiplicity of overlapping identities is an advance, intersectional theorists still subscribe to a view that identity work is liberating rather than an entrapment of modernism. We subscribe to this latter view, which sees the preoccupation with identity as turning people in on themselves and reducing the 'other' to that which can simply confirm the self's own image of itself (Levinas 1986; Knights 2006).

The chapter is organized as follows. First we provide some detail of how we conducted the survey together with a brief rationale for the project. We then proceed to the survey, examining positivist, interpretivist, and critical literatures in turn before discussing an alternative posthumanist feminism.

Search Methodology

Our focus for analysis is empirical studies of diversity in organizations that have been published, as journal articles, from the beginning of twenty-first century until the year 2013. We used the following databases to locate the articles: *Science Direct, Scopus*, and *Sci Topics*. The most common key words of our search were: *Managing Diversity, Diversity in Organizations, Diversity and its Management*. Our first search resulted in some 250 articles. Many of these articles dealt with areas not relevant for our purposes, such as medicine, the arts, and technology. Therefore, we refined our search, using the following criteria: articles on 'diversity in organizations' and empirical articles. Our final selection consisted of approximately 100 articles that were published within the set time period. Around 40 per cent of these journal articles were the most recent publications—published from the year 2007 to the year 2013. Apart from these newer publications on diversity in organizations, we included as well a few studies (approximately ten) focusing on diversity in organizations that were published before the year 2000—as a way of contextualizing our own study. We also looked at a number of studies that, on examination, were rather peripheral to our main focus, so that in total we have consulted around 180 studies.

The results discussed in this chapter reflect our interpretation of the primary theoretical and methodological foci of these articles. Our interpretation is, in turn, based on our previous readings and knowledge and 'engagement' with the reviewed literature. Identifying the range of analytical frameworks and their epistemological and methodological roots through a literature review is one conventional way of developing a research field, as did Burrell and Morgan (1979) and Morgan (1980) in relation to organization studies. In the field of gender and organization, a number of authors have also sought to classify the different approaches (see, for example, Acker 1990; Hartsock 1995; Rantalaiho and Heiskanen 1997; Alvesson and Billing 1999; Calás and Smircich 2006).

More broadly, in the area of diversity at work, authors have identified different political (Lorbiecki and Jack 2000) and paradigmatical (Nemetz and Christensen 1996; Omanović 2011) standpoints within the research field. Drawing on Burrell and Morgan's work on paradigmatic differences, Nemetz and Christensen (1996) identify two opposing beliefs (underlying paradigms) about multiculturalism: one polarity is labelled the sociology of regulation (or functionalism) and the other is described as the sociology of radical change (radical structuralism). By setting these views in relation to DM, the authors present two ways of action regarding potential (societal and organizational) responses to difference. For example, the functionalist view seeks to induce change through problem-solving and building consensus from within the boundaries of existing authority and control, while the structuralist view sees social change as possible only by revolution, which shifts power from the oppressor to the oppressed. Lorbiecki and Jack (2000) also reviewed the DM literature, but their focus is changes within the fields. The results of their study is the identification of four overlapping turns—demographic, political, economic, and critical—regarding the focus in the diversity in organizations research. Finally, Omanović's (2011) study investigates how diversity is being represented in the management and organization literature. In particular, the author focuses on the identification and examination of researchers' ontological and epistemological assumptions—which results in four philosophical traditions in the literature: *the positivist, the interpretative, the discursive*, and *the critical-dialectic*. Our study builds on this approach, but sees the discursive and the critical-dialectic as part of a critical tradition that we seek to contribute to through developing a more embodied analysis of difference within diversity. We also challenge some 'critical research' on diversity in organizations by asking questions: In what way is 'critical research' on diversity in organizations *transformative*? Does this research, as well as mainstream managerial approaches, stabilize the conditions of possibility of disadvantage and discrimination? We turn now to the material from our literature survey.

The Positivist Tradition(s)

Diversity in management research, following the positivist tradition(s), mostly documents the *relationships* between 'diverse workforces', their various characteristics/dimensions (such as race, ethnicity, gender, age, disability, sexual orientation, and national origin), and their *effects*. The themes of these articles are the following: goal orientation (e.g. Pieterse, van Knippenberg, and Ginkel 2011); performance (e.g. Richard 2000; Dwyer, Richard, and Chadwick 2003; Kidder et al. 2004; Shoobridge 2006; Roberson and Park 2007); projects (e.g. Bhadury, Mighty, and Damar 2000; Wang et al. 2006); teams (e.g. Watsona, BarNir, and Pavur 2005); innovativeness (Kearney and Gebert 2006); greater decision-making and problem-solving capability (e.g. Cunningham 2011); organizational commitment (e.g. Kirby and Richard 2000); corporate social orientation (e.g. Smith et al. 2004); diversity as strategy (Thomas 2004); cultural differences (Tung and Quaddus 2002); firm value (e.g. Johnston and Malina 2008); and 'successful buyer–seller relationships' (e.g. Bush and Ingram 2011).

The 'diversity' definitions sometimes refer to other characteristics/dimensions than those listed—such as '*deep-level diversity*', which includes, for example, personality, information, attitudes, and values (Phillips and Loyd 2006; Pieterse, van Knippenberg, and Ginkel 2011); differences in business *practices* by foreign and local companies (Mohr and Puck 2005); and differences amongst companies in different societal contexts, such as Japan and South Korea (Magoshi and Chang 2009). The major research interests in these studies are the potential (economic) benefits of certain characteristics/dimensions of diversity for organizations and companies.

This stream of research, which is strongly *social psychological in perspective*, focuses on concepts such as *social identity* and *social categorizations* that suggest that people use predominantly cognitive categories to distinguish themselves and others like them (e.g. Eckel and Grossman 2005; Sawyer, Houlette, and Yeagley 2006; Klein et al. 2011; Østergaarda, Timmermans, and Kristinsson 2011). This research also draws on the *similarity/attraction concept*, which argues that individuals are more attracted to people like themselves (e.g. Shore et al. 2009; Pieterse, van Knippenberg, and Ginkel 2011) and the *uncertainty reduction concept* (e.g. Bush and Ingram 2011) where individuals negatively stereotype different or deviant others in order to reduce uncertainty about them (Bush and Ingram 2011). The assumptions underlying much of this research is that people cooperate better with those who are like themselves and, consequently, homogeneity in work groups or teams is generally viewed as facilitating productivity more than heterogeneity. This conflates a tendency for people to feel more comfortable with others that they know with a fear of difference, whereas familiarity may have no connection to difference and diversity.

The *information/decision-making concept* has also informed this stream of research. However, unlike the *similarity/attraction concept* and the *uncertainty reduction concept*—the mentioned differences amongst team members (e.g. nationalities, genders, and ages), in combination with an open diversity climate, are generally seen to have positive effects for organizations. The assumption is that differences between team members, for instance, in terms of knowledge, experiences, and perspectives lead to better decisions (e.g. Shore et al. 2009; Pieterse, van Knippenberg, and Ginkel 2011), and (if successfully managed) diverse workforces can have positive (economic) effects for companies.

Other researchers of the positivist tradition view the effects of diverse workforces as both positive and negative. For instance, Østergaarda, Timmermans, and Kristinsson

(2011) argue that employee diversity should generally have a positive effect on innovation but may also generate conflict. In their study of the effects of gender diversity on firm performance within the managerial ranks, Dwyer, Richard, and Chadwick (2003) draw on *contingency and configurational* approaches in their hypothesis that heterogeneity is beneficial for unstructured, novel tasks but not for routine tasks. Supporting these approaches, results from their research show that the effect of gender diversity at the management level is conditional on the company´s strategic orientation, the organizational culture, and/or their mutual interaction.

Finally, Pieterse, van Knippenberg, and Ginkel (2011) adopt *the socially shared cognition perspective* in their study that focuses on 'deep level diversity' (e.g. differences in personalities, attitudes, and values). They claim that the 'mental representations', or understanding of the team and its tasks, tend to determine how team members interact and perform their tasks. In other words, the team's homogeneous or heterogeneous composition is of less importance in conditioning the individual's engagement than is her/his mental representation of the task.

In literature within the positivist tradition, the goal of researchers is typically to identify human differences (e.g. gender, age, race, and ethnicity) and behavioural difference (e.g. attitudes and values) using the following traditional organizational concepts: *management* and *leadership* (e.g. Dwyer, Richard, and Chadwick 2003; Bogaert and Vloeberghs 2005; Klein et al. 2011); *project management* (e.g. Bhadury, Mighty, and Damar 2000; Wang et al. 2006); *innovation* (e.g. Auh and Bulent Menguc 2005; Østergaarda, Timmermans, and Kristinsson 2011); *teamwork* (e.g. Sawyer, Houlette, and Yeagley 2006; Pieterse, van Knippenberg, and Ginkel 2011; Luis 2012); *team identity* (e.g. Eckel and Grossman 2005); *strategy* (e.g. Fink and Pastore 2003; Cunningham 2011); *communication* (e.g. Dinsbach, Feij, and de Vries 2007); *international joint ventures* (e.g. Mohr and Puck 2005); and *organizational commitment* (e.g. Magoshi and Chang 2009).

In this research, 'diversity' and specific or related concepts, such as *diversity structure* (e.g. Sawyer, Houlette, and Yeagley 2006), *cultural diversity* (e.g. Lauring 2009), and *diversity climate and international language management* (Lauring and Selmer 2012) seem of interest mostly for corrective purposes in organizations. In other words, if management make some adjustments in employee structure (or in the composition, behaviour, and attitudes of teams and their members) and/or open the organizational climate more to 'diversity', then positive (economic) effects are likely to occur.

There is also some positivist tradition research that focuses on *human resource (HR) management* topics such as gender and age differences in recruitment (e.g. Pinar et al. 2011) and in (sales) training (e.g. Bush and Ingram 2011). Other studies focus on the acquisition of human capital by creating a 'diverse workforce' (e.g. Auh and Bulent Menguc 2005), and on different work arrangements that are more friendly/open to diversity practices (e.g. Fink and Pastore 2003).

Much of the research examined so far indicates a strong functionalist/positivist orientation where the belief is that social research can emulate natural science in identifying quantifiable independent and dependent variables to produce causal analyses which can be applied to develop practices to facilitate the orderly functioning of a healthy society.

In pursuit of these scientistic aims (Schroyer 1975),[1] researchers invariably deploy survey methods (e.g. questionnaires, scenarios, and experiments based on laboratory studies) and samples of several hundred or even thousands of informants. In addition, where researchers recognize the failure of survey data to reflect the meaning that respondents attach to different issues, they deploy a combination of interviews, observations, and/or secondary data (e.g. Härtel 2004; Roberson 2006; Süß and Kleiner 2007; Magoshi and Chang 2009).

The majority of these positivist-oriented studies ask research questions that result from the identification of gaps in the literature, a practice that has been heavily criticized for its failure to challenge assumptions that underlie the existing approaches (Sandberg and Alvesson 2011). One example is Dinsbach, Feij, and de Vries's (2007) study of the relationship between unequal treatment, content-related communication, and job attitudes amongst ethnic minority and majority employees. Once the gaps are identified, the researchers pose a number of hypotheses.[2] They then test the hypotheses against their empirical data. They construct their questionnaires according to certain theoretical framework(s)/perspective(s). For instance, Dinsbach, Feij, and de Vries (2007) are inspired by organization socialization theories in which they identify various domains (e.g. 'role clarity', 'task mastery', and 'social integration'). They then use these domains to measure some key variables (e.g. 'the content-related communication'). The questionnaires are thus directly related to these domains and variables, while the alternative responses are often constructed as five-point scales (e.g. from 1/none/ to 5/a lot/). In short, different dimensions of 'diversity' are objectified and then transformed into operational and measurable variables.

The positivist researchers then analyse the results using different analytical techniques, such as multiple, hierarchical, and logistical regression (e.g. Cunningham 2011; Pieterse, van Knippenberg, and Ginkel 2011); econometric (e.g. Østergaarda, Timmermans, and Kristinsson 2011); or by using a mathematical equation (e.g. Auh and Bulent Menguc 2005).

These studies present suggestions for future research that are informed by precisely the same epistemology and methods as the researchers have used, but that can fill in the gaps. For example, Dinsbach, Feij, and de Vries (2007) recommend that future studies take a longitudinal design to determine the causal directions of the relationships identified in their own study. Such future research recommendations are also often motivated by the ambition to generalize results relating to the larger sphere of how DM can improve organizational performance.

---

[1] This term is used to describe research that fails to recognize the ontological discontinuity between natural and human phenomena (Douglas 1970) insofar as, with respect to the latter, interpretation occurs not just among the researchers but also among the researched, and this renders causal analysis problematic.

[2] For instance: 'Ethnic minority employees report less content-related communication and less positive job attitudes than ethnic majority employees' (Dinsbach, Feij, and de Vries 2007: 727).

While a majority of these studies are located in the United States (e.g. Mollica, 2003; McKay, 2008), there are also a number of studies set in other locations: Härtel (2004) in Australia; Dinsbach, Feij, and de Vries (2007) and Pieterse, van Knippenberg and Ginkel (2011) in the Netherlands; Süß and Kleiner (2007, 2008) in Germany; Pinar and colleagues (2011) in Turkey; Bogaert and Vloeberghs (2005) in Belgium; and Magoshi and Chang (2009) in Japan and South Korea. Insofar as these researchers minimize the importance of location, they typically neglect the geographical and historical context of their research. DM is thus assumed to have universal application regardless of historical time, geographical space, or local context. However, in some studies (e.g. Süß and Kleiner 2007; Magoshi and Chang 2009; Pinar et al. 2011) practices are partly contextualized by descriptions of recent discussions regarding the development of DM in the local situation in the studied contexts. For instance, unlike the starting point for DM in the research from the United States (racial discrimination), the starting point for DM in Germany (Süß and Kleiner 2007) and in Japan and South Korea (Magoshi and Chang 2009) was the problem of equal employment opportunities for men and women. Although this kind of contextualization helps to better understand the starting points for DM in these specific societal contexts, these researchers have, somehow, a static view of the selected contextual factors. For instance, in the Süß and Kleiner (2007) study, there is no clear evidence of how the specific context of Germany influences the ideas about, and the interests in, DM in the examined (210) companies and vice versa during the particular time period. Thus, these societal and organizational contexts are treated as stable or rather as facts—thus unchangeable over time.

The Interpretative Tradition(s)

There are several similarities between positivist and interpretative traditions, for both are inclined to address the effects of diversity, such as its commercial benefits, more than the conditions of life that make stereotyping possible and damaging to its victims. For example, Rao (2012) studied religious diversity and its *impact* in the Indian workplace, while Shachaf's (2008) exploratory study focuses on the *effects* of cultural diversity and information and communication technology (ICT) on virtual (or ad hoc) teams.

A second similarity with the studies inspired by the positivist tradition(s) is that research in the interpretative tradition(s) is also motivated by the identification of gaps in the literature. Such gaps provide the starting points for the formulation(s) of research questions. For instance, Shachaf (2008) motivates her research interest by the lack of empirical findings that support the relationship between cultural diversity and effectiveness. Freeman and Lindsay (2012) have also noted that little research addresses the expatriate experience of ethnic diversity in the host country. Therefore, to address this gap, they studied how Australian expatriate managers *interpret* their experience of working in an ethnically diverse workplace in Malaysia.

While not always explicit, the third similarity between these two traditions is that they tend to be concerned with managerial problems and the organizational life of executives. These interpretative-oriented researchers also discuss the results of their studies in terms of managerial implications such as managing (and valuing) workforce diversity (Gilbert and Ivancevich 2000; Ivancevich and Gilbert 2000), preventing conflicts (Rao 2012), and increasing team cohesiveness (Shachaf 2008).

There are, however, several fundamental differences in research methodologies between studies in the positivist tradition(s) and those in the interpretative tradition(s). On the one hand, the important issue for some researchers in the positivist tradition(s) is the *measurement* of the *effects* of diversity on organizational performance, whereas in the interpretative tradition(s) many researchers are more concerned to *understand the meaning(s)* of diversity. When the latter study diversity, they also draw on different concepts. These concepts include the following: sense-making (e.g. how people make sense of the business case for diversity; see Omanović 2002); managing (cultural) diversity (e.g. Foster 2005; Foster and Harris 2005; Subeliani and Tsogas 2005); ethnic minority women's experiences of stereotypes in predominantly white, Western organizations (Kamenou, Watt, and Fearfull 2006); understanding teamwork across national and organizational cultures (Gibson and Zellmer-Bruhn 2001), and a culture of diversity in sport workplaces (Doherty et al. 2010); exploring hospital managers' perceptions of age as an employee attribute (Furunes and Mykletun 2007); focusing on *understanding* the relationships between diversity and team *effectiveness* (Shachaf 2008); and *interpreting* the expatriate managers' experience of working in an ethnically diverse workplace abroad (Freeman and Lindsay 2012).

Thus, unlike researchers in the positivist tradition(s), most researchers in the interpretative tradition(s) are interested in documenting and studying how participants perceive, understand, interpret, or make sense of diversity. These researchers usually take qualitative approaches, often inspired by ethnographic methods that involve non-participant/participant observation techniques as well as the more conventional ways of accessing empirical material through interviews (e.g. 'semi-structured', 'in-depth', and/or 'open-ended') and archival documentary materials.

For instance, Shachaf's (2008) study was based on forty-one interviews with global virtual team members (sixteen face-to-face interviews and twenty-five telephone interviews) conducted in a nine-month period, while Doherty and colleagues (2010) conducted personal interviews with eleven employees in athletic departments. In this research, the interviewees are sometimes selected by the so-called 'snowballing' technique. Furunes and Mykletun (2007), as an example, use this technique when they asked those they interviewed for recommendations of other potential interviewees (see also Chapter 26, this volume).

Some researchers also use *interview protocols/guides* with open-ended questions based on their research questions and their literature review. The empirical data are then often separated for analysis using various *coding techniques*. Such coding techniques are used to identify central terms/categories and subcategories (e.g. Shachaf 2008), or to eliminate statements 'that seize the invariant constituents of the phenomenon' (Freeman and Lindsay 2012: 6).

Thus, the sampling in interpretative tradition(s) studies generally requires fewer informants because, unlike the positivist tradition(s) studies, it makes no claim to be representative of a population.[3] Rather, it seeks to provide analytical or theoretical generalizations (Mayring 2007).

The Critical Tradition(s)

Unlike the positivist/functionalist traditions(s), and in part the interpretative tradition(s), the critical tradition(s) are not as well represented in the diversity literature for organizations. However, it is important to emphasize that the critical tradition(s)—in particular, the discursive one—is becoming increasingly attractive to researchers in this field (see Omanović 2011). We identified two critical perspectives that we label as *the (critical) discursive tradition* and *the critical-dialectic tradition*. These two traditions, although they have some points in common with the interpretative tradition(s)—for example, the view that diversity is socially constructed—are still fundamentally different from the interpretative tradition(s); for instance, in the design of research projects and in the study of the idea of diversity. In addition, there are also differences between studies inspired by the critical discursive tradition and those inspired by the critical dialectic tradition.

The (Critical) Discursive Tradition

Research adopting a discursive perspective has developed ever since the linguistic turn in social science, where it was recognized that because interpretations of social reality are always mediated through language, discursive practices need to be a central focus of research. The critical discursive approach, however, generates three central arguments against uncritical and apolitical approaches to discourse analysis in diversity research (Zanoni et al. 2010: 13–14). First, that it has subscribed to a positivist and 'fixed' conception of identity that is readily represented and measured as something 'objective' and an essential feature of the subject. Second, it has primarily drawn upon the discipline of social psychology that privileges interpersonal interactions and, in so doing, neglects institutional and organizational relations. Third, and partly as a result, it neglects a conception of power/knowledge relations (Foucault 1980, 1982), and how these constitute

---

[3] The absence of representativeness is set against a view that positivist claims are often exaggerated, since, outside of large-scale surveys, rarely do they secure fully stratified random samples. In all research, however, research access often determines the sample more than strict statistical procedures.

discourses and subjectivities that reflect and reproduce systems of inequality (Knights and Kerfoot 2004).

The critical discursive approach began by challenging the tendency for DM to deflect attention from the inequalities of power associated with different dimensions of diversity (Zanoni et al. 2010: 9). Among other things, critical discursive research seeks to interrogate these underlying assumptions to expose conflicting interests, contradictions, and discrepancies in the narratives and discursive practices. Research has been conducted across a wide range of countries and, of course, different cultures have an impact on perceptions of, and interventions on, diversity. Jack and Lorbiecki (2007), for example, discovered some major discrepancies between national identities and organizational globalization strategies in relation to UK DM initiatives. Meriläinen and colleagues (2009) demonstrated the effects of the institutionalized societal discourse of gender equality on 'DM' in Finland-based companies. In a case study of a Belgian company, Zanoni and Janssens (2004, 2007) critically examined diversity activities and the extent to which employees participated in their control.

A central feature of all discursive approaches is the importance of language and communication in constituting any phenomenon (Westwood and Linstead 2001; Ashcraft, Kuhn, and Coreen 2009). Without such communications, inequality around diversity would exist in a vacuum and intervention to modify or eradicate its negative effects would be impossible, as Jack and Lorbiecki (2007) discovered when researching how different forms of control and resistance to diversity initiatives were exercised in organizations. Also it is important that organizations do not just become insular with regard to exploiting the 'business case' but also provide alternative understandings, especially in communicating their diversity initiatives to the wider society (Litvin 2006).

However, it is also the case that DM can often provide moral support at a distance yet fail to address 'some of the more contentious and uncomfortable aspects of workforce diversity' (Dick and Cassell 2002: 973) and especially power relations. In what she calls 'commodity diversity', Swan (2010) demonstrated how a diversity poster generated visual images that produce a racial ideology, thus reinforcing unequal power in organizations. Her concern with the shift to discourse was how it can marginalize the examination of images that can be equally productive of organizational inequalities.

However, not all theorists referring to the critical discursive traditions are negative about DM, even when the 'business case' is pre-eminent. For instance, in a study of the Dutch police force, Boogaard and Roggeband (2010) found that an initiative introducing 'multicultural skills' for executive officers benefited ethnic minorities, because they were often seen to be culturally in tune rather than requiring specific training. Also, gender inequality was challenged when the force recognized the importance of good interpersonal and communication skills within police work since these were deemed to be less demanding for women. The authors did not reflect on the sense in which, although advantaging specific minorities and women, these practices also reinforced stereotypes that could, in other circumstances, backfire to generate or reinforce diversity inequalities. In a similar vein, even though there were significant dilemmas that remained unresolved, Schwabenland (2010) found that, in the voluntary sector, the potential tensions between moral issues and business rationales could be reconciled when utilitarian objectives were achieved through diverse employees but within the context of a 'commitment to social justice' (Tomlinson and Schwabenland 2010: 113).

While there has only been space to review a selection of the studies in the critical discourse tradition, it is clear that they offer a methodological approach different from both non-discursive (the positivist and interpretative traditions) and discursive research on diversity in organizations. This is equally the case with the critical dialectical tradition to which we now turn.

The Critical Dialectical Tradition

Some parts of the critical tradition take their impetus from the philosophical discourse of Hegel, with his dialectical view that the opposition of thesis (a positive assertion or theory) and antithesis (the negation of the thesis) are resolved in a synthesis that combines the most positive elements of both in a perfect reconciliation of historically obdurate and unyielding conflicts. Hegel was somewhat opportunistic by declaring that his society (Prussia in the 1830s) was the apotheosis of his dialectical theory of progress, thus legitimizing and justifying the absolute rule of Frederick William III (Popper 1947). Marx, on the other hand, reversed this argument. He emphasized instead that societies would not reach the perfect synthesis without a social revolution. Such revolution would, according to Marx, lead first to a regime (communism) as oppressive as the capitalist order it overthrew, but that eventually a liberated form of society called socialism would prevail, so constituting the perfection Hegel was premature in accepting. Given the conflict and opposition that inequality around diversity fosters and fabricates, a dialectical approach would seem to provide an appropriate framework for diversity research.

In organization studies, this perspective has been and continues to be used: with a focus on the dynamics of processes of organizational change (Groleau, Demers, and Engeström 2011), explaining how institutional contradictions create space for organizational changes (Sharma, Lawrence, and Lowe 2010) and providing insight into role change as processes by focusing both on institutional embeddedness and transformational agency (Burns and Baldvinsdottir 2005). Also from this perspective, the notion of resistance and control is viewed as mutually constitutive and socially produced in daily organizational life (Mumby 2005), in corporate culture as corporate hegemony (Ogbor 2001), and in corporate–social enterprise collaborations as shaped processes (Di Domenico, Tracey, and Haugh 2009). An ambition in the dialectical-inspired studies is to bring about alternative practices/praxes to existing structures of domination (e.g. Barros 2010; Foster and Wiebe 2010).

The critical dialectical perspective has also been applied in studies on diversity and its management (Omanović 2009, 2013). These studies build upon several of the mentioned discursive studies, while going beyond them at certain crucial points. Following Benson's (1977, 1983) application of dialectical reasoning for studying organizations,

Omanović (2009, 2013) sought to develop the analysis in relation to his research on diversity and its management. Omanović's (2009) examination of the social production of ideas of diversity in two social-historical contexts (the United States and Sweden) shows how diversity and its management are mediated by social-historical relationships that reflect their ongoing construction, but are neither fixed realities nor immune to human intervention and change.

In a more recent study, Omanović (2013) described how managers of diversity at a large manufacturing company in Sweden prioritized some ideas on diversity and ignored or marginalized others. This study focused on the dynamics in play by which acceptable ideas on 'diversity' are socially produced and become normative in time. However, such ideas can also be challenged because they are, as this study shows, preliminary and changeable choices between 'given' and alternative (although suppressed) ideas about, and interests in, diversity.

In order to examine ideas about and interests in diversity (and its management) as a critical-dialectical and social-historical process, Omanović (2009, 2013) used an ethnographic methodology in both studies. This methodology incorporates some elements of a critical orientation in ethnography (see Thomas 1993), such as the focus on diversity in terms of injustices (e.g. discrimination and marginalization) and domination (e.g. particular sectional interests related to diversity). The data came from archival research, in-depth (ethnographic) interviews, and detailed participant observations.

Thus, like the critical discursive tradition studies, from the critical dialectical tradition, diversity and its management are viewed and studied as socially constructed processes that are far from neutral, since they have strong incitements towards a business rather than a human rights rationale. Also, both of these critical perspectives point out the importance of historically constructed relations of *dominance* and *subordination* that have certain impacts on particular groups of people.

However, discursive studies (unlike the critical dialectical studies) often fall short of understanding how production processes over particular interests are formed and maintained, in and through organizational events unfolding over time. One explanation for this is that discursive studies rely primarily on interviews and documents rather than observations. As a result, despite challenging and focusing critically on managerial discourses, these studies tend to leave unattended actual *relational dynamics* in the workplace—dynamics that, through power/knowledge relations (Foucault 1980), tend to reinforce rather than challenge inequalities and discriminations at work.

In contrast, critical dialectical research follows both historical and real-time activities and discourses by organizational participants. The focus is on organizational change (e.g. focusing both on multiple power interests that shape the production of diversity and alternative social 'realties') without presuppositions about how the process will unfold. For instance, Omanović's (2013) study follows the activities in a manufacturer's project of promoting diversity practices and policies during a three-year period. The focus is on key participants' ideas, (opposing) interests, and actions regarding 'diversity' in the project, as well as contradictions and some ideas and activities of other organizational members who are 'touched' by the diversity programme.

To sum up, the critical dialectical perspective, unlike the other perspectives discussed above, offers an alternative view on 'diversity in organizations'—by understanding diversity as a socio-historical process, which is driven by contradictions. Identifying alternative social 'realities' and exploring their potential to redefine the production of diversity are important aspects of the dialectical perspective. From a critical dialectic perspective, the criticism of existing social arrangements, the search for alternatives, and the active mobilization of institutional agents are seen as potentially emancipatory and transformative. However, the precise forms through which these different diversity practices are produced cannot be predicted in advance.

Following the line of reasoning of the critical perspectives we have discussed, a particularly relevant area for a future research on diversity in organizations would be to focus more directly on the marginalized actors who are often identified as the subjects of diversity. How do these actors learn that social/business arrangements do not meet their interests? When do they stop taking their reality for granted? What are the consequences of such awareness? Do they mobilize other similarly situated actors to take collective action for organizational change? In short, how can we bring about real emancipatory/transformative organizational praxes? In pursuing such research it would be of value to consider some more radical and embodied approaches to diversity that have emanated from posthumanist feminism and philosophies of the body.

Discussing Posthumanist Feminism as an Alternative

The methodological perspectives on diversity that we have examined so far either follow a scientistic/positivist, a phenomenological/interpretivist, or a social constructionist/discursive and dialectical approach(es). While there are other potential alternatives, such as critical realism and postcolonial theory, space restricts us here to examining a new wave of feminism and anti-racism. This draws on a philosophically grounded posthumanist materialism that, through the philosophies of Deleuze (2005) and Deleuze and Guattari (1988), for example, generates a discourse that attempts to transform prevailing subjectivities (Grosz 1994, 2005). It seeks to transcend the limitations of unilinear, disembodied, and dualistic thinking as reflected, to a greater or lesser degree, in both the establishment and critical traditions of scientific and humanistic theory. Grosz rethinks the sense of what it is to be a human subject (subjectivity) through re-theorizing the body in ways that depart from both the Cartesian mind–body dualism and the Freudian conscious–unconscious mind binary. These binaries or dualisms generally involve an understanding of humans in terms of a separation between their minds or consciousness and their unconscious bodies, but also invariably a privileging of rationality over embodied experience. It is associated with the domination of cognition over emotion that is reflective of white masculine control and mastery of the 'other' or that which is outside of the self (i.e. subordinates, women, non-white, alternative sexualities, and the environment). This is a way of relating to the world that has been heavily criticized by feminists (e.g. Game 1991; Clough 1992; Grosz 2005).

Also drawing on Deleuze and Guattari (1988) and Foucault (1977), in affirming the body and embodied relations as necessary conditions for ethical relations, Braidotti (2011) criticizes the way in which, within binary thinking, language dominates experience. This has produced a social constructivist discourse that is negative (Braidotti 2011: 122) insofar as it assumes that individuals crave social recognition (identity) to overcome a 'lack' or sense of emptiness in their lives (Lacan 1977). This occurs because, in having been separated from the mother, children miss the embodied security of nurturing and cannot replace this through the demands of the father, since these tend to be cold, rational, and full of expectations of competitive performance and success. Chasing the recognition of others through achievement, competitive success, and the accumulation of those things that are valued in society (e.g. wealth, status, and power) can drive us all to expend enormous energy and creativity. However, the project of securing an identity can be self-defeating, because we cannot guarantee that others will confirm the image we seek from them.

It has also been argued that identity politics and the preoccupation with securing the self through social confirmations is heavily gendered, in the sense of being a rational teleological project of subjects dominated by masculine discursive power that affects both women and men as well as those outside conventional sexual identities (Knights 2015). Moreover, what is of particular importance for our purposes is that identity politics often leads to in-group/out-group stereotyping that easily slides into embittered war-like relations, especially where identity is threatened by the mere presence of the other (Ziarek 2001: 74).

One of the most important targets of posthumanist material methodologies is a critique of binary thinking, particularly with regard to mind/body, rational/emotion, gender, race, age, and ability binaries. While those concerned with diversity and anti-discrimination have perhaps always attempted to be non-dualistic, often they have slipped into treating different genders, races, and other discriminated targets in a binary fashion, partly because of taking for granted white, masculine Western values, a problem frequently addressed by postcolonial theory (Mohanty 1995; Lewis and Mills 2003; cf. Chibber 2013). To avoid this, posthumanist feminists have turned to a neglected seventeenth-century philosopher—Spinoza. His monist methodological framework, by definition, avoids any reification of dualistic distinctions and the elevation of one side of a binary over its 'other' to develop a celebration of difference and an ethics of affect (Gatens 1996, 1997; Gatens and Lloyd 1996) where difference is not merely respected at a distance but reflects a bodily and ethical engagement.

There are a range of other theorists that draw on Levinas (1986) and Foucault (1977, 1997) to advance non-dualistic and ethical approaches to diversity (in organizations and society) that are also political (McCallum 1996; Ziarek 2001), or generate an ethics of generosity, responsibility, and resistance (Diprose 2002; Pullen and Rhodes 2010; 2014). The value of this literature is that it gives diversity studies a new lease of life in putting centre stage what has always been implicit—a concern with the body, and an embodied ethics, which has been either neglected altogether or taken for granted in the theory and practice of diversity.

These deliberations are important for diversity studies because invariably, especially with respect to gender, it is discourses of masculinity that elevate cognitive consciousness above the body, emotion, and the unconscious, the latter of which are deemed to reflect the female sex and often racial minorities. These approaches believe less in a technical intervention in the form of specific methodologies so much as inviting students and scholars of diversity to examine the epistemological and ontological assumptions of their work and transforming them where they are dualistic and disembodied. It means being more 'open' or 'generous' (Diprose 2002) to others who are different, rather than seeking to define them in our own image or treating them instrumentally as a means to our own pursuits. It is about transforming the subjectivity of ourselves as researchers so as to give space to difference as an embodied and ethical relationship to the world. As a result, we would be more self-reflexive in our engagements with others in everyday life as well as in research, so as not to reproduce the very discriminations and stereotyped identities that our research aims to dissolve. For, in the absence of transforming subjectivity to displace these binaries and to restore embodied ethicality, diversity in organizations and society can only end up being mismanaged (Knights and Omanović 2013). Insofar as many of the approaches discussed in the positivist and interpretivist sections are managerialist, they necessarily treat diversity as an object to be managed so there is a binary between the manager and the managed. It is therefore important for us to move beyond managing diversity and its entrapment within binary thinking, so as to understand and engage with those who are different and do not automatically serve as a mirror image of ourselves.

One implication of this kind of approach to diversity is that, instead of seeking to capture diversity as a set of objectivations ascribed to different subjects, we need to interrogate the power relations and the various contexts through which this knowledge is produced and look at how diverse subjects are constituted. Without this interrogation, 'diversity research can only produce dislocated knowledge that is unaware of the conditions of its own production' (Ahonen et al. 2014: 8). Methodologically, this means challenging the stereotypes that research on diversity in organizations and its management often reproduces through discourses of diversity. Instead, we can begin to treat diversity as a discourse itself (Ahonen et al. 2014: 3), which can be critiqued insofar as it is a form of governance designed to engineer and advance some mythical infinite human potential (Costea, Amiridis, and Crump 2012).

Traditional, and even some critical, understandings of diversity tend to take identity for granted and are largely oblivious of the extent to which it is one of the most prevalent conditions of the possibility of discrimination. It is so insofar as the pursuit of identity ordinarily involves negation as a means of elevating the self over the 'other'. This occurs through treating the other person or object as an instrumental resource for securing the self in a socially confirmed identity. That is to say, the other is of little more significance than as a mirror for confirming the self (Knights 2015), and what does not do so must be seen as deviant and treated as an object of discrimination. Consequently, the 'otherness' of the Other (Levinas 1991) has to be tamed, minimized, or controlled if it is to fulfil its requirements of providing social confirmation of the self. It has to be reduced to being the Same as the self—like me (Knights 2006, 2015). In terms of diversity, this often takes the form of 'othering' as a way of undermining and stigmatizing those (e.g. women, ethnic minorities, the young or the old, sexualities that deviate from heterosexual normativity or homosociality, etc.) that appear to be outside and a challenge to dominant white, masculine, heterosexual norms. In short, masculine logocentric or legislative reason (Derrida 1982) reduces the 'feminine' to an absent or wholly subordinate 'other': the dividing practices stigmatize difference by elevating normalized over deviant subjects and discourses (Foucault 1982), and seeking to secure or maintain a stable identity demonizes rather than celebrates difference (Knights and Kerfoot 2004).

The implications of this alternative approach to studying diversity at work is that we seek to pursue a less disembodied methodology. Although some methodology texts are more focused on reflexive research approaches, where embodied engagement might be seen as a requirement, books such as Alvesson and Deetz's (2000) *Critical Management Research*, Alvesson and Sköldberg's (2003) *Reflexive Methodology*, and Aull Davies's (2008) *Reflexive Ethnography* offer no significant mention of the body or embodiment. Alvesson and Sköldberg's (2003) sub-chapter on feminist methodology does discuss the role of gendered experiences, feelings, and emotions in doing research and reflecting about the research process, but no attention is given to the embodied and visceral aspects of such experiences, feelings, and emotions. Aull Davies acknowledges the importance of personal and cultural reflexivity and the need to reflect about socio-historical context and disciplinary belonging. In arguing for a 'continuing reflexive awareness' (Aull Davies 2008: 23), emphasis is on the fundamental reflexivity of research in general and ethnographic research in particular. While acknowledging that the researcher's presence affects the social reality it is claimed merely to describe, this is largely discussed in cognitive terms. Consequently, the researcher and the researched remain disembodied in such texts, and the rationale and implications of our alternative approach to diversity is that this undermines the very objectives that are being sought in studying diversity and difference.

Conclusion

In this chapter a diverse range of analytical frameworks and their epistemological and methodological roots subscribed to by researchers of diversity have been examined critically and challenged in relation to the assumptions they frequently deploy explicitly or implicitly. Our concern is that the research on diversity in organizations has prevailingly been less concerned with disrupting than with reproducing the stereotypes that condition the possibility of treating diversity in organizations (and society) as a problem to be managed. While it may be expected that mainstream managerial approaches would be less likely to challenge the ways in which diversity discourses actually produce knowledge, we find that even some critical approaches can be equally as guilty of reproducing the conditions of possibility of disadvantage and discrimination. Some of these critical studies frequently fail to question the assumptions about subjectivity that render their representations possible, and they tend to reproduce linear, disembodied, and dualistic representations of diversity. For this reason, we turned to some alternative scholars within posthumanist feminism, where there is an attempt to transcend the masculinity of linear rational thinking with respect to diversity in organizations and society. We concluded that what is needed is a fresh look at methodology, so as to develop embodied methods that focus on the thinking, feeling, and acting body as prominently as on the mind, cognition, and rationality when examining diversity practices and discourses.

This focus could help to develop an understanding even further of the contradictions and tensions underlying representations of diversity so as to facilitate research with a potential for advancing organizational transformations that undermine historical and systematic disadvantage. Whether such change is likely depends, of course, also on the researchers themselves, who may or may not subscribe to our critical politics of intervention to be more open and may find it more comfortable to follow establishment traditions of research methodology, together with strategies that appeal to prevailingly (rational) managerialist aims and objectives.

References

Acker, J. (1990). Hierarchies, jobs, bodies: a theory of gendered organizations. *Gender & Society* 4(2): 139–58.
Ahonen, P., Tienari, J., Meriläinen, S., and Pullen, A. (2014). Hidden contexts and invisible power relations: a Foucauldian reading of diversity research. *Human Relations*, 67(3): 263–86.
Alvesson, M. and Billing, Y. D. (1999). *Kön och organisation*. Lund: Studentlitteratur.
Alvesson, M. and Deetz, S. (2000). *Doing Critical Management Research*. London: SAGE Publications Ltd.
Alvesson, M. and Sköldberg, K. (2003). *Reflexive Methodology: New Vistas for Qualitative Research*. Thousand Oaks, CA: SAGE.
Ashcraft, K., Kuhn, T. R., and Coreen, F. (2009). Constitutional amendments: 'materializing' organizational communication. *Academy of Management Annals*, 3(1): 1–64.
Ashkanasy, N., Härtel, C., and Daus, C. (2002). Diversity and emotion: the new frontiers in organizational behaviour research. *Journal of Management* 28(3): 307–38.
Auh, S. and Bulent Menguc, B. (2005). Top management team diversity and innovativeness: the moderating role of interfunctional coordination. *Industrial Marketing Management* 34: 249–61.
Aull Davies, C. (2008). *Reflexive Ethnography: A Guide to Researching Selves and Others*. London: Routledge.
Bagilhole, B. (2009). *Understanding Equal Opportunities and Diversity*. Bristol: The Policy Press.
Barros, M. (2010). Emancipatory management: the contradiction between practice and discourse. *Journal of Management Inquiry*, 19(2): 166–84.

Benson, J. K. (1977). Organizations: a dialectical view. *Administrative Science Quarterly* March (22): 1–22.
Benson, J. K. (1983). A dialectical method for the study of organizations. In G. Morgan (ed.), *Beyond Methods: Strategies for Social Research*. Beverly Hills, CA: SAGE Publications, 331–46.
Bhadury J., Mighty, E. J., and Damar, H. (2000). Maximizing workforce diversity in project teams: a network flow approach. *Omega*, 28: 143–53.
Bogaert, S. and Vloeberghs, D. (2005). Differentiated and individualized personnel management: diversity management in Belgium. *European Management Journal* 23(4): 483–93.
Boogaard, B. and Roggeband, C. (2010). Paradoxes of intersectionality: theorizing inequality in the Dutch police force through structure and agency. *Organization*, 17(1): 53–75.
Bordo, S. (1990). Feminism, postmodernism and gender-scepticism. In L. Nicholson (ed.), *Feminism/Postmodernism*. New York: Routledge, 133–76.
Braidotti, R. (2011). *Nomadic Theory: The Portable Rosi Braidotti*. New York: Columbia University Press, Kindle Edition.
Burns, J. and Baldvinsdottir, G. (2005). An institutional perspective of accountants' new roles: the interplay of contradictions and praxis. *European Accounting Review*, 14(4): 725–57.
Burrell, G. and Morgan, G. (1979). *Sociological Paradigms and Organizational Analysis*. Gateshead: Athenaeum Press Ltd.
Bush, V. D. and Ingram, T. N. (2011). Building and assessing cultural diversity skills: implications for sales training. *Industrial Marketing Management*, 30: 65–76.
Calás, M. and Smircich, L. (2006). From the 'women's point of view' ten years later: towards a feminist organization studies. In S. R. Clegg, C. Hardy, T. B. Lawrence, and W. R. Nord (eds.), *Handbook of Organization Studies*. London: SAGE, 284–346.
Chibber, V. (2013). *Postcolonial Theory and the Specter of Capitalism*. London: Verso.
Clough, P. T. (1992). *The End(s) of Ethnography: From Realism to Social Criticism*. Newbury Park, CA: SAGE.
Costea, B., Amiridis, K., and Crump, N. (2012). Graduate employability and the principle of potentiality: an aspect of the ethics of HRM. *Journal of Business Ethics*, DOI 10.1007/s10551-012-1436-x.
Crenshaw, K. (1991) Mapping the margins, intersectionality, identity, and violence against women of color', *Stanford Law Review*, 43: 1241–99.
Cunningham, G. B. (2011). The LGBT advantage: examining the relationship amongst sexual orientation diversity, diversity strategy, and performance. *Sport Management Review*, 14: 453–61.
Deleuze, G. (2005). 'Ethology: Spinoza and us'. In M. Fraser and M. Greco (eds.), *The Body: A Reader*. London and New York: Routledge, 58-61.
Deleuze, G. and Guattari, F. (1988). *A Thousand Plateaus: Capitalism and Schizophrenia*, tr. B. Massumi. London: The Athlone Press.
Derrida, J. (1982) *Margins of Philosophy*, tr. A. Bass. Chicago: University of Chicago Press.
Dick, P. and Cassell, C. (2002). Barriers to managing diversity in a UK constabulary: the role of discourse. *Journal of Management Studies*, 39: 7.
Di Domenico M. L., Tracey, P., and Haugh, H. (2009). The dialectic of social exchange: theorizing corporate–social enterprise collaboration. *Organization Studies*, 30(8): 887–907.
Dinsbach, A. A., Feij, J. A., and de Vries, R. E. (2007). The role of communication content in an ethnically diverse organization. *International Journal of Intercultural Relations* 31: 725–45.

Diprose, R. (2002) *Corporeal Generosity: On Giving with Nietzsche, Merleau-Ponty and Levinas.* New York: SUNY.
Doherty, A., Fink, J., Inglis, S., and Pastore, D. (2010). Understanding a culture of diversity through frameworks of power and change. *Sport Management Review*, 13: 368–81.
Douglas J. D. (ed.). (1970). *Understanding Everyday Life.* London: Routledge.
Dwyer, S., Richard, O. C., and Chadwick, K. (2003). Gender diversity in management and firm performance: the influence of growth orientation and organizational culture. *Journal of Business Research*, 56: 1009–19.
Eckel, C. C. and Grossman, P. J. (2005). Managing diversity by creating team identity. *Journal of Economic Behavior & Organization*, 58: 371–92.
Fine, M. G. (1996). Cultural diversity in the workplace: the state of the field. *The Journal of Business Communication*, 33(4): 485–502.
Fink, J. S. and Pastore, D. L. (2003). Managing employee diversity: perceived practices and organisational outcomes in NCAA Division III athletic departments. *Sport Management Review*, 6: 147–68.
Foster, C. (2005). Implementing diversity management in retailing: exploring the role of organisational context. *International Review of Retail, Distribution and Consumer Research*, 15(4): 471–87.
Foster, C. and Harris, L. (2005). Easy to say, difficult to do: diversity management in retail. *Human Resource Management Journal*, 15(3): 4–17.
Foster, W. M. and Wiebe, E. (2010). Praxis makes perfect: recovering the ethical promise of critical management studies. *Journal of Business Ethics*, 94(2): 271–83.
Foucault, M. (1977). *Language, Counter-Memory, Practice.* Ithaca, NY: Cornell University Press.
Foucault, M. (1980). *Power/Knowledge*, ed. C. Gordon. Brighton: Harvester Press.
Foucault, M. (1982). The subject and power. In H. Dreyfus and P. Rabinow (eds.), *Michel Foucault: Beyond Structuralism and Hermeneutics.* New York: Harvester Press, 208-226.
Foucault, M. (1997). *Ethics: Subjectivity and Truth.* London: Allen Lane.
Freeman, S. and Lindsay, S. (2012). The effect of ethnic diversity on expatriate managers in their host country. *International Business Review*, 21: 253–68.
Furunes, T. and Mykletun, R. J. (2007). Why diversity management fails: metaphor analyses unveil manager attitudes. *Hospitality Management*, 26: 974–90.
Game, A. (1991). *Undoing the Social.* Milton Keynes: Open University Press.
Gatens, M. (1996). *Imaginary Bodies: Ethics, Power and Corporeality.* London: Routledge.
Gatens, M. (1997). Through a Spinozist lens: ethology, difference, power. In P. Patton (ed.), *Deleuze: A Critical Reader.* Oxford: Blackwell, 162–87.
Gatens M. and Lloyd, G. (1996). *Collective Imaginings: Spinoza, Past and Present.* London and New York: Routledge, Kindle edition.
Gibson, C. B. and Zellmer-Bruhn, M. E. (2001). Metaphors and meaning: an intercultural analysis of the concept of teamwork. *Administrative Science Quarterly*, 46: 274–303.
Gilbert, J. A. and Ivancevich, J. M. (2000). Valuing diversity: a tale of two organizations. *Academy of Management Executive*, 14(1): 93–105.
Groleau, C., Demers, C., and Engeström, Y. (2011). Guest editorial. *Journal of Organizational Change Management*, 24(3), 330–2.
Grosz, E. (1994). *Volatile Bodies: Toward a Corporeal Feminism.* Bloomington, IN: Indiana University Press.
Grosz, E. (2005). From 'intensities and flows'. In T. Atkinson (ed.), *The Body: Readers in Cultural Criticism.* Basingstoke: Palgrave Macmillan, 142–55.

Härtel, C. E. J. (2004). Towards a multicultural world: identifying work systems, practices and employee attitudes that embrace diversity. *Australian Journal of Management*, 29(2): 189–200.

Hartsock, N. C. M. (1995). The feminist standpoint: developing the ground for a specifically feminist historical materialism. In N. Tuana and R. Tong (eds.), *Feminism and Philosophy*. Boulder, CO: Westview Press, 35–47.

Hekman, S. J. (1999). *The Future of Differences: Truth and Method in Feminist Theory*. Oxford: Polity Press.

Ivancevich, J. M. and Gilbert, J. A. (2000). Diversity management time for a new approach. *Public Personnel Management*, 29(1): 75–92.

Jack, G. and Lorbiecki, A. (2007). National identity, globalization and the discursive construction of organizational identity. *British Journal of Management*, 8: S79–S94.

Janiewski, D. (1995). Gendering, racializing and classifying: settler colonization in the United States, 1590–1990. In D. Stasiulis and N. Yuval-Davis (eds.), *Unsettling Settler Societies: Articulations of Gender, Race, Ethnicity and Class*. London: SAGE Publications, 71–89.

Johnston, D. and Malina, M. A. (2008). Managing sexual orientation diversity: the impact on firm value. *Group Organization Management*, 33(5): 602–25.

Johnston, W. B. and Packer, A. H. (1987). *Diversity Workforce 2000: Work and Workers for the 21st Century*. Indianapolis, IN: Hudson Institute.

Kamenou, N., Watt, H., and Fearfull, A. (2006). Ethnic minority women: a lost voice in HRM. *Human Resource Management Journal*, 16(2): 154–72.

Kearney, E. and Gebert, D. (2006). Does more diversity lead to more innovativeness? An examination of the critical role of leadership. Paper presented at IFSAM VIIIth World Congress, 28–30 September, Berlin, Germany.

Kelly, E. and Dobbin, F. (1998). How affirmative action become diversity management. *American Behavioral Scientist*, 41(7): 960–84.

Kidder, D. L., Lankau, M. J., Chrobot-Mason, D., Kelly, A., Mollica, K. A., and Friedman, R. A. (2004). Backlash toward diversity initiatives: examining the impact of diversity program justification, personal and group outcomes. *The International Journal of Conflict of Management*, 15(1): 77–102.

Kirby, S. L. and Richard, O. C. (2000). Impact of marketing work-place diversity on employee job involvement and organizational commitment. *The Journal of Social Psychology*, 140(3): 367–77.

Klein, K. J., Knight, A. P., Ziegert, J. C., Lim, B. C., and Saltz, J. L. (2011). When team members' values differ: the moderating role of team leadership. *Organizational Behavior and Human Decision Processes*, 114: 25–36.

Knights, D. (2006). Passing the time in pastimes, professionalism and politics: reflecting on the ethics and epistemology of time studies. *Time and Society*, 15(3): 251–74.

Knights, D. (2015). Binaries need to shatter for bodies to matter: do disembodied masculinities undermine organizational ethics? *Organization*, 22(2): 200–16.

Knights, D. and Kerfoot, D. (2004). Between representations and subjectivity: gender binaries and the politics of organizational transformation. *Gender, Work and Organization*, 11(4): July: 430–54.

Knights, D. and Omanović, V. (2013). Diversity management or mismanaging diversity: reflections on re-covering difference in organization studies. Presented at the APROS Conference, 15 Tokyo 15–17 February. To be published as: (Mis)managing diversity: exploring the dangers of diversity. *Management Orthodoxy Equality Diversity and Inclusion: An International Journal*, 2016.

Kurowski, L. L. (2002). Cloaked culture and veiled diversity: why theorists ignored early us workforce diversity. *Journal of Management History*, 40(2): 183–91.

Lacan, J. (1977). *Écrits: A Selection*. London: Tavistock.

Lauring, J. (2009). Managing cultural diversity and the process of knowledge sharing: a case from Denmark. *Scandinavian Journal of Management*, 25: 385–94.

Lauring, J. and Selmer, J. (2012). International language management and diversity climate in multicultural organizations. *International Business Review*, 21: 156–66.

Levinas, E. (1986). in Face to Face with Levinas. Edited by Cohen, R.A., Albany, NY: State University of New York Press.

Levinas, E. (1991). *Otherwise than Being or Beyond Essence*. Dordrecht: Kluwer Academic Publishers.

Lewis, R. and Mills, S. (2003). *Feminist Postcolonial Theory: A Reader*. New York: Routledge.

Litvin, D. (2000). *Defamiliarizing Diversity*. Amherst, MA: Isenberg School of Management.

Litvin, D. (2006). Diversity: making space for a better case. In Pringle J. K. and Prasad P. (eds.), *Handbook of Workplace Diversity*. Thousand Oaks, CA: SAGE Publications Inc, 75-94.

Lorbiecki, A. and Jack, G. (2000). Critical turns in the evolution of diversity management. *British Journal of Management*, 11(Special Issue): S17–S31.

Luis, J. (2012). Diversity and internationalization: the case of boards and TMT's. *International Business Review*, 21(1): 1–12.

Lynch, F. R. (1997). *The Diversity Machine: The Drive to Change the 'White Male Workplace'*. New York: The Free Press.

McCallum, E. L. (1996). Technologies of truth and function of gender in Foucault. In S. J. Hekman (ed.), *Feminist Interpretations of Michel Foucault*. University Park, PA: Pennsylvania State University Press.

McKay, P. F. (2008). Mean racial-ethnic differences in employee sales performance: the moderating role of diversity climate. *Personnel Psychology*, 61: 349–74.

Magoshi, E. and Chang, E. (2009). Diversity management and the effects on employees' organizational commitment: evidence from Japan and Korea. *Journal of World Business*, 44: 31–40.

Mayring, P. (2007). On generalization in qualitatively oriented research. *Forum Qualitative Sozialforschung/Forum: Qualitative Social Research*, 8(3), Art. 26, <http://nbn-resolving.de/urn:nbn:de:0114-fqs0703262>, accessed 28 August 2013.

Meriläinen S., Tienari, J., Katila, S., and Benschop, Y. (2009). Diversity management versus gender equality: the Finnish case. *Canadian Journal of Administrative Sciences*, 26(3): 230–43.

Mohanty, C. T. (1995). Feminist encounters: locating the politics of experience. In L. Nicholson and S. Seidman (eds.) *Social Postmodernism: Beyond Identity Politics*. Cambridge: Cambridge University Press, 68-86.

Mohr, A. M. and Puck, J. F. (2005). Managing functional diversity to improve the performance of international joint ventures. *Long Range Planning*, 38: 163–82.

Mollica, K. A. (2003). The influence of diversity context on white men's and racial minorities' reactions to disproportionate group harm. *The Journal of Social Psychology*, 143(4): 415–31.

Morgan, G. (1980). Paradigms, metaphors, and puzzle solving in organization theory. *Administrative Science Quarterly*, 25: 605–22.

Mumby, D. K. (2005). Theorizing resistance in organization studies: a dialectical approach. *Management Communication Quarterly*, 19(1): 19–44.

Nemetz, P. and Christensen, S. (1996). The challenge of cultural diversity: harnessing a diversity of views to understand multiculturalism. *Academy of Management Review*, 21(2): 434–62.

Nkomo, S. M. and Cox, Jr, T. (1996). Diverse identities in organizations. In S. Clegg and C. Hardy (eds.), *The Handbook of Organization Studies*. Thousand Oaks, CA: SAGE Publications, 338–56.

Noon, M. (2007). The fatal flaws of diversity and the business case for ethnic minorities. *Work, Employment and Society*, 2(4): 773–84.

Noon, M. (2010). The shackled runner: time to rethink positive discrimination? *Work, Employment and Society*, 24(4): 728–39.

Nussbaum, M. (1992). Human functioning and social justice: in defence of Aristotelian essentialism. *Political Theory*, 20(2): 202–46.

Ogbor, J. O. (2001). Critical theory and the hegemony of corporate culture. *Journal of Organizational Change Management*, 14(6): 590–608.

Omanović, V. (2002). Constructing the business case for diversity. Paper presented at 'Meeting Ourselves and Others:Perspectives in Diversity Research and Diversity Practices', Göteborg, Sweden, 29–31 August.

Omanović, V. (2006). *A Production of Diversity: Appearances, Ideas, Interests, Actions, Contradictions and Praxis*. Gothenburg: BAS Publishing.

Omanović, V. (2009). Diversity and its management as a dialectical process: encountering Sweden and the U.S. *Scandinavian Journal of Management*, 25(4): 363–73.

Omanović, V. (2011). Diversity in organizations: a critical examination of the assumptions about diversity and organizations in 21st century management literature. In E. Jeanes, D. Knights, and P. Y. Martin (eds.), *Handbook of Gender, Work and Organization*. London: Wiley, 315–32.

Omanović, V. (2013). Opening and closing the door to diversity: a dialectical analysis of the social production of diversity. *Scandinavian Journal of Management*, 29(1): 87–103.

Østergaarda C. R., Timmermans, B., and Kristinsson, K. (2011). Does a different view create something new? The effect of employee diversity on innovation. *Research Policy*, 40: 500–9.

Phillips, K. W. and Loyd, D. L. (2006). When surface and deep-level diversity collide: the effects on dissenting group members. *Organizational Behavior and Human Decision Processes*, 99: 143–60.

Pieterse, A. N., van Knippenberg, D., and Ginkel, W. P. (2011). Diversity in goal orientation, team reflexivity, and team performance. *Organizational Behavior and Human Decision Processes*, 114: 153–64.

Pinar, M., McCuddy, M. K., Birkan, I., and Kozak, M. (2011). Gender diversity in the hospitality industry: an empirical study in Turkey. *International Journal of Hospitality Management*, 30: 73–81.

Popper, K. R. (1947). *The Open Society and Its Enemies*. London: Routledge.

Powell, N. G. (1993). *Women and Men in Management*. Thousand Oaks, CA. SAGE Publications.

Pullen, A. and Rhodes, C. (2010). Gender, ethics and the face. In P. Lewis and R. Simpson (eds.), *Concealing and Revealing Gender*. Basingstoke: Palgrave, 233–48.

Pullen, A. and Rhodes, C. (2014). Corporeal ethics and the politics of resistance in organizations. *Organization*, 21(6): 782–96.

Rantalaiho, L. and Heiskanen, T. (1997). Persistence and change of gendered practices. In L. Rantalaiho and T.Heiskanen (eds.), *Gendered Practices in Working Life*. New York: St. Martin's Press, 7–23.

Rao, A. (2012). Managing diversity: impact of religion in the Indian workplace. *Journal of World Business*, 47(2): 232–9.

Rhodes, C. (2012). Ethics, alterity and the rationality of leadership justice. *Human Relations*, 65(10): 1311–31.
Richard, O. C. (2000). Racial diversity, business strategy, and firm performance: a resource-based view. *Academy of Management Journal*, 43(2): 164–77.
Roberson, Q. (2006). Disentangling the meanings of diversity and inclusion in organizations. *Group and Organization Management*, 31(2): 212–36.
Roberson, Q. M. and Park, H. J. (2007). Examining the link between diversity and firm performance: the effects of diversity reputation and leader racial diversity. *Group & Organization Management*, 32(5): 548–68.
Robinson, G. and Dechant, K. (1997). Building the business case. *Academy of Management Executive*, 11(3): 21–31.
Sandberg, J. and Alvesson, M. (2011) Ways of constructing research questions: gap-spotting or problematization? *Organization*, 18(1): 23–44.
Sawyer, J. E., Houlette, M. A., and Yeagley, E. L. (2006). Decision performance and diversity structure: comparing faultlines in convergent, crosscut, and racially homogeneous groups. *Organizational Behavior and Human Decision Processes*, 99: 1–15.
Schroyer, T. (1975). *The Critique of Domination: The Origins and Development of Critical Theory*. New York: Beacon Press.
Shachaf, P. (2008). Cultural diversity and information and communication technology impacts on global virtual teams: an exploratory study. *Information & Management*, 45: 131–42.
Sharma, U., Lawrence, S. and Lowe, A. (2010). Institutional contradiction and management control innovation: a field study of total quality management practices in a privatized telecommunication company. *Management Accounting Research*, 21(4): 251–64.
Shoobridge, G. E. (2006). Multi-ethnic workforce and business performance: review and synthesis of the empirical literature. *Human Resource Development Review*, 5(1): 92–137.
Shore, L. M., Chung-Herrera, B. G., Dean, M. A., Ehrhart, K., Jung, D. I., Randel, A. E., and Gangaram Singh, G. (2009). Diversity in organizations: where are we now and where are we going? *Human Resource Management*, 19: 117–33.
Smith, W. J., Wokutch, R. E., Harrington, K. V., and Dennis, B. S. (2004). Organizational attractiveness and corporate social orientation: do our values influence our preference for affirmative action and managing diversity? *Business & Society*, 43(1): 69–96.
Styhre, A. and Eriksson-Zetterquist, U. (2008). Thinking the multiple in gender and diversity studies: examining the concept of intersectionality. *Gender in Management: An International Journal*, 23(8): 567–82.
Subeliani, D. and Tsogas, D. (2005). Managing diversity in the Netherlands: a case study of Rabobank. *International Journal of Human Resource Management*, 16(5): 831–51.
Süß, S. and Kleiner, M. (2007). Diversity management in Germany: dissemination and design of the concept. *International Journal of Human Resource Management*, 18: 1934–53.
Süß, S. and Kleiner, M. (2008). Dissemination of diversity management in Germany: a new institutionalist approach. *European Management Journal*, 26: 35–47.
Swan, E. (2010). Commodity diversity: smiling faces as a strategy of containment. *Organization*, 17(1): 77–100.
Taylor, C. (1995). Building a business case for diversity. *Canadian Business Review*, 22(1).
Thomas, D. A. (2004). *Diversity as Strategy*. Boston, MA: Harvard Business School (EBSCOhost).
Thomas, J. (1993). *Doing Critical Ethnography*. London: SAGE.

Thomas, Jr, R. R. (1990). From affirmative action to affirming diversity. *Harvard Business Review*, 68: 107–17.

Thomas, Jr, R.R. (1991). *Beyond Race and Gender*. New York: AMACOM.

Tomlinson F and Schwabenland, C. (2010). Reconciling competing discourses of diversity? The UK non-profit sector between social justice and the business case. *Organization*, 17(1): 101-121.

Tung, L. L. and Quaddus, M. A. (2002). Cultural differences explaining the differences in results in GSS: implications for the next decade. *Decision Support Systems*, 33: 177–99.

Wang, E. T. G., Wei, H. L., Jiang, J. J., and Klein, G. (2006). User diversity impact on project performance in an environment with organizational technology learning and management review processes. *International Journal of Project Management*, 24: 405–11.

Watsona, W. E., BarNir, A., and Pavur, R. (2005). Cultural diversity and learning teams: the impact on desired academic team processes. *International Journal of Intercultural Relations*, 29: 449–67.

Westwood, R. I. and Linstead, S. (2001). Language/organization: introduction. In R. I. Westwood and S. Linstead (eds.), *The Language of Organization*. London: SAGE, 1–19.

Zanoni, P. and Janssens, M. (2004). Deconstructing difference: the rhetoric of human resource managers' diversity discourses. *Organization Studies*, 25(1): 55–74.

Zanoni, P. and Janssens, M. (2007). Minority employees engaging with (diversity) management: an analysis of control, agency, and micro-emancipation. *Journal of Management Studies*, 44(8): 1371–97.

Zanoni, P., Janssens, M., Benschop, Y., and Nkomo, S. (2010). Unpacking diversity, grasping inequality: rethinking difference through critical perspectives. *Organization*, 17(1): 9–29.

Ziarek, E. P. (2001). *An Ethics of Dissensus: Postmodernity, Feminism and the Politics of Radical Democracy*. Stanford, CA: Stanford University Press.

CHAPTER 5

REFLECTIONS ON DIVERSITY AND INCLUSION PRACTICES AT THE ORGANIZATIONAL, GROUP, AND INDIVIDUAL LEVELS

RUTH SESSLER BERNSTEIN, MARCY CRARY, DIANA BILIMORIA, AND DONNA MARIA BLANCERO

Introduction

WITH increasing globalization, immigration, and changing demographics, workplaces are increasingly heterogeneous in nature. These changes are challenging organizations to harness the power of diversity by adopting practices of inclusion that improve and sustain performance outcomes at the organizational, group, and individual levels—creating a diversity dividend (Van Knippenberg and Haslam 2003), which we define as the positive outcomes associated with harnessing and leveraging the social identities and resources of diverse individuals and workgroups. In the present chapter, we provide our reflections on the practices that are being employed by organizations to diversify the workplace and maximize the potential for a diversity dividend by practices of inclusion. We first briefly review empirical findings in the extant literature on the performance outcomes of diverse workgroups. Next, we draw on our own research, as well as extant literature, to discuss diversity and inclusion practices at the organizational, group, and individual levels that engender a diversity dividend. Our discussion shows that achieving beneficial outcomes from diversity is dependent on a variety of practices of diversity and inclusion occurring at a multitude of levels—organizational, group, and individual.

Workplace diversity in the United States has evolved from meeting quotas dictated by federal law with regard to the current focus on inclusion, reducing tensions, and contributing to organizational success. Unfortunately, diversity in the workplace remains an enigma, sometimes supporting and sometimes undermining performance outcomes. Therefore, diversity management (DM) remains an enduring issue within organizational life. It concerns individual identity formation and group processes, as well as efforts at the organizational level to become inclusive in order to enhance business performance. *Diversity* has multiple interpretations, from simple demographic diversity (sometimes referred to as numerical diversity or representative diversity based on both ascribed (e.g. race, gender) and acquired (e.g. knowledge, skills) characteristics), to meaningful, deep-level, intercultural interactions that enable individuals to learn from one another and build intercultural skills (Stangor et al. 1992; Harrison, Price, and Bell 1998). Based on extant conceptualizations in the literature, *inclusion* refers to an individual's or subgroup's sense of efficacy, belonging, and value in a work system (cf. Roberson 2006; Bernstein and Bilimoria 2013).

Extant Findings on the Outcomes of Diverse Workgroups

Despite substantial research assessing the effects of diversity on organizational and group performance, these studies have produced inconsistent results (see Milliken and Martins 1996; Horwitz and Horwitz 2007; Van Knippenberg and Schippers 2007; Joshi and Roh 2009). Diverse groups have been shown to outperform homogeneous groups in some studies (e.g. Cox, Lobel, and McLeod 1991), while in others homogeneous groups outperformed heterogeneous groups (e.g. Pelled 1996). The only thing we know for sure is that we have limited understanding as to how, why, and when diversity impacts outcomes (Van Knippenberg and Schippers 2007; Joshi, Liao, and Roh 2011; Guillaume et al. 2013) or which DM practices are most effective (Guillaume et al. 2013).

Horwitz and Horwitz's (2007) meta-analysis determined that group bio-demographic diversity had an adverse impact on group outcomes (e.g. Byrne 1971; Tajfel and Turner 1986), and that varying member characteristics such as age, ethnicity, and expertise may be negatively associated with performance outcomes (Milliken and Martins 1996). Horwitz and Horwitz (2007) concluded that simply increasing the amount of visible diversity in teams did not necessarily maximize the benefits of diversity in teams. However, task-related diversity positively related to the quality and quantity of team performance, suggesting that creating high-performing teams with members who have task-relevant heterogeneity is much more important than focusing on bio-demographic attributes. While this may make sense, our multicultural society demands the integration of demographically diverse groups.

Despite this vast amount of research, the inconsistency in the findings leads us to agree with Roberson (2006: 234) that, 'The management of diversity is more complex than is currently articulated in both practitioner and scholarly research... there is a critical difference between merely having diversity in an organization's workforce and developing the organizational capacity to leverage diversity as a resource...' Thus, achieving positive diversity performance outcomes is complex, and involves a multitude of approaches at the organizational, group, and individual levels. Without concerted effort and attention to the practices of inclusion, diversity may create negative performance outcomes, and lead individuals to experience tension and discomfort when interacting with diverse others (Crisp and Turner 2011). In the rest of this chapter, we reflect on a number of effective inclusion practices that have been empirically shown to improve organizational performance and achieve the diversity dividend. We begin at the level of organizational practices, by discussing effective practices of diversity and inclusion empirically observed in research studies we have conducted within samples of universities and non-profit boards of trustees. Next, at the group level, drawing on research conducted by us and that in other extant literature, we examine specific diversity and inclusion practices which impact group cohesiveness and outcomes. Finally, drawing on our own and extant research, we delve into the individual level and examine individuals' development of competence for engaging with and managing social identity dynamics in the workplace.

REFLECTIONS ON ORGANIZATION-WIDE PRACTICES OF DIVERSITY, EQUITY, AND INCLUSION

In this subsection, we review effective practices of diversity, equity, and inclusion at the organizational level by drawing on recent efforts of faculty workforce diversification among leading universities in the United States, supported by the National Science Foundation's (NSF's) *ADVANCE* initiative. The *ADVANCE* institutional transformation programme has been in place since 2001, and its goals are to catalyse the transformation of academic work environments in US higher education institutions in ways that enhance the participation and advancement of women in science and engineering. In a study of nineteen US universities that constituted the first two cohorts of *ADVANCE* funding, Bilimoria and Liang (2012) identified two major clusters of practices aimed at improving gender equity, diversity, and inclusion: (a) workforce diversification practices—initiatives to diversify the faculty workforce and enhance the career trajectories of women and underrepresented minority faculty at every stage of the academic pipeline; and (b) organizational culture enhancement practices to improve extant institutional systems, policies, and climate by enhancing equity and inclusion. We describe each of these practices in more detail in the following paragraphs.

Embracing diversity is a central, defining characteristic that leads to the development of attitudes and skills that help translate the organization's values into effective practices, leading to desirable outcomes (Groggins and Ryan 2013). In the case of the *ADVANCE* universities, *workforce diversification practices* included three aspects: (a) practices to increase the inflow of women and minority faculty into the pipeline, such as through active search and recruitment, mentoring and training; (b) practices to equip women and minority faculty to successfully progress in the academic pipeline, such as through regular career development workshops; and (c) initiatives to improve the institutional systems, structures, and practices related to key academic career transition points in the pipeline. Examples of the latter included training and development interventions in the institution's extant recruitment, advancement, and retention decision processes, aimed at informing the persons undertaking such decisions about their unconscious biases, changing their approaches and attitudes towards diverse others, and making their ways of operating more transparent, participative, and accountable. As Kulik and Roberson (2008) indicated, training supervisors and decision makers is an important step in creating a culture that welcomes and supports diversity.

The second emphasis of *ADVANCE* institutional transformation focused on *practices that make the organizational culture more equitable and inclusive*, in terms of creating performance standards that apply to everyone, fostering high-quality relations, being attentive to the meaning and significance of people's diverse identities, and making all employees feel valued and respected. The creation of a positive diversity climate, where employees feel supported and the impediments to career advancement of diverse individuals are eliminated, may be facilitated by human resource (HR) policies that encourage open lines of communication among employees (Singh, Winkel, and Selvarajan 2013). The *ADVANCE* institutions undertook many initiatives to change their organizational cultures and create positive diversity climates (cf. Guillaume et al. 2013). Four initiatives most frequently used to improve the micro (departmental) climate across *ADVANCE* universities were: faculty climate surveys and feedback, small funding opportunities for departmental transformation, facilitated microclimate interventions, and leadership development and climate awareness training of department chairs. Faculty climate surveys were one of the most widely implemented strategies across *ADVANCE* sites. The core climate variables that were investigated in the climate surveys included treatment by colleagues/supervisors, recognition, respect, collegiality, expectations, sense of being valued, fit, exclusion, spousal employment, childcare responsibilities, job/career satisfaction, resource equity and access, service and teaching loads, and time allocation. *ADVANCE* universities also focused on improving the macro institutional (school/college and university) climate. These institutions worked on enhancing overall school/college- and campus-wide awareness of gender equity and institutional climate through establishing campus-wide advisory councils on women and minorities, undertaking salary equity and laboratory space equity studies, bringing distinguished senior women scholars on visits to campus, undertaking gender equity awareness training for non-faculty campus constituencies such as students, holding climate awareness workshops for faculty and administrators through interactive theatre presentations, instituting family-friendly and academic career flexibility policies, enacting childcare initiatives, and targeting the increase of women in administrative (department chair and dean) and faculty leadership (endowed chair) positions.

Two recent studies of American non-profit organizations (Bernstein and Davidson 2012; Buse, Bernstein, and Bilimoria 2014) examined the impact of specific organizational-level *practices that demonstrate organizational commitment to diversity and inclusion*. These practices include diversity statements or policies, committees or taskforces dedicated to diversity and inclusion, diversity training for board members, organizational efforts to recruit from communities of colour, and integration of diversity into the organization's core mission and values. Bernstein and Davidson (2012) determined that the adoption of such diversity-focused practices had no direct impact on organizational performance, but significantly influenced the adoption of inclusive behaviours by board members, including reaching a consensus about the value and benefits of expanding the diversity of the board and developing an inclusive culture and inclusive board dynamics. Buse, Bernstein, and Bilimoria (2014) found that board inclusion practices (such as valuing the contributions of diverse members in the board's tasks, including diverse members in developing the board's most important policies, and ensuring diverse members are influential in the board's routine activities) partially mediated the relationship between board gender and racial/ethnic diversity on the one hand, and the performance of effective non-profit governance on the other.

In summary, results from NSF *ADVANCE* institutions (Bilimoria, Joy, and Liang 2008; Bilimoria and Liang 2012) as well as non-profit board studies (Bernstein and Davidson 2012; Buse, Bernstein, and Bilimoria 2014) indicate that effective diversity and inclusion practices at the organizational level include practices of workforce diversification, practices that make the organizational culture more equitable and inclusive, and practices that demonstrate the organization's commitment to diversity and inclusion.

Reflections on Group-Level Practices of Diversity and Inclusion

The literature suggests that achieving positive performance outcomes from diversity and inclusion is not going to occur without the adoption of deliberate practices. When work groups foster environments that promote high-quality relationships and learning, diversity may be appreciated as a resource, not an impediment to the organization, potentially enhancing performance (Ely, Padavic, and Thomas 2012). In this section we reflect on a number of empirically derived practices that we recommend in order to stimulate positive outcomes at the group level.

Shared purpose and common goals within groups enable members to build common bonds, goals, and values with others in the group, consistent with Brint's (2001) view that community members' common experiences enable the development of bonding ties and concern for one another. Focus on a common purpose allows group members to share attitudes, personal beliefs, and values associated with deep-level diversity (Stangor et al. 1992). When individuals are motivated by the purpose of the group, members develop a strong group social identity (Tajfel and Turner 1986), are less focused on individualistic or personal benefits (Lembke and Wilson 1998), and are more willing to change personal perspectives (Tajfel 1982). According to Gaertner and Dovidio (2000), organizational purpose expands members' identity beyond the self to the organization. Bernstein and Salipante's (2010) study of college students determined that students who were members of voluntary or co-curricular groups with a strong organizational purpose were more likely to experience deep-level, meaningful interactions that led to them experiencing behavioural comfort (the felt ease, safety, and self-efficacy of interacting appropriately with diverse others) when interacting with dissimilar students. The strength of common mission, interests, and shared purpose of the organization enables individuals to place a high priority on group performance and success, as opposed to dwelling on differences within the group.

Inclusive welcoming practices, consistent with the concept of opportunity (Allport 1954), positively impacts members' ability to meet and befriend diverse others. Welcoming is one of the organizational practices identified by Bernstein and Salipante (2011) in enabling diverse group members to achieve behavioural comfort. Welcoming practices convey to all potential members that the group is accepting of diverse individuals. Welcoming practices vary depending on the type of group and age of the members, but may include ice-breakers, time with other members, information sharing, team building exercises, and so on. When effective, welcoming practices facilitate inclusive socialization and fellowship, which promote organizational identity and a personal sense of belonging.

Practices of optimal contact, interaction structuring and social integration refer to deliberate actions that promote positive group member interactions. Rosenblatt, Worthley, and MacNab (2013: 358) refer to Allport's (1954) concept of optimal contact as involving 'a number of conditions, including equal status among participants, common goals, personalized contact, and support of the contact by authorities'. *Optimal contact practices* may be translated in workplace environments as practices of mentoring, coaching, and sponsoring; affinity or employee resource groups; dialogue groups; and personal or professional training and development workshops. For example, core groups at Digital Equipment Company (Walker and Hanson 1992), key identity groups at Merck (Park 2008), identity group task forces at IBM Corporation (Thomas 2004) are examples of organizations hosting and resourcing spaces for recognizing and honouring diverse social identities.

Interaction structuring practices similarly focus on deliberately planning activities and forums for positive interaction (Bernstein and Salipante 2011). One such method is re-categorization, which occurs when in-group and out-group members realign themselves as belonging to a common group with a superordinate goal (Gaertner and Dovidio 2000). This change enables diverse individuals to maintain their original identities, while allowing an individual's sense of self to be 'based on symbolic attachment to the group as a whole' (Roccas and Brewer 2002: 89). Since socializing is the strongest predictor of positive intercultural interactions (Saenz, Ngai, and Hurtado 2007), purposefully engineering activities to maximize constructive social interactions among members is beneficial. Other practices of interaction structuring include rotating committee assignments and leadership positions to maintain equal member status, adoption of practices that encourage voice, participation in decision-making, and reduced reliance on hierarchy, which contributes to a strong group identity and mutual respect (Shore et al. 2011). When such practices are successful, hierarchy, subgroup homogeneity, and cliques are minimized.

Social integration practices (e.g. providing mentors for new members and planning recreational social activities) enable diverse individuals to interact together; however, these interactions must not only include contact time but be positive and meaningful as well. Simply experiencing interactions with diverse others does not guarantee that the interactions will not be negative, contributing to increased tension and distrust among group members. Thoughtfully planned social integration, fellowship, or 'fun' practices create the right kind of interactions for building closer relationships between group members (Dumas, Phillips, and Rothbard 2013).

Both interaction structuring and social integration practices are predicated on the premise that that group members often base their initial categorization of other group members on stereotypes determined by surface-level biological characteristics (e.g. Harrison et al. 2002). Harrison and colleagues (2002) pursue the idea that initial stereotypes are later moderated with deeper-level knowledge of attitudinal, belief, and value similarities, enabling interactions to transition from surface-level to deep-level diversity. The element of time spent together is critical since 'negative affective outcomes of diversity in observable attributes [surface-level diversity] appear to decrease with the amount of time that the group stays together' (Harrison et al. 2002: 415–16). However, poorly managed group tensions may simply increase with tenure (Watson, Johnson, and Merritt 1998), contributing to negative group performance. Therefore, optimal contact, interaction structuring, and social integration practices must be carefully designed and evaluated over time so that they encourage learning about and from diverse others as part of a multipronged effort to promote inclusion.

Practices fostering a sense of belonging or group acceptance constitute the next aspect of effective diversity and inclusion practices. The desire to belong drives people to seek frequent, positive interactions with others within a stable, long-term, and caring context (Baumeister and Leary 1995). This results in people becoming attached to one another through their common connections to social groups, balancing their sense of uniqueness and belongingness (Shore et al. 2011). While no single practice may foster a sense of belonging or group acceptance, workgroups enable all members to achieve 'insider' or 'owner' status, potentially by adopting resolution procedures; facilitating communication; providing opportunities for influence in decision-making; enabling access to the information, resources, and networks necessary for effective job performance; affording access to opportunities for advancement and career development; and providing freedom from stereotyping (e.g. Roberson 2006; Bilimoria, Joy, and Liang 2008). In a recent study of non-profit boards, minority members perceived inclusion when the board as a whole functioned without using insensitive or offensive comments or jokes, board members shared power, communications were geared to all members, inclusivity was discussed and acted upon, and minority members were treated equally (Bernstein and Bilimoria 2013).

Recent research has also examined the optimal environmental conditions for working with identity dynamics in organizational life. Bodenhausen (2010: 12) noted that: '... working environments need to be engineered in way that promote the recognition and valuing of complex social identities, allowing for group members to experience social self-verification within the group'. An important group condition in this regard is *psychological safety*. Debebe (2011) describes the qualities of holding environments or nurturing spaces for meaning-making and transformational growth in the context of a women's leadership development programme. Foldy, Rivard, and Buckley (2009) describe the critical role of experiences of safety for learning in racially diverse groups. High-quality relationships are associated with a sense of psychological safety (Carmeli, Brueller, and Dutton 2009). When psychological safety is present in a workgroup, diverse members are empowered to participate fully, bringing their different social identities to the table. For example, Bernstein and Salipante's (2010) qualitative examination of university students found that inside the psychologically safe environment of a voluntary association (where they felt welcomed, shared goals, and participated in interaction structuring practices) students were able to move beyond political correctness and build friendships while simultaneously learning about each other. Outside of the voluntary association, however, political correctness made the students fearful of asking potentially sensitive questions that could be misinterpreted or cause embarrassment to themselves or those with whom they were engaging.

In summary, the results of studies at the group level indicate the usefulness of certain group-level practices in achieving the diversity dividend: the practices of shared purpose, inclusive welcoming, interaction structuring, social integration, and optimal contact, fostering a sense of belonging or group acceptance, and psychological safety.

Reflections on the Development of Individual-Level Diversity Competence in the Workplace

In the preceding sections we have reflected on how organizations and groups can optimize cross-identity differences to build more inclusive work environments. However, organization-level and group-level practices will have little effect if individuals do not have the capabilities to take advantage of them. The individual capacities and competencies of organizational members are the underpinning of successful diverse and inclusive workgroups and organizations. Thus, in this section we turn our attention to the individual level, and consider how individuals develop their understandings about their own and others' social identities and learn how to navigate social identity issues in the workplace.

Here we focus on social identities that are ascribed (e.g. gender, race, etc.) and used in categorizing ourselves and others. We recognize that social identities are developed and fashioned within the context of multiple self-identities, including those defined through occupational, career, organizational roles, and so on in organizational settings. We join with theorists and researchers who frame the management of social identities in the workplace as a social construction process—for example, an active ongoing negotiation project (e.g. Kreiner, Hollensbe, and Sheep 2006), 'identity work' (e.g. Kreiner, Hollensbe, and Sheep 2009), 'identity as problem and project' (Alvesson, Ashcraft, and Thomas 2008), or a self-navigational challenge (Roberts and Creary 2013). As Roberts (2005: 685) notes, 'In a diverse society, all organizational members must learn how to effectively navigate their interactions with people from different cultural backgrounds so that they can build credibility, form high-quality relationships, and generate high performance outcomes with their constituents.' The reality of our having multiple, intersecting identities that may be altered in their saliency across different contexts is part of the complexity and challenge of managing our social identities in the workplace.

We are particularly interested in the challenge of how a single identity category can dominate one's sense of social identity. 'A given identity [may] trump other potential identities, remaining salient in most circumstances while other identities fall off the radar screen ... so only the dominant category retains the power to define the individual's social identity ... From the perceiver's perspective, category dominance would be reflected in routinely relying on the same category dimension(s) when construing and reacting to others' (Bodenhausen 2010: 5). Therefore, understanding how individuals 'construct' their own social identities and those of others becomes important for knowing how to support individuals' development towards the management of the complexity of identity issues that can arise in organizational settings. Questions that concern us include: How do people learn to work with the complexity of the issues that present themselves in a diverse workplace? How do individuals learn to understand and navigate intergroup issues that arise from differences in social identity, the dynamics of political correctness, stereotype, or identity threats/tensions/abrasions (cf. Petriglieri 2011) and learn to leverage diversity for optimal results in the organization?

Of particular interest are *individuals' orientations to learn about diverse social identities when they are in a majority group position*—that is, when they are members of the demographically typical group in the workplace. Engaging demographically typical members of an organization, particularly leaders, can be a critical part of successful organizational diversity change initiatives (e.g. Davidson 2011). For example, in their study of barriers to the inclusion and advancement of women faculty in science and engineering schools, Bilimoria, Joy, and Liang (2008) argue that it is essential to have the participation of dominant group members in these university change initiatives. These authors cite Dominquez (1992: 436) 'It's not women's inabilities that prevent their advancement, but rather their male managers' or peers' inabilities to deal with someone who is different and may not fit the paradigm.' Within the complexity of our multiple, intersecting identities, it can be especially hard to be conscious of our majority-based identities and how they shape our experiences, perspectives, and abilities to effectively engage across different identities in work situations (Debebe and Reinert 2014).

Organizational cultures can shape members' identity consciousness and experiences. In their research on diversity climate, Hofhuis, van der Zee, and Otten (2012: 970) point out, 'An organization characterized by low openness to and appreciation of diversity may stimulate in-group projection, meaning that majority members may view the organization as synonymous with the majority's cultural group. In this situation, majority members may take their cultural background for granted, as they are rarely confronted with it in the workplace.' Learning as a dominant group member to be effective in one's cross-identity work relationships entails encountering moments in which one feels the presence of diversity-related intrapersonal or interpersonal disturbances such as identity abrasions (Ely, Meyerson and Davidson 2006), stereotype threats (Roberson and Kulik 2007), or intergroup anxiety in responses to out-group members (e.g. Plant and Devine 2003). Effective social identity engagement requires learning how to move beyond positions of silence (Davidson and Proudford 2007) or protective hesitations (Thomas 2001) when operating out of the salience of one's dominant identity in a workplace interaction.

In addition, an individual's *general orientation towards learning* contributes to the development of his or her diversity competence. Foldy, Rivard, and Buckley (2009) argue that individuals who are able to engage with high, as compared with low, learning frames can help a group work more productively with the differences that surface among its members: '... team members' high learning frames are helpful here as well: Members believe they can learn from others; they see differences of opinion as something to actively debate and integrate. If members believe that their discomfort with risky topics signals a learning opportunity, they are more likely to tolerate it. High learning frames authorize reflection about one's own point of view and curiosity about others' (Foldy, Rivard, and Buckley 2009: 33). Other individual-level factors may be enablers or barriers to optimizing within/across identity work relationships (see Cox 1993). For example, Homan and colleagues (2008) found that *openness to experience* was an individual difference variable that has important implications for the functioning of diverse teams. They cite Flynn's (2005) research, showing that this factor had significant impact on individuals' receptivity to stereotype disconfirming information and had positive effects on attitudes towards minority members.

Interest and motivation to become aware of one's unconscious bias and privilege can contribute to developing more effective cross-identity work relationships (e.g. McIntosh 1988). Extant research demonstrates how individuals' unconscious bias impacts their attitudes and behaviours towards different others, mirroring societal biases (Greenwald et al. 2009). Buttner, Lowe, and Billings-Harris's (2006) study of diversity activities in a university found that awareness of racial privilege was associated with more support for diversity in the leadership of the institution.

Attitudes towards institutional diversity efforts also affect how individuals build competency with diversity and inclusion. Employees' level of support for diversity work in organizations may impact the effectiveness of institutional initiatives, for example through their endorsements (Avery 2011) or through composition beliefs that favour a group's diversity (Van Knippenberg and Haslam 2003). In their research on who shows interest in learning about diversity in organizational settings, Kulik and colleagues (2007) found that individuals with high versus low competence levels around diversity exhibited more interest in taking advantage of diversity training in the organization.

Beliefs about whether human attributes are fixed or changeable also contribute to shaping individuals' engagement with social identity differences at work. Molden and Dweck (2006) have studied the effects of differing lay beliefs about personality in relation to assumptions about whether human attributes are fixed entities that are not subject to personal development or whether human attributes can develop and change incrementally through a person's efforts. They found that the meanings created by these two different beliefs can have profound effects on social perception and social information processing. In their experiments on the challenges of stereotype threat for student performance, they found that, 'Several other interventions or experimental manipulations that have successfully alleviated the detrimental effects of stereotype threat also appear to orient students away from an entity theory, with its emphasis on judgment and toward an incremental theory, with its emphasis on learning' (Molden and Dweck 2006: 195). In related work, Bodenhausen (2010: 5) cites studies that provide evidence that 'individuals who endorse essentialist beliefs in a general way tended to endorse stereotypes about a number of different social groups'.

In their research on identifying and training cross-cultural management skills, Mor, Morris, and Joh (2013) highlight the importance of *cultural metacognition* for cross-cultural management skills—which can be seen to parallel skills needed to work across race, ethnicity, gender, and other identity differences. The ability to think about one's thinking and be self-reflexive can underlie successful cross-cultural work relationships. As Mor, Morris, and Joh (2013: 453) note, 'Metacognitive strategies enable successful intercultural collaborations.' Chua, Morris, and Mor (2012: 116) propose from their research findings that '... managers adept at thinking about their cultural assumptions (cultural metacognition) are more likely than others to develop affect-based trust in their relationships with people from different cultures, enabling creative collaboration'.

Research on different kinds of social identity development highlights the *ability of individuals to move through stages of awareness and knowledge related to different social identities* (for example, Cross 1971 on black identity; Helms 1990 on white identity; Carnes, Handlesman, and Sheridan 2005 on gender; or Wishik and Peirce 1995 on sexual orientation). What does research on stage theory tell us about what helps individuals' progress in their awareness, and what instigates movement towards the capabilities of the higher stages? Progression in one's understanding of social identities and experiences with diversity can be linked with opportunities for the development of greater cognitive flexibility. Crisp and Turner (2011) explored the preconditions and processes through which people cognitively adapt to the experience of social and cultural diversity—in perceiving others who are multicultural and/or being multicultural themselves. They argue that, '... positive psychological and behavioral outcomes will be observed only when social and cultural diversity is experienced in a way that challenges stereotypical expectations and that when this precondition is met, the experience has cognitive consequences that resonate across multiple domains' (Crisp and Turner 2011: 242). Based on an extensive review of research across multiple disciplines, Crisp and Turner propose a model of cognitive adaptation that includes the following 'positive' progression through diversity experiences by an individual: (1) the diversity experience takes a form that involves stereotypic inconsistencies; (2) the perceiver is motivated and able to engage in elaborative processing to resolve the stereotypic inconsistencies; (3) the perceiver engages in a process of inconsistency resolution involving stereotype suppression and generative thought; (4) their multiple diversity experiences result in repeated engagement of the inconsistency resolution process; and (5) the perceiver develops generalized cognitive flexibility characterized by spontaneous inhibition of stereotype-based knowledge and generative thought.

In summary, many factors influence the development of individual diversity and inclusion competencies—what we have referred to as individual-level capacity building for the engagement and management of social identity dynamics in the workplace. These include: individuals' orientations to learn when they are working from a dominant group position and their general learning orientation, their openness to experience, their interest and motivation to become aware of their own unconscious bias and privilege, their attitudes towards institutional diversity work, their beliefs on whether human attributes are fixed or changeable, their cultural metacognition, and their ability to move through stages of awareness and knowledge related to different social identities.

Conclusion

Reaping the diversity dividend is catalysed by the organization's, group's, and individual's capacities to engage constructively and generatively with diverse others. On a day-to-day basis, individuals frequently work in diverse groups, each with its unique social identity dynamics. Interactions with diverse others must function in order to promote, instead of hinder, desired individual, group, and organizational processes and outcomes. In this chapter we have drawn on our own research and extant literature to discuss various practices of diversity and inclusion at the organizational, group, and individual levels that have the potential to generate a diversity dividend—that is, to generate positive outcomes from harnessing and leveraging the social identities and resources of diverse individuals and workgroups. A summary of these diversity and inclusion practices is provided in Table 5.1.

For analytic purposes, we have discussed the diversity and inclusion practices separately at the organizational, group, and individual levels in this chapter. Clearly, however, the practices within and across the different levels are interrelated and interdependent.

Table 5.1 Summary of practices at the organizational, group, and individual levels that cumulatively engender a diversity dividend

Organization-Level Practices	Workgroup-Level Practices	Individual-Level Competencies

• Workforce diversification practices
  ○ Increasing the inflow of diverse employees
  ○ Equipping diverse employees to succeed
  ○ Improving the institutional systems, structures, and practices related to key career transition points for diverse employees
• Practices that make the organization more equitable and inclusive
  ○ Creating performance standards that apply to everyone
  ○ Providing equal access to resources, networks, and opportunities for all employees
  ○ Creating a culture that is supportive of the meaning and significance of people's diverse identities
• Practices that demonstrate organizational commitment to diversity and inclusion
  ○ Diversity and inclusion statements or policies
  ○ Committees or taskforces dedicated to diversity and inclusion
  ○ Diversity and inclusion training initiatives
  ○ Organizational efforts to recruit from communities of colour
  ○ Integration of diversity and inclusion into the organization's core mission and values
	• Shared purpose and common goals
	  ○ Expands members' identity beyond the self to the organization
	  ○ Increases likelihood of experiencing deep-level, meaningful interactions
	  ○ Enables individuals to place a high priority on group performance and success
	• Inclusive welcoming practices
	  ○ Conveys to potential members that the group is accepting of diverse individuals
	  ○ Facilitates inclusive socialization and fellowship
	• Practices of optimal contact, interaction structuring, and social integration
	  ○ Adopt actions that promote positive group member interactions
	  ○ Create equal status among participants
	  ○ Establishing practices which promote social integration
	• Practices fostering a sense of belonging or group acceptance
	  ○ The desire to belong drives people to seek frequent, positive interactions with others in a stable, long-term, and caring environment
	  ○ Group enables members to find common connections and achieve insider status
	• Practices ensuring psychological safety
	  ○ Foster high-quality relationships among diverse individuals
	  ○ Empower diverse members to participate fully, bringing their different social identities to the table
		• Recognition of and interest in engaging with multiple, intersecting identities in the workplace
		  ○ Ability to move through stages of awareness and knowledge related to different social identities
		  ○ Develop awareness of effect of one's majority vs minority group status in situation
		  ○ Willingness to engage vs back off when faced with identity abrasions
		• General orientation towards learning and openness to experience
		  ○ Beliefs that human attributes are changeable vs fixed
		• Cultural metacognition
		  ○ Interest and motivation to become aware of one's unconscious bias and privilege
		  ○ Reflection on one's own and others' assumptions and points of view
		• Interest in institutional diversity efforts

Various studies examining interventions to promote diversity and inclusion support our conclusion that a dynamic portfolio of simultaneous, varied, and multi-level practices can cumulatively transform organizations to become more diverse, equitable, and inclusive (Hogue and Lord 2007; Bilimoria and Liang 2012). Since 'simplistic, ad hoc, or piecemeal solutions cannot eradicate systematic, historical and widespread... underrepresentation and inequities' (Bilimoria and Liang 2012: 206), wide and deep change is required at all levels—organizational, workgroup, and individual—to harvest the full potential of diversity and reap the diversity dividend. Efforts are simultaneously needed to transform organizational systems, structures, and cultures, improve workgroup norms and practices, and strengthen the capacity of individuals to engage and manage social identity dynamics in the workplace. Through these multi-level efforts *all* employees can fully participate, contribute, and develop, enabling their organizations to achieve goals of effectiveness by reaping a diversity dividend.

Clearly, much needs to be done in order to more fully understand how to optimize diversity in organizations and create an inclusive culture. The study of effective practices at all system levels—organizational, group, and individual—can continue to marry the knowledge of practitioners and academic researchers. It would be useful to develop case studies of individuals who are perceived as 'diversity competent' or 'behaviourally comfortable' within cross-identity relationships, or case studies of work groups and organizations that are experienced as inclusive, in order to further our understanding of the key factors contributing to effective outcomes from diversity. Additionally, more research is needed to advance our understanding of how majority group members can contribute to optimizing the diversity dividend in their work settings. An example of this is a recent study of how men engage in organizational gender initiatives to stimulate organizational change (Prime, Moss-Racusin, and Foust-Cummings 2009). Finally, even though additional research is necessary, there is still enough known that organizations can take proactive steps to increase inclusion. The multi-level practices discussed in this chapter and summarized in Table 5.1 can be employed to gain a diversity dividend.

References

Allport, G. W. (1954). *The Nature of Prejudice*. Reading, MA: Addison-Wesley.
Alvesson, M., Ashcraft, K. L., and Thomas, R. (2008). Identity matters: reflections on the construction of identity scholarship in organization studies. *Organization*, 15(1): 5–28.
Avery, D. R. (2011). Support for Diversity in organizations: a theoretical exploration of its origins and offshoots. *Organizational Psychology Review*, 1(3): 239–56.
Baumeister, R. F. and Leary, M. R. (1995). The need to belong: desire for interpersonal attachments as a fundamental human motivation. *Psychological Bulletin*, 117(3): 497.
Bernstein, R. S. and Bilimoria, D. (2013). Diversity perspectives and minority nonprofit board member inclusion. *Equality, Diversity and Inclusion: An International Journal*, 32(7): 636–53.
Bernstein, R. S. and Davidson, D. (2012). Exploring the link between diversity, inclusive practices, and board performance: an analysis of the National BoardSource Nonprofit

Governance Index. In *Annual Conference of the Association for Research on Nonprofit Organizations and Voluntary Action, Washington, DC.*

Bernstein, R. S. and Salipante, P. (2010). Feeling comfortable with pluralistic diversity. Paper presented at the Academy of Management, Montreal, Canada.

Bernstein, R. S. and Salipante, P. (2011). The impact of non-diversity-focused organizational practices on intercultural behavioral comfort. Paper presented at the Academy of Management, San Antonio, TX.

Bilimoria, D. and Liang, X. (2012). *Gender Equity in Science and Engineering: Advancing Change in Higher Education*. New York: Routledge.

Bilimoria, D., Joy, S., and Liang, X. (2008). Breaking barriers and creating inclusiveness: lessons of organizational transformation to advance women faculty in academic science and engineering. *Human Resource Management*, 47(3): 423–41.

Bodenhausen, G. V. (2010). Diversity in the person, diversity in the group: challenges of identity complexity for social perception and social interaction. *European Journal of Social Psychology*, 40: 1–16.

Brint, S. (2001). Gemeinschaft revisited: a critique and reconstruction of the community concept. *Sociological Theory*, 19(1): 1–23.

Buse, K., Bernstein, R. S., and Bilimoria, D. (2014). The influence of board diversity, board diversity policies and practices, and board inclusion behaviors on nonprofit governance practices. *Journal of Business Ethics*, 1–13.

Buttner, E. H., Lowe, K. B., and Billings-Harris, L. (2006). The influence of organizational diversity orientation and leader attitude on diversity activities. *Journal of Managerial Issues*, 15(3): 356–71.

Byrne, D. (1971). *The Attraction Paradigm*. New York: Academic Press.

Carmeli, A., Brueller, D., and Dutton, J. E. (2009). Learning behaviors in the workplace: the role of high-quality interpersonal relationship and psychological safety. *Systems Research and Behavioral Science*, 26: 81–98.

Carnes, M., Handelsman, J., and Sheridan J. (2005). Diversity in academic medicine: the stages of change model. *Journal of Women's Health*, 14(6): 471–5.

Chua, R. V. J., Morris, M. W., and Mor, S. (2012). Collaborating across cultures: cultural metacognition and affect-based trust in creative collaboration. *Organizational Behavior and Human Decision Processes*, 118: 116–31.

Cox, T. H. (1993). *Cultural Diversity in Organizations: Theory, Research and Practice*. San Francisco, CA: Berrett-Koehler.

Cox, T. H., Lobel, S. A., and McLeod, P. L. (1991). Effects of ethnic group cultural differences on cooperative and competitive behavior on a group task. *Academy of Management Journal*, 34(4): 827–47.

Crisp, R. J. and Turner, R. N. (2011). Cognitive adaptation to the experience of social and cultural diversity. *Psychological Bulletin*, 13(2): 242–66.

Cross, W. E. (1971). The Negro-to-black conversion experience. *Black World*, 20(9): 13–27.

Davidson, M. N. (2011). *The End of Diversity as We Know It*. San Francisco, CA: Berrett-Kohler.

Davidson, M. N. and Proudford, K. L. (2007). Cycles of resistance: how dominants and subordinates collude to undermine diversity efforts in organizations. In K. Thomas (ed.), *Diversity Resistance in Organizations: Manifestations and Solutions*. Hillsdale, NJ: Lawrence Erlbaum Associates, 249–72.

Debebe, G. (2011). Creating a safe space for women's leadership transformation. *Journal of Management Education*, 35(5): 679–712.

Debebe, G. and Reinert, K. A. (2014). Leading with our whole selves: a multiple identity approach to leadership development. In M. L. Miville and A. D. Ferguson (eds.), *Handbook of Race-Ethnicity and Gender in Psychology*. New York: Springer, 271–93.

Dominquez, C. M. (1992). The glass ceiling: paradox and promises. *Human Resource Management*, 31: 385–92.

Dumas, T. L., Phillips, K. W., and Rothbard, N. P. (2013). Getting closer at the company party: integration experiences, racial dissimilarity and workplace relationships. *Organization Science*, 24(5): 1377–401.

Ely, R. J., Meyerson, D. E., and Davidson, M. N. (2006). Rethinking political correctness. *Harvard Business Review*, 84(9): 78–87.

Ely, R. J., Padavic, I., and Thomas, D. A. (2012). Racial diversity, racial asymmetries, and team learning environment: effects on performance. *Organization Studies*, 33(3): 341–62.

Flynn, R. J. (2005). Having an open mind: the impact of openness to experience on interracial attitudes and impression formation. *Journal of Personality and Social Psychology*, 88: 816–26.

Foldy, E., Rivard, P., and Buckley, T. (2009). Power, safety, and learning in racially diverse group. *Academy of Management Learning and Education*, 8(1): 25–41.

Gaertner, S. L. and Dovidio, J. F. (2000). *Reducing Intergroup Bias: The Common Ingroup Identity Model*. Brandon, VT: Psychology Press.

Greenwald, A. G., Poehlman, T. A., Uhlmann, E. L., and Banaji, M. R. (2009). Understanding and using the Implicit Association Test: III. Meta-analysis of predictive validity. *Journal of Personality and Social Psychology*, 97(1): 17–41.

Groggins, A. and Ryan, A. M. (2013). Embracing uniqueness: the underpinnings of a positive climate for diversity. *Journal of Occupational and Organizational Psychology*, 86(2): 264–82.

Guillaume, Y. R., Dawson, J. F., Woods, S. A., Sacramento, C.A., and West, M.A. (2013). Getting diversity at work to work: what we know and what we still don't know. *Journal of Occupational and Organizational Psychology*, 86(2): 123–41.

Harrison, D. A., Price, K. H., and Bell, M. P. (1998). Beyond relational demography: time and the effects of surface-and deep-level diversity on work group cohesion. *Academy of Management Journal*, 41(1): 96–107.

Harrison, D. A., Price, K. H., Gavin, J. H., and Florey, A. T. (2002). Time, teams, and task performance: changing effects of surface-and deep-level diversity on group functioning. *Academy of Management Journal*, 45(5): 1029-1045.

Helms, J. E. (1990). *Black and White Racial Identity: Theory, Research and Practice*. New York: Greenwood Press.

Hofhuis J., van der Zee, K. I., and Otten, S. (2012). Social identity patterns social identity patterns in culturally diverse organizations: the role of diversity climate. *Journal of Applied Social Psychology*, 42(4): 964–89.

Hogue, M. and Lord, R. G. (2007). A multilevel, complexity theory approach to understanding gender bias in leadership. *Leadership Quarterly*, 18: 370–90.

Homan, A. C., Hollenbeck, J. R., Humphrey, S. E., Van Knippenberg, D., Ilgen, D. R., and Van Kleef, G. A. (2008). Facing differences with an open mind: openness to experience, salience of intragroup differences, and performance of diverse work groups. *Academy of Management Journal*, 51(6): 1204–22.

Horwitz, S. K. and Horwitz, I. B. (2007). The effects of team diversity on team outcomes: a meta-analytic review of team demography. *Journal of Management*, 33(6): 987–1015.

Joshi, A. and Roh, H. (2009). The role of context in work team diversity research: a meta analytic review. *Academy of Management Journal*, 52: 599–628.

Joshi, A., Liao, H., and Roh, H. (2011). Bridging domains in workplace demography research: a review and reconceptualization. *Journal of Management*, 37(2): 521–52.

Kreiner, G. E., Hollensbe, E. C., and Sheep, M. L. (2006). Where is the 'me' among the 'we'? Identity work and the search for optimal balance. *Academy of Management Journal*, 49: 1031–57.

Kreiner, G. E., Hollensbe, E. C., and Sheep, M. L. (2009). Balancing borders and bridges: negotiating the work-home interface via boundary work tactics. *Academy of Management Journal*, 52: 704–30.

Kulik, C. T. and Roberson, L. (2008). Diversity initiative effectiveness: what organizations can (and cannot) expect from diversity recruitment, diversity training, and formal mentoring programs. In A. Brief (ed.), *Diversity at Work*. Cambridge: Cambridge University Press, 265–317.

Kulik, C. T., Pepper, M. B., Roberson, L., and Parker, S. K. (2007). The rich get richer: predicting participation in voluntary diversity training. *Journal of Organizational Behavior*, 28: 753–69.

Lembke, S. and Wilson, M. G. (1998). Putting the 'team' into teamwork: alternative theoretical contributions for contemporary management practice. *Human Relations*, 51(7): 927–44.

McIntosh, P. (1988). *White Privilege and Male Privilege: A Personal Account of Coming to See Correspondences through Work in Women's Studies*. Wellesley College, Center for Research on Women.

Milliken, F. J. and Martins, L. L. (1996). Searching for common threads: understanding the multiple effects of diversity in organizational groups. *Academy of Management Review*, 21(2): 402–33.

Molden, D. C. and Dweck, C. S. (2006). Finding 'meaning' in psychology: a lay theories approach to self-regulation, social perception and social development. *American Psychologist*, 61(3): 192–203.

Mor, S., Morris, M., and Joh, J. (2013). Identifying and training adaptive cross-cultural management skills: the crucial role of cultural metacognition. *Academy of Management Learning and Education*, 12(3): 453–75.

Park, A. (2008). Making diversity a business advantage. *Harvard Business Review*, April: 1–5.

Pelled, L. H. (1996). Demographic diversity, conflict and work group outcomes: an intervening process theory. *Organization Science*, 7: 615–31.

Petriglieri, J. L. (2011). Under threat: responses to and the consequences of threats to individuals' identities. *Academy of Management Review*, 36(4): 641–62.

Plant, E. A., and Devine, P. G. (2003). The antecedents and implications of interracial anxiety. *Personality and Social Psychology Bulletin*, 29: 790–801.

Prime, J., Moss-Racusin, C. A, and Foust-Cummings, H. (2009). *'Engaging men in gender initiatives: Stacking the deck for success'*. New York: Catalyst. Downloaded on May 20, 2015 from <http://www.catalyst.org/knowledge/engaging-men-gender-initiatives-stacking-deck-success>.

Roberson, L. and Kulik, C. T. (2007). Stereotype threat at work. *Academy of Management Perspectives*, 21(2): 24–40.

Roberson, Q. M. (2006). Disentangling the meanings of diversity and inclusion in organizations. *Group and Organization Management*, 31(2): 212–36.

Roberts, L. M. (2005). Changing faces: professional image construction in diverse organizational settings. *Academy of Management Review*, 30(4): 685–711.

Roberts, L. M. and Creary, S. J. (2013). 'Navigating the self' in diverse work contexts. In Q. M. Roberson (ed.), *The Oxford Handbook of Diversity and Work*. New York: Oxford University Press, 73–97.

Roccas, S. and Brewer, M. B. (2002). Social identity complexity. *Personality and Social Psychology Review*, 6(2): 88–106.

Rosenblatt, V., Worthley, R., and MacNab, B. (2013). From contact to development in experiential cultural intelligence education: the mediating influence of expectancy disconfirmation. *Academy of Management Learning and Education*, 12(3): 356–79.

Saenz, V. B., Ngai, H. N., and Hurtado, S. (2007). Factors influencing positive interactions across race for African American, Asian American, Latino, and white college students. *Research in Higher Education*, 48(1): 1–38.

Shore, L. M., Randel, A. E., Chung, B. G., Dean, M. A., Ehrhart, K. H., and Singh, G. (2011). Inclusion and diversity in work groups: a review and model for future research. *Journal of Management*, 37(4): 1262–89.

Singh, B., Winkel, D. E., and Selvarajan, T. T. (2013). Managing diversity at work: does psychological safety hold the key to racial differences in employee performance? *Journal of Occupational and Organizational Psychology*, 86(2): 242–63.

Stangor, C., Lynch, L., Duan, C., and Glass, B. (1992). Categorization of individuals on the basis of multiple social features. *Journal of Personality and Social Psychology*, 62(2): 207.

Tajfel, H. (1982). Social psychology of intergroup relations. *Annual Review of Psychology*, 33(1): 1–39.

Tajfel, H. and Turner, J. C. (1986). The social identity theory of intergroup behavior. In S. Worchel and W. G. Austin (eds.), *Psychology of Intergroup Relations*, 2nd edn. Chicago: Nelson-Hall, 7–24.

Thomas, D. A. (2001). The truth about mentoring minorities: race matters. *Harvard Business Review*, 79(4): 98–112.

Thomas, D. A. (2004). Diversity as strategy. *Harvard Business Review*, September: 98–108.

Van Knippenberg, D. A. A. N. and Haslam, S. A. (2003). Realizing the diversity dividend: exploring the subtle interplay between identity, ideology, and reality. In S. A. Haslam, D. van Knippenberg, M. J. Platow, and N. Ellemers (eds.), *Social Identity at Work: Developing Theory for Organizational Practice*. New York/Hove: Psychology Press, 61–77.

Van Knippenberg, D. A. A. N. and Schippers, M. C. (2007). Work group diversity. *Annual Review of Psychology*, 58: 515–41.

Walker, B. A. and Hanson, W. C. (1992). Valuing differences at digital equipment corporation. In S. E. Jackson (ed.), *Diversity in the Workplace: Human Resource Initiatives*. New York: Guilford Press, 119–37.

Watson, W. E., Johnson, L., and Merritt, D. (1998). Team orientation, self-orientation, and diversity in task groups: their connection to team performance over time. *Group and Organization Management*, 23(2): 161–88.

Wishik, H., and Peirce, C. (1995). *Sexual Orientation and Identity: Heterosexual, Lesbian, Gay and Bisexual Journeys*. Laconia, NH: New Dynamics Publication.

CHAPTER 6

REFRAMING DIVERSITY MANAGEMENT

ALEX FARIA

Introduction

Diversity management (DM) is a concept that was created in the United States in the first years of the post-Cold War neoliberal era by the field of management and organization studies (MOS) to tackle discrimination in employment and the workplace at a time when state-based multiculturalism and corresponding affirmative action policies were phasing out and postcolonial/decolonial initiatives and demands were growing (Wallerstein 1998; Young 2003; Dussel 2012). Managing diversity within organizations means acknowledging and valuing differences, such as race and gender, and moving towards cultural pluralism from a cosmopolitan and pro-diversity perspective of globalization (Robinson and Dechant 1997). Although (or perhaps because) it has been critically described as a politically correct concept (Lorbiecki and Jack 2000) which is good for employers but not for employees (Wrench 2005), many researchers in MOS from different parts of the world describe DM nowadays as a body of knowledge and practices which adds sustainable value by fostering inclusion and enhancing organizational performance (Cooke and Saini 2010; Ferdman and Deane 2014). From a decolonial perspective, we face a rather curious situation: while few authors criticize the ethnocentric stance of DM (e.g. von Bergen, Soper, and Foster 2002; Faist 2009; Holvino and Kamp 2009; Jonsen, Maznevski, and Schneider 2011; Metcalfe and Woodhams 2012), the concept is being transformed into a type of global idea within MOS, in the non-Western world in general (e.g. Howie 2007; Shen et al. 2009; Gotsis and Kortezi 2015) and, in particular, in so-called emerging economies or markets (Horwitz and Budhwar 2015).

Unlike those who understand that decoloniality is a future-oriented project, this chapter shows that the US-led concept of DM has appropriated in a particular way the basic tenets of diversality or pluriversality that have been put forward by the decolonial literature. Pluriversality is not Eurocentric relativism, but a decentred epistemology and cosmology enunciated by those who have been transformed into 'different' by coloniality which proposes a 'universal project of delinking from modern rationality and building other possible worlds' (Mignolo 2007: 498). In other words, pluriversality is a way 'to imagine a future that is not the future that those in Washington, or London, or Paris, or Berlin would like the people of the world to have' (Mignolo 2007: 498) through the mobilization of 'a network of local/global histories constructed from the perspective of a politically enriched alterity' (Escobar 2007: 183), which brings together all those who have been contacted in various ways by modernity/coloniality and 'emphasizes dialogue as the route to adjudicate [the colonial] difference' (Alcoff 2012: 66).

Analysis of the trajectory of globalization of the concept of DM shows that diversality has been appropriated and reworked in a particular way by Eurocentric universality within the post-Cold War context of global coloniality. The resulting US-led 'global' DM embodies a perspective of diversality informed by Eurocentric universalism—that is, universal diversity—which is based on the selective inclusion of certain sub-knowledges informed by diverse diversity(ies) and the classification of radical ones as a kind of essentialist counter-knowledge. We posit that a major challenge for academics and non-academics alike in different parts of the world – and particularly in so-called emerging economies – is to foster the co-construction of diversality and diversity as concepts not to be classified as essentialist counter-knowledge. Unlike those who enact decoloniality as a future-oriented project we argue that decoloniality and diversality have coexisted asymmetrically with coloniality and universality since the creation of the colonial difference by Eurocentric universalism—that is, 'the differential time-space where a particular region becomes connected to the world-system of colonial domination' (Moraña, Dussel, and Jáuregui 2008: 6). Accordingly, the reframing of DM requires decolonizing the darker side of US-led global DM and highlighting both the bright side of diversality (i.e., DM otherwise) and the complex dynamic involving the decolonial design of diverse diversity(ies), the hegemonic US-led (Eurocentric) design of universal diversity, and the ambivalent design put forward by emerging economies. Such reframing of DM might evolve in parallel with the co-construction of a pluriversal rather than US-led 'global' field of MOS and create better conditions of possibility for a world in which many worlds and knowledges could coexist (Mignolo 2011a).

ON DIVERSITY, MANAGEMENT, AND KNOWLEDGE(S)

The concept of DM was created in the first years of the post-Cold War neoliberal era in the United States, in tandem with the advance of the US-led neoliberal globalism, the phasing out of state-based multiculturalism and corresponding affirmative action policies, and the rise of postcolonial/decolonial initiatives and demands worldwide (Wallerstein 1998; Young 2003; Dussel 2012). It is arguable that its creation by the field of MOS in the United States was triggered by the advance of post-Reagan neoliberalism and the corresponding interest of US large corporations in taking the lead in the management of an unprecedented degree of diversity of markets, workplaces, and cultures or worlds (Thomas 1990).

Following a pioneering critical examination in the late 1990s (Prasad and Mills 1997), other critical researchers pointed out in the early 2000s that DM was a politically correct concept (Kersten 2000; Lorbiecki and Jack 2000) which overshadowed the enduring tensions between 'managers of diversity' and the 'diverse managed' within organizations and society at large (Blommaert and Verschueren 1998), and was good to employers but not to employees (Wrench 2005). This US-led concept was exported worldwide with considerable success from the mid-1990s, and then turned into a kind of global concept within MOS and also in the non-Western world—in particular in so-called emerging economies (Howie 2007; Shen et al. 2009; Gotsis and Kortezi 2015). The concept was enacted in a particular way in the US as the post-Cold War order was allegedly moving towards a clash of civilizations (Huntington 1993) rather than postcolonial cosmopolitanism in a global scale (Giddens 1990).

DM was portrayed by critical management authors in the early 2000s as one of the conditions of an era they describe as global colonialism (Banerjee and Linstead 2001). In sharp contrast with the notion of global cosmopolitanism espoused by US-led literatures on globalization and MOS, Banerjee and Linstead argue that neoliberal globalization is a broader colonial order which, instead of just imposing commonality, homogeneity, and convergence around the world, mobilizes difference, diversity, and divergence from a hegemonic perspective. They conclude that diversity of race, ethnicities, and nationalities within such era of global colonialism/neoliberalism 'has to be "managed" for the market economy to function smoothly' on a global scale (Banerjee and Linstead 2001: 702).

Managing diversity within an era of global colonialism involves the mobilization of several mechanisms of inclusion informed by a 'revolutionary' design of discriminatory tolerance (Blommaert and Verschueren 1998). In other words, it involves a kind of 'revolutionary' reworking of the Eurocentric design of DM which was inaugurated in the fifteenth century. It means departing from a sort of monolithic Eurocentric universalism towards a sort of pro-diversity cosmopolitan Eurocentric universalism led by the United States, the lonely superpower with a face of benign hegemon (i.e., an all-powerful state whose power is experienced on a global scale not only through political-economy and military intervention, but also through the realm of cultural ideas and practices).

Arguably, global colonialism enables and requires the sheer hegemon to develop mechanisms of DM based on processes of exclusionary inclusion. This connects to a number of diverse factors related to the evolving of neoliberalism that include: the deepening of the crisis of the US-led Eurocentric neoliberal order (Duménil and Lévy 2012); the spread of inequality in a global scale (Piketty 2014); the growing distance between north and south and the haves and have nots (Banerjee, Carter, and Clegg 2009); the rise and dissemination of decolonial ideas and practices (Escobar 2004); the ascension (or resurgence) of China through a kind of neoliberal market-oriented socialism with

Chinese characteristics and informed by peace-oriented foreign policies (Harvey 2007); the ascension of so-called emerging economies and, correspondingly, of non-white leaders within institutions of global governance created by the West (Hurrell 2007); the rise of voices from peripheries within the US-led 'global' academy in general (Alatas 2006; Mignolo 2011a) and within the US-led 'global' field of MOS in particular (Ibarra-Colado 2006; Tsui 2009; Mir and Mir 2013). In other words, global colonialism/neoliberalism conveys a number of incentives and justifications for the hegemon to develop a kind of 'global' DM (i.e. DM supported and enlarged by 'revolutionary' mechanisms of inclusion which are exclusionary).

Not surprisingly, the concept of global colonialism has been rather ignored by the DM literature. Even less surprisingly, the concept of global coloniality put forward by decolonial authors from Latin America has also been ignored by corresponding debates. Informed by the colonial difference and by a historical perspective of *longue durée*[1]—which does not take the post-Cold War global neoliberalism to be a sort of discontinuity—decolonial literature from Latin America responded to the US-led celebratory accounts on globalization by arguing for the displacement of the long-standing hegemony of Eurocentric universality by pluriversality or diversity. Unlike colonialism, which is commonly understood as a specific political or cultural condition or epoch involving nations and peoples, coloniality is conceived as a hegemonic 'matrix of knowledge, power, and being' which has shaped the modern/colonial world system (Maldonado-Torres 2012: 2). Coloniality survives colonialism in its diverse manifestations. It refers to long-standing and profound patterns of colonial power which define culture, labour, racial, gender and intersubjective relations, and knowledge production well beyond the strict limits of more typical colonial space-time settings. Coloniality has been kept alive 'in books, in the criteria for academic performance, in cultural patterns, in common sense, in the self-image of peoples, in aspirations of self, and so many other aspects of our modern experience... [in sum] we breathe coloniality all the time and every day' (Maldonado-Torres 2007: 243).

In response to the celebratory pro-diversity knowledge on globalization produced by a growing number of knowers in/from the Euro-American world—who described it as the ultimate stage of Eurocentric liberalism— led by the United States from a 'revolutionary' perspective of cosmopolitanism (i.e. to be enjoyed by the entire postcolonial and postmodern world)—decolonial accounts produced by 'sub-knowers' (especially those who were included by the US-led 'global' academia) portrayed globalization as the radicalization of the darker side of over five centuries of Eurocentrism. More specifically 'sub-knowers' from Latin America embraced a long trajectory of decoloniality to describe globalization not as global colonialism/neoliberalism but as an era of

---

[1] The *longue durée* is a term from the French Annales School of History and refers to a long period of historical structuring of events that influence numerous aspects of ongoing events, for example, in this case, the influence of European colonization of the Americas and the consequent structuring of various societies as captured in the term Latin America.

coloniality on a global scale—that is, globalization is global coloniality (Mignolo 2000; Escobar 2004; Grosfoguel 2007).

The aggressive expansion of US-led neoliberal capitalism towards the rest of the world since the early 1970s (Stone and Kuznick 2012) led decolonial authors to already define globalization in the early 1990s as racialism/imperialism in disguise (Dussel 1993; Quijano 1993). The corresponding sub-knowledge posits that this design of global coloniality, which on the surface seems to be 'revolutionary' and informed by diversality or pluriversality, represents the radical *universalization* of the matrix of coloniality of knowledge, power, and being which was inaugurated in the end of the fifteenth century (Quijano 2007). In other words, globalization means the radicalization of the *longue durée* of Eurocentric modernity/coloniality initiated in 1492 with the conquest of America and establishment of a modern/colonial world-system based on racial, economic, and epistemic segregations (Mignolo 2011b).

Decolonial authors also point out that such radicalization of over five centuries of Eurocentric modernity may lead to either further radicalization or a potential transition towards a non-Western world order informed by decolonial ideas and practices on a global scale (Dussel 1997; Escobar 2004). In other words, they argue that such radicalism represents a major challenge, but also a major opportunity for the advance of decoloniality on a global scale—that is, towards 'a deeply negotiated reality that encompasses many heterogeneous cultural formations—and of course the many shades in between' (Escobar 2007: 181).

What we are saying is that, from a decolonial perspective, DM is not a novel concept created by the US-led field of MOS within an era of US-led neoliberal globalization or global colonialism/neoliberalism as sharply pointed out by Banerjee and Linstead. DM is an enduring body of practices and knowledges which has fostered the supremacy of Eurocentrist modernity over the last five centuries of modernity/coloniality. As there is no modernity without coloniality (Dussel 1994; Mignolo 2000; Quijano 2000), such radical universality of US-led Eurocentric modernity—that is, global coloniality—implies both the advance of decolonial 'DM' (or DM otherwise) and the corresponding mobilization of further and more powerful and inclusive mechanisms of DM on a global scale. In other words, global coloniality involves the reworking of Eurocentric DM through its radical *universalization* and systematic attempts to transform it into a kind of an hegemonic design of hyper-management of diversity/(de)coloniality.

Overall, such hegemonic design involves the radical mobilization of mechanisms of subalternization of knowledges and practices (Spivak 1988) developed by peoples and countries marked by the colonial difference. In more specific terms, it involves the radicalization of mechanisms of co-optation and containment (through appropriation, translation and detainment) of decolonial diversality and respective alternatives to the *longue durée* of Eurocentric modernity. In sum, the advance of global coloniality involves an unprecedented apparatus of DM and knowledge management dedicated to the hyper-management not only of the corresponding advance of non-hegemonic decolonial movements and knowledges on a global scale (Suárez-Krabbe 2013) but in particular the ascension of a particular non-Western or de-Westernizing hegemonic order as a result of the rise of so-called emerging economies (Hurrell 2013; Mignolo 2014).

Back in history the creation of the US-led concept of DM in the early post-Reagan years has been accompanied by the creation of anti-essentialist radical knowledge and policies in the United States, directed towards not only the rest of the world (Huntington 1993) but also emerging economies in general and China in particular (Layne 1993). In accordance with such a body of warfare-oriented knowledge, decolonial sub-knowers and the corresponding literature from Latin America have been classified as a serious threat to cosmopolitanism—the so-called Hispanic challenge (Huntington 2004)—and used as a resource of legitimation to the further *universalization* of the US-led concept of DM and the mobilization of a complex apparatus of knowledge management with no precedent within the *longue durée* of over five centuries of Eurocentric coloniality.

Decolonial authors describe coloniality as constitutive rather than derivative of modernity; in other words, coloniality is the inseparable and darker side of Eurocentric modernity. Decolonial authors add that one of the main features of the *longue durée* of modernity/coloniality is the negation of the negation of the non-Western other (Moraña, Dussel, and Jáuregui 2008). As pointed out by decolonial authors, such colonial matrix of power, knowledge and being (Quijano, 2000) has become virtually invisible to the distracted eyes created by modernity/coloniality. Even when the articulation of the colonial matrix of power surfaces, 'it is explained through the rhetoric of modernity that the situation can be "corrected" with "development", "democracy", a "strong economy", etc.' (Mignolo 2005: 11). Such systematic negation of negation explains, for example, why modern critical theory overlooks the fact that coloniality (or different manifestations of colonialism involving nations and peoples) is not a by-product of Eurocentric modernity (Escobar 2007). Modern capitalism does not lead to colonialism as a by-product, because without colonialism and corresponding racial distinction between conquerors and conquered there would be no modern capitalism in the first place (Dussel 1994; Quijano 2000, 2007). In other words, decolonial literature suggests that the supremacy of Eurocentric modernity is informed by a kind of essentialism which has been negated by Eurocentric academia and by the US-led 'global' academia. Those processes of negation have been accompanied by a design of construction of 'universal' knowledge based on hegemonic mechanisms of exclusionary inclusion of academics themselves. The acknowledgement of the negation of the subhuman other within the US-led 'global' academia is becoming even harder to achieve—at the same time, it is becoming even harder to sustain for and by an enlarging community of 'free' academics. In other words the evolving of the US-led 'global' academia involves a rather complex interplay of both coloniality and decoloniality on a global scale.

In the past, such patterns of negation involved not only the extermination or segregation of the 'different'—that is, those who were classified as non-humans or subhumans—but also the supposedly benevolent engagement of knowers with them. The corresponding mechanisms of DM have become invisible to academics in particular, and civil society in general, due to the prevalence of the idea that a major distinguishing feature of the West is its capacity of creation and free dissemination of disinterested and disembodied knowledge—that is, modern knowledge—informed by humanness and universality (Amin 2009). Nevertheless, it is the controversial engagement of Eurocentric knowers with sub-knowledges and sub-knowers—across the colonial difference through mechanisms of domination, seduction and exploitation—that has permitted the creation and dissemination of supposedly disinterested and disembodied 'universal' knowledge by Eurocentric modernity, as illustrated by the contemporaneous concept of DM. In the words of Grosfoguel (2011: 5):

> [In] the same way as the European industrial revolution was achieved on the shoulders of the coerced forms of labor in the periphery, the new identities, rights, laws, and institutions of modernity such as nation-states, citizenship and democracy were formed in a process of colonial interaction with, and domination/exploitation of, non-Western people.

Such design of knowledge production and management through co-optation and containment, however, remains negated in the 'global' academia and overlooked in the colonial world partially because of the hegemonic power of Eurocentrism and the virtual impossibility of challenging the corresponding apparatus of knowledge management still controlled by conquerors.

From a decolonial perspective DM is therefore as controversial and powerful as the concept of development; the latter described by the decolonial literature as 'multiscale hegemonic process that . . . [as such] is constantly transformed and contested' (Escobar 2008: 129–30). Both these ideas, with their focus on otherness, have been transformed into organized bodies of knowledge in the United States, involving not only mechanisms of co-optation and containment of sub-knowledges and sub-knowers (Maldonado-Torres 2005; Saldívar 2011), but also an opposition to (even more) radical bodies of knowledge and practices focused on otherness produced by conquerors. No wonder it is fairly accepted nowadays by the US-led 'global' academia that DM is a major source of sustainable development (Banks 2009). The concept of development is based on the controversial Eurocentric idea that those who classify themselves as superiors have the natural power and right to know and classify the others; the latter must move from such a position of inferiority and backwardness towards the standard of civilization achieved by the former—what decolonial authors call the 'developmentalist fallacy' (Dussel 1997). Development was turned in the US into a powerful and seductive body of knowledge and practices within the Cold War period—and still is (Escobar 2008)— for partially challenging the Eurocentric darker side of modernity/coloniality; that is, it challenges imposing an unjust world order in much the same way as European colonialism did. The idea of development put forward in the United States opposed European theorists and practitioners who defended the mobilization of war as the solution to eliminate part of the 'problematic' growing population of the Third World (see Sauvy 1952). Accordingly, it is arguable that development is a US-led 'revolutionary' concept which fostered the engagement with sub-knowledges informed by diversality through mechanisms of co-optation and containment mobilized by a powerful knowledge management apparatus.

In response to the rather understandable and enduring negation of the negation by the US-led 'global' academia contemporaneous development projects have been correctly portrayed by decolonial authors from Latin America as 'a "neo-colonial pact" between international capital and national elites that has perpetuated relations of international dependency and social inequality in the region' (Moraña, Dussel, and Jáuregui 2008: 14). However, it is arguable that the US-led science of development conveys a 'revolutionary' pro-diversity stance for opposing a powerful warfare-oriented body of knowledge and practices (what might be called 'darkest' side of modernity/coloniality), which stands for the elimination of the different through the mobilization of war. This partially explains why the corresponding unjust and racist division of labour involving the First-Third World in the production and diffusion of knowledge has been negated since then within and around academic circles (Pletsch 1981; Escobar 2004).

Supported by centuries of Eurocentric universalism and backed by the fear that the Third World would 'naturally' join the communist empire in a fatal war against Western civilization (Stone and Kuznick 2012), the US-led field of development enabled First World countries to classify themselves as developed rather than 'colonial' or 'imperial', and Third World countries to classify themselves as underdeveloped rather than as eternal barbarian enemies which should be partially eliminated by imperial modern states through the mobilization of radical warfare-oriented knowledge and practices. Through mechanisms of co-optation and containment of sub-knowledges informed by diversality, this US-led body of knowledge, as a successful case of reworking of Eurocentric DM, 'enabled' the subhuman 'other' to evolve from a position of backwardness or underdevelopment towards the standards of modernization In practice, as enunciated by decolonial sub-knowers, Western knowledge on development was also mobilized to perpetrate and justify practices of both covert and overt violence against the 'different' or 'diverse' (Fanon 1963). In response to those practices undertaken in the name of progress, and as a result of the many 'political and cultural struggles arising from the promises [development] makes and rarely fulfils' (Escobar 2008: 129), sub-knowledges and practices informed by radical engagement with diversality or pluriversality gained strength throughout Latin America—as philosophy of liberation, theology of liberation, and dependence theories. Interestingly, this body of sub-knowledges, which provided justification for elimination or violent conversion of Third World peoples through the mobilization of warfare-oriented mechanisms of knowledge management in name of national/international security (see Bilgin and Morton 2002), also provided ground for the emergence of a kind of 'new' decolonial scholarship by Latin American sub-knowers, published in English in the United States in the 1990s (Escobar 1995, 2004; Moraña, Dussel, and Jáuregui 2008).

The US-led concept of DM has taken an even more inclusive and pro-diversity stance, also in response to the extraordinary advance of postcolonial and decolonial initiatives and demands during the Cold War (Young 2003). To some extent, the critical and decolonial literatures on development informed by diversality were incorporated and rearticulated by this 'new' US-led concept, which opposed the reworking of post-Cold War radical warfare-oriented theories and practices. In other words, the US-led concept of DM is also a knowledge-based and 'revolutionary' artefact grounded on a hierarchical and racist rearticulation of Eurocentric ideas of sameness and otherness (Escobar 1991), whose main feature is the 'legitimate' mobilization of more inclusive US-led mechanisms of co-optation and containment of decolonial sub-knowledges informed by diversality. Decolonial analysis of the *longue durée* of Eurocentric modernity/coloniality has shown that the use of force and warfare-oriented mechanisms is crucially important, but not so effective as the use of knowledge-based mechanisms (Dussel and Ibarra-Colado 2006; Mignolo 2011b). Selective engagement with sub-knowledges and sub-knowers for the construction and justification of both more radical and more inclusive bodies of Eurocentric knowledge has informed the mobilization of an increasingly complex apparatus of knowledge management. Overall such apparatus informs the growing effectiveness of both knowledge-based and warfare-oriented mechanisms of global coloniality.

The reinforcement of knowledge-based mechanisms by the only superpower with undisputable military power in the post-Cold War era has been instrumental in offsetting the mobilization of warfare-based mechanisms of global coloniality. More inclusive knowledge-oriented mechanisms have provided further conditions for US-led Eurocentric universality not only to co-opt and contain decolonial sub-knowledges, but also to foster the advance of the decolonial literature (Escobar 2004; Mendieta 2009). Arguably, the creation of the US-led concept of DM, and the rearticulation of corresponding mechanisms of management of diversity within an area of global coloniality, have been informed by decolonial advances during the Cold War period and the production of decolonial literature from Latin America in the United States from the 1990s.

Back in history once again, the creation of specialized fields of knowledge on otherness in the past—for instance, anthropology and area studies—involved the engagement of knowers with sub-knowledges and sub-knowers and the classification of certain sub-knowledges as radical. As a sort of third space—using in a particular way the postcolonial terminology provided by Bhabha (1994)—those fields of knowledge required the co-optation and containment of sub-knowledges and sub-knowers informed by diversality. This design of knowledge management was formally inaugurated by the Eurocentric modern state with the creation of Eurocentric social sciences in the nineteenth century (Wallerstein 1997). The creation of Eurocentric (or ethno-)social sciences by the modern state and its diffusion towards other parts of Europe were marked by asymmetrical encounters between the *humanitas* and the *anthropos* (or humans and subhumans) in the colonial world and the mobilization of analogous mechanisms of knowledge management in Southern Europe. Through co-optation and containment social sciences managed to displace competing knowledges in Europe and forge its hegemonic position throughout the continent (Santos 2009). Such engagement with diversality informs the negation of the negation by the Eurocentric academy and the classification of Eurocentric knowledge as 'universal' also by the conquered. For example, the field of anthropology was formally created and presented and taken as a pro-diversity advance within social sciences by both knowers and sub-knowers. In the United States this complex dynamics involving coloniality and decoloniality presented itself as even more 'revolutionary' as social science was framed in the 1960s as an opposition to the warfare-oriented area studies (Bilgin and Morton 2002).

In other words, it is fairly true that the contemporaneous concept of DM and the field of development studies are US-led bodies of knowledge informed by the broad idea that 'others' (classified as subhumans or non-humans by Eurocentric universal knowledge) are inferiors. Nevertheless it is arguable that both are 'revolutionary' for opposing more radical warfare-oriented bodies of knowledge which say that those others are a permanent threat to the (Hegelian) historical path of humanity towards progress. Therefore, a major issue not to be negated by the US-led 'global' academia is that decolonial sub-knowledges classified as radical have been instrumental to the creation and justification of those radical warfare-oriented bodies of knowledge and, correspondingly, to the reinforcement of mechanisms of negation of the negation of the subhuman other within and around the 'global' academia. Managing diversity involves not only the subalternization of sub-knowledges and voices (Spivak 1988), but also internal struggles involving opposite bodies of knowledge within the inner realms of the US-led Eurocentric knowledge management apparatus. The marginal position of the work of Frantz Fanon within US-led postcolonial theory literature (McLeod 2000), and the rise of academic discourses of human rights in tandem with the deployment of neoliberal warfare-oriented mechanisms in Latin America throughout the 1970s (Mignolo 2009), illustrate such pattern of DM.

The radicalization of Eurocentric modernity within an era of global coloniality has hence been marked by further engagement of the hegemon with a wider range of sub-knowledges informed by diversality. Supposedly informed by 'essentialism' and resentment against civilizing universalism and cosmopolitanism, sub-knowledges classified as radical became instrumental to the co-optation and appropriation of sub-knowledges informed by diversality, to the legitimation of warfare-oriented mechanisms of coloniality, and to the justification of reinforcement of the knowledge management apparatus controlled by the supremacy.

Such evolving of global coloniality and corresponding mechanisms of DM has been marked by the reinforcement of radical warfare-oriented bodies of knowledge and more aggressive appropriation of decolonial sub-knowledges. The next section, 'Diversity, Globalization, and Post-9/11', shows that the dynamic involving coloniality and decoloniality which has informed the evolving of the US-led concept of globalization is crucially important to the understanding of the trajectory of globalization of the US-led concept of DM.

Diversity, Globalization, and Post-9/11

The creation of the US-led concept of DM has evolved in tandem with a complex process of construction of a radical pro-diversity idea of globalization in the United States. The emerging US-led globalization literature put together new global fields and universal fields of knowledge which were turned in a controversial fashion into global sub-fields, namely as global strategy, global economy, global management, and so on. Championed by so-called globalization studies, this new body of knowledge was advertised and taken by many as 'revolutionary' for embracing a worldview that challenged the dominant warfare-oriented literature produced and carefully managed mainly by the field of international relations throughout the Cold War period. Such revolutionary ideas became instrumental not only in disseminating on a global scale a pro-diversity understanding of globalization, but also in managing the proliferation of sub-knowledges from peripheries in opposition to the inauguration of the unipolar world by the lonely superpower (Gill and Mittelman 1997; Munck 2007; Mignolo and Escobar 2010). The dissemination of such pro-diversity and cosmopolitan ideas of globalization by the lonely superpower was also accompanied by controversial foreign policies which aimed to replace so-called defensive internationalism with affirmative internationalism—that is, 'no longer coordination of the major capitalist powers under American dominance against a common enemy, the negative task of the Cold War, but an affirmative ideal—the reconstruction of the globe in the American image' (Anderson 2002: 24).

The universalization of such pro-diversity globalization literature was accompanied by ethnic-oriented military interventions aimed to manage diversity—in particular the 'ethnic wars' against the so-called ethnic state in Kosovo and Bosnia. It was also accompanied by attempts at military containment of the spread of alter-movements, which were framed as counter-movements, in response to the increasing asymmetry between First and Third Worlds, the rise of inequality on a global scale triggered by the massive globalization of the US-led post-Reagan neoliberal order, and the emergence of corresponding decolonial sub-knowledges on globalization informed by diversality (Escobar 2004). No wonder the decolonial literature defined globalization in the first years of the post-Cold War period as the radicalization of the Eurocentric racist matrix of coloniality of power, knowledge, and being, which was inaugurated in 1492 with the conquest and discovery of the America rather than with the fall of the Berlin Wall and the ultimate triumph of Western liberalism (Quijano 1993).

In the United States the context was not very favourable towards the decolonial accounts of globalization informed by diversality and enunciated by sub-knowers from Latin America. At that time, state-based multiculturalism was portrayed in the United States as responsible for the de-Westernization of the country, and a serious threat to Western interests in general for its corrosive effects on US foreign policies and erosion of American values and creeds from within (Huntington 1993). Multiculturalists in general were described by radical warfare-oriented theorists of globalization as 'ethnocentric separatists who see little in the Western heritage other than Western crimes... Their mood is one of divesting Americans of the sinful European inheritance and seeking redemptive infusions from non-Western cultures' (Schlesinger 1992: 66–7, 102).

The so-called thesis of the clash of civilizations was enunciated in 1993 by a prominent Harvard scholar of the warfare-oriented tradition in development studies and international relations. He portrayed the West as a major victim, rather than beneficiary, of pro-diversity globalization. He then affirmed the post-Cold War period would replace the clash of ideologies championed by the United States and the Soviet Union with an inevitable clash of civilizations on a global scale (Huntington 1993). In 1989, this same author criticized the rise of pro-diversity globalization discourses in the United States based on the thesis of the end of history and the general idea that the end of the Cold War meant that bad things were coming to an end. Instead, he argued that 'the end of the Cold War does not mean the end of political, ideological, diplomatic, economic, technological, or even military rivalry among nations' and then concluded that 'to hope for the benign end of history is human. To expect it to happen is unrealistic. To plan on it happening is disastrous' (Huntington 1989: 29). The resulting fear, shared by the rest of the world, of the subordination of pro-diversity discourses to the construction of US supremacy informed by warfare-oriented ideas within a supposedly hyper-anarchical world—that is, marked, for instance, by the emergence of fundamentalism Islam, the rise of East Asia, and the new geopolitical configuration of Russia and Eastern Europe as major threats to the West—triggered the production and dissemination of alternative sub-knowledge on globalization in Asia which also challenged the pro-diversity literature reproduced by the US-led 'global' academia in the making, as illustrated in the following passage:

> In key Western capitals there is a deep sense of unease about the future. The confidence that the West would remain a dominant force in the 21st century, as it has for the past four or five centuries, is giving way to a sense of foreboding that forces like the emergence of fundamentalist Islam, the rise of East Asia and the collapse of Russia and Eastern Europe could pose real threats to the West. A siege mentality is developing. Within these troubled walls, Samuel P. Huntington's essay 'The Clash of Civilizations?' is bound to resonate. It will therefore come as a great surprise to many Westerners to learn that the rest of the world fears the West even more than the West fears it, especially the threat posed by a wounded West. (Mahbubani 1993: 10)

In accordance with the US-led concept of DM informed by diversality in a particular way, different perspectives on globalization could coexist within the hegemonic realm of US-led globalization studies. Globalization views from the periphery were not eliminated or rejected; rather, they were included and presented as sub-knowledges by the 'non-global' field of globalization studies (Mittelman 2000: 917) and corresponding knowledge management apparatus. Those sub-knowledges reinforced the idea that, as an explanatory phenomenon, globalization should be portrayed as not having a centre of power; in other words, globalization was portrayed as epiphenomenon beyond the control of any powerful actor. Accordingly, the more radical bodies of US-led warfare-oriented knowledge on globalization—informed, for instance, by the end of history thesis (Fukuyama 1989) and by the clash of civilizations thesis (Huntington 1993)—were accompanied by the ascension of more malleable pro-diversity bodies of knowledge in the United States, informed by the notion of 'cultural globalization' (e.g. Jameson and Miyoshi 1998).

Through a systematic process of appropriation and transformation of certain ideas into knowledge, and the corresponding mobilization of an unprecedented knowledge management apparatus, globalization was turned into a new and complex phenomenon of ultimate importance for individuals, societies, and the world, not only in economic, but also in political and cultural terms (e.g. Giddens 1990; Hirst and Thompson 1999; Held and McGrew 2000). Informed by diversality in a particular way this US-led globalization literature aimed to offset the negative connotations given to difference, diversity, and otherness in the 'past'. Diverse conceptualizations were fostered in order to establish a hegemonic understanding of globalization informed by an apparently cosmopolitan pro-diversity design by the US-led 'global' academia. In practice, all nations and peoples had to converge 'on one narrative of progress, based on Western, liberal democratic models and functionalist bureaucracies' (Clegg and Carter 2008: 272).

Critical views on globalization were published in English and classified as sub-knowledges. Informed by the thesis 'of clash of civilizations, the sub-knowledges which were classified as radical became instrumental in justifying the radical *universalization* of the US-led field of globalization studies and the concept of DM. As in any hegemonic design, such control was far from absolute. In response, intellectuals from Asia and Africa delinked from Western counterparts and joined sub-knowers from Latin America, who interpreted globalization as the radicalization of the Eurocentric project and the most obvious signal of the crisis of five centuries of Eurocentrism (Quijano 1993). Intellectuals in Asia framed the mismatch between pro-diversity globalization discourses and US foreign policies as a clear sign that Eurocentric liberalism was the next to collapse after the fall of Marxism (Umehara 1992). Globalization was interpreted by other intellectuals in Africa as a violent era of marginalization of communities without precedents that would lead the region to silent resistance and eventual revolution (Cheru 1997). As warfare-oriented theories of globalization were reinforced and justified, the US-led pro-diversity globalization literature became 'a core dictum in the prescriptions of management gurus, and a catch-phrase for journalists and politicians of every stripe' (Hirst and Thompson 1999: 1).

The darker face of DM and globalization studies resurged more overtly in the aftermath of the events of 9/11, with the corresponding revival of Huntingtonian racialism (Hurrell 2013). In tandem with the rise of more radical bodies of knowledge and displacement of the less radical ones, new mechanisms of knowledge management aimed to deter sub-knowledges and respective 'sub-knowers', for global security motives, have been added to the hegemonic mechanisms of co-optation and containment of sub-knowledges which informed the trajectory of 'globalization' of US-led globalization knowledge until the events of 9/11. The construction of the so-called 'global' social sciences became a chief component of the global war on terror inaugurated by George W. Bush (Shaw 2003), with corresponding implications within the US-led field of MOS (Faria, Ibarra-Colado, and Guedes 2010; Guedes and Faria 2010). Globalization was rearticulated in response to a growing number of anti-globalizers who announced its obsolescence (Held and McGrew 2007) and transformed into an extremely powerful northern theory which helped construct and disseminate a misleading 'social world read through the metropole—[i.e.] not read through the metropole's action on the rest of the world' (Connell 2011: 45). In response to such radicalization and the reinforcement of mechanisms of negation of the negation within the 'global' academy, decolonial authors pointed out knowledge as the most effective resource of decoloniality in a global scale: 'the most radical struggles in the twenty-first century will take place on the battlefield of knowledge and reasoning' (Mignolo 2005: 100; see also Mignolo and Schiwy 2003).

Informed by the rise of radical warfare-oriented theories focused on otherness, some analysts classified sub-knowledges in general as counter-knowledge or anti-West conspiracy theories. Although this post-9/11 literature does not equal such counter-knowledge with terrorism and transnational violence, some authors agree that the main characteristic of counter-knowledge produced in parts of the rest of the world is to 'hold extremist groups together and push them in a more extreme and sometimes violent direction' (Bartlett and Miller 2010: 5).

In contrast with academic and non-academic discourses informed by the pro-diversity globalization literature affirming that we all live in a postmodern and postcolonial world marked by the free flow of knowledge worldwide, those post-9/11 happenings made clear the prevalence of the Eurocentric racial design of universality in the contemporaneity, as repeatedly denounced by sub-knowers from Latin America (e.g. Mignolo 2000; Escobar 2004; Ibarra-Colado 2006). With the shift of knowledge-based mechanisms of global coloniality from market-oriented motives towards security-oriented ones (Mignolo 2002), the events of 9/11 were described by the decolonial literature, in a more radical tone, not as a threat to civilization but as 'the first wake-up call and not only for globalization but for cosmopolitanism as well' (Mignolo 2011b: 15). The following passage illustrates the essentialist feature attributed to US-led globalization by post-9/11 radical decolonial sub-knowledge:

> With the conquest of the societies and the cultures which inhabit what today is called Latin America, began the constitution of a new world order, culminating, five hundred years later, in a global power covering the whole planet. This process implied a violent concentration of the world's resources under the control and for the benefit of a small European minority and above all, of its ruling classes. Although occasionally moderated when faced with the revolt of the dominated, this process has continued ever since. But, now during the current crisis, such concentration is being realized with a new impetus, in a way perhaps even more violent and on a much larger, global scale. The 'Western' European dominators and their Euro-North American descendants are still the principal beneficiaries, together with the non-European part of the world not quite former European colonies, Japan mainly, and mainly their ruling classes. The exploited and the dominated of Latin America and Africa are the main victims. (Quijano 2007: 168)

In the name of global security, and with a tight control of the process of construction of the 'global' social sciences, developed countries enlarged their right to know the 'other' and produce and disseminate universal knowledge. In other words, the Eurocentric assumption that all societies, groups, or communities are 'knowable in the same way and from the same [i.e. metropolitan] point of view' (Connell 2011: 44) was reinforced and negated further rather than dismantled. This post-9/11 big picture has informed not only the trajectory of radical *universalization* of the pro-diversity globalization literature but also the 'globalization' of the US-led concept of DM. As developing countries and an increasing population of 'suspicious' inferiors around the world (also within the United States and Europe) were forced to replace sub-knowledges with universal knowledge proper, the decolonial literature rose on a global scale (e.g. Lionnet and Shih 2011; Maldonado-Torres 2012; Ndlovu-Gatsheni 2013). Decoloniality presented itself neither as relevant only to Latin America nor as an abstract anti-West universal to be imposed worldwide, but as an epistemic option informed by diversality which might become universal by connecting 'similar colonial experiences in different colonial histories, whether in the rest of the Americas, in Asia, or in Africa' (Mignolo 2002: 246).

In parallel, China has led the controversial path towards the constitution of a non-Western (Ikenberry 2011) or de-Westernized world order (Mignolo 2011a) through its growing participation, along with other emerging economies, with Western institutions of global governance (Hurrell 2013), development projects in Africa and Latin America (Mignolo 2014), and also the US-led global social sciences in the making (Alatas 2006). This was accompanied by the ascension of the Chinese threat literature in the United States and the corresponding reinforcement of foreign policies based on the peaceful rise framework by China (and other emerging economies). With the resurgence of Huntingtonian racialism, the fear that so-called emerging economies—in particular China—would inevitably lead the world to a situation of non-peaceful developments was institutionalized within the US-led field of globalization studies (Mearsheimer 2006). The literature on Islamophobia as a form of cultural and epistemic racism also saw a rise (Grosfoguel 2012).

In parallel to the growing participation of Chinese scholars and institutions in the construction of the US-led global field of MOS (e.g. Tsui 2009), decolonial sub-knowers from Latin America followed a radical path by portraying the field as 'one of the most important forms of epistemic coloniality of the last 150 years . . . a strategic knowledge aimed at the maintenance and reproduction of the colonial difference in the context of globalization, legitimating to some extent the corporate domination of the world economy' (Ibarra-Colado 2006: 468), and pointing out the growing number of (neo-) imperial interventions in Latin America and Africa disguised as management and organization affairs (see Cooke and Faria 2013).

Interestingly, the rise of radical decolonial accounts has also been accompanied not only by the reinforcement of warfare-oriented knowledge and practices, but also by a growing number of victims of US-led eurocentrism in the United States and Europe, and an increasing number of peripheral voices from within the US-led 'global' academia, who stand for the decolonization of the world in general and of knowledge in particular—in particular the field of MOS..

This rather complex and ambivalent picture is illustrated by the literature, which portrayed the advances of *buen vivir* (i.e. living well) in Ecuador and Bolivia as a concrete alternative to development interventions in the region and to the radicalization of global coloniality (Walsh 2010; Mignolo 2014). In response to the increasing importance of warfare-oriented knowledge focused on the advance of decoloniality in general and of emerging economies in particular *buen vivir* was also celebrated by decolonial MOS sub-authors from emerging economies as a kind of DM otherwise (e.g. Ibarra-Colado 2010; Misoczky 2011; Cooke and Faria 2013). *Buen vivir* became a focus for heated and unjustified criticism within academic and non-academic circles in the US-led fields of development studies and globalization studies: whereas warfare-oriented radical bodies of knowledge classified it as a global threat (Huntington 2004; see also Borón 2013), authors and experts in sustainable development, together with local elites, appropriated it (Walsh 2010) and took a less radical stance by classifying *buen vivir* 'as a mystical return to an indigenous past, lacking any practical strategy' (Gudynas 2011: 445). In other words, the different versions of *buen vivir* practised in the Andean regions of Latin America—accompanied by controversies and debates (see Walsh 2010; Escobar 2012; Quijano 2012; Borón 2013; Vanhulst and Beling 2014)—was addressed by decolonial sub-knowledge from an anti-development perspective which was appropriated by colonial mechanisms of co-optation and containment of sub-knowledges. In the end, such radical response helped reinforce the trajectories of 'globalization' of US-led 'revolutionary' conceptualizations of development, globalization and DM from a perspective of universal diversity rather than decolonial diversity.

The ambivalent support provided by Chinese institutions and organizations to *buen vivir* in Latin America, as part of foreign policies in the region informed by the peaceful rise framework (Foot 2006), and the controversial appropriation of *buen vivir* by sustainable development theories and local elites in Ecuador and Bolivia, have been accompanied by more radical arguments from decolonial sub-authors (e.g. Quijano 2012) who extended the debates in Latin America on whether or not emerging economies could be taken as part of the decolonial turn informed by diversality (Mignolo 2011a; Borón 2013). These radical accounts became instrumental for warfare-oriented knowers to claim once again that decolonial sub-knowledges and sub-knowers are informed by essentialism, barbarism, or anti-cosmopolitanism.

The engagement of Chinese organizations with the concept of DM and *buen vivir* to differentiate from US-led 'global' development and management frameworks and justify its development interventions in Africa and Latin America—as perhaps a sort of Eurocentric DM or neocolonialism with Chinese characteristics—was accompanied by many criticisms from the growing US-led China threat literature (Alden and Large 2011). Those debates informed by different appropriations of diversality have been rather ignored but had an indirect influence on the literature in Latin America with different interpretations of DM put forward by MOS authors from emerging economies from Latin America (e.g. Alves and Galeão-Silva 2004; Romero 2004; Pereira and Hanashiro 2010; Jabbour et al. 2011).

It is arguable hence that the trajectory of 'globalization' of the US-led concept of DM has been informed by the complex interplay of global coloniality and decoloniality at large but not managed as such by the proponents of decolonial diversality and DM otherwise. This complex picture gives support to our argument that the decolonial reframing of DM in and from emerging economies requires specific efforts in the co-construction, together with the proponents of a US-led global field of MOS, the concept of diversality and, therefore, of a pluriversal field of MOS.

The tacit and ambivalent engagement of China with the global war on terror when US unilateralism was formally inaugurated in the post-9/11 period (Foot 2006) illustrates the chief importance for emerging economies to engage and manage with diligent care the complex interplay involving global coloniality and decoloniality at large. Hence, a first major challenge for reframing DM is to highlight the bright side of decolonial diversality and its radical opposition to warfare-oriented knowledge and practices. This would enable academics of the US-led 'global' academy and a growing number of victims of global coloniality to enact the chief importance of decolonial diversality in the creation of US-led 'revolutionary' concepts as globalization, development and DM itself and the respective trajectories of 'globalization'. A second major challenge is to investigate, particularly (but not only) in emerging economies, mechanisms of knowledge management based on co-optation and containment of diversality which inform the US-led 'global' concept of DM.

Such decolonial reframing of DM requires academics and non-academics to engage the growing population of victims of US-led global coloniality and to prioritize the careful management—for instance, by embracing the peaceful rise framework mobilized by China in recent decades—the complex dynamics involving the decolonial design of diverse diversity(ies), the US-led (Eurocentric) design of universal diversity, and the ambivalent designs put forward by emerging economies.

Final Considerations

DM is a Eurocentric constitutive component of modernity/coloniality informed by decolonial diversality, which was reworked in the United States in the early 1990s within an era of global coloniality. The US-led concept of DM embodies a 'revolutionary' rearticulation of the Eurocentric design of universality—which in the past has been one of the major tools for both extermination and effective conversion of inferiors and natives towards Eurocentric standards of universal modernity and civilization through different mechanisms of knowledge management and selective engagement with diversality and diverse diversity(ies)—from a 'revolutionary' perspective marked by the opposition to radical warfare-oriented knowledges and practices focused on otherness. Its creation and 'globalization' over recent decades have been supported by complex mechanisms of hyper-management of diversity which involve appropriation, co-optation, and containment of decolonial sub-knowledges and sub-knowers.

This chapter argues that the trajectory of 'globalization' of the US-led concept of DM has been informed by both the deepening and widening of global coloniality and the corresponding advance of a non-Western or de-Westernized world order, and also of decolonial sub-knowledges and practices in a global scale. This picture illustrates the complex dynamics involving the decolonial design of diverse diversity(ies), the US-led (Eurocentric) design of universal diversity, and the ambivalent designs put forward by emerging economies. In other words, such US-led 'global' DM embodies a complex and asymmetric interplay of different understandings, appropriations, and reworkings of universality, diversality, and diversity that should be further examined by the field of MOS.

The decolonial reframing of DM is needed, as illustrated by our analysis of the ambivalent trajectory of 'globalization' of this US-led concept over recent decades. Such decolonial reframing requires our engagement with the peaceful rise framework for the co-construction of concepts of diversity and diversality not to be classified as essentialist anti-cosmopolitan counter-knowledge by the US-led hegemonic apparatus of knowledge management. Highlighting the bright side of decolonial diversality and promoting the engagement of so-called emerging economies in investigations and the management of the complex interplay of global coloniality and decoloniality at large are major challenges for an enlarging community of academics and non-academics who wish to foster a pluriversal field of MOS which is in the making.

References

Alatas, F. (2006). *Alternative Discourses in Asian Social Science: Responses to Eurocentrism.* London: Sage.

Alcoff, L. (2012). Enrique Dussel's transmodernism. *Transmodernity: Journal of Peripheral Cultural Production of the Luso-Hispanic World*, 1(3): 60–8.

Alden, C. and Large, D. (2011). China's exceptionalism and the challenges of delivering difference in Africa. *Journal of Contemporary China*, 20(68): 21–38.

Alvarez, D. (2001). Of border-crossing nomads and planetary epistemologies. *CR: The New Centennial Review*, 1(3): 325–43.

Alves, M. and Galeão-Silva, L. (2004). A crítica da gestão da diversidade. *Revista de Administração de Empresas*, 44(3): 20–9.

Amin, S. (2009). *Eurocentrism: Modernity, Religion, and Democracy: A Critique of Eurocentrism and Culturalism.* New York: Monthly Review Press.

Anderson, P. (2002). Internationalism: a breviary. *New Left Review*, 14: 5–25.

Banerjee, S. and Linstead, S. (2001). Globalization, multiculturalism and other fictions: colonialism for the new millennium? *Organization*, 8(4): 683–722.

Banerjee, S., Carter, C., and Clegg, S. (2009) Managing globalization. In M. Alvesson, H. Willmott, and T. Brigham (eds.), *Handbook of Critical Management Studies.* Oxford: Oxford University Press, 186–212.

Banks, J. (2009). Diversity and Citizenship Education in Multicultural Nations. *Multicultural Education Review*, 1(1): 1–28.

Bartlett, J. and Miller, C. (2010). *The Power of Unreason: Conspiracy Theories, Extremism and Counter-Terrorism*. London: Demos.

Bhabha, H. K. (1994). *The Location of Culture*. New York: Routledge.

Bilgin, P. and Morton, A. (2002). Historicizing representations of 'failed states': beyond the Cold-War annexation of the social sciences? *Third World Quarterly*, 23(1): 55–80.

Blommaert, J. and Verschueren, J. (1998). *Debating Diversity: Analyzing the Discourse of Tolerance*. London: Routledge.

Borón, A. (2013). *América Latina en la Geopolítica del Imperialismo*. Buenos Aires: Ediciones Luxemburg.

Cheru, F. (1997). From silent revolution and the weapons of the weak: transformation and innovation from below. In S. Gill and J. Mittelman (eds.), *Innovation and Transformation in International Studies*. Cambridge: Cambridge University Press, 153–69.

Clegg, S. and Carter, C. (2008). The sociology of global organizations. In G. Ritzer (ed.), *The Blackwell Companion to Globalization*. London: Routledge, 272–98.

Connell, R. (2011). *Southern Theory*. London: Polity Press.

Connell, R. (2012). A iminente revolução na teoria social. *Revista Brasileira de Ciências Sociais*, 27(80): 9–20.

Cooke, B. and Faria, A. (2013). Development, management and North Atlantic imperialism: for Eduardo Ibarra Colado. *Cadernos EBAPE*, 11(2): 1–15.

Cooke, F. and Saini, D. (2010). Diversity management in India: a study of organizations in different ownership forms and industrial sectors. *Human Resource Management*, 49(3): 477–500.

Duménil, G. and Lévy, D. (2012). *The Crisis of Neoliberalism*. Cambridge, MA: Harvard University Press.

Dussel, E. (1993). Eurocentrism and modernity. *Boundary 2*, 20(3): 65–76.

Dussel, E. (1994). *1492. El descubrimiento del Otro. Hacia el origen del mito de la Modernidad*. La Paz: Plural Editores, Colección Academia.

Dussel, E. (1997). *Filosofía de la Liberación*. Ciudad de Mexico: Edicol.

Dussel, E. (2012). Transmodernity and interculturality: an interpretation from the perspective of philosophy of liberation. *Transmodernity*, 13: 28–59.

Dussel, E. and Ibarra-Colado, E. (2006). Globalization, organization and the ethics of liberation. *Organization*, 13(4): 489–508.

Escobar, A. (1991). Anthropology and the development encounter: the making and marketing of development anthropology. *American Ethnologist*, 18(4): 658–82.

Escobar, A. (1995). *Encountering Development*. Princeton, NJ: Princeton University Press.

Escobar, A. (2004). Beyond the Third World: imperial globality, global coloniality and anti-globalisation social movements. *Third World Quarterly*, 25(1): 207–30.

Escobar, A. (2007). Worlds and knowledges otherwise: the Latin American modernity/coloniality research program. *Cultural Studies*, 21(2–3): 179–210.

Escobar, A. (2008). Development, trans/modernities, and the politics of theory. *Focaal—European Journal of Anthropology*, 52: 127–35.

Escobar, A. (2012). Una minga para el posdesarrollo. *Signo y pensamiento*, 30(58): 278–84.

Faist, T. (2009). Diversity: a new mode of incorporation? *Ethnic and Racial Studies*, 32(1): 171–90.

Fanon, F. (1963). *The Wretched of the Earth*. New York: Grove.

Faria, A., Ibarra-Colado, E., and Guedes, A. (2010). Internationalization of management, neoliberalism and the Latin America challenge. *Critical Perspectives on International Business*, 6(2/3): 97–115.

Ferdman, B. and Deane, B. (eds.) (2014). *Diversity at Work: The Practice of Inclusion*. San Francisco, CA: Jossey Bass.

Foot, R. (2006). Chinese strategies in a US-hegemonic global order: accommodating and hedging. *International Affairs*, 82(1): 77–94.

Fukuyama, F. (1989). The end of history? *The National Interest*, 16: 3–18.

Giddens, A. (1990). *The Consequences of Modernity*. Stanford, CA: Stanford University Press.

Gill, S. and Mittelman, J. (eds.) (1997). *Innovation and Transformation in International Studies*. Cambridge: Cambridge University Press.

Gotsis, G. and Kortezi, Z. (2015). *Critical Studies in Diversity Management Literature*. Rotterdam: Springer.

Grosfoguel, R. (2007). The epistemic decolonial turn: beyond political economy paradigms. *Cultural Studies*, 21(2–3): 211–23.

Grosfoguel, R. (2011). Decolonizing post-colonial studies and paradigms of political-economy: transmodernity, decolonial thinking, and global coloniality. *Transmodernity*, 1(1): 1–18.

Grosfoguel, R. (2012). The multiple faces of Islamophobia. *Islamophobia Studies Journal*, 1(1): 9–33.

Gudynas, E. (2011). Buen vivir: today's tomorrow. *Development*, 54(4): 441–7.

Guedes, A. and Faria, A. (eds.) (2010). *International Management and International Relations*. London: Routledge.

Harvey, D. (2007). *A Brief History of Neoliberalism*. Oxford: Oxford University Press.

Held, D. and McGrew, A. (2000). *An Introduction to the Globalization Debate*. Cambridge: Polity Press.

Held, D. and McGrew, A. (2007). *Globalization/Anti-Globalization*. London: Polity Press.

Hirst, P. and Thompson, G. (1999) *Globalization in Question*, 2nd edn. Cambridge: Polity Press.

Holvino, E. and Kamp, A. (2009). Diversity management: are we moving in the right direction? Reflections from both sides of the North Atlantic. *Scandinavian Journal of Management*, 25(4): 395–403.

Horwitz, F. and Budhwar, P. (2015). *Handbook of Human Resource Management in Emerging Markets*. London: Edward Elgar.

Howie, L. (2007). The terrorism threat and managing workplaces. *Disaster Prevention and Management*, 16(1): 70–8.

Huntington, S. (1989). No exit: the errors of endism. *The National Interest*, 17: 3–11.

Huntington, S. (2004). The Hispanic challenge. *Foreign Policy*, 141(2): 30–45.

Huntington, S. P. (1993). The clash of civilizations? *Foreign Affairs*, 72(3): 22–49.

Hurrell, A. (2007). *On Global Order*. Oxford: Oxford University Press.

Hurrell, A. (2013). Narratives of emergence: rising powers and the end of the Third World? *Revista de Economia Política*, 33(2): 203–21.

Ibarra-Colado, E. (2006). Organization studies and epistemic coloniality in Latin America: thinking otherness from the margins. *Organization*, 13(4): 463–88.

Ibarra-Colado, E. (2010). La modernidad y sus dilemas en la era del mercado: ¿Hay algún futuro posible? *Psicoperspectivas*, 9(2): 158–79.

Ikenberry, G. J. (2011). The future of the liberal world order: internationalism after America. *Foreign Affairs*, 90(3): 56–68.

Jabbour, C., Gordono, F., Oliveira, J., Martinez, J., and Battistelle, R. (2011). Diversity management: challenges, benefits, and the role of human resource management in Brazilian organizations. *Equality, Diversity and Inclusion: An International Journal*, 30 (1): 58–74.

Jameson, F. and Miyoshi, M. (eds.) (1998). *The Cultures of Globalization*. Durham, NC: Duke University Press.

Jonsen, K., Maznevski, M., and Schneider, S. (2011). Diversity and its not so diverse literature: an international perspective. *International Journal of Cross Cultural Management*, 11(1): 35–62.

Kersten, A. (2000). Diversity management: dialogue, dialectics and diversion. *Journal of Organizational Change Management*, 13(3): 235–48.

Layne, C. (1993). The unipolar illusion: why new great powers will rise. *International Security*, 17(4): 5–51.

Lionnet, F. and Shih, S. (eds.) (2011). *The Creolization of Theory*. Durham, NC: Duke University Press.

Lorbiecki, A. and Jack, G. (2000). Critical turns in the evolution of diversity management. *British Journal of Management*, 11(s1): S17–S31.

McLeod, J. (2000). *Beginning Postcolonialism*. Manchester: Manchester University Press.

Mahbubani, K. (1993). Dangers of decadence: what the rest can teach the West. *Foreign Affairs*, 72: 10–14.

Maldonado-Torres, N. (2005). Decolonization and the new identitarian logics after September 11: Eurocentrism and Americanism against the new barbarian threats. *Radical Philosophy Review*, 8(1): 35–67.

Maldonado-Torres, N. (2007). On the coloniality of being: contributions to the development of a concept. *Cultural Studies*, 21(2–3): 240–70.

Maldonado-Torres, N. M. (2012). Decoloniality at large: towards a trans-Americas and global transmodern paradigm. *Transmodernity*, 1(3): 1–10.

Mearsheimer, J. (2006). China's unpeaceful rise. *Current History*, 105(690): 160–9.

Mendieta, E. (2009). From imperial to dialogical cosmopolitanism? *Ethics & Global Politics*, 2(3): 241–58.

Metcalfe, B. and Woodhams, C. (2012). Introduction: new directions in gender, diversity and organization theorizing: re-imagining feminist post-colonialism, transnationalism and geographies of power. *International Journal of Management Reviews*, 14(2): 123–40.

Mignolo, W. (2000). The many faces of cosmo-polis: border thinking and critical cosmopolitanism. *Public Culture*, 12(3): 721–48.

Mignolo, W. (2002). The Zapatista's theoretical revolution: its historical, ethical and political consequences. *Review (Fernand Braudel Center)*, 25(3): 245–75.

Mignolo, W. (2005). *The Idea of Latin America*. Oxford: Blackwell Publishing.

Mignolo, W. (2007). Delinking: the rhetoric of modernity, the logic of coloniality and the grammar of de-coloniality. *Cultural Studies*, 21(2/3): 449–514.

Mignolo, W. (2009). Who speaks for the 'human' in human rights? *Hispanic Issues On Line*, 5(1): 7–24.

Mignolo, W. (2011a). *The Darker Side of Western Modernity*. Durham, NC, and London: Duke University Press.

Mignolo, W. (2011b). Cosmopolitan localism: a decolonial shifting of the Kantian's legacies. *Localities*, 1: 11–45.

Mignolo, W. (2014). Democracia liberal, camino de la autoridad humana y transición al vivir bien. *Sociedade e Estado*, 29(1): 21–44.

Mignolo, W. and Escobar, A. (eds.) (2010). *Globalization and the Decolonial Option*. London: Routledge.

Mignolo, W. and Schiwy, F. (2003). Transculturation and the colonial difference: double translation. In T. Maranhão and B. Streck (eds.), *Translation and Ethnography: The Anthropological Challenge of Intercultural Understanding*. Tuscon: The University of Arizona Press: 3–29.

Mir, R. and Mir, A. (2013). The colony writes back: organization as an early champion of non-Western organizational theory. *Organization*, 20(1): 91–101.

Misoczky, M. (2011). World visions in dispute in contemporary Latin America: development x harmonic life. *Organization*, 18(3): 345–63.

Mittelman, J. H. (2000). Globalization: captors and captive. *Third World Quarterly*, 21(6): 917–29.

Mittelman, J. H. (2002). Globalization: an ascendant paradigm? *International Studies Perspectives*, 3(1): 1–14.

Moraña, M., Dussel, E., and Jáuregui, C. (2008). Colonialism and its replicants. In M. Moraña, E. Dussel, and C. Jáuregui (eds.), *Coloniality at Large*. Durham, NC: Duke University Press. 1–22.

Munck, R. (2007). *Globalization and Contestation*. London: Routledge.

Ndlovu-Gatsheni, S. (2013). The entrapment of Africa within the global colonial matrices of power Eurocentrism, coloniality, and deimperialization in the twenty-first century. *Journal of Developing Societies*, 29(4): 331–53.

Pereira, J. and Hanashiro, D. (2010). Ser ou não ser favorável às práticas de diversidade? Eis a questão. *Revista de Administração Contemporânea*, 14(4): 670–83.

Piketty, T. (2014). *Capital in the Twentieth First Century*. Cambridge, MA: Belknap Press.

Pletsch, C. (1981). The three worlds, or the division of social scientific labor, circa 1950–1975. *Comparative Studies in Society and History*, 23(4): 565–90.

Prasad, P. and Mills, A. (1997). Managing the organizational melting pot: dilemmas of diversity at the workplace. In P. Prasad, A. Mills, M. Elmes, and A. Prasad (eds.), *Managing the Organizational Melting Pot: Dilemmas of Workplace Diversity*. Newbury Park, CA: Sage, 3–27.

Quijano, A. (1993). América Latina en la economía mundial. *Problemas del desarrollo*, 24(95): 43–59.

Quijano, A. (2000). Coloniality of Power, Ethnocentrism and Latin America. *Neplanta*, 1(3): 533–80.

Quijano, A. (2007). Coloniality and modernity/rationality. *Cultural Studies*, 21(2–3): 168–78.

Quijano, A. (2012). Bien Vivir: entre el desarrollo y la des/colonialidad del poder. *Viento Sur*, 122: 46–56.

Robinson, G. and Dechant, K. (1997). Building a business case for diversity. *Academy of Management Executive*, 11(3): 21–31.

Romero, E. (2004). Hispanic identity and acculturation: implication for management. *Cross-Cultural Management: An International Journal*, 11(1): 61–72.

Saldívar, J. (2011). Conjectures on 'Americanity' and Junot Díaz's 'Fukú Americanus' in *The Brief Wondrous Life of Oscar Wao*. *The Global South*, 5(1): 120–36.

Santos, B. (2009). A non-occidentalist West? Learned ignorance and ecology of knowledge. *Theory, Culture & Society*, 26(7–8): 103–25.

Sauvy, A. (1952) 'Trois mondes, une planète' (three worlds, one planet). *L'Observateur*, 14 August.

Schlesinger, A. (1992). *The Disuniting of America: Reflections on a Multicultural Society*. New York: W. W. Norton.

Shaw, M. (2003). The global transformation of the social sciences. In M. Kaldor, H. Anheier, and M. Glasius (eds.), *Global Civil Society Yearbook*. London: Sage, 35–44.

Shen, J., Chanda, A., D'Netto, B., and Monga, M. (2009). Managing diversity through human resource management: an international perspective and conceptual framework. *International Journal of Human Resource Management*, 20(2): 235–51.

Spivak, G. C. (1988). *Can the Subaltern Speak?* Basingstoke: Macmillan.

Stone, O. and Kuznick, P. (2012). *The Untold History of the United States*. New York: Gallery Books.

Suárez-Krabbe, J. (2013). Democratising democracy, humanising human rights: European decolonial social movements and the 'alternative thinking of alternatives'. *Migration Letters*, 10(3): 333–41.

Thomas, R. (1990). From affirmative action to affirmative diversity. *Harvard Business Review*, March/April: 107–18.

Tsui, A, (2009). Editor's introduction—autonomy of inquiry: shaping the future of emerging scientific communities. *Management and Organization Review*, 5(1): 1–14.

Umehara, T. (1992). Ancient Japan shows post-modernism the way. *New Perspectives Quarterly*, 9(10): 12–28.

Vanhulst, J. and Beling, A. (2014). Buen vivir: emergent discourse within or beyond sustainable development? *Ecological Economics*, 101: 54–63.

Von Bergen, C. W., Soper, B., and Foster, T. (2002). Unintended negative effects of diversity management. *Public Personnel Management*, 31(2): 239–51.

Wallerstein, I. (1997). Eurocentrism and its avatars: the dilemmas of social science. *Sociological Bulletin*, 46(1): 21–39.

Wallerstein, I. (1998). The rise and future demise of world-systems analysis. *Review*, 21(1): 103–12.

Walsh, C. (2010). Development as Buen Vivir: institutional arrangements and (de)colonial entanglements. *Development*, 53(1): 15–21.

White, S. (2002). Thinking race, thinking development. *Third World Quarterly*, 23(3): 407–19.

Wrench, J. (2005). Diversity management can be bad for you. *Race & Class*, 46(3): 73–84.

Young, R. (2003). *Postcolonialism: A Very Short Introduction*. Oxford: Oxford University Press.

PART II
EPISTEMOLOGICAL PLURALITY

CHAPTER 7

ADVANCING POSTCOLONIAL APPROACHES IN CRITICAL DIVERSITY STUDIES

GAVIN JACK

Introduction

SINCE the mid-1990s there has been significant growth in the volume of research conducted about diversity management (DM) (Oswick and Noon 2014). This corpus of research includes critical diversity studies, a growing number of conceptual essays, empirical studies, special issues (for instance, Calás, Holgersson, and Smircich 2009; Miller, Mills, and Helms Mills 2009; Zanoni et al. 2010; Metcalfe and Woodhams 2012), research monographs, and edited collections that collectively question the underlying assumptions, and social and organizational effects, of DM. Now a well-established area of critical management thinking, there seems to be 'something in the air' (Calás, Holgersson, and Smircich 2009: 351) amongst scholars that the field of critical diversity studies needs to 'move on'. Whether that 'something' is hope and excitement, or exasperation and disenchantment, is hard to grasp with any great precision. That said, there are recent calls by leading scholars to 'revitalize the field' (Ahonen et al. 2013: 263), and to 'reimagine' wider (orthodox and critical) gender and diversity scholarship beyond its dominant 'western epistemological frames' (Metcalfe and Woodhams 2012: 123–4). According to Zanoni and colleagues (2010: 10): 'After a decade of critical diversity studies, it is time, we believe, for the critical diversity community to take stock of the new theoretical insights that have emerged and to initiate a new conversation on where our work should go from here.'

Postcolonial theory is a potentially powerful tool for critical analyses of workplace diversity—given its focus on culture, difference, power, and racial inequality—and is now an important frame for critical organizational analysis. It is a vast terrain of scholarly work, with no single epistemological, political, or ethical perspective on the historical analysis of the colonial encounter, or on the critique of new and continuing forms of neocolonialism and imperialism in contemporary workplaces. Yet, with a few notable and insightful exceptions (Prasad 2006; Kalonaityte 2010), postcolonial theory is underdeployed and selectively represented in critical scholarship on workplace diversity despite calls for its use (Prasad, Pringle, and Konrad 2006). As such, there is significant opportunity to respond to Zanoni and colleagues' call for a 'new conversation' in critical diversity scholarship through a broader and deeper engagement with postcolonial theory.

To facilitate a new conversation, this chapter is organized into three key sections, following the introduction. The first section situates critical diversity studies within the broader historical emergence of DM theory and practice. It selectively outlines key criticisms of the practitioner-driven, US-originated discourse of managing diversity, and its export and appropriation. The second section provides a brief synopsis of postcolonialism and core concepts, as well as the very small number of existing critical studies of workplace diversity that draw upon it. The third section recommends two scholarly texts that provide significant food for thought with regard to future conversations about the development of postcolonial perspectives for critical diversity studies. These texts encourage researchers to engage more closely with psychoanalytic *and* discursive variants of postcolonial theory (especially as they pertain to the study of racism) (Hook 2012), and to consider how the genre of 'Southern Theory' (Connell 2007) could be used to reconfigure the Eurocentrism of the global social sciences (mainstream and critical diversity studies included).

A Brief Survey of Critical Diversity Studies

According to Zanoni and colleagues (2010: 9), critical diversity studies 'emerged in the mid-1990s as a reaction to the re-appropriation of equal opportunities by business through the notion of diversity'. To understand the key themes of critical diversity studies, therefore, one needs to historicize them in the dominant narrative about the emergence and spread of the managing diversity perspective and the associated business case framework. Whilst critical diversity studies can be read as a response to the rise of DM, Zanoni and colleagues' (2010) review essay also clarifies the fact that understanding this scholarly subfield requires locating it as part of the broader multidisciplinary and multiparadigmatic terrain of gender and diversity research (Metcalfe and Woodhams 2012). That is to say, DM, and critical studies of it, are just one manifestation of gender and diversity research. Bearing this in mind, this section is structured using Kalonaityte's (2010) schematization of contemporary research on workplace diversity into two major areas: (mainstream and critical) research on the business case for diversity in respect of its implementation and internationalization; research 'beyond' the business case.

The Implementation and Internationalization of the Business Case for Diversity

According to the dominant and familiar historical narrative (see, notably, Kelly and Dobbin 1998, for one of the earliest accounts of this narrative; see also Sinclair 2000; Omanović 2009), DM emerged as a discourse and set of human resource (HR) practices in late 1980s/early 1990s corporate America, spearheaded by leading practitioners, key practitioner/trade articles, and management consulting frameworks (Thomas 1990; Cox and Blake 1991; Cox 1993; Gardenswartz and Rowe 1993; Thomas and Ely 1996; Robinson and Dechant 1997; Dass and Parker 1999). Its rise is typically portrayed as the other side of the coin of the decreasing popularity of affirmative action (AA) approaches to tackling issues of underrepresentation and discrimination in the workplace. Holvino and Kamp (2009: 396), for instance, described how DM was distinctively 'presented as an alternative to its prior AA and EEO [equal employment opportunity] legal and moral predecessors, steeped in rationales of competitive advantage, human resource utilization, and the "business imperative" to enhance global productivity and profitability'. This putative shift from AA/EEO to DM in the US was predicated on a number of intersecting contextual factors, including:

- *Demographic change.* The Workplace 2000 Report (Johnston and Packer 1987) predicted, fallaciously as it turned out (Edelman, Fuller, and Mara-Drita 2001), that 'by 2000 only 15% of new entrants to the US workforce would be US-born white males' (Oswick and Noon 2014: 24).
- The *politicization* of AA/EEO. According to Kelly and Dobbin (1998), AA was increasingly conceived as an overtly political, exclusionary, costly, and unpopular activity during the Reagan-era 1980s in elite government and corporate circles, weakened by poor legal enforcement and judicial support. Valuing and then managing diversity, by contrast, was hailed as a distinctive, more inclusive, future-oriented, and voluntarist *management* discourse, which 'both stated and implied ... that the equal opportunity approach is backwards, less developed, not adapted to current organizational needs and unfairly selective in those it assists' (Oswick and Noon 2014: 25). DM was a less controversial pill for large corporates to swallow than AA (Lorbiecki and Jack 2000).

The management/managerialist element noted above is crucial, as it appealed to the idea that differences could be managed, and the (financial) contribution to the firm's bottom line measured through the rubric of the business case. Managing cognitive or demographic diversity—whether of individuals or teams—promised significant organizational dividends, and triggered a surge of predominantly positivist and social psychological (as well as cognitive) academic research into the dynamics affecting the relationship between chosen types/dimensions of diversity, process-, or performance-related outcomes, and the role of a battery of mediating and moderating variables (see, for instance, Jehn,

Northcraft, and Neale 1999; Pelled, Eisenhardt, and Xin 1999; Richard 2000; Benschop 2001). Crucially, the basis for conceiving human differences also (putatively; see Liff 1997) shifted with practitioner interest in diversity from the social group (typical in AA/EEO practice) to an array of individual demographic and non-demographic differences. Difference was now a manageable commodity and researchable artefact. After its inception in the US, DM spread and gained popularity with practitioners and scholars across several parts of the globe, notably the UK, Canada, Australia, and Western Europe. Research on the internationalization of DM has underscored—not surprisingly—that its US underpinnings are not cross-nationally applicable (see, for instance, Jones, Pringle, and Shepherd 2000; Boxenbaum 2006; Risberg and Søderberg 2008). What counts as a diverse workforce, and on what basis, then, differs from one (national) context to another, in accordance with demographic and historical specificities (e.g. connected with patterns of migration, and histories of colonialism/imperialism).

Critical diversity studies emerged as a response to a variety of different concerns regarding the intentions, assumptions, and effects of this new 'diversity discourse' (Sinclair 2006), in particular its business case element and managerialist ideology, the reification of difference by researchers and practitioners, and its contextually specific meanings. Wrench (2007) provides a comprehensive review of the different forms of critique that developed. He labels these non-fundamental, equal opportunities, and fundamental critiques (see Table 7.1), according to their underlying paradigm and/or constituent political position. Non-fundamental critiques inspect some of the 'origins, philosophy or claims' (Wrench 2007: 88) of DM, but do not fundamentally undermine the notion that it has intrinsic value for organizations. That is to say, they 'do not lead to the implication that diversity management is intrinsically wrong—only that *bad* diversity management is wrong' (Wrench 2007: 95; italics in original).

Equal opportunities critiques point to the costs of adopting DM approaches (e.g. the undermining of the moral imperative to tackle workplace discrimination) rather than AA/EEO approaches to employment equity, with Wrench (2007: 101) noting that, 'The diversity approach has been criticised for allowing people to choose the parts of the diversity mix that they like, and under-emphasizing or disguising what they don't like.' Scholars have cautioned against a key element of the dominant narrative—that DM and its focus on the individual represents a new and distinctive approach to workplace diversity and anti-discrimination that has eclipsed EEO approaches. As Oswick and Noon (2014: 27) suggest, 'at organizational level (sic) this [DM] often amounted to little more than repackaged EO/AA practices' (see also Kirton and Greene 2005; Tomlinson and Schwabenland 2010; Tatli 2011).

Wrench's final category covers fundamental critiques (from both the left and the right of the political spectrum) which 'question the whole basis and existence of diversity management' (2007: 103). Fundamental critiques from the right argue that it is a mutation of identity politics, still in the tradition of EEO (despite appearances) and overreaching social engineering that represents 'a threat to the values of the generic liberalism enshrined in modern American law and culture' (Lynch 1997, quoted in

Table 7.1 Overview of critiques of diversity management

Type of critique	Example of criticism
Non-fundamental	DM serves sectional interests. The benefits of DM are overstated and overgeneralized. Professional practice and implementation of DM initiatives are characteristically poor.
Equal opportunities	DM undermines trade union and legal approaches to tackling discrimination and racism: it replaces the moral imperative of fairness and justice with the business case and thus depoliticizes difference. DM is a soft option that fails to tackle enduring organizational problems, notably racism.
Fundamental	DM is an exercise in reification and trades on essentializing, *a priori*, immutable, reductionist, and one-dimensional views of (ethnic and cultural) difference. Criticism from the left: DM overlooks the structural relations that create racial inequality; discrimination and racism persist despite DM; DM accommodates the dominant group and obscures inequity whilst promulgating a rhetoric of equality. • DM thus naturalizes a new type of management control that obfuscates its own complicity in organizational practices of inclusion and exclusion • 'For many of its critics, DM has served to eliminate discussions of power and systemic oppression, along with associated concepts such as hierarchy, privilege, equity, discrimination and organizational justice' (Holvino and Kamp 2009: 396) Criticism from the right: DM is unnecessary social engineering that curtails individual freedoms

Source: Adapted from Wrench (2007).

Wrench 2007: 107). From the left, fundamental critiques cover a wider variety of criticisms, and form the foundation for what I would loosely call 'first-wave' critical diversity studies (see, for instance, Humphries and Grice 1995; Cavanaugh 1997; Linnehan and Konrad 1999; Litvin 1997; Prasad and Mills 1997; Dickens 1999; Kersten 2000; Lorbiecki and Jack 2000; Sinclair 2000. For more recent critical diversity studies see, for instance, Hoobler 2005; Janssens and Zanoni 2005; Ahmed and Swan 2006; Jones and Stablein 2006; Noon 2007; Metcalfe and Woodhams 2008; Perriton 2009; Swan 2010; Zanoni 2010; Özbilgin and Tatli 2011). Zanoni and colleagues' (2010) critical reflections on DM, and specifically dominant social psychological research approaches, synthesize three criticisms: a 'positivistic ontology of identity' (Zanoni et al. 2010: 13) which has the effect of 'naturalizing identities into objective entities, rather than acknowledging their socially constructed nature' (Zanoni et al. 2010: 13); underappreciating the role of context (specifically societal and organizational contexts) in moulding what diversity means; and, an 'inadequate theorization of power'

(Zanoni et al. 2010: 14). Elaborating the latter point, they explain (Zanoni et al. 2010: 14) that:

> The micro-lens of social psychology leads to an explanation of identity-based power inequality exclusively as the result of individual discriminatory acts originating in universal cognitive processes [...]. Such acts are disembedded from the greater context of historically determined, structurally unequal access to and distribution of resources between socio-demographic groups.

This first wave of critical diversity studies, then, is largely focused on critiques of the business case, and the production of analyses (often using variants of discourse analysis; see, for instance, Litvin 1997; Kirby and Harter 2003; Ahmed 2007; Ostendorp and Steyaert 2009; Christiansen and Just 2012) that illuminate the power dynamics and effects of diversity discourse. However, Zanoni and colleagues' (2010) review also notes a number of diversity studies beyond the business case, connecting DM to broader gender and diversity research which precedes, exists alongside, and informs critical diversity scholarship.

Research Beyond the Business Case: Towards Second-Wave Critique?

Two recent review articles demonstrate the vast scope of gender and diversity research, and the intersection with critical diversity studies. With regard to the former, Metcalfe and Woodhams (2012) make it clear that DM research sits alongside a number of scholarly interests in diversity, many of which have a longer lineage. They describe current gender and diversity research as comprising studies of: women in management; gender and organization theory; social constructionism/critical management studies/intersectionality; critical men's studies; and critical race studies. Zanoni and colleagues' (2010) synthesis of key streams of critical diversity studies illuminates cross-over with the broader terrain described by Metcalfe and Woodhams. They summarize these streams as:

- Discourse studies of the construction of identities and differences, and of socio-demographic groups.
- 'Agent-centred' perspectives on minority group members' own identity work and construction of positive professional identities in workplace settings, and modes of resistance to inequality.
- Studies of men and masculinities, and whiteness in organizations.
- Intersectionality studies, and their origin in black feminist scholarship.
- Renewal of a critical sociological lens on socio-demographic group research. For instance, they cite Acker's (2006) work on inequality regimes and Essed's (1991) notion of micropractices of everyday racism as good exemplars.
- Studies of diversity in specific geographical, cultural, or historical contexts, including that of globalization.

Despite expansion in the interests of the broader terrain of gender and diversity research, and the concomitant growth of critical work on DM, recent reviews suggest that critical diversity studies is in need of reinvigoration. Perhaps what is needed, then, is a 'second wave' of critique to address the concerns of these recent reviews. Ahonen and colleagues (2013: 278), for example, propose that the field needs to develop better understandings of 'how context matters in terms of power'. Metcalfe and Woodhams (2012) articulate a further challenge for the broader field of gender and diversity research: to tackle its Eurocentrism and to enable a greater plurality of voices to be heard in research. This latter point is significant in light of Zanoni and colleagues' (2010: 17) view that 'much remains to be done to come to grips with the dynamics of power and diversity in organizations operating within a globalized world'. They call for a 'new conversation on where our work should go from here' (Zanoni et al. 2010: 10) and suggest a future agenda for critical diversity studies comprising: more empirical work; studies of those labelled 'diverse'; research, especially in discourse studies, that goes beyond textual representation, and considers the visual domain; linking (diversity) discourses with social practices; searching for new emancipatory forms of organizing. I would add to this agenda the need for further development of the theoretical base for critical diversity studies and, in this respect, deeper engagement with postcolonialism.

POSTCOLONIAL THEORY AND DIVERSITY MANAGEMENT

This section presents a brief synopsis of postcolonialism and some of its core analytic concepts, and outlines the key insights of the very small number of existing postcolonial pieces on workplace diversity.

Postcolonialism

It is beyond the scope of this chapter to provide an exhaustive review of a complex body of scholarship like postcolonialism: it is not a homogenous area of enquiry, with a singular mode of theoretical and political analysis. Instead, it is contested scholarly terrain that spans multiple disciplines, with different and competing analytical variants connected to poststructuralist, psychoanalytical, historical materialist, and feminist theory, amongst others (for good introductions, see Moore-Gilbert 1997; Young 2001). For the purposes of this chapter, I am guided by a useful umbrella definition by Prasad (2006: 123), who describes postcolonialism as:

> [A]n attempt—from an intellectual perspective that insists upon, among other things, a persistent interrogation of Eurocentrism—to take stock of the

consequences of the fateful colonial encounter between the West and the non-West and, in so doing, 'to investigate the complex and deeply fraught dynamics of modern Western colonialism and anti-colonial resistance, and the ongoing significance of the colonial encounter for people's lives both in the West and the non-West'.

Postcolonial writers recognize the formal imperial expansion of a number of European nations—and the brutal violence, racism, and dispossession of land often associated with it—as constitutive of Western modernities.[1] Though primarily pursued to build an economic system in which colonies would provide factors of production and markets for finished goods for industrializing Western Europe (Young 2001), colonization was also an important exercise in cultural imperialism (Said 1993). That is to say, it was also a matter of: '[...] the desire for, and belief in, European cultural dominance—a belief in a superior right to exploit the world's resources [...]. Ultimately [...] it was the control of the means of representation rather than the means of production that confirmed the hegemony of the European powers in their respective empires' (Ashcroft, Griffiths, and Tiffin 2000: 127).

Postcolonial theory is thus centrally concerned with issues of culture, knowledge, power, and representation, and understanding how cultural and racial difference and inequality are produced and experienced. Colonizers were in the business of 'civilising the natives', of inculcating modernity, order, and progress, and 'cleansing' the natives of their cultural impurities (McClintock 1995). Cultural imperialism was propagated by a belief that it was a colonizer's moral duty to carry out these tasks, since it was he (sic) who possessed superior knowledge and cultural traditions. A linear teleology of progress underpins this ideological artifice, where the West stands as the vanguard of history replacing the histories and subjectivities of others trapped in tradition (Chakrabarty 2000). Naming and challenging this problem of *Eurocentrism*—the assumption of the superiority of 'European' civilization and the positing of a universalizing, yet ultimately parochial, 'European' history as the centre against which all other histories are articulated and judged—is a key task of postcolonial scholars. The adjective 'European' is in quote marks to acknowledge that the Europe in Eurocentrism refers not so much to the geographical entity. Rather, Mufti's (2005: 474; italics in the original) definition of Eurocentrism clarifies that:

> The modes of cultural authority that the idea of Europe regulates are *Western* in an encompassing sense, underwriting narratives of American universalism as well as those of a uniquely Europe polity and culture in the geographically specific sense. It is the social and cultural force of this idea of Europe in intellectual life, as in the phenomenal world of global power relations [...].

---

[1] There is no singular form of colonization; different imperial powers pursued their colonial ambitions in different ways depending on location. Colonization is typically defined as the physical occupation by a foreign power of domestic land; it is one, amongst many, examples of how imperial power can be exerted (Young 2001).

Postcolonial organizational scholars have pursued keenly the analysis of Eurocentrism at work both within scholarly disciplines (for instance, comparative and international management; see Jack and Westwood 2009), and in business and organizational practices, such as the transfer of management knowledge from Western to non-Western corporate settings (Frenkel 2008; Mir and Mir 2009). Broadly speaking, scholars have used postcolonial modes of analysis (usually informed by the work of Edward Said, Homi Bhabha, or both) to identify, in contemporary business practice and research, examples of cultural imperialism underpinned by assumptions of the superiority of Western modes of management and organization, and the concomitant denigration or marginalization of non-Western/Indigenous knowledge systems (Prasad 2003, 2012; Özkazanç-Pan 2008).

Edward Said's (1978) *Orientalism: Western Conceptions of the Orient* is considered a foundational text for postcolonial theory and analysis. It presents an analysis of how (mainly nineteenth-century—although Orientalism can be viewed in much earlier cultural artefacts—) Western scholars and others (including travel writers, artists, curators, administrators, philologists, historians) constructed their object of study—the Orient (referring to the Middle East and North Africa)—through a series of classifications, categories, and visual imagery. For Said (indebted to Foucault and to Gramsci), Orientalism is not a set of methods for neutrally and accurately describing the contours of a pre-existing reality called 'the Orient'; rather, it is an exercise in othering and a discursive formation that simultaneously produces and naturalizes knowledge of the Self and the Other (the Occident and the Orient), whilst erasing the ideological practices that make this possible in the first place. Central to Said's colonial discourse analysis (as it would become named) is an exposition of the hierarchical system of colonialist binaries (e.g. that positions the West as active, civilized, developed, masculine, scientific, and thus superior, vis-à-vis the non-West as passive, primitive/savage, backward, feminine, superstitious, and thus inferior (Prasad 1997)) that generate *colonial subjectivities* through which both the colonizer and the colonized would be hailed to know themselves. As Brantlinger (1985) points out, these binaries often circulated via colonial myths (e.g. the myth of the 'lazy native' (Alatas 1977)) that both projected European fears and (gendered and sexualized) desires onto the Other, and 'blam[ed] the victim' (Brantlinger 1985: 198) for their own colonization.

A key criticism (amongst others; see Young 2001) of Said's text is that it lacks appropriate acknowledgement of the multiple forms of resistance to colonization and cultural imperialism, and the unsettled nature of colonial subjectivities. On the one hand, anti-colonialist scholarship (notably associated with Marxist perspectives) draws attention to the multiplicity of armed and violent as well as pacifist struggles against imperial forces in a variety of locations (Young 2001). On the other hand, psychological and notably psychoanalytic accounts (for instance, in the early anti-colonialist writings of Frantz Fanon (1952/86), or Jean-Paul Sartre (which combined Marxism with phenomenology), or the later Lacanian-inspired work of Homi Bhabha) have noted the complex psychological dynamics and *ambivalences* of the colonial encounter, which mean that colonial subjectivities can never be fixed, secure, or fully finished. Prakash (1999) describes the encounter as a tension zone in which colonial discourses led a discordant life of dominance associated with paradox and subterfuge, and in which the intersubjective and interdependent qualities of the colonizer–colonized relationship are masked. Through scholars' subsequent use of Said and Bhabha, Foucauldian ideas on discourse and the disciplinary subject (and associated concepts of knowledge, governmentality, and biopolitics) and Lacanian ideas on identification and the psychoanalytic subject (and associated concepts of desire, fantasy, and hybridity) have become sedimented in postcolonial theory (amongst others, of course).

Despite the prefix post- (in postcolonialism),[2] Orientalist binaries, colonial myths, and other forms of racism, violence, and oppression associated with colonialism continue to exist (even since the formal independence of many formerly colonized countries); it is sometimes referred to under the banner of neocolonialism (Young 2001). It is these legacies of colonization (notably the perpetuation of Eurocentrism and colonial subjectivities), as well as new modes of economic and cultural imperialism, that have spurred the interests of postcolonial organizational scholars in recent years. However, organizational scholars have been selective in borrowing from the complex terrain of postcolonial theory in the parent disciplines in the humanities. For instance, in the editorial essay to a recent special issue on postcolonial organizational analysis, we noted *inter alia* the relative lack of analysis of the continuing psychological impact and affective nature of neocolonial relations, and discussion of the relationship between postcolonial theory and Indigenous knowledge systems (Jack et al. 2011). To that list of underexplored issues, we should add workplace diversity.

Postcolonial Perspectives on Workplace Diversity

In critical diversity studies, there are very few extended engagements with postcolonialism and its implications, even though it has been noted as an important theoretical resource in workplace diversity research (Prasad, Pringle, and Konrad 2006). The few treatments that do exist are reflective of the dominant reception of postcolonialism in organizational research, insofar as they are concerned (conceptually and/or empirically) with themes of cultural and racial difference, Eurocentrism and ambivalence, and the continuing production of colonial binaries in managing workplace diversity.

The most extended conceptual analysis of DM from a postcolonial perspective is a chapter by Anshuman Prasad (2006) in the *Handbook of Workplace Diversity*. In it, he

---

[2] Early debate in the field focused on whether the prefix (post-) should be used at all in relation to colonialism, and what difference adding a hyphen would make to the word post-/colonialism. On the one hand, scholars agree that, despite formal independence, old structures and practices of colonialism continue and mutate (and can be referred as 'neocolonialism'). As for the hyphen, it is sometimes used by writers who wish to denote 'postcolonial' in purely temporal terms; in other words, to refer to the time period after formal independence, but certainly not to imply that colonial forms would simultaneously disappear overnight.

argues that postcolonialism and its focus on 'analyses of social and cultural marginality' is pertinent to diversity scholars 'because the project of workplace diversity is linked to ameliorating the condition of those on the margins of the organization' (Prasad 2006: 125). In the contexts of the US and Europe (to which Prasad broadly refers in his chapter),[3] this link reflects the manner in which 'workplace diversity initiatives often tend to be viewed as organizational reform projects that would *empower* marginalized groups, and bring them to a position of equality with the white privileged groups' (Prasad 2006: 135; italics in the original). Drawing upon Said's hierarchy of colonial binaries (1978), and Bhabha's concepts of ambivalence and the colonial stereotype (1983), Prasad offers a critical interpretation of this 'positive' view of diversity initiatives (though he does not negate the potential for initiatives to have some beneficial results for marginalized groups).

In short, he argues that diversity initiatives are, despite appearances, designed to *sustain* (rather than dismantle) the (racial) binaries that enable the reproduction of hierarchical relations of privilege and subordination. The complex manner in which the management of workplace diversity operates to generate such a conservative outcome is, according to Prasad (2006: 136), 'traceable, in part, to the continuing imprint of such colonialist schizophrenia'. On the one hand, such 'schizophrenia' is manifest in contradictory beliefs and attitudes, for example, surrounding the 'Latinization' of US society, where 'Latin people are seen by (neo-)colonial discourse as being weak, lazy and shiftless but, *at the same time*, also as capable of swamping the Anglo culture of America and sapping its cultural strength' (Prasad 2006: 136; italics in the original). Such ambivalent beliefs, and associated emotions including fear and/or loathing, prompt a dominant group response of discursive 'repair and maintenance work' (Prasad 2006: 136), in which linguistic tropes are used to propagate and normalize difference. Colonization—and the advantages that dominant groups extract from it—requires ongoing maintenance (especially in contexts of demographic and social change), and this is effected through the promulgation of group differences based on binary oppositions which ensure '*continued* access to groups of people (e.g. cultures, subcultures, etc.) that may be seen in *need* of help' (Prasad 2006: 135). To quote Prasad:

> [I]t would appear to be in the interest of the white privileged groups that diversity initiatives designed to help marginalized groups be also *designed*, wittingly or unwittingly, to fail (and/or to discursively produce 'new' marginal groups in continuing *need* of help) and, in so doing, leave the hierarchical force of the said system of binaries relatively intact. [...] As a corollary to this, we might also expect that, in general, diversity initiatives would be unlikely to include elements that could seriously disturb the stability of the binaries in question. (Prasad 2006: 135)

---

[3] Note that Prasad is looking at diversity in terms of social groups and social justice primarily with regard to the US context. He does not make claims to cover non-US contexts, and there is little mention of the individualism that is often associated with US DM discourse.

Prasad draws out two implications for critical diversity researchers. First, research on failed diversity initiatives needs to explore how *failure* was designed into the programme in the first place; second, research on the *value* of diversity initiatives needs to explore the extent to which they 'destabilize the binaries under consideration' (Prasad 2006: 136).

In this latter regard, a study from Sweden by Kalonaityte (2010) offers empirical insights into how 'organisations contribute to the creation and maintenance of disadvantaged identity categories through organizing' (Kalonaityte 2010: 34). The setting for this study is a municipal adult education school which has an active pro-DM framework with respect to its employees and students, most of whom are immigrants to Sweden. In this case study, therefore, DM refers to ethnic diversity, and the integration (or otherwise) of immigrants into the organization. Kalonaityte conceptualizes DM in terms of organizational 'identity work' and 'internal border control' (referring to the processes and practices that dominant groups use to police boundaries, exclude minority groups, and thus maintain hierarchies). Her work echoes and extends Prasad's concerns with empirical evidence (generated via interviews, observation, and documentary evidence) and a more fully fleshed Bhabhaian postcolonial perspective.

In terms of the latter, she combines Bhabha's writing on ambivalence, with his ideas on nation and narration (1990, 1994), notably the distinction he draws between the pedagogical and the performative elements of narrative. She uses this writing on 'national culture', since the identity work going on in the empirical setting pertains precisely to the role of diversity initiatives in reproducing a particular version of Swedish national identity. The pedagogical are the 'preferred' elements of a nation's narrative, typically treated as static representations of a kind of national essence. The performative points to the daily lived realities of the nation, and the various deviations or inconsistencies that problematize the notion of a 'culturally pure' national identity. The constant unsettling of the pedagogical by the performative has consequences for social action: it leads to the search for ever new forms of boundary maintenance and new 'national symbols to maintain the hierarchical relation between cultures' (Kalonaityte 2010: 39). As such:

> The concept of ambivalence puts the spotlight on the discursive crisis in the assumedly stable collective cultural identity [...]. In other words, ambivalence needs to be treated as a record of the ongoing resistance to the dominant cultural imperatives and as a pointer in how oppressive discourses can be dismantled. (Kalonaityte 2010: 39)

The task for the organizational analyst is to identify the living tensions and inconsistencies between these elements in relation to diversity initiatives, and to conceive of them as forms of resistance to the ongoing maintenance of racial hierarchies in organizational settings. Through her interview data, for instance, Kalonaityte gives examples of how one dominant (white) racial group employee in the school reached for an essentialist idea of Swedish national culture (based around certain 'core values' such as equality and responsibility) to simultaneously construct a privileged self-identity and a culturally inferior, non-Swedish immigrant identity. This was a common pattern across the employee interviews, but so too were a number of contradictions in these self-representations. For example, one interview demonstrated inconsistency in the expression of democracy as a cultural value that underpins a putatively superior Swedish cultural identity (which immigrants are, per force, imagined to lack). Whilst democracy may be valued in rhetoric, Kalonaityte's study illustrates how it was curtailed in an everyday classroom context (of mainly adult immigrant students) by silencing alternative points of view during class discussion. For this author: 'The contribution of the postcolonial lens in the study of workplace diversity lies in the conceptual space it provides for rendering visible, and legitimizing, non-traditional forms of resistance to hierarchical differentiation of cultural identities' (Kalonaityte 2010: 31).

While the works of Prasad and Kalonaityte represent postcolonial analyses specifically of workplace diversity (where organizations can be viewed as 'containers' of diverse members), there are two scholarly pieces from the broader domain of gender and diversity research which merit mention. Both recommend and use (in different ways) postcolonial perspectives—and, more specifically, postcolonial feminist perspectives—to provoke researchers to become more reflexive about their underlying cultural and epistemological perspectives in the context of 'global' management research. In their editorial introduction to a special issue on new directions in gender, diversity, and organization theorizing, for instance, Metcalfe and Woodhams (2012: 124) argue that the field is constrained by its dominant 'western epistemological assumptions' and that these 'western perspectives of gender and diversity theorizing are limited when evaluating contemporary, global, social and organizational change'. They call for a reimagination of gender and diversity research, one specifically attuned to a number of intersecting themes connected to globalization and global social capital, 'so as to challenge western ideologies and create space for envisioning new trajectories of gender, diversity, organization and management development' (Metcalfe and Woodhams 2012: 130).

This involves two key elements. First, greater dialogue with global stakeholders, between theories and theorists located in the global north and the global south, and 'giving voice' (sic) to scholars from Africa, the Middle East, and Latin America. Second, developing a theoretical model that draws on three areas of interdisciplinary enquiry to address social justice issues on a global scale. The three areas are: postcolonialism, gender and development; geography and place; transnationalism and global movements. As for Özkazanç-Pan (2012), she illuminates how researchers conducting fieldwork in international (management) settings can use the postcolonial feminist concepts of subalternity, reflexivity, and representation to address the risk of reproducing and reinscribing inappropriate and imperious Western assumptions and research approaches. She encourages researchers to ask themselves: 'For whom do "we" produce knowledge? and what are the consequences of such claims of knowledge?' (Özkazanç-Pan 2012: 582).

In sum, postcolonialism is a well-established, theoretically diverse, and politically contested multidisciplinary field of study in the humanities and social sciences, but it has yet to be fully engaged as a framework for critical diversity studies. As such, there are many opportunities to advance postcolonial perspectives in critical diversity studies. But how should we go about this task?

ADVANCING POSTCOLONIAL PERSPECTIVES IN CRITICAL DIVERSITY STUDIES

A common strategy for making suggestions about how a scholarly field should broach its future is to generate a manifesto of new topics, methodological approaches, and research settings, or return to familiar ones with fresh eyes. I would like offer a different approach. Rather than detail a future agenda for postcolonialism and critical diversity studies, I will instead recommend two texts that offer fresh and multidisciplinary perspectives on postcolonial thinking. Insights contained in these texts carry implications for recommended future objects of diversity research, as well as for diversity researchers themselves.

South African psychoanalyst Derek Hook's (2012) book, *A Critical Psychology of the Postcolonial: The Mind of Apartheid*, begins with excerpts from the Apartheid Archive Project. These excerpts bear witness to the manner in which privileged white representations constitute the black Other as an object of both disgust and desire, of hate and admiration, of intense bodily repugnance and repressed sexual desire. Hook refers to such (strongly) ambivalent and visceral responses to, and imaginaries of, the Other as 'extra-discursive' components of racism, with two significant implications for postcolonial analysis in his home discipline of psychology. First, discourse analytical approaches (e.g. Wetherell and Potter 1992; LeCouteur and Augoustinos 2001) (a popular alternative to standard cognitive or social psychological perspectives) offer necessary but incomplete insights into the nature of racism. Second, an alternative theory needs to attend to multiple analytical domains. Specifically, it needs to recognize and explain the relationship between the psychological/subjective/unconscious and the social/structural/ideological, all domains in which (ambivalent and incomplete) racial subjectivities are produced and experienced. Based on these parameters, Hook draws upon psychoanalytic, anti-colonial, and postcolonial writings to generate what he calls a 'psychopolitical' theory of (post)colonial racism with respect to apartheid (and post-apartheid) South Africa. He describes his approach thus, because he considers it 'a form of critique in which we not only place the psychological within the register of the political, but [...] in which the political is also [...] approached through the register of the psychological' (Hook 2012: 40).

The careful complexity of Hook's theory cannot be adequately represented in this short section. However, my own reading of what is distinctive and thus singularly valuable to critical diversity work about his psychopolitical theory is that it draws from *inter alia* and pushes beyond Bhabha's and Fanon's (a central figure in Hook's thought) explanation of the paranoid-schizophrenic generative structure of colonial subjectivation.[4] His theory of colonial racism—and thus a novel critical perspective on workplace diversity and racial discrimination—is that it is generated by disavowing the incommensurabilities that are attendant to ego–bodily relations and three different registers of colonial experience (the corporeal, the psychical, the symbolic).

Beyond this singular theory, Hook's book provides considerable food for thought for critical diversity scholars. It reminds us that the continuing legacies and mutating forms of colonialism and cultural imperialism are a present, yet often hidden and unacknowledged, reality in many organizations, especially those located in formerly colonized locations, or for organizational members from such locations working in (formerly colonial/imperial) metropolitan contexts. As Frosch notes in his introduction to Hook's text: 'colonialism forges patterns of social and psychological practice that persist into the "post" era, often as hidden chains still binding colonized and colonizers to their past' (Hook 2012: ix). Frosch thus reminds us that colonialism is not solely discernible in observable artefacts like written and spoken texts that are ripe for discourse analysis, but also requires other analytical methods to bear witness to experiences beyond the domain of representation. As such, it is vital that critical diversity and postcolonial scholars remind themselves of the importance of colonial psychology (and associated research methods), and the operations of the unconscious in structuring workplace diversity, alongside continuing scholarly interests in discourse analyses. There is a potential danger that we might lose sight of this domain, given the recommendations for more organizational-level/structural analysis in diversity research (Zanoni et al. 2010), or deeper engagement with Foucault's concepts of governmentality and biopolitics (Ahonen et al. 2013). Working with Hook's psychopolitical approach also offers a means of responding to the selective attention of postcolonial organizational analysts as regards the affective domain of colonization.

Furthermore, Hook's treatment of a number of psychoanalytic anti- and postcolonial thinkers—whose works (notably Fanon's) are yet to be fully embraced in organizational analysis—offers a rich resource for extending Prasad's and Kalonaityte's work with and beyond that of Homi Bhabha. On the one hand, Hook's discussion of Bhabha's essay on the colonial stereotype (e.g. with notable reference to the concepts of fetish, condensation, replacement) and his close and critical reading of Fanon (e.g. with notable reference to the concepts of divided colonial subjectivities, trauma, libidinal economy, paranoid-schizophrenia) should enable future researchers to generate even more finessed explanations of the 'designed failure' (as noted by Prasad) and the empirical 'contradictions' of and resistances to (as noted by Kalonaityte) diversity initiatives. Hook's discussions thus aid a postcolonial interpretation of the constant disappointments and mixed results (Bell and Berry 2007) associated with voluntary DM initiatives (and perhaps therefore the shift away from diversity to inclusion discourse noted by Oswick and Noon 2014), and the persistent presence of racism in organizations, despite legal measures.

---

[4] With the notable assistance of Kristeva's (1982) concept of the abject, Žižek's (1993) work on ideology and political fantasy, Biko's (1978) political work in the Black Consciousness movement in South Africa, and Manganyi's (1981) phenomenological work on ego–body relations.

Australian sociologist Raewyn Connell's (2007) book *Southern Theory: The Global Dynamics of Knowledge in Social Science* is a second text that can spark provocative conversations about the possibilities of decolonizing (mainstream and critical) workplace diversity research, generating greater epistemic diversity (as recommended by Metcalfe and Woodhams 2012) in the field, and learning from Indigenous knowledge systems. This is certainly not the only text of relevance to these concerns; indeed, there are ongoing conversations within postcolonial organizational analysis (notably, for instance, on the implications of the Latin American decolonial paradigm for postcolonial research (Faria et al. 2013)) and Indigenous social science research methods (Smith 1999; Denzin, Lincoln, and Smith 2008) that should also be drawn upon to a greater extent in critical diversity studies. However, Connell's text is distinctive; to engage with Connell, first of all, is to participate in an ambitious and challenging discussion about 'a new path for social theory that will help social science to serve democratic purposes on a world scale' (2007: vii). The point of departure for this call to a new path is her view that:

> [S]ocial science is, at best, ambiguously democratic. Its dominant genres picture the world as it is seen by men, by capitalists, by the educated and affluent. Most importantly, they picture the world as seen from the rich capital-exporting countries of Europe and America—the global metropole. (Connell 2007: vii)

Her book demonstrates how this dominant 'world-picturing' of social science from the global north has produced a core-periphery system, and an associated inequality in the global division of intellectual labour between (crudely put) theory production in the global north and data collection elsewhere. Connell offers a number of suggestions to reconfigure this status quo, and a discussion of the epistemological, institutional, and practical challenges involved. Her primary recommendation is for social science researchers—especially those located in the global north—to recognize, read, and learn from the genre of (what she calls) 'Southern Theory' (i.e. theoretical and empirical knowledge about social experience produced in semi-peripheral and peripheral locations of the contemporary world system) and thus to 're-picture' global social science from the starting point of the global majority world (i.e. the 'two-thirds world' (Esteva and Prakash 1998), whose perspectives are marginalized through the export and adoption of mainstream/northern social theory). To do so is to acknowledge that: 'colonised and peripheral societies produce social thought *about the modern world* which has as much intellectual power as metropolitan social thought, and more political relevance' (Connell 2007: xii; italics in the original).

To illustrate the rich theoretical and empirical insights into the (neocolonial) modern world of 'Southern Theory', she outlines and discusses a number of authors and anti-colonial/postcolonial texts located in countries, regions, and continents (including postcolonial Africa, modernizing Iran, Latin America, India) that have experienced colonization or foreign imperialism, and where the resultant economic and cultural dependency has been challenged. As well as the substantive insights into the struggles and complexities of relations of dependency, she draws out lessons from these texts about the conditions of possibility (enablers and constraints) for (re)asserting Indigenous knowledges as forms of intellectual and political resistance, and for the development of autonomous indigenous intellectual disciplines. Whilst endorsing the importance of the latter, she recognizes a logical impossibility: academic disciplines in postcolonial peripheral locations, and local knowledge systems, are already cultural hybrids and translated objects, precisely because of the colonial encounter, not culturally 'pure' systems of knowledge waiting to be resurrected or developed. To recognize these relational conditions of knowledge, and their epistemological complexities, is the starting point for conversations between theories and theorists in the global north and south, and for 'giving voice' (sic) to scholars on the periphery of the system (cf. Metcalfe and Woodhams 2012).

That said, there are simpler, practical steps (recommended by Connell) that critical diversity researchers located in core, semi-, and peripheral locations can take to generate new conversations, including: practices of connection (travel, publication, and network formation), especially between scholars located in the global south; collective learning and 're-tooling' scholars (especially early career scholars) in the centre (e.g. setting readings from multiple locations, or encouraging students to learn the languages in which those different readings were originally written); self-reflection (e.g. considering what material interests shape our scholarly interests, and the role of performance management discourse and incentives in driving our research).

Despite the many insightful and provocative elements of Connell's argument, it could be extended further by drawing clearer lines to existing work on Indigenous research paradigms and methodologies. Social scientific methodology and research design issues are not addressed in much detail in Connell. Bagele Chilisa's (2012) *Indigenous Research Methodologies*, written for students, offers an excellent introduction into 'the meaning of postcolonial indigenous research methodologies and philosophies' (Chilisa 2012: 97). She outlines two distinct but interconnected ways of conceiving such methodologies: as 'the indigenization of conventional research and [as] a relational indigenous research paradigm'. She defines the former approach in the following way:

> An indigenization process challenges researchers to invoke indigenous knowledge to inform ways in which concepts and new theoretical frameworks for research studies are defined, new tools of collecting data developed, and the literature base broadened, so that we depend not only on written texts but also on the largely unwritten texts of the formerly colonized and historically oppressed peoples. (Chilisa 2012: 101)

Whilst her book goes on to articulate how this might be accomplished, it is also clear that this is an approach not without its problems, both epistemological and political. In the latter regard, simply 'inserting an indigenous perspective into one of the major research paradigms may not be effective because it is hard to remove the underlying epistemology and ontology on which the paradigms are built' (Chilisa 2012: 108). Politically, such an approach could be viewed as assimilationist in effect, integrating or subsuming a marginalized knowledge system into a dominant one, and/or as denying the irreducible difference of alternative belief systems.

The second approach—respecting and learning about relational indigenous postcolonial paradigms—emphasizes both the relational and intersubjective ontologies of chosen indigenous belief systems and the development of methodological approaches framed by indigenous terms of reference. Whilst relational ontologies challenge a number of fundamental assumptions about the nature of human relations in workplace diversity research, together with indigenous methodologies, they offer radically different paradigms for the pursuit of critical diversity studies.

Conclusion

This chapter set out to ignite interest in postcolonial analyses in critical diversity studies as a way of responding to recent calls for new conversations in the field regarding 'where to next'. Following selective reviews of critical diversity studies, postcolonialism, and critical diversity studies based on postcolonial thinking, the final section of 'Advancing Postcolonial Perspectives in Critical Diversity Studies' recommended two texts which provide multiple avenues for provoking postcolonial conversations of distinctive relevance to workplace diversity research. To conclude this chapter, two key recommendations can be drawn. First, critical diversity scholars might undertake a closer engagement with psychoanalytic *and* discursive variants of postcolonial theory (Hook 2012) to generate complex understandings of the psychological dimensions of (post)colonial subjectivities and the persistence of racism in organizations. Second, scholars might also consider the merits of 'Southern Theory' (Connell 2007) (and Indigenous research paradigms) in order to move beyond the noted Eurocentric limits of existing gender and diversity research.

References

Acker, J. (2006). Inequality regimes: gender, class, and race in organizations. *Gender and Society*, 20(4): 441–64.
Ahmed, S. (2007). The language of diversity. *Ethnic and Racial Studies*, 30(2): 235–56.
Ahmed, S. and Swan, E. (2006). Doing diversity. *Policy Futures in Education*, 4(2): 96–100.
Ahonen, P., Tienari, J., Meriläinen, S., and Pullen, A. (2013). Hidden contexts and invisible power relations: a Foucauldian reading of diversity research. *Human Relations*, 67(3): 263–86.
Alatas, S. H. (1977). *The Myth of the Lazy Native*. London: Frank Cass.
Ashcroft, B., Griffiths, G., and Tiffin, H. (2000). *Post-Colonial Studies: The Key Concepts*. London: Routledge.
Bell, M. P. and Berry, D. P. (2007). Viewing diversity through different lenses: avoiding a few blind spots. *Academy of Management Perspectives*, 21(4): 21–5.
Benschop, Y. (2001). Pride, prejudice and performance: relations between diversity, HRM and performance. *International Journal of Human Resource Management*, 12(7): 1166–81.
Bhabha, H. (1983). The other question. *Screen*, 24(6): 18–35.

Bhabha, H. (ed.) (1990). *Nation and Narration*. London: Routledge.
Bhabha, H. (1994). *The Location of Culture*. London and New York: Routledge.
Biko, S. (1978). *I Write What I Like*. London: Bowerdean.
Boxenbaum, E. (2006). Lost in translation: the making of Danish diversity management. *American Behavioral Scientist*, 49(7): 939–48.
Brantlinger, P. (1985). Victorians and Africans: the genealogy of the myth of the Dark Continent. *Critical Inquiry*, 12: 166–203.
Calás, M. B., Holgersson, C., and Smircich, L. (2009). Diversity management? Translation? Travel? *Scandinavian Journal of Management*, 25: 349–51.
Cavanaugh, J. M. (1997). (In)corporating the other? Managing the politics of workplace difference. In P. Prasad, A. J. Mills, M. Elmes, and A. Prasad (eds.), *Managing the Organizational Melting Pot: Dilemmas of Workplace Diversity*. Thousand Oaks, CA: Sage, 31–53.
Chakrabarty, D. (2000). *Provincializing Europe: Postcolonial Thought and Historical Difference*. Princeton, NJ: Princeton University Press.
Chilisa, B. (2012). *Indigenous Research Methodologies*. Thousand Oaks, CA: Sage.
Christiansen, T. J. and Just, S. N. (2012). Regularities of diversity discourse: address, categorization, and invitation. *Journal of Management & Organization*, 18(3): 398–411.
Connell, R. (2007) *Southern Theory: The Global Dynamics of Knowledge in Social Science*. Sydney: Allen & Unwin.
Cox, T. and Blake, S. (1991). Managing cultural diversity: implications for organizational competitiveness. *Academy of Management Executive*, 5: 45–56.
Cox Jr, T. (1993). *Cultural Diversity in Organizations: Theory, Research and Practice*. San Francisco, CA: Berrett-Koehler.
Dass, P. and Parker, B. (1999). Strategies for managing human resource diversity: from resistance to learning. *Academy of Management Executive*, 13(2): 68–80.
Denzin, N. K., Lincoln, Y. S., and Smith, L. T. (eds.) (2008). *Handbook of Critical and Indigenous Methodologies*. Thousand Oaks, CA: Sage.
Dickens, L. (1999). Beyond the business case: a three-pronged approach to equality action. *Human Resource Management Journal*, 9: 9–19.
Edelman, L. B., Fuller, S. R., and Mara-Drita, I. (2001). Diversity rhetoric and the managerialization of the law. *American Journal of Sociology*, 106(6): 1589–641.
Essed, P. (1991). *Understanding Everyday Racism: An Interdisciplinary Theory*. Newbury Park, CA: Sage.
Esteva, G. and Prakash. M. S. (1998). *Grassroots Post-Modernism: Remaking the Soil of Cultures*. London: Zed Press.
Fanon, F. (1952/86). *Black Skin White Masks*. London: Pluto.
Faria, A., Wanderley, S., Reiz, Y., and Celano, A. (2013). Can the subaltern teach? Performativity otherwise through anthropophagy. In V. Malin, J. Murphy, and M. Siltaoja (eds.), *Getting Things Done*. Dialogues in Critical Management Studies, vol. 2. Bingley: Emerald Group Publishing, 205–24.
Frenkel, M. (2008). The multinational corporation as a third space: rethinking international management discourse on knowledge transfer through Homi Bhabha. *Academy of Management Review*, 33(4): 924–42.
Gardenswartz, L. and Rowe, A. (1993). *Managing Diversity: A Complete Desk Reference and Planning Guide*. Alexandria, VA: Society for Human Resource Management.
Holvino, E. and Kamp, A. (2009). Diversity management: are we moving in the right direction? Reflections from both sides of the North Atlantic. *Scandinavian Journal of Management*, 25: 395–403.

Hoobler, J. M. (2005). Lip service to multiculturalism: docile bodies of the modern organization. *Journal of Management Inquiry*, 14: 49–56.

Hook, D. (2012). *A Critical Psychology of the Postcolonial: The Mind of Apartheid*. London and New York: Routledge.

Humphries, M. T. and Grice, S. (1995). Equal employment opportunity and the management of diversity: a global discourse of assimilation? *Journal of Organizational Change Management*, 8(5): 17–33.

Jack, G. and Westwood, R. (2009). *International and Cross-Cultural Management Studies: A Postcolonial Reading*. Basingstoke: Palgrave Macmillan.

Jack, G., Westwood, R., Srinivas, N., and Sardar, Z. (2011). Broadening, deepening and re-asserting a postcolonial interrogative space in organization studies. *Organization*, 18(3): 275–302.

Janssens, M. and Zanoni, P. (2005). Many diversities for many services: theorizing diversity (management) in service companies. *Human Relations*, 58(3): 311–40.

Jehn, K. A., Northcraft, G. B., and Neale, M. A. (1999). Why differences make a difference: a field study of diversity, conflict, and performance in workgroups. *Administrative Science Quarterly*, 44: 238–51.

Johnston, W. and Packer, A. (1987). *Workforce 2000: Work and Workers for the Twenty-First Century*. Indianapolis, IN: Hudson Institute.

Jones, D. and Stablein, R. (2006). Diversity as resistance and recuperation: critical theory, post-structuralist perspectives and workplace diversity. In A. M. Konrad, P. Prasad, and J. K. Pringle (eds.), *Handbook of Workplace Diversity*. London: Sage, 145–66.

Jones, D., Pringle, J., and Shepherd, D. (2000). Managing diversity meets Aotearoa/New Zealand. *Personnel Review*, 29(3): 364–80.

Kalonaityte, V. (2010). The case of vanishing borders: theorizing diversity management as internal border control. *Organization*, 17(1): 31–52.

Kelly, E. and Dobbin, F. (1998). How affirmative action became diversity management. *American Behavioral Scientist*, 41: 960–84.

Kersten, A. (2000). Diversity management: dialogue, dialectics and diversion. *Journal of Organizational Change Management*, 13(3): 235–48.

Kirby, E. L. and Harter, L. M. (2003). Speaking the language of the bottom-line: the metaphor of 'managing diversity'. *International Journal of Business Communication*, 40(1): 28–49.

Kirton, G. and Greene, A.-M. (2005). *The Dynamics of Managing Diversity: A Critical Approach*, 2nd edn. Oxford: Elsevier Butterworth-Heinemann.

Konrad, A. M., Prasad, P., and Pringle, J. K. (eds.) (2006). *Handbook of Workplace Diversity*. London: Sage.

Kristeva, J. (1982). *The Powers of Horror: An Essay on Abjection*. New York: Columbia University Press.

LeCouteur, A. and Augoustinos, M. (2001). The language of racism and prejudice. In M. Augoustinos and K. J. Reynolds (eds.), *Understanding Prejudice, Racism and Social Conflict*. London: Sage, 215–30.

Liff, S. (1997). Two routes to managing diversity: individual differences or social group characteristics. *Employee Relations*, 19(1): 11–26.

Linnehan, F. and Konrad, A. (1999). Diluting diversity: implications for intergroup inequality in organizations. *Journal of Management Inquiry*, 8: 399–414.

Litvin, D. (1997). The discourse of diversity: from biology to management. *Organization*, 4(2): 187–209.

Lorbiecki, A. and Jack, G. (2000). Critical turns in the evolution of diversity management. *British Journal of Management*, 11: 17–31.

Lynch, F.R. (1997). 'The diversity machine'. *Society*, 34(5): 32-45.

McClintock, A. (1995). *Imperial Leather: Race, Gender and Sexuality in the Colonial Conquest*. New York and London: Routledge.

Manganyi, N.C. (1981). *Looking through the Keyhole: Dissenting Essays on the Black Experience*. Johannesburg: Ravan.

Metcalfe, B. D. and Woodhams, C. (2008). Critical perspectives in diversity and equality management. *Gender in Management: An International Journal*, 23(6): 377–81.

Metcalfe, B. D. and Woodhams, C. (2012). Introduction: new directions in gender, diversity and organization theorizing—re-imagining feminist post-colonialism, transnationalism and geographies of power. *International Journal of Management Reviews*, 14: 123–40.

Miller, G. E., Mills, A. J., and Helms Mills, J. (2009). Introduction: gender and diversity at work: changing theories. Changing organizations. *Canadian Journal of Administrative Sciences*, 26: 173–5.

Mir, R. A. and Mir, A. (2009). From the colony to the corporation: studying knowledge transfer across international boundaries. *Group & Organization Management*, 34(1): 90–113.

Moore-Gilbert, B. (1997). *Postcolonial Theory: Contexts, Practices, Politics*. London and New York: Verso.

Mufti, A. (2005). Global comparativism. *Critical Inquiry*, 31(2): 472–89.

Noon, M. (2007). The fatal flaws of diversity and the business case for ethnic minorities. *Work, Employment & Society*, 21: 773–84.

Omanović, V. (2009). Diversity and its management as a dialectical process: encountering Sweden and the U.S. *Scandinavian Journal of Management*, 25: 352–62.

Ostendorp, A. and Steyaert, C. (2009). How different can differences (be)come? Interpretative repertoires of diversity concepts in Swiss-based organizations. *Scandinavian Journal of Management*, 25: 374–84.

Oswick, C. and Noon, M. (2014). Discourses of diversity, equality and inclusion: trenchant formulations or transient fashions? *British Journal of Management*, 25: 23–39.

Özbilgin, M. and Tatli, A. (2011). Mapping out the field of equality and diversity: rise of individualism and voluntarism. *Human Relations*, 64(9): 1229–53.

Özkazanç-Pan, B. (2008). International management meets 'the rest of the world'. *Academy of Management Review*, 33(4): 964–74.

Özkazanç-Pan, B. (2012). Postcolonial feminist research: challenges and complexities. *Equality, Diversity and Inclusion: An International Journal*, 31(5–6): 573–91.

Pelled, L. H., Eisenhardt, K. M., and Xin, K. R. (1999). Exploring the black box: an analysis of work group diversity, conflict, and performance. *Administrative Science Quarterly*, 44: 1–28.

Perriton, L. (2009). 'We don't want complaining women!' A critical analysis of the business case for diversity. *Management Communication Quarterly*, 23: 218–43.

Prakash, G. (1999). *Another Reason: Science and the Imagination of Modern India*. Princeton, NJ: Princeton University Press.

Prasad, A. (1997). The colonizing consciousness and representations of the other: a postcolonial critique of the discourse of oil. In P. Prasad, A. J. Mills, M. Elmes, and A. Prasad (eds.), *Managing the Organizational Melting Pot: Dilemmas of Workplace Diversity*. Thousand Oaks, CA: Sage, 285–311.

Prasad, A. (ed.) (2003). *Postcolonial Theory and Organizational Analysis: A Critical Engagement*. New York: Palgrave Macmillan.

Prasad, A. (2006). The jewel in the crown: postcolonial theory and workplace diversity. In A. M. Konrad, P. Prasad, and J. K. Pringle (eds.), *Handbook of Workplace Diversity*. London: Sage, 21–44.

Prasad, A. (ed.) (2012). *Against the Grain: Advances in Postcolonial Organization Studies*. Malmo: Liber & Copenhagen Business School Press.

Prasad, P. and Mills, A. J. (1997). From showcase to shadow: understanding the dilemmas of managing workplace diversity. In P. Prasad, A. J. Mills, M. Elmes, and A. Prasad (eds.), *Managing the Organizational Melting Pot: Dilemmas of Workplace Diversity*. Thousand Oaks, CA: Sage, 3–30.

Prasad, P., Pringle, J., and Konrad, A. M. (2006). Examining the contours of workplace diversity: concepts, contexts, and challenges. In A. M. Konrad, P. Prasad, and J. K. Pringle (eds.), *Handbook of Workplace Diversity*. London: Sage, 1–22.

Richard, O. (2000). Racial diversity, business strategy, and firm performance: a resource-based view. *Academy of Management Journal*, 43(2): 164–77.

Risberg, A. and Søderberg, A.-M. (2008). Translating a management concept: diversity management in Denmark. *Gender in Management*, 23(6): 426–41.

Robinson, G. and Dechant, K. (1997). Building a business case for diversity. *Academy of Management Executive*, 11(3): 21–31.

Said, E. (1978). *Orientalism: Western Conceptions of the Orient*. London: Penguin.

Said, E. (1993). *Culture and Imperialism*. London: Vintage.

Sinclair, A. (2000). Women within diversity: risks and possibilities. *Women in Management Review*, 15(5/6): 237–46.

Sinclair, A. (2006). Critical diversity management in Australia: Romanced or co-opted?. In A. M. Konrad, P. Prasad, and J. K. Pringle (eds.), *Handbook of Workplace Diversity*. London: Sage, 511–30.

Smith, L.T. (1999). *Decolonizing Methodologies: Research and Indigenous Peoples*. London and Dunedin: Zed Books and University of Otago Press.

Swan, E. (2010). Commodity diversity: smiling faces as a strategy of containment. *Organization*, 17(1): 77–100.

Tatli, A. (2011). A multi-layered exploration of the diversity management field: diversity discourses, practices and practitioners in the UK. *British Journal of Management*, 22: 238–53.

Thomas, D. A. (1990). From affirmative action to affirming diversity. *Harvard Business Review*, 68: 107–17.

Thomas, D. A. and Ely, R. (1996). Making differences matter. *Harvard Business Review*, 74: 79–90.

Tomlinson, F. and Schwabenland, C. (2010). The UK non-profit sector between social justice and the business case. *Organization*, 17(1): 101–21.

Wetherell, M. and Potter, J. (1992). *Mapping the Language of Racism: Discourse and the Legitimation of Exploitation*. Hemel Hempstead: Harvester-Wheatsheaf.

Wrench, J. (2007). *Diversity Management and Discrimination*. Aldershot: Ashgate.

Young, R. J. C. (2001). *Postcolonialism: An Historical Introduction*. Oxford: Blackwell.

Zanoni, P. (2010). Diversity in the lean automobile factory: doing class through gender, disability and age. *Organization*, 18(1): 105–27.

Zanoni, P., Janssens, M., Benschop, Y., and Nkomo, S. (2010). Unpacking diversity, grasping inequality: rethinking difference through critical perspectives. *Organization*, 17(1): 9–29.

Žižek, S. (1993). *Tarrying with the Negative: Kant, Hegel, and the Critique of Ideology*. Durham, NC: Duke University Press.

CHAPTER 8

A POSTCOLONIAL DECONSTRUCTION OF DIVERSITY MANAGEMENT AND MULTICULTURALISM

ANNA-LIISA KAASILA-PAKANEN

Introduction

In this chapter, I offer an analysis of multiculturalism in diversity management (DM) research. I consider DM research as a practice that relies on an underlying multiculturalist discourse, and I highlight the problematic nature of this connection. Within studies of cultural diversity, the deep complexity of multiculturalism is rarely articulated. I suggest that the postcolonial integration of the two perspectives, multiculturalism and DM, has important implications for theory building and research on workplace diversity. Appropriating Saidian critique and Bhabha's conceptual resources, this chapter demonstrates how postcolonial insights can be used to deconstruct the ontological and epistemological character of DM and to create new key concepts for understanding workplace diversity.

Although the introduction of postcolonialism as a theoretical location for interrogating management and organization studies (MOS) is often traced back to Prasad's (1997) well-known analysis of the diversity industry (Jack et al. 2011), the scarceness of diversity research informed by postcolonial thought underscores the idea that the full potential of postcolonial theory has not yet been explored within diversity scholarship itself. Apart from Prasad's (1997, 2006) and Prasad and Prasad's (2002) influential works, few studies have specifically addressed diversity issues through the postcolonial lens, the most recent examples being the studies of Schwabenland and Tomlinson (2008), Kalonaityte (2010), and Leonard (2010). According to Prasad (2006: 125), postcolonial insights are useful for diversity researchers because the colonial encounter has significantly shaped Western perceptions of its 'others' (other races, ethnicities, and cultures). Helping to think how hierarchies have been articulated and negotiated, postcolonialism has come to touch on the social differentiations that constitute the modernity of everyday life, not just the specific classes, peoples, or regions to which colonial discourses are most obviously tied (Bhabha 1995). Therefore, it can be used as a framework to explore power relations in wider contexts, as in this chapter.

Using Said's (1978) idea of fixed cultural essence and representations, in this chapter I develop a particular argument to describe how the current multicultural approach of DM is saturated with neocolonial assumptions of individual's and culture's natural positions as stable parts of a society. The tendency to oversimplify culture and to see representations of difference through binary lenses as mirroring some sort of authentic cultural character that sets one apart from the other is criticized. What I suggest is that, through the celebrated discourse of multiculturalism, managing cultural diversity comes to intervene in the reproduction of inequalities and the established social order in organizations. The main argument is that, based on multiculturalism, organizational diversity becomes represented through simplistic, historically bounded, and fixed categorizations of identity and culture that reinforce cultural and racial otherness.

To go beyond mere critique and offer a way forward, I introduce Bhabha's (1994, 2007) notion of the third space as an attempt to rethink the concepts of culture and cultural identities within DM. Through the non-essentialist starting point that the concept of the third space offers, I sketch an alternative approach to the largely US-based research tradition that derives from a business-oriented social psychological paradigm of diversity research. I demonstrate how, through the outlined third space, there is a new way to theorize culture and the individual's relation to it, provided that we are able to tolerate the passing of a social value system based on grand oppositions (Bhabha 1996). This requires a form of cultural value recognized by cultural difference, not by cultural diversity. What is emphasized is that culture cannot be represented by single definitions because it is constantly in the process of 'becoming'—being negotiated, (re)interpreted, and challenged by the agency produced in language and interaction through the hybrid third space.

Proposing a postcolonial understanding of the construction of subjectivity, otherness, and the experience of culture in agency, the analysis I present contributes to the research stream of critically informed diversity studies and the emergent discussions on negotiated and flux notions of culture within diversity scholarship. In critical diversity scholarship, the controversial and even oppressive nature of the concept of DM has been articulated on many occasions since the 1990s (e.g. Nkomo and Cox 1996; Litvin 1997; Prasad and Mills 1997; Blommaert and Verschueren 1998) and the early 2000s (e.g. Lorbiecki and Jack 2000; Lorbiecki 2001; Zanoni and Janssens 2004, 2007; Litvin 2006; Prasad 2006). These interventions have led to a serious questioning of 'diversity' and its 'management', through which a need to move beyond the current articulations of the dilemmas surrounding the theme has been emphasized by Calás, Holgersson, and Smircich (2009). The publication of special issues (see Calás, Holgersson, and Smircich 2009) dedicated to critically informed diversity research in journals such as *Gender in Management* (vol. 23/2008), *Scandinavian Journal of Management* (vol. 25/2009), *Gender, Work and Organization* (vol. 17/2010), and *Organization* (vol. 17/2010), serves as an accurate example of the fervency with which controversies related to diversity have been explored in recent organizational scholarship.

While exploring various questions of diversity in organizations, the critical research tradition has produced a comprehensive mapping of: the US-based origins of the concept of diversity (e.g. Risberg and Søderberg 2008; Holvino and Kamp 2009; Omanovic 2009); the traditional conceptualization of diversity within the mainstream literature (e.g. Litvin 1997; Konrad 2003; Zanoni and Janssens 2004; Janssens and Zanoni 2014); the juxtaposition of the managerial business rationale and social justice approaches to diversity (e.g. Holvino and Kamp 2009; Tomlinson and Schwabenland 2010); the evolution of the concept over the past two decades (e.g. Lorbiecki and Jack 2000); and the transformation and the mobility of the complex global phenomenon to local contexts (e.g. Risberg and Søderberg 2008; Klarsfeld 2009; Lauring 2009; Omanovic 2009; Ostendorp and Steyaert 2009). As this recent research interest proves, the critical research stream of organizational diversity is currently well established, but the discourse has not yet come to include issues of multiculturalism.

In many countries, societal debates on diversity have been going on for some time now under the label of the 'rise and fall of multiculturalism', and the need for alternative and more sustainable ways to accommodate diversity has been identified (Kymlicka 2010). Given that it has been the same state-sponsored concept of multiculturalism, aiming at preserving different cultures without interfering with the smooth functioning of society, that has formed the basis for corporate multiculturalism and diversity (Banerjee and Linstead 2001: 702), it is no surprise that the concepts have also been confronted by severe challenges at the organizational level. According to Prasad, Pringle, and Konrad (2006), cultural pluralism, a built-in feature of multiculturalism, has been shown to lead to struggles over cultural spaces in organizations as well as in societies. From the point of view of this chapter, the concept of multiculturalism, and cultural diversity itself, can be seen as problematic, because it merely means recognizing pre-given cultural contents and customs and representing the rhetoric of a separation of totalized cultures that remain untouched by the interrelations of their historical locations, guarding the myth of a unique collective identity (Bhabha 2007: 50). In light of this interpretation, a new form of understanding, if not a dismissal, of the concepts of multiculturalism and diversity is needed. Before engaging in the presented agenda of the chapter, I provide a short description of the connection between DM and multiculturalism, because this is necessary for providing the context out of which my argument emerges. I also give a brief account of the identified connection and its relation to critical diversity studies and to the aims of this chapter.

Diversity Management as Multiculturalist Discourse

Despite the obvious resemblance of the connotations associated with the terms 'diversity' and 'multiculturalism', DM and multiculturalism have not been extensively linked (exceptions being Banerjee and Linstead 2001; Shimoni and Bergmann 2006; Nkomo and Hoobler 2014). Although without explicit connection, since the late 1980s, multiculturalism and DM have merged together as integrated paradigms of workplace diversity research. Whereas the term multiculturalism has been more frequently applied in sociology and public policy, given the same pressure exerted by major demographic changes, the management literature came to adopt the slightly broader term of diversity (Nkomo and Hoobler 2014). Cox and Blake's (1991) highly influential (see citation index of Oswick and Noon 2014: 33) publication on managing cultural diversity, which provides a clear connection between effective DM and the creation of a multicultural organization for achieving competitive advantage (see also Cox 1991), stands as an example of, and an incentive for, the complementary development of these discourses. Also exemplary of the research that relies on the business rationale behind diversity, Cox and Blake (1991: 52) state that 'Organizations wishing to maximize the benefits and minimize the drawbacks of diversity... must create "multicultural" organizations.' Furthermore, the text establishes a connection between national competitiveness and multiculturalism (Cox and Blake 1991: 50), bringing together the societal and corporate discourses of multiculturalism.

Omanovic (2009) states that, in past decades, the concept of DM has been advocated especially by US-based scholars (e.g. Thomas 1990, 1991; Cox 1994; Thomas and Ely 1996). In the context of the global economy, this approach has proposed managing diversity as a company initiative motivated by economic imperatives of productivity, competitive advantage, and profitability (e.g. Risberg and Søderberg 2008; Holvino and Kamp 2009; Lauring 2009; Omanovic 2009). For Banerjee and Linstead (2001), this traditional business case for diversity functions as an example of how diversity, in terms of race, ethnicities, and nationalities, has been reduced to something that must be 'managed' for the sake of pursuing the market opportunity. This emphasis on the economic benefit of DM has guided its development into a somewhat rigid, essentialist, and procedure-driven issue (Ghorashi and Sabelis 2013), affecting the way cultural diversity and its implications for organizations became understood through multiculturalism.

Thus, a particular connection can be found between the business-oriented social psychological paradigms of diversity and multiculturalism that are now discussed as interlocking discourses. The reductionist view of cultural diversity that this chapter challenges has its basis in this research tradition, which understands multiculturalism as consisting of fixed, observable, and measurable categories. Despite its important and still effective role in the development of workplace diversity research, it has been observed that this research tradition has resulted in a limited understanding of diversity and the processes leading to inequalities (Zanoni et al. 2010). Nkomo and Hoobler's (2014) findings, which indicate that diversity research from the present era exhibits strong inertia (particularly in its epistemology, which seems to lag behind recent ontological developments of the field), support the continuing influence of the business case and the multiculturalist approach to diversity. Nkomo and Hoobler (2014: 254) suggest that even when the terminology may be new, for example, inclusion instead of equal opportunity (EO) or DM (as in Shore et al. 2011, see also Oswick and Noon 2014), the focus on the business case and firm practices has remained the same—research continues to focus on trying to link the presence of persons with certain demographic characteristics to performance, and answering the question of how persons from various racioethnic groups can best work together towards efficiency and productivity.

With specific regard to the study of cultural, racial, or ethnic diversity in organizations, in addition to Cox and Blake (1991), other foundational works in the described tradition include the studies of Gomez-Mejia and Palich (1997), Richard (2000), and Richard and colleagues (2004). In Oswick and Noon's (2014) extensive bibliometric analysis of management publications on diversity, equality, and inclusion over a forty-year period, from 1970 to 2010, all these studies are ranked within the top twenty of the most popular works on diversity. The distinct and lasting popularity of the four studies mentioned, which are pinpointed with the amount of total citations, the average citations per year, and the patterns of citation (Oswick and Noon 2014), can be seen as indicative of the collective research interest in the field of cultural diversity. As exemplified in the works of Cox and Blake (1991), Gomez-Mejia and Palich (1997), Richard (2000), and Richard and colleagues (2004), the continuous meta-level trend of academic interest in the study of cultural diversity through multiculturalism has been in: (1) emphasizing cross-cultural differences through cross-national comparisons and ethnic group differences through intra-national comparisons; (2) using particular surface level or observable characteristics to identify cultural diversity; (3) and then tautologically using these characteristics as a proxy for persons' perspectives, belief systems, networks, and affiliations.

The research tradition that derives from the four studies has made significant contributions to the way culture and cultural identities have become understood within the field. The nature of this tradition has evoked a very narrow understanding of culture as a stable coherent entity often tied to a place with an essential connection to people's identities in that location. Based on the identified connection with the business case for diversity, the language of multiculturalism, by necessity, has been coloured by cultural categorizations, generalizations, and distances—because diversity needed to be determined by the used measurement scales to provide the objective evidence of its effects on the bottom-line performance of the company (e.g. Richard 2000).

In the critical diversity literature, particular attention has been paid to expressing the paradigmatic pitfalls of the dominant research practice described—a practice that derives from a positivist ontology of naturalized and fixed identities and that has largely ignored the role of specific contexts and theorizations of power in addressing diversity (Zanoni et al. 2010: 13–14). For this chapter, being rooted in this tradition of critical diversity scholarship means understanding diversity and difference as culturally, socially, and historically (re)produced phenomena that, therefore, need to be examined within specific socio-political and geographic regions as well as within specific organizational contexts and processes that reflect and enact structural power relations (e.g. Metcalfe and Woodhams 2008; Zanoni et al. 2010; Janssens and Zanoni 2014). However, to establish the interconnection between the multiculturalist paradigm and its implications for managing diversity, I address multiculturalism by concentrating specifically on the inescapable, underlying essential assumptions embedded in the notion at the conceptual level, prior to its local interpretations and enactments in social contexts. It should be noted that, for the purposes of this chapter, this approach has been intentional, and the chapter recognizes that the interconnection and its implications take various forms of operation that depend on organizational and national contexts.

In critical diversity research, the idea of discursive, emergent, and relational identities is firmly accepted. Drawing on different theoretical positions, many recent studies (e.g. Jack and Lorbiecki 2007; Bendl, Fleischmann, and Walenta 2008; Boogaard and Roggeband 2010; Essers, Benschop, and Doorewaard 2010; Holvino 2010; Kalonaityte 2010; Leonard 2010; Tomlinson 2010; Van Laer and Janssens 2014) have approached organizational diversity and difference from a perspective that acknowledges the multiple and shifting nature of identities and denies the existence of a fully constituted, distinct identity, an authentic self. Identities are recognized not as matters of 'having' but instead as discursive processes of 'becoming' (Zanoni et al. 2010). By adopting the underlying ontology, it should be clear that a similar understanding of culture not as 'being' but as something diffuse, heterogeneous, and negotiated, infused with contestation and power relations (Jack et al. 2008: 875), would be adopted. Yet, to be able to discuss, in terms of 'multicultural', whether in a critical vein or not, the concept of multiculturalism itself, determines the use of an essentializing vocabulary that unavoidably fixes cultural positions. As elaborated, this is mainly due to the historical baggage of the research tradition that the term has come to carry. Having identified this discontinuation, and hoping to break the scholarly silence on the fluid notions of culture in the discussions of organizational diversity, I concentrate on analysing the organizational implications of this omission.

Postcolonial Critique of Diversity Management and Multiculturalism

My theoretical argumentation builds on the assumption that the current diversity discourse, in its devotion to the idea of multiculturalism, is still based on essentialist ontological assumptions (Litvin 1997) that echo representationalist and universalizing categorizations and the desire to 'know the other' raised in the analysis of colonial discourse (Said 1978). In his analysis, Said (1978) highlights the role of power relations in constructing postcolonial subjectivity, in which the notion of the Other is inseparable from the Self. Said's paradigmatic work *Orientalism* (1978) examines how non-Western otherness is constructed through a set of representations that are commonly circulated within the written work of the Western intellectual, aesthetic, scholarly, and cultural tradition. These texts, and the accompanying categories, classifications, and images that were utilized in producing accounts of the West's others, are addressed as ontological assumptions, epistemological practices, and cultural constructions that serve to create the texts' object of study, not as neutral descriptions of reality as they most often became understood to be (Jack and Westwood 2009: 21–2). In his exploration, Said (1978) emphasizes the questionability of objective and non-political (Western) knowledge in general and, in particular, in the case of producing a veridical discourse of the Orient/Other. In Said's analysis, the discourse of Orientalism and the cultural dominance of the West are tightly intertwined with Euro-Atlantic material and political interests, and the maintenance of asymmetrical power relations between the Orient and Occident, the non-West and West.

According to Said (1978: 7), the discourse of Orientalism constantly reifies the asymmetry of power by means of its strategy of positional superiority, 'which puts the Westerner in a whole series of possible relationships with the Orient without ever losing him the relative upper hand'. Said (1978: 2) describes how the distinction between the Occident and the Orient is seen as an ontological and epistemological difference that relies on the idea of essential and fixed identities. Throughout Said's analysis, examples are given of the binary opposites and historical generalizations that were used to justify the colonial dominance of the non-West. Prasad (1997) has done an extensive listing of these colonial binaries (e.g. civilized/primitive, masculine/feminine, scientific/superstitious, nation/tribe, developed/backward) through which the non-West became portrayed around the theme of inferiority with fixed essence.

It is important to note that Said's interpretation of the constructed binaries concerns not only the Other but also the self-image of the West itself. Orientalism has been described as a process of othering in which the construction of the self is dialectically achieved through the simultaneous construction of the Other (Jack and Westwood 2009: 22). The mutually constitutive role that representations play can be understood through the circularity that surrounds the concept of difference as something that mediates between the binaries and, in doing so, holds apart while holding together (Kwek 2003: 126). As Prasad (1997: 289) asserts, the colonial discourse, therefore, not only naturalized or essentialized the subjectivities of the colonized but also of the colonizers—'the Orient has helped to define Europe (or the West) as its contrasting image, idea, personality, experience' (Said 1978: 1–2). Jack and Westwood (2009: 22) explain how, in the process of naturalization, the ideological practices required to produce the representations of the Other are erased and the knowledge of the Other that is produced is made to appear as a form of truth. Hall (1997: 245) understands naturalization as a representational strategy designed to stop the inevitable 'slide' of meaning and secure so-called discursive closure to fix difference, to secure it in its place.

It is exactly this attempt to fix difference, to 'contain everyone in their place, easily identifiable, and attached to the specificity' (Calás, Holgersson, and Smircich

2009: 351) for which I see the discourse of multiculturalism, and cultural diversity, as responsible. Enabling the objectification, reduction, and displacement of ideas and understandings, the feature of containment, which is inherent in the mutually defining role of representations, creates the precise borders that include/exclude one from the other (Kwek 2003: 126). Containment is inseparably linked to the essentializing logic of representations and Orientalist processes of othering. Building on the established connection between Western management discourses and colonialism, and especially the way that the binaries have been used to construct the static historicity and dichotomy of subjectivities, it can be stated that culture has been reified as a fixity of ideas and values that simply exist (Kwek 2003) and define the behaviour of people within certain national or ethnic borders. Therefore, I suggest that the discourse of multiculturalism, acknowledging and advancing the idea of separate and pure cultures, is yet another legacy of the colonial mindset.

To illustrate the connections between the representationalist and universalizing tendencies of DM and multiculturalism, we need to pay attention to the location of the emergence of these discourses and to their way of confronting difference. As identified, DM was established mainly as a result of US-based economic concerns for productivity, competitive advantage, and profitability in the name of national and corporate competitiveness. The business rhetoric was soon adopted by international companies (Van Dijk, Van Engen, and Paauwe 2012), through which the discourse spread to other Western countries where it was seen as somewhat universal, until the critical problematizations of this development (see, e.g., Jones, Pringle, and Shepherd 2000; Metcalfe and Woodhams 2008; Calás, Holgersson, and Smircich 2009; Holvino and Kamp 2009; Calás et al. 2010). The universalizing tendency of management discourses in general has been brought forward and linked to the position of the West's strength and the politicization of knowledge by postcolonial organizational scholars (e.g. Kwek 2003; Ibarra-Colado 2006; Westwood 2006; Nkomo 2011). Regarding this tendency, the discourse of diversity makes no exception. As Said (1978) has elaborated with regard to the concept of positional superiority, colonial discourse strongly advocated the superiority of Western thoughts and practices (cultural, scientific, and other) that were universalized as a common norm against which others became compared. Thus, despite the fact that DM can be quite precisely located in a particular geographical, historical, and ideological context (e.g. Risberg and Søderberg 2008; Holvino and Kamp 2009; Omanovic 2009), in its devotion to universal applicability a resemblance to colonial discourse can be observed.

It should be emphasized that DM research, due to its origins, is based on a practice of comparison, on a deviation from the (Western) norm (see also Zanoni et al. 2010: 13). As a specifically Western discourse, DM can be seen to be effective in controlling its others to gain various types of information—information deriving from diversity, which, as a matter of course, has meant deviation—to support the management decisions to increase corporate financial performance (Richard 2000). Drawing on Calás (1992), Zanoni and colleagues (2010) have noted that, in the act of comparison, the other is constructed as the object of study and discursively constituted as marginal. Thus, the comparative nature of DM and multiculturalism contributes to the creation of its others, silencing the others, and more broadly, politics of knowledge (Said 1978) through the representational strategies by which the comparison is made possible.

The representational nature of DM research is observable in its way of confronting difference through categorizations that rely on essential identities (e.g. Litvin 1997, 2002; Zanoni and Janssens 2004; Zanoni et al. 2010; Ghorashi and Sabelis 2013). I argue that the essentialist perception of difference present in the studies that derive from the positivist social psychological approach to diversity can be seen to derive from similar representational practices used in colonial discourse, where the difference of the West's others became reduced to a set of fixed historical generalizations (Said 1978). As exemplified in the beginning of the chapter through the foundational works on cultural diversity in organizations, the common practice of utilizing particular fixed characteristics to identify diversity and then applying these reduced characteristics as a group essence, explanatory variables for the study in question, is an illustration of this tendency. In addition, the representational practices apparent in DM connect to the field's universalizing impulse that is made possible through homogenizing difference (Westwood 2006). Westwood (2006: 96–7) has offered an explanation of how Western practice, while claiming to examine and report on difference, actually avoids and reduces it into sameness by subjugating encountered differences to the West's pre-existing codes and categories, that is, stereotypes. Additionally, Kwek (2003: 135) has criticized the way representations subjugate, homogenize, and essentialize difference simply because it threatens boundaries. According to Prasad (1997: 294), in the discourse of colonialism, reducing the difference of the Other into a sameness was an attempt to reduce the threat of the Other by constituting it in terms of images that were already familiar to the colonizing consciousness (see also Kwek 2003; Westwood 2006).

To clarify, I see the discourses of diversity and multiculturalism intertwined in the process of producing otherness and stereotypes through the way their theories categorize difference by means of essentialized identities tied to a stable cultural heritage. With the stagnant cultural essence, an idea deriving from 1950s cultural anthropology (e.g. Bjerregaard et al. 2009), positivist and functionalist approaches have persisted up to this day in the research on organizational diversity (e.g. Nkomo and Hoobler 2014; Oswick and Noon 2014). Through these approaches, the multiculturalist diversity discourse supports a language based on binary categorizations that were created in colonial representations. In specific relation to the study of cultural diversity, the use of cultural dimensioning and measurements of cultural distances (e.g. Hofstede 1980, 1991) illustrate the linkage between colonial representational strategies and stereotyping that is present in the research practice of the field. Gomez-Mejia and Palich's (1997) study, in which, typical of the tradition, cultural polarity is expected to be the prevailing condition between universalized categories of difference (West and East/North and South), stands as an early archetype of this tendency within the business paradigm.

One of the drawbacks of the current discourse of multiculturalism—questions of inclusion are largely overshadowed by the question of recognizing difference and managing it—follows from the expectation of fixed binary differences between cultures.

With its representational and ethnocentric practice, the idea of multiculturalism has proven to be excellent at containing everyone in their place and facilitating the reproduction of dominant categories that reify the global hierarchy within approaches to diversity in organizations. It has been demonstrated that there is a considerable gap between the ideal of multiculturalism and the actual ideology of cultural pluralism that often ends up reinforcing the stereotypes and the marginalizing tendencies it is designed to counteract (Huggan 2001). In this analysis, I have aimed to illustrate how this actually happens by showing how, despite the celebratory rhetoric of multiculturalism with its mosaics, rainbows, and quilts (Prasad and Mills 1997), the discourse can be highly effective in circulating stereotypical views of different cultures and their members. Thus, the analysis offers one explanation for the counterproductivity of classical DM practices that build on the social psychological research paradigm, which aims to correct individuals' stereotypes and prejudices (e.g. Janssens and Zanoni 2014).

Having said that, the explanation is incomplete without clarifying that I regard the stereotypes and prejudices encountered in organizations not as the problem but as the easily detected consequence of the actual problem—the emphasis that multiculturalism and its static view of culture place on cultural purity and historic heritage (Bhabha 2007). Prasad (1997: 304) has emphasized how discourses saturate us—they provide us the everyday language, the idioms, and the vocabulary for speaking and thinking. As postcolonialism suggests, the West's language, idioms, and vocabulary for addressing difference are deeply rooted in the colonial encounter. The way that everything non-Western (people, civilizations, cultures) became conceptualized as not just something different from but less than the Western ideal (e.g. Said 1978; Prasad 1997, 2006; Jack and Westwood 2009) has affected the way otherness is perceived. Thus, genuinely valuing differences and working towards the equalization of organizational power relations can only begin when we relinquish our ideas not only of authentic selves, but also of the authenticity of cultures and constructed cultural polarities.

FROM MULTICULTURALISM TO CULTURAL DIFFERENCE THROUGH THE THIRD SPACE

The idea of the border between self and other is pivotal in postcolonial studies (Ashcroft, Griffiths, and Tiffin 2007), in terms of its totalizing and essentializing nature. To go beyond the essentialism present in the dominant multicultural approach in diversity studies, I am taking advantage of how borders can also be seen as liminal and ambivalent spaces that challenge the fixities and binary systems from within the spatial boundary itself (Bhabha 2007). Similarly, within the critical DM discourse, Bendl, Fleischmann, and Walenta (2008) have proposed how dimensions or categories seen as permanent and static can be opposed by the constitutive dynamics that define them. The implication is that borders can actually function as inclusive as much as exclusive factors between individuals and cultures within organizations, which opens up a space for the shattering of the foundations of the hierarchical power positions of self and other as the fundamental entities of organizational life, as identified by Ghorashi and Sabelis (2013).

For Barth (1982: 15), border-construction processes function as cultural markers between groups, and it is the boundary itself that defines the group, not the actual culture that it encloses. Bhabha (2007: 50) has also drawn attention to the frequent way in which the emergence of problems in cultural interaction are only recognized at the significatory boundaries of cultures, where meanings and values are (mis)read. For Bhabha, culture only emerges as problematic when there is a loss of meaning in the contestation and articulation of everyday life between group (class, gender, race, nation) boundaries—yet, the limit of culture is rarely theorized as a problem of the enunciation of cultural difference. Theorizing multiculturalism more closely from the liminal and ambivalent spaces of boundary-crossings, an implicit shift of focus from cultural diversity to cultural difference occurs. The shift is enforced because the Bhabhaian view (2007: 49–50) conceptualizes cultural diversity as an epistemological object, an object of empirical knowledge that represents culture through the language of universality and social generalization, whereas cultural difference can be seen as a process of signification through which statements on culture form culture as knowledgeable and differential, bringing cultural authority into existence only at the ambivalent moment of its enunciation.

Instead of holding on to the exoticism of multiculturalism or the diversity of cultures, I emphasize respecting cultural difference, which restores the ontological principles of this chapter to the indeterminacy of meanings constructed through difference and deferral. Through the examination of cultural difference, the Bhabhaian perspective brings into focus the ambivalence of cultural authority, the attempt to dominate in the name of a cultural supremacy even though it is produced only at the moment of differentiation (Bhabha 2007: 51). Thus, the concept of cultural difference underscores the ambivalence of cultural authority, weakening 'the homogenizing effects of cultural symbols and icons by questioning our sense of the authority of cultural synthesis in general' (Bhabha 2007: 52). In Bhabha's approach, the ambivalence of colonial discourse appears in the cultural interpretation itself, in which the production of meaning occurs through a hybrid third space: because the interpretation is never simply an act of communication between the I and You present in the statement, the production of meaning requires that these two places are mobilized through an unconscious relation that the third space introduces (Bhabha 2007: 53). It is the third space of enunciation that, therefore, challenges the structure of meaning and reference, destroying the form of representation through which culture is seen as a unifying force authenticated and kept alive by the shared history and national tradition of the people (Bhabha 2007: 54).

Leaning on the presented understanding of culture and the formation of the third space interrogates the traditional concept of culture advocated by multiculturalism. Culture and its relation to the homogenizing historical past as the main source of one's cultural identity, as 'being' something, is clearly incompatible with these ideas, which focus on the processes produced in the articulation of cultural differences and the need to think beyond narratives of originary subjectivities. Through conceptualizations of the third space, we have the opportunity to understand why hierarchical claims of the inherent originality or purity of cultures are untenable, as we come to acknowledge that all cultural statements and systems are contracted in this ambivalent space of enunciation (Bhabha 2007: 55). The fluctuation and fragmentation of cultural meanings and symbols is ensured by the third space, which constitutes the discursive conditions for articulating cultural differences, demonstrating 'that even the same signs can be appropriated, translated, rehistoricized and read anew' (Bhabha 2007: 55).

Acknowledging the 'newness' and unknown present in the third space triggers a clarification of the problematic analytical logic of multiculturalism in diversity scholarship that enforces hegemonic social structures based on the clear-cut division between self and other, and the fixed assumptions of the representatives of different cultural groups. Achieving an alternative starting point for theorizing cultural diversity in organizations requires an approach that is willing to accept and engage in the unknown present in cultural interaction and organizational structures that allow the legitimacy of hybrid (cultural) subject positions to exist and develop through the interaction of individuals in the in-between spaces of different discursive fields. This highlights the theorizations of the transverse linkages and interrelations of the subject positions available for individuals to identify themselves with, to shatter the one-dimensional power relations and dominant patterns of othering. Foundational prerequisites for this type of approach can be found in the third space, thus leading us to see the concept of liminality as the main tool for challenging organizational boundaries by rethinking them as in-between spaces that function as the conditions of existence for altering the fixed subject positions of the organizational actors of today.

As noted earlier in this section, Bhabha's (2007: 56) view on the subjectivities formed in the in-between spaces of difference—where it is *neither the one nor the other* that carries the meaning of culture but rather the area of 'inter', of translation and negotiation—reminds us of poststructuralist understanding of meanings, which are always deferred (e.g. Hall 1993; Ashcroft, Griffiths, and Tiffin 2007). Elaborating the idea of deferral, Ashcroft, Griffiths, and Tiffin (2007) note that, in the third space, as a space of hybridity itself, cultural meanings and identities always contain the traces of other meanings and identities. The third space can therefore be compared to this space of deferral and endless possibilities for interpretation, which proves that cultural difference should never be treated as simple and static, but rather as an ever-changing, ambivalent process of interpretation (Ashcroft, Griffiths, and Tiffin 2007: 53). For Bhabha (2007: 56), it is the fragmented space of enunciation that holds the potential to understand culture free from the essentializing logic of multiculturalism, which turns our attention to our willingness to acknowledge this instability and the unknown present in the production of hybrid cultural meanings.

The presented indeterminacy of hybrid and ambivalent cultures erodes the ground under the current multicultural paradigm of DM. As stated, identities can be understood as processes of 'becoming', as multiple and shifting, not as something that already exists, but instead as something that belongs to the future as much as to the past (Hall

1993: 225). According to Bhabha (2007: 10), this same newness is always present in the borderline work of culture where the encountered new is not part of the continuum of the past and present, simply repeating the already known and articulated past, but instead is the product of a cultural translation that recreates the past as an unpredictable liminal space that both initiates and temporarily pauses the act of the present. Thus, it should be noted that the newness created in cultural encounters, as it is understood here, is not a merger or a combination of the old perspectives but rather something totally new, produced in the moment. In the field of management, culture is rarely conceptualized as an ongoing process of interpretation, although the similar logic behind how culture and identities could both be understood as processes of the future and 'becoming' is apparent.

Why are these presented conceptualizations of culture, cultural meanings, and subjectivity and otherness meaningful for DM? According to Shimoni and Bergmann (2006), those researchers, practitioners, and organizations that base their work on coherent definitions of culture presented by the multicultural approach are unable to recognize the instances of cultural interpretation and hybridization, resulting in an insufficient ability to understand and work with cultures. Bhabha (2007) suggests that the process of hybridization destabilizes the difference and binary division of identities and cultures in liminal spaces, thereby overturning the current homogenizing cultural order and focusing our attention on the actual cultural encounter and its interpretation, which has the potential to bring out the complexity of cultural meanings in organizations without essentializing or estranging them from the context in which they were produced. Therefore, this alternative way of theorizing cultural positions enables an opportunity to engage in cultural interaction from an approach that can offer more realistic explanations of how cultural meanings come to guide the decisions and sense-making of organizational actors and, consequently, organizational thinking and processes.

Towards a Reconstructed Research Practice of Diversity

In the presented analysis, I have exposed the complexities of theorizing DM and its specific relation to multiculturalism through the postcolonial lens. I have made explicit the problematic relationship between representations, the presumptions of difference, and locating cultural identities in geopolitical places, compelling a reconsideration of the ontological and epistemological premises of DM. I used the concept of subjectivity as an entrance point to explain exclusion, inequalities, and institutionalized power relations in organizations. As shown in the previous section, in Bhabha's perspective, subjects are formed in-between the sum of the parts of difference (Bhabha 2007: 2). These parts of difference, such as race, gender, or class, affect the way otherness is perceived in encountering difference in organizations because, in that process, one must face the ambivalence of his or her own identifications. The ambivalence in the structure of identification is to be found in the in-between, 'where the shadow of the other falls upon the self', creating the categories of cultural difference that we enunciate (Bhabha 2007: 85). Thus, it is to be emphasized that, although subjectivity is constructed in relation to the Other, neither one can exist as pure, free from the shadow of its oppositional counterpart. The interplay between the two is never total because they are both present in one another, which challenges all claims of fixed polarities and originary pasts and, therefore, the basic principles of multiculturalism.

From theorizations of the third space, it is possible to go beyond the dominant discourses of othering in addressing cultural difference in organizations, but because the acceptance of the unstable and unknown aspects of cultural production actually poses a threat to one's comfortable and stabilized worldview and sense of self, it becomes a matter of whether we are willing to encounter the other in ourselves and rethink our own position within the play of power. Janssens and Zanoni (2014: 327) have stated that organizations tend to copy social structures, including unequal categorical relations, from other locations, such as broader societal discourses, because they are familiar and thus decrease individuals' transaction costs of learning them. As no organization is an island (Holvino and Kamp 2009), the prominent neocolonial societal discourses that strongly dictate the construction of otherness and subjectivity through binaries and borders are firmly intertwined with organizational discourses that encourage the majority of organizational actors to protect the so-called purity of their cultural identities. This subsequently works to prevent members of certain cultural groups from achieving 'full subjectivity' (concept of Zanoni and Janssens 2004; Janssens and Zanoni 2014).

I should note that I do not use theorizations of the third space to propose a starting point where one would intentionally try to create this liminal space for better understanding other perspectives or position oneself 'in someone else's shoes'. Instead, my intention has been to give a description of the alteration of cultural positions and meanings that occurs in interaction. The presented perspective, starting from the premises of cultural difference, brings us to the third space, which can be understood as creating a bridge between seeming opposites and enabling encounters between individuals—not representatives of certain groups—who are free from preset cultural interpretations, thus producing cultural (subject) positions outside the normalizing order of multiculturalism and, therefore, opening equal access to full subjectivity for all members of organizations. With the approach's ability to question fixed cultural positions and revise the hegemonic discourses that we enact, the development of more inclusive forms of organizing is possible, with the emphasis on the agency of an individual in an in-the-moment interaction in which cultural hierarchies and social norms can be challenged through the continuous (re)production of our own subjectivity and cultural meanings.

Three reasons can be identified that summarize the value of the postcolonial perspective in advancing the theoretical development of cultural difference in organizations. First, the presented perspective reveals the multiculturalist agenda as affirming Western hegemony and capitalist interests in the way it implicitly affects the social order in organizations. Second, the perspective criticizes the essentialist and fixed notions of culture and cultural identities most often conceptualized through the reductionist dimensions that are most familiar to us. Third, it emphasizes flux cultural meanings produced in the moment. Thus, these postcolonial insights open up new avenues for analysing cultural difference, through which hierarchical social structures can be challenged and all members of organizations, regardless of their cultural, ethnic, or racial background, can be acknowledged through their individuality as full subjects.

The presented approach, which focuses on expanding our understanding of culture and cultural identities in organizational settings, calls for a change in the way that cultural difference is articulated in diversity scholarship. As the main implication of the presented analysis for advancing the study of cultural diversity in organizations, I suggest that future research should concentrate on giving voice to organizational actors as individuals, not as representatives of categories produced by the normalizing force of dominant discourses. To change the way that culture and cultural identities have become conceptualized through the multiculturalist approach, the unheard stories of individuals in the liminal spaces of multiple subject positions across the levels of organizations should be brought forward to elucidate the processes of forming hybrid cultural identities and culture in agency. It is seldom that these stories find their way in through the dominant multiculturalist paradigm of diversity studies, and, consequently, the complexity of cultures and subjectivity formations is downplayed.

The proposed research direction would enable bringing in the excluded others as employees, full subjects, in DM, which is seen as a key condition for equality (Janssens and Zanoni 2014: 12). Highlighting the downside of considering others as members of cultural groups and then associating certain characteristics to the entire group, Ghorashi and Sabelis (2013: 81) note that this 'prevents us from looking at individuals in their context, from accepting different interpretations of culture, from cultures changing over time, and most importantly, from questioning our own repertoires with regard to cultural exchange', which leads to a reinforcement of the hidden hierarchies inherent in categorizations. Thus, the objectives of giving voice to the suggested alternative stories of organizational actors are: (1) to facilitate a change from the multiculturalist paradigm that (re)produces organizational inequalities to transform the understanding of social relations based on binaries; and (2) to bring focus to the interaction taking place in cultural encounters, rather than having it on the generalized representations of the other.

Based on this chapter's analysis, I suggest, most simply, that there is a need to shift the focus of the research on cultural difference in organizations away from the equation of culture with physical place or origin and from pre-given fixed categories of nation, race, and ethnicity, to multiple subject positions produced in language and interaction. It is to be noted that producing cultural meanings in the third space and questioning organizational boundaries from within the very premises of their existence can be understood on many levels of analysis, not just on the individual level. The meaning of group, organizational, and societal levels is important for avoiding the way in which the social psychological paradigm of diversity research explains unsuccessful diversity initiatives by concentrating on individual cognition (Zanoni et al. 2010; Janssens and Zanoni 2014) and, as frequently suggested within critical diversity scholarship, for avoiding the interpretation that individual-level changes alone could change the institutionalized mechanisms of exclusion without the alteration of broader systemic structures.

Reflecting on the third space approach, which offers an option for rejecting the institutionalized categorical identity positions offered by neocolonial discourse, I suggest that the understanding of cultural difference and inequalities in organizations will be further enhanced by perspectives that: (1) focus on identifying other (than multiculturalism) institutionalized practices within DM research that create and reify asymmetrical power relations between different cultural groups in organizations; (2) explain how these identified practices are reinforced by consequential organizational processes; and (3) explicate the multiple connections of these organizational processes and dynamics to the broader contemporary societal contexts dictated by globalized capitalism. Of course, if one wished to be more optimistic in mapping the future directions of research on cultural difference in organizations (cf. Holvino and Kamp 2009), one could start from the reversed themes of the presented directions by: (1) focusing on identifying and providing an outline of those practices of diversity research that are seen to advocate cultural equality in organizations; (2) explaining the organizational processes that help to foster those practices; and (3) explicating the multiple connections of those organizational processes and dynamics that can also be seen to generate and foster empowerment and emancipation in the broader context of globalized capitalism.

Concluding Remarks

I would like to conclude this chapter by recalling that all research on cultural difference is necessarily saturated with cultural assumptions. I have written this chapter from the location of a Finnish business school, as a woman who was born, and has lived and been educated mostly in Finland. Therefore, the institutional and societal contexts of my location should be considered as conditions that have enabled and influenced the produced text and the nature of the presented viewpoints. Writing from this position, I have argued that the controversies that have risen from the traditional way of managing diversity become less surprising when we unravel the conceptual foundations of the concept of multiculturalism behind the dominant research paradigm. In contrast to its formal ambition, the celebration of the concept of multiculturalism can be seen to uphold and create the segregation of the privileged and the disempowered, people who are set apart by fixed cultural positions and fictional representations in organizational contexts. Accordingly, if we do not relinquish the categorizing and hierarchical structures the current understanding of multiculturalism leans towards, it is probable that cultural relations will continue to be a source of organizational controversy well into the future.

Acknowledgements

I would like to thank Inge Bleijenbergh and Albert J. Mills for their valuable comments on earlier versions of this chapter, as well as the Eudaimonia Research Center (University of Oulu) for funding this research. The main ideas of this chapter were first presented at the 30th EGOS Conference, Rotterdam, July 2014. I would also like to acknowledge the conference audience, whose questions and comments helped me to develop the thoughts presented here.

References

Ashcroft, B., Griffiths, G., and Tiffin, H. (2007). *Post-Colonial Studies: The Key Concepts*, 2nd edn. (eBook). Taylor & Francis e-Library: Taylor & Francis.
Banerjee, S. B. and Linstead, S. (2001). Globalization, multiculturalism and other fictions: colonialism for the new millennium? *Organization*, 8: 683–722.
Barth, F. (1982). Introduction. In F. Barth (ed.), *Ethnic Groups and Boundaries: The Social Organization of Culture Difference*. Oslo: Universitetsforlaget, 9–38.
Bendl, R., Fleischmann, A., and Walenta, C. (2008). Diversity management discourse meets queer theory. *Gender in Management*, 23: 382–94.
Bhabha, H. K. (1994). *The Location of Culture*. London: Routledge.
Bhabha, H. K. (1995). Translator translated: interview with cultural theorist Homi Bhabha by W. J. T. Mitchell. *Artforum International Magazine*, 33: 80–4.
Bhabha, H. K. (1996). Unpacking my library... again. In I. Chambers and L. Curti (eds.), *The Post-Colonial Question: Common Skies, Divided Horizons*. London: Routledge, 199–211.
Bhabha, H. K. (2007). *The Location of Culture*. New York: Routledge.
Bjerregaard, T., Lauring, J., and Anders, K. (2009). A critical analysis of intercultural communication research in cross-cultural management. *Critical Perspectives on International Business*, 5: 207–28.
Blommaert, J. and Verschueren, J. (1998). *Debating Diversity: Analysing the Discourse on Tolerance*. London: Routledge.
Boogaard, B. and Roggeband, C. (2010). Paradoxes of intersectionality: theorizing inequality in the Dutch police force through structure and agency. *Organization*, 17: 53–75.
Calás, M., Holgersson, C., and Smircich, L. (2009). 'Diversity management?' Translation? Travel? *Scandinavian Journal of Management*, 25: 349–51.
Calás, M., Smircich, L., Tienari, J., and Ellehave, C. F. (2010). Editorial. Observing globalized capitalism: gender and ethnicity as an entry point. *Gender, Work and Organization*, 17: 243–7.
Calás, M. B. (1992). An/other silent voice? representing 'Hispanic woman' in organizational texts. In A. J. Mills and P. Tancred (eds.), *Gendering Organizational Analysis*. Newbury Park, CA: Sage, 201–21.
Cox, T. (1991). The multicultural organization. *Academy of Management Executive*, 5: 34–47.
Cox, T. (1994). *Cultural Diversity in Organizations: Theory, Research and Practice*. San Francisco: Berret-Koehler.

Cox, T. and Blake, S. (1991). Managing cultural diversity: implications for organizational competitiveness. *Academy of Management Executive*, 5: 45–56.

Essers C., Benschop, Y., and Doorewaard, H. (2010). Female ethnicity: understanding Muslim immigrant businesswomen in the Netherlands. *Gender, Work and Organization*, 17: 320–39.

Ghorashi, H. and Sabelis, I. (2013). Juggling difference and sameness: rethinking strategies for diversity in organizations. *Scandinavian Journal of Management*, 29: 78–86.

Gomez-Mejia, L. and Palich, L. (1997). Cultural diversity and the performance of multinational firms. *Journal of International Business Studies*, 28: 1–36.

Hall, S. (1993). Cultural identity and diaspora. In J. Rutherford (ed.), *Identity: Community, Culture, Difference*. London: Lawrence & Wishart, 222–37.

Hall, S. (1997). The spectacle of the 'other'. In S. Hall (ed.), *Representation: Cultural Representations and Signifying Practices*. London: Sage, 223–90.

Hofstede, G. (1980). *Culture's Consequences: International Differences in Work-Related Values*. Beverly Hills, CA: Sage.

Hofstede, G. (1991). *Cultures and Organizations: Software of the Mind*. London: McGraw-Hill.

Holvino, E. (2010). Intersections: the simultaneity of race, gender and class in organization studies. *Gender, Work and Organization*, 17: 248–77.

Holvino, E. and Kamp, A. (2009). Diversity management: are we moving in the right direction? Reflections from both sides of the North Atlantic. *Scandinavian Journal of Management*, 25: 395–403.

Huggan, G. (2001). *The Postcolonial Exotic*. London: Routledge.

Ibarra-Colado, E. (2006). Organization studies and epistemic coloniality in Latin America: thinking otherness from the margin. *Organization*, 13: 463–88.

Jack, G. and Lorbiecki, A. (2007). National identity, globalization and the discursive construction of organizational identity. *British Journal of Management*, 18: 79–94.

Jack, G. and Westwood, R. (2009). *International and Cross-Cultural Management Studies: A Postcolonial Reading*. New York: Palgrave Macmillan.

Jack, G., Calás, M., Nkomo, S., and Peltonen, T. (2008). Critique and international management: an uneasy relationship? *Academy of Management Review*, 33: 870–84.

Jack, G., Westwood, R., Srinivas, N., and Sardar, Z. (2011). Deepening, broadening and re-asserting a postcolonial interrogative space in organization studies. *Organization*, 18: 275–302.

Janssens, M. and Zanoni, P. (2014). Alternative diversity management: organizational practices fostering ethnic equality at work. *Scandinavian Journal of Management*, 30: 317–31.

Jones, D., Pringle, J., and Shepherd, D. (2000). 'Managing diversity' meets Aotearoa/New Zealand. *Personnel Review*, 29: 364–80.

Kalonaityte, V. (2010). The case of vanishing borders: theorizing diversity management as internal border control. *Organization*, 17: 31–52.

Klarsfeld, A. (2009). The diffusion of diversity management: the case of France. *Scandinavian Journal of Management*, 25: 363–73.

Konrad, A. M. (2003). Special issue introduction: defining the domain of workplace diversity scholarship. *Group and Organization Management*, 28: 4–17.

Kwek, D. (2003). Decolonizing and re-presenting culture's consequences: a postcolonial critique of cross-cultural studies in management. In A. Prasad (ed.), *Postcolonial Theory and Organizational Analysis: A Critical Engagement*. New York: Palgrave Macmillan, 121–46.

Kymlicka, W. (2010). The rise and fall of multiculturalism? New debates on inclusion and accommodation in diverse societies. *International Social Science Journal*, 61: 97–112.

Lauring, J. (2009). Managing cultural diversity and the process of knowledge sharing: a case of Denmark. *Scandinavian Journal of Management*, 25: 385–94.

Leonard, P. (2010). Organizing whiteness: gender, nationality and subjectivity in postcolonial Hong Kong. *Gender, Work and Organization*, 17: 340–58.

Litvin, D. R. (1997). The discourse of diversity: from biology to management. *Organization*, 4: 187–209.

Litvin, D. R. (2002). The business case for diversity and the 'iron cage'. In B. Czarniawska and H. Höpfl (eds.), *Casting the Other*. London: Routledge, 160–84.

Litvin, D. R. (2006). Diversity: making space for a better case. In A. M. Konrad, P. Prasad, and J. K. Pringle (eds.), *Handbook of Workplace Diversity*. Thousand Oaks, CA: Sage, 75–94.

Lorbiecki, A. (2001). Changing views on diversity management: the rise of the learning perspective and the need to recognize social and political contradictions. *Management Learning*, 32: 345–61.

Lorbiecki, A. and Jack, G. (2000). Critical turns in the evolution of diversity management. *British Journal of Management*, 11: 17–31.

Metcalfe, B. D. and Woodhams, C. (2008). Critical perspectives in diversity and equality management. *Gender in Management*, 23: 377–81.

Nkomo, S. (2011). A postcolonial and anti-colonial reading of 'African' leadership and management in organization studies: tensions, contradictions and possibilities. *Organization*, 18: 365–86.

Nkomo, S. and Cox, T. (1996). Diverse identities in organizations. In S. Clegg and C. Hardy (eds.), *The Handbook of Organization Studies*. Thousand Oaks, CA: Sage, 338–56.

Nkomo, S. and Hoobler, J. (2014). A historical perspective on diversity ideologies in the United States: reflections on human resource management research and practice. *Human Resource Management Review*, 24: 245–57.

Omanovic, V. (2009). Diversity and its management as dialectical process: encountering Sweden and the U.S. *Scandinavian Journal of Management*, 25: 352–62.

Ostendorp, A. and Steyaert, C. (2009). How different can differences be(come)? Interpretative repertoires of diversity concepts in Swiss-based organizations. *Scandinavian Journal of Management*, 25: 374–84.

Oswick, C. and Noon, M. (2014). Discourses of diversity, equality and inclusion: trenchant formulations or transient fashions? *British Journal of Management*, 25: 23–39.

Prasad, A. (1997). The colonizing consciousness and representations of the other: a postcolonial critique of the discourse of oil. In P. Prasad, A. J. Mills, M. Elmes, and A. Prasad (eds.), *Managing the Organizational Melting Pot: Dilemmas of Workplace Diversity*. Thousand Oaks, CA: Sage, 285–311.

Prasad, A. (2006). The jewel in the crown: postcolonial theory and workplace diversity. In A. M. Konrad, P. Prasad, and J. K. Pringle (eds.), *Handbook of Workplace Diversity*. London: Sage, 121–44.

Prasad, A. and Prasad, P. (2002). Otherness at large: identity and difference in the new globalized organizational landscape. In I. Aaltio and A. J. Mills (eds.), *Gender, Identity and the Culture in Organizations* (eBook). Taylor & Francis e-Library: Taylor & Francis, 57–71.

Prasad, P. and Mills, A. J. (1997). From showcase to shadow: understanding the dilemmas of managing workplace diversity. In P. Prasad, A. J. Mills, M. Elmes, and A. Prasad (eds.), *Managing the Organizational Melting Pot: Dilemmas of Workplace Diversity*. Thousand Oaks, CA: Sage, 3–30.

Prasad, P., Pringle, J. K., and Konrad, A. M. (2006). Examining the contours of workplace diversity. In A. M. Konrad, P. Prasad, and J. K. Pringle (eds.), *Handbook of Workplace Diversity*. London: Sage, 1–22.

Richard, O. (2000). Racial diversity, business strategy, and firm performance: a resource-based view. *Academy of Management Journal*, 43: 164–77.

Richard, O., Barnett, T., Dwyer, S., and Chadwick, K. (2004). Cultural diversity in management, firm performance, and the moderating role of entrepreneurial orientation dimensions. *Academy of Management Journal*, 47: 255–66.

Risberg, A. and Søderberg, A. (2008). Translating a management concept: diversity management in Denmark. *Gender in Management*, 23: 426–41.

Said, E. (1978). *Orientalism*. London: Routledge & Kegan Paul.

Schwabenland, C. and Tomlinson, F. (2008). Managing diversity or diversifying management? *Critical Perspectives on International Business* 4: 320–33.

Shimoni, B. and Bergmann, H. (2006). Managing in a changing world: from multiculturalism to hybridization: the production of hybrid management cultures in Israel, Thailand, and Mexico. *Academy of Management Perspectives*, 20: 76–89.

Shore, L. M., Randel, A. E., Chung, B. G., Dean, M. A., Holcombe Ehrhart, K., and Singh, G. (2011). Inclusion and diversity in work groups: a review and model for future research. *Journal of Management*, 37: 1262–89.

Thomas, R. R. (1990). From affirmative action to affirming diversity. *Harvard Business Review*, 68: 107–17.

Thomas, R. R. (1991). *Beyond Race and Gender*. New York: AMACOM.

Thomas, R. R. and Ely, R. J. (1996). Making differences matter: a new paradigm for managing diversity. *Harvard Business Review*, 74: 79–90.

Tomlinson, F. (2010). Marking difference and negotiating belonging: refugee women, volunteering and employment. *Gender, Work and Organization*, 17: 278–96.

Tomlinson, F. and Schwabenland, C. (2010). Reconciling competing discourses of diversity? The UK non-profit sector between social justice and the business case. *Organization*, 17: 101–21.

Van Dijk, H., Van Engen, M., and Paauwe, J. (2012). Reframing the business case for diversity: a values and virtues perspective. *Journal of Business Ethics*, 111: 73–84.

Van Laer, K. and Janssens, M. (2014). Between the devil and the deep blue sea: exploring the hybrid identity narratives of ethnic minority professionals. *Scandinavian Journal of Management*, 30: 186–96.

Westwood, R. (2006). International business and management studies as an orientalist discourse: a postcolonial critique. *Critical Perspectives on International Business*, 2: 91–113.

Zanoni, P. and Janssens, M. (2004). Deconstructing difference: the rhetoric of human resource managers' diversity discourses. *Organization Studies*, 25: 55–74.

Zanoni, P. and Janssens, M. (2007). Minority employees engaging with (diversity) management: an analysis of control, agency and micro-emancipation. *Journal of Management Studies*, 44: 1371–9.

Zanoni, P., Janssens, M., Benschop, Y., and Nkomo, S. (2010). Unpacking diversity, grasping inequality: rethinking difference through critical perspectives. *Organization*, 17: 9–29.

CHAPTER 9

QUEER PERSPECTIVES FUELLING DIVERSITY MANAGEMENT DISCOURSE

Theoretical and Empirical-Based Reflections

REGINE BENDL AND ROSWITHA HOFMANN

INTRODUCTION

DIVERSITY and diversity management (DM) have become more central to organization studies. Scholarly research presents the pros and cons of DM (Metcalfe and Woodhams 2008; Zanoni et al. 2010) and various studies highlight the importance of unveiling hegemonic patterns in organizations with regard to different diversity categories (e.g., 'gender',[1] 'sexual orientation', 'ethnicity', 'age', 'religion', 'disability') (Konrad, Prasad, and Pringle 2006). However, as demonstrated by the extant scholarly literature on the (re-) production of diversity categories in organizational contexts, not all diversity categories have received the same attention in the past. DM discourse shows that theoretical concepts and strategies often neglect issues of 'sexual orientation' or 'sexuality',[2] and unwittingly reinforce patterns of exclusion in organizational practice, although 'sexuality' has been on the organizational discourse research agenda for over twenty-five years (Hearn et al. 1989; Martin and Collison 2000; Brewis, Tyler, and Mills 2014; Colgan and Rumens 2015). From our point of view, at least two reasons exist for this phenomenon: first, organizations are often still considered to be sexless and gender-neutral. As a consequence, 'sexual orientation'—despite being part of the anti-discrimination

---

[1] The use of quotation marks signals that these categories are considered to be social constructions and therefore not naturally given and fixed.

[2] In this chapter, the term 'diversity management discourse' subsumes DM research and practices, though excludes the discussion of discourse theories.

legislation in many countries—is deemed to be a mere 'private matter' and not a category of social stratification which impacts employees, organizational culture, processes, and structures. Second, DM practices suffer from the general problem of categorical diversity approaches, which mask the fluidity, intersectionality, and the connectedness of (legally) fixed diversity categories such as 'sex', 'gender', and 'sexual orientation'. The aim of this chapter is to consider the diversity category 'sexual orientation' within a broader theoretical framework, by highlighting the constitutive connectedness between 'sex', 'gender', and 'sexuality'. We will use queer theoretical concepts to give insight into the normative intersections of 'sex', 'gender', and 'sexuality' and, thus, heteronormative phenomena in DM discourse. This will allow a serious engagement with 'sexual orientation', and, in particular, heterosexuality as a social institution in DM discourse. In other words, this chapter highlights the interventional and transformative potential of queer theory as an approach to DM discourse. For this purpose, we first present core queer-theoretical concepts, followed by a literature overview on the treatment of such concepts in DM research. Next, we exemplify this discussion with an exploration of multinational corporations (MNCs) and their codes of conduct (CoCs), identifying the reproduction of hetero- and cisnormative patterns as well as opportunities for change. Finally, we conclude with recommendations for DM research and practice.

Queer Theory as a Multifaceted Theoretical Concept

The term queer theory serves to describe a growing body of theoretical and political concepts,[3] which are connected in terms of their radical critique of essentialist and dualistic constructions of 'sex' and 'gender'. This includes the exploration of hetero- and cisnormativities, and thus the idea of fixed 'gender identities', 'sexual identities', and 'sexual orientations'. Scholars of queer theory are also concerned with materialities (not only of the bodies), and the normalizing power of capitalism and its particular mode of neoliberalism (Binnie 2010). Queer theory owes this focus to the experience of people who were excluded from society and also from liberation movements, such as lesbian and gay communities due to their 'sexual orientation', their 'gender identity', and/or their 'sexual identity'. As a consequence, queer theory is deeply rooted in social movements like the Stonewall movement (Duberman 1994), the Women of Color movement (Crenshaw 1991) and the 'AIDS Coalition to Unleash Power' movement (ACT UP) (Jagose 1997; Hall and Jagose 2013: xvi) in the USA during the 1970s and 1980s. Currently, it highlights the multifaceted theoretical work behind diverse political endeavours all over the world in fighting forms of societal, social, and economic exclusion that are grounded in the

---

[3] Teresa de Lauretis coined the term for a conference in 1990 and used it in her publication: de Lauretis (1991).

normative intersection of 'sex', 'gender', and 'sexuality', and in single-issue identity politics. Its academic roots are strongly connected with Gayle S. Rubin (1975, 1984), Michel Foucault (1979), Adrienne Rich (1980), Judith Butler (1990, 1993), Eve Kosofsky Sedgwick (1991), Michael Warner (1993), Judith/Jack Haberstam (1998), Lisa Duggan (2003), and Sara Ahmed (2006)—to name only a few scholars. Queer theoretical concepts that are addressed in this chapter are the heterosexual matrix (Butler 1990), performativity (Butler 1990), heteronormativity (Warner 1993), homonormativity (Duggan 2003), and cisnormativity (Bauer et al. 2009). We use these concepts to show how 'sex', 'gender', and 'sexuality' are regulated in organizations by practices of DM under neoliberal conditions.

Queer scholarship and activism is multifaceted, but there is some common ground: queer thinkers start from the premise that dual categorizations like 'sex' (man/women), 'gender' (male/female), and 'sexuality' (heterosexuality/homosexuality) are results of social and cultural processes and not 'naturally' given characteristics of human beings. From a queer point of view, the hegemonic perspective of a dualistic sex/gender system (Rubin 1984) and 'heterosexuality' as the norm in terms of desire, is a positing which is constitutive for identity formations as well as for societal power relations and institutions (Lorber 1995). The *heterosexual matrix* (see Figure 9.1) describes this specific but normative relationship between 'sex' (female/male), 'gender' (feminine/masculine), and 'heterosexuality' as the norm which keeps hierarchical gender relations stable and obstructs the chance of unequal societal, social, and organizational structures and processes (Hofmann 2014).

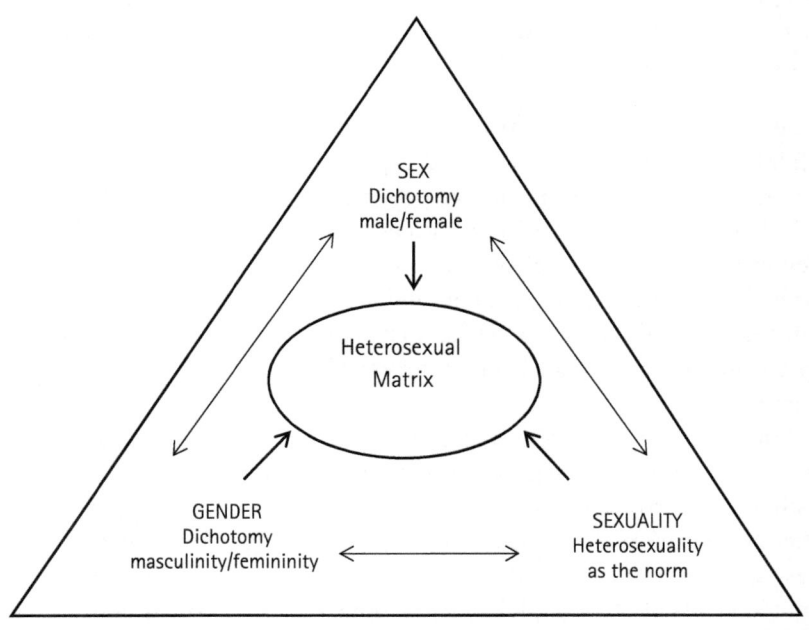

FIGURE 9.1 The heterosexual matrix: the normative entanglement of 'sex–gender–sexuality' (own figure).

In addition, the heterosexual matrix is built on the construction of *cisgender*. This term denotes 'individuals who have a match between the gender they were assigned at birth, their bodies, and their personal identity' (Schilt and Westbrook 2009).

Hence, from a queer theoretical perspective the heterosexual matrix has to be considered as a power structure which not only shapes identities—by socially valuing and rewarding personal adjustments to the norm—but also the social and economic structures of societies, their institutions (e.g. laws, relationships, rules of social appreciation, etc.), and, last but not least, organizations. It constitutes and reinforces organizational structures, processes, and cultures in which a normative relation between 'heterosexuality' and 'cisgender' is reproduced. This leads to multiple exclusions of those who do not accept gendered expectations or fixed identities, who present their 'sexual' and 'gender identities' or 'sexual orientations' in a fluid and non-normative way, whether these people define themselves as lesbian, gay, bisexual, heterosexual (Jackson 2006), cissexual, intersexual, transsexual, transgender, or in any other way.

From a scholarly perspective, the heterosexual matrix opens up the possibility of exposing the heteronormative culture of organizations:

> By *heteronormativity* we mean the institutions, structures of understanding and practical orientations that make heterosexuality seem not only coherent—that is, organized as a sexuality—but also privileged. Its coherence is always provisional, and its privilege can take several (sometimes contradictory) forms: unmarked, as the basic idiom of the personal and the social; or marked as a natural state; or projected as an ideal or moral accomplishment. It consists less of norms that could be summarized as a body of doctrine than of a sense of rightness produced in contradictory manifestations—often unconscious, immanent to practice or to institutions. (Berlant and Warner 1998: 548; my italics).

This heteronormative power structure is continuously stabilized by reiterated acts which fulfil the norm and the connected expectations (Pringle 2008). Through these acts of reiteration, the heteronormative power structure historically became a quasi-'natural' phenomena—a part of the 'human condition' which is hard to question. Butler describes these acts of reiteration as gender *performativity* (Butler 1990), which coin societal discourses on 'sex', 'gender', and 'sexuality'. Butler and other scholars (e.g. Diedrich et al. 2013) also point to the fact that alternative forms of gender performance and expression can disturb and alter discourses and social realities as well as variances in the reiterative acts.

Queer theory and queer political practices aim to foster the analysis of normative structures and non-normative gender expression in order to transgress and transform the existing power structures related to 'sex', 'gender', and 'sexuality'. Queer scholars have often been criticized for their fixation on the 'sex-gender-sexuality-relation', but in the last decade they have broadened these perspectives, and apply queer approaches to examine aspects of other exploitative relations such as classism or racism (see also Halberstam et al. 2005; Kulpa and Mizielińska 2011; Mesquita et al. 2013). Researchers are also engaged with cultural aspects of exploitative relations, as Sharma (2009: 5) indicates, for example: 'I understand heteronormativity to refer to those norms related to gender and sexuality which keep in place patriarchy and compulsory heterosexuality as well as other systems and ideologies related to power such religious fundamentalism, casteism, the class system and so on.' Such a perspective makes the queer concept applicable to other dual and hierarchical (= binary) orders.

This work is important for the development of differentiated DM and organizational discourses, as it allows a shift from the individual perspective to exploitative relationships in the global markets of organizations. Therefore, the growing body of queer theoretical work dealing with the exploitative, commodifying, and regulating impact of economic neoliberalism on 'gender' and 'sexual identities' is of similar importance to a radical reflection of DM discourse. Furthermore, the self-reflection of queer politics, which is often accused of fuelling a neoliberal system and culture (Winnubst 2012), should also be included here. In this context, Duggan (2003) identified *homonormativity* as one effect of heteronormativity. Homonormativity describes the assimilation of heteronormative (institutional and material) ideals and values into individual identities of socially stigmatized people such as lesbians and gays, as well as non-heteronormative heterosexuals (Duggan 2003). Duggan points out that lesbians, gays, bisexuals, or trans, by best mimicking heteronormative and (economic) performance standards through 'self-techniques' (Foucault 2010), are trapped by the desire of recognition and the corresponding promise of equal rights. Ironically, this promise has a stabilizing character for the hierarchical heteronormative power structure and will, therefore, never be kept. In addition, those individuals who are unable or unwilling to meet the related heteronormative and performative expectations, and thus do not become 'normalized', stay at the bottom of this hierarchy and remain excluded.

To sum up, the application of queer theoretical concepts raises issues and questions concerning modes of categorization and normalization, as well as the reiteration of gender dichotomies in organizations, processes of de/stabilization of the heteronormative matrix, and self-techniques in a neoliberal context. From a queer perspective, destabilizing heteronormative socio-political, working, and life conditions would open new possibilities for the emergence of more inclusive societies, with organizational and DM discourse where the term 'inclusion' describes organizational practices which interrupt hetero- and cisnormativity.

This short overview highlights the main potential of queer theory for organizational discourse in general and DM discourse in particular. The next section gives an insight into the present application of queer theoretical concepts in DM research.

APPLICATION OF QUEER THEORY IN DIVERSITY MANAGEMENT RESEARCH

Queer theoretical thinking has not only been adopted in feminist studies, cultural studies, sociology, and political science, but also in organization studies (e.g. Parker 2001, 2002; Linstead and Pullen 2006; Schilt and Connell 2007; Thanem 2011).

With regard to the DM discourse, our literature review shows that the studies carried out in this area are limited in number,[4] and divided into two subject areas.[5] Texts on the *micro* level address the individual experiences and identity of sexual minorities within organizations. Texts on the *meso* level focus on how organizations are dealing with 'sexual orientation' and 'sexual identities', though a DM perspective is often lacking. On the other hand, the latter scrutinize DM practices explicitly, by not only focusing on the diversity categories of 'gender' and 'sexual orientation', but on other diversity categories as well. Table 9.1 shows how the selected texts adopted queer theoretical aspects in terms of these two levels, including which research methods were used and which perspectives the texts offer for the exploration of CoCs later in this chapter. We have excluded those texts from the table which cite texts on queer theory but do not apply queer theory at all (for example, Bell and Hartmann 2007; Neal 2010; Mkono 2010; Christiansen and Just 2012).

Application on the Micro Level

These texts refer to specific queer concepts: Lewis (2009) explicitly mentions 'heteronormative power structures' in her empirical work on lesbian police officers. Bowring and Brewis (2009) embed their work in Butler's concept of the heterosexual matrix for their investigation on how lesbians and gays manage their non-hegemonic identity within organizations. According to their research results, power effects are obvious when lesbians and gays do not fulfil expectations concerning appearance or relationships. Ward and Winstanley (2003) examine the role of silence in the creation of social identities in organizations. For this, they combine the concept of the power–knowledge regime of 'compulsive heterosexuality' (see Butler 1990; Seidman 1997) with a discursive method, following Foucault's work on discourses on sexuality (Foucault 1979). Common to these three texts is the use of queer theoretical insights on heteronormative power relations in context with lesbian and gay identity. Creed and Scully (2000) go a step further, referring to queer theory when highlighting the multiplicity and ambiguity of LGBT identities. In fact, for all these texts, queer

---

[4] The literature review was conducted by searching in the ABI/Inform literature database for reviewed journal articles with the following keywords in title or abstract: queer theory and diversity, management and queer theory, managing diversity and queer, managing diversity and queer theory. Fifteen articles were considered as being relevant for the discussed topic, all of which deal with queer theory and (diversity) management. Thus, this body of literature gives an insight into how queer theory is applied within organization studies in general, and DM discourse in particular.

[5] Due to the queer critique of the imagination of fixed identities and of the exclusive character of identity politics, research focusing on single identity groups such as lesbians, gays, bisexuals, or trans (LGBT) has not been addressed in the literature review. Nevertheless, from the authors' point of view, it is not a question of *either* queer *or* LGBT studies: the growing body of LGBT research is of enormous importance in terms of socio-political and organizational transformations.

Table 9.1 Diversity management and queer approaches

	Queer concepts applied but reproducing existing identity categories	Queer concepts applied for dissolving identity categories	Methods applied in the included texts	Aspects relevant for empirical analysis of CoC
Micro level (individual)	Lewis (2009) Bowring and Brewis (2009) Ward and Winstanley (2003) Creed and Scully (2009)	Sardy (2001)	• Qualitative interviews • Narrative interviews • Semi-structured interviews • Partial observation • Auto-ethnography • Focus groups • Discourse analysis	• Power effects of the heterosexual matrix • Multifaceted nature of silence • Intragroup diversity among LGBT/multiple identities • Questioning fixed identities—using lesbian and gay only as self-identification not as group identification
Meso level (organizational discourse)	Chapman and Gedro (2009)	Lee, Learmonth, and Harding (2008) Parker (2001) Parker (2002) Tyler and Cohen (2008)	• In-depth interviews • Case studies • Qualitative interviews • Text/film analysis	• Suggestions how to contribute to new knowledge on LGBT in HRD • Mode of analysis—diverse reading strategies, multiple interpretative stances • Focus on gender performativity and the desire of recognition in the workplace
Meso level (DM discourse)		Bendl, Fleischmann, and Walenta (2008) Bendl, Fleischmann, and Hofmann (2009) Just and Christiansen (2012)	• Deconstruction	• Linkage between diversity management and queer approaches • Heterosexuality as unmarked norm • Critical questioning of DM discourse • DM as performance • Deferral of discourse in order to dissolve identity categories

theoretical concepts are explicitly constitutive in highlighting the power effects of heteronormativity for certain identity groups. But all these texts remain in the reproduction of the binaries of heterosexuality and homosexuality.

In contrast to these texts, Sardy (2001) refers to queer theoretical concepts by rejecting the term 'homosexual' as essentialistic. In his analysis of the experiences of queer people in an urban organization (Las Vegas) he refers to people who 'disagree with the manner in which heterosexuality is constructed' (Sardy 2001: 182). In fact, the author points to the potential of queer theory for challenging identity constructions and binary oppositions, and for uncovering heteronormative practices.

Application on the Meso Level: Organizational Discourse

In their reflections on queering in the human resource development (HRD) curriculum, Chapmans and Gedro (2009) use queer theory as a critical method of questioning normality and identity in organizations, but still assert the idea of fixed identities such as lesbians and gays. Other texts take a more radical approach: in their research on public administration, Lee and colleagues (2008: 149) understand queer theory 'as a set of political/politicized practices and positions which resist normative knowledge and identity [...]', which has emancipatory and explanatory power. In their case study, they explicitly use queer theory to identify norms that govern identities, highlighting that which is either allowable or unspeakable within those norms. In his conceptual texts, Parker (2001, 2002) connects queer theory with managing and organizing. Based on Butler and Sedgwick, he addresses management as a form of performance—a form of doing. Similar to Parker, Tyler, and Cohen (2008: 113) focus on 'the organizational performance and management of gender in accordance with the terms of the heterosexual matrix'. By analysing the BBC comedy series *The Office* as a popular cultural text, the authors highlight the critical insights and some of the limitations of queer theory. Tyler and Cohen (2008: 114) embed their work explicitly in Butler's work on performativity, in particular the heterosexual matrix as 'an ontological-epistemic schema that frames particular (binary and hierarchical) configurations of the relationship between sex, gender and desire as normative [...]' in organizations and their management. They therefore present queer theory as a 'mode of critique' that disrupts and disturbs doings, and invites a critical reflection of the relationship between management, normative masculinity, and the desire for recognition, which constitutes 'viable subjectivity' in organizations.

Application on the Meso Level: Diversity Management Discourse

Some texts apply queer theory to interrogate DM discourse. For example, Bendl, Fleischmann, and Walenta (2008) explain how queering is especially well suited for unpacking DM discourses' implicit assumptions about identity constructions. In order to show queer theory's potential for questioning heteronormative and hierarchical structures, the authors refer to the heterosexual matrix, performativity, and heteronormativity. For the authors, queer theory allows: (1) the conceptualization of heterosexuality as an unmarked norm that governs social practices; (2) the questioning of essentialist notions and fixed identities; and (3) the dismantling of invisibilities or representations which neither refer to term A (the norm) nor term not-A (the other). In the same vein as Parker (2001, 2002), they suggest the following key approaches: to examine more deeply the term 'diversity manager', to de- and reconstruct DM practices, and to interrogate DM discourse in these terms. Furthermore, Bendl, Fleischmann, and Hofmann (2009) present a deconstructive three-step analysis for reading the CoCs of multinational companies. This is based on the heterosexual matrix and heteronormativity, in order to assess the assumption that—even for organizations in which DM procedures have been implemented—stereotyping and exclusion by categorization and heteronormativity are discursively kept in place. First by defining marked and unmarked terms, then by unveiling binaries (hierarchy and duality), and, finally, by shifting the dual, hierarchical, and heteronormative limits, the authors demonstrate that queer approaches support the disclosure of unmarked heteronormative constructions of DM strategies, and thus expose the reproduction of heteronormativity and hegemonic managerial elites in multinational companies.

To sum up, this insight into the literature on the micro and meso level shows that queer theory is often applied as a method of critique, addressing power relations and their discriminatory effects on certain identity groups, such as lesbians and gays. However, its full potential—in terms of questioning and deconstructing the heterosexual matrix and the idea of fixed identities—is rarely applied. Therefore, the listed aspects must be considered in order to draw upon the full potential of queering in the empirical analysis of CoCs in the section 'A Queer-Theoretical Analysis of Codes of Conduct':

- the relational connection between 'sex', 'gender', and 'sexuality';
- modes of categorizations (fixed identities) and references to intragroup diversity/multiple identities;
- manifestations of the heterosexual matrix/hetero- and cisnormativity;
- potential power effects of the heterosexual matrix;
- modes of silencing of non-normative existences; and
- deferral of discourses.

With our analysis of CoCs—which serves as an example for the 'critical tradition of diversity management discourse' (see Chapter 4, this volume)—we apply a queer perspective in the interrogation of underlying heteronormative assumptions in CoCs to expose conflicting interests, contradictions, and discrepancies in the discursive practices of DM.

A Queer-Theoretical Analysis of Codes of Conduct

The following analysis of CoCs from twenty European and US-based globally acting corporations sets out to explore whether CoCs reproduce hetero-/cis- and homonormative patterns, despite the fact that a DM policy exists in these corporations. It focuses on possible hetero- and cisnormative relations in the reproduction of notions of 'sex', 'gender', and 'sexual orientation', as well as on any signs of transgression.

The CoCs of MNCs often incorporate the corporations' DM policies, and thus reflect DM as one of the corporation's practices (see, for example, Mor Barak 2011) related to corporate governance and Corporate Social Responsibility Initiatives (CSR initiatives). The Organisation for Economic Co-operation and Development (OECD) defines CoCs as 'commitments voluntarily made by companies, associations or other entities, which put forth standards and principles for the conduct of business activities in the marketplace' (OECD 2001: 3). Analyses show that CoCs reflect the diversity of organizations, which differ, for example, in terms of size, regional and cultural affiliation, (business) sector and history of leadership (Gilman 2005). On the one hand, CoCs are very diverse in their content and the variety of issues included, which are not only of concern to the general public (such as consumer protection, environmental issues, and standards of labour), but also to stakeholders and shareholders (e.g. internal control and risk of liability, and insurance of compliance with the law). On the other hand, CoCs differ in their degree of detail and transparency concerning the information provided on certain elements of the document, but their economic motivations are mostly clear (e.g. compete successfully, be a trustworthy supplier with good reputation, etc.) (see Pelfrey and Peacock 1991; Farrell and Farrell 1998; OECD 2001). For at least two reasons, CoCs are of interest to the DM discourse. First, as an artefact they are mirroring the discursive practices, power structure, and culture of an organization (see Bendl, Fleischmann, and Hofmann 2009: 629) and, second, by functioning as a set of standards and principles which summarize values and set out rules to guide present and future actions, CoCs influence individual decisions and behaviours (Farrell and Farrell 1998). As such, CoCs produce their own meaning of 'sex', 'gender', 'gender identities', 'sexual orientation', and 'sexual identities', which they establish as relevant not only for individuals' actions and behaviours but also for organizational structures, processes, and cultures, as well as identities. In other words, CoCs generate power processes of normalization within the organization which are fuelled by the norms that they inhabit.

For this analysis, the CoCs of the following US- and European-based corporations have been included: ArcelorMittal, Continental, Daimler, Delhaize Group, Deutsche Bank, Deutsche Post, GDF Suez, Siemens, Unilever, Veolia (all European-based), and Coca-Cola Company, Chevron, General Electric, Google, Exxon, Microsoft, IBM, Johnson & Johnson, P&G, and Walmart (all US-based). We chose corporations featured on the Fortune 500 and Handelsblatt lists which had over 100,000 employees, branch offices in four continents, and both a DM and an inclusion policy mentioned on their corporation website. The CoC also had to be available on the website. Out of this sample we have then selected the twenty corporations (ten US-based, ten European-based) with the biggest number of employees. The CoCs were downloaded in January 2013.

Analytical Framework

The methodological application of queer theoretical concepts is a challenge, although queer theoretical approaches do not imply specific methods. Due to their epistemological roots, queer modes of analysis are mostly based on variations of discourse analysis (see e.g. Sedgwick 1985) and deconstructive approaches (see e.g. Lorber 1996). As Graham (2010: 185) points out, 'we must be aware of what a method constitutes as well as what it excludes and fails to materialize, for methods are not only revelatory, they are also *productive* devices'. Thus, for our queer analysis, we conceptualized DM as performative and CoCs as one effect of the performative act. In order to avoid pre-categorizations, we used a grounded theory-oriented method of text analysis based mostly on in-vivo coding; we did all the coding by ourselves and synchronized our codes as we coded the texts separately.

As mentioned, this empirical analysis addresses the reproduction and transgression of hetero- and cisnormative structures and cultures in organizations. Due to the results of the literature review and the aim of revealing the potential of queer concepts in DM discourse, the analysis is conducted with the following questions in mind: Are there patterns of reproduction in terms of 'sex', 'gender', and 'sexuality' dichotomies and hetero-/cisnormativity? How do the CoCs conceptualize the relation of 'sex–gender–sexuality'? Do the CoCs produce manifestations of, or space for, alternative constructions of 'sex–gender–sexuality?' What does it mean to become an anti-discrimination and inclusive organization from a queer perspective in terms of not reproducing hetero- and cisnormative structures, and what is needed in order to do so?

The coding process resulted in forty-seven codes which refer to the relation of 'sex', 'gender', and 'sexuality' in the twenty organizations. For this publication we chose nine core codes which portray constructions and intersections of 'sex', 'gender', and 'sexuality' and related (non-)hetero- and cisnormative patterns. These codes are 'sex', 'gender', 'gender identity', 'gender expression', 'sexual identity', 'relationships', 'health and safety', 'laws, regulations, principles, policies and values', and 'business case of diversity management'.

Findings

Sex–Gender–Sexuality

Most of the corporations included a list of diversity categories in their CoC. These lists should demonstrate which social categories are protected against discrimination and/or should be addressed by the inclusion policies. As Table 9.2 shows, six out of ten CoCs from the European-based corporations have 'sex' or 'gender' in the list of diversity categories; two of the European-based corporations refer to 'sex' in their CoC and four to 'gender'. In comparison, six out of ten US-based corporations refer to 'sex' and four to 'gender'. With regard to 'gender identity', only one of the European CoCs refers to this category compared with five of the US CoCs. Four US organizations also mention 'gender expression'.

For the analysis of the entanglement of the constructions, the co-occurrence of codes is also of interest. It has to be noted that 'sex', 'gender', and 'gender identity' co-occur in the same context in different combinations and also with 'gender expression' and 'sexual orientation'.

With regard to the detailed description of 'sex' and 'gender', six out of ten CoCs from the European-based corporations do not use personal pronouns which would allow identification of a reference to women and men or female and male. This conceals the nature of the gender relation in the CoCs. The four CoCs which have a gender-inclusive language reproduce a dichotomy by referring to women and men only, for example: 'In addition, every Senior Officer must familiarize herself/himself with the written description of the Company's disclosure controls and procedures and its internal controls provided by the Company' (Daimler), or 'You are not permitted to search only for male applicants nor may You reject the applications of female applicants just because they are female because this is discrimination on the basis of gender. Your search must be focused on the qualifications, skills, and experiences of the candidates and how they meet the essential functions of the position, without regard to the candidate's gender' (Continental). In fact, no European- or US-based CoC produces a language which goes beyond the binary (dichotomy and hierarchy) of gender to offer additional gender representations and identities. One CoC explicitly problematizes a hierarchy of gender with man/males as the 'norm' and woman/female as the 'other' as follows 'You are searching for a candidate to hire a sales manager for the sales department. You believe that sales business is "male business" and ask Yourself if You can consider only male applicants for the sales manager position' (Continental).

In the US-based organizations more personal pronouns (seven out of ten, but mainly in examples) are applied but, like the European CoCs, they construct employees as female or male and do not mention other genders, although some of the CoCs mention gender identity as a diversity dimension which should be protected against discrimination.

Interestingly, some CoCs do not include 'sexual orientation' in their explicit listing of diversity categories (e.g. 'gender', 'race', 'age', 'disability', 'religion', etc.) towards which a discriminatory practice or any other unlawful basis will not be tolerated. With regard to the European-based CoCs, only three have included 'sexual orientation' in their list of diversity categories (see Table 9.2), but these CoCs have a more extensive list of diversity categories, going far beyond the six diversity categories ('gender', 'age', 'sexual orientation', 'disability', 'religion', 'ethnicity') protected by the EU Antidiscrimination Directive (RL 2000/78/EG). These CoCs also list, for example, pregnancy, veteran status or marital status, language, and national origin, as well as citizenship, aptitude,

Table 9.2 Sex, gender, and sexual orientation in the CoCs

Company	Sex	Gender	Gender identity	Sexual identity	Gender expression	Sexual orientation
Europe-based	2	4	1	1	–	3
US-based	6	4	5	–	4	8

ancestry, and worldview. Furthermore, certain diversity categories are made even more precise, for example, physical or mental disability, religion and religious beliefs. One of the European-based corporations' CoCs does not refer to 'sexual orientation', but lists 'sexual identity' amongst the diversity categories: 'We work together with individuals of various ethnic backgrounds, cultures, religions, ages, disabilities, races, sexual identity, world view and gender' (Siemens).

The US-based organizations show a different picture. Eight out of ten mention 'sexual orientation' in the list of diversity categories, although no US law on the federal level provides protection for this diversity dimension. The companies seem to react to protection laws, including sexual orientation, on the US state level and laws in other countries such as European Union (EU) member states.

Some European CoCs do not refer explicitly to sexual orientation, but make, for example, general statements which may either include or exclude sexual orientation: 'This principle governs our Group's policy on the respect for private life and diversity, the fight against discrimination and the prevention and punishment of bullying and harassment' (GDF Suez), or 'In addition to providing equal employment opportunity, it is also the Corporation's policy to undertake special efforts to [...] foster a work environment free from sexual, racial, or other harassment' (Exxon).

With regard to the structure of the text, both the European- and US-based CoCs refer to 'sexual orientation' directly in connection with anti-discrimination (local laws, national standards). Furthermore, some European CoCs indirectly link 'sexual orientation' with local cultures. In the majority of the twenty codes, 'sexual orientation' represents one criterion of anti-discrimination amongst others (e.g. 'gender', 'race', 'religion', etc.).

In terms of 'sexuality', the CoCs refer mainly to those contexts where negative behaviour (e.g. 'unwelcome sexual advances') towards any person, either inside (employees) or outside the organizations (customers, suppliers, partners) should be avoided, for example 'In no case may information be retrieved or transmitted that furthers or incites racial hatred, glorification of violence or other criminal acts, or contains material which is sexually offensive within the respective culture' (Siemens), or 'This includes harassment based upon gender, race, ethnicity, religion, sexual orientation, age, pregnancy, national origin, veteran or marital status, disability, or other characteristics or categories protected by law. Harassment can be verbal, non-verbal, or physical in nature and can take many forms, including behavior that offends, threatens, or disturbs others or which creates an unpleasant or hostile environment' (Delhaize Group). All in all, these results show that most of the CoCs have adopted the triangle of 'sex–gender–sexuality'. However, even though the CoCs mean to apply it with an anti-discriminative appeal, its application reproduces binaries. But the results demonstrate also that its application and meaning is context-dependent in terms of place, law, organizational culture, and so on.

Relationships

The construction of relationships represents an important indicator of an organization's social order. The CoCs address different forms of relationships, and at times these go beyond familial or private relationships by also including business partners; for example: 'They should disclose any relationship with persons or firms with whom we do business ("business partners"), which might give rise to a conflict of interest, to a supervisor. Such relations include in particular a relationship by blood or marriage, partnership, participation or an investment in business partners' (Deutsche Post). Additionally, the CoCs mention, for example, 'family members', 'spouse', 'brother', 'sister', 'friends', 'biological parent', 'adoptive parent', and 'close relatives or partners which can be linked by relationships of blood' or 'partnership'. One CoC from a US corporation even refers explicitly to these 'significant others': 'same or opposite sex domestic partner'. In this context, we tend to believe that this designation is meant to refer to a lesbian, homosexual, and so on, partner. However, considered closely, it could also refer to a person with which the employee lives but does not have a sexual relationship. Altogether, the CoCs consider all partnerships to be a factor for their financial and moral well-being but, except for one cooperation, in terms of private couples the CoCs reproduce heterosexual relationships.

Health and Safety

With regard to health and safety perspectives, most of the CoCs (eight European-based corporations and seven US corporations) refer to workplace health and safety policies/regulations which are not only concerned with physical ('accident rates', 'accident prevention', 'ban of illegal drugs', 'work instructions', 'physical wellbeing of employees', etc.), but also with psychological ('no threatening and intimidating behaviour', 'secure and positive working climate', 'psychological wellbeing of employees') notions. Some CoCs also subsume health and safety perspectives under security issues. However, an employee's sense of safety is also of concern with regard to the exposure of sexual orientation or sexual identity, and in terms of protection when reporting cases of harassment, violence, or retaliation. Therefore, some of the companies have anti-violence, anti-harassment, and anti-retaliation policies in place, but link them only implicitly to health and safety issues. This shows that CoCs do not explicitly consider sexual orientation and identity as safety issues.

Laws, Regulations, Principles, Policies, and Values

The CoCs address the corporations' internal and external stakeholders and refer to internal policies as well as external regulations and laws. Internal policies are self-defined principles such as 'instructions of management', 'accounting and auditing standards', 'data protection guidelines and policies', and 'corporate rules, standards and instructions', for example. As external sources, the CoCs state general policies such as 'applicable governmental law, rules and regulations', 'jurisdictions in which the country operates', 'existing legal framework', 'respective local laws', 'laws, rules and standards on ethics and compliance produced not only by international, federal, national and local bodies, but also by professional bodies'. More specified external sources are, for example, 'United Nation's Global Compact', 'Principles of the United Nations Global Pact', 'Anticorruption and Bribery Law', 'ISO 14000', 'export and import laws', 'trade law', 'human rights', 'customs law and regulations'. Apart from the fact that the CoCs advise all corporations' stakeholders to comply with these principles, regulations, and laws, the CoCs set up values to which all the stakeholders should adhere: 'Fairness', 'integrity', 'respect', 'trust', 'to act ethically' and 'responsibility'. However, the content used to outline the meaning of these values causes the CoCs to merge them somewhat, in a way that, to some extent, they use one value to explain another value. For example, trust is defined in terms of integrity and respect ('Integrity and respectful behaviour towards one another are indispensable prerequisites for trust', Deutsche Bank), respect in terms of integrity, fairness, and respect ('Arcelor Mittal expects us to preserve the quality of our customer relations by maintaining business relationships that are based on integrity, fairness and mutual respect', ArcelorMittal), and integrity in terms of fairness and respect ('As a Company and as individuals, we must commit ourselves to treat each other in a fair, respectful and honest manner', Delhaize Group).

But, in explaining their values, the CoCs also go beyond such tautological constructions. For example, the emphasis on the value 'respect' lies on 'no harassment (including workplace bullying, unwelcome sexual advances, unwanted physical contact, propositions or a working environment poisoned with harassing jokes, words and demeaning comments)', 'dignity in all circumstances and their differences and cultures' and 'for different cultures and sensitive manner in order to build trust and credibility', as well as 'local cultures and understand issues of communities'. In fact, the CoCs display the business case as well as the moral case of DM.

Business Case of Diversity Management

'We see employee diversity as a guiding principle in our employment policy. This means promoting the diversity and heterogeneity of the individuals in the company in order to attain the highest possible productivity, creativity and efficiency' (Deutsche Post)—this and similar statements, such as: 'Unilever is committed to diversity in a working environment where there is mutual trust and respect and where everyone feels responsible for the performance and reputation of our company' (Unilever) introduce the business case for DM in the CoCs (two European-based corporations and six US corporations). In reference to business cases, the CoCs do not mention diversity dimensions in detail, but the reader can assume that all diversity dimensions, which are enumerated elsewhere in the CoC, are considered to contribute to the business case.

Discussion

To begin with, our applied methodology has unavoidable limitations: CoCs are only one artefact within organizations, and therefore the findings mirror only one of the ways in which organizations construct their normative systems. For a deeper analysis, the CoC must be placed in a broader managerial, sectoral, and social context. However, despite this, our analysis of the CoCs of MNCs which have DM practices in place allows some deductions regarding how the corporations (re)produce the relationship between 'sex', 'gender', and 'sexual orientation'. In the empirical data, we identified the following patterns of reproduction of 'sex', 'gender', and 'sexuality' dichotomies and hetero- and cisnormativity:

> The representation of 'sex', 'gender' and 'gender identity' shows that some organizations do not distinguish between 'sex' as the biological (woman/man) and 'gender' as the social (male/female) representation of gender. Otherwise, both 'sex' and 'gender' are present as terms in every CoC. But the use of personal pronouns he/she and the lack of other gender and sexual identities shows that the companies reproduce a dualistic sex–gender system. A more inclusive solution could be a reference that employees may choose how they want to be addressed in their gender and sexual identity (as he or she or in another way or only by their name without using a gendered personal pronoun). Additionally, it becomes evident that organizations relate to different anti-discrimination laws, in which different reasons for discrimination are mentioned which have effects for the setup of the CoC. In the EU, 'sexual orientation' constitutes part of the list, while in the USA this is not the case on the level of the federal law, but is present in some state laws.[6] From this point of view the results are surprising: Only three European-based companies have 'sexual orientation' in their list of diversity dimensions compared to eight US-based companies. One reason for this may be the differing degrees to which companies have to apprehend sanctions, which are comparatively more serious in the USA than in the EU.

What is remarkable in this context is that a CoC from one of the European-based corporations refers to 'sexual identity' and not to 'sexual orientation'. This may be an indicator that organizations are beginning to recognize the public discussion on 'sexual identities', but it may also be a result of different translations of the notion of 'sexual orientation', as described in the EU directive 2000/78/EG, in national law.[7] Either way, the application of the term 'sexual identity' allows the whole person and not only their sexual orientation to be addressed.

---

[6] See e.g. <http://www.eeoc.gov/employees/> (accessed 21 August 2014).
[7] See, for example, the Equality Act 2010 of the UK (<http://www.legislation.gov.uk/ukpga/2010/15/section/4> (accessed 21 August 2014)), where gender reassignment and sexual orientation are mentioned separately. Concerning different translations: in the Austrian anti-discrimination law (Gleichbehandlungsgesetz—GlBG) sexual orientation is mentioned, while in the German law (Allgemeines Gleichbehandlungsgesetz—AGG) sexual orientation is translated as *sexuelle Identität*, which includes not only sexual orientations like homosexuality, bisexuality, and heterosexuality, but also transsexuality.

However, independent of whether 'sexual orientation' is mentioned explicitly or implicitly, the structures of the CoCs show that 'sexual orientation' and sexual behaviour (e.g. romantic relationships, sexual activities, sexually explicit language, or sexual advances) are considered as risks to the organization, and thus have to be kept under control (see Foucault 1978). This is also the case when companies portray relationships between their employees outside of the company setting. Relationships are considered as potentially hazardous, as they are mainly mentioned in the context of conflicts of interest, which can be broadly subsumed under the term 'insider information'.

The data also shows traces of hetero- and cis-normative patterns. The CoCs do not always mention 'sex' and 'gender,' (see Table 9.2), but in the cases where they do—mostly in examples—they do so in a dichotomic way. In not one of the twenty CoCs is the connection between 'sex', 'gender', and 'sexuality' explicitly considered. As a consequence, the dichotomic view of the hetero- and cisnormative 'sex–gender' concept has not been transcended by, for example, mentioning transpersons or examples of non-normative gender expression. In addition, it remains unclear as to whether 'heterosexuality' is included under 'sexual orientation', and whether the organizations only refer to 'the other', not normative sexual orientations such as 'homosexuality' or 'bisexuality'. Last but not least, the CoCs consider sexual matters primarily as a risky terrain which has to be controlled.

Regarding to the (legal) forms of partnership, some CoCs also mention 'registered partner', 'adoptive child', 'child (regardless of the marital status of the parents)', 'member of families or persons living with us or with whom we are associated, or in any other manner'. Implicitly, these terms may go beyond traditional heterosexual living arrangements and may consider the fact that not all employees live according to heteronormative patterns. But the CoCs do not mention non-heterosexual partners explicitly, as in the way heterosexual partners are mentioned. By referring only implicitly to non-heterosexual partners (except for one CoC), the CoC makes them the 'other', which may also work as a process of silencing.

Of interest in this context is also the fact that the CoCs mention relationships mainly in terms of conflicts of interest, as stated. We therefore would assume that the focus of the CoCs is not on the form of sexuality and actual sexual arrangements in the relationship (whether it be homosexual or heterosexual) per se, but on the employees' (competing) bonds of trust between the company and the people that they live with. In contrast, relationships are not mentioned in the context of corporate organizational culture or corporate values; such a perspective nourishes our assumption that the corporations do not explicitly connect the relations of 'sex', 'gender', and 'sexuality' with organizational culture. As a consequence, the powerful arrangement of 'sex', 'gender', and 'sexuality' is not a subject of organizational change.

To secure the economic bottom line is one of the main goals for a corporation, but, from an equality and inclusion perspective, the CoCs show that their interest is primarily in the business case of DM for all forms of relationships. Being inclusive in such a context is largely related to preventing the organization from any kind of—mostly financial—damage. With regard to the presence of 'sex' and 'gender' alongside the near-absence of 'sexual orientation' and, in particular, the absence of a reference to gay, lesbian, queer, and so on, sexual relationships, the CoCs constitute that only a heteronormative structure can contribute to the business case of DM. In terms of relationships, then, the corporations' interest in inclusion goes only as far as the point at which the bottom line can be secured.

This is also the case when it comes to laws, regulations, principles, and policies. The CoCs make clear that compliance is imperative in order to avoid negative consequences for the business. For this reason, the relevant regulations are defined very well. Compared to this, values such as 'fairness', 'integrity', 'respect', 'trust' and 'acting ethically', and 'responsibility', which should build the cultural and moral basis for action, remain in the texts as a state of common sense. From a queer perspective, this is a core issue. Whereas laws and so on are results of societal negotiations, and organizational decisions connected with sanctions are considered as binding, values are indicators of normative orientations and, therefore, much more contested. For example, we have to ask how fairness is related to justice (e.g. Fraser 2008); what does integrity and acting ethically mean when dealing with non-conforming gender identities? How can trust be built under hetero- and cisnormative structures and processes, and what does responsibility mean for an inclusive organization? In addition, values not connected with an idea of inclusion and self-reflection, such as 'trust' and 'responsibility', define the cultural frame only for 'fitting' and 'passing', which foster modes of assimilation in a homonormative way.

In relation to the question of how far companies connect 'sex', 'gender', and 'sexuality' with other issues in their CoC, the data show that, besides the association of 'sex', 'gender', and 'sexuality' and their relationship with risk, such connections are rare. Explanations of what a positive working climate, security, and health mean in terms of a diversity of sex–gender and sexuality would foster a more inclusive approach.

To sum up: our analysis of CoCs shows that laws and regulations, as well as societal movements with their negotiations on norms, have an influence on organizations. But within the CoCs, the companies barely produce manifestations of non-normative, alternative constructions of 'sex', 'gender', and 'sexuality'. According to their CoCs, the corporations still seem to be far from a relational perspective on 'gender–sex–sexual orientation' and a non-hetero- and cisnormative approach. Although some of the CoCs do mention 'gender identity', 'gender expression', and 'sexual identity', their situatedness shows no transfer to organizational life. In addition, the interconnectedness of 'sex', 'gender', and 'sexuality', and the powerful effects of this connection, remain hidden. From this perspective, CoCs are a means of enforcing the organizational rules and of establishing the predictability of employees' behaviour in reproducing hetero- and cisnormative power relations.

Conclusion

From a queer perspective, what does it mean to be an anti-discrimination and inclusive organization, which does not reproduce hetero- and cisnormative structures? And what is required in order to become such an organization? Although the analysis shows that the corporations more or less uphold hetero- and cisnormative structures in their CoCs by not addressing the powerful effects of hetero- and cisnormativity, the CoCs also offer a transformational potential. For example, there are possibilities for exemplifying the connections between hetero- and cisnormative structures and processes in descriptions of situations where organizational members have to act in a certain way to fulfil the requirements of the CoC. It could also be shown how non-normative gender expression can be handled within the organization, or which problems, for heterosexuals and LGBTIQ,[8] arise from gender norms. There are some further challenges for the practice of DM in dealing with the entanglement of 'sex', 'gender' and 'sexuality' and the intersections with other social categories, such as, for example, controversies in terms of LGBTIQ's rights and religion, or dealing with multi-discrimination such as the 'lesbian double gazed class ceiling' (Miles 2008). From a queer perspective it is therefore important that organizations disclose their knowledge on normative constructions when defining their normative orientations in the CoC. This could help to make visible the possibilities for those agencies aiming for inclusion.

With regard to organizational discourse, queer analysis makes it possible to show how the powerful normative connection between 'sex', 'gender', and 'sexuality' is oftentimes neglected. As a consequence, when organizational research deals with the discrimination of queer employees, it reduces them to sexual objects by referring only to sexual orientation, but making no reference to gender and sexual diversity beyond the norm. Queer-oriented analyses have the potential to make visible the idea that heterosexuality is not addressed as the norm explicitly, but reproduced performatively by the display and presentation of couples/gendered pairs in the workplace. In addition, with its focus on exploitative relations, queer perspectives are not only restricted to the individual level but include societal inequalities (classism, racism, intersectionalities, etc.), which are reproduced in organizations. Queer notions also have the power to defer the organizational discourse as they shift the perspective from 'sex', 'gender', and 'sexual orientation' to 'gender identities' and 'gender expressions', as well as to 'sexual identities' and 'sexual expressions'. Thus, organizational analyses with such stances of deferral do not only break the silence and bring 'the others', who have been rendered invisible, into the centre of the discussion, but also open up space for new and more inclusive organizational practices by addressing hetero- and cisnormativity and their excluding effects.

By fuelling the DM discourse with critical perspectives, scholars and practitioners can search for knowledge, resources, and networks for deconstructing and destabilizing hetero- and cisnormativity. By reflecting and answering the following questions, for example, they can open a door to a deferral of the existing DM discourse: Where and how have I come across the concept of hetero- and cisnormativity in research, organizational practices, and private life? How does hetero- and cisnormativity affect my research methodologically and empirically? How does it influence organizational

---

[8] LGBTIQ = lesbians, gays, bisexuals and transgender, intersexuals, queers.

practices in my context? Where do I experience limits caused by hetero- and cisnormativity. And, last but not least, if I have found a way to overcome hetero- and cisnormativity in my field, what strategy can I recommend to my colleagues?

REFERENCES

Ahmed, S. (2006). *Queer Phenomenology: Orientations, Objects, Others*. Durham, NC: Duke University Press.

Bauer, G. R., Hammond, R., Travers, R., Kaay, M., Hohenadel, K., and Boyce, M.(2009). 'I don't think this is theoretical; this is our lives': how erasure impacts health care for transgender people. *Journal of the Association of Nurses in AIDS Care*, 20(5): 348–61.

Bell, J. M. and Hartmann, D. (2007). Diversity in everyday discourse: the cultural ambiguities and consequences of 'happy talk'. *American Sociological Review*, 72(6): 895–914.

Bendl, R., Fleischmann, A., and Hofmann, R. (2009). Queer theory and diversity management: reading codes of conduct from a queer perspective. *Journal of Management and Organization*, 15(5): 625–38.

Bendl, R., Fleischmann, A., and Walenta, C. (2008). Diversity management discourse meets queer theory. *Gender in Management: An International Journal*, 23(6): 382–94.

Berlant, L. and Warner, M. (1998). Sex in public. *Critical Inquiry*, 24(2): 547–66.

Binnie, J. (2010). Queer theory, neoliberalism and urban governance. In R. Leckex and K. Brooks (eds.), *Queer Theory: Law, Culture, Empire*. Abingdon: Routledge, 21–36.

Bowring, M. and Brewis, J. (2009). Truth and consequences: managing lesbian and gay identity in the Canadian workplace. *Equal Opportunities International*, 28(5): 361–77.

Brewis, J., Tyler, M., and Mills, A. (2014). Sexuality and organizational analysis—30 years on: editorial introduction. *Organization*, 21(3): 305–11.

Butler, J. (1990). *Gender Trouble: Feminism and the Subversion of Identity*. London: Routledge.

Butler, J. (1993). *Bodies That Matter: On the Discursive Limits of 'Sex'*. New York: Routledge.

Chapman, D. and Gedro, J. (2009). Queering the HRD curriculum: preparing students for success in the diverse workforce. *Advances in Developing Human Resources*, 11(1): 95–108.

Christiansen, T. J. and Just, S. N. (2012). Regularities of diversity discourse: address, categorization, and invitation. *Journal of Management & Organization*, 18(3): 398–411.

Colgan, F. and Rumens, N. (2015). Understanding sexual orientation at work: Introduction. In F. Colgan and N. Rumens (eds.), *Sexual Orientation at Work: Contemporary Issues and Perspectives*. New York: Routledge, 1–27.

Creed, D. and Scully, M. (2000). Songs of ourselves: employees' deployment of social identity in workplace encounters. *Journal of Management Inquiry*, 9(4): 391–412.

Crenshaw, K. (1991). Mapping the margins: intersectionality, identity politics, and violence against women of color. *Stanford Law Review*, 43(6): 1241–99.

De Lauretis, T. (1991). Queer Theory: Lesbian and Gay Sexualities. Special issue of *Differences: A Journal of Feminist Cultural Studies*, 3(2).

Diedrich, A., Eriksson-Zetterquist, U., Ewertsson, L., Hagberg, J., Hallin, A., Lavén, F., Lindberg, K., Raviola, E., Rindzeviciute, E., and Walter, L. (2013). *Exploring the Performativity Turn in Management Studies*. Gothenburg Research Institute, GRI-rapport 2013:2. Available at: <https://www.academia.edu/4782559/Exploring_the_Performativity_Turn_in_Management_Studies> (accessed 28 August 2014).

Duberman, M. (1994): *Stonewall*. New York: Plume.

Duggan, L. (2003). *The Twilight of Equality? Neoliberalism, Cultural Politics, and the Attack on Democracy.* Boston, MA: Beacon Press.

Farrell, H. and Farrell, B. J. (1998). The language of business codes of ethics: implications of knowledge and power. *Journal of Business Ethics*, 17(6): 587.

Foucault, M. (1978). *Dispositive der Macht. Über Sexualität, Wissen und Wahrheit.* Berlin: Merve.

Foucault, M. (1979) [1976]. *The History of Sexuality*, vol. 1: *An Introduction.* London: Viking.

Foucault, M. (2010). *The Government of Self and Others: Lectures at the Collège de France 1982–1983*, ed. Arnold I. Davidson, tr. Graham Burchell. New York: Palgrave Macmillan.

Fraser, N. (2008). *Scales of Justice: Reimagining Political Space in a Globalizing World.* Cambridge: Polity Press.

Gilman, S. C. (2005). Ethics codes and codes of conduct as tools for promoting an ethical and professional public service: comparative Successes and Lessons. Available at: <http://www.oecd.org/mena/governance/35521418.pdf> (accessed 28 August 2014).

Graham, M. (2010). Method matters: ethnography and materiality. In K. Browne and C. Nash (eds.), *Queer Methods and Methodologies.* Farnham: Ashgate, 183–194.

Halberstam, J. (1998). *Female Masculinity.* Durham, NC: Duke University Press.

Halberstam, J., Muñoz, J. E., and Eng, D. L. (eds.) (2005). What's queer about queer studies now? *Social Text*, 84/85.

Hall, D. E. and Jagose, A. (2013). Introduction. In D. Hall and A. Jagose (eds.), *The Routledge Queer Studies Reader.* Abingdon: Routledge, xiv–xx.

Hearn, J., Sheppard, D. L., Tancred-Sheriff, P., and Burrell, G. (eds.) (1989). *The Sexuality of Organization.* London: Sage.

Hofmann, R. (2014). Organisationen verändern Geschlechterverhältnisse?! Queer-theoretische Perspektiven für eine geschlechtergerechte Entwicklung von Organisationen. In M. Funder (ed.), *The Gender Cage—Revisited. Handbuch zur Organisations- und Geschlechterforschung.* Baden-Baden and Mannheim: Nomos, 387–410.

Jackson, S. (2006). Interchanges: gender, sexuality and heterosexuality: the complexity (and limits) of heteronormativity. *Feminist Theory*, 7(1): 105–21.

Jagose, A. (1997). *Queer Theory: An Introduction.* New York: New York University Press.

Just, S. N. and Christiansen, T. (2012). Doing diversity: text–audience agency and rhetorical alternatives. *Communication Theory*, 22: 319–37.

Konrad, A. M., Prasad, P., and Pringle, J. K. (2006). *Handbook of Workplace Diversity.* London: Sage.

Kulpa, R. and Mizielińska, J. (eds.) (2011). *De-Centering Western Sexualities.* Farnham and Burlington: Ashgate.

Lee, H., Learmonth, M., and Harding, N. (2008). Queer(y)ing public administration. *Public Administration*, 86(1): 149–67.

Lewis, A. P. (2009). Discourses of change: policing, sexuality, and organizational culture. *Quantitative Research in Organizations and Management*, 4(3): 208–30.

Linstead, S. and Pullen, A. (2006). Gender as multiplicity: desire, displacement, difference and dispersion. *Human Relations*, 5(9): 1287–310.

Lorber, J. (1995). *Paradoxes of Gender.* New Haven, CT, and London: Yale University Press.

Lorber, J. (1996). Beyond the binaries: depolarizing the categories of sex, sexuality, and gender. *Sociological Inquiry*, 66(2): 143–59.

Martin, P. Y. and Collison, D. L. (2000). Gender and sexuality in organizations. In M. M. Ferree, J. Lorber, and B. B. Hess (eds.), *Revisioning Gender.* Walnut Creek, CA: AltaMira Press, 285–310.

Mesquita, S., Wiedlack, M. K., and Lasthofer, K. (2013). *Import-Export-Transport: Queer Theory, Queer Critique and Activism in Motion*. Vienna: Zaglossus.

Metcalfe, B. D. and Woodhams, C. (2008). Guest editorial: critical perspectives on diversity and equality management. *Gender in Management*, 23(6): 1754–2413.

Miles, N. (2008). *The Double-Glazed Ceiling: Lesbians in the Workplace*. London: Stonewall.

Mkono, M. (2010). An analysis of Zimbabwean hotel managers' perspective on workforce diversity. *Tourism and Hospitality Research*, 10(4): 301–10.

Mor Barak, M. E. (2011). *Managing Diversity: Toward a Globally Inclusive Workplace*. London: Sage.

Neal, M. (2010). When Arab-expatriate relations work well. *Team Performance Management*, 16(5/6): 242–66.

OECD (Organisation of Economic Co-operation and Development) (2001). Codes of Corporate Conduct: Expanded Review of their Contents. OECD Working Papers on International Investment, 2001/06, OECD Publishing. Available at: <http://dx.doi.org/10.1787/206157234626> (accessed 19 August 2014).

Parker, M. (2001). Fucking management: queer, theory and reflexivity. *Ephemera*, 1(1): 36–53.

Parker, M. (2002). Queering management and organization. *Gender, Work and Organization*, 9(2): 146–66.

Pelfrey, S. and Peacock, E. (1991). Ethical codes of conduct are improving. *Business Forum*, 16(2): 14–17.

Pringle, J. K. (2008). Gender in management: theorizing gender as heterogender. *British Journal of Management*, 19(s1): S110–S119.

Rich, A. (1980). Compulsory heterosexuality and lesbian existence. *Signs: Women: Sex and Sexuality*, 5(4): 631–60.

Rubin, G. S. (1975). The traffic in women: notes on the 'political economy' of sex. In R. Reiter (ed.), *Toward an Anthropology of Women*. New York: Monthly Review Press, 157–210.

Rubin, G. S. (1984). Thinking sex: notes for a radical theory of the politics of sexuality. In C. S. Vance (ed.), *Pleasure and Danger: Exploring Female Sexuality*. Boston, MA: Routledge, 267–319.

Sardy, R. (2001). Queering Las Vegas: personal experience stories of gay men. *Management*, 4(3): 175–83.

Schilt, K. and Connell, C. (2007). Do workplace gender transitions make gender trouble? *Gender, Work and Organization*, 14(6): 597–618.

Schilt, K. and Westbrook, L. (2009). Doing gender, doing heteronormativity: 'gender normals', transgender people, and the social maintenance of heterosexuality. *Gender & Society* 23(4): 440–64.

Sedgwick, E. K. (1985). *Between Man: English Literature and Male Homosocial Desire*. New York: Columbia University Press.

Sedgwick, E. K. (1991). *Epistemology of the Closet*. Berkeley, CA: University of California Press.

Seidman, S. (1997). *Difference Troubles*. Cambridge: Cambridge University Press.

Sharma, J. (2009). Reflections on the construction of heteronormativity. *Development*, 52(1): 52–5.

Thanem, T. (2011): Embodying transgender in studies of gender, work and organization. In E. Jeanes, D. Knights, and M. P. Yancey (eds.), *Gender, Work and Organization Handbook*. Oxford: Wiley, 199–204.

Tyler, M. and Cohen, L. (2008). Management in/as comic relief: queer theory and gender performativity in *The Office*. *Gender, Work and Organization*, 15(2): 113–32.

Ward, J. and Winstanley, D. (2003). The absent presence: negative space within discourse and the construction of minority sexual identity in the workplace. *Human Relations*, 56(10): 1255–90.

Warner, M. (1993): *Fear of a Queer Planet: Queer Politics and Social Theory*. Minneapolis, MN: University of Minnesota Press.

Winnubst, S. (2012). The queer thing about neoliberal pleasure: a Foucauldian warning. *Foucault Studies*, 14: 79–97.

Zanoni, P., Janssens, M., Benschop, Y., and Nkomo, S. M. (2010). Guest editorial: unpacking diversity, grasping inequality: rethinking difference through critical perspectives. *Organization*, 17(1): 9–29.

CHAPTER 10

AMBIGUOUS DIVERSITIES

Practices and Perceptions of Diversity Management

ANNETTE RISBERG AND SINE NØRHOLM JUST

INTRODUCTION: IS AMBIGUITY GOOD FOR DIVERSITY?

DIVERSITY management (DM) is a multifarious academic and practical field; there are many different theoretical rationales and principles for engaging with diversity and many different practical takes on DM. One could argue that it is only fitting for a field that explicitly aims at enhancing organizational diversity to be diverse in and of itself; however, the literature tends to speak of the multiplicities as ambiguities and to view them as problems rather than resources (Liff and Wajcman 1996; Nkomo and Cox 1996; Dick and Cassell 2002). Sidestepping the discussion of whether the theoretical and practical ambiguities of DM are inherently good or bad, we begin from the assumption that ambiguity is an unavoidable and constitutive condition of organizational practices, generally, and practices of diversity, specifically. Our main argument, then, is that the value of ambiguity for DM cannot be assigned *a priori*; it must be studied in and through managerial practices and employee perceptions. Does ambiguity lead to better or worse conditions for practising diversity? This is a question to be studied in its specific instantiations, not to be settled as a matter of scholarly sentiment or managerial temperament.

In this chapter we offer a framework for such study, exploring various expressions of ambiguity in theoretical terms and presenting empirical illustrations of how ambiguities are practised and perceived by managers and employees. We suggest three categories of ambiguity which may be used to express and analyse diversity in organizations: strategic ambiguity, contradiction, and ambivalence. Furthermore, we exemplify each through an illustrative case study (conducted by one of the authors, Annette Risberg) of diversity practices in a Swedish municipality. The case study was conducted between April 2008 and December 2010 and based on observations (of daily work, events, training, and diversity and equality committees' meetings), semi- and unstructured interviews, and internal material (e.g. annual reports, diversity plans, personnel surveys). All observation notes and interviews have been transcribed and the texts have been analysed to identify common and particular themes. In this chapter, the results of the analysis will be used to illustrate our theoretical arguments (see Stake 1994 for a discussion of illustrative cases).

While our main purpose is to present a conceptual and methodological framework that begins from the assumption of ambiguity as an unavoidable condition of DM, we also wish to suggest whether and how expressions of ambiguity may foster new and more inclusive practices of diversity. That is, given the constitutive condition of ambiguity, which expressions of it are likely to produce more positive effects and which might tend to be detrimental to diversity? In order to realize these goals, we substantiate the claim that ambiguities are inherent in the theory and practice of DM, before moving on to presenting and illustrating our conceptual framework for investigating expressions of ambiguity. In a final section, we discuss the implications of our framework (and our illustrative findings) for future studies and practices of DM.

Ambiguities of Diversity Management

The field of DM is riddled with ambiguities. What is, for instance, the rationale behind diversity initiatives: the need to comply with legal requirements, the desire to uphold moral standards, or the endeavour to achieve economic goals (e.g. Thomas 1992; Özbilgin et al. 2008; Mensi-Klarbach 2012)? While these three reasons are not mutually exclusive, they point to quite different goals and standards for measuring success and, hence, may lead to considerable uncertainty about which specific practices to pursue. At the conceptual level, DM straddles a number of binaries: difference/equality, structure/actor, group/individual, and problem/potential (Cox and Blake 1992; Liff 1997; Litvin 1997; Lorbiecki and Jack 2000). Here, the individual scholar or manager is seemingly faced with a choice: For instance, should diversity initiatives aim at promoting difference or at ensuring equality? Or could they actually do both? These basic ambiguities foster a practical problem of choosing between various approaches that either pertain to affirmative action (AA) or equal opportunities (EO) (Liff and Wajcman 1996; Holvino and Kamp 2009). Is it necessary to opt for one or the other? Or is it possible to treat some groups/individuals in special ways while ensuring that everyone has the same chances? Could it even be said that we need to treat people differently in order to give them the same treatment? Here, we will briefly unfold how the ambiguities of DM are usually handled or smoothed over, and then go on to discuss the possibility of viewing the ambiguities as not only inherent to DM, but potentially beneficial to it. This entails a reconceptualization of ambiguity and a presentation of its analytical implications, resulting in our suggested framework for studying ambiguous diversity.

The ambiguities of DM are often solved by opting for one of the rationales, one side of the binaries, and one of the practical approaches. A perfect duality may be achieved by placing the rationales of legal and moral responsibility in one camp and the rationale of economic potential in another, as the first two view diversity efforts as an obligation whereas the last sees it as an opportunity (Risberg and Søderberg 2008). Thus, one camp emphasizes the legal or moral commitment of organizations to protect and enhance differences. This camp suggests that organizations can become more diverse by using AA programmes to reduce institutional and structural barriers that hinder certain social groups from gaining access to and thriving within organizations (see, e.g., Benschop 2001; Ahmed 2007; Ahonen et al. 2014). The other camp deals with the 'business case' for DM: how organizations can gain economic benefits by promoting equality and focusing on the potentials of individual actors through EO initiatives (see, e.g., Gilbert, Stead, and Ivancevich 1999; Friday and Friday 2003; Maxwell 2004). Thus, the tensions of DM can seemingly be solved by simply placing oneself in one camp or the other.

However, there is an increasing and fundamental recognition within (studies of) DM that this route is untenable; instead, it is suggested than one must engage with the ambiguities that arise from combining various rationales and approaches (Syed and Kramar 2009; Tomlinson and Schwabenland 2010; Danowitz and Hanappi-Egger 2012). In practice, however, the need for clarity all too often wins out, leading companies to focus on, for instance, including more women as a group through one initiative (i.e. quotas) and developing the talent of individual women in another initiative (i.e. talent management or mentor schemes) without regard for the ambiguities that may arise from the combination of initiatives. The ambiguity of DM could, for instance, appear in the following way: when women as a group are seen as in need of help to gain access to the upper echelons of organizations, this might rub off on the subsequent careers of individual women. Promotion of a woman could, in this context, be perceived as a result of organizational support rather than of personal achievements. Conversely, the inclusion of women might not take the form of a full-blown AA scheme (i.e. quotas) for fear of neglecting the potentials and competencies of the individual (i.e. not choosing 'the best person for the job'). The result of not addressing these and similar tensions would be that neither collective initiatives to promote women as a group, nor plans to develop individual women's careers are implemented fully; the organization, as well as the women involved, remain caught in a double-bind between group characteristics and individual propensities (Tienari and Nentwich 2012: 116–17).

The problems of DM, then, may be said to arise from the way the ambiguities are predominantly handled rather than from the ambiguities themselves. This has led to calls for more systematic or comprehensive approaches that allow each specific diversity initiative to be aligned with, and embedded within, an overarching company strategy. DM, on this count, is first and foremost a matter of general organizational cultural change and only subsequently a question of specific organizational practices (Gilbert, Stead, and Ivancevich 1999).

Potentials of Ambiguity: A Framework for Studying Ambiguous Diversity

We suggest that embracing the ambiguity of DM may facilitate the cultural change that is needed if specific diversity initiatives are to succeed. Thus, we seek to radicalize the burgeoning recognition that ambiguity is not only unavoidable, but also necessary for successful DM. Diversity is inherently ambiguous, and one misses the chance for creating more inclusive practices, more room for the expression of difference, if one does not embrace, perhaps even seek to enhance, this ambiguity. Thinking of ambiguity as a potentially productive force, however, demands a reconsideration of the concept that moves beyond its common-sense and usually negative connotations of equivocation and misunderstanding. Thus, we will now turn to conceptualizing ambiguity and setting up an analytical framework for the study of ambiguous diversity practices. The remaining issue of whether and how diversity practices may actually prosper from ambiguity is partially addressed in and through the illustrative case, but also taken up for more direct consideration in our concluding discussion.

Ambiguity may be defined as a state of indeterminateness or plurality. If a situation, practice, or utterance is ambiguous, it does not have a single specified meaning, but is open to various interpretations. The concept of ambiguity is itself ambiguous: there are many different definitions and meanings of ambiguity in the relevant literature (Risberg 1999). As we have seen, ambiguity is often perceived to be a problematic or abnormal situation in the literature on DM, and this also goes for some of the scholarly discussions of the concept as such: an ambiguous situation may be viewed as something that should be avoided or resolved (e.g. McCaskey 1982; Thomas 1988). However, we begin from the assumption that ambiguity is a constitutive feature of human interaction (Martin 1992; Meyerson 1994). Noting that ambiguity is inherent to discursive and social practices also means moving beyond the issue of whether ambiguity is good or bad; in itself, ambiguity is neither. It is, instead, a non-normative condition of possibility that may have both positive and negative effects through the concrete expressions and practices it elicits. Thus, the analytical task is to determine the forms and effects of ambiguous expressions, and we aim to provide a framework for studying and determining these.

We may begin to grasp the potential of ambiguity as a means of expressing and fostering diversity by noting its affinity with the concept of 'queerness', which points to the possibility of performing existing norms differently, of queering them through '… an attitude of unceasing disruptiveness' as Parker (2002: 148) puts it. Queerness, then, is a theoretical and political stance that refuses to accept reified meanings and identity positions, insists on the contingent and constructed—ambiguous—nature of what is currently taken for granted, and seeks out potentials for alternative meanings and practices (Butler 1993: 19). Although it is important to note the link between queer theory and an activist stance on (non-heterosexual) identity politics, we follow Rand's (2008) lead in detaching queerness from specific identity positions and highlighting its general 'undecidability'. Rather than being a quality of certain individuals and groups, queerness is a characteristic of sense-making per se; it is 'the lack of a necessary or predictable relation between an intending agent and the effects of an action' (Rand 2008: 298). Or, to put it bluntly, queerness is ambiguity.

Relating ambiguity to queerness in Rand's sense of the word brings us closer to an understanding of the potential of ambiguity. Queer or ambiguous expressions have many possible meanings, rather than one intended and/or predictable effect; they hold up the possibility of indeterminate agency, of repeating existing and recognizable norms with a difference, of bringing about change from within. In order to unpack this claim, let us look closer at the concept of agency and its link to ambiguity. Here, the question of how individual expressions of identity relate to general norms takes centre stage; according to the theory of performativity, to which the notion of queerness is intimately connected, individual performances of identity are recognizable because they rely on and reproduce a limited number of existing norms. Yet the norms do not exist outside of their expression and, hence, depend upon their reiteration for continued effect (Butler 1993). This is what creates the possibility of queerness, of repetition with a difference, or, in Allen's (1998: 463) words: 'the very fact that it is *necessary* for norms to be reiterated or cited by individuals in order for them to maintain their efficacy indicates that we are never completely determined by them'. From this perspective, blatant rejections or negations of existing norms will not result in recognizable expressions of identity, but more subtle, nuanced, ambiguous expressions offer agential potentials whose effects are not given, whose resulting subject positions are not pre-determined.

The potential of ambiguity, understood as a 'queer form', is that it holds indeterminate agency and, hence, may rework the relationships between existing norms and their expressions, opening up new opportunities for performing identity within given social contexts. In order to explore whether and how this potential may be realized, we introduce three ambiguous forms whose ability to enhance, but also hinder, diversity are explored through our illustrative analyses: strategic ambiguity, contradiction, and ambivalence.

Strategic Ambiguity

The notion of strategic ambiguity was first presented by Eisenberg (1984) as a strategic use of communication to enable multiple interpretations. Davenport and Leitch (2005) call this a ' "space" in which multiple interpretations by stakeholders are enabled and to which multiple stakeholder responses are possible' (Davenport and Leitch 2005: 1604). Eisenberg (1984) established three central characteristics of strategic ambiguity: (1) it promotes unified diversity; (2) it facilitates organizational change; and (3) it amplifies existing resource attribution and preserves privileged positions. For our purpose, the first two characteristics are particularly relevant.

Strategic ambiguity, the proponents of this form assert, may be used as a way to attain organizational goals by reaching unified diversity. Thus, leaving messages open to multiple interpretations may allow people to hold different views or opinions while continuing to work towards a common or overall goal. When strategic ambiguity is used, for example, in organizational goals and mission statements, 'it is... not the case that people are moved toward the same views (in any objectively verifiable sense) but rather that the ambiguous statement of core values allows them to maintain individual interpretations while at the same time believing that they are in agreement' (Eisenberg 1984: 231). The main argument for the potential positive effects of strategic ambiguity is that it allows for creativity and flexibility. Thus, strategic ambiguity may enhance the possibility of diversity within organizations generally speaking, but can also be linked directly to DM, in that it may be a device for using the ambiguities that are built into the concept of diversity productively. It is likely that contesting views towards diversity are held in the organization. It may be that diversity is understood differently by different individuals or in different organizational units, or even that it is resisted. If used strategically, such ambiguity may be to the advantage of the organization as well as its members, leading not to resistance, but to the possibility of working together while maintaining—perhaps, even promoting—difference.

Strategic ambiguity, then, tends to be used in organizational missions, goals, values, and plans enabling conflicting interpretations to exist simultaneously and allowing diverse groups to work together (Eisenberg and Witten 1987). Eisenberg (1984) posits that concretely stated organizational goals are ineffective; ambiguously stated goals, missions, and plans, on the contrary, foster the productive existence of multiple viewpoints in an organization. He further claims that it is 'a political necessity to engage in strategic ambiguity so that different constituent groups may apply different interpretations to the symbol' (Eisenberg 1984: 231). Research on strategic ambiguity finds that it is a valuable political resource, as it enables the mobilization of collective action and change where organizational constituents hold different interests (Jarzabkowski, Sillince, and Shaw 2010), and it could thus be useful in implementing diversity in organizations. Diversity and equality work in organizations is not always accepted by the organizational actors, and too clear and open goals may lead to the mobilization of dissent (Eisenberg 1984; Davenport and Leitch 2005). On the other hand, ambiguous statements could enable people to agree on the symbol of diversity even if they disagree on the specific means and ends of DM. Ambiguity, then, could be used strategically to foster agreement that diversity is something we should strive for without limiting specific interpretations of what it may mean. A typical example of this would be to write diversity policies in a general and abstract manner that allows the interpretation of what diversity is and how to achieve it to be negotiated locally by the involved stakeholders (Davenport and Leitch 2005). Specifically, statements such as 'we value diversity' or 'we see difference as an asset' are ambiguous enough to be open to different interpretations. For example, they could be seen as maintaining tensions between expressions of moral support for diversity and articulations of the economic benefits of diversity. Strategic ambiguity could also be used as a way to move diversity efforts forward or even redirect them without losing the sense of commonality and continuity; the symbol ('diversity') would remain the same, but its ambiguous expression allows for gradual change in its interpretation over time (Eisenberg 1984). For instance, the diversity categories that are in focus may vary over time, and by being strategically ambiguous in the general definition of diversity, the organization creates the possibility for shifting or new categories to be emphasized as the work moves along. A current practical example of this is the rising focus on lesbian, gay, bisexual, and transgender (LGBT) issues in many organizations' diversity work; the general definition of diversity usually remains the same, but the scope of the concept is broadened or earlier emphases (typically, gender and ethnicity) are downplayed or displaced.

Strategic ambiguity, however, is not only viewed as a positive resource: Abdallah and Langley (2014) discuss what they term the double edge of strategic ambiguity, pointing to the pitfalls as well as the potentials. Whereas strategic ambiguity may hold great potential, as Eisenberg points out and we have sought to illustrate, it may also cause confusion and even lead to what Denis and colleagues (2011) call escalating indecision. According to Abdallah and Langley (2014), the results depend on how the receiver of the message interprets it. They draw on de Certeau, presenting organizational members as consumers of strategy discourse who are free to 'creatively consume it in multiple and sometimes unexpected ways' (Abdallah and Langley 2014: 236). Individual readings may be productive and constructive or constraining and disabling. Abdallah and Langley conclude that strategic ambiguity does offer all the benefits laid out by Eisenberg (1984); in particular it may be very useful to launch new initiatives and to initiate change. Sooner or later, however, constraints are likely to (re)occur as the outcomes of divergent interpretations become clearer, but this does not mean that strategic ambiguity becomes less important, only that the strategic process of (dis)ambiguation enters another cycle.

Moving to our illustrative analysis, the diversity practices in our case organization exemplify how a lack of strategic ambiguity may have negative effects of less, rather than more, room for diversity. In the municipality, the diversity goals were very explicit and specific, often presented in terms of measurable key performance indicators (KPIs); they were non-ambiguous. A specific example is the stipulated political goal that the backgrounds of the employees in the organization should reflect the ratio of inhabitants with a foreign background in the municipality, or, on a more local level, that the number of male employees should increase in the kindergartens. These political goals proved to be difficult to put into practice at local organizational levels: because they were so specific, they actually became ambiguous in the sense that local managers could not work out how to use them locally. Here, the ambiguities were not strategic, but actually resulted from the intended clarity of the goals. As a consequence, unproductive ambiguities arose between clear goals and less distinct practices; the goals were intended to promote structural diversity, but managers simply did not know how to move from structure to actor—they did not feel empowered to adapt the goals to their own contexts, nor to deal with individual cases on an individual level.

The relationship between organizational goals and practices was ambiguous in a number of ways, but none of them were very productive, and some had rather negative consequences. One could say that the goals were both too clear and too ambiguous at the same time, or to put it differently, strategic ambiguity was not in place. First, and somewhat surprisingly, the very specific goals were barriers to the practice of diversity; they did not create room for local and individual interpretations and creative solutions. That is, the goals were not expressions of strategic ambiguity in the positive sense. Second, the specific diversity goals were sometimes misinterpreted in an even more specific direction than intended; this shows that employees, because of the seeming clarity of the goals, were seeking the 'official' interpretation (which they sometimes got wrong) rather than promoting the interpretation that would be most productive in their own work. For example, one unit with a focus on community work interpreted the political goal of reflecting the backgrounds of the inhabitants as if the unit had to reflect the backgrounds of the inhabitants in the neighbourhood that was specifically targeted by the community work. A dominant ethnic group in the neighbourhood had low levels of education and some individuals were even illiterate. The unit manager asked how he could find enough qualified job candidates within that ethnic group to meet the goal. One possible answer to this problem could be to initiate special educational programmes for the relevant groups, yet such bridges between structural inequalities and context-specific solutions were not made. Thus, the goals may have been operationalized and, to some extent, realized, but employees carried them out mechanically and/or grudgingly, rather than practising them in a personalized and creative manner. Indeed, the very focus on being able to measure diversity was at the heart of the problem; a measure is a number that can be reached once and for all, a 'head count' rather than a dynamic, open-ended practice. In sum, one could say that the goals became barriers for all forms of non-measurable diversity work, and many managers did not know how to conduct diversity initiatives in the required direct and directly measurable way.

As our illustrative case shows, too clear diversity goals may work as an impediment for the goals' potential to be fulfilled. In large organizations (such as our municipality, with approximately 20,000 employees), it will never be possible to agree on one understanding of diversity nor to find diversity goals that can apply equally to all operations. Instead, strategic ambiguity may be a way to enable diversity in organizations where different interpretations of diversity occur, but also where resistance against diversity exists. It could be used initially to launch the notion of diversity in the organizations, but as the diversity work proceeds, at least part of the work might call for less ambiguous discourse, which could lead to disambiguation, but also to new rounds of strategically ambiguous expressions. Rather than having a political goal point out a certain number of a certain category, the municipal political goal could have been more abstract; that is, more ambiguous, allowing for the local organizational units to provide their own interpretations of the overall goal. Likewise, the KPIs could have been replaced by more practical suggestions of how to become a more equal and inclusive organization.

Contradiction

Broadly speaking, contradiction, as conceptualized by Renegar and Sowards (2009), is linguistic opacity; Renegar and Sowards suggest (2009: 2) that what may be seen as an irreconcilable clash between two opposed principles, positions, or practices could, in fact, '...foster agency in social, political, and collaborative contexts'. 'Rather than condemning the rhetorical practice of contradiction', they argue, we should view it as 'a strategic and agential orientation that enables marginalized perspectives to find voice' (Renegar and Sowards 2009: 3). Contradiction, then, is here conceptualized as a way of introducing a new or subversive idea or position by relating it with its opposite. Applying this conceptualization to DM suggests that we can play 'diversity' and 'management' against each other. Some scholars (most notably Kirby and Harter 2001) have argued that DM is, in some respects, a contradiction in terms, since 'management' always implies some form of regulation, control, and/or ordering that can hardly be seen as conducive for diversity. Whereas Kirby and Harter (and other scholars that point to the same tension, e.g., Bendl, Fleischmann, and Hoffman 2009) are critical towards the diversifying potential of (any form of) management, Renegar and Sowards' take on contradiction suggests that the very strain between the two terms of 'diversity', on the one hand, and 'management', on the other, could also become a strategy for bringing diversity into the field of management, for enabling a discussion and a possible change process that would otherwise be inconceivable. While the current tendency may be for management to overrule diversity, the contradictory relationship works both ways, so to speak, and is not necessarily to the disadvantage of diversity. Subversive groups or individuals, then, could use an initially delimiting contradiction as a means of voicing their own views and bringing more diversity into management and organizations.

Whereas contradictions are usually seen as logical dead ends or fallacies, they can be used productively as an ambiguous form that is particularly suited for overcoming dichotomies and limited choices. That is, contradiction may be used as a starting point for thinking about alternatives to the two seemingly exclusive and exclusionary options or for discovering ways of merging the opposites (Renegar and Sowards 2009). Moving from the general articulation of DM to its underlying principles, this could, for instance, involve dissolution of the tendency to focus either on individuals or groups, EO or AA, the business case or the moral arguments. DM, it could be claimed, is all of these things at once, and while that may seem (indeed, be) conceptually messy, it is also helpful, since it creates the potential for new and unthought-of concepts and practices. Ultimately, the messier, more logically inconsistent the concept, the more potential for change and for forging new pathways. The conceptual contradictions of DM, then, could be seen as resources to be explored, rather than as obstacles to be overcome.

Moving from theory to practice, contradiction as a specific mode of articulating ambiguity may contribute positively to DM in two respects: first, it may help recover/uncover the social contradictions and conflicts of interest that DM, in a sense, sets out to unveil and address, but may end up obfuscating or even reproducing (Kersten 2000). Thus, DM with its claims to (establish) 'colour-blindness', 'gender equality', and the like may, in fact, blind itself to the persistent inequality of, and discrimination against, people who represent minorities within organizational settings. Saying 'we do not discriminate' does not (necessarily) do away with discrimination, and contradiction may be a particularly effective way of pointing to gaps between organizational talk (e.g. 'we value difference') and practices (e.g. upholding a homogenous workforce). Contradiction, then, can serve to raise awareness of the structural differences that DM initiatives leave intact and the conflicts of interest associated with these differences (e.g. male members of the organization might have to give up some privileges if 'gender equality' were to become rigorously enforced). Second, contradictions may not only serve as a means of promoting collective interests, but are also '... useful rhetorical tools for negotiating complex lives in a complicated world' (Renegar and Sowards 2009: 3) that may help individuals to construct and come to terms with their own multiple and strained identities. Thus, contradictions are apt tools for bringing in and acting out the intersectionalities that comprise one's (social) identity (Staunæs 2003); for instance, a female manager might describe herself as an 'insider–outsider' (which is, in specific rhetorical terms, an oxymoron, a condensed contradiction) and use this as a privileged position for analysing (and changing) the social setting (Naples 1996; see also the section 'Ambivalence' in this chapter).

It is not enough, however, to raise awareness if the identified problems are not dealt with; nor is it sufficient to point to intersectionalities if these are not given room to flourish. Our illustrative case will here be used to show how contradictions point to weaknesses in current diversity work, but will also show that the inability to deal with these weaknesses leads to ambiguity with a negative effect on the organization. In one of the organizational units of the municipality, much of the diversity work was delegated to a diversity committee responsible for coordinating the diversity work. Thus, the diversity committee should serve as an engine for this work, and at the same time act as an expert. Moreover, the committee was expected to initiate and execute the active diversity work in each department. To put it differently, the members of the committee were given the responsibility for the diversity work in the organizational unit. At the same time, however, the members of the committee all had ordinary full-time jobs elsewhere in the unit. While the committee was given a lot of responsibility, it had neither the resources nor the mandate to actually make decisions and plan for the diversity activities. For each and every activity, the committee members needed to request permission and, frequently, resources. And often the answer was no, you may not do this. There was a clear contradiction between what the committee was meant to do and what it could do. When the committee members pointed out this contradiction to the management of the unit, the management failed to do anything about it. This led to stress and a feeling of despair among the committee members.

This example points to a negative consequence of ambiguity based on the fact that the organizational structures were not aligned with the way the diversity work was meant to be conducted. A conclusion is that, not surprisingly, managers need to create structures that enable the practices they want to promote; otherwise, the resulting ambiguity will be restrictive, rather than enabling the agency of individual employees. For instance, if diversity training is prioritized by the top management, they should also make sure that it is possible for the unit managers to train the personnel during work time without jeopardizing daily operations. The experienced discrepancy between the stipulated responsibilities of the diversity committee and its actual inability to act was contradictory, and while members of the committee were able to point this out, they could not use the contradiction productively. They could articulate the existence of structural barriers, but could not change them. On a more positive note, the employees' expressions of the contradiction might serve as a first awareness-raising initiative that could (if one accepts that the municipality is actually committed to diversity) eventually change the structures (or put the hypocrisy of the organization on display). What is more, the contradiction might allow for various decentralized actions; in a structurally complex organization such as the municipality, the diversity practices might be diverse themselves, leaving room to adapt the diversity work to local structures. While this does not help the specific diversity committee much in overcoming the contradiction between its nominal responsibilities and its actual resources, it suggests that the most important diversity work goes on at the specific sites where the diversity goals should be realized, rather than in a committee setting that is structurally and practically unable to implement the goals into the day-to-day operations of the municipality. Perhaps, then, a greater potential exists at the nexus of the overall goals and specific practices.

In sum, contradiction offers the possibility of negotiating tensions between identity and difference, of maintaining and using those tensions creatively, rather than dissolving them or having them fall on one side or the other of the contradictory pair(s). When the contradiction is one between articulated goals and structural realities, as in our case, individual (and collective) actors may not be able to do much more than point to the limitations of their own agencies. But even such limited criticism of (and, possibly, resistance to) the organizational 'powers that be' could create the initial impetus for reconfiguring the structures and relations of those powers.

Ambivalence

Renegar and Sowards's contradictions are primarily linked with a bottom-up or subversive approach, where marginalized groups can point out structural differences and discriminations and individuals can construct complex identities. In contrast, Eisenberg's strategic ambiguity has an instrumental top-down and possibly unethical flavour (Davenport and Leitch 2005: 1606), meaning that it is primarily a managerial tool for securing and maintaining 'unity in diversity'. Meyerson and Scully (1995) offer a strategy for expressing ambiguity that is positioned midway between bottom-up (and, perhaps, reformative) and top-down (possibly conservative) uses of ambiguity: ambivalence. Ambivalence, Meyerson and Scully suggest, enables 'tempered radicals' to identify with the organizations of which they are members, as well as with very different, perhaps opposed, groups, communities, and/or causes (Meyerson and Scully 1995: 588). The dual identity of ambivalence may enable organizational unity and diversity simultaneously, and provide a means for different individuals to not only enter organizational settings on their own terms, but also to diversify organizations from within.

In the context of DM, the position of 'tempered radicals' may be occupied by both diversity managers, who seek to diversify organizations through policies, strategies, and initiatives, and subjects of diversity, who live and breathe diversification every time they enter the organizational context. Both are 'change agents' who may use their professional and/or personal ambivalence (oftentimes diversity managers are themselves representatives of one minority group or another) as a means of overcoming resistance to change. Meyerson and Scully offer two main advantages of the ambivalent subject position, corresponding to two ways in which ambivalence may be advantageous to DM. First, the ambivalent subject position offers a more detailed account of and way of harnessing the insider–outsider position (or 'outsider within' in Meyerson and Scully's terms): 'While insider status provides access to opportunities for change, outsider status provides the detachment to recognize that there even is an issue or problem to work on' (Meyerson and Scully 1995: 589). The insider–outsider, then, may use his or her ambivalent position to advocate diversity (or, indeed, other kinds of organizational change) in a form that is recognizable to those who would otherwise not see a need for change or, indeed, be resistant to it. Second, the ambivalent stance of the tempered radical may act as a bridge between advocates of the status quo and advocates of more radical change, thus mediating between the various factions of the organization—and in so doing he or she can both be critical towards and in favour of more conservative and more radical positions (Meyerson and Scully 1995: 589). This provides a good starting point for sustainable diversification processes because it offers the possibility of reflecting upon all the various interests and positions of the organization, thereby setting goals upon which everyone can agree, and providing steps towards these goals that take their starting points not only in the dominant organizational consensus, but also in the existing opposition.

Let us turn to our illustrative case one last time to see how ambivalence can play out in an organizational setting. As mentioned, the municipality had an overly clear political goal regarding the reflection of the ethnic background of inhabitants. When middle managers attempted to fulfil this goal, and when organizational members tried to make sense of it, ambiguous interpretations arose that were turned into ambivalence by some middle managers, who thereby became tempered radicals. In their local interpretations, managers agreed with the goal as such, but they initially had difficulties in understanding how it should—and could—be fulfilled at the local level. As mentioned, the goal was sometimes interpreted as if employees with a foreign background had to be proportionally represented at each organizational level and in each unit, although this was not its original meaning, according to the politicians who drew up the goal. The meaning of the goal was thus ambiguous, and the local interpretations meant that it became a barrier to the work practices or caused frustration because it was difficult to fulfil. Some units, however, used this ambiguity productively instead of reducing it in unfruitful ways. One example was to make a local interpretation of the goal as it related to local operations. For instance, one of the local units doing community work aimed at developing a poor neighbourhood with a high degree of immigrant inhabitants. By employing people with many different backgrounds (educational, professional, national, religious)—instead of the type of backgrounds stipulated by the political goal—the employees of the unit developed innovative projects and solutions. For example, an immigrant man with a doctoral degree in nuclear physics worked with a project on immigrant role models for school pupils, and a woman with no formal training, but with a great deal of social work experience collaborated with real estate owners in the neighbourhood to improve the living conditions as well as the quality of the housing. The local manager said that it was due to the diverse background of people (as opposed to a more uniform group of employees trained as social workers who would normally do this kind of job) that the unit was very successful. This example points to ways in which ambivalence may lead to stronger agency and nuanced negotiations of identities.

At a more general level, some managers saw diversity as a specific resource to their operations, and this meant that they became more successful in achieving the diversity goals. However, in doing so, the managers applied a logic that was different from the dominant logic of the municipality—one closer to the business case than the moral case for diversity—even though the moral case was what had been officially sanctioned by the municipality. These managers became tempered radicals who espoused the official goals of the organization, but used alternative logics to make sense of them and/or found different practices to realize them. The ambivalent stance of these managers meant that they both took on more personal agency and became better able to realize organizational goals.

While it is arguably not the best solution that managers work on the basis of a logic that is different from that of the organization to achieve organizational goals, the example nevertheless points to the potentials of ambiguity in a general sense, and of ambivalence more specifically. When diversity is seen as a resource to the operations rather than a goal to be achieved, it becomes possible to maintain and promote diverse identities and different practices, to cultivate ambivalent stances to the benefit of the organization. This final illustration points to the potential of ambiguity for promoting diversity. Understood as an open-ended practice that allows individuals to maintain their ambivalence(s) towards the organization, while at the same time allowing the organization to prosper from the employees' precarious stances, ambiguity may create room for diversity as both a managerial tool and a liberating project. By being positioned in the middle of the other two strategies (and possibly drawing on both), ambivalence may seem to provide the best option for using ambiguity productively to enhance diversity in organizational settings. However, this does not mean that strategic ambiguity and contradictions cannot also become productive; rather, what is indicated is that all three forms need to be present—and be put to use by organizational members in various positions—if ambiguous expressions of diversity are to enable new and better practices of diversity.

Conclusion

DM is inherently ambiguous. Through our theoretical framework and empirical illustrations, we have suggested some of the ambiguous aspects of diversity and its management. We have also focused on the potentials of strategic ambiguity, contradiction, and ambivalence in terms of creating more room for diversity practices as related to the stated goals and existing structures of our case organization.

Strategic ambiguity seems to be a necessity in writing diversity goals, as too clear and specific goals leave little room for localized interpretations and actions. Diversity is contextual and must be understood within the organizational as well as societal context. Our case is an example of how the context of a large organization, with many different daily operations requiring employees with different competencies and backgrounds, affects how diversity can be understood and practised.

For DM to work, the overall organizational diversity policies and goals must be ambiguous to allow for local translations. In our case, we saw that the very specific goals, and especially the focus on measurability, often had adverse effects, particularly with regard to the limitations of what diversity might mean and what social categories might be included. In the municipality, diversity was mostly reduced to a question of ethnicity or gender, whereby other types of diversity, especially intersectionalities between diversity categories, were ignored.

Contradiction is probably unavoidable when diversity and its management are introduced in an organization; existing structures will usually present barriers to the suggested practices of (promoting) diversity. Our case has, however, illustrated that contradictions can have both positive and negative consequences. A contradiction can be the signal needed to raise awareness about inequalities and covert discrimination taking place in the organization. And pointing out a contradiction could become an opportunity for the organization to become more inclusive if it is willing to listen. Contradictions, then, may present opportunities for addressing existing tensions between stated goals of inclusion and existing structural limitations on individual agencies, but they must be harnessed by individuals as a means of raising awareness, and organizations must respond positively to the raised challenges if the potential is to be realized.

Ambivalence seems to be the expression of ambiguity with the greatest potential for creating positive effects because it allows the organizational members to negotiate their identities in and through practice. When organizational members act as tempered radicals, they turn ambiguities into resources which enable more diversity and allow for more benefits of diversity. Having said this, we would like to emphasize that ambivalence is unlikely to arise if other expressions of ambiguity are not at hand. For example, strategic ambiguity may be a necessary means of creating room for the exercise of ambiguity, for the negotiations of identities to take place. And contradiction may be a way of creating ambiguity from the bottom up if organizational leaders do not create sufficient ambiguity strategically. In our case, for instance, the expressions of contradictions—however exasperated they may have been—enabled tempered radicals, represented by middle management, to promote practices of diversity through expressions of ambivalence, despite the non-ambiguous diversity goals of the top management.

In sum, what we have sought to demonstrate in both theory and practice is that and how ambiguity may work to provide enhanced opportunities for diverse and diversifying organizational practices. When understood as a defining feature of all organizations, however, ambiguity is neither inherently good nor bad, and we have illustrated the fact that it may have both positive and negative effects. Further research, as well as experiments with diversity practices, may shed light on the specific ways in which ambiguity may be employed so as to avoid its possible delimiting consequences and provide the basis for more open and inclusive practices and perceptions of organizational diversity. Ambiguous diversity, then, is not something that can be achieved once and for all, or that organizations can ever be finished with. On the contrary, it is an open stance which organizations and their members alike could apply to enable the ever-unfolding negotiations of collective interests and individual needs.

References

Abdallah, C. and Langley, A. (2014). The double edge of ambiguity in strategic planning. *Journal of Management Studies*, 51(2): 235–64.
Ahmed, S. (2007). The language of diversity. *Ethnic and Racial Studies*, 30(2): 235–56.
Ahonen, P., Tienari, J., Meriläinen, S., and Pullen, A. (2014). Hidden contexts and invisible power relations: a Foucauldian reading of diversity research. *Human Relations*, 67(3): 263–86.
Allen, A. (1998). Power trouble: performativity as critical theory. *Constellations*, 5(4): 456–71.
Bendl, R., Fleischmann, A., and Hofmann, R. (2009). Queer theory and diversity management: reading codes of conduct from a queer perspective. *Journal of Management and Organization*, 15(5): 625–38.
Benschop, Y. (2001). Pride, prejudice and performance: relations between HRM, diversity and performance. *International Journal of Human Resource Management*, 12(7): 1166–81.
Butler, J. (1993). Critically queer. *GLQ: A Journal of Gay and Lesbian Studies*, 1(1): 17–32.
Cox, T. H. and Blake, S. (1992). Managing cultural diversity: implications for organizational competitiveness. *Academy of Management Executive*, 5(3): 45–56.
Danowitz, M. A. and Hanappi-Egger, E. (2012), Diversity as strategy. In M. A. Danowitz, E. Hanappi-Egger, and H. Mensi-Klarbach (eds.), *Diversity in Organizations: Concepts and Practices*. Basingstoke: Palgrave Macmillan, 137–60.
Davenport, S. and Leitch, S. (2005). Circuits of power in practice: strategic ambiguity as delegation of authority. *Organization Studies*, 26(11): 1603–23.
Denis, J.-L., Dompierre, G., Langley, A., and Rouleau, L. (2011). Escalating indecision: between reification and strategic ambiguity. *Organization Science*, 22(1): 225–44.
Dick, P. and Cassell, C. (2002). Barriers to managing diversity in a UK constabulary: the role of discourse. *Journal of Management Studies*, 39(7): 953–76.
Eisenberg, E. M. (1984). Ambiguity as strategy in organizational communication. *Communication Monographs*, 51(3): 227–42.
Eisenberg, E. M., and Witten, M. G. (1987). Reconsidering openness in organizational communication. *Academy of Management Review*, 12(3): 418–26.
Friday, E. and Friday, S. S. (2003). Managing diversity using a strategic planned change approach. *Journal of Management Development*, 22(10): 863–80.
Gilbert, J. A., Stead, B. A., and Ivancevich, J. M. (1999). Diversity management: a new organizational paradigm. *Journal of Business Ethics*, 21(1): 61–76.

Holvino, E. and Kamp, A. (2009). Diversity management: are we moving in the *right* direction? Reflections from both sides of the North Atlantic. *Scandinavian Journal of Management*, 25(4): 395–403.

Jarzabkowski, P., Sillince, J. A., and Shaw, D. (2010). Strategic ambiguity as a rhetorical resource for enabling multiple interests. *Human Relations*, 63(2): 219–48.

Kersten, A. (2000). Diversity management: dialogue, dialectics and diversion. *Journal of Organizational Change Management*, 13(3): 235–48.

Kirby, E. L. and Harter, L. M. (2001). Discourses of diversity and the quality of work life: the character and costs of the managerial metaphor. *Management Communication Quarterly*, 15(1): 121–7.

Liff, S. (1997). Two routes to managing diversity: individual differences or social group characteristics. *Employee Relations*, 19(1): 11–26.

Liff, S. and Wajcman, J. (1996). 'Sameness' and 'difference' revisited: which way forward for equal opportunity initiatives?. *Journal of Management Studies*, 33(1): 79–84.

Litvin, D. R. (1997). The discourse of diversity: from biology to management. *Organization*, 4(2): 187–209.

Lorbiecki, A. and Jack, G. (2000). Critical turns in the evolution of diversity management. *British Journal of Management*, 11: 17–31.

McCaskey, M. B. (1982). *The Executive Challenge: Managing Change and Ambiguity*. Marshfield, MA: Pitman.

Martin, J. (1992). *Cultures in Organizations: Three Perspectives*. New York: Oxford University Press.

Maxwell, G. (2004). Minority report: taking the initiative in managing diversity at BBC Scotland. *Employee Relations*, 26(2): 182–202.

Mensi-Klarbach, H. (2012). Diversity management: the business and moral cases. In M. A. Danowitz, E. Hanappi-Egger, and H. Mensi-Klarbach (eds.), *Diversity in Organizations: Concepts and Practices*. Basingstoke: Palgrave Macmillan, 63–89.

Meyerson, D. (1994). Interpretations of stress in institutions: the cultural production of ambiguity and burnout. *Administrative Science Quarterly*, 39(4): 628–53.

Meyerson, D. and Scully, M. A. (1995). Tempered radicalism and the politics of ambivalence and change. *Organization Science*, 6(5): 585–600.

Naples, N. A. (1996). A feminist revisiting of the insider/outsider debate: the 'outsider phenomenon' in rural Iowa. *Qualitative Sociology*, 19(1): 83–106.

Nkomo, S. M., and Cox, T. (1996). Diverse identities in organizations. In S. R. Clegg, C. Hardy, and W. R. Nord (eds.), *Handbook of Organization Studies*. London: Sage, 338–56.

Özbilgin, M. F., Mulholland, G., Tatli, A., and Worman, D. (2008). *Managing Diversity and the Business Case*. London: Chartered Institute of Personnel and Development.

Parker, M. (2002). Queering management and organization. *Gender, Work and Organization*, 9(2): 146–66.

Rand, E. J. (2008). An inflammatory fag and a queer form: Larry Kramer, polemics, and rhetorical agency. *Quarterly Journal of Speech*, 94(3): 297–319.

Renegar, V. R. and Sowards, S. K. (2009). Contradiction as Agency: self-determination, transcendence, and counter-imagination in third-wave feminism. *Hypatia*, 24(2): 1–20.

Risberg, A. (1999): *Ambiguities Thereafter: An Interpretive Approach to Acquisitions*. Lund: Lund University Press.

Risberg, A. and Søderberg, A.-M. (2008). Translating a management concept: diversity management in Denmark. *Gender in Management: An International Journal*, 23(6): 426–41.

Stake, R. E. (1994). Case studies. In N. K. Denzin and Y. S. Lincoln (eds.), *Handbook of Qualitative Research*. Thousand Oaks, CA: Sage, 236–48.

Staunæs, D. (2003). Where have all the subjects gone? Bringing together the concepts of intersectionality and subjectification. *NORA—Nordic Journal of Feminist and Gender Research*, 11(2): 101–10.

Syed, J. and Kramar, R. (2009). Socially responsible diversity management. *Journal of Management and Organization*, 15(5): 639–51.

Thomas, H. (1988). Policy dialogue in strategic planning: talking our way through ambiguity and change. In L. R. Pondy, R. J. Boland, and H. Thomas (eds.), *Managing Ambiguity and Change*. New York: John Wiley & Sons, 51–77.

Thomas Jr, R. R. (1992). Managing diversity: a conceptual framework. In S. E. Jackson (ed.), *Diversity in the Workplace: Human Resources Initiatives*. New York: Guilford Press, 306–17.

Tienari, J. and Nentwich, J. (2012). The 'doing' perspective on gender and diversity. In M. A. Danowitz, E. Hanappi-Egger, and H. Mensi-Klarbach (eds.), *Diversity in Organizations: Concepts and Practices*. Basingstoke: Palgrave Macmillan, 109–34.

Tomlinson, F. and Schwabenland, C. (2010). Reconciling competing discourses of diversity? The UK non-profit sector between social justice and the business case. *Organization*, 17(1): 101–21.

CHAPTER 11

INDIVIDUALS, TEAMS, AND ORGANIZATIONAL BENEFITS OF MANAGING DIVERSITY

An Evidence-Based Perspective

EDDY S. NG AND JACQUELINE STEPHENSON

One of the most salient trends of the twenty-first century is the increasing diversity in the workforce as a result of worker immigration. Immigrants make up a significant percent of the workforce in Australia (32.8%), Canada (22.4%), New Zealand (21.9%), the United States (13.3%), the United Kingdom (8.7%), and other Organisation for Economic Co-operation and Development (OECD) nations (Belot and Hatton 2012). Despite the promise of a competitive advantage, employers are grappling with how best to manage diversity to enhance organization performance (Kochan et al. 2003; Jayne and Dipboye 2004; Kearney and Gerbert 2009). Researchers have touted that workforce diversity, when properly managed, improves business performance because of a greater utilization of talents, and also because firms can reach out to a broader and more diverse customer base (Cox and Blake 1991; Robinson and Dechant 1997). Others, however, are sceptical of this claim, pointing to the contingent and short-term nature of the 'business case', and the inability to quantify the benefits of workforce diversity (Dickens 1999; Noon 2007). The findings from studies documenting the direct effects of workforce diversity on performance have been mixed and inconclusive (van Dick et al. 2008; Pitts and Wise 2010). This chapter attempts to reconcile these seemingly contradictory studies by adopting an evidence-based approach to investigate the benefits of managing diversity at the individual, team, and organization levels. We first provide a brief commentary on the definitions of diversity in the workplace. We then review existing theoretical frameworks on the proposed benefits of diversity. Next, we examine existing empirical evidence on the benefits of managing diversity at the individual, team, and organizational levels, based on existing studies that have been published in this domain. We also document how, when, and under what conditions diversity enhances performance at the individual, team, and organization levels. Where possible, we identify the policies and practices that are effective at promoting a more diverse workforce, and also those that can enhance the benefits of diversity.

Definitions of Diversity

Diversity, in its most basic form, refers to differences among people, which includes attributes that may be used to differentiate one person from another (Williams and O'Reilley 1998). Examples of such differences include, but are not limited to, age, gender, race, ethnicity, (dis)ability, sexual orientation, religion, social class, education/function, national origin, and language (see Kossek, Lobel, and Brown 2005). There are many typologies which have been used to classify people together as distinct groups, the most common being cultural differences (Richard 2000; Shore et al. 2009), physical differences, including appearance and (dis)ability (Woodhams and Danieli 2000; Olkin 2002; McLaughlin, Bell, and Stringer 2004; James 2007), and inherent differences (e.g. age and race) (see Bohm et al. 2011; Stone and Tetrick 2013; Andrevski et al. 2014). These differences may also be grouped into two primary categories: surface-level and deep-level diversity (Harrison, Price, and Bell 1998). Surface-level diversity attributes encompass age, race, and sex (see Tajfel and Turner 1986; Phillips, Northcraft, and Neale 2006), while deep-level attributes include one's personality, values, beliefs, attitudes, and mental models (see Bell 2007). For the purpose of this chapter, we will focus on gender and racial diversity, since they are more prevalent and present significant challenges to organizations and employers in light of an influx of women into the labour market, and worker immigration (Burke and Ng 2006), although logically and theoretically, other forms of diversity, such as age, nationality, and the others identified here, would also apply. We also use the terms ethnic diversity, racial diversity, and cultural diversity interchangeably.

Theoretical Frameworks

The term 'managing diversity' (MD) was popularized by Thomas (1990) to refer to management practices that aim to harness the benefits of a heterogeneous workforce. It includes espousing an official policy on diversity, active recruitment of minority group members, training and development of minority employees, examining compensation for fairness, and holding management accountable for diversity goals (Ng 2008). Managing diversity is also differentiated from affirmative action (AA), in that it is a voluntary corporate approach to dealing with increasing heterogeneity in the workplace, rather than being mandated by the government (Ng and Burke 2005). As a result, managing diversity is seen as less controversial than AA, since there is no quota or numerical targets to fulfil (Ng and Burke 2005).

Multiple theoretical perspectives have been advanced on the benefits of managing diversity. Thomas (1990) first suggests that AA is outmoded, as the emphasis in recent years is for managers to tap into the potential capacities of everyone. This perspective is seen as more inclusive than AA because everyone, including the white male majority, is encouraged to contribute to their fullest potential to maximize organizational effectiveness. Thomas (1990) argues that managing diversity is better than AA because it focuses on leveraging on the benefits of diversity rather than trying to gain the same level of efficiency as a homogeneous workforce. As a result, employers can gain a competitive advantage when everyone in the workforce performs to his or her own potential.

Following Thomas (1990), Cox (1993) proposes that individual differences among diverse employees can serve to enhance creativity and improve problem-solving in workgroups. According to the 'value-in-diversity' hypothesis, workforce diversity when properly managed, can lead to group and organizational processes that enhance overall firm performance. The benefits which may be realized by firms include attracting talent from across different cultural groups, greater marketing success, and better retention of employees, thus also contributing to cost savings for employers. The value-in-diversity hypothesis has been the catalyst in promulgating the business case for diversity, and has also spawned numerous studies in both experimental and field studies (which will be discussed in the section titled 'Effect of Diversity on Group and Team Performance').

Thomas and Ely (1996; see also Ely and Thomas 2001) propose three paradigms for managing diversity, which are related to organizational performance. Under the 'discrimination and fairness' perspective, the goal for diversifying the workforce is to increase the underrepresentation of minority groups with little to no connection to work outcomes. In the past, this has been the predominant approach for firms when dealing with an increasingly diverse workforce. Under the 'access and legitimacy' perspective, firms are actively managing diversity, but only to access the marketplace and gain legitimacy with diverse customers. However, according to Thomas and Ely (1996), this perspective is short term in focus and utilizes the benefits of diversity at the margins. Employers do not incorporate the value of diversity into the core functions of the firm. The third paradigm, 'integration and learning' is about infusing diversity into organizational processes and using diversity as a resource for organizational change and renewal. This approach is seen as more enduring because it links diversity to work processes. Thomas and Ely's three paradigms for managing diversity have also been widely cited in academic literature (Mannix and Neale 2005; Carroll and Shabana 2010; Zanoni et al. 2010; Shore et al. 2011; Guillaume et al. 2013).

Apart from Cox's (1993) value in-diversity hypothesis and Thomas and Ely's (1996) paradigms for managing diversity, other theoretical perspectives document the impact of workforce diversity on performance. Richard (2000), drawing on Barney's (1991) resource-based theory, argues that workforce diversity can be a strategic advantage when firms are able to capitalize on the value of its diverse workforce, and to create a diverse workplace that is rare and difficult to imitate. Ortlieb and Sieben (2013) similarly propose a typology for managing diversity based on resource-based theory, to take advantage of the human capital among diverse group members. In this view, workforce diversity is seen as an economic resource that can provide firms with a competitive advantage, under the right conditions.

Stakeholder theory argues that diversity should be a concern for managers and firms because of instrumental and normative reasons (Berman et al. 1999). Under the instrumental perspective, employers manage diversity because of the economic benefits that accrue to the firm. In the normative view, firms should manage diversity out of a moral obligation because it is the right thing to do. The stakeholder perspective considers the 'treatment of women and minorities' as employees and stakeholders who can affect a firm's social and corporate performance (Agle, Mitchell, and Sonnenfeld 1999). Firms gain legitimacy with investors and customers when employees are treated fairly and equitably, thus leading to greater firm profitability (Donaldson and Preston 1995).

Research in corporate governance has documented that the presence of women on corporate boards leads to greater monitoring of firm behaviour and, consequently, better firm performance (Campbell and Mínguez-Vera 2008; Bernardi, Bosco, and Columb 2009; Boulouta 2013). Likewise, studies conducted in the public sector have found that having women in government leads to lower corruption (Sung 2012). Although a majority of studies have focused on the gender-ethical orientation link, other dimensions of diversity such as culture and nationality have also been linked to greater firm ethical orientation and performance (Ben-Amar et al. 2013; Hafsi and Turgut 2013). It is likely that the greater diversity of viewpoints and constructive conflicts that arise from diverse group members may lead to better decision-making (de Wit, Greer, and Jehn 2012). Suffice to say, firms with diverse boards also benefit from enhanced firm reputation as they gain legitimacy with customers and investors (Bear, Rahman, and Post 2010).

Our review of the major theoretical frameworks suggests that workforce diversity has the potential to provide organizations with a source of competitive advantage. However, in order to realize this potential, employers and managers will need to proactively manage the differences arising from a diverse workforce (Cox and Blake 1991). As Thomas (1990) noted, the goal is to harness the benefits of diversity beyond what can be accomplished by a homogeneous workforce. Furthermore, employers that are able to infuse diversity into core organizational processes will reap greater benefits than those who simply utilize them at the margins (Ely and Thomas 2001). When firms hire from a diverse workforce, they also gain diverse viewpoints leading to more ethical decision-making. Firms also benefit from enhanced reputation for social responsibility and gain legitimacy with customers, resulting in overall improved performance. Given the promise on the benefits of a diverse workforce, the following sections review how managing diversity can benefit individuals, teams, and organizations.

Benefits of Managing Diversity on Individuals

Literature on diversity management (DM) has focused on improving individual and group effectiveness to improve overall firm performance.[1] However, comparatively little research has been undertaken to examine how diversity programmes affect individual outcomes. On this basis, we document how DM can assist individuals in attaining individual career goals, and consequently contribute to their career outcomes and satisfaction.

Equal Employment Opportunity and Affirmative Action

One focus of managing diversity in organizations is to increase the representation of minority group members to achieve a demographically diverse workforce (Thomas and Ely 1996; Ely and Thomas 2001). In this regard, public policies such as equal employment opportunity (EEO) and AA are useful and effective instruments to increase the number of women and minority groups in the workforce. EEO refers to regulations prohibiting employers from using an individual's immutable characteristics as their criteria for making employment decisions (Holzer and Neumark 2006), while AA refers to situations where preference is given to individuals if they are members, of an underrepresented group for employment (see Brown, Langer, and Stewart 2012). Although EEO and AA programmes are often differentiated from managing diversity, in reality they are a part of a firm's broader efforts to manage diversity (Mighty 1996). For example, Canadian firms which have to comply with AA often refer to it as DM (Ng 2005). In general, EEO and AA are legally mandated, while DM represents voluntary efforts to manage diversity by the employers (Agocs and Burr 1996).

Studies have shown that AA practices do affect the employment outcomes for women and minorities. For example, Konrad and Linnehan (1995) found that, in the American manufacturing and service sector, AA is associated with positive employment outcomes for women and minorities. Likewise, Holzer and Neumark (2000) reported that AA increased employers' use of targeted human resource (HR) practices, to hire more women and minorities into organizations. Furthermore, Ng and Burke (2010) found that senior management (e.g. CEOs) are more likely to pay attention to and commit to managing diversity when they are required to comply with AA mandates. In Canada,

---

[1] DM includes a range of diversity practices, such as diversity policy statements, active recruitment, training and development, compensation, management accountability, and community support, all of which are considered to be essential in the advancement of women and minorities (Konrad and Linnehan 1995).

the threat of fines and negative publicity may also compel employers to increase the number of women and minority group members (Taggar, Jain, and Gunderson 1997).

Moreover, it has been suggested that when AA is replaced by a meritocracy-based policy, as in the case of California in 1996, employment of women and minorities dropped sharply as a result (Myers 2007). The effectiveness of AA policies in increasing the employment of women and minorities has been documented in Australia (French and Strachan 2007), Canada (Haq and Ng 2010), New Zealand (Edgar 2001; Hyman 2008), India (Saha 2012), and South Africa (Horwitz and Jain 2011), although at varying levels of success in different countries, and for different groups.

Career Advancement and Pay Equity

EEO and AA programmes have been instrumental in advancing and promoting the careers of women and minority groups. Kurtulus (2012) reported that AA has been responsible for the increasing share of women and minorities in high-paying occupations over a thirty-one-year period in the US. Similarly, women assumed greater executive roles in government and exercised as much influence as men in the US public sector as a result of AA (Dolan 2004). Therefore, it should be no surprise that organizations that have to comply with AA see the strongest effects in the number of women and minorities in management. When the different types of AA programmes are considered, firms that assign accountabilities for diversity to managers (e.g. setting goals and timetables, assessing progress) were found to be more effective than programmes that address managerial bias or social isolation of minorities (Kalev, Kelly, and Dobbin 2006).

Additionally, Hakim (2006) credits AA for the progress of women's career advancement. Although the occurrence of women (and minorities) in senior and executive-level positions is still rare, due to limited experience (resulting in part from a lack of mid-level managerial experience), AA programmes ensure that women (and minorities) gain the experience necessary for assuming senior positions in the future. In other words, increasing the number of women and minorities in the pipeline will inevitably lead to increases in female and minority representation in management and senior-level positions. Countries such as Norway, which mandates the number of women on corporate boards (quotas) also reported more women in management (Matsa and Miller 2011, 2013).

Many jurisdictions, such as Canada and Europe, put in place pay equity or equal pay policy as a part of their AA legislation (Rubery and Fagan 1994; Singh and Peng 2010). Pay equity essentially requires that employers pay women and men the same wages for performing the same job, while equal pay dictates that employers pay women the same as men for performing work of comparable worth or value. Pay equity policy has been largely responsible for pay increases for women, especially in the public sector, and for narrowing the pay gap. According to Singh and Peng (2010), the wage gap decreased from 38 per cent to 29 per cent, from 1988 to 2008 (a twenty-year period) in Canada.

Career Satisfaction

Career satisfaction relates to an individual's career attainment in terms of goals, progression, income, and development. In Canada, Yap and colleagues (2010) found that racial minorities in managerial and professional jobs reported lower satisfaction than whites because their human capital is frequently undervalued and underutilized. This finding is not surprising, given that minority employees' qualifications and work experience, particularly among immigrants, are often devalued or discounted when they are acquired abroad (Esses et al. 2007). When individuals are dissatisfied with their careers, on account of prejudice and discrimination, they are more likely to report lower job satisfaction, have less commitment to their work, perform more poorly, and be more likely to engage in withdrawal behaviours (e.g. absenteeism and turnover) (Hughes and Dodge 1997; McKay et al. 2007; McKay, Avery, and Morris 2008; Antecol and Cobb-Clark 2009).

In this regard, EEO and AA programmes may be helpful in promoting perceptions of justice and in creating a more inclusive climate among women and minorities at the individual level. Likewise, AA in the public sector moderates minority employees' job satisfaction, which in turn lowers turnover intentions (Choi 2009). Furthermore, an appreciation of diversity can lead to employee well-being (e.g. less stress and a better work/life balance), and a greater commitment to their team members (Lehmann-Willenbrock, Lei, and Kauffeld 2012). Thus, there is evidence to suggest that AA programmes promote minority employees' career satisfaction and individual work performance (Gonzalez and DeNisi 2009; Triana, Garcia, and Colella 2010).

In sum, DM practices such as EEO and AA programmes are responsible for ensuring the representation of women and racial minorities. When managers are held accountable for diversity goals, minorities are also more likely to be promoted into management. This is important, because they gain the experience and acquire management experience necessary for promotion to senior management levels. DM through pay equity legislation is also responsible for reducing the pay gap between women and men.

IMPACT OF MANAGING DIVERSITY ON TEAM AND GROUP OUTCOMES

When individuals feel valued, they are more likely to be committed to the team and to the organizations for which they work (Hopkins, Hopkins, and Mallette 2001). Therefore, it should come as no surprise that women and minorities value employer efforts to manage diversity in the workplace (Kossek and Zonia 1993). On this basis, firms that are able to manage the diversity in terms of communication, cohesion, and intra-group conflict are more likely to reap the benefits from diversity. However, the context and conditions in which diverse work groups are required to perform also have an impact on overall group processes and team performance (see Jehn and Bezrukova 2004; Joshi and Roh 2009).

Effect of Diversity on Group and Team Performance

Research findings on the effects of workgroup diversity have related to team performance, despite the value-in-diversity arguments. In a laboratory study in the US, Watson, Kumar, and Michaelsen (1993) reported that homogeneous workgroups outperformed culturally diverse workgroups on problem-solving and idea generation at the initial stages of the task. However, performance differences disappeared after seventeen weeks when diverse workgroups were able to work out their communication challenges. However, it is unclear if diverse teams were able to outperform homogeneous teams over a longer period of time, although Ng and Tung (1998) did find diverse workgroups outperformed homogenous workgroups in a field study involving multicultural bank branches across different financial measures. In a subsequent study, based on a US sample, Watson, Johnson, and Merritt (1998) reported that team orientation vis-à-vis self-orientation predicted team performance, with diverse teams outperforming homogeneous teams initially and homogenous teams outperforming diverse teams subsequently. Thus, findings on realizing the gains from the value-in-diversity hypothesis at the group and team level remain largely mixed and contingent upon a number of factors.

Diversity Beliefs

A number of other studies have shown that the processes and dynamics within diverse workgroups can affect their performance. Van Dick and colleagues (2008) reported that when individual team members believe that diversity is good for achieving team goals (i.e. pro-diversity beliefs), they are more likely to identify as a group, share information with each other, and intend to stay as a group. Groups that hold pro-diversity beliefs also performed better, although groups that hold pro-similarity beliefs (i.e. preferring group members who are demographically similar) did not have poorer performance (Homan et al. 2007). Foldy (2004) suggests that individual beliefs about diversity may moderate the relationship between team diversity and performance. Van Knippenberg, van Ginkel, and Homan (2013) similarly propose that diversity mindsets (mental beliefs about diversity), moderate the diversity–performance link. Based on these studies, there is evidence to suggest that positive beliefs about diversity, which promotes diverse team efficacy, may be key to unlocking the performance of diverse workgroups.

Task Types

The types of tasks required of diverse workgroups also appear to have an effect on their team performance. Accordingly, diversity is expected to provide teams with greater creativity and innovation, but diverse teams also suffer from poorer communication, a lack of cohesion, and intra-group conflicts. Nouri and colleagues (2013) reported that team diversity was beneficial for creative-type tasks (e.g. idea generation) when tight coordination and shared understanding among team members are relatively less important. In another study, Woehr, Arciniega, and Poling (2013) reported similar observations, and concluded that less diversity in teams is suited for tasks with process outcomes, since there is more team cohesion and less conflict. Furthermore, the benefits of diversity (e.g. creativity) accrue to teams with highly interdependent outcomes and low longevity, since they are more likely to avoid groupthink (Schippers et al. 2003). In this regard, team performance is highly dependent on the types of tasks and outcomes that are expected of teams with diverse and homogeneous team members.

Levels of Diversity

Additionally, the composition of diverse teams also affects the outcomes of diverse workgroups. Richard, Kochan, and McMillan-Capehart (2002) propose that the relationship between diversity and performance is curvilinear. The curvilinear relationship represents the tension that exists between the positive and negative effects of diversity. As the level of diversity increases, the benefits that accrue to groups also increase. As an example, Konrad, Kramer, and Erkut (2008) found that having three women on corporate boards appears to be most helpful to realize the gains from diversity (one or two female directors are tokens and less effective). Once the optimal level of diversity has been attained, groups will begin experiencing diminishing returns from diversity. Drawing from societal-level studies, when a neighbourhood becomes increasingly more diverse, citizens reported that their interactions with dissimilar others occur less often and they also have less trust for each other (Putnam 2007; Stolle, Soroka, and Johnston 2008). In this instance, the benefits from diversity may be eroded by weakening relationships and trusts among diverse group members, as is often documented in social network studies (McFadyen and Cannella 2004; Chen and Gable 2013).

Diversity Fault Lines

Diversity in teams may also create fault lines, which are 'hypothetical dividing lines that may split a group into subgroups based on one or more [demographic] attributes' (Lau and Murnighan 1998: 328). In other words, members in diverse groups divide themselves into homogeneous subgroups, which can threaten the gains from diversity. Strong fault lines increase the potential for dissensus with demographically dissimilar others, which could lead to 'behavioural disintegration' (Li and Hambrick 2005: 800). Members from this smaller subgroup may also receive less internal support and experience more opinion suppression, leading to reduced confidence and effectiveness (Lau and Murnighan 1998). Meyer and Schermuly (2012) reported that pro-diversity beliefs, task motivation, and communication about task information help lessen the fault-line strength. Likewise, Sawyer, Houlette, and Yeagley (2006) found that diverse cross-cutting teams (where race crosses job functions), and team members not pre-disposed to pre-task discussions (which facilitated necessary discussions) outperformed homogeneous teams. The fault line may be diminished when no clear subgroups exist, or weakened when members are required to interact with each other more extensively prior to task.

Top Management Teams

A critical area for examining group or team diversity is within top management teams (TMTs), as top executives make decisions that directly impact firm performance (Homberg and Bui 2013). Studies have shown that various dimensions of diversity on corporate boards lead to greater degree of internationalization (Kaczmarek and Ruigrok 2013), greater product diversification (Hutzschenreuter and Horstkotte 2013), greater innovation (Mihalache et al. 2012), and overall firm performance (Nielsen and Nielsen 2013). Group processes such as fault lines also affect TMTs. For example, task-related diversity lessens the fault-line strength, while demographic diversity (i.e. race) strengthens TMT fault lines (Hutzschenreuter and Horstkotte 2013). The presence of women also contributes to the informational and social diversity on TMTs, which leads to firm performance, particularly for innovative firms (Dezsö and Ross 2012).

In sum, diversity at the team or group level has the potential to benefit organizations. However, the types of task, a belief in (the benefits of) diversity, and the composition of the teams are all crucial in realizing the potentials from team diversity. In this regard, it is crucial for managers and team leaders to create teams with three or more minority group members (or women), and to weaken any potential fault lines (by having greater diversity). Firms also benefit when TMTs are diverse.

Impact of Diversity on Organizational Outcomes

The impact of diversity at the organizational level receives the most attention in research studies, since top executives are most likely to pay attention to the instrumental benefits derived from a diverse workforce (Ng and Wyrick 2011). Despite the impetus to manage diversity at the individual and group or team levels, evidence on the diversity–organizational performance link has not yet been conclusively established, as evidenced by the conflicting findings from empirical research (Shore et al. 2009; Roberge and van Dick 2010). This is likely because the ability of a firm to capitalize on its diverse workforce is dependent on a host of factors, such as a firm's strategic orientation, TMT diversity, and firm leadership, as well as policies and practices that are related to DM.

Strategic Orientation

Richard (2000) reported that the link between workforce diversity and firm performance is contingent upon a firm's strategic orientation. Workforce diversity contributed to employee productivity, return on equity, and market performance, but only for firms with a growth orientation. In another study, conducted in the US, Richard and colleagues (2003) reported that employee diversity enhanced the performance of firms that are pursuing an innovative strategy. Diversity in TMTs similarly affected the innovation outcomes and firm performance for firms with an innovative orientation (Mihalache et al. 2012). Taken together, these findings suggest that firms pursuing growth and innovation strategies are more likely to be able to capitalize on the gains from diversity, particularly when creativity and innovation, as well as access to the market, are considered to be essential for firm success.

Leadership

Although workforce diversity, when properly managed, is expected to lead to improved firm performance (Cox 1993), the role of leaders and managers in capitalizing on those benefits cannot be underestimated. Ayoko and Konrad (2012) demonstrate that effective leadership could reduce task and relationship conflicts in diverse teams, which are related to morale and group performance. Likewise, Muchiri and Ayoko (2013) found that transformational leadership style plays a moderating role in eliciting greater organizational citizenship behaviour and productivity among women in diverse work units. Ng and Sears (2012) similarly reported that transformational leaders, and transactional leaders with relatively high age or social values, are related to the number of diversity practices implemented in a firm (see also Ng (2008) on other individual characteristics that are hypothesized to predict CEO motivation to manage diversity). The number of diversity practices have been found to be related to the employment outcomes for women and minorities (Konrad and Linnehan 1995). CEOs are more likely to be motivated to manage diversity when they see an instrumental link to workforce diversity. Researchers have variously attempted to document the relationship between workforce diversity and firm financial returns (Weigand 2007), as well as stock prices (Wright et al. 1995), to establish the diversity–financial success link, with positive results

Diversity-Related Policies and Practices

Research has also shown that DM practices contribute to firm performance above and beyond high performance work systems (Armstrong et al. 2010). In the US public sector, diversity policies and practices enhanced the performance of government agencies (Choi and Rainey 2010). Western-based multinational corporations (MNCs) were more likely to adopt strategic HR management practices that promote a diverse workforce than Eastern-based (e.g. Indian and Chinese) firms, given the link to firm financial performance (Cooke and Saini 2010). As we mentioned in the section titled 'Equal Employment Opportunity and Affirmative Action', Konrad and Linnehan (1995) reported that HR policies and practices must specifically target women and minorities in order for them to be effective. Kalev, Kelly, and Dobbin (2006) found creating accountability to be crucial for ensuring representation of women and minorities in management. Likewise, Ng and Sears (2010) found bias-free selection to have the greatest influence on the promotion of minorities into management ranks, because of the possibility of adverse impact in selection practices. Thus, in order for firms to capitalize on the benefits of diversity, the 'right' context-dependent HR policies and practices must be in place, to ensure that the potential advantages associated with workforce diversity are maximized, while the potential disadvantages are minimized.

In sum, having the right leaders (e.g. CEOs) and strategic orientation (e.g. growth- or innovative-oriented firms) is helpful for organizations to reap the benefits of a diverse workforce. Furthermore, the right HR management practices can reduce adverse impact and increase the number of minorities in management. Taken together, DM has the potential to contribute to overall firm performance.

Conclusion

Although the benefits of workforce diversity are promising for organizations and employers, research on its direct effect on individual, team, and organizational performance have not been conclusively established. This chapter reviews existing research and documents how, when, and under what conditions diversity enhances performance at the individual, team, and organization levels. We also identify several policies and practices which are effective when promoting a more diverse workforce, as well as those that enhance the benefits of diversity.

Our review suggests that the positive effects of diversity on performance at all levels are present, but they are established only under the appropriate conditions. According to the resource-based view, firms must be able to create a diverse workforce in order to capitalize on its benefits. In this regard, EEO and AA programmes appear helpful in increasing the employment of women and minorities. When individuals feel valued and are treated fairly, they are also more likely to perform on the job, report greater career satisfaction, and contribute to a firm's success. At the team level, an understanding of group-level processes and dynamics is key to ensuring that communication barriers, cohesion, and intra-group conflicts arising out of diversity are minimized. Holding pro-diversity (or pro-similarity) beliefs, types of team tasks, group composition, the levels of diversity, as well as team fault lines, individually and jointly contribute to, or distract from, team performance. These processes also have an impact in the TMTs, with firm performance consequences. At the organizational level, firm strategy and leadership are crucial for firms to capitalize on the benefits of employee diversity. Employers must also have HR policies and practices that are inclusive to encourage everyone to contribute to their fullest potential. A number of such types of practices have already been identified in multiple studies referenced in this chapter. As workforce diversity becomes an imperative with the emergence of globalization and worker immigration, we surmise that organizations which pay attention to issues of diversity will reap the potential benefits that are associated with it.

In closing, we suggest a few avenues for future research to extend our knowledge on the benefits that can be derived from a diverse workforce. First, based on our review, the impetus for managing diversity appears to be driven by the business case. Therefore, it remains unclear if organizations and employers will devote resources to manage diversity in the absence of instrumental benefits. On this basis, we suggest that future research on managing diversity be extended to the public service and non-profit sectors. The findings could inform researchers and practitioners on other potential benefits that could be realized from managing a diverse workforce across different organizations and settings. Second, while it is evident that senior leadership commitment is crucial for an organization's diversity efforts, it is unlikely that the leaders themselves will be responsible for implementing an organization's diversity strategies. Thus, greater research attention should be focused on the individual (e.g. AA officer) who is charged with managing diversity. In this regard, it is important to study the role and characteristics of the AA officer, in order for diversity programmes to be successfully implemented. Furthermore, the relationship between an organization's leader and the AA officer (e.g. direct reporting relationship) should also be explored. Third, there has been a suggestion that the relationship between diversity and performance is curvilinear (Richard, Kochan, and McMillan-Capehart 2002). In other words, increasing levels of diversity is will bring about diminishing marginal benefits to team and group performance. However, it is unclear what level of diversity is optimal for work teams, and comparatively little research has been conducted in this area. Thus, it would be fruitful to investigate the levels of diversity that would be associated with maximum team performance.

REFERENCES

Agle, B. R., Mitchell, R. K., and Sonnenfeld, J. A. (1999). Who matters to CEOs? An investigation of stakeholder attributes and salience, corporate performance, and CEO values. *Academy of Management Journal*, 42(5): 507–25.

Agocs, C. and Burr, C. (1996). Employment equity, affirmative action and managing diversity: assessing the differences. *International Journal of Manpower*, 17(4): 30–45.

Andrevski, G., Richard, O. C., Shaw, J. D., and Ferrier, W. J. (2014). Racial diversity and firm performance: the mediating role of competitive intensity. *Journal of Management*, 40(3): 820–44.

Antecol, H. and Cobb-Clark, D. (2009). Racial harassment, job satisfaction, and intentions to remain in the military. *Journal of Population Economics*, 22(3): 713–38.

Armstrong, C., Flood, P. C., Guthrie, J. P., Liu, W., MacCurtain, S., and Mkamwa, T. (2010). The impact of diversity and equality management on firm performance: beyond high performance work systems. *Human Resource Management*, 49(6): 977–98.

Ayoko, O. B. and Konrad, A. M. (2012). Leaders' transformational, conflict, and emotion management behaviors in culturally diverse workgroups. *Equality, Diversity and Inclusion: An International Journal*, 31(8): 694–724.

Barney, J. (1991). Firm resources and sustained competitive advantage. *Journal of Management*, 17: 99–120.

Bear, S., Rahman, N., and Post, C. (2010). The impact of board diversity and gender composition on corporate social responsibility and firm reputation. *Journal of Business Ethics*, 97(2): 207–21.

Bell, S. T. (2007). Deep-level composition variables as predictors of team performance: a meta-analysis. *Journal of Applied Psychology*, 92(3): 595.

Belot, M. V. and Hatton, T. J. (2012). Immigrant selection in the OECD. *The Scandinavian Journal of Economics*, 114(4): 1105–128.

Ben-Amar, W., Francoeur, C., Hafsi, T., and Labelle, R. (2013). What makes better boards? A closer look at diversity and ownership. *British Journal of Management*, 24(1): 85–101.

Berman, S. L., Wicks, A. C., Kotha, S., and Jones, T. M. (1999). Does stakeholder orientation matter? The relationship between stakeholder management models and firm financial performance. *Academy of Management Journal*, 42(5): 488–506.

Bernardi, R. A., Bosco, S. M., and Columb, V. L. (2009). Does female representation on boards of directors associate with the 'most ethical companies' list? *Corporate Reputation Review*, 12(3): 270–80.

Bohm, S., Baumgartner, M. K., Divertmann, D. J., and Kunze, F. (2011). Age diversity and its performance implications: analysing a major future workforce trend. In S. Kunisch, S. Boehm, and M. Boppel (eds.), *From Grey to Silver: Managing the demographic change successfully*. Berlin and Heidelberg: Springer, 121–41.

Boulouta, I. (2013). Hidden connections: the link between board gender diversity and corporate social performance. *Journal of Business Ethics*, 113(2): 185–97.

Brown, G. K., Langer, A., and Stewart, F. (2012). Affirmative action: foundations, contexts and debates. In G. K. Brown, A. Langer, and F. Stewart (eds.), *Affirmative Action in Plural Societies (International experiences)*. Basingstoke: Palgrave Macmillan, 1–23.

Burke, R. J. and Ng, E. (2006). The changing nature of work and organizations: implications for human resource management. *Human Resource Management*, 16(2): 86–94.

Campbell, K. and Mínguez-Vera, A. (2008). Gender diversity in the boardroom and firm financial performance. *Journal of Business Ethics*, 83(3): 435–51.

Carroll, A. B. and Shabana, K. M. (2010). The business case for corporate social responsibility: a review of concepts, research and practice. *International Journal of Management Review*, 12(1): 85–105.

Chen, L. and Gable, G. G. (2013). Larger or broader: performance implications of size and diversity of the knowledge worker's egocentric network. *Management and Organization Review*, 9(1): 139–65.

Choi, S. (2009). Diversity in the US federal government: diversity management and employee turnover in federal agencies. *Journal of Public Administration Research and Theory*, 19(3): 603–30.

Choi, S. and Rainey, H. G. (2010). Managing diversity in U.S. federal agencies: effects of diversity and diversity management on employee perceptions of organizational performance. *Public Administration Review*, 70(1): 109–21.

Cooke, F. L. and Saini, D. S. (2010). Diversity management in India: a study of organizations in different ownership forms and industrial sectors. *Human Resource Management*, 49(3): 477–500.

Cox, T. H. (1993). *Cultural Diversity in Organizations: Theory, Research and Practice*. San Francisco, CA: Berrett-Koehler.

Cox Jr, T. H. and Blake, S. (1991). Managing cultural diversity: implications for organizational competitiveness. *The Executive*, 5(3): 45–56.

De Wit, F. R. C., Greer, L. L., and Jehn, K. A. (2012). The paradox of intragroup conflict: a meta-analysis. *Journal of Applied Psychology*, 97(2): 360–90.

Dezsö, C. L. and Ross, D. G. (2012). Does female representation in top management improve firm performance? A panel data investigation. *Strategic Management Journal*, 33(9): 1072–89.

Dickens, L. (1999). Beyond the business case: a three-pronged approach to equality action. *Human Resource Management Journal*, 9(1): 9–19.

Dolan, J. (2004). Gender equity: illusion or reality for women in the federal executive service? *Public Administration Review*, 64(3): 299–308.

Donaldson, T. and Preston, L. E. (1995). The stakeholder theory of the corporation: concepts, evidence. *Academy of Management Review*, 20(1): 65–91.

Edgar, F. (2001). Equal employment opportunity: outcomes in the New Zealand public service. *New Zealand Journal of Industrial Relations*, 26(2): 217–26.

Ely, R. J. and Thomas, D. A. (2001). Cultural diversity at work: the effects of diversity perspectives on work group processes and outcomes. *Administrative Science Quarterly*, 46(2): 229–73.

Esses, V. M., Dietz, J., Bennett-Abuayyash, C., and Joshi, C. (2007). Prejudice in the workplace: the role of bias against visible minorities in the devaluation of immigrants' foreign-acquired qualifications and credentials. *Canadian Issues*, Spring: 114–18.

Foldy, E. G. (2004). Learning from diversity: a theoretical exploration. *Public Administration Review*, 64(5): 529–38.

French, E. and Strachan, G. (2007). Equal opportunity outcomes for women in the finance industry in Australia: evaluating the merit of EEO plans. *Asia Pacific Journal of Human Resources*, 45(3): 314–32.

Gonzalez, J. A. and DeNisi, A. S. (2009). Cross-level effects of demography and diversity climate on organizational attachment and firm effectiveness. *Journal of Organizational Behavior*, 30(1): 21–40.

Guillaume, Y. R., Dawson, J. F., Woods, S. A., Sacramento, C. A., and West, M. A. (2013). Getting diversity at work to work: what we know and what we still don't know. *Journal of Occupational and Organisational Psychology*, 86(2): 123–41.

Hafsi, T. and Turgut, G. (2013). Boardroom diversity and its effect on social performance: conceptualization and empirical evidence. *Journal of Business Ethics*, 112(3): 463–79.

Hakim, C. (2006). Women, careers, and work-life preferences. *British Journal of Guidance & Counselling*, 34(3): 279–94.

Haq, R. and Ng, E. S. (2010). Employment equity and workplace diversity in Canada. In A. Klarsfeld (ed.), *International Handbook on Diversity Management at Work: Country Perspectives on Diversity and Equal Treatment.* Cheltenham: Edward Elgar, 68–82.

Harrison, D.A., Price, K.H. and Bell, M.P. (1998). Beyond relational demography: time and the effects of surface-and deep-level diversity on work group cohesion. *Academy of Management Journal,* 41(1): 96–107.

Holzer, H. J. and Neumark, D. (2000). What does affirmative action do? *Industrial & Labor Relations Review,* 53(2): 240–71.

Holzer, H. J. and Neumark, D. (2006). Equal employment opportunity and affirmative action. In W. Rodgers (ed.), *Handbook on the Economics of Discrimination.* Northampton, MA: Edward Elgar, 260–87.

Homan, A. C., van Knippenberg, D., Van Kleef, G. A., and De Dreu, C. K. (2007). Bridging faultlines by valuing diversity: diversity beliefs, information elaboration, and performance in diverse work groups. *Journal of Applied Psychology,* 92(5): 1189–99.

Homberg, F. and Bui, H. T. M. (2013). Top management team diversity: a systematic review. *Group & Organization Management,* 38(4): 455–79.

Hopkins, W. E., Hopkins, S. A., and Mallette, P. (2001). Diversity and managerial value commitment: a test of some proposed relationships. *Journal of Managerial Issues,* 13(3): 288–306.

Horwitz, F. M. and Jain, H. (2011). An assessment of employment equity and broad-based black economic empowerment developments in South Africa. *Equality, Diversity and Inclusion: An International Journal,* 30(4): 297–317.

Hughes, D. and Dodge, M. A. (1997). African American women in the workplace: relationships between job conditions, racial bias at work, and perceived job quality. *American Journal of Community Psychology,* 25(5): 581–99.

Hutzschenreuter, T. and Horstkotte, J. (2013). Performance effects of top management team demographic faultlines in the process of product diversification. *Strategic Management Journal,* 34(6): 704–26.

Hyman, P. (2008). Pay equity and equal employment opportunity in New Zealand: developments 2006/2008 and evaluation. *New Zealand Journal of Employment Relations* (Online), 33(3): 1–15, <http://www.nzjournal.org/NZJER33(3).pdf> (accessed 18 May 2015).

James, H. R. (2007). If you are attractive and you know it, please apply: appearance-based discrimination and employers' discretion. *Valparaiso University Law Review,* 42(2): 629–74.

Jayne, M. E. A. and Dipboye, R. L. (2004). Leveraging diversity to improve business performance: research findings and recommendations for organisations. *Human Resource Management,* 43(4): 409–24.

Jehn, K. A. and Bezrukova, K. (2004). A field study of group diversity, workgroup context, and performance. *Journal of Organizational Behavior,* 25(6): 703–29.

Joshi, A. and Roh, H. (2009). The role of context in work team diversity research: a meta-analytic review. *Academy of Management Journal,* 52(3): 599–627.

Kaczmarek, S. and Ruigrok, W. (2013). In at the deep end of firm internationalization. *Management International Review,* 53(4): 513–34.

Kalev, A., Kelly, E., and Dobbin, F. (2006). Best practices or best guesses? Assessing the efficacy of corporate affirmative action and diversity policies. *American Sociological Review,* 71(4): 589–617.

Kearney, E. and Gerbert, D. (2009). Managing diversity and enhancing team outcomes: the promise of transformational leadership. *Journal of Applied Psychology,* 94(1): 77–89.

Kochan, T., Berzrukova, K., Ely, R., Jackson, S., Joshi, A. John, K., Leonard, J., Levine, D., and Thomas, D. (2003). The effects of diversity on business performance: report of the diversity research network. *Human Resource Management*, 42(1): 3–21.

Konrad, A. M. and Linnehan, F. (1995). Formalized HRM structures: coordinating equal employment opportunity or concealing organizational practices? *Academy of Management Journal*, 38(3): 787–820.

Konrad, A. M., Kramer, V., and Erkut, S. (2008). Critical mass: the impact of three or more women on corporate boards. *Organizational Dynamics*, 37(2): 145–64.

Kossek, E.E., Lobel, S.A., and Brown, A.J. (2005), Human resource strategies to manage workforce diversity. In A. M. Konrad, P. Prasad, and J. M. Pringle (eds.), *Handbook of Workplace Diversity*. Thousand Oaks, CA: Sage, 54–74.

Kossek, E. E. and Zonia, S. C. (1993). Assessing diversity climate: a field study of reactions to employer efforts to promote diversity. *Journal of Organizational Behavior*, 14(1): 61–81.

Kurtulus, F. A. (2012). Affirmative action and the occupational advancement of minorities and women during 1973–2003. *Industrial Relations*, 51(2): 213–46.

Lau, D. C. and Murnighan, J. K. (1998). Demographic diversity and faultlines: the compositional dynamics of organizational groups. *Academy of Management Review*, 23(2): 325–40.

Lehmann-Willenbrock, N., Lei, Z., and Kauffeld, S. (2012). Appreciating age diversity and German nurse well-being and commitment: co-worker trust as the mediator. *Nursing and Health Sciences*, 14(2): 213–20.

Li, J. and Hambrick, D. C. (2005). Fractional groups: a new vantage on demographic faultlines, conflict, and disintegration in work teams. *Academy of Management Journal*, 48(5): 794–813.

McFadyen, M. A. and Cannella Jr, A. (2004). Social capital and knowledge creation: diminishing returns of the number and strength of exchange relationships. *Academy of Management Journal*, 47(5): 735–46.

McKay, P. F., Avery, D. R., and Morris, M. A. (2008). Mean racial-ethnic differences in employee sales performance: the moderating role of diversity climate. *Personnel Psychology*, 61(2): 349–74.

McKay, P. F., Avery, D. R., Tonidandel, S., Morris, M. A., Hernandez, M., and Hebl, M. R. (2007). Racial differences in employee retention: are diversity climate perceptions the key? *Personnel Psychology*, 60(1): 35–62.

McLaughlin, M. E., Bell, M. P., and Stringer, D. Y. (2004). Stigma and acceptance of persons with disabilities: understudied aspects of workforce diversity. *Group & Organisation Management*, 29(3): 302–33.

Mannix, E. and Neale, M. A. (2005). What differences make a difference? The promise and reality of diverse teams in organisations. *Psychological Science in Public Interest*, 6(2): 31–55.

Matsa, D. A. and Miller, A. R. (2011). Chipping away at the glass ceiling: gender spillovers in corporate leadership. *The American Economic Review*, 101(3): 635–9.

Matsa, D. A. and Miller, A. R. (2013). A female style in corporate leadership? Evidence from quotas. *American Economic Journal: Applied Economics*, 5(3): 136–69.

Meyer, B. and Schermuly, C. C. (2012). When beliefs are not enough: examining the interaction of diversity faultlines, task motivation, and diversity beliefs on team performance. *European Journal of Work and Organizational Psychology*, 21(3): 456–87.

Mighty, E. J. (1996). Factors affecting the adoption of employment equity: an example from Canada. *Equal Opportunities International*, 15(5): 1–27.

Mihalache, O. R., Jansen, J. J. J. P., Van Den Bosch, F. A. J., and Volberda, H. W. (2012). Offshoring and firm innovation: the moderating role of top management team attributes. *Strategic Management Journal*, 33(13): 1480–98.

Muchiri, M. K. and Ayoko, O. B. (2013). Linking demographic diversity to organisational outcomes: the moderating role of transformational leadership. *Leadership & Organization Development Journal*, 34(5): 384-406.

Myers, C. K. (2007). A cure for discrimination? Affirmative action and the case of California's proposition 209. *Industrial and Labor Relations Review*, 60(3): 379–96.

Ng, E. S. W. (2005). Employment Equity and Organizational Diversity Performance: The Role of CEOs' Characteristics and Commitment. Unpublished doctoral dissertation. McMaster University, Ontario, Canada.

Ng, E. S. W. (2008). Why organizations choose to manage diversity? Toward a leadership-based theoretical framework. *Human Resource Development Review*, 7(1): 58–78.

Ng, E. S. W. and Burke, R. J. (2005). Person–organization fit and the war for talent: does diversity management make a difference? *The International Journal of Human Resource Management*, 16(7): 1195–1210.

Ng, E. S. W. and Burke, R. J. (2010). A comparison of the legislated employment equity program, federal contractors program, and financial post 500 firms. *Canadian Journal of Administrative Sciences*, 27(3): 224–35.

Ng, E. S. W. and Sears, G. J. (2010). The effect of adverse impact in selection practices on organizational diversity: a field study. *International Journal of Human Resource Management*, 21(9): 1454–71.

Ng, E. S. W. and Sears, G. J. (2012). CEO leadership styles and the implementation of organizational diversity practices: moderating effects of social values and age. *Journal of Business Ethics*, 105(1): 41–52.

Ng, E. S. W. and Tung, R. L. (1998). Ethno-cultural diversity and organizational effectiveness: a field study. *International Journal of Human Resource Management*, 9(6): 980–95.

Ng, E. S. W. and Wyrick, C. R. (2011). Motivational bases for managing diversity: a model of leadership commitment. *Human Resource Management Review*, 21(4): 368–76.

Nielsen, B. B. and Nielsen, S. (2013). Top management team nationality diversity and firm performance: a multilevel study. *Strategic Management Journal*, 34(3): 373–82.

Noon, M. (2007). The fatal flaws of diversity and the business case for ethnic minorities. *Work, Employment and Society* 21: 773.

Nouri, R., Erez, M., Rockstuhl, T., Ang, S., Leshem-Calif, L., and Rafaeli, A. (2013). Taking the bite out of culture: the impact of task structure and task type on overcoming impediments to cross-cultural team performance. *Journal of Organizational Behavior*, 34(6): 739–63.

Olkin, R. (2002). Could you hold the door for me? Including disability in diversity. *Cultural Diversity and Ethnic Minority Psychology*, 8(2): 130–7.

Ortlieb, R. and Sieben, B. (2013). Diversity strategies and business logic: why do companies employ ethnic minorities? *Group & Organization Management*, 38(4): 480–511.

Phillips, K. W., Northcraft, G. B., and Neale, M. A. (2006). Surface-level diversity and decision making in groups: when does deep-level similarity help? *Group Processes and Inter Group Relations*, 9(4): 467–82.

Pitts, D. W. and Wise, L. R. (2010). Workforce diversity in the new millennium: prospects for research. *Review of Public Personnel Administration*, 30(1): 44–69.

Putnam, R. D. (2007). E pluribus unum: diversity and community in the twenty-first century: the 2006 Johan Skytte prize lecture. *Scandinavian Political Studies*, 30(2): 137–74.

Richard, O., McMillan, A., Chadwick, K., and Dwyer, S. (2003). Employing an innovation strategy in racially diverse workforces: effects on firm performance. *Group & Organization Management*, 28(1): 107–26.

Richard, O. C. (2000). Racial diversity, business strategy, and firm performance: a resource-based view. *Academy of Management Journal*, 43(2): 164–77.

Richard, O. C., Kochan, T. A., and McMillan-Capehart, A. (2002). The impact of visible diversity on organizational effectiveness: disclosing the contents in Pandora's black box. *Journal of Business and Management*, 8(3): 265–91.

Roberge, M. and van Dick, R. (2010). Recognizing the benefits of diversity: when and how does diversity increase group performance? *Human Resource Management Review*, 20(4): 295–308.

Robinson, G. and Dechant, K. (1997). Building a business case for diversity. *The Academy of Management Executive*, 11(3): 21–31.

Rubery, J. and Fagan, C. (1994). Equal pay policy and wage regulation systems in Europe. *Industrial Relations Journal*, 25(4): 281–92.

Saha, S. K. (2012). Relationship between managerial values and hiring preferences in the context of the six decades of affirmative action in India. *Equality, Diversity and Inclusion: An International Journal*, 31(2): 176–97.

Sawyer, J. E., Houlette, M. A., and Yeagley, E. L. (2006). Decision performance and diversity structure: comparing faultlines in convergent, crosscut, and racially homogeneous groups. *Organizational Behavior and Human Decision Processes*, 99(1): 1–15.

Schippers, M. C., Den Hartog, D. N., Koopman, P. L., and Wienk, J. A. (2003). Diversity and team outcomes: the moderating effects of outcome interdependence and group longevity and the mediating effect of reflexivity. *Journal of Organizational Behavior*, 24(6): 779–802.

Shore, L. M., Randel, A. E., Chung, B. G., Dean, M. A., Ehrhart, K. H., and Singh, G. (2011). Inclusion and diversity in work groups: a review and model for future research. *Journal of Management*, 37(4): 1262–89.

Shore, L. M., Chung-Herrera, B. G., Dean, M. A., Ehrhart, K., Jung, D. I., Randel, A. E., and Singh, G. (2009). Diversity in organisations: where are we now and where are we going? *Human Resource Management Review*, 19(2): 117–33.

Singh, P. and Peng, P. (2010). Canada's bold experiment with pay equity. *Gender in Management*, 25(7): 570–85.

Stolle, D., Soroka, S., and Johnston, R. (2008). When does diversity erode trust? Neighborhood diversity, interpersonal trust and the mediating effect of social interactions. *Political Studies*, 56(1): 57–75.

Stone, D. L. and Tetrick, L. E. (2013). Understanding and facilitating age diversity in organisations. *Journal of Managerial Psychology*, 28(7–8): 725–8.

Sung, H. E. (2012). Women in government, public corruption, and liberal democracy: a panel analysis. *Crime, Law and Social Change*, 58(3): 195–219.

Taggar, S., Jain, H. C., and Gunderson, M. (1997). The status of employment equity in Canada: an assessment. International Industrial Relations Association, 49th Annual Proceedings, 331–9, Madison, WI: Industrial Relations Research Association.

Tajfel, H. and Turner, J. C. (1986). The social identity theory of inter-group behavior. In S. Worchel and L. W. Austin (eds.), *Psychology of Intergroup Relations*. Chicago: Nelson-Hall, 7–24.

Thomas, D. A. and Ely, R. J. (1996). Making differences matter. *Harvard Business Review*, 74(5): 79–90.

Thomas, R. R. (1990). From affirmative action to affirming diversity. *Harvard Business Review*, 68(2): 107–17.

Triana, M. D. C., Garcia, M. F., and Colella, A. (2010). Managing diversity: how organizational efforts to support diversity moderate the effects of perceived racial discrimination on affective commitment. *Personnel Psychology*, 63(4): 817–43.

Van Dick, R., Van Knippenberg, D., Hägele, S., Guillaume, Y. R., and Brodbeck, F. C. (2008). Group diversity and group identification: the moderating role of diversity beliefs. *Human Relations*, 61(10): 1463–92.

Van Knippenberg, D., van Ginkel, W. P., and Homan, A. C. (2013). Diversity mindsets and the performance of diverse teams. *Organizational Behavior and Human Decision Processes*, 121(2): 183–93.

Watson, W. E., Johnson, L., and Merritt, D. (1998). Team orientation, self-orientation, and diversity in task groups: their connection to team performance over time. *Group & Organization Management*, 23(2): 161–88.

Watson, W. E., Kumar, K., and Michaelsen, L. K. (1993). Cultural diversity's impact on interaction process and performance: comparing homogeneous and diverse task groups. *Academy of Management Journal*, 36(3): 590–602.

Weigand, R. A. (2007). Organizational diversity, profits and returns in U.S. firms. *Problems and Perspectives in Management*, 5(3): 69–83, 138.

Williams, K. Y. and O'Reilley, C. A. 1998. Demography and diversity in organizations: a review of 40 years of research. *Research in Organizational Behavior*, 20: 77–140.

Woehr, D. J., Arciniega, L. M., and Poling, T. L. (2013). Exploring the effects of value diversity on team effectiveness. *Journal of Business and Psychology*, 28(1): 107–21.

Woodhams, C. and Danieli, A. (2000). Disability and diversity: a difference too far? *Personnel Review*, 29(3): 402–17.

Wright, P., Ferris, S. P., Hiller, J. S., and Kroll, M. (1995). Competitiveness through management of diversity: effects on stock price valuation. *Academy of Management Journal*, 38(1): 272–87.

Yap, M., Cukier, W., Holmes, M. R., and Hannan, C. (2010). Career satisfaction: a look behind the races. *Relations Industrielles*, 65(4): 584–608.

Yap, M., Holmes, M. R., Hannan, C., and Cukier, W. (2010). The relationship between diversity training, organizational commitment, and career satisfaction. *Journal of European Industrial Training*, 34(6): 519–538.

Zanoni, P., Janssens, M., Benschop, Y., and Nkomo, S. M. (2010). Unpacking diversity grasping inequality: rethinking difference through critical perspectives. *Organisation*, 17(1): 9–29.

CHAPTER 12

ORGANIZATIONAL BENEFITS THROUGH DIVERSITY MANAGEMENT

Theoretical Perspectives on the Business Case

KELLY DYE AND GOLNAZ GOLNARAGHI

ORIGINATING in the United States in the 1990s (Lorbiecki and Jack 2000; Kochan et al. 2003; Litvin 2006), the business case for diversity is essentially a managerially driven, economic argument for improving organizational outcomes through investment in diversity management (DM) initiatives (Litvin 2006; Tomlinson and Schwabenland 2010). The business case *attempts* to quantify the benefits of effectively managing diversity and links DM strategies such as 'the recruitment, selection, development and retention of a diverse workforce to business goals, labour market shifts, globalization and competitive advantage (Yakura 1996)' (in Kossek, Lobel, and Brown 2006: 53). The use of the word 'attempt' is intentional as the quantification of benefits is problematic, as will be discussed below in the section 'What is the Business Case for Diversity?'.

This chapter explores the business case for diversity as it is situated within the broader discourse of DM. Of interest is the 'making of meaning' in terms of how arguments in support of DM are communicated and thus legitimized. Language is an important tool for 'the analysis of social organization, social meanings, power, and individual consciousness' (Weedon 1993: 21), as it is through language that meaning is constructed. This is supported by Alvesson and Karreman (2000: 1128), who contend 'language, put together as discourses, arranges and naturalizes the social world in a specific way and thus informs social practices'. It is through an examination of discourse that we hope to better understand the business case for diversity and the subsequent making of meaning.

Although this chapter is dedicated to the specifics of the business case for diversity, a brief discussion of its origins within the evolution of the broader discourse of DM seems appropriate.

The Evolution of Diversity Management

Lorbiecki and Jack (2000) suggest that the evolution of DM is best described by four overlapping turns, each with their own dominant discourse. The first such turn, the demographic turn, was a product of influential studies such as *Workforce 2000* (Johnson and Packer 1987), which suggested that the demographic face of the American workforce would be dramatically changed by the year 2000. The predominantly white, male-dominated workforce would become more diverse, and representations by women, African Americans, Hispanics, Native Americans, and other visible minority groups would increase dramatically, to the point where they become the majority. Stated simply, the demographic make-up of the United States was changing and the need to 'manage' this diversity was deemed essential (Hall and Parker 1993; Cox 1994; Kelly and Dobbin 1998; Dolan and Giles-Brown 1999; Barak 2000; Berger 2001; Von Bergen, Soper, and Foster 2002). The assumption here was that if organizations did not accommodate this demographic shift through appropriate recruitment, management, and retention of diverse employees, their competitiveness would suffer (Wrench 2005). Similar changes were happening in the Canadian and UK workforces, thus ushering in what became known as the demographic imperative to manage diversity (Cox and Blake 1991). Many argue that this first turn was responsible for the emergence of organizations' focus on diversity and the need to manage it.

Steeped in an almost palpable fear of the change in demographics, the language of this turn includes a focus on labour force, participation rates, immigration, minority groups, and the notion of the 'visible minority'. Central to the discourse were issues of sex and race and, as a result, much of the focus was on the representation of women and non-white members of the workforce. This resulted in greater numbers of women and non-white men and women in organizations, and legislative attempts to 'equal out the numbers'. Other underrepresented groups were less present in the discourse.

The second turn, according to Lorbiecki and Jack (2000), was political in nature and resulted in a focus away from affirmative action (AA) programmes in the United States and employment equity programmes in Canada and the United Kingdom, which were all experiencing considerable backlash caused by feelings of reverse discrimination and the perception that hiring was based on factors other than merit. Instead of 'counting people who look different' (Ahmed 2007: 240), the focus of DM initiatives changed. This was mirrored by a change in the discourse. Essentially, DM became more 'palatable' by focusing on language around inclusion, equity, and fairness (Lorbiecki and Jack 2000).

Interestingly, in many cases, the worker became 'disembodied' or 'sexless' (Acker 1990) in an attempt to demonstrate that organizational actors were not making decisions based on sex or gender—at least not overtly. Within this discourse, references were made to 'the employee' rather than men and women, and overt discrimination was deemed taboo.

However, this change in discourse was met with some scepticism as many were still reeling from perceived (or real) injuries felt as a result of AA and employment equity. Some felt the change in language was really about political correctness and that the programmes presented under this guise were nothing more than 'politically correct' continuations of AA and employment equity agendas (Wise and Tschirhart 2000). Indeed, in some instances this was very much the case. This proved to be a significant challenge when implementing diversity initiatives, and resulted in many less-than-successful attempts to manage diversity (Caudron 1998; Kelly and Dobbin 1998; Von Bergen, Soper, and Foster 2002).

The third turn is where our interest, for the purpose of this chapter, begins, as it was the harbinger of the business case for diversity. This turn, deemed the economic turn by Lorbiecki and Jack (2000), was quite dramatic and bespoke of the need for organizations to embrace and manage diversity or perish at the hands of competitors who had already begun to do so, in an increasingly competitive, global marketplace. According to Lorbiecki and Jack (2000), 'These economic arguments were highly seductive as they tapped into the existing fear that traditional monocultural organizations were no longer effective in meeting the demands of a global marketplace' (s21). As a result, the bottom line became the focus and is at the core of the business case for diversity.

The DM climate had changed. Fuelled by globalization and demographic shifts, and in response to failed diversity initiatives couched in notions of multiculturalism and equity as a moral imperative, there was a general sentiment that, as stated by Kevin Sullivan, vice president of Apple Computer, 'initiatives must be sold as business, not social work' (in Ivancevich and Gilbert 2000: 79). A common sentiment, it was evident that 'arguments for inclusive and non-discriminatory employment practice based on the rationale of "equal opportunity" [had] proved insufficiently convincing' (Tomlinson and Schwabenland 2010: 103).

Accompanied by a change in rhetoric (Gilbert, Stead, and Ivancevich 1999; Kochan et al. 2003; Tomlinson and Schwabenland 2010), the business case for diversity gained ground in the 1990s, and became what some claim is the most enduring argument for the need to manage diversity. What marks this turn is the key role of top management in situating managing diversity as a strategic element, linked to organizational performance (Wrench 2007).

Indeed, many DM initiatives today still cling to the discourse of diversity as imperative for growth and success. Redolent of the arguments put forth for any new initiative within organizations, the business case discourse is riddled with references to competitive advantage, return on investment, profits, and market share. Within this greater discourse, we find language around globalization, innovation, customer service, and stakeholder engagement. A more thorough review of the business case follows.

What is the Business Case for Diversity?

The business case for diversity suggests that improvements in productivity and profitability can be achieved by having, and effectively managing, a more diverse workforce and by creating a culture that embraces differences (Cox 1994; Robinson and Dechant 1997; Lorbiecki and Jack 2000). In essence, improvements to the bottom line can be gained by managing diversity through various strategic and human resource (HR) initiatives aimed at changing organizational culture and managing people 'so that the potential advantages of diversity are maximized while its potential disadvantages are minimized' (Cox 1994: 11). Accordingly, the business case 'legitimized organizational scrutiny of employees' responses to differences, and suggested that there were ways of changing them if responses were deemed "improper"' (Lorbiecki and Jack 2000). In essence, DM became 'programmable' (Lorbiecki and Jack 2000), and the end goal of these programmes was organizational performance.

This focus on bottom line and strategy was a dramatic change from the equity-centred discourse found in the political turn discussed. As explained by Litvin (2006), 'One makes the business case to demonstrate to members of the organization that they should engage in diversity work for pragmatic, financial, *business* reasons' (Litvin 2006: 75), not social justice reasons.

Although not immediately evident in most DM initiatives centred on the business case, at the core is the need to convince others (usually those holding power and control over resources) that DM is essential, thus legitimizing it (Kochan et al. 2003; Litvin 2006; Tomlinson and Schwabenland 2010). As indicated by Robinson and Dechant (1997: 21), 'Just as the head of Research and Development must present a compelling, fact-based business case to top management to gain the necessary commitment and resources from the organization to pursue a product initiative, so too must the head of Human resources develop a case for diversity integration based on the competitive edge gained by optimizing the people resources of the firm.' Consistent with capitalist agendas, the business case for diversity implies that decisions made by organizations, and the subsequent utilization of resources, must be made in the best interest of stockholders, and that HR can be controlled and optimized through DM. As indicated by Tomlinson and Schwabenland (2010), the business case 'reinforce[s] the view that [diversity] is something that needs to be justified and advocated in order to "get through" various points of resistance (Ahmed, 2007)' (in Tomlinson and Schwabenland 2010: 105).

Some argue that the business case provides space for social justice issues such as inclusion and the reduction of prejudice (Tomlinson and Schwabenland 2010). Proponents of this line of thought suggest that there is a need to create more harmonious and equitable workplaces if the financial benefits of diversity are actually to be realized. They suggest that, more than just ensuring women and minorities have equal access to positions and promotions within organizations, as AA programmes seem to typify, diversity-management programmes should focus on: '(1) increasing sensitivity to cultural differences; (2) developing the ability to recognize, accept, and value diversity; (3) minimizing patterns of inequality experienced by women and minorities; (4) improving cross-cultural interactions and interpersonal relationships among different gender and ethnic groups; and (5) modifying organizational culture and leadership practices' (Soni 2000: 396). It is important to note that these arguments, which appear to be couched in social justice issues and engage a social justice discourse, are often presented as necessary for organizational performance improvements. The bottom line *is* the bottom line in many such business case arguments.

Within the business case for diversity, a number of arguments link DM initiatives with firm strategy, HR practices, and, ultimately, performance. Most include the following claims (or variations thereof) about the benefits of effectively managing diversity:

- Attracting and retaining top talent.
- A reduction in costs associated with not managing diversity effectively.
- The ability to better represent an increasingly diverse consumer group.
- Enhanced creativity/innovation and decision-making.

The Ability to Attract and Retain Top Talent

The business case relies heavily on the notion that employees, especially top performers, want to work for organizations that value diversity. They want to be part of inclusive organizations that actively engage with members of minority groups and offer opportunities, benefits, and accommodation for diverse needs. It also suggests that failing to value diversity prevents the organization from having access to an important pool of 'stars', and much is made of the competition for talent (Robinson and Dechant 1997; Tomlinson and Schwabenland 2010). Organizations that remain homogeneous are at risk of drawing from a smaller labour talent pool (Wrench 2007).

This argument has garnered considerable attention and, as a result, there are countless 'Top Employer' competitions, awards, and published lists. These include: Canada's Best Diversity Employer, the Top 50 Employers for Women (UK), Top Employers for Canadians Over 40, the Stonewall Top 100 Employers 2013 (self-reported as 'the definitive list of Britain's most gay-friendly workplaces'), and The DiversityInc Top 50 Companies for Diversity (USA), among many others. A quick review of such lists and awards reveals a discourse that includes emphasis on inclusive workplaces, work–life balance, inclusive benefits, the celebration of diversity, and diversity strategy.

Reduced Costs Associated with *Not* Managing Diversity Effectively

Focused solely on the bottom line, this argument makes no allusions to social justice agendas—if organizations wish to save money on litigation and HR complaints, as well as maintain customers, diversity needs to be managed effectively (Bell, Connerley, and

Cocchiara 2009). Several assumptions are central to this argument. First, it is assumed that poorly managed diversity will result in an increase in discrimination-based lawsuits (Robinson and Dechant 1997). On the other hand, employees will not sue employers or 'waste' resources on grievances if diversity is well managed. Second, this justification for effectively managing diversity assumes that employees will have higher rates of absenteeism and turnover if diversity is not well managed (Robinson and Dechant 1997). The final assumption is that customers care enough about the ethics of the organizations they patronize to base their consumption on whether an organization receives bad publicity. Bad management of diversity leads to lawsuits, bad publicity, and reputations as poor employers, which all contribute to a reduced bottom line.

This argument does have the benefit of good optics, as some of the outcomes are more visibly linked to the bottom line than in the other arguments. Whereas it is difficult to quantify whether an organization has attracted top talent because of its diversity initiatives, it is easier to assess whether litigation costs, incidents of harassment, and the amount of bad publicity have gone up or down.

Better Representation of an Increasingly Diverse Consumer Group

As the face of the workforce changed, so did the face of the consumer. As consumers become more diverse in race, ethnicity, age, and gender, they represent an important market opportunity for organizations. This business case argument suggests that a more diverse workforce is better able to represent a diverse group of customers in terms of product offerings, sales, and customer service (Cox and Blake 1991; Cox 1994; Williams and O'Reilly 1998; Bell, Connerley, and Cocchiara 2009), and is thereby able take advantage of the opportunity to attract and retain more customers (Tomlinson and Schwabenland 2010). Instead of diversity acting as a liability and barrier, under this argument it is seen as a desirable trait and positive asset (Wrench 2005) that offers valued intelligence to organizations.

In response to this particular argument, it is not unusual to see firms hiring employees that they feel most 'resemble' their clients for sales and customer service positions, both at home and abroad. This argument relies on the assumption that minority group membership makes one an expert in how to best serve other members of that minority group. It is assumed that employees who are demographically similar to consumers may have an easier time understanding their preferences, behaviours, and needs. For example, Pepsi's 2001 diversity push required that half of all new hires be women or ethnic minorities in order to help the company better understand customer tastes and behaviour as it strived to target new market segments (Slater, Weigand, and Zwirlein 2008). It also suggests that customers prefer to be sold products and serviced by members of the groups to which they perceive they belong. This argument holds broad appeal and often appears on websites and publicly available marketing and reporting materials. Customers like to see that effort is being made to meet their specific needs and shareholders like to see efforts being made to increase market share. It is within the discourse of this argument that we see an emphasis on customer service and stakeholder engagement.

Enhanced Creativity/Innovation and Decision-Making

This argument stems from that belief that more diverse organizations, and especially more diverse teams, result in better decision-making, creativity/innovation, and problem-solving (Cox 1991, 1994; Cox and Blake 1991; Robinson and Dechant 1997; Williams and O'Reilly 1998; Bell, Connerley, and Cocchiara 2009). Citing the benefits of multiple perspectives and diversity in experiences, it is thought that a more diverse workforce is better able to analyse problems and generate more creative solutions, thus giving the organization a competitive advantage and driving business innovation and growth (Robinson and Dechant 1997; Tomlinson and Schwabenland 2010).

What is perhaps most interesting about this argument is its focus on the benefits of alternative perspectives, as reflective of its diverse employees (Tomlinson and Schwabenland 2010). This is a slight shift away from more traditional understandings of diversity, as well as other arguments within the business case, that focus on those elements of diversity which can be seen—sex, ethnicity, ability, and so on. In doing so, one could argue that this shift creates space within the business case discourse for other important forms of diversity and encourages divergent thinking. Rather than simply being 'managed', this perspective suggests that employees who challenge established practices and offer unique and interesting ideas should be embraced. Whether this is put into practice is another matter entirely.

DOES THE BUSINESS CASE DELIVER?

Despite the enduring nature and widespread use of the business case to promote and support DM initiatives, research conducted on the benefits does not reveal a clear picture in terms of the measurable impact on the bottom line (Kossek, Lobel, and Brown 2006). At best, the research is incomplete and contradictory (Kochan et al. 2003). One of the reasons for this incomplete picture is the difficulty in, and failure of organizations to, measure the impact of their own diversity initiatives. For example, a study of US colleges and universities found that many of the institutions studied had 'invested substantial resources in (diversity workshops) without seeing or seeking any empirical assessment of return on their investment' (McCauley, Wright, and Harris 2000: 11). Another US study found that only 30 per cent of the organizations who conduct diversity training go on to measure resulting behaviour at work (Carnevale and Stone 1994). This is consistent with other findings discussed in the literature (Rynes and Rosen 1994; Kelly and Dobbin 1998; Ivancevich and Gilbert 2000; McCauley, Wright, and Harris 2000). It appears that although many North American organizations are committing considerable resources (Von Bergen, Soper, and Foster 2002) to managing diversity, the effectiveness of these projects is often not being measured. Given the nature of the business case, it seems paradoxical that few organizations actually measure their 'return on investment' when it comes to diversity initiatives.

The indirect nature of the relationship between diversity initiatives and firm performance is partly to blame for the dearth of measurements of success for many diversity initiatives (Kochan et al. 2003). The relationship between good HR practices and the bottom line is complex and indirect. Although one might hypothesize that creating an inclusive organization leads to the hiring of top performers, which in turn leads to better performance, it is not a direct relationship that can be easily measured (Kochan et al. 2003).

The incompleteness is further exacerbated by the lack of research on actual organizations, as opposed to experimental research commonly used to assess whether diverse teams make better or more creative decisions (Kochan et al. 2003; Wrench 2005). The Diversity Research Network, a consortium of researchers dedicated to the study of the relationships between gender and racial diversity and firm performance (Kochan et al. 2003: 5), found that 'There is little research conducted in actual organizations that addresses the impact of diversity or diversity-management practices on financial success.' In an attempt to remedy this, the consortium conducted a multi-firm study of the effects of gender and racial diversity on firm performance. They found few positive *or* negative direct effects of diversity on performance, although they did gain some insight into the nuances of more diverse groups (Kochan et al. 2003).

The research results that we do have are contradictory. For example, Cox and Blake (1991) contend that their results demonstrate a positive net effect on the bottom line, and McLeod, Lobel, and Cox (1996) contend that there is evidence to suggest that increased diversity results in greater creativity. Similarly, Watson, Kumar, and Michaelsen (1993) found that heterogeneous groups are better at problem-solving than more homogenous groups. Other studies have also found racial diversity to positively influence organizational outcomes, especially where there is a strong emphasis on innovation (Richard et al. 2003). On the other hand, von Bergen, Soper, and Foster (2002) contend that unintended consequences of DM actually increase costs, and others have found that diverse workplaces experience more conflict and reduced cohesion (Tajfel and Turner 1979). Williams and O'Reilly (1998) found that racial diversity has a negative impact within the firm. Finally, several studies have resulted in the conclusion that there simply is not much hard evidence to support the claims that DM improves firm performance (Kochan et al. 2003; Wrench 2007).

THE CRITICAL TURN IN DIVERSITY MANAGEMENT

According to Lorbiecki and Jack (2000), the fourth turn is the critical turn in DM, which resulted from the plethora of challenges encountered by those attempting to manage diversity. It is here that we find many of the critiques of the business case for diversity, which focus on its ideological assumptions, located within a functionalist paradigm, thus privileging management interests (Tomlinson and Schwabenland 2010). Critical studies have attempted to destabilize the common-sense, taken-for-granted ways of thinking about the business case for diversity. Such efforts attempt to 'create possibilities for the construction and practice of alternative discourses about people, diversity and organizations' (Litvin 2006: 80).

Several themes that critique the business case discourse are evident and are discussed in the sections that follow.

Discourse of Control

A number of scholars have interrogated the business case discourse's practical implications and strong linkages to organizational performance (Prasad and Mills 1997; Lorbiecki and Jack 2000; Kirby and Harter 2003; Noon 2007). For example, Kirby and Harter (2003) suggest that the language of the bottom line and competitive advantage serve to frame diversity in the workplace in the interest of management. This is supported by Litvin (2006: 86), who contends that the managerial focus evident in the business case discourse is based in 'a normalized Mega-discourse that enshrines the achievement of organizational economic goals as the ultimate guiding principle and explanatory device for people in organizations'. Lorbiecki and Jack (2000) further suggest that the business case for diversity can be viewed as an instrument that uses employee diversity as a means for achieving economic end goals. Because of its managerial approach, this instrumental use of a diverse workforce as a way of achieving financial goals is possible through control and compliance, thus restricting diversity as opposed to setting it free (Christiansen and Just 2012).

The business case discourse values difference within the workforce based on how it contributes to the bottom line. The notion of 'valuing diversity' within this discourse becomes diluted, and inextricably links contributions to organizational goals (Tomlinson and Schwabenland 2010). This is supported by Zanoni and Janssens (2004), who found that HR managers are less interested in demographic differences, and are more focused on how these differences can be used to attain organizational goals. According to the same study, 'diversity is conceived in a very selective and instrumental way with reference to the productive process in the specific organizational context' (Zanoni and Janssens 2004: 71). The findings suggest that the business case discourse of diversity is a discourse of control. Drawing on the assumptions of human capital theories, members of the workforce are treated as assets and economic resources (Prasad and Mills 1997) with potential value to the organization when organizational goals are met. According to Litvin (2006: 87), within this discourse, 'the colourful chaos of human diversity disappears into a synchronized, mutually indistinguishable chorus, whose members' only purpose is to function as instrumental, interchangeable cogs in the profit-making machine'. Thus, the organization appears to take centre stage within the business case discourse, while the diverse workforce fades in the shadows.

Denies Agency and Full Subjectivity

In order to limit potential backlash and resistance from dominant groups in the workplace, diversity is defined more broadly within the business case discourse (Zanoni and Janssens 2004). As Litvin (2002) suggests, this conceptualization of diversity within the business case discourse implicitly assumes that specific groups are not targeted, as it moves beyond race and gender to target all members of the workforce. This broad conceptualization conveys that all group members (including the dominant) can participate without feeling threatened (as implied by the equal opportunity (EO) and AA approaches) (Mirchandani and Butler 2006). However, where diversity is defined within this discourse, it tends to encompass fixed representations by constructing employees in demographic categories portrayed as obvious, natural, and immutable (Lorbiecki and Jack 2000). Difference is seen within static and mutually exclusive traits, and organizations fail to take into consideration 'the ways in which individuals' social locations are embedded within multiple and interconnected norms around gender, race, class, ability and sexuality' (Mirchandani and Butler 2006: 482). Zanoni and Janssens (2004) found that HR managers construct employees solely as members of reference groups deemed to be relevant to the organization (i.e. gender and culture). This construction is problematic as these fixed singular identities fail to recognize the fluidity and hybridity of identities within organizations (Mirchandani and Butler 2006). What is more, such constructions of identity groups fail to represent difference in individual terms with situational and contextual considerations in mind. Such a construction is further problematic as diversity is conceptualized as being different from the norm: the white, heterosexual, Western, middle/upper-class abled men (Zanoni et al. 2010). Thus, those who manage are privileged subjects and those constructed as different are managed and denied agency and full subjectivity (Zanoni and Janssens 2004).

Dilution of Racism and Discrimination

According to critical scholars, the business case discourse silences discrimination, racism, unequal power relations, and other conflicts that are rampant in the workplace (Prasad and Mills 1997). Wrapped in a HR management discourse, critics of the business case discourse argue that racism and discrimination need to be combatted against and not managed (Wrench 2007). Further, with its happy rhetoric and inclusive approach, the business case discourse dilutes racism and discrimination by mixing policies related to traditionally excluded groups with those of all groups, potentially failing to address crucial hard elements required to address systemic inequities within organizations. These critics argue that the business case for diversity does not challenge these conflicts, but serves to facilitate existing hierarchies and unequal power relations privileging management interests.

A number of critical scholars have turned to postcolonial theory for new discursive accounts of diversity in the workplace (Prasad 1997, 2006; Prasad and Prasad 2002; Munshi 2005), because of the particular attention given to processes of Western knowledge construction which stereotype and subordinate the other (Lorbiecki and Jack 2000). Munshi (2005) draws from Prasad's (1997) analysis to make a case for using colonialism as a sense-making framework in order to surface power dynamics, inequalities, and the mission to manage, control, and help save the other. Prasad (1997: 305), in his analysis of workplace diversity, has shown that 'the discourse of workplace diversity is inextricably (and fatally) linked with the discourse of colonialism'. Prasad suggests that diversity is viewed as something that needs to be managed to keep the non-Western other (namely immigrants and visible minorities) under control—their treatment resembling that of the colonized other. Drawing on the business case for diversity discourse, 'diversity becomes the *cause* of organizational problems, and, therefore, needs to be *managed* by the controlling elite for the sake of goal achievement and profitability' (Munshi 2005: 58). In essence, the business case for diversity calls for the need to capitalize on diverse and top talent to drive bottom-line results and competitive advantages. In the quest for organizational performance, minority groups remain at the margins, and are capitalized upon for financial gains. The imprint of the colonial doctrine is visible, as these organizational programmes serve to guide and develop the other in their civilizing mission and implement control over the other to drive performance (Prasad 1997, 2006).

Contextual Considerations of the Business Case Discourse

Critical scholars have also argued that demographic, historical, social, institutional, and geopolitical contexts impact our understandings of diversity within the workplace and yet are dangerously absent from the business case discourse. A number of researchers have examined diversity discourses within their contexts, problematizing and challenging the dominant business case conceptualization of DM (Zanoni et al. 2010). Several of these studies suggest that diversity as business case discourse is featured most strongly in the management discourse of multicultural societies such as the United States, United Kingdom, Canada, and Australia. While it is argued that US-based multinational corporations (MNCs) have played an important role in transferring the business case discourse to other national and local contexts, differences exist across national boundaries. Singh and Point (2004, 2006) show, in their analysis of corporate websites in Europe, that UK-based firms embrace the US model most readily amongst all the countries examined. The United Kingdom has followed the American tradition more closely than other European countries (Wrench 2007). Other studies have shown that

DM within European contexts is very different from discourses engaged in the United States, Canada, and the United Kingdom (Singh and Point 2004, 2006; Meriläinen et al. 2009; Barbosa and Cabral-Cardoso 2010). Within a Portuguese context, Barbosa and Cabral-Cardoso (2010) found that foreign-owned companies are most eager to publicize their equity and diversity initiatives. Conversely, Portuguese-owned companies do not appear to have a policy on diversity and equity, particularly where they are targeting a local audience (Barbosa and Cabral-Cardoso 2010). In their analysis of Finnish companies, Meriläinen and colleagues (2009) and Singh and Point (2006) found that the business case discourse has not gained a strong foothold in Finland, as it is ignored on most Finnish corporate websites.

Adopting a universal business case discourse is problematic given the different paradigms between countries in North America and those in Europe when it comes to diversity (Wrench 2007). The North American paradigm reflects a history of immigrant absorption and policies rooted in anti-discrimination and fairness (Wrench 2007), whereas the European paradigm differs across national boundaries. Various studies have shown differences and variations across Europe in awareness levels 'of racial discrimination in employment, in the definition of it as a problem issue, and in the experience in organizational policies to combat it' (Wrench 2007: 39).

Relationship between the Business Case and Social Justice Discourses

A number of scholars, such as Ahmed (2007) and Tomlinson and Schwabenland (2010), suggest that a relationship exists between the social justice and business case discourses. However, the nature of the relationship remains unclear and is a matter of debate amongst diversity scholars (Tomlinson and Schwabenland 2010). For example, while some argue that an overreliance on the business case absolves organizations from social justice obligations (Prasad and Mills 1997; Bell, Connerley, and Cocchiara 2009), others contend that the business case makes room for social justice issues in an otherwise profit-driven world (Soni 2000; Tomlinson and Schwabenland 2010). For example, Ahmed's (2007) work suggests that some practitioners use the diversity business case (and economic language) when appealing to senior managers to enable social justice and transformation within organizations. It is also argued that both discourses have an important role to play in achieving social justice aims, even within profit-driven organizations. Ahmed (2007) suggests that practitioners without a political purpose for social change should choose the appropriate discourse based on what works best for each audience in order to drive action. Therefore, 'the business model and the social justice model are used together, or there is a switching between them, which depends on a judgement about which works when, and for whom' (Ahmed 2007: 242). By switching between these models and attaching them to words valued by the organization, practitioners make diversity appealing for uptake. *Saying* one will implement the business case for diversity, does not necessarily equate to *undertaking* the business case for diversity. Social change and action is enabled depending on how the discourses are taken up within organizations and by whom.

Litvin (2006) takes a more disruptive position. Given the lack of solid empirical evidence related to the efficacy of the business case discourse (Kochan et al. 2003), she argues that the reframing of the business case discourse is simplistic, and does not allow for new ways of talking and thinking about diversity. According to her, perhaps it starts with new discourses rooted in different conceptualizations of the origins and purpose of organizations and the employees that are found within them (Litvin 2006). Perhaps these new discourses rest on the ideas of justice, equity, and basic employee rights, and new conceptualizations of how organizations view their purpose in relation to the lives of their members (Litvin 2006).

Positions on the business case versus the social justice case are polarized, and research on the relationships between the two discourses is scant. A review of the extant literature leaves one amid a sea of debate with very little reconciliation. The question, as posed by Tomlinson and Schwabenland (2010), remains: Are the two discourses oppositional or can they can they be reconciled? While reaching a conclusion in this regard is beyond the scope of this chapter, a better understanding of the tensions and relationships between the business case and social justice discourses is warranted. This understanding is of particular interest given the fact that the efficacy and endurance of the business case are central to this chapter.

In an effort to better understand the tensions and relationships between these discourses, a small study was undertaken which examines organizations labelled by one agency as 'Canada's Best Diversity Employers'. This annual list is created to acknowledge and celebrate those organizations 'that have exceptional workplace diversity and inclusiveness programs' (<http://www.canadastop100.com/diversity/>). For the purposes of the Best Diversity Employer designation, organizations are evaluated in terms of their diversity initiatives aimed at five employee groups, including: women; visible minorities; persons with disabilities; Aboriginal peoples; and lesbian, gay, bisexual, and transgendered/transsexual (LGBT) peoples. It was acknowledged that this focus on only five groups (and the labelling of employees according to seemingly obvious, natural, and immutable groupings) is in itself problematic. However, it was felt that such a list provides a snapshot of mainstream 'doing' (Prasad and Mills 1997) of DM.

The 2013 list contains fifty-five organizations and can be found in Table 12.1. For the purposes of the current study, the list was refined by examining the mission and values statements of all fifty-five organizations. Those that contained an emphasis on diversity in either statement (indicated by the use of words such as diversity, inclusion, equity, and various other forms of these words) were included in the study. It was anticipated that organizations publish their mission and values statements on their website as an important strategy for communicating their identity to stakeholders. While some researchers have suggested that the mission and/or value statements may not always be directly linked to organizational practice (Helms-Mills 2006), others have argued that

Table 12.1 2013 Canada's best diversity employers

Accenture Plc
Agrium Inc.
Amex Canada Inc.
BC Hydro
Boeing Canada Operations Limited
Bombardier Inc.
British Columbia Institute of Technology
Business Development Bank of Canada
Cameco Corporation
Cargill Limited
Centre for Addiction and Mental Health
CIBC/Canadian Imperial Bank of Commerce
Corus Entertainment Inc.
Dalhousie University
Dentons Canada LLP
ENMAX Corporation
Ernst & Young LLP
Health Canada/Santé Canada
Hewlett-Packard Canada Co.
Home Depot Canada, The
Information Services Corporation/ISC
Jazz Aviation LP
KPMG LLP
Loblaw Companies Limited
McCarthy Tétrault LLP
Manitoba, Government of
Manitoba Hydro
Mount Sinai Hospital
National Bank Financial Group
New Directions for Children, Youth, Adults and Families Inc.
Newalta Corporation
Northwest Territories, Government of the
Ontario Public Service
Ottawa, City of
PricewaterhouseCoopers LLP
Procter & Gamble Inc.
Rogers Communications Inc.
Saskatoon, City of
SaskPower
SaskTel
SGI/Saskatchewan Government Insurance
Shaw Communications Inc.
Shell Canada Limited
Stikeman Elliott LLP
TD Bank Group

(continued)

Table 12.1 (Continued)

TELUS Corporation
TransCanada Corporation
University of Toronto
University of Victoria
Vancouver, City of
VIHA/Vancouver Island Health Authority
William Osler Health System
Workers' Compensation Board of Manitoba
Xerox Canada Inc.
YMCA of Greater Toronto

misleading mission and value statements can be damaging to a firm's reputation and credibility—important issues in stakeholder management (Mahon and Wartick 2003). Therefore, it was deduced that organizations which place DM at the core of their mission and values statements would prove to be rich arenas for study. Twenty-two organizations indicated an emphasis on diversity in such statements. Of these, eleven were for-profit organizations and eleven were non-profit and/or government organizations. Table 12.2 lists the organizations included in the study.

The intent of the study was to explore the discourses being used by these organizations to celebrate or 'sell' their emphasis on diversity, and the relationships between the discourses therein. In each case, the HR, corporate social responsibility, and diversity web pages were examined for mentions of diversity and the organizations' reasons for and commitment to diversity initiatives. That data was collected and content analysed.

Business Case Most Dominant Discourse for Most Companies

The first step in the analysis was to identify the most dominant discourses. Overall, the business case discourse was, by far, the most dominant discourse in both profit-driven and not-for-profit-oriented organizations alike. Indeed, twenty-one of the twenty-two organizations analysed engaged the business case discourse, thus supporting the aforementioned suggestion that the business case for diversity may well be the most enduring argument for effectively managing diversity. The business case discourse was engaged in ways that are consistent with the main arguments outlined in the first section of this chapter, 'The Evolution of Diversity Management'. For example, diversity was linked to a multicultural discourse and the assertion that diverse customers are best represented by a diverse workforce. It is suggested that only through the diversity of employees can organizations supply products, services, and customer care that meet the needs of different client or customer groups. This was consistent for both for-profit or non-profit

Table 12.2 For-profit and non-profit companies selected for study

For-profit companies
Accenture Plc
Cameco Corporation
Dentons Canada LLP
Hewlett-Packard Canada Corp
Jazz Aviation LP
Loblaw Companies Limited
McCarthy Tétrault LLP
Rogers Communication Inc.
Stikeman Elliott LLP
TD Bank Group
TransCanada Corporation

Non-profit companies
Dalhousie University
Health Canada
Information Services Corporation (ICS)
Manitoba, Government of
Ontario Public Service
Saskatoon, City of
University of Toronto
University of Victoria
William Osler Health System
Workers' Compensation Board of Manitoba
YMCA of Greater Toronto

organizations. The organizations studied also explained the benefits of drawing ideas from a diverse group of employees, and the richness in ideas, approaches, and experiences, leading to creative and innovative solutions to business challenges.

This reliance on economic discourses, situated within a managerialist agenda, is worrisome for critics. They question leaving issues of employment equity in the hands of managers, and suggest that this focus on the business case absolves organizations of their moral responsibility and other worthwhile endeavours that do not directly tie to financial performance and labour market conditions (Prasad and Mills 1997; Bell, Connerley, and Cocchiara 2009). It is not surprising that this discourse does not sit well with the ideals of equity, fairness, and social justice (Tomlinson and Schwabenland 2010). It is argued that the underlying dominant business case is more consistent with a liberal economic discourse, focused on responding to individual needs as opposed to equalizing differences between groups (Wrench 2007). Critics argue that DM has moved EO away from its intended moral and ethical intensions and the quest for egalitarianism, towards a business strategy (Wrench 2007).

Social Justice Discourse Strongest in Non-Profit Organizations

The social justice discourse was particularly strong in the non-profit organizations studied. As noted by Tomlinson and Schwabenland (2010), this is not surprising given the fact that social justice is often central to the mandates of such organizations. They suggest that increasing demands by funders for 'cost-effective and professional management' (Tomlinson and Schwabenland 2010: 102), coupled with the expectation 'to adopt a "business-like" approach' (Tomlinson and Schwabenland 2010: 107) may be at the heart of the adoption of the business case discourse. The existence of the social justice discourse was anticipated but, although much should be made of its presence and more research on this is warranted, this is beyond the scope of this chapter. Of more interest is the application of the social justice discourse and the resultant relationships between the business case and social justice discourses.

Relationship between Business Case and Social Justice Discourses

An attempt was made to tease out the relationships between these two discourses. This was particularly interesting in cases where both the business case discourse and the social justice discourse played a significant role. This occurred in fifteen of the twenty-two organizations analysed (five for-profit and ten non-profit). The 'employment equity as mandated' discourse was also evident and appeared in seven of the eleven for-profit organization websites. This is not surprising given that many of these organizations are federally regulated and are required, by law, to have employment equity programmes. What may be surprising is the manner in which the discourses were engaged. Our snapshot approach does not lend itself to an analysis of rationales behind, or orders of adoption of, the discourses. However, careful review of language use is telling and leads to some compelling questions.

One that is of interest is the inclusion of social justice arguments, alongside business case arguments, within some of the for-profit organizations:

> At TD, we believe that diversity is key to our success in the competitive global marketplace... As part of our team, you will be treated fairly and recognized and rewarded for your ability. You'll have access to opportunity for career growth and personal development. You'll work in a culture that actively supports respect; where the fundamental values of diversity and inclusion are ingrained and promoted in our corporate policies and principals.[1]

---

[1] TD Bank Group; see <http://www.td.com/careers/why-td/diversity/diversity.jsp>.

From this quote, it is evident that a space has been carved out within the business case for social justice issues, but it appears that this is an effort to attract and retain the most productive employees—or star performers. It is with regard to this goal that we see organizations engage in discussions of inclusion, EO employers, justice, fairness, and opportunity for all.

It is becoming more common for companies to promote equality and diversity together (Tomlinson and Schwabenland 2010). Carving out a space for social justice within the business case discourse supports claims that diversity builds on equality and facilitates advocacy on behalf of a broader range of employees (Tomlinson and Schwabenland 2010). This argument begs the question of whether organizations recruit, develop, and promote on the basis of competence, group membership, or possibly both. By carving out a space for both discourses, focus and attention continue to be placed on categories of people argued to be historically excluded: 'The privileges of inclusion may be delivered to a more diverse group than in the past' (Wrench 2007: 110). The business case and social justice discourses are used, as Wrench (2007: 110) states, to legitimize recruitment efforts and DM under a 'natural functioning of a market comprised of individuals aspiring for' access and upward mobility within organizations.

There is evidence of the reliance on both the business case and social justice discourses by non-profit-oriented organizations, which is consistent with the findings of Tomlinson and Schwabenland (2010). In their study of UK non-profit organizations, they too found that 'the idea of the business case does seem to have taken hold in the voluntary sector' (Tomlinson and Schwabenland 2010: 117). For example, in many cases this study found that organizations present a compelling social justice argument for DM, which is immediately followed by a business case argument:

> By providing a safe working environment and a manager who demonstrates the importance of diversity, employees with varied backgrounds can become more comfortable within the workplace. This encourages employees to be actively involved in the workplace, as well as share and discuss work issues and ideas with each other, leading to increased satisfaction levels of employees, as well as higher productivity and quality results.[2]

> UVic is committed to equity, diversity, social justice and fostering a welcoming and diverse learning, teaching and working environment. These are essential elements in achieving excellence in research and education.[3]

Tomlinson and Schwabenland (2010), in their examination of the tensions between the social justice and business case discourses, concluded that the instrumental aspect (i.e. the business case) could never be completely dismissed, 'because the demands on organizations imposed by their goals, performance expectation and limited resources

---

[2] Government of Manitoba; see <http://www.gov.mb.ca/govjobs/government/emplequity.html>.
[3] University of Victoria.

shape and constrain how diversity is produced and practised (Janssens and Zanoni 2005)' (in Tomlinson and Schwabenland 2010: 118).

The tensions presented by the use of these two discourses raise important questions. Could social justice discourses be presented solely for the purpose of making the business case more compelling? If this is the case, what does this mean for both the social justice and business case discourse? For example, does the presence of the business case undermine social justice arguments? One could argue that the social justice discourse is being co-opted (Dye and Mills 2011) to achieve business case ends. Such co-optation is not uncommon (Dye 2011; Dye and Mills 2011), and may be a skilful attempt to engage the competing discourse in a way that dilutes it and renders it 'accomplished', thus requiring no further action. As discussed by Humphries and Grice (1995), where organizations use the business case and social justice discourses together, it is feared that 'discourse of diversity is the discourse of pragmatics clothed in the garments borrowed from "the discourse of equity"... contemporary preferences for an economic pragmatism in the promotion of EEO and AA may mean that in the future communities may have little or inadequate labour regulation and limited practice in public resistance to unfair exclusion from employment opportunities' (Humphries and Grice 1995: 31). Although a closer examination of the co-optation of discourse is beyond the scope of this chapter, it is, nonetheless, important to consider this if we are to truly understand the complexities of the business case. Suffice it to say that the discourse of the business case for DM is a complicated one, including social justice language within a more dominant discourse of profit and market share.

Conclusion

Simply stated, the business case for diversity is a utilitarian, managerial argument that promises quantifiable organizational benefits for those organizations that can effectively 'manage' their diversity. Although some decry the business case's position as firmly planted within the functionalist paradigm, and assert that it privileges and universalizes managerial interests (Tomlinson and Schwabenland 2010), others feel that the business case, with its broad definitions of diversity and its focus on culture change and inclusivity, has made room for social justice aims and outcomes. Whatever the sentiment, the business case discourse has endured.

Given the paucity of concrete evidence, some might consider it hard to understand the enduring nature of the business case. If there is little empirical evidence to support the business case, and some evidence to the contrary, why is it that organizations continue to rely on the business case discourse to support their diversity initiatives? One could argue that the business case offers logical arguments for diversity initiatives that, at face value, seem to make sense—the arguments are intuitive and simple; therefore, practitioners continue to trot out the business case whenever there is a need to defend old diversity programmes or legitimize new ones. Or do organizations cling to the business case in order to maintain power and privilege in the face of more diverse workplaces? Or perhaps the business case discourse is simply a vehicle through which managers and CEOs can be convinced to commit resources to initiatives that are really trying to 'do the right thing'. If this is true, should we *not* use the business case in order to affect change? Or, finally, is it simply another fad that has incredible staying power, feeds the coffers of diversity gurus and consultants, and is continuously taught in business schools, despite contradictory evidence? Much has been written about such fads and fashions (see Dye, Mills, and Weatherbee 2005; Weatherbee, Dye, and Mills 2008) and their enduring nature (i.e. Maslow's Hierarchy of Needs and Lewin's Three Stage Model of Change). The motivations behind the continued reliance on the business case remain unclear and warrant further research.

Regardless of the intentions behind the reliance on the business case, it is important to consider both the intended and unintended consequences of doing so. Careful review of work that is critical of the business case brings to light some important questions. For example, what happens when diversity, as a means to a business end, is not economically viable (Christiansen and Just 2012)? Or what happens when diversity, focused on economic benefits, is vulnerable to market challenges? Could it be that the fight for discrimination and racism will only be given importance when there is a business reason for doing so? As stated by Wrench (2003: 10), within the business case discourse, racism and discrimination are 'indeed argued to be unacceptable, but only when it is recognized that the outcome leads to inefficiency in the utilization of human resources'. Furthermore, does the business case absolve organizations of moral responsibilities and ethical behaviour? Does bottom line trump moral obligations? And finally, does a continued emphasis on categories of difference only serve to reify otherwise non-existent boundaries and positions of power? It seems that there is much work to do if we are to truly understand the business case for diversity and the multitude of contradictions that it brings.

References

Acker, J. (1990). Hierarchies, jobs, bodies: a theory of gendered organizations. *Gender and Society*, 4(2): 139–58.

Ahmed, S. (2007). The language of diversity. *Ethnic and Racial Studies*, 30(2): 235–56.

Alvesson, M. and Kärreman, D. (2000). Varieties of discourse: on the study of organizations through discourse analysis. *Human Relations*, 53(9): 1125–49.

Barak, M. (2000). The inclusive workplace: an ecosystems approach to diversity management. *Social Work*, 45: 339 - 353

Barbosa, I. and Cabral-Cardoso, C. (2010). Equality and diversity rhetoric: one size fits all? Globalization and the Portuguese context. *Equality, Diversity and Inclusion: An International Journal*, 29(1): 97–112.

Bell, M., Connerley, M., and Cocchiara, F. (2009). The case for mandatory diversity education. *Academy of Management Learning & Education*, 8(4): 597–609.

Berger, N. (2001). Musavi-Lari: an experimental exercise in diversity awareness. *Journal of Management Education*, 25: 737–45.

Carnevale, A. and Stone, S. (1994). Diversity: beyond the golden rule. *Training & Development*, 48: 22–39.

Caudron, S. (1998). Diversity watch. *Black Enterprise*, 28: 141–4.

Christiansen, T. J. and Just, S. N. (2012). Regularities of diversity discourse: address, categorization and invitation. *Journal of Management & Organization*, 18(3): 398–411.

Cox, T. (1991). Managing cultural diversity: implications for organizational competitiveness. *Academy of Management Executive*, 5(3): 45–56.

Cox, T. (1994). *Cultural Diversity in Organizations*. San Francisco, CA: Berrett-Koehler Publishers.

Cox, T. and Blake, S. (1991) Managing cultural diversity: implications for organizational competitiveness. *The Executive*, 5(3): 45–56.

Dolan, J. and Giles-Brown, L. (1999). Realizing the benefits of diversity: a wake-up call. *The Public Manager: The New Bureaucrat*, 28: 51–4.

Dye, K. (2011). Holding our words against us: cooptation of the feminist discourse to perpetuate ethnic discrimination. Critical Management Studies Conference, Naples, Italy, July.

Dye, K. and Mills, A. J. (2011). Dueling discourses at work: upsetting the gender order. *Canadian Journal of Administrative Sciences*, 28: 427–39.

Dye, K., Mills, A. J. and Weatherbee, T. G. (2005). Maslow: man interrupted—reading management theory in context. *Management Decision/Journal of Management History*, 43(10): 1375–95.

Gilbert, J. A., Stead, B. A., and Ivancevich, J. M. (1999). Diversity management: a new organizational paradigm. *Journal of Business Ethics*, 21(1): 61–76.

Hall, D. and Parker, V. (1993). The role of workplace flexibility in managing diversity. *Organizational Dynamics*, 22: 4–18.

Helms-Mills, J. (2006). Organizational change and representations of women in a North American utility company. *Gender, Work and Organization*, 12(3): 242–69.

Humphries, M. and Grice, S. (1995). Equal employment opportunity and the management of diversity: a global discourse of assimilation. *Journal of Organizational Change Management*, 8(5): 17–32.

Ivancevich, J. and Gilbert, J. (2000). Diversity management: time for a new approach. *Public Personnel Management*, 29: 1.

Johnson, W. and Packer, A. (1987). *Workforce 2000: Work and Workers for the Twenty-First Century*. Indianapolis, IN: Hudson Institute.

Kelly, E. and Dobbin, F. (1998). How affirmative action became diversity management. *The American Behavioral Scientist*, 41: 960–84.

Kirby, E. and Harter, L. (2003). Speaking the language of bottom-line: the metaphor of 'managing diversity'. *The Journal of Business Communication*, 40(1): 28–49.

Kirby, S. and Orlando, R. (2000). Impact of marketing work-place diversity on employee job involvement and organizational commitment. *The Journal of Social Psychology*, 140: 367–77.

Kochan, T., Bezrukova, K., Ely, R., Jackson, S., Joshi, A., Jehn, K., Leonard, J., Levine, D., and Thomas, D. (2003). The effects of diversity on business performance: report of the diversity research network. *Human Resource Management*, 42: 3–21.

Kossek, E., Lobel, S. A., and Brown, J. (2006). Human resource strategies to manage workforce diversity. In A. Konrad, P. Prasad, and J. Pringle (eds.), *Handbook of Workplace Diversity*. London: Sage, 53–74.

Litvin, D.R. (2002). The business cage for diversity and the 'iron cage'. In Czarniawska, B. and Höpfl, H. (eds.) *Casting the Other: The Production and Maintenance of Inequalities in Work Organizations*. London: Routledge, 160–84.

Litvin, D. (2006). Diversity: making space for a better case. In A. Konrad, P. Prasad, and J. Pringle (eds.), *Handbook of Workplace Diversity*. London: Sage, 75–94.

Lorbiecki, A. and Jack, G. (2000). Critical turns in the evolution of diversity management. *British Journal of Management*, 11(s1): s17–s31.

Lowery, M. (1995). The war on equal opportunity. *Black Enterprise*, 25: 1–5.

McCauley, C., Wright, M., and Harris, M. (2000). Diversity workshops on campus: a survey of current practice at U.S. colleges and universities. *College Student Journal*, 34: 100.

McLeod, P., Lobel, S., and Cox, T. (1996). Ethnic diversity and creativity in small groups. *Small Group Research*, 2(27): 248–64.

Mahon, J. F. and Wartick, S. L. (2003). Dealing with stakeholders: how reputation, credibility and framing influence the game. *Corporate Reputation Review*, 6(1): 19–35.

Meriläinen, S. T., Tienari, J., Saija, K., and Benschop, Y. (2009). Diversity management versus gender equality: the Finnish case. *Canadian Journal of Administrative Sciences*, 26(3): 230–43.

Mirchandani, K. and Butler, A. (2006). Beyond inclusion and equity: contributions from transnational anti-racist feminism. In P. Prasad, A. J. Mills, E. Michael, and A. Prasad (eds.), *Handbook of Workplace Diversity*. Thousand Oaks, CA: Sage.

Munshi, D. (2005). Through the subject's eye: situating the other in discourses of diversity. In G. Cheney and G. Barnett (eds.), *International and Multicultural Organizational Communication*. Cresskill, NJ: Hampton Press Inc., 45–70.

Noon, M. (2007). The fatal flaws of diversity and the business case for ethnic minorities. *Work, Employment & Society*, 21: 773–84.

Prasad, A. (1997). The colonizing consciousness and representations of the other. In P. Prasad, A. J. Mills, M. Elms, and A. Prasad (eds.), *Managing the Organizational Melting Pot: Dilemmas of Workplace Diversity*. Thousand Oaks, CA: Sage, 285–311.

Prasad, A. (2006). The jewel in the crown: postcolonial theory and workplace diversity. In P. Prasad, A. J. Mills, E. Michael, and A. Prasad (eds.), *Handbook of Workplace Diversity*. Thousand Oaks, CA: Sage.

Prasad, A. and Prasad, P. (2002). Otherness at large: identity and difference in the new globalized organizational landscape. In I. Aaltio-Marjosola and A. J. Mills (eds.), *Gender, Identity and the Culture of Organizations*. London: Routledge, 57–71.

Prasad, P. and Mills, A. J. (1997). From showcase to shadow: understanding the dilemmas of managing workplace diversity. In P. Prasad, A. J. Mills, M. Elmes, and A. Prasad (eds.), *Managing the Organizational Melting Pot: Dilemmas of Workplace Diversity*. London: Sage, 3–27.

Richard, O., McMillan, A., Chadwick, K., and Dwyer, S. (2003). Employing and innovation strategy in racially diverse workforces: effects on firm performance. *Group & Organization Management*, 28(1): 107–26.

Robinson, G. and Dechant, K. (1997). Building a business case for diversity. *Academy of Management Perspective*, 11(3): 21–31.

Rynes, S. and Rosen, B. (1994). What makes diversity programs work. *HR Magazine*, 39: 67.

Singh, V. and Point, S. (2004). Strategic responses by European companies to the diversity challenge: and online comparison. *Long Range Planning* 37: 295–318.

Singh, V. and Point, S. (2006). (Re)Presentation of gender and ethnicity in diversity statements on European company websites. *Journal of Business Ethics*, 68: 363–79.

Slater, S. F., Weigand, R. A., and Zwirlein, T. J. (2008). The business case for commitment to diversity. *Business Horizons*, 51: 201–9.

Soni, V. (2000). A twenty-first-century reception for diversity in the public sector: a case study. *Public Administration Review*, 60: 395–408.

Tajfel, H. and Turner, J. C. (1979). An integrative theory of intergroup conflict. In W. G. Austin and S. Worchel (eds.), *The Social Psychology of Intergroup Relations*. Monterey, CA: Brooks/Cole), 7–27.

Tomlinson, F. and Schwabenland, C. (2010). Reconciling competing discourses of diversity? The UK non-profit sector between social justice and the business case. *Organization*, 17: 101–21.

Von Bergen, C., Soper, B., and Foster, T. (2002). Unintended negative effects of diversity management. *Public Personnel Management*, 31: 239–51.

Watson, W. E., Kumar, K., and Michaelsen, L. K. (1993). Cultural diversity's impact on interaction process and performance: comparing homogeneous and diverse task groups. *The Academy of Management Journal*, 369(3): 590–602.

Weatherbee, T. G., Dye, K., and Mills, A. J. (2008). There's nothing as good as a practical theory: the paradox of management education. *Management and Organizational History*, 3(2): 147–59.

Weedon, C. (1993). *Feminist Practice and Poststructuralist Theory*. Oxford: Blackwell.

Williams, K. Y. and O'Reilly, C. A. (1998). Demography and diversity in organisations: a review of 40 years of research. In B. M. Staw and L. L. Cummings (eds.), *Research in Organizational Behaviour*, Vol. 20. Greenwich: JAI Press, 77–140.

Wise, L. and Tschirhart, M. (2000). Examining empirical evidence on diversity effects: how useful is diversity research for public-sector managers. *Public Administration Review*, 60: 386–94.

Wrench, J. (2003). Resituating culture: reflections on diversity, racism, gender and identity in the context of youth. Council of Europe and European Commission Research Seminar, Budapest, Hungary, June.

Wrench, J. (2005). Diversity management can be bad for you. *Race & Class*, 46(3): 73–84.

Wrench, J. (2007). *Diversity Management and Discrimination: Immigrants and Ethnic Minorities in the EU*: Aldershot: Ashgate.

Zanoni, P. and Janssens, M. (2004). Deconstructing difference: the rhetoric of human resource managers' diversity discourse. *Organization Studies*, 25(1): 55–74.

Zanoni, P., Janssens, M., Benschop, Y., and Nkomo, S. (2010). Unpacking diversity, grasping inequality: rethinking difference through critical perspectives, *Organization*, 17(1): 1–21.

> # PART III
>
> # DIVERSITY OF EMPIRICAL METHODS

CHAPTER 13

EXPLAINING DIVERSITY MANAGEMENT OUTCOMES

What Can Be Learned from Quantitative Survey Research?

SANDRA GROENEVELD

INTRODUCTION

THE purpose of this chapter is to provide an overview of the role of quantitative survey research in the field of diversity management (DM) in organizations. Surveys are data collection methods and techniques which involve asking individuals questions in order to produce statistics about characteristics of a population (Fowler 2009). These characteristics may not only involve socio-demographic characteristics, but also opinions, attitudes, and preferences, which makes survey research a very popular research method in the social sciences. However, since diversity-related research questions are often complex and multilayered, they will not so quickly be associated with statistics, except perhaps for the monitoring of the representation of minority groups. Therefore, before going through the findings of survey research in the field, I will briefly explain the fit between survey research and the study of DM in detail.

In this chapter, DM is delimited to *policies and interventions* that organizations develop and implement for *managing a diverse workforce*. I define diversity as all the characteristics in which individuals may differ, although the policies examined in the studies reviewed in this chapter usually focus on socio-demographic groups, such as women and men, persons with different ethnic backgrounds, ages, disabilities, and sexual orientations. Part 1 of this *Handbook* has already outlined the shift from equal opportunity (EO) policies to DM, the accompanying change in policy orientations and what this has meant for organizational diversity practices. Broadly speaking, EO policies are primarily motivated by social justice arguments, while DM is more strongly linked to the business case of diversity (Kirton and Greene 2010; also Chapter 12, this volume). Notwithstanding the fact that policies that would once have fallen under the label of EO policy are now incorporated in the DM practices in organizations (see, for example, Kellough and Naff 2004), DM is targeted at bringing about the added value of diversity for business-related objectives, rather than having an exclusive and explicit aim to combat inequalities and discrimination in the workplace. This shift in focus in organizational practice is reflected in academic literature. Since the 1990s, a line of research has emerged focusing on this business case of diversity, which tries to disentangle the processes that foster or hamper the realization of the potential benefits of diversity for organizations. Many of these processes involve attitudes and behaviours of employees, leading scholars to examine work-related outcomes of diversity on the individual level and on the level of the work group, often by surveying employees (see Chapter 5, this volume).

Survey research on DM and its outcomes is emerging. Whereas these research efforts are certainly inspired by the findings of previous studies on diversity and their outcomes, I believe that the growing body of survey research on human resource (HR) management, work-related outcomes, and performance has been another important driver of survey research into DM outcomes. In fact, survey research fits very well with the examination of the incidence and outcomes of management policies and practices, since employees themselves are the best source of information in finding out about the practice of management and whether this influences their attitudes and perceptions. The employee outcomes central to these studies, such as job satisfaction, work motivation, commitment, and turnover are, furthermore, often considered important predictors of employee, team, and organizational performance.

The chapter is organized as follows. The next section provides an overview of recent research articles on DM and its outcomes, using survey research methods. I will distinguish between organizational surveys and employee surveys, and discuss the main findings and the contributions of these studies to our knowledge about DM outcomes. The chapter proceeds with an example of a recent survey research study among public sector employees in the Netherlands. While explaining the design and results of this study, specific advantages and disadvantages of survey research will be touched upon. I will then go deeper into four main weaknesses of current survey research on DM outcomes, and identify the main gaps in our knowledge that need to be addressed in future research. A research agenda for future survey research on DM outcomes will be outlined in the concluding section.

Overview of the Field

In view of this chapter's focus on studies inspired by the business case of diversity since the mid-1990s, I start with a brief discussion of survey research that has been conducted with the aim of identifying factors that foster or hamper diversity outcomes which boost organizational performance, the so-called diversity dividend.

Work Group Diversity Outcomes

Several theoretical and review studies published since the mid-1990s have shown that, from an organizational perspective, work group diversity may have both positive and negative outcomes. Milliken and Martins's (1996) review of the management literature identifies possible mediating factors between different types of diversity, and individual-level, group-level, and organizational-level outcomes. Their study identifies four common consequences of diversity that affect diversity outcomes, positively or negatively: affective consequences, cognitive consequences, symbolic consequences, and communication-related consequences. By distinguishing between different mediating factors, this much cited review article offers a first explanation for previous inconsistent findings on the diversity and performance relationship. Van Knippenberg, de Dreu, and Homan (2004) amended this study by identifying two dominant perspectives in the diversity and performance literature, highlighting positive cognitive processes related to diversity and negative affective processes respectively. Their categorization and elaboration model (CEM) integrates an information and decision-making perspective, and a social categorization perspective, on diversity. Their model shows that there are several mediating and moderating factors simultaneously at play that hamper or foster productive processes in diverse work groups.

What both these two key articles have in common is that they point at the underlying *mechanisms* through which diversity outcomes come about. Following these two studies, many empirical studies have been conducted focusing on one or more factors making up or influencing these processes, and amending previous studies on direct effects. Empirical studies of work group diversity outcomes can be mainly found in the domain of social and organizational psychology. Survey research techniques are an important part of the two types of research strategies that are most commonly used in this field: experimental designs (laboratory experiments and field experiments in which surveys are administered to members of the control and treatment groups) and field studies (case studies of organizations within which work groups and/or individual employees are surveyed) (see, for example, the meta-analytical studies of Bell et al. (2011) and Horwitz and Horwitz (2007) for an overview).

Identifying mediators and moderators in the diversity and performance relationship provides management practice with possible intervention points. For instance, recent studies emphasize the need to create organizational climates that are inclusive of all employees as a necessary condition for realizing the potential benefits of work group diversity (Shore et al. 2011; Ashikali and Groeneveld 2015). The emerging literature on inclusiveness essentially built on a integration-and-learning perspective on workforce diversity, which 'links diversity to work processes—the way people do and experience the work—in a manner that makes diversity a resource for learning and adaptive change' (Ely and Thomas 2001: 240). Shore and colleagues (2011: 1265) argue that 'diverse work groups that adopt an Integration-and-Learning perspective incorporate both uniqueness (through viewing diversity as a resource) and belongingness (through members feeling valued and respected)'.

Using a survey completed by 1324 employees working in 100 departments of a regional site of a large biomedical company, Nishii (2013) examined the benefits of an inclusive climate in gender-diverse work groups. This study is one of the few that empirically examines and validates the measurement of climate for inclusion. Nishii (2013: 1766) finds evidence for a moderating role of climate within the relationships between gender diversity, conflict, and satisfaction: '[B]oth relationship and task conflict were significantly lower in gender diverse groups with high climate for inclusion than in diverse groups with low climate for inclusion. [...] [T]he negative association between relationship conflict and satisfaction disappears when climate for inclusion is high.'

Other research articles in this strand of research adopt organizational and managerial characteristics, such as leadership and HR policies, as contextual factors in their models, explaining the diversity and performance relationship. An increasing focus on the role of leadership can be observed, which is very relevant to the study of DM. By explicitly examining the influence of managing practices, these studies go beyond studying outcomes of diversity as such. In their study of sixty-two research and development (R&D) teams, Kearney and Gebert (2009) draw on the processes identified in the CEM model and find that transformational leadership fosters elaboration processes and collective team identification of diverse teams. Nishii and Mayer (2009), in their study of 4500 employees within 348 supermarket departments, find that the role of leadership is important for creating patterns of inclusion within diverse work groups, and thus for reducing employee turnover. Both studies are good examples of the use of survey research methods and techniques with a large sample size on both the work group and individual level, and of the use of advanced statistical techniques to analyse the hypothesized relationships between diversity, leadership, and performance. I will come back to these methodological issues later on in this chapter.

Articles that examine the moderating role of HR and diversity policies in the relationship between diversity and its work-related outcomes are by far the least common. For example, Jehn and Bezrukova (2004) examine training-oriented and diversity-oriented HR practices as moderators of the diversity and performance relationship. Their study shows that training and diversity-oriented HR practices do not affect the performance of demographically diverse groups. Furthermore, and again contrary to what had been expected, training and diversity-oriented HR practices negatively affect the performance of work groups that are diverse in level of education. However, although their study is quantitative as to research technique (a field study of one organization within which a large number of work groups are examined), they did not use survey research techniques.

Diversity Management Outcomes

Despite the growing body of literature on the relationships between diversity in organizations or work groups and outcomes on the individual level (job satisfaction, motivation, turnover intention), the team level (conflicts, cohesion, performance), and the organizational level (turnover, performance), not much is known about whether and how DM affects these relationships. So far, more general research questions about the extent to which DM succeeds in producing desirable outcomes have not been answered either. All in all, compared to the studies of diversity outcomes, (survey) research into the outcomes of DM is more recent and still fewer in number, and is based in multiple disciplines. It is fragmented and characterized by multiple theories, methodologies, and measurements (Foster Curtis and Dreachslin 2008; Guillaume et al. 2014).

The conceptualizations and measurements of DM particularly vary. This may impair the reliability and validity of the findings. Whereas DM is generally distinguished from EO and affirmative action (AA) policies, what exactly DM entails remains unclear. Some studies take a comprehensive view of DM by including both policy and management programmes and practices aimed at both the attraction and management of a diverse workforce. For example, Pitts (2009: 330) states that DM encompasses 'elements of both affirmative action/EEO and diversity management programs. These programs [...] consider all diversity-related processes and programs under a large diversity management umbrella.' In contrast, other studies focus on specific DM programmes, policies, practices, or interventions. Some of these studies depart from an organizational policy approach and examine the effectiveness of specific diversity policies. Others explicitly take a management focus and conceptualize DM by focusing on management practices targeted at a diverse workforce within organizations. All in all, the variety in approaches to DM adopted in these studies explains the inconsistency in the field and impedes research progress.

In the remainder of this section, two types of survey research into DM outcomes are briefly discussed. First, a short overview will be given of survey research among organizations which mostly take a policy approach to DM. Second, studies based on employee surveys are discussed. These increasingly take a management approach.

Organizational Surveys

To my knowledge, the study of Rynes and Rosen (1995) is the first, and one of the very few, organizational surveys on diversity-related issues in organizations. It examines what factors affect the adoption of diversity training and its perceived effectiveness by surveying 785 HR professionals. This study explicitly draws on HR management studies and studies on diversity outcomes. It shows that only one third of respondents perceived the adopted diversity training in their organization as successful, although, at the same time, the results indicate a change in employee attitudes to diversity, with more positive attitudes after training. Unfortunately, the study adopts a general and subjective measurement of perceived training success, by asking respondents to evaluate the overall success of the diversity training on a five-point scale. Hence, conclusions on the precise outcomes cannot be drawn.

Other studies, based on organizational surveys, are more explicit about the outcome variable, but in doing so seem to move away from the business case approach of diversity. Instead, they assess diversity policy effectiveness by examining its impact on minority representation. Although employment equity and inclusion may be considered necessary conditions for the business case of diversity being realized, these studies do not assess to what extent and in what way DM may positively affect the diversity and performance relationship. For example, Naff and Kellough (2003: 1307) assess the effectiveness of DM programmes of US federal agencies by examining the relationship between five components of DM programmes and three indicators of success or failure: promotions, dismissals, and turnover. Based on a survey of 160 federal agencies and subagencies (Kellough and Naff 2004), it is concluded that, all in all, these programmes have barely had any effect on these outcome indicators.

Kalev, Dobbin, and Kelly (2006) examine the effects of seven diversity programmes on the proportion of native and ethnic minority men and women in management. Their study combines administrative data from the annual equal employment opportunity (EEO) reports US private employers are required to file, with an organizational survey among a random sample of establishments in this dataset of the Equal Employment Opportunity Commission, comprising of all EEO reports in the period 1971–2002. Their findings point at the importance of assigning responsibility for diversity: 'Structures that embed accountability, authority, and expertise (affirmative action plans, diversity committees and taskforces, diversity managers and departments) are the most effective means of increasing the proportions of white women, black women, and black men in private sector management' (Kalev, Dobbin, and Kelly 2006: 612). However, even the most effective programmes still have only modest effects on the representation of women and ethnic minorities in managerial positions.

Based on a comparable database of annual EEO reports in the Netherlands, Stijn Verbeek and I examined the effects of diversity programmes on the representation of ethnic minorities in Dutch organizations (Groeneveld and Verbeek 2012; Verbeek and Groeneveld 2012). We concluded that assigning responsibility can be evaluated most positively, even when, in the short span of a year, effects of separate policies on ethnic minority representation are absent (Verbeek and Groeneveld 2012). In addition, policy programmes targeted at managing a diverse workforce do show modest positive effects on ethnic minority representation in the course of a year, whereas more traditional EEO programmes targeted at the influx of ethnic minorities into the organization do not show any effect (Groeneveld and Verbeek 2012).

Employee Surveys

One of the earliest studies I encountered that uses survey research techniques among employees to examine DM outcomes draws both substantively and methodologically on the field studies on diversity outcomes mentioned. Gilbert and Ivancevich (2001) examine the effects of DM on work group attachment and organizational commitment of employees by comparing two organizations, one that could be considered as exemplary with respect to DM and a second organization with less DM efforts, and those primarily motivated by EEO. In both organizations, a sample of employees was surveyed with respect to attitudinal attachment. Results suggest that DM contributes to the attachment of both majority and minority employees.

The publication of the Diversity Research Network on the effects of diversity on business performance can be placed in the same research tradition and is frequently cited (Kochan et al. 2003). While, in fact, the relationship between diversity and business performance is central to this study, it explores the way in which, among others, HR policies and practices produce beneficial outcomes of diversity, by focusing on the moderating role of the organizational context. The study initially aimed at including a large number of organizations but instead ended up with four case study reports of four organizations, which were also reported in separate publications (see, for example, Jehn and Bezrukova 2004). Some case studies use secondary analyses of existing employee surveys. For that reason I discuss this publication here. The case studies largely draw on the field studies on diversity outcomes, as discussed, and draw on a management approach to diversity. In so doing, this publication can be considered a marker in the evolution of diversity and performance studies, and a starting point for employee surveys on DM and its business-related outcomes.

In addition to variation regarding conceptualization and measurement of DM, the survey research on DM and business-related outcomes uses different outcome indicators. The majority of studies use one or more work-related outcomes which have proven to be predictors of employee performance, such as job satisfaction, work motivation, and organizational commitment. Some also include a measure of performance, but, given the survey research methodology, based on respondents' perceptions of work group or organizational performance.

Most studies are, again, US-based. Public management scholars in particular have examined DM outcomes, probably since public organizations face a double DM challenge: on the one hand, being a model employer providing employees with a fair workplace and, on the other, managing a diverse workforce in such a way that it improves performance (Groeneveld and Van de Walle 2010). The majority of publications examine DM outcomes in US federal agencies, use the same dataset, the Federal Human Capital Survey, and, as a consequence, apply the same measurement of DM (Choi 2009; Pitts 2009; Choi and Rainey 2010, 2014). The studies show that there is a positive link between DM, job satisfaction, and perceived work group performance (Pitts 2009). Furthermore, DM affects these outcomes more strongly for women and ethnic minorities compared to men and natives. Choi (2009) and Choi and Rainey (2010) examine DM as a moderator affecting the relationship between diversity and affective outcomes (job satisfaction and turnover intentions) and perceived performance. Their results show that DM is particularly effective in managing racially diverse work groups. Analysing the same dataset, Choi and Rainey (2013) find that DM affects job satisfaction more strongly in the presence of fair organizational procedures. However, ethnic minority employees have lower levels of job satisfaction in the presence of a combination of

DM and fair organizational procedures. Probably this is due to the 'identity blindness' that fair organizational procedures tend to imply. In such an organizational environment, ethnic minority employees may feel their uniqueness inadequately recognized, while, at the same time, they may have high expectations in this regard given the organization's efforts in managing diversity.

Employee surveys among a representative sample of the workforce in a specific sector or country are relatively uncommon. Using an internet panel survey among a representative sample of Dutch public sector employees, I found positive relationships between DM policies and practices, and employee retention (Groeneveld 2011). I will discuss this survey in more detail in the next section. Houkamau and Boxall (2011), in their telephone survey of 500 New Zealand workers, examined employees' perceptions of, and responses to, DM in their organizations. Their results show that employees who perceive more DM practices in their organization are more satisfied with their job, are more committed, and have higher levels of trust in their employer.

All in all, previous survey research among employees has predominantly found positive effects of DM policies and practices on employee outcomes and perceptions of performance, although effects may vary across groups and are dependent on the context and measurement of both DM and its outcomes. And yet little is known about how effects of DM can be explained. Following research on the diversity and performance relationship, as discussed in the previous section, 'Diversity Management Outcomes' research on DM outcomes should focus more on the impact DM has on the mediating and moderating factors this research has already identified. In doing so, it will help us understand when and why some programmes are successful, while others are not. For example, if DM programmes are perceived to be favouring specific groups in an organization, this could reinforce categorization processes. This may explain backlash effects of DM comparable to those found in previous studies on attitudes towards AA programmes (Harrison et al. 2006). If, on the other hand, DM programmes are helpful tools in the hands of managers, enabling them to achieve an inclusive organizational climate, social categorization processes could be countered, and information and decision-making processes enhanced (Ashikali and Groeneveld 2015).

Diversity Management Outcomes: Survey Research among Dutch Public Sector Employees

Several of my own studies on DM outcomes have been based on an employee survey among a representative sample of Dutch public sector employees in 2010 and 2011 (Celik, Ashikali, and Groeneveld 2011, 2013; De Ruijter and Groeneveld 2011; Groeneveld 2011; Ashikali and Groeneveld 2015). Both the 2010 and 2011 editions were based on an internet panel with employees who had agreed to participate in the research. Their agreement was asked for in a large-scale survey project among Dutch public sector workers, which was based on a probability sample of over 100,000 public sector employees. The questionnaire contains items on DM, diversity policies, diversity attitudes and beliefs, attitudes towards diversity policies, leadership, employee outcomes such as job satisfaction, commitment, and turnover, and performance. In spring 2013, the research was replicated and the questionnaire elaborated, with, among others, items on inclusive organizational climate added.

The results show that employment equity policies targeted at specific minority groups are most commonly used in their organization, although frequently combined with policies that can be labelled as DM. Employees, on average, have positive attitudes towards diversity and diversity policies, although some differences between public subsectors can be observed. It seems that in sectors with organizations that are most engaged in DM and policies, employees are more doubtful about the value and effectiveness of DM and policies (De Ruijter and Groeneveld 2011). Furthermore, it is concluded that policies targeted at managing diversity effectively, in particular training and development trajectories aimed at creating an inclusive culture, show the strongest associations with positive employee outcomes, such as increased work motivation and commitment, and organizational outcomes, such as a more positive diversity climate (Celik, Ashikali, and Groeneveld 2011, 2013; De Ruijter and Groeneveld 2011).

Compared to native Dutch employees, ethnic minority employees have a more positive attitude to DM and policies, and are more positive about potential positive effects of diversity (diversity beliefs). However, the relationship between the perceived *presence* of DM in the organization and employee outcomes does not differ across groups (Groeneveld 2011). As such, we do not have any signals of backlash effects occurring.

In order to *explain* the DM and employee outcome relationship, we examined the mediating role of leadership and perceived inclusiveness of organizational climate. It was hypothesized that employee perceptions of DM are affected by the behaviours of direct supervisors (Purcell and Hutchinson 2007). The supervisor also influences the perceived inclusiveness of the organizational culture, for supervisors can be considered the agents of creating inclusiveness (Nishii and Mayer 2009; Shore et al. 2011). In particular, a transformational leadership style of direct supervisors is expected to be supportive, since this style balances attention for individual growth and inspiration and for collective endeavours of the work group or organization.

The results show that the relationship between perceived DM and commitment and retention of employees is mediated by the inclusiveness of the organizational culture (Ashikali and Groeneveld 2015). We also found evidence that diversity policies that are targeted at creating an inclusive organizational climate affect perceived inclusiveness of the organizational climate and employee outcomes particularly positively (Celik, Ashikali, and Groeneveld 2013). Finally, a transformational leadership style by the direct supervisor contributes to the positive outcomes of DM (Ashikali and Groeneveld 2015). These studies confirm the importance of targeting diversity interventions at the development of an inclusive organizational culture and accompanying leadership behaviours, in order to maintain and effectively manage a diverse public sector workforce.

The external validity of these survey studies among a representative sample of Dutch public sector employees is relatively high, particularly when compared to qualitative case studies. In addition, by unravelling the causal chain between DM and employee outcomes we shed light on possible explanatory factors involved. However, the cross-sectional design limits the possibilities of making causal inferences. Moreover, our results have all been based on employee perceptions of all variables. Although the construct validity of the variables involved has been tested, the analysis in this study is undoubtedly partly influenced by *common method bias* (Podsakoff et al. 2003; Meier and O'Toole 2013). Common method bias exists 'when some of the common variation between two concepts is a function of the common measurement and/or source used to gather the data' (Meier and O'Toole 2013: 431). It yields systematic measurement errors and may inflate relationships between variables. DM, transformational leadership, and organizational culture were measured by perceptions of individual employees in one questionnaire, together with the dependent variable. The observed variances therefore will be partly due to having a common respondent and a common item context. These and other methodological issues related to doing survey research on DM outcomes are dealt with in the next section.

Methodological Issues in Survey Research in the Study of Diversity Management Outcomes

The four methodological issues I will discuss in this section underlie debates about the usefulness of survey research in the study of diversity, but often remain implicit. I will illustrate them by examples from survey studies on DM outcomes. All four issues are related to the *validity* of studies based on survey methods.

External Validity: The Role of Context

Survey research as a quantitative research strategy is generally strong with regard to external validity compared to qualitative research strategies, albeit, of course, to the degree that a representative sample of the population is being analysed. Statistical generalization implies that findings that were based on analyses of a sample are generalized to the population. The question arises, however, regarding to what extent findings can actually be generalized. Studies on diversity outcomes are commonly case studies in which survey research techniques are used to examine attitudes and behaviour of employees in different work groups in one or more organizations. External generalizability is then restricted to the specific context of the case. Furthermore, the organizational context is often only used post hoc to interpret the findings or to provide explanations for their deviation from findings in previous studies (compare Joshi and Roh 2009).

The review of studies on DM outcomes reveals that survey research techniques are used to examine the attitudes and behaviour of employees in a wider context compared with the studies on diversity outcomes (Pitts 2009; Groeneveld 2011). However, whereas these samples allow generalization to a population of employees across organizational contexts (but in a specific sector or country), such studies do suffer from problems with regard to the content and internal validity of the research results. These issues will be discussed in the next section, 'Content and Construct Validity'.

Content and Construct Validity

Diversity-related concepts are often complex, multilayered, and multi-interpretable. The review of survey research studies in this chapter reveals that a validated measurement of diversity policies and DM has not yet been developed. Although employees themselves are a valuable source of information in finding out about the practice of management, when measuring DM by surveying employees several problems arise. First, the construct validity of existing measurements may be questioned. If we take, for example, the measurement applied in the Federal Human Capital Survey, on which several research articles have been based (Choi 2009; Pitts 2009; Choi and Rainey 2010, 2013), DM is measured by a three-item measure on a five-point Likert-type scale:

1. Supervisors/team leaders in my work unit are committed to a workforce representative of all segments of society.
2. Policies and programmes promote diversity in the workplace (for example, recruiting minorities and women, training in awareness of diversity issues, mentoring).
3. Managers/supervisors/team leaders work well with employees of different backgrounds.

The researchers have tried to provide a broad conception of DM, but, in doing so, essentially different concepts have been put together in one measure. In fact, policies (item 2), management practices (item 1), and their effectiveness (item 3), are combined within this single measure. The measure is, most of the time, labelled as DM, although Pitts (2009) also refers to measuring a 'diversity culture' when using this measurement. Replicating this measurement in a Dutch context, the items showed only moderate correlations, resulting in a low reliability of the scale in contrast to the high alpha scores found in the US context. Related to this, what DM or diversity policies mean to respondents may be context-dependent. If a sample of a national workforce is surveyed, respondents are employed in a variety of work group and organizational settings.

The substance, but also the meaning, of certain policies may very well differ across these settings. Likewise, they mean different things in different national contexts.

Second, what policies or management activities mean to individual employees may be different from what executive management or HR professionals have intended. Wright and Nishii (2007), for example, distinguish between intended, actual, and perceived human resources management (HRM) policies, a distinction that is taken up by many scholars to explain how HRM, work-related outcomes, and performance are linked. Applied to diversity policies and management, their model assumes that diversity policy and management practices actually implemented by managers can be different from those intended when formulated at the organizational level. Perceived practices result from the interpretation of the actual policy by individual employees. These perceptions may affect employee outcomes that, in turn, affect organizational performance.

Internal Validity: Multi-Level Theories Require Multi-Level Research Designs

The links between work group diversity, DM, and their outcomes are expected to be influenced by several mediating and moderating factors. Furthermore, these hypothesized mediating processes occur across different levels: the organizational level (at which diversity policies are formulated), the work group or team level (at which supervisors implement diversity policies and at which consequences of diversity actually occur), and the individual level (at which diversity as well as policies targeted at work group diversity are perceived). In the recent years, HRM scholars have been analysing the mediating processes between HRM and performance across different levels (Wright and Nishii 2007). The distinction between intended, actual, and perceived diversity policies, as discussed, implies that we need theories that link these multiple levels of analysis. Multi-level theories are an important step forward and require *multi-level designs*, with data collection on the distinguished levels of analysis. So far, however, most survey research designs only include one level of analysis.

Internal Validity: Causal Relationships and Common Method Bias

Another advantage of a multi-level design with data collection on different levels is the assurance of independent measurements of independent and dependent variables. In this way, problems associated with *common method bias* can be prevented (Podsakoff et al. 2003; Meier and O'Toole 2013). Studies on the relationships between DM and their outcomes that are based on a survey of either managers or employees, often suffer from biases as a result of having a common respondent and a common item context. Common method bias may lead to spurious results, to the extent that the error in the measurement of DM is related to the error in the measurement of its outcomes. For example, managers may overestimate both their DM efforts and their performance. Likewise, employees' general attitudes towards their work context may affect their perceptions of both DM initiatives and its outcomes. Related to this, a more general concern is that self-reported outcomes in surveys are often inflated (Horwitz and Horwitz 2007).

Common method bias can be a problem in survey research on diversity outcomes, since my review showed that, in studies that actually found positive relationships between DM and favourable outcomes, both independent and dependent variables are measured by surveying the same respondents. Multi-level designs may solve this by measuring the independent and dependent variables separately, for instance by measuring DM at the organizational level, DM practices at the level of the work unit by surveying direct supervisors and perceptions, and outcomes at the level of employees.

Conclusion: New Avenues for Survey Research on Diversity Management Outcomes

This chapter has focused on what survey research has recently contributed to our knowledge of DM outcomes. To this end it provided an overview of recent survey research articles on DM outcomes. This review revealed inconsistent results: whereas organizational surveys have yielded inconclusive findings with regard to the outcomes of diversity policies and management, employee surveys have generally shown positive relationships between diversity policies and management and employee outcomes. The inconsistency of the findings was then further explained by discussing four main methodological weaknesses of current survey research practice in the field of DM. These methodological issues may have severe implications for the substantive conclusions that can be drawn, and lead us to identifying the main gaps in our knowledge.

First, as can be derived from the review of studies in this chapter, research progress is impeded by the lack of consistency in the measurement of the central concepts. Survey research should particularly allow for reliable measures, as well as developing and testing the construct validity of the measurements. Research on DM would very much benefit from efforts to develop measurements of DM and related concepts, and to validate measurements across contexts.

Second, problems related to the internal validity of existing survey research on diversity outcomes brings us to more thoroughly examining why-questions: Why would DM yield positive or negative outcomes? Studies based on organizational surveys and those based on employee surveys both have their strengths and weaknesses, but both particularly fall short in *explaining* DM outcomes, as this would require insight in intermediate processes that diversity and DM imply across levels in organizations. Diversity processes occur at several levels of analysis: the individual, dyad, work group, and organizational level, but multi-level studies are still few in number (Jackson, Joshi, and Erhardt 2003). Multi-level designs may better capture the cross-level interactions diversity-related processes yield. Following multi-level studies on diversity outcomes and the increasing number of multi-level studies in the field of HRM and performance studies on DM outcomes would profit from multi-level designs. Given the statistical techniques that are currently available, it can be expected that multi-level studies will emerge in the field of DM.

Third, existing multi-level studies on diversity outcomes generally focus on the individual and work group level within a specific organizational context. For explaining DM outcomes, the inclusion of the organizational level as a source of variance would, however, be of theoretical importance. A recent example of such a study is based on a survey among 155,922 employees across 395 health-care organizations in England (King et al. 2012). Results show that the extent of diversity training in organizations affects ethnic minorities' experiences of discrimination. Personal experiences of employees with diversity training lead to higher job satisfaction, whereas the organizational prevalence of diversity training as such does not have an effect.

Finally, this example also shows that survey research, in principle, allows for a wider scope compared to other research methods. The problems related to external validity that were discussed in this chapter draw our attention to when-questions: When or under what conditions and in what contexts does DM lead to positive or negative outcomes? In order to answer this question, survey research methods could be used to measure DM outcomes across contexts, be it across national contexts, sectors, or organizations.

If survey research on DM outcomes acknowledges current drawbacks and tries to reduce its potential sources of error, as I have outlined, I believe the strengths of survey research on DM outcomes would be fully utilized and its potential contribution to the field realized. In more general terms, survey research on DM outcomes, in my opinion, would profit from combining insights from the literature on diversity outcomes with those from the literature on the HRM and performance relationship. Furthermore, I would substantially build on the work of Benschop (2001), who, in her qualitative case study research, developed a theoretical model incorporating these insights. Now, more than ten years later, both literatures provide extensive theoretical work that enable us to amend and fine-tune this model, as well as survey research and statistical techniques to put it to the test. Developing survey research in this direction would improve our understanding of 'what works' (Pitts and Wise 2010). It would not only contribute to academic work on DM outcomes, but also be beneficial for managers confronted with the challenge of managing a diverse work group effectively.

References

Ashikali, T. and Groeneveld, S. (2015). Diversity management in public organizations and its effect on employees' affective commitment: the role of transformational leadership and

the inclusiveness of the organizational culture. *Review of Public Personnel Administration*, 35(2): 146–68.
Bell, S. T., Villado, A. J., Lukasik, M. A., Belau, L., and Briggs, A.L. (2011). Getting specific about demographic diversity variable and team performance relationships: a meta-analysis. *Journal of Management*, 37(3): 709–43.
Benschop, Y (2001). Pride, prejudice and performance: relations between HRM, diversity and performance. *International Journal of Human Resource Management*, 12(7): 1166–81.
Celik, S., Ashikali, T., and Groeneveld, S. (2011). De invloed van diversiteitsmanagement op de binding van werknemers in de publieke sector. De rol van transformationeel leiderschap. *Tijdschrift voor HRM*, 14(4): 32–57.
Celik, S., Ashikali, T., and Groeneveld, S. (2013). Diversiteitsinterventies en de binding van werknemers in de publieke sector. De rol van een inclusieve organisatiecultuur. *Gedrag & Organisatie*, 26(3): 329–52.
Choi, S. (2009). Diversity in the US federal government: diversity management and employee turnover in federal agencies. *Journal of Public Administration Research and Theory*, 19: 603–30.
Choi, S. and Rainey, H. G. (2010). Managing diversity in U.S. federal agencies: effects of diversity and diversity management on employee perceptions of organizational performance. *Public Administration Review*, 70(1): 109–21.
Choi, S. and Rainey, H. G. (2013). Organizational fairness and diversity management in public organizations: does fairness matter in managing diversity? *Review of Public Personnel Administration*, 34(4): 307–31.
De Ruijter, S. and Groeneveld, S. (2011). *Diversiteit binnen de publieke sector. Een kwantitatief onderzoek naar de ervaringen van werknemers in de publieke sector met diversiteit en diversiteitsbeleid* [Diversity in Public Sector Organizations: A Quantitative Survey on Employee Perceptions of Diversity and Diversity Management]. The Hague: Ministerie van Binnenlandse Zaken en Koninkrijksrelaties.
Ely, R. J. and Thomas, D. A. (2001). Cultural diversity at work: the effects of diversity perspectives on work group processes and outcomes. *Administrative Science Quarterly*, 46(2): 229–73.
Foster Curtis, E. and Dreachslin, J. L. (2008). Diversity management interventions and organizational performance: a synthesis of current literature. *Human Resource Development Review*, 7(1): 107–34.
Fowler, F. J. (2009). *Survey Research Methods*, 4th edn. Thousand Oaks, CA: Sage.
Gilbert, J. A. and J. M. Ivancevich (2001). Effects of diversity management on attachment. *Journal of Applied Social Psychology*, 31(7): 1331–49.
Groeneveld, S. (2011). Diversity and employee turnover in the Dutch public sector: does diversity management make a difference?. *International Journal of Public Sector Management*, 24(6): 594–612.
Groeneveld, S. and Van de Walle, S. (2010). A contingency approach to representative bureaucracy: power, equal opportunities and diversity. *International Review of Administrative Sciences*, 76(2): 239–58.
Groeneveld, S. and Verbeek, S. (2012). Diversity policies in public and private sector organizations: an empirical comparison of incidence and effectiveness. *Review of Public Personnel Administration*, 32(4): 353–81.
Guillaume, Y. R. F., Dawson, J. F., Priola, V., Sacramento, C. A., Woods, S. A., Higson, H. E., Budhwar, P. S., and West, M. A. (2014). Managing diversity in organizations: an

integrative model and agenda for future research. *European Journal of Work and Organizational Psychology*, 23(5): 783–802.

Harrison, D. A., Kravitz, D. A., Mayr, D. M., Leslie, L. M., and Lev-Arey, D. (2006). Understanding attitudes toward affirmative action programs in employment: summary and meta-analysis of 35 years of research. *Journal of Applied Psychology*, 91(5): 1013–36.

Horwitz, S. K. and Horwitz, I. B. (2007). The effects of team diversity on team outcomes: a meta-analytic review of team demography. *Journal of Management*, 33(6): 987–1015.

Houkamau, C. and Boxall, P. (2011). The incidence and impacts of diversity management: a survey of New Zealand employees. *Asia Pacific Journal of Human Resources*, 49(4): 440–60.

Jackson, S. E., Joshi, A., and Erhardt, N. L. (2003). Recent research on team and organizational diversity: SWOT analysis and implications. *Journal of Management*, 29(6): 801–30.

Jehn, K. A. and Bezrukova, K. (2004). A field study of group diversity, workgroup context, and performance. *Journal of Organizational Behavior*, 25(6): 703–29.

Joshi, A. and Roh, H. (2009). The role of context in work team diversity research: a meta-analytical review. *Academy of Management Journal*, 52(3): 599–627.

Kalev, A., Dobbin, F., and Kelly, E. (2006). Best practices or best guesses? Assessing the efficacy of corporate affirmative action and diversity policies. *American Sociological Review*, 71: 589–617.

Kearney, E. and Gebert, D. (2009). Managing diversity and enhancing team outcomes: the promise of transformational leadership. *Journal of Applied Psychology*, 94(1): 77–89.

Kellough, J. E. and Naff, K. C. (2004). Responding to a wake-up call: an examination of federal agency diversity management programs. *Administration & Society*, 36(1): 62–90.

King, E. B., Dawson, J. F., Kravitz, D. A. and Gulick, L. M. V. (2012). A multilevel study of the relationships between diversity training, ethnic discrimination and satisfaction in organizations. *Journal of Organizational Behavior*, 33(1): 5–20.

Kirton, G. and A. Greene (2010). *The Dynamics of Managing Diversity: A Critical Approach*. Oxford: Elsevier/Butterworth-Heinemann.

Kochan, T., Bezrukova, K., Ely, R., Jackson, S., Joshi, A., Jehn, K., Leonard, J., Levine, D., and Thomas, D. (2003). The effects of diversity on business performance: report of the diversity research network. *Human Resource Management*, 42(1): 3–21.

Meier, K. J. and O'Toole, L. J. (2013). Subjective organizational performance and measurement error: common source bias and spurious relationships. *Journal of Public Administration Research and Theory*, 23(2): 429–56.

Milliken, F. and Martins, L. (1996). Searching for common threads: understanding the multiple effects of diversity in organizational groups. *Academy of Management Review*, 21(2): 402–33.

Naff, K. C. and Kellough, J. E. (2003). Ensuring employment equity: are federal diversity programs making a difference? *International Journal of Public Administration*, 26(12): 1307–36.

Nishii, L. H. (2013). The benefits of climate for inclusion for gender diverse groups. *Academy of Management Journal*, 56(6): 1754–74.

Nishii, L. H. and Mayer, D. M. (2009). Do inclusive leaders help to reduce turnover in diverse groups? The moderating role of leader–member exchange in the diversity to turnover relationship. *Journal of Applied Psychology*, 94(6): 1412–26.

Pitts, D. W. (2009). Diversity management, job satisfaction, and performance: evidence from U.S. federal agencies. *Public Administration Review*, 69(2): 328–38.

Pitts, D. W. and Wise, L. R. (2010). Workforce diversity in the new millennium: prospects for research. *Review of Public Personnel Administration*, 30(1): 44–69.

Podsakoff, P. M., MacKenzie, S. B., J.-Y. Lee, and Podsakoff, N. P. (2003). Common method biases in behavioural research: a critical review of the literature and recommended remedies. *Journal of Applied Psychology*, 88(5): 879–903.

Purcell, J. and Hutchinson, S. (2007). Front-line managers as agents in the HRM performance causal chain: theory, analysis and evidence. *Human Resource Management Journal*, 17(1): 3–20.

Rynes, S. and Rosen, B. (1995). A field survey of factors affecting the adoption and perceived success of diversity training. *Personnel Psychology*, 48: 247–70.

Shore, L. M., Randel, A. E., Chung, B. G., Dean, M. A., Ehrhart, K. H. and Singh, G. 2011. Inclusion and diversity in work groups: a review and model for future research. *Journal of Management*, 37(4): 1262–89.

Van Knippenberg, D., Dreu, de, C. K. W., and Homan, C. (2004). Work group diversity and group performance: an integrative model and research agenda. *Journal of Applied Psychology*, 89(6): 1008–22.

Verbeek, S. and Groeneveld, S. (2012). Do 'hard' diversity policies increase ethnic minority representation? An assessment of their (in)effectiveness using administrative data. *Personnel Review*, 41(5): 647–64.

Wright, P. M. and Nishii, L. H. (2007). *Strategic HRM and Organizational Behavior: Integrating Multiple Levels of Analysis*. Center for Advanced Human Resource Studies (CAHRS): CAHRS Working Paper Series.

CHAPTER 14

CHALLENGES AND OPPORTUNITIES

Contextual Approaches to Diversity Research and Practice

JANET PORTER AND ROSALIE HILDE[1]

INTRODUCTION

It is not unusual to hear concerns that organizational diversity literature is over-weighted in positivist research and that managerialist approaches dominate diversity management practice (Nkomo and Cox 1996; Dickens 1999; Janssens and Zanoni 2005; Willmott 2005; Nkomo and Stewart 2006; Noon 2007; Hart 2010; McMahon 2010). Management of diversity in organizations has been found to be coupled with improvement of business efficiency variables (Dickens 1999; Noon 2007; Hart 2010), maintenance of organizational economic performance (Janssens and Zanoni 2005; McMahon 2010), and the normalization of organizational members to reduce conflict and to maintain control (Nkomo and Cox 1996; Willmott 2005; Nkomo and Stewart 2006). Paradoxically, researchers have found that diversity management programmes exist in organizations alongside with discrimination (Nkomo and Stewart 2006).

A second broad criticism is that social psychology frameworks (e.g., social identity theory) dominate theoretical approaches in this body of work. Researchers have paid much attention to understanding the constructions of identities of social demographic categories such as race or gender. Over time, scholars have reflected on two key problems resulting from this over-focus. In the first instance, concentration on one or two identities ignores multiple interacting and conflicting identities in individuals' actions (McCall 2005; Bagilhole 2010). Secondly, focus on individual identity tends to underplay

---

[1] This chapter was an equal collaboration between the two authors.

or to neglect the effects of other levels of analysis such as organization and organizing processes (Ashcroft 2004; Martin 2006). Scholars such as Zanoni et al. (2010: 12) agree that predominance of social psychological approaches in this literature has resulted 'in a narrow understanding of the processes leading to inequality, namely one that largely overlooks structural, context-specific elements'.

In this chapter we focus on three calls for future diversity research that emanate from the above general criticisms. The first call is for more enquiry that is multi-level in analysis, reflecting the view that individuals with intersecting multiple identities are situated within multiple organizational, institutional, and social structures (Zanoni et al. 2010). Secondly, there is a call for more study of subtle linguistic and non-linguistic mechanisms of discrimination in the workplace. This includes inter-individual focus such as inter-individual incivility (Cortina 2008) or everyday examples of social exclusion (Van Laer and Janssens 2011). It can also include the observation, documentation, and analysis of formal and operationalized organizational processes that produce inequalities in workplaces (Janssens and Zanoni 2005) or 'the means by which groups are able to secure their vested interests within the organizational structure' (Mumby 1987: 117). The last call we wish to note emanates from the observation that diversity research and practices often serves to perpetuate the status quo (Grimes 2002). This articulates as the need for diversity research design to more deeply problematize basic assumptions—such as the origins of diversity concepts (Nkomo and Stewart 2006), the assumptions of diversity management pedagogy (Litvin 1997), or the unquestioned social constructions of organizations. Over the years, scholars have noted that too few diversity studies address the intents of these calls empirically (Nkomo and Cox 1996; Nkomo and Stewart 2006; Zanoni et al. 2010).

Our aim in this chapter is to demonstrate that textual analysis methodologies have much potential to serve this assembly of identified needs. For researchers in non-positivist and non-essentialist theoretical positions, textual analysis can be used to produce expository diversity studies that are empirical, contextual, and situational, with multi-levels of analysis. Critical approaches using textual analysis add the benefit of a problematized status quo, challenging assumptions of both management researchers and practitioners. When one has specific, concrete, and numerous details about how power within organizations is created, organized, structured, distributed, entrenched, enacted, resisted, or challenged, one can see how asymmetrical differences in power and inequities are subtly and, in some cases, invisibly produced among and between social groups. Textual analysis can serve to illuminate the enactment of injustice on individuals by other individuals, by organizing processes unintentionally or unknowingly designed to be unfair, or by institutional discrimination. These illuminations can, in turn, be used to create awareness, strategies for resistance, provocation for change, and improvement in sets of evidence for legal cases, challenges, and settlements—the banes of every human resource department.

This chapter assists those interested in organizational diversity studies. We wish to offer understanding beyond functionalist and interpretive approaches in order to actively challenge the assumptions underlying traditional organizational diversity management theory and practice. To that end, we will first discuss, in the broadest sense, what textual analysis is, what it has to offer, and its disparate uses in organizational diversity research. Then we will highlight findings in diversity research that show the different ways in which textual analysis produces specific but wide-ranging examples of how asymmetry in social groups in organizations is created. Next we present and explore in detail the use of Laclau and Mouffe's (1985) discourse theory and the application of Helms Mills et al.'s (2010) critical sensemaking in the context of studying diversity in organizations. We believe that these two approaches offer much potential for delivering specific, contextual, empirical, and multi-level analysis, exploring how asymmetry in social groups is simultaneously and mutually constructed by individuals and by organizational structures.

Textual Analysis in Different Theoretical Perspectives

Human actions, it has been argued (Weick 1995; Weick, Sutcliffe, and Obstfeld 2005), are not based on people's knowledge, but rather on whether they can make sense of the information presented to them. Textual analysis is one method that researchers can use to explore how people do this, by studying human interaction with, and response to, information in the form of language, symbols, and sign systems. Understandably then, the range of textual data that can be used is quite broad. Data may include, but are not limited to, written material, spoken words, pictures, symbols, artefacts (Phillips and Hardy 2002), as well as cartoons (Hardy and Phillips 1999), metaphor (Morgan 2006), photographs (Bell 2012), fiction, stories, and narratives (Mumby 1987; Flyvjberg 2001; Czarniawska-Joerges 2004; Czarniawska 2006), films (Bell 2008), advertisements (Royo-Vela et al. 2007), or TV programmes (Fairclough 2003).

The textual analysis approach to research is evident throughout many epistemological positions and appears in many different research traditions. In positivist and post-positivist quantitative content analysis, individual texts are coded and categorized for purposes of correlation or prediction. In the interpretive paradigm, textual analysis can be used to understand individual construction and interpretation of a past situation or event (Cox and Hassard 2007) with an unproblematic view of the status quo (Burrell and Morgan 1979). Critical perspectives and related inquiry problematize the status quo by exposure and critique of existing realities and, depending on the perspective, consideration how alternative realities can be emancipatory (Gergen and Thatchenkery 1996). In these two non-positivist and non-essentialist perspectives, textual methodologies appear as analysis of, for example, documents, discourse, conversation, life histories, narrative, or rhetoric (O'Connor 1995; Bryman et al. 2011). In the critical perspectives (including critical theory, feminism, and post-structuralism), different epistemological beliefs produce different methodological uses of textual analysis. Researchers in this tradition problematize existing processes, practices, and texts and may advocate for fundamental change in organizational, institutional, or societal structures. Textual approaches can include examination and deconstruction of text for alternative meanings, hidden assumptions, and/or power relations in context (Bryman et al. 2011), production of alternative texts (Calás and Smircich 1991), or reproduction of texts from opposing assumption bases (Martin 1990). Simply put, a researcher who is positioned in a non-positivist and non-essentialist framework performs textual analysis in order to call out and to debate different interpretations that might be made of a particular set of texts (McKee 2003). If taken as systems of interpretation and organizing processes (Vibert 2004), text can plausibly represent, for example, how institutions function (Smith 2001), how collective identity is accomplished (Garfinkel 1967; Scott 1994), or 'the social relations of which we are practitioners' (Smith 1983: 322).

Choosing to collect a variety of types of data strengthens representations of interactions between individuals, groups, and organizations (Helms Mills, Thurlow, and Mills 2010) and improves arguments about the resulting implications (Flyvjberg 2001; Smith 2001). A multiplicity of texts and different levels of analysis and maintenance of contextual data provides specific examples and helps support localized and relevant arguments about where change is needed or can occur in organizations. Lastly, when a wide variety of texts are studied across and between organizing processes and between groups, this may help shift the managerialist approach to diversity management to one that is less focused on how to get individuals to conform and one that is more introspective about how organizing processes embed discriminatory workplace practices. The next section discusses how textual analysis has been used in non-positivist/non-essentialist and critical perspective organizational diversity research.

Textual Analysis in Organizational Diversity Research

Both non-positivist/non-essentialist and critical theoretical perspectives employing textual analysis are useful in revealing important facets of diversity in organization and management. Discourse analysis, conversation analysis, narrative analysis, rhetorical analysis, or contextual analysis (sometimes a grounded theory approach) are commonly used textual analysis methodologies for organizational diversity research rooted in these two positions. In non-positivist/non-essentialist positions, studies are expository—designed to show and understand how individuals make sense of and react to their experiences. These positions tend to problematize gaps in applications of theory, absence of a certain type of methodology, or empirical terrains that have been under-explored, or missed completely. Herbert (1990), for example, uses Levinson's clinical/biographical interview method to capture the psychosocial developmental periods of black male entrepreneurs, in order to add to the literature of experiential differences between white and black adults and between white and black male entrepreneurs. Pio (2005) uses interviews with South-Asian female immigrants to New Zealand, with a grounded theory approach to qualitative analysis, to interpret the *bricolage* of ethnic identity construction within the context of immigration policy and management of a diverse workforce. Similarly, Liversage (2009) evaluates the narratives of high-skilled female immigrants for identity-challenging difficulties during attempts to access job markets in Denmark. The professional identities of the respondents were challenged by difficulties in accessing their original professions, with some reporting fall-back to traditional social roles such as mother and housewife. Studies in this perspective are situational and empirical. They are contextual in that broader institutional or societal themes are mentioned, albeit for information purposes rather than textual analysis. Data collection is usually via interviews with individuals. The text that is evaluated is the language expressed by the respondents, as reflected by and through the researchers.

In diversity studies rooted in critical perspectives, the exploration of language and its uses similarly figures prominently. In one strand, researchers employing textual analysis have challenged the very construction of the knowledge of diversity. Zanoni and Janssens (2004) use critical analysis of discourse and the use of rhetoric to make visible the diversity discourses expressed in interviews of human resources managers. The authors explore the definitions of diversity as found in three types of texts within the mainstream literature: practitioners' articles and books on diversity management, chapters on diversity in organizational behaviour handbooks, and academic articles researching the effects of diversity in organizations. They question the nature of the managers' narrowly defined construct of diversity and link this construct to power exerted in managerial relations. On the same note, Litvin (1997) traces the origins and assumptions of workforce diversity discourse in organizational behaviour textbooks back to its underlying roots in essentialist thought.

Other critical studies focus on language-based practices within organizations. Van Laer and Janssens (2011) go deep into the language of discrimination by exploring subtle verbal mechanisms of social exclusion uttered by Flemish Belgian majority professionals as reported by minority professionals of Turkish or Maghrebi descent in interviews, using critical discourse analysis. Menard-Warwick (2008) use Fairclough's critical discourse analysis to locate the hidden assumptions of ESL (English as a Second Language) teachers with respect to Latina immigrant women. This critical ethnographic study discursively analysed a linguistic practice of positioning Latina immigrant students in an ESL programme essentially as homemakers, employable as domestic servants.

A third strand of critical diversity studies focuses on studying language-based individual resistance to various forms of discrimination in organizations. For example, Essers and Benschop's (2009) study shows the intersection and agency of entrepreneurship, gender, and religion identity of Muslim women of Moroccan or Turkish origin as these women established self-employment in the Netherlands. The authors used qualitative content (thematic) analysis of life story interview material. Bell et al. (2003) use conversation analysis to compare and contrast silence and voice as resistance strategies used by black and white women in reaction to injustice and hierarchy in workplaces.

Malhi and Boon (2007) employ rhetorical and critical discourse analysis in interviews with South Asian Canadian women to show themes of resistance and understanding in incidents of covert 'democratic' racism in Canadian workplaces. In an inductive (grounded) approach, with ethnographic and interview material, Denissen (2010) documents resistance and strategic adjustment in tradeswomen's responses to normative constructions of gender enacted in the male-dominated building industry. Pullen and Simpson (2009) use a feminist post-structuralist perspective to explore the discursive and disruptive 'doing and undoing' of gender identity (West and Zimmerman 1987; West and Fenstermaker 1995; Gherardi 2003) by males in the female-dominated nursing and primary school teaching professions. Narrations of lived experience were evaluated to understand how men managed gender identity differences (Otherness) in these areas of feminized work.

A Call for Multi-Level Approaches in Organizational Diversity Research

So far, we have drawn attention to many diversity studies using textual analysis that explicitly problematize the presence of discriminating attitudes and behaviours of organization members and explore other members' responses. These studies are similar in the collection of linguistic data at the individual level, with analysis at the individual, group, or broader cultural level. We can see the numerous and varied reports of ways that discrimination and resistance in organizations manifest between individuals of different social groups. However, as mentioned in the introduction, diversity scholars are calling for studies that are situational, empirical, contextual, *and multi-level*. Asymmetrical differences in power and inequities are subtly and, in some cases, invisibly produced among and between social groups and individuals. They are also structured, distributed, entrenched, enacted, and produced by organizing processes unintentionally or unknowingly designed to be unfair or administered as such. The delivery of knowledge of diversity in organization is arguably incomplete in specific contexts as few studies in its canon consider structure and the interactions with individuals thereof. More simply, in a practical sense, it is difficult to prove systematic and actionable injustice in organizations if one only speaks about data that relates strictly to individuals' experiences of discrimination.

By using the term *multi-level*, we mean combining individual respondent data with other levels of analysis. This can be done in many different ways. Textual analysis can be used to show the impacts of everyday practice, which comprises both linguistic and non-linguistic activity (Boréus 2006). In one example, Fletcher (1999) job-shadowed several female engineers in their roles as project managers or team members in a US high-tech company. Fletcher found that the women engineers and their practices of relational work (calling on, for example, skills of empathy, collaborative behaviour, and actions supportive of teamwork) had been 'disappeared'; that is, the types of relational work required to move work smoothly through an organization was either not noticed, not valued, or ignored. In a different example, McCoy and Masuch (2007) use institutional ethnography to explore foreign credential recognition in Canada from the standpoint of immigrant women with post-secondary degrees and non-regulated professional employment backgrounds. Interviews, observation, and document analysis are used to explain social and institutional influencers of the respondents' everyday experience. Two sets of interviews are used—one with the immigrant women and another with local service providers and government officials. Ethnographic observation and discourse and document analysis contribute to locating the experience of these immigrant women in larger sets of societal and institutional formations. This permits McCoy and Masuch to present not only findings but also recommendations for directions in immigration policy development and services. These studies both model systems as social constructions that establish, maintain, and control organizational, institutional, and societal structures. Studies of this nature can focus on organizational processes, policies, and procedures that contribute to non-language-based discrimination, such as exclusion from important meetings or discussions (Boréus 2006).

As with any methodology, consideration of multi-level textual analysis by researchers should be accompanied by sensitivity to some of the issues that critics of textual analysis studies raise. One important criticism is that specific textual data is often overemphasized as the basis for analysis (Merquior 1985; Fairclough 2003). This will be somewhat alleviated through the inclusion of diversity of texts as well as the researcher's careful consideration and explanation of text selection. Will analysis closely focus on a specific text as in Martin (1990) or on a wider range of documents as in Smith (1990, 2001)? See Alvesson and Karreman (2000) for a useful discussion of text selection. Secondly, Phillips and Hardy (2002) comment that many researchers who use textual analysis in fact only link text and context, omitting an exploration of the role of the discourse of which the text is a part. This may be because establishing boundaries and deciding how to interface into historical and societal context are difficult theoretical concepts. Every theorist has an opinion—Laclau and Mouffe say everything is discourse, Fairclough, Wodak, and Meyer argue for discourse interfacing into social and historical context, and Helms Mills argues for a multilayered approach with an emphasis on agency and social accomplishment. The researcher then grapples with where to gather texts, which texts to include or exclude, and how to explain their choices to other scholars. We recommend that the researcher develops a carefully supported and plausible position on text selection that is sustained and consistent throughout the work. The researcher should also consider, as mentioned previously, the danger that individual identity work and frameworks of discursive psychology theory can be overemphasized. This begs the question of methodological choice of unit of analysis: individuals, groups, organizations, institutions, social movements, or rules and routines. Lastly, transference of theoretical conceptualizations to empirical applications through methodology and data collection can be problematic. For some theoretical frameworks of textual analysis neither numerous empirical examples nor broad sets of methodological guidelines exist (Howarth 2000). However, this does not release the researcher from a fully explained approach (Jorgensen and Phillips 2002) that delivers against the research question. As in all research, ontological, epistemological, and methodological choices should be congruent, transparent, and reflexive.

At this point, we wish to introduce two relatively overlooked textual analysis methodologies that we believe provide situational, contextual, empirical, and multi-level approaches to studying diversity, its effects, and its management in organizations. Our next two sections explore this claim.

Two Critical Approaches to Textual Analysis

We believe that we have demonstrated the usefulness of textual analysis methodologies in the study of diversity in workforces. We argue that when both linguistic and non-linguistic practices are studied across individual, group, organization, and societal levels, we can more clearly see and understand how realities of diversity are constructed. By implication, this opens possibilities of problematizing deeper and further into areas that are not within legitimate reach of the researcher when the unit of analysis is restricted to one level or when only linguistic (or non-linguistic) practices are studied.

Our purpose in this section is to provide two in-depth examples of textual analysis methodologies that we hope meet this standard. Laclau and Mouffe's discourse theory and Helms Mills' critical sensemaking method (CSM) are similar in that they emanate from the common philosophical position that reality is socially constructed. These critical approaches problematize the status quo, are multi-level in approach, and include analysis of linguistic and non-linguistic practices. In contrast, Laclau and Mouffe's work is socio-political while CSM has its roots in social psychology. The two empirical examples discussed here employ different approaches to collecting linguistic data; one mainly uses interviews, and the other uses public records of group data. There is also a wide range of non-linguistic practices in both examples. By reading this section, we hope that the reader gains further insight into the usefulness and flexibility of textual analysis methodologies in diversity study and agrees with our opinion that both these approaches have attributes that can enrich this body of work. We will now discuss our examples.

Laclau and Mouffe's Discourse Theory and the Concept of Hegemony

Laclau and Mouffe (1985) construct their theory of discourse by combining and modifying aspects of Marxism (a theory of the social), structuralism (a theory of meaning), and Saussurian linguistics (Jorgensen and Phillips 2002), along with adoption and adaptation of Foucauldian discursive concepts and Gramsci's conceptualization of hegemony. In de Saussure's signification of language theory, an 'element' is a sign that has multiple (*polysemic*) meanings. When the potential for multiple meanings of an element is tied down to only one meaning, as determined by the presence and position of other signs and the relations among these signs, this element has been reduced to a *moment*. A *nodal point* is a moment that has *privilege*; it has particular influence in ordering relations among the gathered signs. A nodal point appears as a sign that is universally structured, thereby providing a taxonomizing (Harding 2005) or organizing process. As privileged signifiers, nodal points serve to stabilize terms, phrases, concepts, and identities into systems of meaning (Solomon 2009). Examples of nodal points include 'health' in the context of the British National Health System (Harding 2005) or 'body' in the context of Western or Eastern medicine (Phillips and Hardy 2002). Whereas a nodal point is temporarily fixed, a *floating signifier* is a sign whose meaning is a site of struggle. In Laclau and Mouffe's discourse theory, an *articulation* is any practice that establishes a set of relations among elements, creating differential positions between elements, reducing the elements to moments where 'all identity is relational and all relations have necessary character' (Laclau and Mouffe 1985: 106). The structured reality emanating from a set of articulatory practices is called a *discourse*, such as the discourses of management (Spicer and Böhm 2007). The infinite set of possibilities of meaning that naturally challenges moments and articulations is denoted as the *field of discursivity*. The meaning encompassed by a moment, an identity, an articulation, or a discourse must have limits in order to be coherent. Therefore frontiers are established between what is meant and what is not meant. These frontiers are dynamic sites of tension, the constant threat of nodal points by antagonistic differences of meaning, establishing the terrain of political struggles for meaning.

In these tension-filled dances between floating signifiers and nodal points, the discursive formations *are* the data and the analysis is the study of the frontiers of tensions. Although the conceptualization of organizational space as political has been used and/or referenced in many diverse academic areas (Carpentier 2005; Harding 2005; Meriläinen et al. 2008; Solomon 2009; van Bommel and Spicer 2011; Herschinger 2012; Kenny and Scriver 2012;), specific use of Laclau and Mouffe's discourse theory is not often found in organizational studies (Willmott 2005). In one recent example, Thomas and Hewitt (2011) study the discursive construction of professional work, combining aspects of Laclau and Mouffe's theoretical positioning with that of Fairclough, Chouliaraki, and Bhabha. Spicer and Böhm (2007) studied the rise of four different kinds of resistance movements, arguing first that they serve to disrupt the hegemonic discourse of management, and second that modes of resistance must be multiple and diverse.

Sparse use of Laclau and Mouffe's framework in organizational diversity studies (see, for example, Hearn's (2004) theoretical essay on conceptualizations of masculine identity) is noteworthy given that Laclau and Mouffe's discursive-based concept of hegemony offers diversity researchers a basis for analysing *how* a political space becomes hegemonized. In order to declare a space as hegemonized, Laclau (2000) specifies four conditions. We will explain the four conditions and then connect hegemony with the study of diversity. Hegemony first requires the condition of asymmetry or unevenness of power between discourses. Asymmetry is created by a growing surplus of differences in meaning and difficulties in trying to fix these meanings in a stable articulation (Laclau and Mouffe 1985). This produces tensions and antagonistic forces that will challenge established frontiers of meaning within a political space. In order to satisfy the second condition of hegemony, there must exist opposing floating signifiers that thwart or prevent the existing meanings from staying intact. In the third condition of hegemony, there is production of tendentially empty (biased and ambiguous) signifiers that either will enable the reconstitution of established meanings or create new ones. This re-establishes a frontier or division of a single political camp into two opposing fields. Lastly, the universalized empty signifiers are taken as common sense, or the constitution of a social ordering; the universalized empty signifiers make reality appear objective and natural (Jorgensen and Phillips 2002). It is through the presence of these four hegemonic conditions within discursive formations that alternative understandings of the world are suppressed, leading to antagonisms for the establishment of dominant meanings and the naturalization of single perspectives.

Clegg (2001) argues that the innovation of the four conditions of hegemony allow us to focus on the forms that hegemony takes rather than on the content of the ideas of the specific political space. This vantage point can be very helpful with research questions in general (see, for example, Herschinger's (2012) study on United Nations discourses on international terrorism and the drugs trade). Moreover, this framework has potential in diversity research. Instead of isolating the conditions that are produced by the hegemonies, and studying how people feel about these conditions, we can look at how the antagonisms arise in the discourse, the ways in which the antagonisms are resolved, and the effects on the discourses thereafter. In her doctoral dissertation (Porter 2013), the first co-author studied empirical linguistic and non-linguistic mechanisms of antagonisms and hegemonies of sexual harassment and sexual discrimination discourse in a Canadian professional engineering association, using the four conditions of hegemony. The author first described the broader discursive formations that organize the localized notion of the profession of engineering in the province of Ontario. As the outcome of many interacting discursive formations, the profession's legislated principle of self-regulation simultaneously constructed a political space and created an eagle's eye view into many linguistic and non-linguistic processes of the association. The author was then able to empirically observe how antagonisms, which articulated discourses of sexual harassment and sexual discrimination of female engineers in engineering workplaces, were formed and positioned at the frontiers of dominant meanings in the local professional association setting. The author could then see and represent the clashing of nodal points and floating signifiers as the engineering association and its women engineers action committee worked through proposals to declare sexual harassment and sexual discrimination in the profession as contraventions of the association's established code of ethics and guidelines of professional practice. The formations and mechanisms of hegemony were present and apparent in both linguistic and non-linguistic data. This enabled the author to conclude that the antagonisms that arose indeed challenged sedimented meanings but were ultimately insufficient to bring significant and sustained change to poor female representation in the local setting of the engineering profession.

In conclusion, the underuse of Laclau and Mouffe's innovation in diversity research is curious, given its capacity to show how dominant meanings are set and maintained in place, how antagonisms arise and challenge, and how the field of discursivity resolves to relative, if temporary, stability. The study of the mechanisms of hegemony in local contexts is useful in that it can expand understanding about existing linguistic and non-linguistic forms of power, in turn serving to broaden strategies for additional and diversified antagonisms. This form of textual analysis methodology makes possible theoretical and empirical contributions to the domain of diversity research in organizations.

Using Critical Sensemaking as a Method of Analysis

Similar to Laclau and Mouffe's goals of untangling complex phenomena and associated power relations, critical sensemaking also digs deeply into context. In this section, we will discuss what the critical sensemaking perspective is, how it works as an analytical method, and its value to researchers who are interested in understanding complex issues surrounding human organizations and diversity. Later in this section, we will briefly discuss some of its drawbacks.

The critical sensemaking perspective (Helms Mills, Thurlow, and Mills 2010), as a poststructuralist lens, can aid in understanding the ongoing interconnected relationships among the micro- (the sensemaker), the meso- (organizational rules), and the macro-elements (the social context) of social interaction. Critical sensemaking is sometimes mistaken as a branch of Weick's (1995) sensemaking that merely deals with *micro* aspects (such as the sensemaker) of critical issues. In fact, this is a methodology that focuses on four clusters of elements: (1) the socio-psychological processes in which people engage (Weick 1995, 2001); (2) the organizational rule(s) within which people make sense (Mills and Murgatroyd 1991); (3) the discursive processes involved in making sense (Foucault 1979); and (4) the sedimented, formative context that serves as the broader social framework in which people interact (Unger 1987a, 1987b, 1987c). However, there has been little discussion of the *application* of critical sensemaking perspective as a method of analysis. Our goal is to provide a sense of how the critical sensemaking perspective can be used as a textual analytical approach in diversity research.[2]

The four clusters of interconnected elements should neither be used separately, nor is sensemaking a simple process where a clear division can be drawn between elements. The elements are simultaneously processing and mediating each other while a person is making sense of his/her situation. Therefore, the framework cannot be restricted to a four-step analysis, nor can each element be used as a stand-alone tool. Guided by the complex elements of critical sensemaking, the researcher's role is to see how sense and organization emerge when a story begins to come together and identities begin to make sense. The

---

[2] A full discussion of critical sensemaking perspective is available in Helms Mills et al. (2010).

identities and the actions of the informants provide a sense of narrative rationality, and the researcher then connects plot and character from the data (Cunliffe and Coupland 2012). This of course requires a repetitive approach, to create and confirm themes (or concepts) for interpretation. Specific attention is given to understanding discursive elements that surface in the data and how they are relevant to the lived experience of the actors (and their agency). Such analysis is not a bounded process; rather, this is a multi-dynamic disorganized situation, particularly in the beginning. It involves a close, line-by-line reading of the text and a noting of the thoughts, ideas, impressions, feelings, and initial interpretations that the text (broadly defined) evokes. Researchers then develop and refine these interpretations, attempting to move away from descriptive to more conceptual and thematic levels of analysis. The goal is to derive a collection of themes that have enough particularity to be grounded and enough abstraction to be conceptualized.

Critical sensemaking is particularly concerned with how the sensemaker's view of agency in context is fleshed out from the text. Agency is broadly defined as 'the ways in which human beings make sense of their life-worlds and the options and restrictions within them' (Tomkins and Eatough 2012: 13). In other words, it refers to a person's ability to act, to choose, and to take action. The key is to pay special attention to the elements of critical sensemaking: both organizational rules and the intersection of formative contexts and other discursive practices (discourses) that are involved in the sensemaking process of each actor (Mills and Murgatroyd 1991; Helms Mills, Thurlow, and Mills 2010; Thurlow 2010). Moreover, hierarchical divisions and labels adopted in the social construction processes also help in locating *voices* and dominant discourses (Foucault 1982; Knights 1992). From there, researchers can conceptualize the process of sensemaking that reveals the forms of micro-politics of resistance that engage at the individual level (Mills and Helms Mills 2004). The value of the critical sensemaking methodology lies in its ability to conceptualize the magnitude of the combined effects and interactions across the various clusters of elements. Because of its emphasis on agency, a critical sensemaking approach helps us to explore how and why some (but not all) experiences become subjectively meaningful for the sensemakers.

One way in which to make a complex approach comprehensible is to develop a metaphorical analytical framework for data analysis (e.g. Figure 14.1), a way of mapping out the interconnected relationships of the clusters of elements.

In the study illustrated in Figure 14.1, for instance, the framework helps researchers to look through the informants' eyes. Imagine a professional immigrant's sense of his/her situation is intensified by the shock of realizing that his/her past experience and education are not recognized in the quest for employment. During the sensemaking process, s/he tries to regain a sense of control, searching for meanings and directions. The meanings are mediated by the unseen organizational rules and institutional discourses (of the multi-ethnic service organization) that simultaneously inform and are informed by the formative context and societal discourse. It is important to note that, to a certain extent, agency shapes discourse and discourse shapes agency (Hardy and Phillips 1999); thus some are more constrained by or resistant to the contextual elements at the individual level than others.

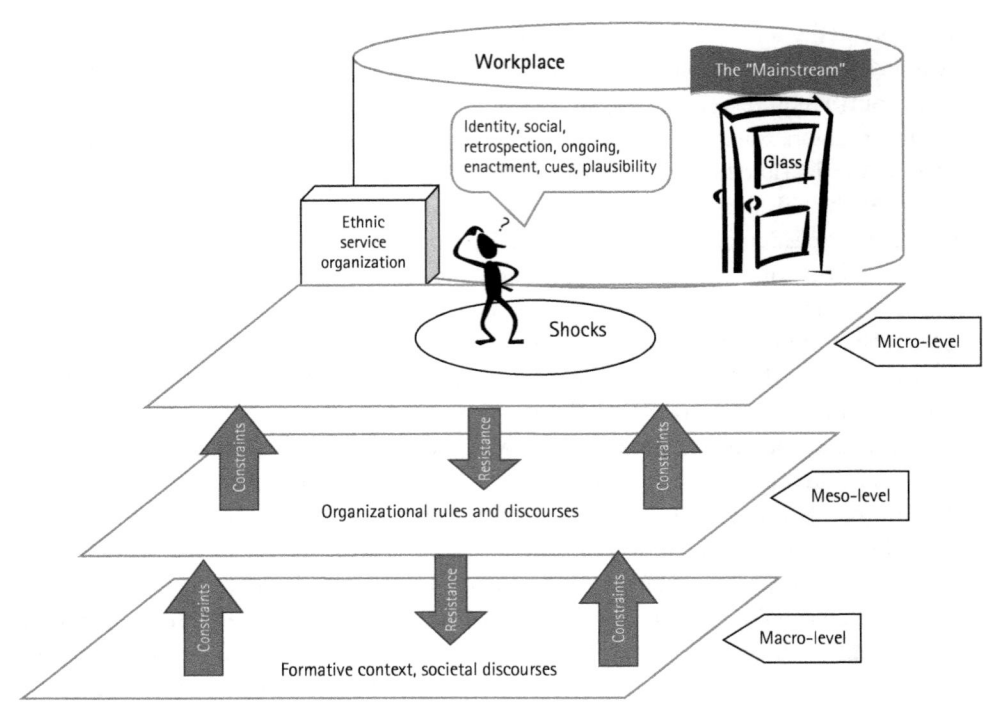

FIGURE 14.1 Immigrant workplace experience in Canada.

Source: Hilde 2013.

When the second author was working with the informants' data, she initially thought that the immigrant workplace experience could result from individual sensemaking—a socio-psychological process—and that this might be why some are more successful than others in the Canadian workplace. However, the framework led her to consider the idea of history—the formative context (one of the critical sensemaking elements)—such as the history of immigrants in Canada. From there, she realized that racism was deeply embedded in the Canadian context, especially during the time when Chinese workers were building the Canadian Pacific Railway. Further, the framework drew her to investigate various organizational rules from a single organization to an entire institutional field, considering both written and unwritten documents. Critical sensemaking also brings the idea of agency to the centre of the analysis, to explain why the same event could have different interpretations. Other textual analysis approaches that deal with single-level analysis could have oversimplified the phenomenon.

Owing to the capability and the approach of critical sensemaking—that is, that it requires researchers to dig into the historical and/or systemic issues and explains the value of agency in the process—this researcher (the second co-author) was able to pull together a wider picture of power relations, such as how government has treated the widely accepted discriminatory practice of positioning local experience and educational qualifications as 'normal'. Instead of enforcing legislation against discrimination, the government has treated such discriminatory practice as a 'normal' social issue that immigrants must face. Further, the government uses funding requirements to control ethnic service organizations in order to legitimize this agenda, reinforcing the restrictions on immigrants' access to the workplace. This allows employers, at the institutional level, to escape the accusation that they have discriminatory practices; they can comfortably reproduce rules that hinder the workplace opportunities of immigrants. At the micro-level of sensemaking (agency), some immigrants were able to push against the powerful discursive context through micro-processes of resistance as they reconceptualized their own identities. Hence, the second author contends that the sense that immigrants make at the level of micro-politics is crucial to the opportunities they are able to find (Hilde 2013).

Critical sensemaking is a powerful tool but also a difficult one to learn and use. With fewer than a dozen empirical studies available for reference (Helms Mills, Thurlow, and Mills 2010), it is extremely hard for novice researchers to master the wide range of elements and concepts in a short period of time. Hence, the depth and breadth of the approach are its strengths but also its weaknesses. Researchers need to deal with epistemological and ontological issues, and to determine whether the diverse elements of the methodology are compatible with the phenomena under investigation. Depending on the problem at hand, pulling all elements together can be far from easy. In attempting to make a significant contribution to the operational side of the critical sensemaking approach, the second author has had to confront several issues of analysis and definition. For example, it is not always clear when and where formative contexts influence ongoing senses of a situation or how their embeddedness in current practices could be revealed. Nor, in the multi-level approach, is it easy to unravel aspects of each level to develop a plausible account. Nonetheless, through the process, researchers can gain greater understandings of the usefulness and challenges of using the critical sensemaking approach as a method of analysis. Owing to all these complexities and perhaps owing to the small word limit prescribed by journals for publishing articles, critical sensemaking may be a less easily accessed methodological approach for researchers when compared to a single-level textual analysis.

Conclusion

Textual analysis methodologies are undoubtedly complex and complicated. It takes time and effort to gather, prepare, and analyse data. By the same token, these methodologies are flexible; a vast array of texts can be gathered and analysed in many different ways. These approaches can show *in situ* the many ways in which organizing processes produce and reproduce asymmetrical differences between and among social groups. They can serve to expand currently held views of diversity in organizations.

They can be used to explore existing theoretical and empirical terrains in new ways. They can also help to open new terrains of research. Lastly, expanding the range of methodologies used in diversity research will enhance the repertoire of strategies available to organizations to acknowledge, embrace, and develop diverse and inclusive workforces.

References

Alvesson, M. and Karreman, D. (2000). Varieties of discourse: on the study of organizations through discourse analysis. *Human Relations*, 53: 1125–49.

Ashcroft, K. L. (2004). Gender, discourse, and organization: framing a shifting relationship. In D. Grant, C. Hard, C. Oswick, and L. Putman (eds.) *The Sage Handbook of Organizational Discourse*. London: Sage, 275–98.

Bagilhole, B. (2010). Applying the lens of intersectionality to UK equal opportunities and diversity policies. *Canadian Journal of Administrative Sciences/Revue Canadienne des Sciences de l'Administration*, 27: 263–71.

Bell, E. (2008). *Reading Management and Organization in Film*. Basingstoke: Palgrave Macmillan.

Bell, E. (2012). Ways of seeing organisational death: a critical semiotic analysis of organisational memorialisation. *Visual Studies*, 27: 4–17.

Bell, E. L. J. E., Meyerson, D., Nkomo, S., and Scully, M. (2003). Interpreting silence and voice in the workplace: a conversation about tempered radicalism among black and white women researchers. *Journal of Applied Behavioral Science*, 39: 381–414.

Boréus, K. (2006). Discursive discrimination. *European Journal of Social Theory*, 9: 405–24.

Bryman, A., Bell, E., Mills, A. J., and A. R. Yue (2011). *Business Research Methods*. Toronto: Oxford University Press.

Burrell, G. and Morgan, G. (1979). *Sociological Paradigms and Organisational Analysis: Elements of the Sociology of Corporate Life*. London: Gower.

Calás, M. B. and Smircich, L. (1991) Voicing seduction to silence leadership. *Organization Studies (Walter de Gruyter GmbH & Co.KG.)*, 12: 567–601.

Carpentier, N. (2005). Identity, contingency and rigidity. *Journalism*, 6: 199–219.

Clegg, S. (2001). Changing concepts of power, changing concepts of politics. *Administrative Theory & Praxis*, 23: 126–50.

Cortina, L. M. (2008) Unseen injustice: incivility as modern discrimination in organizations. *Academy of Management Review*, 33: 55–75.

Cox, J. W. and Hassard, J. (2007). Ties to the past in organization research: a comparative analysis of retrospective methods. *Organization*, 14: 475–97.

Cunliffe, A. and Coupland, C. (2012). From hero to villain to hero: making experience sensible through embodied narrative sensemaking. *Human Relations*, 65: 63–88.

Czarniawska-Joerges, B. (2004). *Narratives in Social Science Research*. London and Thousand Oaks, CA: Sage.

Czarniawska, B. (2006). Doing gender unto the other: fiction as a mode of studying gender discrimination in organizations. *Gender, Work and Organization*, 13: 234–53.

Denissen, A. M. (2010). The right tools for the job: constructing gender meanings and identities in the male-dominated building trades. *Human Relations*, 63: 1051–69.

Dickens, L. (1999). Beyond the business case: a three-pronged approach to equality action. *Human Resource Management Journal*, 9: 9–19.

Essers, C. and Benschop, Y. (2009). Muslim businesswomen doing boundary work: the negotiation of Islam, gender and ethnicity within entrepreneurial contexts. *Human Relations* 62: 403–23.

Fairclough, N. (2003). *Analysing Discourse*. London and New York: Routledge.

Fletcher, J. K. (1999). *Disappearing Acts: Gender, Power, and Relational Practice at Work*. Cambridge, MA: The MIT Press.

Flyvjberg, B. (2001). *Making Social Science Matter: Why Social Inquiry Fails And How It Can Succeed Again*. Cambridge: Cambridge University Press.

Foucault, M. (1979). *Discipline and Punish: The Birth of the Prison*. New York: Vintage.

Foucault, M. (1982). The subject and power. *Critical Inquiry*, 8: 777–95.

Garfinkel, H. (1967) *Studies in Ethnomethodology*. Englewood Cliffs, NJ: Prentice-Hall.

Gergen, K. J. and Thatchenkery, T. J. (1996). Organization science as social construction: postmodern potentials. *Journal of Applied Behavioral Science*, 32: 356–77.

Gherardi, S. (2003). Feminist theory and organization theory: a dialogue on new bases. In: H. Tsoukas and C. Knudsen (eds.) *The Oxford Handbook of Organization Theory*. Oxford: Oxford University Press, 210–36.

Grimes, D. S. (2002) Challenging the status quo?: whiteness in the diversity management literature. *Management Communication Quarterly*, 15: 381–409.

Harding, N. (2005) The inception of the National Health Service: a daily managerial accomplishment. *Journal of Health Organization and Management*, 19: 261–72.

Hardy, C. and Phillips, N. (1999) No joking matter: discursive struggle in the canadian refugee system. *Organization Studies (Walter de Gruyter GmbH & Co.KG.)*, 20: 1–24.

Hart, S. (2010) Self-regulation, corporate social responsibility, and the business case: do they work in achieving workplace equality and safety? *Journal of Business Ethics* 92: 585–600.

Hearn, J. (2004) From hegemonic masculinity to the hegemony of men. *Feminist Theory*, 5: 49–72.

Helms Mills, J., Thurlow, A., and Mills, A. J. (2010) Making sense of sensemaking: the critical sensemaking approach. *Qualitative Research in Organizations and Management: An International Journal*, 5: 182–95.

Herbert, J. I. (1990). Integrating race and adult psychosocial development. *Journal of Organizational Behavior*, 11: 433–46.

Herschinger, E. (2012). 'Hell is the other': conceptualising hegemony and identity through discourse theory. *Millennium—Journal of International Studies*, 41: 65–90.

Hilde, R. (2013). Workplace (In)Equality: Making Critical Sense of Immigrant Experiences in the Canadian Workplace. *Faculty of Business*. Athabasca, AB: Athabasca University, 242.

Howarth, D. (2000). *Discourse*. Buckingham and Philadelphia: Open University Press.

Janssens, M. and Zanoni, P. (2005). Many diversities for many services: theorizing diversity (management) in service companies. *Human Relations*, 58: 311–40.

Jorgensen, M. and Phillips, L. J. (2002). *Discourse Analysis As Theory And Method*. London and Thousand Oaks, CA: Sage.

Kenny, K. and Scriver, S. (2012). Dangerously empty? Hegemony and the construction of the Irish entrepreneur. *Organization*, 19: 615–33.

Knights, D. (1992). Changing spaces: the disruptive impact of a new epistemological location for the study of management. *Academy of Management Review*, 17: 514–36.

Laclau, E. (2000). Identity and hegemony: the role of universality in the constitution of political logics. *Contigency, Hegemony, Universality: Contemporary Dialogues on the Left*. London: Verso.

Laclau, E. and Mouffe, C. (1985). *Hegemony And Socialist Strategy: Towards A Radical Democratic Politics*. London: Verso.

Litvin, D. R. (1997). The discourse of diversity: from biology to management. *Organization*, 4: 187–209.

Liversage, A. (2009). Vital conjunctures, shifting horizons: high-skilled female immigrants looking for work. *Work, Employment & Society*, 23: 120–41.

McCall, L. (2005). The complexity of intersectionality. *Signs*, 30: 1771–1800.

McCoy, L. and Masuch, C. (2007). Beyond 'entry-level' jobs: immigrant women and non-regulated professional occupations. *Journal of International Migration & Integration*, 8: 185–206.

McKee, A. (2003) *Textual Analysis: A Beginner's Guide*, London: Sage.

McMahon, A. M. (2010). Does workplace diversity matter? a survey of empirical studies on diversity and firm performance, 2000–09. *Journal of Diversity Management*, 5: 37–48.

Malhi, R. L. and Boon, S. P. (2007). Discourses of 'democratic racism' in the talk of south Asian Canadian women. *Canadian Ethnic Studies*, 39: 125–49.

Martin, J. (1990). Deconstructing organizational taboos: the suppression of gender conflict in organizations. *Organization Science*, 1: 339–59.

Martin, P. Y. (2006). Practising gender at work: further thoughts on reflexivity. *Gender, Work and Organization*, 13: 254–76.

Menard-Warwick, J. (2008). 'Because she made beds. Every day': social positioning, classroom discourse, and language learning. *Applied Linguistics*, 29(2): 267–89.

Meriläinen, S., Tienari, J., Thomas, R., and Davies, A. (2008). Hegemonic academic practices: experiences of publishing from the periphery. *Organization*, 15: 584–97.

Merquior, J. G. (1985). *Foucault*. London: Fontana/Collins.

Mills, A. J. and Helms Mills, J. (2004). When plausibility fails: towards a critical sensemaking approach to resistance. In R. Thomas AJMJHM (ed.) *Identity Politics at Work: Resisting Gender and Gendered Resistance*. London: Routledge, 141–59.

Mills, A. J. and Murgatroyd, S. J. (1991). *Organizational Rules: A Framework For Understanding Organizational Action*. Milton Keynes: Open University Press.

Morgan, G. (2006). *Images of Organization*. Thousand Oaks, CA: Sage.

Mumby, D. K. (1987). The political function of narrative in organizations. *Communication Monographs*, 54: 113.

Nkomo, S. and Cox, T. J. (1996). Diverse identities in organizations. In S. R. Clegg, C. Hardy, and W. R. Nord (eds.) *Handbook of Organization Studies*. Thousand Oaks, CA and London: Sage, 338–56.

Nkomo, S. and Stewart, M. M. (2006). Diverse identities in organizations. In: S. R. Clegg, C. Hardy, T. B. Lawrence, and W. R. Nord (eds) *The SAGE Handbook of Organization Studies*. 2nd edn. Thousand Oaks, CA and London: Sage, 520–40.

Noon, M. (2007). The fatal flaws of diversity and the business case for ethnic minorities. *Work, Employment & Society*, 21: 773–84.

O'Connor, E. S. (1995). Paradoxes of participation: textual analysis and organizational change. *Organization Studies*, 16: 769–803.

Phillips, N. and Hardy, C. (2002). *Discourse Analysis: Investigating Processes Of Social Construction*. Thousand Oaks, CA: Sage.

Pio, E. (2005). Knotted strands: working lives of Indian women migrants in New Zealand. *Human Relations*, 58: 1277-99.

Porter, J. M. (2013). The hegemonies and antagonisms of sexual harassment and sexual discrimination discourse in a professional engineering association. *Faculty of Business*. St. Albert: Athabasca University.

Pullen, A. and Simpson, R. (2009). Managing difference in feminized work: men, otherness and social practice. *Human Relations*, 62: 561-87.

Royo-Vela, M., Aldás-Manzano, J., Vila-Lopez, N., and Küster-Boluda, I. (2007). Gender role portrayals and sexism in Spanish magazines. *Equal Opportunities International*, 26: 633-52.

Scott, J. W. (1994). Deconstructing equality-versus-difference: or, the uses of poststructuralist theory for feminism. In A. Herrmann and A. J. Stewart (eds.) *Theorizing Feminism: Parallel Trends In The Humanities And Social Sciences*. Boulder, CO: Westview Press, 358-71.

Smith, D. E. (1983). No One Commits Suicide: Textual Analysis of Ideological Practices. *Human Studies*, 6: 309-59.

Smith, D. E. (1990). *Texts, Facts, and Femininity: Exploring The Relations of Ruling*. London and New York: Routledge.

Smith, D. E. (2001). Texts and the ontology of organizations. *Studies in Cultures, Organizations, and Society*, 7: 40.

Solomon, T. (2009). Social logics and normalisation in the war on terror. *Millennium—Journal of International Studies*, 38: 269-94.

Spicer, A. and Böhm, S. (2007). Moving management: theorizing struggles against the hegemony of management. *Organization Studies*, 28: 1667-98.

Thomas, P. and Hewitt, J. (2011) Managerial organization and Professional Autonomy: A Discourse-Based Conceptualization. *Organization Studies*, 32: 1373-93.

Thurlow A. (2010) Critical sensemaking. In A. J. Mills, G. Durepos, and E. Weibe (eds.) *Sage Encyclopedia of Case Study Research*. Thousand Oaks, CA: Sage, 257-60.

Tomkins, L. and Eatough, V. (2014). Stop 'helping' me! Identity, recognition and agency in the nexus of work and care. *Organization*, 21(1): 3-21.

Unger, R. M. (1987a). *False Necessity: Anti-Necessitarian Social Theory in the Service of Radical Democracy*. Cambridge: Cambridge University Press.

Unger, R. M. (1987b). *Plasticity into Power*. Cambridge: Cambridge University Press.

Unger, R. M. (1987c). *Social Theory: Its Situation and Its Task*. Cambridge: Cambridge University Press.

van Bommel, K. and Spicer, A. (2011). Hail the snail: hegemonic struggles in the slow food movement. *Organization Studies*, 32: 1717-44.

Van Laer, K. and Janssens, M. (2011). Ethnic minority professionals' experiences with subtle discrimination in the workplace. *Human Relations*, 64: 1203-27.

Vibert, C. (2004). *Theories of Macro Organizational Behaviour*. Armonk, NY and London: M. E. Sharpe.

Weick, K. E. (1995). *Sensemaking in Organizations*. Thousand Oaks, CA: Sage.

Weick, K. E. (2001) *Making Sense of the Organization*. Victoria: Blackwell.

Weick, K. E., Sutcliffe, K. M., and Obstfeld, D. (2005). Organizing and the process of sensemaking. *Organization Science*, 16: 409-21.

West, C. and Fenstermaker, S. (1995). Doing difference. *Gender and Society*, 9: 8-37.

West, C. and Zimmerman, D. H. (1987). Doing gender. *Gender and Society*, 1: 125-51.

Willmott, H. (2005). Theorizing contemporary control: some post-structuralist responses to some critical realist questions. *Organization*, 12: 747–80.

Zanoni, P. and Janssens, M. (2004). Deconstructing difference: the rhetoric of human resource managers' diversity discourses. *Organization Studies*, 25: 55–74.

Zanoni, P., Janssens, M., Benschop, Y., and Nkomo, S. (2010). Guest editorial: unpacking diversity, grasping inequality: rethinking difference through critical perspectives. *Organization*, 17: 9–29.

CHAPTER 15

IN SEARCH OF THE 'REAL'

The Subversive Potential of Ethnography in the Field of Diversity Management

PAUL MUTSAERS AND MARJA-LIISA TRUX

INTRODUCTION

IN a recent genealogy of diversity management (DM) Vertovec (2012) returned to the emergence of the concept and explored its various affiliations, detours, and associations over the past five decades. In tune with others (e.g. Foldy 2002; Litvin 2006; Zanoni et al. 2010) he observed a well-known transformation in the ideas and practices attached to the concept of diversity; that is, a shift away from diversity as social justice and towards a business rationale (see also Chapter 13, this volume). This positive approach to diversity does not take 'difference as a source of deficiency but of productive relationships' (Blackmore 2006: 183).

Despite the deluge of investments in the appeal of this discourse (i.e. its conceptual origins and developments as well as the consequent social and discursive practices of DM) it is not without its critics. Some have argued that it is simply emphasizing esteem and 'feel-good' measures at the expense of actual amelioration of structural inequality (cf. Vertovec 2012), while others have regarded the 'we-are-all-different mantra' principally as a strategy to fragment the workforce and suppress collective labour action (hence the hostility of trade union officials towards DM in some contexts; cf. Wrench 2005). A focus on deregulated individual accomplishments (e.g. diversity as a business condition for 'high potential leaders' to experience personal challenge and ambition) has substituted collective and orchestrated action (e.g. social movements that organize around wrongs to be righted). While this may strike a disturbing chord for some, it may not do so for others—and the matter remains by and large political.

Dazed by the often fierce debates between advocates of (ostensibly) competing discourses of diversity as a social issue versus diversity as a business case (cf. Tomlinson and Schwabenland 2010)—often backed up with more or less covert political agendas—researchers may run the risk of forgetting to actually study DM and what it means to people. It is precisely this task that we have assigned to ourselves, that is, to open up diversity discourses and find out what really happens *in situ*. Such a concrete task creates a moment that appears rife with ethnographic significance as it is exactly anthropology's analytical edge that allows an escape from ideological argumentations that go in repetitive circles simply because they were started with tools of power rather than tools of inquiry. Such ideological argumentations can be found on both sides of the ideological divide. Scholars such as Noon (2007) attack the logical integrity of business arguments for the compatibility and mutual reinforcement of on the one hand capitalizing on diverse human resources and on the other hand realizing equal opportunities and fairness. Noon says the latter are universal rights whereas the former is contingent upon volatile economic circumstances (e.g. changes in labour or commodity markets). As such, the political statement can be made that an 'overly rational cost–benefit analysis' may give people 'evidence-based arguments for not pursuing [equality] initiatives because it is not in the interest of their business' (Noon 2007: 778; see Carter 2000 for an example within the British National Health Service). And certainly, the same can be said about those who pit their tent on the other side of the divide, like those who take matters of justice, fairness, and equality *cum grano salis* and have an interest in the added value of diversity in terms of, say, high performance systems, creativity, innovation, flexible workforces, or work-related outcomes at large (e.g. Richard 2000; Kochan et al. 2003).

Despite some ethnographically oriented approaches to DM (e.g. Janssens and Zanoni 2005; Zanoni and Janssens 2007; Zanoni 2011), the field remains dominated by academic quarrels over who has the best, preferably meta-analytic, evidence for or against the business case of diversity and its social implications (e.g. Horwitz and Horwitz 2007; Bell et al. 2011; Van Dijk, Van Engen, and Van Knippenberg 2012). We draw on our experiences in both Finland and The Netherlands when we state that DM scholars may tend to lose touch with reality in the workplace. To speak with a Dutch community police officer in Amsterdam, whose statement is the prototype for numerous others: 'What I've never understood is . . . when you look at the enormous investment in diversity, cultural craftsmanship, particularly in these endowed chairs; that is absolutely not corresponding to the things that happen in practice.'

We therefore suggest looking at diversity afresh and studying what it means to people by looking through the eyes of the beholder; that is, by centralizing the addressees of DM initiatives. Were we not to do this, we argue, we would forgo opportunities to take the complexity of DM seriously. In a way, ethnography is complexity and it derives its potential and its capacity of challenging established views, its counter-hegemonic punch, exactly from its openness towards complexity (Blommaert and Dong 2010). Herein lies its subversive potential. We concur with Groeneveld (Chapter 13, this volume) and Porter and Hilde (Chapter 14, this volume) that we can only really grasp the complexity of DM through a multi-level/multi-layer analytical framework. We hope to demonstrate that ethnography has the ability to do so, by emphasizing its capacity to cross organizational domains (and thus levels).

THE EYES OF THE BEHOLDER: ETHNOGRAPHIC INQUIRIES INTO WORKPLACE DIVERSITY

Ethnographic studies in (work) organizations have multiplied since Barley and Kunda published their widely known call for such efforts in 2001. While anthropologists, who have been developing ethnographic styles of social research since the late nineteenth century, have busied themselves largely elsewhere, the 'Western worlds of work' have been examined by other scholars with varying approaches, but often relying on the legacy of ethnography: the credibility of one who 'has been there' using what is termed participant observation. Organization studies and working life studies (e.g. Roy 1954; Burawoy 1979; Hochschild 1983/2003; Kunda 1992; Fine 1996/2008; Orr 1996) have in a way kept open the paths of the Chicago school and early organization studies through the years of macro sociology and institutional studies.[1] The present-day ethnographic landscape is characterized by a burgeoning field of organizational ethnography (see Bate 1997; the *Journal of Organizational Ethnography*; Ybema et al. 2009; Van Maanen 2011; Watson 2011). Over the years much has been gained by a growing body of eye-witness reports of work practices, labour conditions, coping strategies, emotions, and identities, to mention but a fraction of all aspects illuminated by these reports. Some anthropologists have partaken in these activities and the days are certainly gone when anthropologists were only known as the troublemakers who used to raise giggles and irritation—and eventually tired their audiences—with exotic counterexamples from the lives of people far away.

Our attempt requires that we shake off some of the dust people associate with the ethnographies of yore. We are not going to tell you what the Trobrianders do to manage their diversity—although that would be a perfectly legitimate option too; we are going to tell you how employees in a Finnish high-tech company go about having various nationalities in their workplace in the absence of official DM initiatives, and what actually happens in Dutch police departments when people are confronted with certain

---

[1] Interestingly, Down (2012) traces this history all the way back to Engels's 1845 account *The Condition of the Working Class in England*. Some of the very first studies of work were conducted by non-academic journalist or novelist ethnographers and amateurs educated in fields beyond social sciences, among them several adventurous women (Zickar and Carter 2010; Down 2012). A tradition of non-academic, covert fieldwork has been continued by, for example, Wallraff (1985) and Ehrenreich (2001).

DM discourses. What actually happens—not how much of it is believed, hoped, or prescribed to happen according to fixed storylines in the diversity literature.

Ethnography is unique among social science methods as it adopts a holistic view on the people, scenes, and activities observed. Actually, what an ethnographer does in the field is not much different from everyday encounters, only better documented. As any fellow human being, the ethnographer meets Noam, rather than *the work-related attitudes of a male worker in age group A with ethnicity X*. She meets him,[2] he meets her, and they might befriend each other or at least get acquainted. She would get a hint of what his work means to him, what it feels like. Some of her questions would go unanswered. Instead, she would learn the answers to questions she never asked. She might be surprised, baffled, scared, awed, or bewildered by things she did not expect to encounter in the field. She would learn which questions matter to Noam and his colleagues. Re-engaging with people who talk about 'diversity', she would have things to say to them that begin like: 'No, no, you've got it all wrong! That's not the issue...' The experience would have decentred the ethnographer's previous understanding.

Ethnography helps to grasp novel phenomena hitherto unknown, like cultural forms in the Southern Seas or work practices in a new industry. But there is more to its capacity: for the same qualities that facilitate this 'cartography', ethnography is also suited for re-conceptualization, building new vocabulary, and escaping dominant cultural forms. Throughout its history in anthropology, it has been used for subversive purposes in at least two ways: by bringing out the voices of the silenced and marginalized, and by *Verfremdung* or distancing. Hegemonic and taken-for-granted ideas can be put into perspective, questioned, or dwarfed by juxtaposing them to unexpected alternatives and dissident perspectives. As George Marcus (1998) reminds us, this helps to rethink and destabilize established orders.

The two strategies that allow for the subversive potential of ethnography—'distancing' and 'voicing'—prevail in both cases discussed in this chapter, albeit with different accents. The strategy of distancing is most articulated in the Finnish case, in the sense that DM is studied in a context that is actually devoid of DM initiatives or campaigns. During long term fieldwork (1999–2004; see Trux (2010) for a more voluminous report on this period) Marja-Liisa immersed herself in F-Secure, a high-tech organization, where she discovered that members of this organization (software engineers and other employees at the Helsinki headquarters) had developed a passionate anti-diversity-management attitude. They were estranged from diversity discourses and had actually developed alternatives in terms of 'organizational democracy', rendering any specific diversity programme mostly unnecessary.

The strategy of voicing is best visible in the Dutch case, in which Paul looks at two ethnographically reconstructed cases in which ethnic minority police officers are

---

[2] The feminine pronoun is here to help you read the passage without mixing researcher with the researched. It also reflects the original encounter of Marja-Liisa with Noam (pseudonym). Of course, you are also welcome to read into it feminist attempts to counterbalance the overwhelming dominance of masculine subjects in the English language. We sympathize with this.

confronted with certain offshoots of official DM discourses. To understand these cases—one is about a job interview; the other about a fireside meeting between ethnic minority police officers and their deputy district commander—it is important to realize from the outset that 'diversity' is often differentially entextualized in different settings; it actually changes when it 'travels along varying institutional pathways in which its immediate referents vary a lot' (Urciuoli 2010: 49). This happens with what may be coined 'itinerant diversity management'; it changes along the way. For instance, a certain technique or instrument may be developed by a group of consultants, then taught to diversity managers in a certain organization, after which it is disseminated to the team leaders of that particular organization, before it finally reaches those people it was originally meant for. What diversity (management) actually means to people may be learned by studying how the circulation of certain techniques, instruments, or bits and pieces of discourse is experienced and subsequently voiced by the informants. This is done in the study of police officers in the south of The Netherlands (based on Paul's ethnography between 2008 and 2013).

The nature of ethnographic knowledge favours a narrative mode of reporting, in which the researcher is a character among others. To do this in a jointly authored chapter, combining the results of two separate fieldworks, we present both eye-witness stories from The Netherlands and from Finland, each voiced by the ethnographer him/herself, and return to our joined, plural narrator discussion thereafter.

Itinerant Diversity Management of Dutch Police Officers

Quintessential to itinerant diversity management is the difficulty of planning or organizing DM schemes, campaigns, or agendas centrally, as things may change with every transfer (e.g. an exchange between a subcontracted diversity consultant and an in-house diversity expert, or the application of a certain 'diversity product' in practice). This difficulty may be expected to arise easier in complex organizations such as the Dutch police organization, which has been organized on the basis of twenty-six relatively autonomous forces for nearly two decades (since regionalization in 1993 and until nationalization in 2013, when the latest police law was enacted). As a corollary of this difficulty, a plethora of diversity initiatives came to life with some initiatives being purposely engineered by for instance the Board of Chiefs of Police (Raad van Hoofdcommissarissen) and others locally and spontaneously grown. Some do not square with others, and there is a great deal of ambiguity involved in the diversity apparatus of the Dutch police. Decoding this apparatus falls outside the purview of this chapter (others have begun to do so; see Boogaard and Roggeband 2010). My interest lies with the 'domaining effect', as anthropologists (Shore and Wright 2000) have called it; an effect which occurs when a certain logic (or constellation of various concept, i.e. a semantic cluster) typically associated with one domain migrates to another where it receives new operational power, often with unanticipated outcomes (Shore and Wright 2000).

In the two cases that follow I am going to look at the domain crossing of 'diversity' and various other keywords that are easily associated with it by diversity consultants and trainers in The Netherlands ('authenticity', 'open-mindedness', 'extraversion', etc.). The semantic value of these keywords appears obvious at the surface, and yet a great deal of indeterminacy is built into their semiotics (cf. Urciuoli 2010), which only reveals itself after application in real-life settings. What follows is an analysis of itinerant diversity discourses that depart from the Nederlandse Stichting voor Psychotechnieken (the 'Dutch Foundation for Psychotechniques'—NSvP) and arrive at two different police districts within the same police force in the south of The Netherlands.

The NSvP is one of the prime suppliers of diversity instruments to the Dutch police. It is an influential knowledge institute in The Netherlands that works at the junction of organizational psychology, social psychology, and human resource management (HRM) (Strien and van Dane 2001). It is mainly involved in facilitating and conducting research projects, awarding grants, organizing seminars, conferences, and workshops, and in journal and book publications (see <http://www.innovatiefinwerk.nl>). Its partnership with the Dutch police is multiplex, including research projects within the police organization conducted by NSvP associates, endowed chairs within the Dutch Police Academy being held by NSvP members, and so on.

Diversity, Authenticity, Leadership

'Discourse as semiotic production...has a chronotopic character...in that it can be conceptualized as something that "circulates", moves virtually through the time [chrono] and space [tope] of social organization' (Silverstein 2008: 6). What this boils down to, Silverstein continues, is that the usage of language by people in a certain communicative event may connect to the language use of other people on other occasions. This connection is best captured by the term 'interdiscursivity', a sort of 'likeness' between various communicative events. But there is more to it, as interdiscursivity may be actively and strategically deployed by people.

That being said, let us now turn to two text fragments; the first coming from a dissertation that appeared under the supervision of a NSvP board member (and was published on their website), the second coming from the national HR division of the Dutch police (published as an official 'employers' statement'):

> Accommodating authenticity allows for individual differences and "being different" and creates possibilities to experience these differences and let them co-exist, rather than disappear.... More specifically, in diverse working contexts, research shows that when group members give recognition to the unique qualities of other group members, this recognition moderates the relation between diversity and performance.... Creating a working climate that stimulates authentic behaviour

> is contingent upon authentic leadership. Authentic leadership means that managers are a reflection of themselves and are in contact with all dimensions of their self. (Raaijmakers 2008: 92)

> The police organization pursues diversity and this requires a variety and authenticity of leadership in the police organization.... Leaders coach and impassion employees in order to let them excel in things they are good at; this gives employees a chance to act in accordance with their own views... Leaders must be capable of touching upon the authenticity of employees. (Werkgeversvisie Politie 2008: 77–8)

It becomes instantly clear that the two excerpts are lexico-grammatically consonant in the sense that the grammatical mood is declarative in both cases (lacking for instance hedging expressions) and the same words are used (diversity, authenticity, leadership). They seem to fit neatly together and appear to form a coherent whole that encourages the reader to feel at ease with working climates that are characterized by this diversity-authenticity-leadership (DAL) triangle. One would hardly be able to spot possible fissures within this apparently coherent discourse if the analysis were kept within the domains of consultancy, HRM, research, and policy. Stepping outside these domains, however, gives a different impression.

In 2011 the DAL discourse, of which the two excerpts are of course merely exemplary, had had some time to settle in or to sediment, so to speak. It had traversed several police districts, one of which was my fieldwork site in the autumn of that year. While 'shadowing' (cf. Czarniawska 2007) a few team and district leaders for several months, I suddenly found myself in a real-life setting in which the surefire DAL triangle was applied. It was a *P-schouw*, a meeting dedicated to review the district personnel, which is organized periodically by the district commander (DC) and his HR advisor (a *bilateraaltje* in police jargon) to discuss career developments of subordinates as well as other HR-related issues. On the agenda was a job interview the two of them had the other week with an operational leader (a line manager) who had applied for a job as deputy team leader. During the *P-schouw* they were finalizing their decision to reject him, as they deemed him insufficiently authentic and thus unfit as a team leader. When I asked at the end of the *P-schouw* what was meant by 'authenticity', how it would fit the job profile, and how it could be assessed, nerves started to dominate the scene. The HR advisor felt ashamed to confess that it is mostly a gut feeling and that it is applied as a criterion in various ways within the force. However, in separate conversations that I had afterwards with both persons, a different story came to the fore. The HR officer had regained confidence when I asked the same questions:

> Leaders must be themselves, that is, authentic.... In a job interview you are most importantly looking for the true self of a person. And you know what... an answer is not right or wrong—I mean substantively right or wrong. No, it's about how you come to it. This means that you look for who someone really is.

When I asked the DC the same questions, he came up with a specific interpretation of authenticity; that is, being assertive and daring to stand up against superiors. He did not refer to himself, of course, but to the (Turkish) team leader the Surinam-born applicant would come to work as her deputy. I had a lengthy conversation with this team leader, and it turned out that her employment record contained a number of ethnic conflicts, which had her expelled from another police district. According to the DC, she had a 'strong personality' and 'needs to be brought back into balance'. In the end, he carefully opened up about his expectation that a team leader and a deputy both having a migration history would not bring the desired harmony in the (predominantly white) team.

I cannot do otherwise but conclude that in this case an inversion has taken place within the DAL triangle, as authenticity has been inverted from a bedfellow to diversity into its infidel spouse, doing more harm than good. To comprehend what has happened here, I embrace what Urciuoli (2008) has to say about 'strategically deployable shifters' (SDSs). She uses the term to understand the value and function of soft skills in the workplace, a category to which authenticity can easily be said to belong. Such skills (often framed as competences) are characterized by a denotational vagueness—in this case clearly indicated by the various definitions given to authenticity—that is central to their strategic use. In fact, their strategic indexicality (they can easily be aligned with certain organizational values) and denotational vagueness (hard to grasp, multi-interpretable) have an inner connection. The applicant did not protest at the usage of authenticity as a criterion for the vacant job. In an interview I conducted afterwards, he acknowledged the importance of it (who can be against authenticity?). But at the same time he shared with me a concern that going along with the expectations of his superiors would force him into processes of alienation. In that sense, a double inversion took place, as 'authentication' meant alienation for him:

> APPLICANT. I am not willing to change my whole personality. . . . And I said that to the committee. If you're looking for someone who bangs his fist on the table, that's fine. But that's not who I am.
> PAUL. You don't want to change that?
> APPLICANT. NO, BECAUSE I WANT TO BE MYSELF.

Fireplace Sessions

The previous case makes clear what can happen if researchers tend to refrain from studying the offshoots of DM in addition to its official or original discourse(s); that is, if they will not cross domains in their research. This may be unpalatable to purists who want to preserve pure research domains and abstain as much as possible from real-life power struggles, but I believe that in order to study DM for real, a certain amount of ethnographic engagement that revolves around such domaining effects is necessary. Let me turn to a second case in order to further substantiate this claim.

A few years ago (in 2010), I sat together with a deputy district commander to have an informal conversation about the progress of my research. Enthusiastic as always, the DC openly shared her knowledge about the topic (diversity) and told about a fireplace mentoring session she had recently had with five Dutch–Turkish colleagues at a fancy restaurant in an idyllic village close by. Such comfortable fireplace settings—'we have our feet on the table and sit by the fire' (said the DC)—are intended to encourage employees to open up about troubles at work. This time she had invited those five men, because time and again they did not succeed in getting promoted from constable first class (*hoofdagent*) to sergeant (*brigadier*). Their quality and quantity of work was perfectly up to standards (this was confirmed in their job evaluations according to the DC) and yet they were facing a stagnant career (as do many ethnic minorities within the Dutch police; cf. Boogaard and Roggeband 2010). Towards the end of the session the DC concluded that all five of them did a great job, but lacked the communicative and personal skills to make this known to others. They were advised to work on their entrepreneurship, open-mindedness, and flexibility, as these had become key competences within the organization according to the DC.

They had become so, as two years earlier a new diversity initiative had made its appearance within the organization, *politietop divers* (police top diverse), which revolves most of its programmes around the five core competences of the 'multicultural personality questionnaire': cultural empathy, open-mindedness, social initiative, emotional stability, and flexibility (cf. Van der Zee and Van Oudenhoven 2001). This questionnaire was developed by Karin van der Zee (an NSvP expert). Van der Zee had applied this questionnaire in her police research in the south of The Netherlands and *politietop divers* had designed a programme that portrayed these multicultural personality traits as a *sine qua non* of police leadership. Since the five officers pursued promotion to a position that involves leadership (sergeant), the DC's advice makes sense at first sight.

In the winter of 2012–13 I joined one of the session participants for several weeks, being unaware that he was in fact one of the participants. Things fell in place when Talik (pseudonym), during one of our car patrols together, shared his concerns about the career-related hardships of ethnic minorities within the organization. He admitted that he was disappointed about the fireplace session, since nothing was done with it afterwards. Nobody had received feedback, there was no follow-up, and almost three years later all participants still worked as constable first class. 'I had the feeling I was forced to sell myself, which I cannot do; perhaps I should move to a marketplace or something for some time', is what he said while complaining about the self-commodification (Urciuoli 2010) he felt was imposed upon him. Coincidentally, at the end of our time together Talik was in fact promoted to sergeant, although it remained unclear to him and others whether this was a result of the polycentric roadblock that he had prepared for several months and brought to a successful end ('the best one we ever had', according to a colleague) or the empowerment course ('you're the director of your own life') in which he had recently enrolled—and which had originally started as a course for ethnic minorities in particular to work on their auto-regulation and mental resilience.

In any case, it cannot be concluded that compliance with the competences enlisted in the multicultural personality questionnaire gives any guarantee to career advancement (here I take it for granted that participating in an empowerment course fuels such compliance; I was not granted access to these classes owing to privacy issues). After all, another participant in the fireplace session (Fahim; pseudonym) had been doing all the tasks of a sergeant for a year and a half, without getting the official recognition (or salary). When he was dismissed from these tasks, because the organization is obliged to promote him to sergeant after two years of doing the job, he took the initiative to send an email about his ideas on this matter (he was 'open-minded' and 'enterprising'). Not much later he found himself transferred to another post doing one of the most ungrateful routine jobs within the organization. Thus manipulation was a primary managerial strategy and coercion was held in reserve. In an interview Fahim complained about the constant exhaustion and feelings of burn-out he experienced, and confessed he considered leaving the organization owing to the constant pressure he felt to profile himself and because of his nightmarish vision of his dead-end career—despite the numerous personal development plans he was forced to write.

My ethnographic data thus reveal a set of techniques—a multicultural personality questionnaire, a fireplace mentoring session, an empowerment course, personal development plans—that dwell on individual change efforts rather than focusing on the structural impediments of career advancement. Such an emphasis on intrapsychic domains leaves unscathed the work systems, structures, and processes that may continue to produce ethnic inequality in this organization (cf. Bielby 2008). In a way this refers all the way back to what Braverman (1974: 20) said about the convenience of 'assaying not the nature of the work but the degree of adjustment of the worker'. That such an adjustment, if at all necessary, is not that easy only shows when one steps out of the comfort zones of research, consultancy, and HRM and enters the domain of real-life interactions and lived experiences. It might easily be said that Fahim was for a moment simultaneously enterprising and emotionally unstable (he showed upset in the email). What will he score on the multicultural personality questionnaire? Neat discourses of DM do not allow for such internal contradictions to arise, but this does not mean that in practice they may burst into conflict nonetheless. These contradictions become all the more salient when the DAL triangle is revisited. Are police officers not required to be authentic, that is, to reveal themselves?

The Hacker Story—Organizational Democracy as Alternative to Identity Regulation

Around the turn of the millennium, the Finnish economy was undergoing rapid deregulation and internationalization. Immigrants started arriving in larger numbers than ever before and ethnic boundaries (cf. Barth 1969) appeared in workplaces used to dealing only with gender, class, and age as social divides. This development began simultaneously at the lower wage ends of service, such as cleaning, and somewhat higher up among skilled employees, such as software engineers. I (Marja-Liisa) studied both, but in this chapter I will go into the particularities of the latter.

The Wonderland of High Tech

I contacted F-Secure, a medium-sized antivirus company, because of a business magazine article that praised their wonderful DM. As DM was still rare in Finland at the time, the article triggered my curiosity. Upon meeting, the Human Resources (HR) director had to dispel my hopeful anticipations. The journalist in question had simply exaggerated the results of a quick visit and small talk with management and reproduced some standard content from International Human Resource textbooks, letting the discourse stand in the way of reality. It would not happen to me, I decided. 'So you do not care for diversity management? How's that? You still have people here from many countries...?' Yes, there were people with different nationalities, but it was stated with certitude that this was not a problem to anyone. I asked around about other personnel politics: how are people treated relative to their professions and tasks, in terms of power and so on? I dutifully recorded a utopian narrative of happy camaraderie in a hacker's paradise. I was going to check it against what the employees said.

The employees sided with the HR director and shared his account. That is, with minor variations they told the same story of a workplace that was social and tolerant (towards socio-demographic differences but also towards mistakes, for instance). They were enthusiastic about the new technology being invented and about their own role in the digitalization of society. This was in their heyday, just before the IT bubble burst; it was an employees' market. The company would do whatever pleased the people, so it seemed, and managed social identities displeased them. 'In the beginning,' said Delphine (pseudonym), the French-German business-lawyer, 'I had the feeling that I was walking with the French flag attached to my back.' That had ceased by the time of the study, to her great relief. The employees detested the idea of being labelled or having to label their colleagues. The only official step taken in favour, as it might be argued, of diversity was the decision to adopt English as a company language. This is not so trivial a point as it may seem. Most of the "foreigners" would have failed requirements if Finnish had been the lingua franca. Apart from Estonians, very few immigrants can speak Finnish upon arrival. But then again, not every company is part of the global high-tech industry, nor a transnational space which recruits people via the internet.

The workers also confirmed management's discourse on the egalitarian organization. The word they used was 'democracy'; they gave praise to the prevailing 'air of democracy'. In practice this meant that the employees actually had some say in company matters, for example through monthly general meetings and the YT-neuvottelukunta (cooperative council), where elected representatives of the personnel discuss all kinds of company matters with top management. Immigrant employees were members of this body as well as Finns. My interviewees were not naively positive about everything, though; in fact, they criticized the management freely and with gusto, just not in issues related to ethnicity. They had a 'voice' (Bakhtin 1981; Holland et al. 1998) but did not use it in matters relating to ethnicity because, as they put it, it was not an issue.

I started to wonder if a genuine slice of power was not a good substitute for specific diversity programmes. Somewhere after my fifteenth interview and two lively Christmas parties mixing employees with all kinds of backgrounds, I stopped disbelieving my ears, and it dawned on me that demographic heterogeneity in the workplace does not automatically lead to a disaster in the absence of managerial treatment; the latter may actually do more harm than good. At this location, people were capable of treating one another with 'civility' (Gomes, Kaartinen, and Kortteinen 2007) without managerial intervention. Immigrant members offered me positive testimonies of their well-being and satisfaction with the company management and collegial relations among the staff.

One might seek explanations in the fact that many immigrant employees had a European or North American nationality; but then again, so-called 'visible minorities' from Asia were present as well as Russians, the latter in large numbers. Russians have been subjected to collective stigmatization in Finland, based on historical events and their offshoots in present-day ethnicism. Others may seek explanations in the race/class nexus (or ethnicity/class nexus for that matter), as I did myself initially. Sheltered from precarity, F-Securians gained a proper livelihood and reaped the fruits of globalization. But this would not hold much longer.

Downturn

Early in the new millennium the IT sector was sliding into the depths of a recession. The blow on professional pride and a sense of security was hard on the hackers, since they fell from such a height. Many of the ills described by Richard Sennett (2006) became chronic at F-Secure. Layoffs and cuts, followed by sharp increases in productivity demands, the imperative of customer orientation, and the bleak outlook of an employers' market hollowed out their self-confidence. Their efforts to explain and get a hold on the situation ran in many directions. Some blamed themselves, calling the lay offs a 'healthy reminder' (see Ho 2009 for similar findings at Wall Street), others cursed the management for its mistakes and for exaggerating financial rigour at the expense of the human productivity that was needed to rise from stagnation. I continued to observe and to interview, expecting soon to witness anxiety becoming ethicized and scapegoats running to slaughter. It never happened.

In interviews, I never started with the theme of ethnicity but took it up eventually if the interlocutor did not. Usually I had to do it. The word 'diversity' rarely came spontaneously from the lips of anyone in management or on the work floor. Though they knew I was studying ethnicity (or 'multinationality' or 'internationality'), they would continue to talk about their work and what the prospects looked like professionally. Though I embedded all inquiries about subjects and identities in the kind of work that each of them did—most of our conversations concerned professional hopes and worries—it took me a while to see that one of their reasons for stubbornly resisting managerial identity regulation was anchored in their professional subculture. They kept drawing from hacker values. One of these was international solidarity, a cherished theme in their folklore. A foreign colleague could therefore only be foreign in the eyes of local authorities. For fellows, (s)he was a citizen of a hackers' nation, bordering virtual space. Computer experts are members of a truly global network of fellow professionals. Although this subculture is very heterogeneous in its constitutive ingredients (Gere 2002; Coleman and Golub 2008) and has been under severe pressure since economic agendas started to toss it between glory and subjugation (Trux 2008), it persists in its strength.

This does not mean that all could skip merrily off into the sunset. The weak spot in a community of hackers is that not all are hackers proper. Bharat (pseudonym), coming from India, was lonely. His young wife stuck in India with their new-born baby, he spent his evenings and weekends mostly alone, producing articles for Indian papers and writing poems. Being a translator of products and manuals, he did not belong to the hacker's community. Computer specialists have communities of practice and wider networks that spread solidarity and useful resources across borders—but not necessarily to the neighbouring cubicle, occupied by a workmate that does not belong to their own moral community. He or she might be, for instance, a secretary or a localizer – such as Bharat. What's more, Bharat suffered from diffuse insecurity in his dealings with the Finns. He was never quite sure whether his anticipation of a ceiling to his career was attributable to a flat hierarchy, his Indianness, non-hacker identity, (imaginary) insufficient productivity, or perhaps just the difficulty in socializing: 'just because of me they have to talk in English. So you feel like OK, let's not disturb them'. But he never could observe that anything like ethnicity would have affected lay offs or other substantial decisions.

At the end of my fieldwork, the downturn was over, though good times did not return to F-Secure. Some latent sources of cross-cultural friction felt a bit like stones in the shoe, being no more discussed than in the average organization. White-collar immigrants nevertheless continued to spend a fairly comfortable middle-class life with their generally tolerant and 'open-minded' colleagues. I agreed with the HR manager that introducing top-down identity management programmes would probably have worsened the situation.

During a visit I paid to the San Jose subsidiary of F-Secure, in Silicon Valley, California, I witnessed worse outcomes of insecurity. After massive lay offs—and without clear task definitions—the local staff trembled with fear of what was to come next; it was a fear of the Finns. I got the chance to observe structurally ethicized troubles, which produced a taxonomy of two: the Finns and the others. Desperate locals asked me what they should do to make the Finns trust them. What I think is to be learned from the comparison of Helsinki and San Jose is the role of the often underestimated impact of their different statuses. Sales offices tend to have less prestige and fewer resources in the high-tech business than offices which house R&D functions or head offices. The personnel in San Jose had higher levels of turnover and were more precarious. Compared with the peaceful, trustful ambience in Helsinki, it was a whole different world. In Helsinki people stuck to their civility, defending their professional pride and sense of community among hackers, even under conditions of economic pressure. Clearly, whatever it was that prevented the workers from ethnicizing in Helsinki did not reach San Jose, or was not powerful enough against the structural evils they faced.

Organizational Democracy

The notion of 'organizational democracy' has a long pedigree in the social sciences (e.g. Davies 1967; Johnson 2006; Luhman 2006). Much can be said about its disadvantages for workers—it may be deployed to manufacture employee consent, as Burawoy (1979) long ago claimed, without adding much to real improvements in working conditions—as well as about its advantages—particularly when genuine power sharing is involved, such as in the case of labour-managed firms or worker-owned firms (cf. Luhman 2006), where property rights are actually held by workers. This is not the place to substantially add to this literature or make normative judgements. It is the place, however, to juxtapose certain qualities that are ascribed to organizational democracy with features of employee experience at F-Secure, which in turn can render understandable why the promises of top-down administration of identity had zero appeal for the workers.

Certain key characteristics of organizational democracy as described by Luhman (2006, based on a meta-analytic narrative study of ninety-seven works), such as community solidarity, control over tasks, involvement in decision-making processes, access to information, a sense of meaningful work, multiple skills, a concern for equality, task variety, tolerance, and respect were observable at F-Secure. In the experiences of my informants, these elements positively contributed to their life at work. What is more, they were part of a meaningful whole, a profession as a 'form of practical activity' (MacIntyre 1981) with its internal goods, traditions, and community-bound sources of legitimation, which, while they allow for managerial discretion, tend to keep it decent and under collegial scrutiny. Like many software companies, F-Secure had been founded by a handful of friends. At the time of the fieldwork, the company was still owned by the same CEO who, back in the start-up days, used to sit on the floor in monthly meetings if there were not enough chairs. In an analysis à la Jacques Rancière (see Biesta 2010), democratic moments ruptured the 'police order' and replaced dependent emancipation with a more genuine one, as minority members assumed themselves equal and came into presence as subjects of the local politics. 'When Noam brings out his checked notebook,' the HR director described the monthly meetings, 'we can be sure that tough questions will follow.' I argue that the 'air of democracy' so whole-heartedly defended in Helsinki equated pretty much with this short distance between management and staff.

Discussion and Conclusions

What can be learned from comparing the experiences of Dutch police officers and Finnish software engineers? How may this help to make sense of the field of DM? We had a unique opportunity to compare two unexpected ethnographic cases, in two different national contexts, that helped us to separate the rhetorics from the realities in the field of DM. In this sense, our work compares to Legge's (2005) meta-analytic effort within the broader field of human resource management, to which DM owes much of its achievements. Our cases qualify as unexpected because one opened a wedge to analyse the downsides of DM (most scholars have only gone so far as casting light on its suboptimal conditions; inquiries seldom reach into its harmful effects), while the other enabled us to study an organization in the absence of DM. Popular rhetoric has it that DM is either neutral (it has no effects whatsoever) or beneficial (economically or in terms of social equality), but our ethnographies uncover a different reality. With the on-going economic recession in mind, we expect that diversity scholars will have plenty of opportunities to study similar scenarios in the future. Being a typical expenditure of surplus, DM may be past its prime for now and will confront workers in the near future with either its absence or its leftovers; that is, the remains of low budget itineraries.

What caught our attention in comparing the two cases were the different ways in which organizational members' careers were dealt with. In both contexts employees were facing the hard realities of being seen as disposable resources and production costs (under public managerialism, police officers too are said to produce rather than serve). However, in Finland, F-Securians faced this reality with clear sight, without ideological clouds, and actually had a say in their company through the cooperative council (YT-neuvottelukunta) and all the rest of it. The Dutch police officers, on the other hand, felt misled by the soft rhetoric of employee development, participation, voice, and self-efficacy that accompanied (the offshoots of) DM. The occlusive language that was used even succeeded at times in breaking resistance (in the case of the applicant), because the rhetorical composition appeared nice, attractive even, and was cherished. So the larger canvas behind diversity discourses is what we might term an economy of good expectations. Protected within the compounds of consultancy, HRM, and para-academic life, good expectations need not be compromised, the shifting character of 'diversity' need not be confronted, and power asymmetries do not have to become too obvious. But eventually diversity discourses have to break out of these compounds because, by design, their real-life applications are their *raison d'être* (and main source of income). At that moment the charm is broken and it becomes evident that they have multiple meanings and can be strategically deployed. The subversive potential of ethnography resides in its ability to uncover these meanings and shed light on these deployments.

On a more abstract level, it may help to revisit Bauman's *Liquid Modernity* (2000) and interpret the various applied diversity instruments that we have studied as auxiliaries to what he calls 'life-politics', in contradistinction to 'public politics'. Central in his analysis of life-politics is the observation that people who live in this historical form of human cohabitation (liquid modernity) feel constantly coerced into sharing intimacies. 'When public politics sheds its functions and life-politics takes over', Bauman warns, the public sphere is likely to be excavated except for 'the site where private worries are confessed and put on public display' (2000: 51–2). This is exactly what happened in the fireplace session, which can easily be thought of as a Foucauldian technique of avowal (cf. Covaleski et al. 1998). After all, the participants were invited to release all breaks and confess as much as they pleased, but gained nothing thereafter. We therefore concur with Bauman, who follows Ulrich Beck in stating that there are simply 'no effective biographic solutions to systemic contradictions, and so the dearth of workable solutions at [people's] disposal needs to be compensated for by imaginary ones' (2000: 38). But herein lies the rub: the psychotechniques that are produced and circulated by the NSvP are both the instigators of and imagined solutions to the participants' troubles. It is a closed circuit, as various forms of psychometric profiling (cf. DiFruscia 2012) are used to problematize a certain situation (e.g. Dutch–Turkish police officers lack certain personality traits) to which solutions are offered that keep them within the same psychological discourse (e.g. an empowerment course). While such a consistency of diagnosis and solution stands to reason, it may be useful to remind oneself of Marxian dialectics, which urges people sometimes to find solutions to problems. The actual problems of structural discrimination remain in the world of work, waiting to be tackled once resources and attention are liberated from the managerial closed circuit of psychotechniques. Our evidence suggests that solutions to problems of power abuse (such as discrimination) might indeed include some measure of power redistribution.

By putting emphasis on the subversive potential of ethnography we hope to escape from the closed circuit of dominant paradigms and produce more radical innovation (see Chapter 16, this volume). The emergency exit is right around the corner if researchers and organizational members only dare listen to the silenced and sometimes distance themselves from the alleged universal good that DM is nowadays considered to be. A deceptive habit of thought has started to confuse the high moral goal of anti-discrimination with managerial and political practices of DM. Our examples show that managerial regulation of identities in organizations (the activity of DM that actually occurs; see Zanoni and Janssens 2006 for similar conclusions) does not stand the test of function. It does not yield the promised results, neither in equality—as it further burdens the careers of minorities, nor in productivity—as it diverts attention from the quality and quantity of work. The claim of its universality is broken by the counterexample of civility without managerial regulation. Failed practices and circular discourses unlearned, it becomes possible to think afresh: how could organizations allow people to live full professional and human lives?

We conclude in the words of Noam (pseudonym), himself an ethnic minority member:

MARJA-LIISA. So, are you happy about the way that this firm addresses diversity among employees?
NOAM. It doesn't address it in any way.
MARJA-LIISA. Are you happy about that?
NOAM. YEAH, I MEAN BECAUSE I DON'T FEEL THAT I'M DIVERSE.

References

Bakhtin, M. M. (1981). *The Dialogic Imagination. Four Essays by M. M. Bakhtin*, ed. M. E. Holquist. Austin, TX: University of Texas Press.
Barley, S. R. and Kunda, G. (2001). Bringing work back in. *Organization Science*, 12(1): 76–95.
Barth, F. (ed.) (1969). *Ethnic Groups and Boundaries: The Social Organization of Cultural Difference*. Long Grove, IL: Waveland Press.
Bate, S. P. (1997). Whatever happened to organizational anthropology? a review of the field of organizational ethnography and anthropological studies. *Human Relations*, 50(9): 1147–75.
Bauman, Z. (2000). *Liquid Modernity*. Cambridge and Malden, MA: Polity Press.
Bell, S. T., Villado, A. J., Lukasik, M. A., Belau, L., and Briggs, A. L. (2011). Getting specific about demographic diversity variable and team performance relationship: a meta-analysis. *Journal of Management*, 37(3): 709–43.
Bielby, W. (2008). Promoting racial diversity at work: challenges and solutions. In A. Brief (ed.), *Diversity at Work*. Cambridge: Cambridge University Press, 53–86.
Biesta, G. (2010). A new logic of emancipation: the methodology of Jacques Rancière. *Educational Theory*, 60(1): 39–59.
Blackmore, J. (2006). Deconstructing diversity discourses in the field of educational management and leadership. *Educational Management Administration & Leadership*, 34(2): 181–99.
Blommaert, J. and Dong, J. (2010). *Ethnographic Fieldwork: A Beginner's Guide*. Bristol: Multilingual Matters.
Boogaard, B. and Roggeband, C. (2010). Paradoxes of intersectionality: theorizing inequality in the Dutch police force through structure and agency. *Organization*, 17(1): 53–75.
Braverman, H. (1974). *Labor and Monopoly Capital: The Degradation of Work in the Twentieth Century*. New York: Monthly Review Press.
Burawoy, M. (1979). *Manufacturing Consent: Changes in the Labour Process under Monopoly Capitalism*. Chicago: Chicago University Press.
Carter, J. (2000). New public management and equal opportunities in the NHS. *Critical Social Policy*, 20(1): 61–83.
Coleman, E. G. and Golub, A. (2008). Hacker practice: moral genres and the cultural articulation of liberalism. *Anthropological Theory*, 8: 255–77.
Covaleski, M. A., Dirsmith, M. W., Heian, J. B., and Samuel, S. (1998). The calculated and the avowed: techniques of discipline and struggles over identity in big six public accounting firms. *Administrative Science Quarterly*, 43(2): 293–327.
Czarniawska, B. (2007). *Shadowing and Other Techniques for Doing Fieldwork in Modern Societies*. Copenhagen: Copenhagen Business School Press.
Davies, B. (1967). Some thoughts on "organizational democracy". *Journal of Management Studies*, 4(3): 270–81.

DiFruscia, K. T. (2012). Work rage: the invention of a human resource management anti-conflictual fable. *Anthropology of Work Review*, 33(2): 89–100.

Down, S. (2012). A historiographical account of workplace and organizational ethnography. *Journal of Organizational Ethnography*, 1(1): 72–82.

Ehrenreich, B. (2001). *Nickel and Dimed: On (Not) Getting By in America*. New York, Holt.

Fine, G. A. (2008). *Kitchens: The Culture of Restaurant Work*. (2nd edn, orig. publ. 1996.) Berkeley, CA: University of California Press.

Foldy, E. G. (2002). "Managing" diversity: identity and power in organizations. In I. Aaltio and A. J. Mills (eds.), *Gender, Identity and the Culture of Organizations*. London: Routledge, 92–112.

Gere, C. (2002). *Digital Culture*. London: Reaction Books.

Gomes, A., Kaartinen, T., and Kortteinen, T. (2007). Introduction: civility and social relations in South and Southeast Asia. *Suomen Antropologi—Journal of the Finnish Anthropological Society*, 32(3): 4–11.

Ho, K. (2009). *Liquidated: An Ethnography of Wall Street*. Durham, NC, and London: Duke University Press.

Hochschild, A. R. (2003). *The Managed Heart: The Commercialization of Human Feeling*. 2nd edn. Berkeley, CA: The University of California Press.

Holland, D., Lachicotte Jr., W., Skinner, D., and Cain, C. (1998). *Identity and Agency in Cultural Worlds*. Cambridge, MA: Harvard University Press.

Horwitz, S. K. and Horwitz, I. B. (2007). The effects of team diversity on team outcomes: a meta-analytic review of team demography. *Journal of Management*, 33(6): 987–1015.

Janssens, M. and Zanoni, P. (2005). Many diversities for many services: theorizing diversity (management) in service companies. *Human Relations*, 58(3): 311–40.

Johnson, P. (2006). Whence democracy? A review and critique of the conceptual dimensions and implications of the business case for organizational democracy. *Organization*, 13(2): 245–74.

Kochan, T., Bezrukova, K., Ely, R., Jackson, S., Joshi, A., Jehn, K., Leonard, J., Levine, D., and Thomas, D. (2003). The effects of diversity on business performance: reports of the diversity research network. *Human Resource Management*, 42(1): 3–21.

Kunda, G. (1992). *Engineering Culture: Control and Commitment in a High-tech Corporation*. Philadelphia, PA: Temple University Press.

Legge, K. (2005). *Human Resource Management: Rhetorics and Realities*. (Anniversary edn). Basingstoke: Palgrave Macmillan.

Litvin, D. R. (2006). Diversity: making space for a better case. In A. M. Konrad, P. Prasad, and J. Pringle (eds.), *Handbook of Workplace Diversity*. London: Sage, 75–94.

Luhman, J. T. (2006). Theoretical postulations on organizational democracy. *Journal of Management Inquiry*, 15(2): 168–85.

MacIntyre, A. (1981) *After Virtue: A Study in Moral Theory*. London: Duckworth.

Marcus, G. (1998). Critical cultural studies as one power/knowledge like, among, and in engagement with others. In G. Marcus (ed), *Ethnography Through Thick and Thin*. Princeton, NJ: Princeton University Press.

Noon, M. (2007). The fatal flaws of diversity and the business case for ethnic minorities. *Work, Employment & Society*, 21(4): 773–84.

Orr, J. E. (1996). *Talking about Machines: An Ethnography of a Modern Job*. Ithaca, NY: Cornell University Press.

Raaijmakers, M. (2008). *Authentiek Verbinden. Diversiteitsmanagment Vanuit een Veranderkundig Perspectief*. Dissertation available at: <http://www.innovatiefinwerk.nl/sites/innovatiefinwerk.nl/files/field/bijlage/thesis_mirea_raaijmakers.pdf> (accessed 24 July 2012).

Richard, O. C. (2000). Racial diversity, business strategy, and firm performance: a resource-based view. *The Academy of Management Journal*, 43(2): 164–77.

Roy, D. (1954). Efficiency and 'the fix': informal intergroup relations in a piecework machine shop. *American Journal of Sociology*, 60(3): 255–66.

Sennett, R. (2006). *The Culture of the New Capitalism*. New Haven, CT: Yale University Press.

Shore, C. and Wright, S. (2000). Coercive accountability: the rise of audit culture in higher education. In M. Strathern (ed.), *Audit Cultures: Anthropological Studies in Accountability, Ethnics and the Academy*. London and New York: Routledge, 57–89.

Silverstein, M. (2008). Axes of evals: token versus type interdiscursivity. *Journal of Linguistic Anthropology*, 15(1): 6–22.

Strien, P. J. and Van Dane, J. (2001). *Driekwart Eeuw Psychotechniek in Nederland: De Magie van het Testen*. Assen: Koninklijke van Gorcum.

Tomlinson, F. and Schwabenland, C. (2010). Reconciling competing discourses of diversity? The UK non-profit sector between social justice and the business case. *Organization*, 17(1): 101–21.

Trux, M.-L. (2008). Identifying flexibilities. In D. Jemielniak and J. Kociatkiewicz (eds.), *Management Practices in High-Tech Environments*. Hershey: Information Science Reference, 330–50.

Trux, M.-L. (2010). *No Zoo: Ethnic Civility and its Cultural Regulation Among the Staff of a Finnish High-Tech Company*. Dissertation in Acta Universitatis Oeconomicae Helsingiensis 358. Helsinki: Aalto University School of Economics.

Urciuoli, B. (2008). Skills and selves in the new workplace. *American Ethnologist*, 35(2): 211–28.

Urciuoli, B. (2010). Entextualizing *diversity*: semiotic incoherence in institutional discourse. *Language & Communication*, 30: 48–57.

Van der Zee, K. I. and Van Oudenhoven, J. P. (2001). The multicultural personality questionnaire: reliability and validity of self- and other ratings of multicultural effectiveness. *Journal of Research in Personality*, 35(3): 278–88.

Van Dijk, H., Van Engen, M. L., and Van Knippenberg, D. (2012). Defying conventional wisdom: a meta-analytic examination of the differences between demographic and job-related diversity relationships with performance. *Organizational Behavior and Human Decision Processes*, 119(1): 38–53.

Van Maanen, J. (2011). Ethnography as work: some rules of engagement. *Journal of Management Studies*, 48(1): 218–34.

Vertovec, S. (2012). 'Diversity' and the social imaginary. *European Journal of Sociology*, 53(3): 287–312.

Wallraff, G. (1985). *Ganz Unten*. Köln, Kiepenheuer & Witsch. (Published in English as *Lowest of the Low* in 1988.)

Watson, T. J. (2011). Ethnography, reality, and truth: the vital need for studies of 'how things work' in organizations and management. *Journal of Management Studies*, 48(1): 202–17.

Werkgeversvisie Politie (2008). *Een Inspirerend Fundament*. De Bilt: Landelijk Programma HRM Politie.

Wrench, J. (2005). Diversity management can be bad for you. *Race & Class*, 46(3): 73–84.

Ybema, S., Yanow, D., Wels, H., and Kamsteeg, F. (eds.) (2009). *Organizational Ethnography. Studying the Complexities of Everyday Life*. London: Sage.

Zanoni, P. (2011). Diversity in the lean automobile factory: doing class through gender, disability and age. *Organization*, 18(1): 105–27.

Zanoni, P. and Janssens, M. (2006). Diversity management as identity regulation in the post-Fordist productive space. In S. Clegg and M. Kornberger (eds.), *Space, Organizations, and Management Theory*. Malmo: Liber & Cobenhagen Business School Press.

Zanoni, P. and Janssens, M. (2007). Minority employees engaging with (diversity) management: an analysis of control, agency and micro-emancipation. *Journal of Management Studies*, 44(8): 1371–97.

Zanoni, P., Janssens, M., Benschop, Y., and Nkomo, S. (2010). Unpacking diversity, grasping inequality: rethinking differences through critical perspectives. *Organization*, 17(1): 9–29.

Zickar, M. and Carter, N. (2010). Reconnecting with the spirit of workplace ethnography. A historical review. *Organizational Research Methods*, 13(2): 304–19.

CHAPTER 16

COLLECTING NARRATIVES AND WRITING STORIES OF DIVERSITY

Reflecting on Power and Identity in Our Professional Practice

PATRIZIA ZANONI AND KOEN VAN LAER

INTRODUCTION

IT is no coincidence that qualitative research is often branded as a 'craft' (e.g. Golden-Biddle and Locke 1997; Prasad 2005). Indeed, as crafting depends on the embodied 'technical' knowledge and experience of craftsmen and craftswomen, qualitative research is a process which is grounded in knowledge that cannot be (easily fully) codified. And again like crafting, qualitative research involves an intensive creative process that (hopefully) leads to an original (research) product. Rather than embarking on yet another attempt to describe 'how to do' qualitative research, in this chapter, we reflect on our own experiences as qualitative, critical researchers of diversity, who regularly conduct interviews with individuals with diverse socio-demographic profiles in different kinds of jobs. By doing so, we aim to highlight and illustrate the difficulties, dilemmas, considerations, and pragmatism inherent in the craft we practise.

We organize our thoughts along the phases of the research cycle, from our socialization into the academic community, to fieldwork, the writing up of our research, and engaging with our peers in the review process. In each phase, we both reflect on our own experiences, paying particular attention to the micro-politics and identity dynamics in the praxis of qualitative research (Song and Parker 1995; Limerick, Burgess-Limerick, and Grace 1996; Johnson-Bailey 1999; Alvesson and Sköldberg

2000). In diversity scholarship, these micro-politics are exacerbated by the unique intersection of power relations characterizing qualitative research with those related to multiple socio-demographic identities. It is our explicit aim to explore the complexity of this intersection, using our experiences to reflect on important themes and institutionalized practices in qualitative organizational diversity research.

'Learning to Labour': On the Disciplining Effects of Discipline-Specific Methodological Norms

To become management/organization studies scholars, we undergo a process of socialization into academia during which we learn how to 'labour' according to contemporary professional norms (Trowler and Knight 2000; Mendoza 2007; Hakala 2009). Methodological practices represent an important aspect of this socialization process as they reflect the community's scientific preferences constituting its very identity. Methodological norms and practices are powerful instruments of socialization because they define, in a field, whether an activity is 'scientific' or not, and thus whether individuals enacting them are members of the 'scientific community'. Learning to labour therefore entails adopting the professional practices of the professional community, and making the underlying ideology one's own to develop a suitable sense of a professional self (Trowler and Knight 2000; Mendoza 2007; Adler and Harzing 2009).

Patrizia: *Starting my PhD with degrees in international sciences and social and cultural anthropology, and having some prior work experience outside academia, my own socialization into management studies has been one of learning new work practices and re-constructing my professional identity. Due to my working-class family background and left political activism, doing a PhD in business was not an obvious step for me. I gradually rolled into organization studies, picking up professional practices from my supervisor and other scholars around me. When I started reading the diversity literature published in 'quality' management journals, what struck me was the absolute dominance of quantitative studies relying on social psychological theories. The contested world of work and the politics of diversity which I had expected to find were not there. Inequality was represented as the inevitable result of 'natural', if problematic, cognitive processes. 'Real' people from disadvantaged groups were absent, as most studies were populated by numbers referring to individuals in managerial jobs, although historically subordinated groups are most often not managers. As a whole, this literature mystified the politics of diversity and was thus quite boring compared to the anthropological (gender) literature and the Marxist literature I was familiar with.*

My own work on diversity was triggered by my initial puzzlement with the narrow way management seemed to approach socio-demographic identities, both theoretically and methodologically. Monographs on gender from the 1980s (e.g. Cavendish 1982; Cockburn 1983; Ong 1987) and the work of a handful of more critically oriented diversity scholars published in the 1990s (e.g. Calás 1992; Nkomo 1992; Liff and Wajcman 1996; Litvin 1997; Prasad et al. 1997) however gave me hope that diversity research could be done differently. My supervisor had a key role in my socialization process into organization studies, as her knowledge of the field enabled us to write of diversity in ways that were at the same time innovating and yet recognizable for the (then emerging) critical (diversity) community in management. This normative process represents a fundamental aspect of one's professional socialization.

Whereas during my PhD, I enjoyed great freedom concerning theoretical choices, methodological ones were also based on 'strategic' considerations. We excluded a single-case ethnography early on in favour of less risky and more time-efficient qualitative data collection methods, such as extensive semi-structured interviews in multiple organizations. Indeed, methodological choices are typically made bearing existing norms of how much and what type of data is 'desirable', 'necessary', and/or 'acceptable'. Because good organizational research is synonymous with anonymously peer-reviewed research, researchers come to stand under high pressure to conform to existing methodological praxis found in published articles (Willmott 2011). Many choose quantitative methods in order to avoid being excluded on methodological grounds from prestigious institutions such as journals and universities. Alternative methods (e.g. visual methods, auto-ethnography) are rarely used also because there is little expertise available to socialize new scholars into using them and a lack of clear shared standards to judge the quality of the ways they are applied.

Koen: *I started my PhD research immediately after completing a business education which had prepared me to be a manager, rather than to study management or organizations. As I had not been exposed to methodological, epistemological, or ontological debates or trained to do research, my only real point of reference on what it meant to do research was my master's thesis. In it, I used economic theory to study cooperation between political parties and adopted a traditional, positivist qualitative approach based on semi-structured interviews. This experience was important because it taught me that I enjoyed doing research on a topic I believed to be socially and politically relevant. Witnessing the steady rise of the Flemish extreme-right party throughout my youth, I had been increasingly concerned about inequality, discrimination, and racism in society.*

With little prior knowledge about doing research or the academic world, but with a clear 'mission', I underwent the socialization process characterizing the start of each young academic's career. Throughout this process, I engaged in both resistance and conformism, leading to a sort of 'tempered radical' professional identity (Meyerson and Scully 1995), which I have aimed to maintain since. On the one hand, I attempted to resist the dominant instrumental and management-focused approach guiding much research in organization studies (Alvesson and Willmott 2003; Adler et al. 2007), including that of many of my colleagues. On the other hand, I tried to establish a 'competent' professional identity by conforming to the norms and institutionalized practices of academia. I listened to my supervisor's and colleagues' ideas, went through articles in 'top' international journals to gain an understanding of what 'good' journal articles look like and how an academic argument should be crafted, learnt about the 'valued' academic outputs, . . . Perhaps because of my lack of prior knowledge about the academic world, I never really questioned such dominant norms on 'correct academic behaviour'. Finding this balance between resisting and conforming is perhaps the fate of many critical diversity scholars in business faculties. After all, it is only by being not too resistant that it is possible to secure a form of legitimacy and maintain one's professional identity and academic voice.

When deciding which diversity issue I wanted to study, I opted for a topic that was not only academically, but also socially relevant. Given the highly precarious position of individuals of Turkish and Maghrebi descent in Flanders, and feeling it was important to give voice to individuals who clearly do not fit into the existing stereotypes about these ethnic groups as unwilling to participate in 'mainstream' society and as causing social problems, I decided to study the workplace experiences of ethnic minority professionals. I later realized that my focus on professionals was actually largely in line with the diversity literature's preference to study individuals in managerial and professional positions (e.g. Bell and Nkomo 2001; Ahmed 2007; Atewologun and Singh 2010; Özbilgin and Tatli 2011; Kenny and Briner 2013). When I also started doing and supervising research on ethnic minority employees in blue-collar jobs, I realized that perhaps part of the explanation of why—even critically oriented—studies of diversity often investigate managers and other highly skilled professionals, might be found in the pressure on (young) academics to quickly publish as much articles as possible (Archer 2008; Lund 2012). Managers and consultants are often highly articulate and can talk at length about their work and their careers using concepts and terminology that closely reflect our own jargon, which makes it easier to quickly translate their interviews into findings sections, and publishable articles. Still, one can wonder whether such pragmatic considerations, promoted by current academic pressures, do not lead us to ignore the most disenfranchised voices, such as those of recent immigrants working in the most dreadful jobs in our economies.

Similarly, despite continued calls for contextualized and in-depth explorations of diversity processes as they unfold in real-life organizational settings (e.g. Pringle, Konrad, and Prasad 2006; Zanoni et al. 2010), the default option in qualitative research seems to be methods based on semi-structured interviews. An approach which can clearly more easily and quickly be translated into findings sections than more time-intensive ethnographic approaches. I myself also used semi-structured interviews, mainly because it made sense given my research topic, but perhaps also in part because this was the main method of gathering qualitative empirical material I had encountered in the organizational literature on diversity.

'ALICE IN WONDERLAND': ON DISCOVERY, POWER, AND IDENTITY IN THE FIELD

The most exciting yet also somewhat threatening experience for a qualitative researcher is fieldwork. In the field, we enter an 'alien' culture and have to learn to navigate it

(Czarniawska 1998). Whereas the initial immersion in the scientific literature requires us to engage with abstract knowledge, fieldwork makes us aware of our dependence on others to collect 'good' stories, which are indispensable for the writing of good research. It forces us to negotiate our position vis-à-vis others, in a web of power relations, and in the process confronts us in novel ways with ourselves (Song and Parker 1995; Limerick, Burgess-Limerick, and Grace 1996; Czarniawska 1998; Johnson-Bailey 1999;). Arguably, the identity processes and power dynamics occurring in all qualitative research (Limerick, Burgess-Limerick, and Grace 1996; Bhopal 2010) are even more salient in research on diversity, to the extent that this latter precisely aims to investigate the role of social identities in power relations.

Patrizia: *Although the methodological literature stresses the difficulties of accessing organizations and gaining the commitment and the trust of interviewees (Czarniawska 1998), my own experience with recruiting organizations was not too painful. Perhaps this is due to the fact that diversity management was, at the time of my fieldwork (2003–5), gaining increasing popularity in Belgium and that the large companies I studied—an automotive factory, a consulting company, and a hotel—profiled themselves as diversity management pioneers. In each, I had distinct fieldwork experiences resulting from partially different methodological approaches, work processes in the organizations, profiles of the respondents, and life phases I was in at the time of fieldwork.*

In the automotive company, I conducted an ethnographic study including participant observation, extensive interviews, internal documents, and photographs. It was early in my PhD and I had no family obligations. I got up at 5 a.m. to reach the factory before the early shift started or stayed till the late shift ended at 10 p.m. I was struck by the role time and space played in defining people in the factory. Bound to the line, workers were under a self-enforcing time–space discipline. This affected my own fieldwork, as to spend time with workers I had to follow their shifts, stand along them while they were working, or join them in their short breaks. I could interview workers only when they could be substituted on the line, which put both of us under time pressure.

Although the quality of the interviews greatly varied across individuals, young Belgian male workers were especially hard to interview. Possibly they missed a 'right' language to speak with a female interlocutor of about the same age. I tried to keep the conversation as neutral as possible, focusing on 'facts'. Young males with a foreign background were in general more talkative with me, perhaps because my research was about diversity and I shared Italian origins with many of the workers. I had introduced myself as a student and told people that I was studying how people with different cultural backgrounds, men and women, people with different ages, abled and disabled, worked together. While some shop floor supervisors were highly critical of diversity, I learned the most from them, as they were not bound by the line, and made the most time for me. They provided key insights in the factory production system, its social world, and the many inconsistencies between the rhetoric and the reality of factory life.

The fieldwork in the consulting company was a different experience. I autonomously selected respondents from a contact list drawn by the HR unit, mailing and calling them to arrange individual meetings. Here, I had to really push for people to make time for an interview, which made me feel guilty about stealing time from these overworked knowledge workers. As consultants often work at the clients' premises, I conducted observations in the open offices at the company's headquarters only sporadically, between interviews. The articulateness of respondents' narratives compensated somewhat for the lack of observation. Given the highly educated profiles of my respondents and the fact that at the time I was in the last trimester of my first pregnancy, I branded myself as a university researcher rather than as a student, as had been the case in the factory. While, at least for some respondents, my pregnancy might have brought the private too much to the foreground, it perhaps signalled to the respondents that it was legitimate to talk about the difficulties of balancing consulting work and private life, as they tended to talk extensively about this topic.

Fieldwork in the hotel was again quite different. I conducted semi-structured interviews during the summer of 2005. Here too, most of my empirical material was collected through interviews, in multiple languages, although I did some non-participant observation and occasionally had lunch with personnel. I excluded systematic participant observation because that would have meant working in the very early morning, late evening, and/or weekends. This was not feasible given the commute and my at the time six-month-old son.

In the hotel, I had the impression that some of the respondents in lower-rank jobs agreed to be interviewed because their supervisor had asked them. I was aware that these workers were particularly vulnerable, as they have few or no other work alternatives. I felt that many female workers with Asian backgrounds found it particularly uneasy to talk with me. This might have however been caused by language problems or 'cultural' reasons rather than fear. Possibly, they felt that talking about their personal experiences at work with a stranger was out of place. I repeatedly stressed that there was no obligation to be interviewed and reassured them that all information was confidential, but am not sure whether this helped.

My exposure to respondents with very different profiles made me aware of how the modalities of interviewing give us, as researchers, unequal access to respondents and how they themselves, in turn, can be heard by us to different degrees. The more respondents are 'like us', speak the same language, have a high education, and are in jobs allowing them to autonomously manage their time, the more they can relate to us and to our work, anticipate what we want to hear, and help us produce 'good' stories. It is with these respondents that we end up talking longer and are more likely to sympathize with, which makes that their perspectives play a greater role in shaping our own understandings.

Although socio-demographic identities and their intersections are key in negotiating with our respondents roles with which both of us are comfortable, caution remains warranted in interpreting the impact of one's own socio-demographic profile on one's fieldwork. This relation is highly complex and not transparent. The roles I took with my informants were highly diverse and reflected not only my intersecting identities, but also theirs. For instance, as a female researcher, I related quite differently to males that were of my age and males that were older (and they clearly did, too), and age seemed generally more important than ethnic background or organizational rank in shaping the relation. Female interviewees of all ethnic backgrounds and in all organizational ranks often expected I would understand their experiences because of my own gender. As an Italian woman, I was approached by young men from Mediterranean countries in less sexualized ways than by some Belgian ones.

Koen: *I experienced the phase of 'gain accessing' to the field for my PhD research as highly challenging. Part of the difficulties I encountered were the result of the group I had chosen to study. At the time, second-generation ethnic minority professionals of Turkish or Maghrebi descent were a relatively small group, and I had further restricted it by (initially) excluding well-known individuals such as famous politicians or media figures. As is often done to study small, hard-to-reach populations, I relied heavily on snowball or chain referral sampling (Biernacki and Waldorf 1981; Penrod et al. 2003). While this approach was useful to identify respondents, it produced 'false starts' (Biernacki and Waldorf 1981), as I was referred to individuals who did not fit into the sample I had envisioned, leading to uncomfortable situations in which I had to turn them down because they did not have the 'right profile'. I also quickly realized that I risked getting 'stuck' in a circle of friends, with often quite similar experiences. Therefore, I looked for interviewees in different chains of reference, for example by placing calls for participation on websites and making use of my own professional and personal networks.*

Once I had obtained the contact information of a possible interviewee, I had to gain his or her commitment to participate in my research. I experienced this ever-continuing cycle of 'gaining access' as very embarrassing and discomforting. First, because I, an ethnic majority individual, was addressing my potential interviewees as ethnic minority individuals. Although I do not know whether my 'outsider status' influenced this, some did refuse to participate because they did not feel like discussing their experiences as an ethnic minority individual with me. Both to make up for the categorical way I addressed them and to convince them that I had 'good intentions', I always clearly positioned myself in my initial communications as an 'ally', who aimed to question and challenge existing stereotypes and inequalities (Gibson and Abrams 2003). Second, making contact with possible interviewees was an unpleasant phase because, as noted by Limerick, Burgess-Limerick, and Grace (1996), I felt that potential interviewees had strong control over me, as I depended on individuals who did not know me to make time for me and help me advance my research. Luckily, many were willing to participate.

While my interviews were characterized by specific identity processes and power dynamics, which were potentially made more salient by the ethnic (and sometimes gender) difference with my interviewees, I think it is too simplistic to assume that who I am made the interviews 'more difficult'. Rather, I believe that my multiple and intersecting identities influenced the interview process in a number of different and potentially contradicting and unpredictable ways (Song and Parker 1995; Johnson-Bailey 1999; Archer 2002). On the one hand, belonging to the ethnic majority, I grew up with the privilege of lacking the 'insider knowledge' of living as an ethnic minority individual in Flanders, and facing the discrimination and identity challenges it entails. This became painfully clear during one of my first interviews, when an interviewee got mad at me because of a follow-up question I asked concerning her cultural identity. She luckily quickly forgave me and we ended up having a very interesting discussion about the issue. While later interviewees never expressed their frustrations this openly, I might have unwillingly offended others by my questions and choice of words, and by doing so, influenced the answers they gave. Still, some interviewees explicitly stated that they allowed me to ask questions they would normally experience as problematic, precisely because they believed the research I was doing was important. Perhaps surprisingly, I myself sometimes felt very uncomfortable because of statements interviewees made about ethnic minorities, including those from their 'own' ethnic community. For example, one person argued that most individuals of foreign descent were only driven by a desire to earn a lot of money, going as far as calling them 'magpies interested in everything that shines'.

On the other hand, I also noticed that ethnic difference was not only a drawback (Gibson and Abrams 2003; Essers 2009). For example, some interviewees expressed admiration for my interest in diversity and my critical views on the status quo, creating a feeling of mutual respect and common purpose, and helping to push our ethnic difference to the background (Manderson, Bennett, and Andajani-Sutjahjo 2006). This was further strengthened by other common identities, such as our higher educational background, or the fact that some interviewees had attended the university or the faculty where I was working. Furthermore, some seemed to be more comfortable expressing their views on sensitive topics to someone not belonging to their ethnic community, feeling I would be less likely to condemn them for them (Essers 2009). My lack of knowledge generally did not appear to offend the interviewees, as most did not expect this from someone of the ethnic majority. They rather made an extra effort to explain their experiences and opinions in depth and often seemed to perceive me as a sort of pupil (Rhodes 1994), who was there to learn from them, a role which was also hinted at by my age and professional junior status compared to them.

I rarely felt I was in a very clear position of power during the interviews. Not only did interviewees ultimately keep control over how long the interview lasted, whether they answered questions, how much information they shared, but they also occasionally clearly had a message they wanted to communicate through my research (Limerick, Burgess-Limerick, and Grace 1996). On the whole, I ended my period in the field with a sense of gratitude, and a feeling that I was really indebted to the individuals who had told me their stories.

'Lost in Translation': Re-telling Field Stories to an Academic Audience

Once empirical material has been 'harvested' in the field, the challenge for a researcher becomes to weave it into a story that is appealing to an academic public (Van Maanen, 1988; Golden-Biddle and Locke 1997; Rhodes and Westwood 2007; Essers 2009). Some refer to this process as one of translating the received 'gift' (Limerick, Burgess-Limerick, and Grace 1996). Today, producing translations in accordance with the dominant norms of academic writing represents perhaps the most important competence for a scholar. As the publication of scientific articles constitutes the basis on which one's academic performance is evaluated, writing in ways that meet peers' expectations largely defines who belongs to the particular realm of academia (Hardy, Phillips, and Clegg 2001; Archer 2008; Adler and Harzing 2009; Miller, Taylor, and Bedeian 2011; Willmott 2011; Lund 2012).

Patrizia: The origin of an article lies in a hunch: What does this empirical material say that makes me think differently about diversity? As the same material might be exciting and stimulating to different people in different ways, this is only an apparently easy question to answer. It is thanks to our socialization into the academic community that we learn, as individual scholars, to 'see' aspects in data that are likely to speak to the community as a whole. This initial intuition is therefore all but 'free', it is firmly embedded in current debates in the field. Then the tricky task comes of problematizing the existing knowledge on diversity to highlight the necessity of the study, out of which new insight will emerge. This process is commonly referred to as showing the 'gap', an unfortunate quantitative metaphor which evokes the possibility that knowledge gaps can be filled once and for all, and which obscures the rhetorical dimension of constructing the 'gap' in the first place (Golden-Biddle and Locke 1997).

Specific to organization studies is the expectation that empirical pieces make not only an empirical contribution (a quite legitimate enterprise in itself in other disciplines), but also a theoretical one, that is contesting, extending, deepening, and/or refining existing theory. While reducing the risk of purely descriptive papers, the focus on theory building straitjackets empirical research into very specific formats, which pose important problems to critical diversity researchers. First, the need to make a theoretical contribution forces authors to relate their work to the existing research, which functions as a 'benchmark'. Much energy and room is spent portraying one's study as commensurable to such research, contributing to the reproduction of existing dominant paradigms. Even when a piece explicitly aims at contesting it, it has to repeat and refer to the main tenets of the contested paradigm, inadvertently favouring theoretical continuity over more radical forms of innovation (Alvesson and Sandberg 2011). Radical breaks are rare not only because they (rightly) require a thorough knowledge of the existing literature but also, crucially (and less rightly), because they tend to require a central, established position in the field from which one's point can be plausibly made.

Second, building theory from subordinated groups' experiences is particularly arduous because academic knowledge largely reflects the perspectives of dominant groups at work. Meriläinen et al. (2008) have rightly pointed to how the dominant assumption that historically subordinated groups are not representative of the working population entails the disqualification of their experiences as suitable bases to build theory that goes beyond them as a group. Respondents from historically dominant groups are on the contrary assumed to be representative, no questions asked. To highlight that their experiences say something that transcends their socio-demographic specificity, I often choose theoretical approaches that allow showing that individuals from subordinated groups are agents, despite their embeddedness in structures which disfavour them. I try to balance between determinism and excessive agency, avoiding, respectively, victimization or naivety. I do not think of myself so much as 'giving voice' to my respondents, but rather as committed to portraying them as 'full' subjects. Ideally, as in fiction, readers should feel in these individuals' shoes and come to the conclusion that, if they actually were, they would think and act in a similar way. This approach has its drawbacks, the main being that it tends to portray individuals as overly 'strategic', downplaying their weaknesses and inconsistencies. As a result, my subjects might be complex yet rarely weak or inconsistent. This reflects my own understanding of weakness and inconsistency as the luxury of privileged groups, whose subjectivity and agency are not constantly called into question. It therefore reflects them as much as me (Rhodes 2009).

Aware of my own privileged position, while writing, I ask myself whether my work could possibly be used to damage individuals in subordinated positions, for instance through the managerial reappropriation of the identified mechanisms of domination and exploitation (Brewis and Wray-Bliss 2008). Then I console myself thinking that managers surely do not read scientific journals (especially the ones I write in), and that no visibility of my work in the 'real' world out there should be assumed.

Koen: *During the process of translating what we encounter in the field into academic writing, we obviously wield important power. Probably the most important challenge we are faced with is upholding our responsibility to our interviewees and our ambition—despite all the difficulties this might entail (Czarniawska 1999)—to give voice to historically disadvantaged groups, while conforming to the demands of academic writing. These demands force us to reduce our interviewees' stories, lives, and experiences to instruments used to achieve the 'greater goal' of the theoretical contribution. As this is an end that is far removed from their realities, we are actually doing to our interviewees what many of us criticize (diversity) management of doing (e.g. Prasad and Mills 1997; Lorbiecki and Jack 2000; Zanoni and Janssens 2004): using people as 'human resources' to reach our own professional ends. In this process, we might end up acting less as spokespersons, and more as ventriloquists, whose voice is transmitted through the stories of others who seem to be doing the talking (Czarniawska 1999).*

A second way in which the interviewees' voice might get compromised is through the need for translation. As English is currently the lingua franca of the academic world, this forces us to translate interview statements from the language in which they emerged, which obviously leads to a certain loss of meaning and nuance. Of specific concern in this process is my fear that staying too close to the original constructions might result in statements which are grammatically weak or incorrect in English, thereby fuelling the stereotype that my ethnic minority interviewees lack adequate language skills. This issue of language is related to a number of larger points that can be made about writing from a 'peripheral country' in the academic world (Meriläinen et al. 2008). For example, I also struggle with the pressure of adopting concepts which are prevalent in the dominant centres of academia, but completely foreign to the lifeworld of the interviewees. For example, while some have advised me to use the concept of race rather than ethnicity, I feel uncomfortable doing so, as this notion was never used by my interviewees, and has a very negative connotation in my own context. Similarly, I often worry that because of a language error or the use of a concept that has a negative meaning in some contexts but not in mine (e.g. second-generation individual), I might be perceived as uninformed, insensitive, or even racist. I think such points touch upon issues central to our discipline, as they raise the question of how much diversity in language, even if we use English, is allowed to capture the nuances of the context under study, or how strongly we should assimilate to the dominant (language) centre of academia.

Another challenge when writing from the academic periphery concerns the description of the local context, which is obviously key to understanding diversity processes (Pringle 2009; Zanoni et al. 2010). While those writing from a dominant centre of academia have the privilege that their context is relatively well known to outsiders, this is not the case for others, who are forced to extensively detail their setting; or even to convince readers/reviewers that what they are saying is also relevant for other (more 'important') contexts (Meriläinen et al. 2008; Nkomo 2009).

'The Good, the Bad and the Ugly': On the Complex Politics of Reflexivity

Throughout the process of crafting qualitative research of diversity, from learning to labour, to our travels in Wonderland, and the translation into an academic text, researchers reflect on their experiences and attempt to make sense of them (Hardy, Phillips, and Clegg 2001; Macbeth 2001; Pillow 2003). Next to this 'good' dimension, reflexivity also harbours some perils. Especially relevant for diversity research is that reflexivity can be used 'badly' to justify and legitimize one's research by strategically positioning oneself in terms of socio-demographic make-up to claim legitimate authorship (Macbeth 2001; Pillow 2003). Conversely, it can be used in 'ugly' ways to call into question the plausibility and legitimacy of the advanced insights based on researchers' socio-demographic identity rather than based on their capacity to say something meaningful and novel.

Patrizia: *Coming from a discipline such as social and cultural anthropology, which has spent the last decades self-reflecting on its involvement in colonial relations, the cursory reference to the authors' identities at the end of the method section of an article appears quite hollow, not to say thoroughly un-reflexive. Yet the disclosure of one's gender, ethnic background, and age have become common practice, and whenever it is omitted in the original manuscript, it is elicited by reviewers during the peer review process to appear in its final version. Although reviewers might be moved by the noblest motivations, to me this request feels like a obligatory ritual in which authors confess their identity sins and ask for absolution and reviewers, as self-elected Catholic priests, grant it or deny it. Surrealistically, even methodology sections of articles written in post-structuralist traditions are filled with over-simplified and essentializing representations of the authors and their relations with their informants. As Pillow (2003) has convincingly argued, they enact a practice of reflexivity resting on a modernist understanding of the subject: singular, knowable, and fixable.*

These 'coming out' statements are generally written in a defensive mode to curb possible critiques or even to claim a superior ability to understand specific forms of diversity (Patai 1991). However, the assumption that commonality of social identity entails closeness, more equal power relations between researcher and respondents, and thus ultimately access to more 'truthful' empirical material is erroneous. Consider my nationality. Although it most probably helped me make friends in the automotive company, where many workers had Italian origins, it is much less clear how it affected my data collection and interpretation. As an Italian migrant to Belgium, I might for example cope with my own traumatic migration experience and develop a positive identity by adopting Belgian stereotypical negative images of Italians. Or, as a highly educated first-generation woman from Northern Italy, I might have trouble connecting with third-generation, low-educated men with roots in Southern Italy (Bhopal 2010). The possibilities in which multiple identities and their intersections might play a role are countless.

In critical diversity research, the 'bad' of reflexivity too often becomes the 'ugly': because socio-demographic identities and power are the core issue under investigation, identity confessions (or the absence thereof) are commonly played out in the review process. It is not exceptional that reviewers appropriate the information provided by the authors on their socio-demographic profile to de-legitimize their claims or, conversely, to insinuate that their claims are biased due to their specific perspective on the grounds of their undisclosed identities. This is highly problematic in that it shifts the plane of the critique from the plausibility of the offered interpretation to the author as defined by an assumed 'essential' identity. Authors and reviewers belonging to specific socio-demographic groups defend their own exclusive claim to the 'truth' over that group against non-members, with the key difference that authors are expected to come out of the closet and declare their socio-demographic profile while reviewers enjoy the comfort of anonymity. Ironically, this occurs among scholars who all swear to anti-essentialistic conceptualizations of identity. Review processes risk becoming the battlefield for inter-individual identity politics rather than a process that develops ideas.

The perils of current practices of reflexivity extend beyond the critical diversity literature, however. Stressing the partiality and specific positionality of our work might have the (unintended) effect to de-legitimize our scholarship in the eyes of colleagues working in positivistic epistemological traditions, who might reappropriate explicit references to the absence of objectivity to dismiss critical research as unscientific/'untrue'. This critique is not far-fetched; on the contrary, it represents one of the main points of debate between critical realists and post-structuralist scholars within the critical management studies community (Johnson and Duberley 2000).

Despite these fundamental reservations with current practices, a self-reflexive praxis remains key to the profession of qualitative researcher (Brewis and Wray-Bliss 2008). I try to systematically reflect on the process through which my empirical material is generated in my interactions in the field, on how my biography shapes my theoretical preferences and my ability to 'see', as well as on how the review process leaves an indelible mark on my work (for good and for bad). I try to make sense, often post hoc, of my own intuitively enacted positioning strategies vis-à-vis my diverse informants, in order to evaluate their strengths and their weaknesses. I regularly discuss this 'experienced' dimension of research with my peers and junior researchers, attempting to learn from our experiences. In sum, scepticism towards public, lip-service reflexivity, does not exclude engaging in multiple, more 'private' circles of reflexivity that help me understand why we do what we do. To avoid a logic of guilt, confession, and redemption, we need to engage in more thorough self-reflective practices in which we do not feel under any pressure to perform alienating personas to fulfil standardized expectations of distant, anonymous others. Practising reflexivity in this way leads to convenience self-branding, the very negation of reflexivity.

Koen: To me, the 'good' of reflexivity is about fundamentally exploring, acknowledging, questioning, and exposing the way our identities, interests, and politics are present throughout, and shape, the research process, and about being aware of the responsibility we have when we wield the blunt weapon of language, construct reality, and represent others (Pillow 2003; Hibbert, Coupland, and MacIntosh 2010). I consider reflexivity to be especially important as my position as a male, heterosexual individual of the ethnic majority without disabilities grants me forms of advantage and privilege which, especially as a diversity researcher, I simply have to be aware of (Jacques 1997; Kamenou 2007). What I do struggle with is the fact that, when trying to unveil myself from behind a text, I feel that to really account for all elements that have played a role in crafting a specific article, I would need a few pages. How else is it possible to offer a nuanced account of my self in relation to the field, to the interviewees, and to the produced translation? Yet this space is not available in a journal article, as every page devoted to reflexivity is a page that cannot be used to describe findings and develop theory, elements which might ultimately decide the fate of the piece.

As a result of these constraints of the article format, reflexivity often seems to be condemned to become 'the bad', and reduced to positioning the self through a simple list of social identities. While such a 'confession' about the self tells us something about the author, it nevertheless appears to be a superficial gesture. First, authors are not simply determined by their social identities nor can they 'transcend' these social positions by the mere fact of acknowledging them. Second, such confessional tales often only seem to involve a strategic exercise aimed at claiming closeness to the subject and at obscuring the power relations in the research process (Pillow 2003). If we acknowledge this, should we be satisfied with such a relatively meaningless overview of social identities? If we answer this question with 'no', then the more fundamental question becomes: is there room for 'real' reflexivity as long as we're bound by the shackles of the journal article with its strict world limits?

Sadly, I have in the past also been confronted with 'the ugly' of reflexivity. The privileges that I have by virtue of my ethnicity, gender, and sexual orientation occasionally seem to turn into disadvantages when I write about diversity. For example, one of the worst days of my professional life so far must have been when I received a review in which my ethnic background was invoked to question what I wrote and to assert that I seemed to be mocking my interviewees. As someone whose objective it has always been to question ethnic inequality, I experienced these comments as a fundamental challenge to my professional identity. The following days, I thought long and hard about these comments, as they bothered me much more than the rejection of the manuscript. While I certainly could have *phrased certain issues better and in more nuanced ways, I also wondered whether this reviewer would have made such remarks if (s)he had not known my ethnicity, or if I had written more about myself, and extended my reflections beyond some short remarks about my social identities. Perhaps this latter element played a role, and perhaps I simply received the type of response I could expect given the superficial way I had positioned/essentialized myself as an ethnic majority individual. As I continue to ponder on such issues, I fear that truly translating the reflexive processes we go through is almost impossible when writing articles, leaving us stuck with the bad and ugly of reflexivity.*

Conclusion

In this contribution, we have shared our experiences as critically oriented scholars of diversity working with qualitative research methods, mainly interviews. Written in the form of personal accounts, our narratives highlight the power-laden difficulties and dilemmas in our research practice, which we attempt to reflect on and deal with. We hope to have touched upon aspects which are relevant to the experiences of colleagues working on diversity, sharing insights, frustrations, and tricks to get the job done without losing oneself completely in the process. Yet there are obviously no once-and-for-all answers to these problems. As researchers, it is our job to make those calls again and again, evaluating each time the potential consequences, for the good and the bad. Indeed, the reader who is familiar with our work might associate us with those very practices we have contested here. For sure, as writers, reviewers, editors, and perhaps even more as teachers, we are always accomplices in the reproduction of those scientific norms, even when we distance ourselves from them.

Learning to be a 'good' researcher always entails some degree of conformity to the dominant norms in academia (Trowler and Knight 2000; Adler and Harzing 2009; Lund 2012). We continuously negotiate our own identity and position vis-à-vis the scholarly communities to which we belong, our interlocutors in the field, the various audiences we address, and of course ourselves. In each relationship, we carry out intense 'identity work', in which we are disciplined by others, self-discipline ourselves, and, in turn, discipline others around us. Although we do retain some freedom in deciding how faithfully we ultimately conform, methodological norms are generally not radically called into question, as they constitute fundamental aspects of paradigms of scientific investigation. They exert a strong homogenizing force, which steers research away from the 'hands on' data collection strategies that are often called for (Pringle, Konrad, and Prasad 2006; Zanoni et al. 2010) towards traditional quantitative methods and, to a much lesser extent, familiar qualitative methods such as semi-structured interviews.

As critical diversity scholars, we should be wary of norms and practices pressuring us to assimilate to an 'ideal' academic and stimulating the reification of our own and our respondents' identities along essentialist logics (Litvin 1997), two power-laden processes which we commonly deconstruct and criticize in our own scholarly work on diversity.

We should also be aware of how our 'theory building' perspective operates as a powerful mechanism to exclude entire bodies of knowledge which are less 'common currency'—for instance because they do not reflect the experiences of dominant groups, or are not written in English—from organization studies, because they are seen as unsuited to contributing to a shared enterprise of building common knowledge. Little is needed to be perceived and branded as 'niche' and 'marginal', a label which then becomes a self-fulfilling prophecy. We suspect that those exclusions say more about ourselves as organizational scholars than about the excluded, reflecting a double inferiority complex of our discipline, which is condemned to borrow theory from the humanities, where theories are generated, while at once mimicking the methodological precision of the exact sciences, which it will never achieve.

References

Adler, N. J. and Harzing, A.-W. (2009). When knowledge wins: transcending the sense and nonsense of academic rankings. *Academy of Management Learning & Education*, 8(1): 72–95.

Adler, P., Forbes, L., and Willmott, H. (2007). Critical management studies. *The Academy of Management Annals*, 1(1): 119–79.

Ahmed, S. (2007). The language of diversity. *Ethnic and Racial Studies*, 30(2): 235–56.

Alvesson, M. and Sköldberg, K. (2000). *Reflexive Methodology: New Vistas for Qualitative Research*. London: Sage.

Alvesson, M. and Sandberg, J. (2011). Generating research questions through problematization. *Academy of Management Review*, 36(2): 247–71.

Alvesson, M. and Willmott, H. (2003). Introduction. In M. Alvesson and H. Willmott (eds.) *Studying Management Critically*. London: Sage, 1–22.

Archer, L. (2002). 'It's easier that you're a girl and that you're Asian': interactions of 'race' and gender between researchers and participants. *Feminist Review*, 72: 108–32.

Archer, L. (2008). Younger academics' constructions of 'authenticity', 'success' and professional identity. *Studies in Higher Education*, 33(4): 385–403.

Atewologun, D. and Singh, V. (2010). Challenging ethnic and gender identities: An exploration of UK black professionals' identity construction. *Equality, Diversity and Inclusion: An International Journal*, 29: 332–47.

Bell, E. L. J. E. and Nkomo, S. M. (2001). *Our Separate Ways: Black and White Women and the Struggle for Professional Identity*. Boston, MA: Harvard Business School Press.

Bhopal, K. (2010). Gender, identity and experience: researching marginalised groups. *Women's Studies International Forum*, 33: 188–95.

Biernacki, P. and Waldorf, D. (1981). Snowball sampling: problems and techniques of chain referral sampling. *Sociological Methods Research*, 10(2): 141–63.

Brewis, J. and Wray-Bliss, E. (2008). Re-Searching ethics: towards a more reflexive critical management studies. *Organization Studies*, 29(12): 1521–40.

Calás, M. B. (1992). An/other silent voice? Representing 'Hispanic woman' in organizational texts. In A. J. Mills and P. Tancred (eds.), *Gendering Organizational Analysis*. Newbury Park, CA: Sage.

Cavendish, R. (1982). *Women on the Line*. London: Routledge.

Cockburn, C. (1983). *Brothers: Male Dominance and Technological Change*. London: Pluto.

Czarniawska, B. (1998). *A Narrative Approach to Organization Studies.* London: Sage
Czarniawska, B. (1999). *Writing Management.* Oxford: Oxford University Press.
Essers, C. (2009). Reflections on the narrative approach: dilemmas of power, emotions and social locations while constructing life-stories. *Organization,* 16(2): 163–81.
Gibson, P. A. and Abrams, L. S. (2003). Racial differences in engaging, recruiting, and interviewing in African American communities. *Qualitative Social Work,* 2(4): 457–76.
Golden-Biddle, K. and Locke, K. (1997). *Composing Qualitative Research: Crafting Theoretical Points from Qualitative Research.* Thousand Oaks, CA: Sage.
Hakala, J. (2009). Socialization of junior researchers in new academic research environments: two case studies from Finland. *Studies in Higher Education,* 34(5): 501–16.
Hardy, C., Phillips, N., and Clegg, S. (2001). Reflexivity in organization and management theory: a study of the production of the research 'subject'. *Human Relations,* 54(5): 531–60.
Hibbert, P., Coupland, C., and MacIntosh, R. (2010). Reflexivity: recursion and relationality in organizational research processes. *Qualitative Research in Organizations and Management,* 5(1): 47–62.
Jacques, R. (1997). The unbearable whiteness of being: reflections of a pale, stale male. In P. Prasad, A. Mills, M. Elmes, and A. Prasad (eds.), *Managing the Organizational Melting Pot: Dilemmas of Workplace Diversity.* Thousand Oaks, CA: Sage, 80–106.
Johnson-Bailey, J. (1999). The ties that bind and the shackles that separate: race, gender, class, and color in a research process. *Qualitative Studies in Education,* 12(6): 659–70.
Johnson, P. and Duberley, J. (2000). *Understanding Management Research.* London: Sage.
Kamenou, N. (2007). Methodological considerations in conducting research across gender, 'race', ethnicity and culture: a challenge to context specificity in diversity research methods. *International Journal of Human Resource Management,* 18(11): 1995–2009.
Kenny, E. J. and Briner, R. B. (2013). Increases in salience of ethnic identity at work: the roles of ethnic assignation and ethnic identification. *Human Relations,* 66(5): 725–48.
Liff, S. and Wajcman, J. (1996). 'Sameness' and 'difference' revisited: which way forward for equal opportunity initiatives? *Journal of Management Studies,* 33(1): 79–94.
Limerick, B., Burgess-Limerick, T., and Grace, M. (1996). The politics of interviewing: power relations and accepting the gift. *International Journal of Qualitative Studies in Education,* 9(4): 449–60.
Litvin, D. R. (1997). The discourse of diversity: from biology to management. *Organization,* 4(2): 187–209.
Lorbiecki, A. and Jack, G. (2000). Critical turns in the evolution of diversity management. *British Journal of Management,* 11 (Special Issue): S17–S31.
Lund, R. (2012). Publishing to become an 'ideal academic': an institutional ethnography and a feminist critique. *Scandinavian Journal of Management,* 28: 218–28.
Macbeth, D. (2001). On 'reflexivity' in qualitative research: two readings, and a third *Qualitative Inquiry,* 7(1): 35–68.
Manderson, L., Bennett, E., and Andajani-Sutjahjo, S. (2006). The social dynamics of the interview: age, class and gender. *Qualitative Health Research,* 16: 1317–34.
Mendoza, P. (2007). Academic capitalism and doctoral student socialization: a case study. *Journal of Higher Education,* 78(1): 71–96.
Meriläinen, S., Tienari, J., Thomas, R., and Davies, A. (2008). Hegemonic academic practices: experiences of publishing from the periphery. *Organization,* 15(4): 584–97.
Meyerson, D. and Scully, M. (1995). Tempered radicalism and the politics of ambivalence and change. *Organization Science,* 6(5): 585–600.

Miller, A. N., Taylor, S. G., and Bedeian, A. G. (2011). Publish or perish: academic life as management faculty live it. *Career Development International*, 16(5): 422–45.
Nkomo, S. (1992). The emperor has no clothes: rewriting 'race into organizations'. *Academy of Management Review*, 17(3): 487–513.
Nkomo, S. (2009). The seductive power of academic journal rankings: challenges of searching for the otherwise. *Academy of Management Learning & Education*, 8(1): 106–12.
Ong, A. (1987). *Spirits of Resistance and Capitalist Discipline: Factory Women in Malaysia*. Albany, NY: State University of New York Press.
Özbilgin, M. and Tatli, A. (2011). Mapping out the field of equality and diversity: rise of individualism and voluntarism. *Human Relations*, 64(9): 1229–53.
Penrod, J., Bray Preston, D., Cain, R. E., and Starks, M. T. (2003). A discussion of chain referral as a method of sampling hard-to-reach populations. *Journal of Transcultural Nursing*, 14(2): 100–7.
Patai, D. (1991). U.S. academics and third-world women: is ethical research possible? In S. Berger Gluck and D. Patai (eds.), *Women's Words: The Feminist Practice of Oral History*. New York: Routledge, 137–53.
Pillow, W. (2003). Confession, catharsis, or cure? Rethinking the uses of reflexivity as methodological power in qualitative research. *International Journal of Qualitative Studies in Education*, 16(2): 175–96.
Prasad, P. (2005). *Crafting Qualitative Research: Working in the Postpositivist Traditions*. Armonk, NY: M. E. Sharpe.
Prasad, P. and Mills, A. (1997). From showcase to shadow, understanding the dilemmas of managing workplace diversity. In P. Prasad, A. Mills, M. Elmes, and A. Prasad (eds.), *Managing the Organizational Melting Pot: Dilemmas of Workplace Diversity*. Sage: Thousand Oaks, CA: Sage, 3–27.
Prasad, P., Mills, A., Elmes, M., and Prasad, A. (eds.) (1997). *Managing the Organizational Melting Pot: Dilemmas of Workplace Diversity*. Thousand Oaks, CA: Sage.
Pringle, J. K. (2009). Positioning workplace diversity: critical aspects for theory. In M. F. Özbilgin (ed.), *Equality, Diversity and Inclusion at Work: A Research Companion*. Cheltenham: Edward Elgar, 75–87.
Pringle, J. K., Konrad, A. M., and Prasad, P. (2006). Conclusion. reflections and future directions. In A. M. Konrad, P. Prasad, and J. K. Pringle (eds.), *Handbook of Workplace Diversity*. London: Sage, 531–9.
Rhodes, C. (2009). After reflexivity: ethics, freedom and the writing of organization studies. *Organization Studies*, 30(6): 653–72.
Rhodes, C. and Westwood, R. (2007). Letting knowledge go: ethics and representation of the other in international and cross-cultural management. In C. Carter, S. Clegg, M. Kornberger, Laske, S., and Messner, M. (eds.), *Business Ethics as Practice: Representation, Reflexivity and Performance*. Cheltenham: Edward Elgar, 68–83.
Rhodes, P. J. (1994). Race-of-interviewer effects: a brief comment. *Sociology*, 28(2): 547–58.
Song, M. and Parker, D. (1995). Commonality, difference and the dynamics of disclosure in in-depth interviewing. *Sociology*, 29(2): 241–56.
Trowler, P. and Knight, P. T. (2000). Coming to know in higher education: theorising faculty entry to new work contexts. *Higher Education Research & Development*, 19(1): 27–42.
Van Maanen, J. (1988). *Tales of the Field: On Writing Ethnography*. Chicago: University of Chicago Press.
Willmott, H. (2011). Journal list fetishism and the perversion of scholarship: reactivity and the ABS list. *Organization*, 18(4): 429–42.

Zanoni, P. and Janssens, M. (2004). Deconstructing difference: the rhetorics of HR managers' diversity discourses. *Organization Studies*, 25(1): 55–74.

Zanoni, P. and Janssens, M. (2007). Minority employees engaging with (diversity) management: an analysis of control, agency, and micro-emancipation. *Journal of Management Studies*, 44(8): 1371–97.

Zanoni, P., Janssens, M., Benschop, Y., and Nkomo, S. (2010). Unpacking diversity, grasping inequality: rethinking difference through critical perspectives. *Organization*, 17: 1–21.

PART IV
DIVERSITY OF CONTEXTS AND PRACTICES

CHAPTER 17

RETHINKING HIGHER EDUCATION DIVERSITY STUDIES THROUGH A DIVERSITY MANAGEMENT FRAME

MARY ANN DANOWITZ

INTRODUCTION

HIGHER education institutions' efforts to promote equality and become inclusive have increased rapidly since the mid-1990s, although diversity management (DM) is a term that is seldom used in the higher education research and policy literature. At the same time, DM has been one of the driving measures for equity and gender mainstreaming in academe in the European Union. By contrast in the United States (US), the concept of DM is embedded in maximizing diversity's learning benefits for students. As a term originating in the business world, DM may seem a rather loose and even contrived fit in the higher education sector. I contend, however, that the guiding perspectives and action to increase equity and inclusivity in higher education may, in part, explain the limited progress that has been made (Hall, Rosenthan, and Wade 1993). Diversity work in higher education has seldom incorporated multiple, interrelated elements of organizational change processes necessary to fully incorporate the initiatives into a comprehensive organizational change process, and thus transform the overall functioning of a higher education organization in its treatment of diversity (Danowitz and Hanappi-Egger 2012). This perspective leads to the suggestion that an improved way to go forward is to reduce current confusions and misunderstandings regarding efforts to diversify higher education by describing diversity management for that sector. I then use that definition as a framework to analyse the literature on diversity work in higher education institutions (HEIs)—universities as well as institutions that teach specific capacities of higher learning such as colleges and technical training institutes.

I begin by proposing a definition: *diversity management is a concept and process that acknowledges the value of difference and strategically strives through structures and processes to increase inclusion and promote equity among its stakeholders, especially its internal ones, to create added value.* It is a comprehensive form of strategic management from the conceptualization and demonstrated commitment to organizational change through its implementation, evaluation, and adaptation. It is a generic definition for higher education that can be understood as a comprehensive multi-element process within diverse multi-level contexts.

Any analysis of DM in higher education needs to consider differences in histories, cultures, politics, priorities, and rationales among countries. These factors profoundly influence the nature of higher education as a core instrument of the nation state (Clark 1986) and HEIs' responses to diversity to become more inclusive (Ibarra 2001; Allen, Bonous-Hammarth, and Teranishi 2006). For example, France's tradition of strong national control on higher education limits the kinds of higher education institutions; its espoused commitment to *égalité* and *fraternité* higher inclusiveness mainly addresses economically disadvantaged youth (Donahoo 2008). In contrast, the US has a relatively unregulated but market-driven postsecondary higher education sector wherein the fifty states and individual HEIs set most policies (Donahoo 2008). The historical backdrop of racial segregation and more recent legal decisions of the late twentieth century intended to reduce discrimination (Greenberg 2001) have, until recently, prioritized race and gender in equity and diversity efforts (Donahoo 2008). These examples from two nations illustrate the importance of situating DM-related policies and practices in specific national contexts.

Syed and Özbilgin's (2009) multi-level relationality perspective on DM offers a useful lens to locate and understand the national differences and the focus of this chapter on DM at the organizational level of HEIs. Syed and Özbilgin identify multi-level factors to contextualize diversity and equality: the macro-national, meso-organizational, and micro-individual levels of analysis. The national characteristics of France and the US constitute the macro-national level—the all encompassing domain of the legal framework of diversity and equal opportunity, cultural traditions, political ideologies, and other elements of the socio-economic context (Syed and Özbilgin 2009: 2445). The meso-organizational level or intermediate level refers to 'relationships that occur between organizational contexts and component behaviour (individuals, groups and dyads), and examines how those relationships affect outcomes' (Syed and Özbilgin 2009: 2442). The micro-level encompasses issues associated with individuals—aspirations, identity, and agency. Applying Syed and Özbilgin's (2009) relationality perspective to DM in higher education, there are a number of interrelated factors at multiple levels of analysis that influence diversity outcomes in HEIs. While for purposes of practice the levels are interconnected, for purposes of explanation in this chapter they are separated. This is done in order to help understand and manage diversity and organizational change systematically and thoughtfully at the core organizational level where most policies and practices are carried out and diversity work is done—the HEI level.

Defining DM in Higher Education

Aspects of DM have been namelessly used in the higher education literature and thereby creating confusion about what DM means. For example, Bensimon (2004: 45) describes the diversity scorecard as 'an ongoing initiative to foster change in higher education in the United States by helping close the achievement gap for historically under-represented students', a priority for HEIs in the US. Thus, she focuses on an institutional change process that uses data analysis by race, ethnicity, and gender for outcome measures of access, retention (such as pass rates in certain courses) to propose interventions to increase educational outcomes for under-represented groups. She makes an important contribution by offering a DM strategy and process, without naming it, to increase student success and the possibility of widening the analysis to other elements of diversity such as disability or age. The higher education diversity scorecard does not refer to the term DM nor does it consider how DM might apply to staff or the interrelationship between staff and student success and/or other institutional performance indicators. Bensimon's helpful higher education tool to increase diversity and access and student success is somewhat similar to Hubbard's (2004) widely used diversity scorecard, which he describes as a DM resource. Hubbard's diversity scorecard encompasses multiple areas of diversity and their interdependence in business organizations to achieve outcomes including generating revenues from new products, satisfying customers, accelerating new multicultural product development, and acquiring, developing, and retaining strategic skills. A key difference between the two approaches is that Bensimon's (2004) emphasizes one aspect of organizational change and does not use the term DM, whereas Hubbard's scorecard is a multifaceted initiative approach to organizational change initiatives integrated into the business as a whole and refers to it as a DM.

Developing a clearer and more comprehensive definition of higher education DM may reduce current confusions and misunderstandings regarding efforts to diversify higher education that are associated with a lack of a clear definition and purpose for diversity and an absence of explicit goals and processes integrated into the whole organization. Although there will never be one universal definition, it is important to have a common reference for scholars and practitioners through which to analyse the phenomena used, to represent an HEI's change processes to increase diversity and equity and to advocate for support from policymakers, academic leaders, and decision makers in various national and cultural contexts.

The working definition proposed earlier in this chapter de-emphasizes a profit outcome found in the business literature on DM (Danowitz, Hanappi-Egger, and Mensi-Klarbach 2012). Further, the definition in this chapter employs a process perspective with DM comprising an interrelated group of elements that together create an added value for an HEI. The definition stresses 'an organisation's actions towards DM represent its socialized predispositions, and as such reflect the social attitudes directed towards diverse groups of individuals' (Syed and Özbilgin 2009: 2442). It also calls for HEIs to change more than a single component for effective DM (Cao, Clarke, and Lehaney 2003) and accommodates a variety of activities and results. The definition emphasizes the internal organizational environment (curriculum) and stakeholders (academic staff and students), and includes the interaction with the external environment and external stakeholders (such as programmes to increase the access of under-represented youth to a university or to specific fields of study). The interaction with the external context reflects the role of higher education as an instrument of the nation state; often at the centre of the public policy regime.

DM refers to the totality of an organization's efforts to become inclusive and to promote equality (Danowitz, Hanappi-Egger, and Mensi-Klarbach 2012: 153). The definition proposed earlier in this chapter is composed of four elements. *Valuing diversity* refers to awareness, vision, and defining relevant diversity issues. *Strategically strives* refers to a planned, intentional change process, and sustained effort. *Initiatives and structures* refer to processes, actions, practices, and rules. *Added value* refers to outcomes from monitoring, controlling, and evaluating. The definition is intentionally broad to encompass the array of benefits, activities, and results that vary enormously across nations and from institution to institution. I now turn to the higher education diversity research to analyse it from the proposed four element framework.

Method

The research method was a qualitative review of journal articles. An extensive online search of peer-reviewed literature from four databases—the Web of Science, ERIC, PsychINFO, and Public Administration Abstracts was conducted for articles published between 1995 and 2013. An eighteen-year time frame was chosen to provide a reasonable sampling of diversity legislation, policies, and practices across a range of nation states. The key word selection criteria used in the search were: higher, postsecondary and tertiary education, college, diversity, DM, equity, inclusiveness, affirmative action, equal opportunity, gender mainstreaming, and widening access. The search was limited to refereed articles as they are considered to have met the standards of external scrutiny of a community of scholars. The 188 articles were then entered into a reference management system.

A qualitative review of the articles indicates that the literature on diversity work in higher education came from twenty-six countries: Australia, Belgium, Brazil, Canada, Chile, China, Egypt, France, Germany, India, Israel, Italy, Japan, Lebanon, Morocco, New Zealand, Poland, Portugal, South Africa, South Korea, Spain, Sweden, Taiwan, Tunisia, the UK, and the US. Some 136 articles (72 per cent) were from the US. Some eleven (about

6 per cent) were comparative or included multiple countries. Another six (about 3 per cent) featured Australia, making Australia the second best represented county in the data set.[1]

Inductive and deductive processes were used to analyse the articles to identify key concepts and to determine the themes in the works. The two readers independently read and coded each article. The independent judgements between readers were compared to validate the analysis. The few times when judgements differed about an article, two readers re-analysed them and discussed them, and a third reader re-evaluated the criteria and reasoning that had been used to reach a final decision.

Coding Content Framework

A content mapping approach was used in phase one to sort and review key information such as the purpose, research questions, level of analysis, and kinds of literature cited to classify articles. The predominant emergent theme was the clustering of articles at three levels with an additional cluster of articles that were conceptual in nature. Four clusters were identified: *governmental or system level, institution level, social category*, and *conceptual*. The first three of these correspond with Syed and Özbilgin's (2009) macro-national, meso-organizational, and micro-individual relational levels of DM. The few articles that overlapped more than one cluster were categorized in multiple categories. Each of the clusters is briefly described:

- *The governmental or system (macro-national) level cluster* includes fifty-seven (30 per cent) articles that focus on the historical context of social inequality in different nation-states and implications of governmental policies to promote equity and social inclusiveness in higher education. These articles present different aspects of diversity work, such as the emergence of new institutions to widen college access; policies regarding admissions (selection criteria for allowing students to matriculate); changes to increase under-represented groups' attendance at elite institutions; higher education finances and their implications on access; and the impact of the market on higher education in different national economic contexts and research projects to determine the effectiveness of diversity work. Articles from developing nations often addressed internationalization of higher education as a prominent topic for study.
- *The institution (meso-organizational) level cluster* includes 100 (53 per cent) articles that focus on policies, practices, and the implementation of projects in areas of selection and retention of students from minority, under-represented groups,

---

[1] There are five articles from the UK, four from South Africa, four from China, and two from South Korea. There is one article from each of the following countries: Belgium, Brazil, Canada, Chile, Egypt, France, Germany, Italy, Japan, Lebanon, Morocco, New Zealand, Poland, Portugal, Spain, and Tunisia. India, Israel, Taiwan, and Sweden are only featured in comparative pieces.

or historically discriminated groups, and how to effectively recruit and support the career advancement of women and individuals from under-represented groups. Another important topic is changes in curriculum, pedagogy, and how classroom teaching may contribute to student understanding of diversity. Articles in this category also study the perception of diversity held by key internal stakeholders, such as students, faculty members, and administrators, and how potential policy and practice changes could more effectively incorporate stakeholders' perspectives and enhance their experiences.

- *The social categories (micro-individual) cluster* includes thirty-three (18 per cent) articles that primarily examine individual, group, or groups' (identified by a social category such as sex, religion, race/ethnicity, gender identity, or nationality, and age) experiences and perceptions of diversity. These social categories are associated with shared characteristics or experiences in relation to diversity and groups that have historically been excluded from higher education. The groups are often defined simply on demographic characteristics and position, such as women leaders or women in technology and engineering. As policies and programmes influence perceptions and experiences, many of these articles are cross-listed with articles at the institutional level.
- *The conceptual cluster* includes forty-nine (26 per cent) articles that address the value of diversity to higher education, social justice, and higher education's social role, competing views towards affirmative action and positive action, research directions for diversity studies, and organizational factors driving or impeding diversity efforts. Articles in this category attempt to untangle the complexity of the diversity term and phenomenon, and provide theoretical foundations for on-going and future diversity research and practice.

There are twenty-five articles that are rated in one category. An example of a cross-categorized article at the governmental—system (macro-national) level and conceptual level is Deem's (2007) article titled 'Managing a Meritocracy or an Equitable Organization? Senior Managers' and Employees' Views about Equal Opportunities Policies in UK Universities', published in the *Journal of Education Policy*. This article examines the tensions between the prevalent meritocratic institutional culture and the governmental policy supporting diversity in higher education. The conceptual cluster placement is based on an application of a feminist perspective to analyse concepts of excellence, meritocracy, and diversity; its governmental level cluster placement is based on its description of how these concepts are operationally defined and implemented in governmental equity policies such as widening participation and gender mainstreaming.

One conclusion drawn from the review of the literature discussed in this chapter is that the dominant understanding is derived largely from US higher education and Anglosphere countries. Another conclusion is that a great deal has been learned about diversity work at the level of HEIs. Yet, the small number of twenty-five multi-level studies suggests that most articles have been written for a domestic audience and seldom considered the interaction between the legal framework of diversity and equal opportunity, cultural traditions, political ideologies, and other elements of the socio-economic context.

The Institutional Level Analysis

In order to change HEI's structures and cultures to be less discriminatory and more inclusive, it is necessary to revise, at least some, organizational rules and practices (Danowitz and Hanappi-Egger 2012: 138). As the work of teaching and learning and the experiences of faculty and students occur within an HEI (the meso-organizational level), often within a sub-unit of an academic department or institute, the remainder of the chapter describes the 100 articles in the institutional level cluster. The next section describes the analysis of the articles in a DM framework.

The Conceptual Framework

Phase two consisted of determining the key elements of DM that have been researched and whether studies have included multiple elements, which are associated with success rates for organizational change (Cao, Clarke, and Lehaney 2003). The articles were analysed for the four elements derived from the DM definition offered in this chapter: (a) valuing diversity, (b) strategy, (c) initiative or structure, and (d) added value (outcome):

- *The valuing diversity element* encompasses statements about key institutional stakeholders' perceptions on diversity. *Valuing diversity* is the foundation for diversity policy and practices to promote equity and inclusion. The core of valuing diversity is to establish a shared understanding, beliefs, or expectations to further an organizational commitment to equity and diversity among stakeholders (Banks 2009). Yet such a valuing of diversity takes place in the context of the organizational culture and the social attitudes directed towards diverse groups or individuals (Syed and Özbilgin 2009). Attention is directed to the perception of internal stakeholders—administrators, faculty, and students. *Valuing diversity* provides information about how HEIs define diversity, incorporate it into their mission, and communicate and demonstrate a commitment to becoming and being an inclusive organization. Also included is the relationship between individual perceptions of diversity and the organizational discourses of diversity.
- *The strategic planning element* encompasses organizational policies and managerial plans to promote inclusion and equity. Attention is directed to organizational culture and its interaction with diversity policies, plans, and approaches. A specific focus is diversity plans, with their proposed processes, oversight, and the extent of their comprehensiveness.

- *The initiative and structure element* includes a variety of practices designed to increase the representation and success of minority groups in higher education and to develop a more inclusive organization. These practices range from recruitment strategies for members of under-represented groups for faculty and administrative positions and student places, and incorporating equity practices and responsiveness to diversity into teaching and the curriculum.
- *The added value element* examines or measures the outcomes of diversity policies and practices, such as having a diverse faculty and/or diversity among students or success of under-represented students. Many of the studies from the US address the consequences of diversity on student learning because of the need to demonstrate the value of diversity in legal cases. Attention is also directed towards how diversity affects student learning and socialization, including cognitive development, critical thinking, leadership development, and preparation to function effectively in work settings with diverse people and/or cultures.

DM at the HEI Level

Figure 17.1 shows the distribution of articles across the various elements of DM. The first four rows on the bottom of the figure show that slightly more than one-third, thirty-eight, of the 100 articles address one element. Attention was somewhat evenly distributed among the first three elements, with fifteen articles focusing on valuing diversity, twelve articles focusing on strategy, eleven articles focusing on initiative or structure, and no articles focusing on added value.

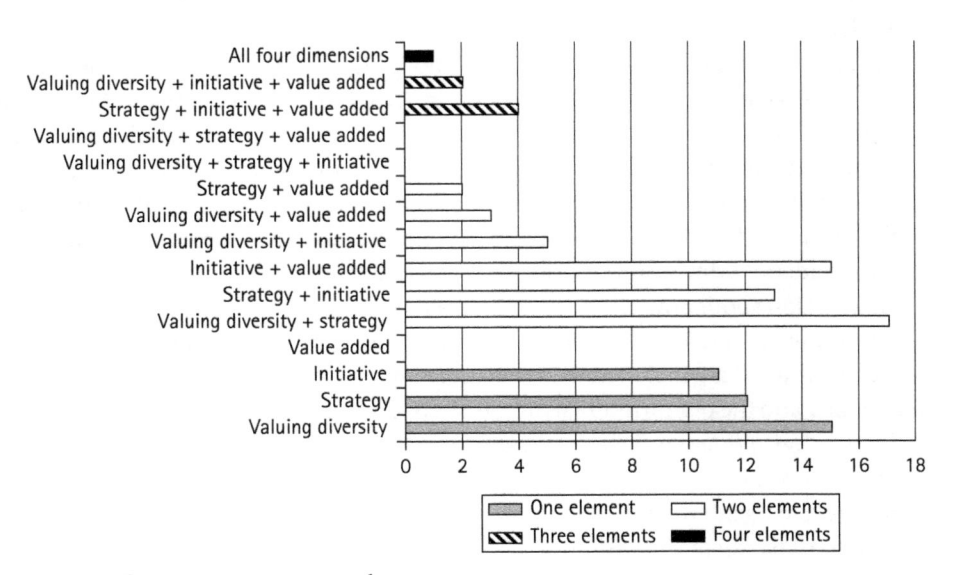

FIGURE 17.1 Diversity management elements.

The next four rows show that slightly more than half (fifty-five) of the articles address two elements of the DM definition. Among these, seventeen include the elements of valuing diversity and strategy; thirteen include strategy and initiatives; fifteen address initiatives and value added; five include valuing diversity and initiatives; three attend to valuing diversity and value added; two focus on strategy and value added.

Very few of the articles take a comprehensive approach or give a full picture of managing diversity, with only six addressing three elements. Two of those articles address strategy, initiative, and value added, and two focus on valuing diversity, initiative, and value added. Only one article addresses all four elements.

The single- or two-element focus of the majority of the articles indicates that most studies break diversity work into small parts and then manage the parts. This is done without regard to how change in one element or area affects the HEI through interactions with other elements or parts of the HEI. These studies focusing on a specific problem or initiative fall short of the ideal of how to manage change to produce measurable impact (Hall, Rosenthal, and Wade 1993) on the HEI through having insufficient breadth or not addressing multiple elements of DM and their relationships. This in turn may help explain why diversity work has often had limited success. Next, a single-element and a four-element article are described to point out the difference in the extent of the comprehensiveness of the treatment of DM.

Single-element Articles

Articles with a single element of DM address one phenomenon, usually in depth and often describing how HEIs define and incorporate diversity into their mission, the organizational policies, and managerial plans in the context of the institutional culture, or a practice to increase diversity. An example of the single dimension article is the Leicht-Scholten, Weheliye, and Wolffram (2009) study of 'Institutionalisation of Gender and Diversity Management in Engineering Education' in the *European Journal of Engineering Education*. The publication provides an in-depth account of the *institutional practices* of gender and DM at a male-dominated German technical university. The authors indicate that the gender and diversity strategy focuses on research and teaching along with organizational human resources development, although the reader is left to speculate what is valued regarding diversity, what strategies are behind the DM initiatives, and what the value-added outcomes are from the institutional practices. Consequently, the article has a narrow rather than comprehensive approach to explicate two concrete measures, the initiatives and structures, developed to increase the participation of women and under-represented groups. The article provides information about the gender and diversity unit and specific measures, including workshops promoting procedural knowledge regarding workplace conflicts, mentoring programmes for seventh to eleventh graders and female graduate students, a lecture series focusing on interdisciplinary studies on gender and diversity, as well as funding to encourage research work on gender and diversity within the institution. The article makes a useful contribution to understanding specific activities to increase diversity. It shows an awareness of the other elements of DM but does not attend to them in detail nor show the inter-relationships between them. For example, missing from the publication is attention to stakeholders other than the rector or to the organizational policies and plans that are behind the efforts to promote equity and inclusion. Also missing is an indication of the measures or actual outcomes of the practices. Thus, there is a fine description of one aspect of DM but the reader is left without knowing what was behind the scenes of the organization to make these initiatives a reality and more importantly what the actual consequences of the initiatives have been and whether they are likely to be sustainable.

Four-element Article

In contrast, the Iverson (2007) 'Camouflaging power and privilege: a critical race analysis of university diversity policies' in *Educational Administration Quarterly* is an exceptional article in that it addresses all four elements of DM to show what HEIs have done and what they need to do in order to improve diversity and inclusion endeavours. The author employs critical race theory to analyse diversity action plans and related activities at twenty US universities. Iverson identifies four predominant frames or rationales that universities use to explain their *valuing diversity*: access, disadvantage, marketplace, and democracy (Iverson 2007: 593). 'For example, university action plans propose to "feed the education pipeline; to open access, to widen the net," and to eliminate barriers and obstacles to increase the "presence" and "prevalence" of people of color...'. The *strategic planning* element of the universities explicitly shows how university administrators, faculty, and students drafting diversity action plans order and constitute the cultural reality for people of colour on campus through the way they write about diversity (Iverson 2007: 588). For example, to reduce harassment and discrimination, institutional strategies may not address the source of the problem—the acts of discrimination. Instead, those strategies might be to 'Create mechanisms to support and protect students who bring allegations of gender, sexual and racial discrimination in order to lessen their vulnerability, fears of reprisals and harassment'. There are many *initiatives and structures* addressed in the article such as diversity in promotional materials to market the university's commitment to diversity, diversifying the curriculum, and creating international programmes. The *value-added element* is substantial in that it shows how diversity action plans may undermine the effectiveness of the policies that set out to promote a diverse and inclusive campus. This can happen through the unintended consequences of reproducing racial inequality by defining the necessary institutional tasks based on white racial experiences. The author concludes by calling upon educators and administrators to re-analyse diversity action plans to reframe their work and identify the roots of problems before developing strategies and initiatives to address them.

Discussion and Implications

In this chapter I have proposed a definition of diversity management modified from the business sector for higher education. It is one through which diversity initiatives can be understood as interrelated elements in an organizational change process. The four elements of the definition were then used as a framework to analyse the literature on diversity work in HEIs to determine what has been studied and to what extent the diversity work has used a comprehensive approach to DM, which has been associated with success in organizational change. Some 188 peer-reviewed articles on diversity work in higher education were analysed. The vast majority of articles are from Anglosphere countries. Those perspectives/biases dominate the knowledge about diversity work in higher education, as in the business sector. The higher education literature analysed seldom attends to the interaction of the multiple levels influencing DM. A few articles address the influence of the government or system level (meta-national) on the HEI level (meso-organizational). Yet most attention focuses solely on the HEI level where policies are enacted and the actual management or implementation of change must occur. An analysis of the 100 HEI level articles using a framework of the four DM elements offered in this chapter: (a) valuing diversity, (b) strategy, (c) initiative or structure, and (d) added value (outcome) and the extent of their treatment of DM indicates that the attention of the majority, fifty-five, of the articles address the interdependence of two elements. The two most frequently combined elements were the valuing diversity (the vision, awareness, and commitment to change) with the strategies guiding and implementing DM and the combination of the actual initiatives with the added value from the initiative. This provides evidence of a limited coupling of multiple elements associated with comprehensive change. This is underscored by only seven of the articles containing three or four of the elements. Consequently, seldom does diversity work entail a comprehensive DM approach.

The review of the articles on DM in higher education suggests that valuable work is taking place to improve equity and inclusivity in higher education, although frequently in a compartmentalized manner; or that is how it is reported. I contend that these narrowly focused studies may be inadequate to sufficiently address the interaction of various elements that influence the complex change processes necessary for HEIs to function more equitably and inclusively.

I have described the article base of diversity work in higher education and proposed a diversity framework and multi-level analysis intended to help researchers and practitioners understand diversity management. My intent is to reduce confusion and misunderstanding about the meaning of DM in higher education and to suggest ways to improve the success of strategies and practices to increase equity and inclusivity. These include taking into account the interaction of contextual levels (Syed and Özbilgin 2009) of HEIs and the multiple elements of diversity management as a strategic organizational change process.

The review is not without limitations. Using only peer-reviewed literature means that many diverse and interesting examples of work have been missed. For example, the key words did not include dimensions of diversity such as nationality, ethnicity, and disability (Kandola and Fullerton 1998), nor books or reports—other significant outlets to improve practice. For example, the Association of American Colleges and Universities has provided a leadership role in making excellence inclusive—a multilayered process to infuse diversity into the institutional core of HEIs in the US (<http://www.aacu.org/compass/inclusive_excellence.cfm>). As the majority of the studies are from the US, individuals searching for research on diversity work must be cautious about a predominant US lens and be diligent when adapting research questions or approaches or applying findings from that nation to others. Moreover, the search is limited to English language journals; therefore, undoubtedly, many important articles published in other languages have been missed. For example, there is a burgeoning literature on diversity in the Scandinavian countries and German-speaking Europe.

In closing, researchers and practitioners may want to validate and/or adapt the multiple level frame and the four-element DM higher education framework proposed in their respective HEIs. They may also want to consider frameworks other than a process approach to investigate and tackle the complexity of the organizational change to reduce inequalities and increase inclusivity. As I have briefly indicated, the proposed framing attempts to transcend a focused or silo emphasis on a strategy or practice to bring about organizational change, but also implies that the processes to achieve more equitable and inclusive HEIs are more complex than the way they have been studied and enacted thus far. In short, the overall aims are to help understand and reduce confusion about diversity management in higher education, encourage creative use of frameworks, and assist improving diversity practices.

Acknowledgement

I wish to thank Difei Li and Trae Brookins* for their generous time and support in this research. * Deceased January 4, 2015.

References

Allen, W., Bonous-Hammarth, M., and Teranishi, R. (2006). *Higher Education in a Global Society: Achieving Diversity, Equity and Excellence*. Amsterdam and London: Elsevier.
Association of American Colleges and Universitites (n.d.). Making excellence inclusive. <http://www.aacu.org/compass/inclusive_excellence.cfm>, accessed 15 October 2014.
Banks, K. H. (2009). A qualitative investigation of white students' perceptions of diversity. *Journal of Diversity in Higher Education*, 2(3): 149–55.
Bensimon, E. M. (2004). The diversity scorecard: a learning approach to institutional change. *Change: The Magazine of Higher Learning*, 36(1): 44–52.

Cao, G., Clarke, S., and Lehaney, B. (2003). A generic critical model of management of change. *Journal of Applied Systems Studies*, 4(1): 4–12.

Clark, B. R. (1986). *The Higher Education System: Academic Organization in Cross-National Perspective*. Berkeley, CA: University of California Press.

Danowitz, M. and Hanappi-Egger, E. (2012). Diversity as strategy. In M. Danowitz, E. Hanappi-Egger, and H. Mensi-Klarbach (eds.), *Diversity in Organizations: Concepts and Practices*. New York: Palgrave Macmillan, 137–160.

Danowitz, M., Hanappi-Egger, E., and Mensi-Klarbach, H. (2012). *Diversity in Organizations: Concepts and Practices*. New York: Palgrave Macmillan.

Deem, R. (2007). Managing a meritocracy or an equitable organization? Senior managers' and employees' views about equal opportunities policies in UK universities. *Journal of Education Policy*, 22(6): 615–36.

Donahoo, S. (2008). Reflections on race: affirmative action policies influencing higher education in France and the United States. *The Teachers College Record*, 110(2): 251–77.

Greenberg, J. (2001). Affirmative action in higher education: confronting the condition and theory. *BCL Rev.*, 43: 521.

Hall, G., Rosenthal, J., and Wade, J. (1993). How to make reengineering really work. *Harvard Business Review*, 71(6): 119–31.

Hubbard, E. (2004). *The Diversity Scorecard: Evaluating the Impact of Diversity on Organizational Performance*. Burlington, MA: Elsevier Butterworth-Heinemann.

Ibarra, R. A. (2001). *Beyond Affirmative Action: Reframing the Context of Higher Education*. Madison: University of Wisconsin Press.

Iverson, S. V. (2007). Camouflaging power and privilege: a critical race analysis of university diversity policies. *Educational Administration Quarterly*, 43(5): 586–611.

Kandola, R. and Fullerton, J. (1998). *Managing the Mosaic: Diversity in Action*, 2nd edn. London: Institute of Professional Development.

Leicht-Scholten, C., Weheliye, A., and Wolffram, A. (2009). Institutionalisation of gender and diversity management in engineering education. *European Journal of Engineering Education*, 34(5): 447–54.

Syed, J. and Özbilgin, M. (2009). A relational framework for international transfer of diversity management practices. *International Journal of Human Resource Management*, 20(12): 2435–53.

CHAPTER 18

GLOBAL DIVERSITY MANAGEMENT

Breaking the Local Impasse

MUSTAFA BILGEHAN ÖZTÜRK, AHU TATLI,
AND MUSTAFA F. ÖZBILGIN

Introduction

THE continually growing literature on diversity management provides a multidimensional set of research emphases, with a sufficiently sophisticated base of theories and ideas now to encompass several milestones in its doxic trajectory (Lorbiecki and Jack 2000). However, the wealth of studies considering diversity management has not yet produced a clear and practical roadmap for improvements, and employees are yet to be free of inequality, exclusion, and marginalization processes, despite virtually all survey evidence indicating that global firms consider diversity of paramount importance, especially in the global domain (Nishii and Özbilgin 2007). The diversity management literature remains a field of contestation, as was first suggested by Linnehan and Konrad (1999), about how best to remedy workplace inequalities, where white, Anglo-Saxon, able-bodied, heterosexual men still enjoy privileged status in corporate hierarchies to the detriment of workers who are not members of this dominant group. Progress on equality, diversity, and inclusion of all employees is still tentative and contingent, despite the advent of a rich range of approaches to diversity management, including ecosystems (Barak 2000), corporate culture (Gordon 1995), micro-emancipation (Zanoni and Janssens 2007), learning (Lorbiecki 2001), relational frameworks (Syed and Özbilgin 2009), Bourdieuan sociology (Tatli 2011), Foucauldian philosophy (Ahonen et al. 2013), and queer theory (Bendl, Fleischmann, and Walenta 2008) perspectives.

Apart from the above-mentioned range of conceptual approaches to diversity management, a plethora of models and frameworks are used to operationalize diversity management priorities. Among these, the strategic model, the process model, and the context model are of particular relevance to global diversity management. The strategic model hinges on shaping diversity management practices through the negotiation of global standardization versus the local customization of policies and frameworks (Brock and Siscovick 2007). The process model of global diversity management, on the other hand, emphasizes the need to take account of varied and multidimensional processes of knowledge management, decision-making, social identification, and so on in the management of diversity issues (Nishii and Özbilgin 2007). Finally, the context model of diversity management encompasses the multi-level, multi-actor nature of the field of diversity relations, and how this may impact upon the management of diversity itself (Joshi and Roh 2009).

Complicating the multifarious approaches to diversity further, there are potentially competing discourses of diversity management (social justice versus the business case), and while it is possible to view this divergence as conflict, we believe that these approaches are actually complementary to one another. Although they may emphasise different motivators for diversity management, this is simply a reflection of the employment landscape where there are multiple reasons why diversity management is beneficial. To clarify our point, in this chapter we take the social justice strand as focusing on fairness concerns as the main driver of the need to ensure team-based or firm-level diversity, with goals of creating fully equal and inclusive environments where individuals with a specific diversity trait (i.e. gender, sexual orientation, race, ethnicity, disability) or an intersection of various diversity traits (for instance, a disabled gay black employee) are safeguarded from discrimination, and are valued and appreciated for their contribution to organizational life. By contrast, the business case for diversity argues that a diverse employee base is essential for business success in a globalizing world, where divergent groups of suppliers and customers have complex needs and requirements that can only be met by an equally multidimensional body of workers. This logic suggests that as diversity is vital for business, good diversity management is in the best interest of firms, and thus once the business case for diversity is proven, it is possible to largely rely on voluntary, firm-initiated solutions to any diversity challenges in day-to-day business life. Rather than seeing these discourses as antagonistic ways of conceiving of diversity management solutions, Tomlinson and Schwabenland (2010) demonstrate that these bifurcations reveal the localized, historicized, and situated uncertainties, obscurities, and multiple workings of local conceptions of equality and diversity. In this sense, for effective, change-inducing diversity management, it is important for diversity managers to be able to foreground localities in the solutions. It is also important for practitioners to have realistic, grounded, solution-based approaches that take account of business sensitivities in the aftermath of a major global downturn.

Implementing global diversity management standards locally is not a straightforward process, as local agents may face socio-political tensions associated with the country in which they operate for a number of reasons (Nishii and Özbilgin 2007). First, there may be local interpretations of the global diversity agenda that differ from the way in which it was construed at the global level. Second, global HR policies of multinational corporations (MNCs) that focus on a specific issue or pillar of diversity may not be as relevant to a given local context. Finally, it may not be obvious exactly how to bring in and implement global diversity management policies at the local level. Thus, discrimination that may be completely unacceptable at the global level may crop up unnoticed in one of many far-reaching localities a global firm encompasses. For instance, in his wide-ranging analysis of the experiences of lesbian, gay, and bisexual (LGB) employees in Turkey, Öztürk (2011) shows that local arms or subsidiaries of otherwise lesbian, gay, bisexual, and transgender (LGBT)-friendly global firms can be just as discriminatory as domestic companies for LGB individuals in Turkey. Therefore, the main global diversity management question may counter-intuitively be precisely about how we resolve local impasses, where the local actors are unwilling to pay attention to diversity concerns or are operating in active resistance against them, and where minorities have declining trust in the relevant institutions' efficacy for providing positive change.

Part of the rationale for this chapter is that there is a great variety of historical contexts and a divergence of local norms, practices, and rules of the game on the ground (Özbilgin 2009), which makes the simplistic one-size-fits-all approach to diversity management models highly suspect. For instance, while market forces, public opinion, and legislation increasingly put pressure on global organizations to have convergent standards and policies of diversity management, we believe this must be tempered with a clear eye to take account of specificities and unique dimensions of various locales. In the aftermath of the global financial crisis and the subsequent recession, trust in institutions and government as well as corporate actors are at a historic low in Europe (Roth 2009). This necessitates that even more care is taken in understanding the needs, requirements, and expectations of local actors in European countries such as the UK, and how diversity management can be calibrated to ameliorate different diversity-related challenges emergent in specific contexts. We believe that this localised perspective avoids the resistance trap, where local actors contest diversity management models imported in a wholesale manner from the global headquarters or, worse yet, a wholly different country with dissimilar structural, institutional, discursive, and normative priorities without adequate attention to local historicity (Ferner, Almond, and Colling 2005).

We suggest in this chapter that it is imperative to make use of diversity toolkits that emerge on the strength of the business case. Such toolkits are, simply put, monitoring tools that assess the deficits in organizational diversity, equality, and inclusion across all levels and areas of operation, and then suggest potential solutions and recommendations to counter discrimination. An effective toolkit would have specific features addressing the local challenges and goals on the ground in order to sustain diversity efforts in a difficult politico-economic environment, where there is much lip service paid to full equality goals, but little fundamental change in the organization of employment relations. Our localized approach hinges on the development and extensive use of diagnostic checks that make sense to the relevant diversity management officers in the field.

The chapter is structured in several sections. We start with an overview of the UK labour market context, which is then followed by a review of the business case arguments drawn from the wider literature in support of organizational diversity. We then draw on an extensive field study of providers and potential users (sixty-two respondents in total) of diagnostics checks in equality and diversity in the UK. Our findings help us to identify success factors for an equality and diversity check, discuss how generic or tailor-made these toolkits should be, and explain the conditions for facilitating the effective adoption and application of diagnostic checks by diversity management officers. By engaging with local circumstances pragmatically, this approach illuminates the adroit use of equality and diversity toolkits to effectuate positive change.

Overview of the UK Labour Market Context

We write this chapter at a time where there are still a potent set of discriminatory trends that afflict the UK labour market. In terms of gender, it has been shown time and again that there is a significant pay disadvantage experienced by women (Harkness 1996; Blackaby, Booth, and Frank 2005; Chevalier 2007), which is exacerbated by gender-based vertical segregation (Conyon and Mallin 1997; Singh and Vinnicombe, 2004; Brammer, Millington, and Pavelin 2007; Martin et al. 2008). Evidence of discrimination against ethnic and racial minorities in UK labour markets has also long been demonstrated (Noon 1993), but barriers persist even despite legal improvements, as there still exists an implementation gap between legislation and practice (Creegan et al. 2003). Furthermore, equality laws are insufficiently sophisticated to deal with more complex cascading of disadvantages such as intersectionality (Healy, Bradley, and Forson 2011), where employees occupy more than one source of difference, such as being an ethnic minority woman employee (Özbilgin et al. 2011). Ethnic and racial minority versus majority tensions are on the increase owing to the recent politicization of the immigration debate in the UK, where the previously liberal views in favour of a strong inward immigration trend, both from the newer European Union (EU) countries as well as non-EU developing countries, is now increasingly vilified (Hopkins 2011). This is a concern as it may strengthen discriminatory trends against ethnic and racial minorities further. Additionally, another changing trend, the ageing population (which is also reflected in the wider socio-geography of the EU), is increasingly recognized as being at the receiving end of subtle but very real discrimination (McVittie, McKinlay, and Widdicombe 2003; Loretto and White 2006). However, in this difficult landscape, perhaps the most silenced and invisibilized employees are sexual and gender identity minorities, who still routinely face a sense of exclusion and a lack of support in the workplace (Wright et al. 2006; Colgan et al. 2007; Colgan and McKearney 2011; Öztürk and Rumens 2014; Öztürk and Tatli forthcoming).

These discriminatory trends are permeating a labour market which inhabits a two-speed economy, with London in the driver's seat imposing disproportionate impact on policy, with its sophisticated services industries, such as finance, legal, marketing and advertising, and technological services. The rest of the country, which had been manufacturing-oriented until its decline (which started with the Thatcherite privatization and de-industrialization policies and continued with the newer trends of international outsourcing and lean employment trends resulting from the globalization of production), poses a continual structural problem for the economy. Given such deep structural challenges, in their desire to attract businesses to the UK and provide a supportive environment for their company operations, successive governments have often adopted a light-touch, business-friendly policy posture towards global companies. This pro-business approach has often resulted in reliance on a voluntaristic approach (Özbilgin and Tatli 2011) as well as a business-shaped and business-driven diversity management agenda for the whole labour market, instead of strong government oversight of business actions that would mandate proactive action on the part of companies to ameliorate equality, diversity, and inclusion challenges in the labour market. This backdrop is a significant basis for our choice of relying on business case arguments to shape equality and diversity tools for company uses. In the absence of a strong legislative environment, business buy-in within the context of the UK is essential to ensure the success of any diversity management initiative.

The Business Case for Organizational Diversity

Diversity is increasingly viewed as an important pillar of firm performance (Richard 2000; Herring 2009; Carroll and Shabana 2010). Organizational interest in harnessing the power of intra-firm diversity can potentially enhance the position of diversity management on the organizational agenda and enable diversity managers to become key players in their organizational settings. In their research on management perspectives in Europe, Calori, Steele, and Yoneyama (1995: 59) indicate that 'top managers identified four common characteristics of management (philosophies and practices) across Europe: an orientation towards people, internal negotiation, managing international diversity and a balance between extremes... Because of the small size of their domestic markets European firms have been forced to look outside at other different markets, and their managers learned to deal with diversity.' Within this context, having effective systems in place to promote equality and diversity would turn the diversity of workforce into a source of competitive advantage and subsequent business success (Soni 2000). In effect, there is a business case for a proactive and voluntary approach on the side of employers to promote diversity and equality in organizations. The business case for equality and diversity is the result of the changing composition of the talent pool as well as the internationalization of business. The main features of the current business environment in the UK in which a diverse workforce may flourish are: changing patterns of labour market demographics, globalization and internalization of business, and changing patterns of work organization, production, and competition (Tatli et al. 2006).

Skill shortages and the ageing population are topical concerns on the UK political as well as industrial relations agenda (Ruhs and Anderson 2010; Shury et al. 2010). Upon the background of demographic changes in the labour market, employers increasingly find themselves in a position to turn to different and previously under-utilized segments of the labour force for recruiting new employees. These segments are generally populated by the individuals disadvantaged in society owing to their age, gender, ethnicity, race, sexual orientation, religion and belief, disability, or minority status. There is also a growing recognition that the retention rates for employees from under-represented groups are lower than the dominant groups in employment (for instance, McKay et al. 2007; Servon and Visser 2011; Wrench 2012). Yet it is predicted that the traditional labour pool made up of white men will not be able to meet the demands of the increasingly international markets, resulting in growing representation of female and non-white employees in the labour market (Gilbert and Stead 1999). The benefits of this transformation are beginning to be experienced already. Using an extensive database, Herring (2009) demonstrates specifically that racial and gender diversity is correlated with a positive upswing in revenues, market share, and profits. There is also research that points out greater diversity at firm level with regard to, for instance, gender is linked to better financial performance (Campbell and Minguez-Vera 2008).

International migration, which appears as another solution to the skills shortages that capture the continent, also promotes the diversification in the labour market. Spatial mobility of not only capital but also labour has become an ordinary phenomenon worldwide, despite the fact that national barriers for labour migration are more rigid. Labour research has long indicated that the brain drain from developing countries to developed countries is a significant trend in the advanced economies (Guellec and Cervantes 2001). In the case of the United Kingdom, the shortage of skilled workers is widely recognized, and the UK government tries to encourage the migration of highly skilled workers. It is argued that with the demise of the homogeneity in workgroups, organizations need to design workforce diversity policies in order to attract and retain a diverse employee base which could serve as a competitive advantage (Shaw 1993; Gilbert and Ivancevich 2000).

As opposed to the relative cultural homogeneity of the enterprises operating in a single country, the internal workforce of multinational corporations (MNCs) consists of the employees from different cultural backgrounds. The external business environment that faces MNCs necessitates responsiveness and flexibility with regard to the cultural contexts in terms of consumers' demand for the products and supply of labour, as well as forming mergers and acquisitions with national companies. From the strategic point of view, workforce diversity of an MNC may provide it with the necessary strengths to deal with the culturally diverse context within which it operates and to implement competitive corporate strategies. Adler and Ghadar (1990: 243) indicate that the emerging circumstances force all multinational companies to 'manage cultural diversity within the organisation as well as between the organisation and its supplier, client, and alliance networks. Attention to cultural differences becomes critical for managing both the firm's organisational culture and its network of relationships outside of the firm'. They further argue that cultural diversity can be used in MNCs 'to differentiate products and services when culturally distinct markets and or workforces must be addressed and as a primary source of new ideas when innovation is needed' (Adler and Ghadar 1990: 253).

Hendry and Pettigrew (1986) state that the internal workforce of a firm is an invaluable strategic resource for gaining and maintaining competitive advantage. In a study of company boards in the UK, it is established that ethnic minority diversity in the boardroom is associated with an appreciably higher market capitalization outcome for the firms involved (Singh 2007). The strong positive relationship between ethnic minority presence in the leadership rungs and positive firm performance is explained through the resource dependency view of the firm. A diverse workforce situated in key positions brings varied layers and types of human and social capital into the strategic mix, which enhances intangible organizational resources to generate non-negligible competitive advantages in the marketplace (Singh 2007).

Creating a team of employees with diverse skills and from different nationalities is increasingly the primary method of enhancing creativity at both individual and organizational levels. However, cross-cultural teams need to be managed effectively in order to reap the benefits of the diverse skills and perspective that is available in the team (Loosemore and Muslmani 1999; Chevrier 2003). The implementation of proactive diversity and equality policies is necessary to transcend the communication problems and conflicts stemming from diversity among employees and to create a trustworthy, inclusive organizational culture that generates feelings of belonging, which in turn enhances the performance, commitment and motivation of different groups of employees.

The organization of work in twenty-first-century global firms has gone far beyond the early twentieth-century Taylorist style of highly planned organization of labour process of the mass production era. The contemporary business environment, which is becoming increasingly dynamic with the rising uncertainty and competition, necessitates corporations to overcome organizational rigidities by developing their capacity to adapt and respond to change through fostering horizontal organizational structures based on diverse teams (Procter and Mueller 2000; Blazevic and Lievens 2002).

As markets expand globally and customer bases become ever more diverse, organizations increasingly need greater diversity in team composition that adequately reflects the diverse customer base that they serve. Ashkanasy, Hartel, and Daus (2002: 328–9) argue that, in the global service-oriented economy, employees' ability to communicate with and respond to the demands of diverse customers and clients is an essential feature of firm survival (Carroll and Hannan 2000; Blazevic and Lievens 2002). Evidence shows that heterogeneous teams have better cognitive and operational performance capacity than their homogeneous counterparts (Page 2007), which form a strong potential causal relationship between workforce heterogeneity or diversity and greater business success. It is argued that workforce diversity enhances the organizational member's capacity for learning (Blazevic and Lievens 2002), thereby providing opportunities for creativity, innovation, problem solving, and adaptability (Gurin, Nagda, and Lopez 2004).

Employers with successful equality and diversity programmes in place are in a more advantageous position to attract and retain the best personnel of scarce skills, because many workers would prefer good practice employers with well-established equality and diversity policies (Woods and Sciarini 1995). As well as recruiting the best personnel in the labour market, employers embracing equality and diversity also spend less on their recruitment efforts. McEnrue (1993) finds that recruitment expenditures of the organizations valuing diversity are significant lower than those organizations which do not. It is also pointed out that equal opportunities and diversity employers suffer less from the costs stemming from high levels of labour turnover and absenteeism, and discrimination lawsuits (Fernandez 1991; Morrison 1992; Cox 1993).

Despite the benefits of workforce diversity for business success, empirical research on the issue displays conflicting results, revealing advantages of diversity on business performance in some studies and disadvantages in others. For instance, some of the potential negative outcomes of diversity include poor employee well-being, low level of team cohesion, tension between and within teams, and communication problems, leading to a decrease in organizational performance and team effectiveness (Thomas and Ely 1996; Robbins 2001; Chevrier 2003). Diversity does not automatically cause better organizational learning, creative brainstorming, higher customer or client satisfaction levels, or better financial performance. As Adler (1986: 118) puts it, 'only if well managed can culturally diverse groups hope to achieve their potential productivity'.

Noon (2007) also suggests that business short-termism and a tendency to narrowly define business value in money terms could mistakenly undervalue the benefits of organizational diversity. In order to reveal the 'creative dimension of diversity' and to avoid the potential conflicts that may stem from having a human resource pool that consists of different nationalities, MNCs need to be able to create a corporate culture valuing, respecting, and learning from diversity. Organizations that embrace the 'equal opportunity climate' and have robust equality and diversity frameworks and programmes take best advantage of their diverse workforce (Knouse and Dansby 2000). For instance, a large-scale survey of organizations in the US finds that an effective diversity management strategy is linked to a significant increase in work-group performance, greater job satisfaction for minority employees, and an elevated overall productivity (Pitts 2009). However, for those organizations which devalue diversity and privilege a white, middle-class, heterosexual, able-bodied man as the implicit model employee, there is the possibility of increased conflict.

METHODOLOGY

Our data collection process was supported by two parallel studies, which we previously conducted for the Equal Opportunities Commission in the UK. First, we performed a consultation exercise on the development of an equality check with the providers of diagnostic checks such as UK equality advocacy bodies working on issues of gender, ethnicity, sexual orientation, disability, and so on, and membership organizations in the UK such as professional bodies that represent Human Resources (HR) officers. During this consultation, we interviewed thirty-four key institutional stakeholders. Second, we identified and carried out interviews with significant employers in public, private, and voluntary sectors in order to map out their approaches to diagnosing inequality in organizational environments. The majority of the private and voluntary sector organizations were large multinationals. The interviews aimed to explore the needs of the potential users of equality checks. In order to increase the number of respondents who were able to comment on the possible approaches for a diagnostic check, we targeted organizations with a commitment to promoting equality and diversity. Twenty-eight interviews were conducted with the HR managers or diversity officers of these organizations. In total, sixty-two interviews lasting around one hour were conducted, tape-recorded, and transcribed verbatim. Three main categories of organizational actors, that is providers of equality check tools, employers, and membership organizations, were included in the study. The organizations participating in the research represented a wide variety of sectors and industries, including recruitment, oil and gas, manufacturing, higher education, defence, banking and finance, retail, energy, and communication.

Views on Diagnostic Equality Checks

Our findings indicate the importance of creating an equality and diversity toolkit that can reduce the burdensome aspects of organizational self-assessments, and that make practical sense in terms of simultaneously covering all the relevant areas of diversity that businesses may have to account for. Situated as they are in businesses that are sensitive to commercial concerns before any other consideration, diversity management officers need tools that will satisfy their organizations by simplifying processes and that will help them in effecting their change agendas by rationalizing their own work burdens:

> A lot of institutions are grappling at the moment with impact assessments in terms of some of the equality legislation, and if you assess your practices in terms of race, then six months later you go back to the same managers and services and say, well, can you assess your practices in terms of disability and then can you do it in terms of gender, it becomes almost like a legislative burden, and I think if there was a general equality check that allowed us or guided us in terms of checking our practises right across the equality and diversity themes, I think that might be more practical in terms of institutions checking their procedures.

Some respondents argued that developers of such a diversity toolkit should be cautious about how they include and balance different strands of diversity. It is now increasingly recognized that making sense of the diversity climate of an organization requires the factoring of multiple strands of diversity into the analysis (Özbilgin et al. 2011). For instance, one of the respondents from the higher education sector thought that equality legislation in the UK is inconsistent with respect to its attention to different strands of diversity. As a result, policies on some diversity strands such as sexual orientation and gender identity remain under-developed. One of the drawbacks of a standardized global HR policy for an MNC is that not only are there differences across national legislative and policy contexts regarding various diversity strands, but also differences appear, sometimes quite strongly, even within a given national context, in the treatment of one diversity strand compared with another. Such complexity across and within nations can potentially create a quagmire if diversity management officers are not empowered and enabled to offer localized equality and diversity initiatives, through the use of, for instance, an equality and diversity toolkit, among other options. Our respondents believed that a new diagnostic check should have a balanced approach in treating different strands of diversity:

> I think it should cover all the diversity scene. So, we know that the legislation is sometimes more involved in some areas such as race and disability than others, but I think it should cover right across the areas such as sexuality and faith.

Yet many of the participants highlighted that the tool should be sensitive about different opportunities and challenges associated with different diversity categories, as well as the unique elements generated by intersections of two or more diversity categories. According to the respondents, there is no consistency in terms of which HR areas are covered more and which areas are covered less, since this is currently dependent on particular firms' differential diversity agendas and what they believe is important for their organization. The participants emphasized the importance of implementing diversity solutions across all aspects of HR throughout the life cycle of employment beginning with recruitment and ranging to promotion to leadership. This is in line with the recent diversity literature's emphasis on holistic and contextual understanding of all aspects of the HR function as they interrelate with diversity (Wrench 2012). The respondents further suggested that while an equality check is primarily a diagnostic tool, it should incorporate possible action points and pathways to improvement for the problems diagnosed. Often, diversity management suffers from ambiguity of objectives and a lack of clarity in terms of positive transformative action, with renewed efforts now focused in the literature on creating a more concrete, action-oriented, principle-specific diversity management (Stahl et al. 2012). The respondents' support and interest in having specific organizational action points in the diagnostic equality check is perhaps a reflection on the ground of this important need:

> I think one of the reasons why employers don't take action now, or as much action as we would like to see on equalities, is that they don't know what to address. So I think developing a good diagnostics toolkit enables them to break down the task that

they face. I think it has to be clear that if employers are going to undertake such an exercise and going through all this toolkit or checklist assessment, if they're not then going to act on it there's no point in it.

The need for an equality and diversity tool that provides organizations with possible action plans and prescriptive logics is particularly acute in organizations, which do not have in-house expertise in tackling diversity challenges. The majority of the respondents were wary that an equality and diversity tool, which does not go beyond diagnosis, may lead to inaction or even negative reaction in organizations with limited resources and expertise for managing diversity. Just as global HR policy of an MNC may be too blunt and generally lacking in terms of expertise of local variations and complexities, it is possible that local HR officers with a finely tuned understanding of their contextual realities may yet be inexpert when it comes to diversity management systems and processes, as in some country settings diversity management as a construct may still be a nascent phenomenon. Thus, resolving the problematic of implementing MNC's global diversity management standards locally may not be as straightforward as simply localizing more. Local agents still need support and enablement, which can come through, in this case, an equality and diversity toolkit that is properly resourced and strategically valued to allow local HR officers to become effective agents.

There was a general agreement that the equality and diversity tool should be integrated into strategic planning if it is be taken seriously at all levels of organization. Yet some others insisted that the employers are best motivated to promote equality and diversity through strong legislative backing. Particularly, the providers of equality tools thought that the absence of strong legal enforcement in the UK leads to the need to develop a business case. Concerns of this type have been raised previously in the literature (Dickens and Hall 2006), and it is telling that they continue to resonate within organizations. As a result, the financial aspect of the equality check implementation is emphasized as a key concern by the respondents. Hence, it is argued that the equality and diversity tool must take account of the opportunity cost of failure to act in support of diversity, as part of constructing a strong business case argument (Robinson and Dechant 1997). As one participant suggested in delineating the crucial role played by business case considerations:

> Commitment from the top to actually do it, if it's labour-intensive to get the staff to do it, collect the data. You need commitment from the department to say 'yes, I will give you two hours of my time to actually go through', preparing to put together evidence to support their statements. First you need commitment from the top to do this, then you need buy-in from the people who are actually going to provide you with information. Because we're all very busy people and we need top management to do this because they believe that this will help our business. Top management also needs to give resources to these departments.

As the quotation above shows, our study found that the equality and diversity tool would need to have an ability to engage other organizational members at different levels through a strong business case. While top management may not have the textured, finely tuned understanding of localized circumstances, they have a key role in the success of diversity initiatives at the local level. Top management commitment and financial backing are needed to activate the local level HR expertise in creating innovative, locally sensitive, more tailor-made solutions appropriate to context. Our data indicate that this symbiotic relationship between the global and local is best activated through the articulation of a business case for diversity agenda, in the local context of the UK, where there is an absence of strong legislative environment and government oversight. A well-made business case is also crucial, as it was thought to be one of the most significant dimensions of acceptance and implementation of the tool:

> You know, businesses still need to function, still need to deliver on their commitments. So the tool needs to actually show that there are benefits. I appreciate that not all the benefits are tangible, but it needs to highlight, you know, what are the long-term intangible benefits. Why should organizations take up this journey, if you like?

This is the idea that aside from the general argument about more meso-linkages between greater diversity and better economic outcomes, there needs to be an emphasis on understanding the exact mechanisms of positive impact through tracing of both tangible and intangible benefits of diversity management, ranging from cognition to learning to performance dynamics of work groups and teams (Kearney, Gebert, and Voelpel 2009; Roberge and van Dick 2010), not to mention the organizational justice benefits (Noon 2007). That is, the local level HR officers often feel the need to show the value of diversity initiatives not just for the resolution of localized issues and challenges, but also for wider organizational outcomes that encompass the global HR policy of MNCs. One way in which this can be achieved is to tie the results of equality and diversity diagnostic checks to wider organizational performance and justice outcomes. The locality argument only works when local HR agents not only argue for equality and diversity solutions which are fit for purpose in their specific contexts, but also robustly explain the potential latent benefits of localized policies upon the global workings of the organization.

Concluding Remarks

Our findings indicate that there is a strong interest in the UK for a high-quality, locally specific, business-sensitive, equality and diversity tool. One of the most important suggestions from our research is that breaking with the past and moving forward into a diversity landscape marked by full equality and inclusion in organizations requires that we implement an evidence-based approach to diversity management. Instead of abstract ideas that might only work in theory or practical ideas translated from a disconnected, super-arching global point of view, the starting point in the diversity management process must hinge on paying attention to a specific locality's issues and problems. This requires understanding the historically and contemporaneously resonant issues on the ground, gathering evidence through a meticulous examination of ground reality, and then attempting to provide diversity management solutions.

Our analysis of the equality and diversity tool suggest that it should be implemented step by step, with a focus on all areas of operation of the organization as well as all aspects of HR processes. This multi-level, multi-area focus is also consistent with the implications of workforce diversity literature in tackling diversity issues (Alcázar, Fernández, and Gardey 2013). Our research also indicates that a sound diagnostic equality check must be able to engage with individual, organizational, and societal concerns, and adopt a multi-level approach, which seeks to reveal the source of diversity challenges in a wider range of constituent fields. This is indicative of the value of a relational approach in the realization of diversity management policies (Jackson and Joshi 2004; Kyriakidou and Özbilgin 2006). With a relational focus here, we emphasize the need to account for overlapping but also competing interests that different diversity management actors in the field may have in trying to reach diversity goals. In other words, we believe that the practice of diversity management is not a monolithic effort in terms of its constituent agents, and thus how their interests relate to and sometimes subsume each other must be accounted for. Local laws, practices, and norms, and global diversity agendas can differ significantly, and understanding how to constantly negotiate the tension requires a delicate balancing act between oppositional forces such as regulation versus voluntarism (Özbilgin and Tatli 2011).

This chapter illuminates the importance of the localized perspective, which is rooted in incorporating the views of the practitioners in the field, in order to empower them, and crucially, rely on their local knowledge of pressures as well as opportunities in dealing with the context-specific challenges in developing robust diversity management solutions. At the level of the locality, this analysis suggests that the needs and expectations of agents on the ground are too complex and variegated for them to be globally determined through standardization-based policies, however well intentioned these may be. The implication of our findings in the global context, as this case indicates, would be the need for MNCs to create company-wide equality policies and procedures, with manoeuvrability left for local actors to adjust intra-policy guidance, without changing the spirit of a given policy, so as to allow them the ability to account for locally specific issues on the ground. The actual act of going out into the field, speaking to professionals situated within both provider and user populations, and identifying their understanding of what would work on the ground to effectuate genuine transformational change formed the key components of this study. Given the ambiguities and challenges surrounding the fortunes of business organizations during a time of deep economic change, we also deemed it crucial to start from an analytical point of view, namely, the business case for diversity, which would be readily intelligible to businesses and respond to their sensitivities. The results of this endeavour provide a strong basis to start reorienting the diversity management literature toward an impact orientation steeped in carefully constructed multidimensional interventions in the form of diversity toolkits designed to effectuate measurable positive change. We believe that the inertia-inducing, macro-stranglehold of history, institutions, and place can be productively disrupted in this manner. However, for such disruption to be effective, diversity managers, organizational change agents and country-level and global strategic policymakers must work in tandem with each other to develop and then, when and where necessary, revise and even tailor diversity management policies. Such multi-level efforts would sustain a beneficial positive feedback loop between the global and the local.

References

Adler, N. (1986). Women in management worldwide. *International Studies of Management and Organization*, 16: 3–32.

Adler, N. and Ghadar, F. (1990). Strategic human resource management: a global perspective. In R. Pieper (ed.), *Human Resource Management in International Comparison*. Berlin: De Gruyter, 235–60.

Ahonen, P., Tienari, J., Meriläinen, S., and Pullen, A. (2013). Hidden contexts and invisible power relations: a Foucauldian reading of diversity research. *Human Relations*, DOI: 10.1177/0018726713491772.

Alcázar, F. M., Fernández, P. M. R., and Gardey, G. S. (2013). Workforce diversity in strategic human resource management models: a critical review of the literature and implications for future research. *Cross Cultural Management: An International Journal*, 20(1): 39–49.

Ashkanasy, N. M., Hartel, C. E. J., and Daus, C. S. 2002. Diversity and emotion: the new frontiers in organisational behaviour research. *Journal of Management*, 28(3): 307–38.

Barak, M. E. M. (2000). The inclusive workplace: an ecosystems approach to diversity management. *Social Work*, 45(4): 339–53.

Bendl, R., Fleischmann, A., and Walenta, C. (2008). Diversity management discourse meets queer theory. *Gender in Management: An International Journal*, 23(6): 382–94.

Blackaby, D., Booth, A. L., and Frank, J. (2005). Outside offers and the gender pay gap: empirical evidence from the UK academic labour market*. *The Economic Journal*, 115(501): F81-F107.

Blazevic, V. and Lievens, A. (2002). Learning during the new financial service innovation process: antecedents and performance effects. *Journal of Business Research*, 57(4): 374–91.

Brammer, S., Millington, A., and Pavelin, S. (2007). Gender and ethnic diversity among UK corporate boards. *Corporate Governance: An International Review*, 15(2): 393–403.

Brock, D. M. and Siscovick, I. C. (2007). Global integration and local responsiveness in multinational subsidiaries: some strategy, structure, and human resource contingencies. *Asia Pacific Journal of Human Resources*, 45(3): 353–73.

Calori, R., Steele, M., and Yoneyama, E. (1995). Management in Europe: learning from different perspectives. *European Management Journal*, 13(1): 58–66.

Campbell, K. and Minguez-Vera, A. (2008). Gender diversity in the boardroom and firm financial performance. *Journal of Business Ethics*, 83(3): 435–51.

Carroll, A. B. and Shabana, K. M. (2010). The business case for corporate social responsibility: a review of concepts, research and practice. *International Journal of Management Reviews*, 12(1): 85–105.

Carroll, G. R. and Hannan, M. T. (2000). *The Demography of Corporations and Industries*. Princeton, NJ: Princeton University Press.

Chevalier, A. (2007). Education, occupation and career expectations: determinants of the gender pay gap for UK graduates*. *Oxford Bulletin of Economics and Statistics*, 69(6): 819–42.

Chevrier, S. (2003). Cross-cultural management in multinational project groups. *Journal of World Business*, 38(2): 141–9.

Colgan, F. and McKearney, A. (2011). Spirals of silence? *Equality, Diversity and Inclusion: An International Journal*, 30(8): 624–32.

Colgan, F., Creegan, C., McKearney, A., and Wright, T. (2007). Equality and diversity policies and practices at work: lesbian, gay and bisexual workers. *Equal Opportunities International*, 26(6): 590–609.

Conyon, M. J. and Mallin, C. (1997). Women in the boardroom: evidence from large UK companies. *Corporate Governance: An International Review*, 5(3): 112–17.

Cox, T. H. (1993). *Cultural Diversity in Organisations: Theory, Research and Practice*. San Francisco, CA: Berrett-Koehler.

Creegan, C., Colgan, F., Charlesworth, R. and Robinson, G. (2003). Race equality policies at work: employee perceptions of the 'implementation gap' in a UK local authority. *Work, Employment & Society*, 17(4): 617–40.

Dickens, L. and Hall, M. (2006). Fairness – up to a point: assessing the impact of new labour's employment legislation. *Human Resource Management Journal*, 16(4): 338–56.

Fernandez, J. P. (1991). *Managing a Diverse Work Force*. Lexington, KY: Lexington Books.

Ferner, A., Almond, P., and Colling, T. (2005). Institutional theory and the cross-national transfer of employment policy: the case of workforce diversity in US multinationals. *Journal of International Business Studies*, 36(3): 304–21.

Gilbert, J. A. and Ivancevich, J. M. (2000). Valuing diversity: a tale of two organisations. *Academy of Management Executive*, 14(1): 93–105.

Gilbert, J. A. and Stead, B. A. (1999). Stigmatisation revisited: does diversity management make a difference in applicant success? *Group and Organisation Management*, 24: 239–56.

Gordon, A. (1995). The work of corporate culture: diversity management. *Social Text*, (44): 3–30.

Guellec, D. and Cervantes, M. (2001). International mobility of highly skilled workers: from statistical analysis to policy formulation. In *International Mobility of the Highly Skilled*. Paris: OECD, 71–98.

Gurin, P., Nagda, B. R. A., and Lopez, G. E. (2004). The benefits of diversity in education for democratic citizenship. *Journal of Social Issues*, 60(1): 17–34.

Harkness, S. (1996). The gender earnings gap: evidence from the UK. *Fiscal Studies*, 17(2): 1–36.

Healy, G., Bradley, H., and Forson, C. (2011). Intersectional sensibilities in analysing inequality regimes in public sector organizations. *Gender, Work and Organization*, 18(5): 467–87.

Hendry, C. and Pettigrew, A. (1986), The practice of strategic human resource management. *Personnel Review*, 15(5): 3–8.

Herring, C. (2009). Does diversity pay? Race, gender, and the business case for diversity. *American Sociological Review*, 74(2): 208–24.

Hopkins, D. J. (2011). National debates, local responses: the origins of local concern about immigration in Britain and the United States. *British Journal of Political Science*, 41(3): 499–524.

Jackson, S. E. and Joshi, A. (2004). Diversity in social context: a multi-attribute, multilevel analysis of team diversity and sales performance. *Journal of Organizational Behavior*, 25(6): 675–702.

Joshi, A. and Roh, H. (2009). The role of context in work team diversity research: a meta-analytic review. *Academy of Management Journal*, 52(3): 599–627.

Kearney, E., Gebert, D., and Voelpel, S. C. (2009). When and how diversity benefits teams: the importance of team members' need for cognition. *Academy of Management Journal*, 52(3): 581–98.

Knouse, S. B. and Dansby, M. R. (2000). Recent diversity research at the defense equal opportunity management institute (DEOMI): 1992–1996. *International Journal of Intercultural Relations*, 24(2): 203–25.

Kyriakidou, O. and Özbilgin, M. F. (eds.) (2006). *Relational Perspectives in Organizational Studies: A Research Companion*. Cheltenham: Edward Elgar.

Linnehan, F. and Konrad, A. M. (1999). Diluting diversity implications for iintergroup inequality in organizations. *Journal of Management Inquiry*, 8(4): 399–414.

Loosemore, M. and Muslmani, H. A. (1999). Construction project management in the Persian Gulf: inter-cultural communication. *International Journal of Project Management*, 17(2): 95–100.

Lorbiecki, A. (2001). Changing views on diversity management: the rise of the learning perspective and the need to recognize social and political contradictions. *Management Learning*, 32(3): 345–61.

Lorbiecki, A. and Jack, G. (2000). Critical turns in the evolution of diversity management. *British Journal of Management*, 11(s1): S17-S31.

Loretto, W. and White, P. (2006), Employers' attitudes, practices and policies towards older workers. *Human Resource Management Journal*, 16(3): 313–30.

McEnrue, M. P. (1993). Managing diversity: Los Angeles before and after the riots. *Organisational Dynamics*, 21(3): 18–29.

McKay, P. F., Avery, D. R., Tonidandel, S., Morris, M. A., Hernandez, M., and Hebl, M. R. (2007). Racial differences in employee retention: are diversity climate perceptions the key? *Personnel Psychology*, 60(1): 35–62.

McVittie, C., McKinlay, A., and Widdicombe, S. (2003), Committed to (un)equal opportunities? 'New ageism' and the older worker. *British Journal of Social Psychology*, 42(4): 595–612.

Martin, L. M., Warren-Smith, I., Scott, J. M., and Roper, S. (2008). Boards of directors and gender diversity in UK companies. *Gender in Management: An International Journal*, 23(3): 194–208.

Morrison, A. M. (1992). *The New Leader: Guidelines on Leadership Diversity in America*. San Francisco, CA: Jossey-Bass.

Nishii, L. H. and Özbilgin, M. F. (2007). Global diversity management: towards a conceptual framework. *The International Journal of Human Resource Management*, 18(11): 1883–94.

Noon, M. (1993). Racial discrimination in speculative application: evidence from the UK's top 100 firms. *Human Resource Management Journal*, 3(4): 35–47.

Noon, M. (2007). The fatal flaws of diversity and the business case for ethnic minorities. *Work, Employment and Society*, 21(4): 773–84.

Özbilgin, M. (ed.) (2009). *Equality, Diversity and Inclusion at Work: A Research Companion*. Cheltenham: Edward Elgar.

Özbilgin, M. and Tatli, A. (2011). Mapping out the field of equality and diversity: rise of individualism and voluntarism. *Human Relations*, 64(9): 1229–53.

Özbilgin, M. F., Beauregard, T. A., Tatli, A., and Bell, M. P. (2011). Work–life, diversity and intersectionality: a critical review and research agenda. *International Journal of Management Reviews*, 13(2): 177–98.

Öztürk, M. B. (2011). Sexual orientation discrimination: exploring the experiences of lesbian, gay and bisexual employees in Turkey. *Human Relations*, 64(8): 1099–118.

Öztürk, M. B. and Rumens, N. (2014). Gay male academics in UK business and management schools: negotiating heteronormativities in everyday work life. *British Journal of Management*, 25(3): 503–17.

Öztürk, M. B. and Tatli, A. (forthcoming). Gender identity inclusion in the workplace: broadening diversity management research and practice through the case of transgender employees in the UK. *International Journal of Human Resource Management*, DOI: 10.1080/09585192.2015.1042902.

Page, S. E. (2007). *The Difference: How the Power of Diversity Creates Better Groups, Firms, Schools and Societies*. Princeton, NJ: Princeton University Press.

Pitts, D. (2009). Diversity management, job satisfaction, and performance: evidence from US federal agencies. *Public Administration Review*, 69(2): 328–38.

Procter, S. J. and Mueller, F. (eds.) (2000). *Teamworking*. London: Macmillan.

Richard, O. (2000). Racial diversity, business strategy and firm performance: a resource-based view. *Academy of Management Journal*, 43(2): 164–77.

Robbins, S. P. (2001). *Organizational Behavior: Concepts, Controversies, Applications*. 9th edn. Upper Saddle River, NJ: Prentice Hall.

Roberge, M. É. and van Dick, R. (2010). Recognizing the benefits of diversity: when and how does diversity increase group performance? *Human Resource Management Review*, 20(4): 295–308.

Robinson, G. and Dechant, K. (1997). Building a business case for diversity. *The Academy of Management Executive*, 11(3): 21–31.

Roth, F. (2009). The effect of the financial crisis on systemic trust. *Intereconomics*, 44(4): 203–8.

Ruhs, M. and Anderson, B. (eds.) (2010). *Who Needs Migrant Workers?: Labour Shortages, Immigration, and Public Policy*. Oxford: Oxford University Press.

Servon, L. J. and Visser, M. A. (2011). Progress hindered: the retention and advancement of women in science, engineering and technology careers. *Human Resource Management Journal*, 21(3): 272–84.

Shaw, M. (1993). Achieving equality of treatment and opportunity in the workplace. In R. Harrison (ed.), *Human Resource Management: Issues and Strategies*. Wokingham: Addison-Wesley Publishing Company.

Shury, J., Winterbotham, M., Davies, B., Oldfield, K., Spilsbury, M., and Constable, S. (2010). National Employer Skills Survey for England 2009: Main Report.

Singh, V. (2007). Ethnic diversity on top corporate boards: a resource dependency perspective. *The International Journal of Human Resource Management*, 18(12): 2128–46.

Singh, V. and Vinnicombe, S. (2004). Why so few women directors in top UK boardrooms? Evidence and theoretical explanations. *Corporate Governance: An International Review*, 12(4): 479–88.

Soni, V. (2000). A twenty-first-century reception for diversity in the public sector: a case study. *Public Administration Review*, 60(5): 395–408.

Stahl, G., Björkman, I., Farndale, E., Morris, S. S., Paauwe, J., Stiles, P., and Wright, P. (2012). Six principles of effective global talent management. *Sloan Management Review*, 53(2): 25–42.

Syed, J. and Özbilgin, M. (2009). A relational framework for international transfer of diversity management practices. *The International Journal of Human Resource Management*, 20(12): 2435–53.

Tatli, A. (2011). A multi-layered exploration of the diversity management field: diversity discourses, practices and practitioners in the UK. *British Journal of Management*, 22(2): 238–53.

Tatli, A., Özbilgin, M., Mulholland, G., and Worman, D. (2006) *Managing Diversity Measuring Success*. CIPD Report. London: Chartered Institute of Personnel Development.

Thomas, D. A. and Ely, R. J. (1996). Making differences matter. *Harvard Business Review*, 74(5): 79–90.

Tomlinson, F. and Schwabenland, C. (2010). Reconciling competing discourses of diversity? The UK non-profit sector between social justice and the business case. *Organization*, 17(1) 101–21.

Woods, R. H. and Sciarini, M. P. (1995). Diversity programs in chain restaurants. *Cornell Hotel and Restaurant Administration Quarterly*, June: 18–23.

Wrench, J. (2012). *Diversity Management and Discrimination: Immigrants and Ethnic Minorities in the EU*. Aldershot: Ashgate.

Wright, T., Colgan, F., Creegany, C., and McKearney, A. (2006). Lesbian, gay and bisexual workers: equality, diversity and inclusion in the workplace. *Equal Opportunities International*, 25(6): 465–70.

Zanoni, P. and Janssens, M. (2007). Minority employees engaging with (diversity) management: an analysis of control, agency, and micro-emancipation. *Journal of Management Studies*, 44(8): 1371–97.

CHAPTER 19

ENTREPRENEURSHIP AND DIVERSITY

DEIRDRE TEDMANSON AND CAROLINE ESSERS

Introduction

TRADITIONAL mainstream entrepreneurship literature tends to emphasize particular psychological traits of entrepreneurs, such as being innovative and creative, possessing the urge for achievement and autonomy, exhibiting risk-taking behaviour and individualism (Thomas and Mueller 2000). The entrepreneurial archetype in this literature is often based on a 'rational' masculine stereotype, assumed to be risk-taking, and conquest, domination, and control focused. This hegemonic entrepreneurial discourse also reproduces the conventional female stereotype as subordinate, supportive, and dependent (Bruni et al. 2004: 186).

Female entrepreneurs and ethnic minority entrepreneurs are, more often than not, either ignored in such normative mainstream entrepreneurship texts, or else depicted as the exotic 'other' entrepreneurs. Many studies develop typologies of female entrepreneurs, either implicitly or explicitly, and authors such as Ahl (2004) and Bruni et al. (2004) have criticized the gender subtext in this style of theorizing, which too often constructs females as the exception, or 'other' entrepreneurs. Research on ethnic minority entrepreneurs tends also to assert that minorities start businesses because they face discrimination in the labour market or because they hold specific values and have access to certain resources, such as close ties and family relations (Bonacich 1973; Portes, Guarnizo, and Haller 2002). This form of analysis focuses in on points of 'difference' and, in doing so, risks reproducing stereotypes rather than disrupting them. Representations of ethnic minority entrepreneurs based on comparisons with a presumed (normative) archetypical entrepreneur can simply perpetuate the relations of power which stem from a preoccupation with othering. The ethnic 'other' is too readily contrasted with other population groups which are alleged to be more culturally focused on performance and therefore presumed to be more 'inclined' to pursue entrepreneurship (McClelland 1987).

This dominant representation of entrepreneurship holds within it an ethnocentric subtext, which implicitly compels businesspeople from minorities to assimilate or Westernize in order to succeed in business (Ogbor 2000). However, Thomas and Mueller (2000) argue that successful entrepreneurs from diverse cultural backgrounds continue to score differently on scales of the more conventionally accepted (Western) entrepreneurial traits. Much of the mainstream entrepreneurship literature suggests that masculinity and Westernness are important to successful entrepreneurship—and this is starkly contrasted with other stereotypes of femininity and non-Westernness.

This chapter aims to extend on other critical entrepreneurship contributions (e.g. but not limited to: Armstrong 2005; Jones and Spicer 2009; Weiskopf and Steyaert 2009; Gross, Sheppes, and Urry 2011) to illustrate and analyse diverse entrepreneurs stemming from diverse contexts. In this chapter, we specifically reject binary and hierarchical ways of reifying and normalizing existing power positions (Wekker and Lutz 2001: 27). We consider that such essentialism creates problematic effects, which, in turn, may result in discriminatory practices by both practitioners and policymakers (Ogbor 2000; Bruni, Gherardi, and Poggio 2004; Essers and Benschop 2007). Instead, we build on more critical accounts of entrepreneurship, to question the often ethnocentrically biased and gendered foundations of entrepreneurial practices in Western society. We incorporate case study material drawn from both our joint and separate empirical fieldwork material, such as studies on Turkish female entrepreneurs in the Netherlands and the UK, and on Aboriginal entrepreneurs in urban and more remote country areas of Australia. We intend to not only demonstrate how 'Other' entrepreneurs have to deal with implicit and explicit prescriptions about what it is to be a successful entrepreneur and how they have to relate to the ethnocentrically and gendered (popular) discourse on entrepreneurship, but also to illustrate how these 'deviant' and less known entrepreneurs 'do entrepreneur*ing*' against the grain, by both implicitly and explicitly inventing and applying particular identity strategies. We reveal new takes on entrepreneurship in action to explore not only new forms of entrepreneurial diversity, but also the diversity of how (and what) entrepreneur*ing* can mean.

In this chapter, we first explore aspects of Indigenous entrepreneurship in Australia, and discuss how entrepreneurial activity in this context can have profound social and political meaning for people who are marginalized and stigmatized yet remain strong in the pursuit of their human right to self-determination on their own lands. We then move on to a comparison of the experiences of female Turkish entrepreneurs in the UK and the Netherlands, discussing the intersectionality of ethnicity, religion, and gender, as well as the different role of the national context in shaping minority entrepreneurial experiences. Both these exemplars deviate from a standard normative view of entrepreneurship as a purely economic activity, and one more often pursued by entrepreneurial Western males. We explore these examples to reveal instead some of the diverse and rich experiences of these entrepreneurial 'Others'.

Indigenous Entrepreneurship

A little-understood phenomenon is the way in which 'entrepreneurs may be more likely to emerge from those groups in society which are deprived or marginal, i.e. groups which are discriminated against, persecuted, looked down upon or exceptionally exploited' (Scase and Goffee 1980: 29). While the study of ethnic minority entrepreneurs is concerned with the economic engagement of immigrant groups new to a particular area, and the diverse forms of social capital such groups may deploy to further their interests in such new contexts (Light 2004), a focus on Indigenous entrepreneurs explores how individuals with a deep and long-standing attachment to their ancestral lands engage in contemporary economic ventures. In this context, Indigenous enterprise development and entrepreneurship is part of a continuum of community-based development which aims to contribute to Indigenous political, social, and economic self-determination (Peredo et al. 2004; Dana and Anderson 2007; Tedmanson 2014).

Indigenous entrepreneurship has both local and global dimensions, and, since the United Nations Declaration of the Rights of Indigenous Peoples in 2007, it has become an area of increasing interest in the field of entrepreneurship studies. We consider it important to first understand the oppressed and often marginalized status of Indigenous populations worldwide, as this is a powerful contextual influence over Indigenous people's economic engagement. Shapero (1975) has explored the notion of the entrepreneur as a 'displaced' person, while others, such as Frederick and Foley (2006), argue that disadvantaged groups, whether Indigenous or non-Indigenous, can improve their economic and social positioning through engagement in entrepreneurial activities (see also: Dana 1995, 2007; Foley 2000, 2006; Sullivan and Margaritis 2000; Anderson 2002; Nnadozie 2002; Dana and Anderson 2007; Lee-Ross and Mitchell 2007; Tedmanson 2014).

Indigenous communities worldwide continue to survive against the harsh and often near genocidal legacies of past (and in some cases continuing) colonial oppressions. Australia's Indigenous peoples fit this worldwide pattern and continue to be the nation's most disadvantaged people,[1] living in the poorest conditions in the poorest urban areas—or, for those in the 'remote' communities in the desert regions of central, northern, and Western Australia, in what are effectively 'Third World' conditions, encircled by the colonizing culture of a globalizing First World nation, 'another country hidden within our borders' (Macklin 2008: 1). Indigenous Australians are overrepresented in the prison system, face high levels of unemployment, have the lowest educational attainment, the highest incidence of chronic disease, the highest rates of infant mortality, a life expectancy some twenty years less than non-Indigenous 'white' Australians, and continue to endure the cumulative, intergenerational effects of invasion, exploitation,

---

[1] The term 'Indigenous' is used to denote the inclusion of both Aboriginal and Torres Strait Islander peoples (who comprise the Indigenous peoples of Australia) whereas the term 'Aboriginal' will elsewhere be used where this refers to Australia's mainland Indigenous peoples who prefer the use of the term 'Aboriginal'.

dispossession, and entrenched racism: 'that such conditions should exist among a group of people defined by race in the 21st century in a developed nation like Australia is a disgrace and should shame us all' (Chivell 2002: 9).

Like those in Latin America, Africa, Canada, New Zealand, and other areas of the South Pacific region, Australia's Indigenous peoples face not only the continuing impact of the colonial past in the neocolonial present, but globalization has also brought greater inequalities in wealth distribution, increased surveillance by governments, the threat of police/military and corporate incursions into Indigenous lands,[2] and either the denigration or appropriation of Indigenous knowledge—ways of being, seeing, doing, organizing. Despite the depravations caused by poverty, poor nutrition, inadequate access to services, alcohol and other substance misuse, and limited access to political power, however, the resilience of Australia's Indigenous cultures continues to defy the political economy of cultural 'genocide' by the dominant state.[3] In such conditions, it can be hard to perceive how entrepreneurship can flourish, yet, following Scase and Goffee (1980), Indigenous entrepreneurship is growing as a field of interest, not only in Australia but also worldwide.

Peredo and Chrisman (2006: 11), for example, suggest that the more 'community-oriented' a population, the more 'they will feel their status and well-being is a function of the reciprocated contributions they make to their community'. Peredo and Chrisman also maintain that this 'community orientation' is a key feature of Indigenous community life worldwide. Similarly, Dana and Anderson (2007: 6) suggest that, 'social organisation among Indigenous people is often based on kinship ties' rather than in response to market needs. This depiction of the communal and socially oriented nature of Indigenous entrepreneurship is a common theme which occurs across the literature in this emerging field of research. Lindsay (2005) argues that Indigenous entrepreneurship is undertaken for the direct benefit of the Indigenous peoples involved in the venture—as a form of Indigenous community economic development that has social as well as economic goals. He connects this 'holistic' view of Indigenous social entrepreneurship with an expression of 'self-determination'. In this way, Lindsay argues (2005: 1) that Indigenous ventures are fundamentally 'entrepreneurial strategies originating in and controlled by the community, and the sanction of Indigenous culture'.

---

[2] On 22 June 2007, the then Australian prime minister announced a national emergency into 'the abuse of children in Indigenous communities in the NT. Amongst these measures was the deployment of the military as well as police and specialist security forces to take over some 60 Indigenous communities in remote areas'.

[3] The 1997 Australian Human Rights and Equal Opportunity Commission report, *Bringing Them Home: National Inquiry into the Separation of Aboriginal and Torres Strait Islander Children from their Families*, found government policies of the time towards Indigenous peoples fell within United Nations' definitions of '*genocide*'. On 13 February 2008, the Australian prime minister formally apologized to Indigenous Australians on behalf of the Australian people for what they had endured during the public policy period known as the 'Stolen Generations'.

There is growing support amongst Indigenous leaders in Australia arguing for an acceleration of Indigenous entrepreneurial effort to help overcome what have been historically (post-European invasion of the continent) intractable levels of Indigenous disadvantage. Prominent Indigenous political spokesperson Noel Pearson (2000), for example, suggests that, in considering problems confronting Indigenous Australians, there has been too much separation of social and economic domains which are, in fact, inextricably related. The disembedding of economic activity from social life creates an artificial notion that the pursuit of economic activity can occur in isolation from considerations of social context. For people living in remote Indigenous communities—which are small and often highly dependent on a state-provided service economy—the opportunities for economic development can be limited. Factors such as historical exclusion from competitive market forces, absence of an economic base, lack of access to skills and training, and tensions between social, cultural, and economic aims are often cited as reasons for the poor prospects of remote Indigenous communities seeking greater market engagement (Tedmanson and Guerin 2011). Altman (2001) suggests, however, that market, state, and customary economies can coexist in many of Australia's remote Indigenous communities, creating a hybrid economy where productive cultural and customary activity intersects with spheres of broader state and market influences. This hybridity enables a diversity of enterpris*ing* effort to emerge.

In summarizing the major research themes in Indigenous entrepreneurial research, Peredo and colleagues (2004: 14) suggest that by far the most dominant research theme is the 'relationship between Indigenous entrepreneurship and Indigenous culture'. Such deep links to cultural values and relational, more communally oriented, forms of exchange and benefit, establish Indigenous entrepreneurial effort as different from, and not confirming to, more orthodox mainstream depictions of entrepreneurship as a form of heroic individualism. Peredo and Chrisman (2006: 19) also argue that Indigenous entrepreneurship may in fact be a way for Indigenous communities to sustain their cultural values, and that 'entrepreneurship may be conducted in a different way in keeping with those values, including a community emphasis, consensus decision-making, and a focus on sharing and cooperation, instead of competition'. Indigenous social entrepreneur*ing*, for example, may have both a market orientation and aim to fulfil a social or cultural purpose—or both. Strengths-based approaches to community development emphasize social 'capital', which can reinforce local talents and build local capacity.

By focusing on local priorities and strengths and assets—rather than perceptions of the 'other' as deficient and disadvantaged—pride, confidence, and motivation can be enhanced. Support for, and facilitation of, locally determined processes stimulates greater participation and lessens dependence on external economic interventions or approaches which aim to 'solve' Indigenous problems by imposing externally designed and driven Eurocentric and mainstream agendas. In collaborative research work with local Indigenous peoples in remote communities, the extent and diversity of entrepreneurial activity can be made more visible and local people can narrate their own forms of entrepreneurship.

Entrepreneurial Aspirations within an Indigenous Cultural Context

In a qualitative participatory action research study conducted in 2008–11 by Banerjee and Tedmanson on stakeholder views of prospects for local entrepreneurial developments on the Anangu Pitjantjatjara Yankunytjatjara (APY) Lands of South Australia,[4] key local Aboriginal (Anangu) informants spoke with great enthusiasm about entrepreneurial ventures stimulating social, cultural, and economic returns to the community. Young people, for example, spoke of their aspirations and hopes:

> I want to learn to run my own business—maybe the shop here. There are no shops or businesses here now—but I would start one, start something at least,—if I can get something going here then it will be good for me but also family...
>
> (Young Indigenous male)

> All my family work in some way—and we still hunt together too—I want to make my own things to sell... maybe punu [traditional Anangu wood carving/craft] and at least then add to supporting my family and helping community here.
>
> (Indigenous male elder)

> I'd like to do people's hair and make-up here; maybe once a week to be open... but we could be a business like in town then... even just once a week or month...
>
> (Young Indigenous female)

Older people focused also on the regenerative power of enterprises to sustain an ongoing desire for connection to country while also fostering engagement with people outside the area:

> I bring tourists here, only a couple at a time, small numbers, but show them my country and tell stories and involve family—pass on culture and leave something here for family... so people can stay on our homeland and not leave for the city...
>
> (Older Indigenous male elder)

> Want to see the community with Anangu serving Anangu... grow our own food and exchange it at maybe markets... We need to teach the culture more to everyone non-Anangu and Anangu—we need to get back to balance!
>
> (Middle-aged Indigenous female)

---

[4] The APY Lands of South Australia are a vast area of the central desert region located within South Australia but bordered by Western Australia and the Northern Territory also, which were handed back to the Aboriginal communities of the region through the historic Anangu Pitjantjatjara Yankunytjatjara Land Rights Act in 1981. A map of this area and information about APY Lands Aboriginal communities is available at: <http://www.anangu.com.au/>.

The entrepreneurial vision of those interviewed always included a combination of both social and economic goals, and usually this was framed within the context of maintaining homeland and community cultural life. Concepts in the international development literature such as 'sustainable livelihoods' provide a framework for analysis that emphasizes the building of community 'assets' in terms of people—not just consumable material goods. Promoting micro-enterprises and local social entrepreneurial ventures are important components of processes that support the recovery of social cohesion and foster its maintenance, and play an often underdiscussed role in strengthening community health and well-being (Tedmanson and Guerin 2011).

On the dark side, however, postcolonial power politics and a 'political economy of whiteness' (Banerjee and Tedmanson 2010: 1) shape the state context within which Indigenous entrepreneurship occurs, and can impede its visibility and control its viability. In analysing the histories of 'settler–native' relations in Australia, Indigenous scholar Moreton-Robinson (2004) shows how the intersection of race and property created and sustained white economic, political, and cultural domination over Indigenous peoples. She argues the hegemonic effects of 'whiteness' served to deny Indigenous sovereignty while legitimating dispossession of Indigenous lands. Thus, 'whiteness' lies at the 'very heart' of the way in which the Australian continent was *un*settled (Tedmanson 2008).

From this theoretical perspective, the 'white' conquerors' lie enabled the founding of an Australian nation specifically built on the dispossession and non-recognition of its Indigenous peoples. Such hegemonic control of the nation's population diversity—and, in particular, its Indigenous peoples, is maintained by keeping economic control and, in effect, marginalizing Indigenous people's entrepreneurial efforts. Yet despite this hegemonic control, the racisms of the dominant nation, and the everyday struggles of the impoverished and poor standard of living that is the lived reality of so many Indigenous peoples, entrepreneurship survives—and in some communities it even continues to thrive.

The potential benefits with respect to enterprise development include building confidence, providing leadership and role modelling, increasing interaction between different groups leading to social harmony, greater social stability derived from feelings of commitment and belonging to the community, and a reduction in dependence on welfare (Fuller, Howard, and Cummings 2003). The key goal expressed by participants in this research project was to develop sustainable entrepreneurial ventures which combined economic, social, cultural, and environmental aims. One of the greatest challenges for Indigenous entrepreneurship is to integrate economic activity with social concerns, cultural priorities, and legal rights within effective governance systems. Given the lack of infrastructure and demand factors, along with community concerns about social, environmental, and economic problems resulting from large-scale economic activity, it may not always be possible to create sustainable for-profit businesses at the onset. Rather, building a social enterprise provides a good opportunity for community members to be involved in business activity, where the goal is to generate revenue rather than profits in a strictly business perspective.

For others, however, entrepreneurship can provide liberation from the difficulties of everyday life. This often-stated dual objective and motivation for Indigenous enterprise activity is cultural *re*building as well as the quest for the general improvement of socioeconomic conditions of family and community (Frederick and Foley 2006; Lee-Ross and Mitchell 2007; Reveley and Down 2009; Banerjee and Tedmanson 2010). One Anangu elder explained his aims to generate a family clan-based cultural enterprise:

> [B]efore I die I want my kids and their kids to know their stories and Tjukurpa [Aboriginal cosmology, spiritual beliefs or 'dreaming'... to understand and have pride in their culture and be able to live off this land right way... and make an income from it... To live independent, not like old days, mission gone, government not helping—the past is gone but we can make it live again new way to hand on down the generations...
>
> (Very old Indigenous male)

Australian Indigenous entrepreneurs who pursue local, national, and international markets in innovative and creative ways, on their own terms, are emerging. The term 'entrepreneurship' has become an iconic mantra in business and management studies, a metaphor for innovative thinking and new ways of 'organizing' economic change across a broad range of settings, spaces, and places. Normative values, however, still shape presumptions about the 'naturalness' of individualism and competition hidden in discourses about entrepreneurial activity and new enterprise creation (Steyaert and Katz 2004). Growth and 'development' is still more often portrayed in terms of wealth generation rather than in socio-political or cultural terms, and most entrepreneurship analyses are informed by Western values and Eurocentric epistemologies, using Western methodologies to reproduce Western theoretical frames of reference (Chakrabarty 2000; Ogbor 2000; Escobar 2001 . By focusing on researching *with* Indigenous entrepreneurs, it becomes possible to see a greater diversity in the range of entrepreneurial effort occurring, and to comprehend more fully the diversity of lived experiences which shape—and are shaped by—the discursive constructions of entrepreneurship and its more heterogeneous potential.

Female Migrant Entrepreneurship

Besides the research on Indigenous entrepreneurs, which contributes much to the literature on diversity in entrepreneurship, studies on female migrant entrepreneurs in Europe enriches this body of literature too. Most studies on ethnic minority entrepreneurship, implicitly or not, concentrate on male entrepreneurs or ignore the roles played by female entrepreneurs in these businesses (Westwood and Bhachu 1987; Essers and Benschop 2007).

Moreover, the popular discourse on entrepreneurship, or the way the public, media, but also traditional entrepreneurship, 'talk' about entrepreneurs and entrepreneurship, seems to be in conflict with the discourse on womanhood. Thus, being a woman and an entrepreneur at the same time results in many tensions (Ahl 2004). Entrepreneurship, and originating from outside Europe (or the West), or being 'non-Western', also seems to be a dichotomy in this popular discourse. And so being a woman of Turkish or Moroccan origin, and an entrepreneur at the same time, is a big challenge for the females that we study: Turkish- and Moroccan-origin female entrepreneurs in Western Europe.

A comparative pilot study was conducted in 2010 (see also Humbert and Essers 2012) to get a first impression on how national opportunity structures in the Netherlands as well as in the UK impact upon the female Turkish entrepreneur's possibilities and chances. Entrepreneurial rates among Turkish migrants in Europe are lower than that of the general population. Yet evidence shows that the number of economically independent female Turkish entrepreneurs is growing. In the Netherlands, only 4 per cent of the population of Turkish origin are entrepreneurs, 18 per cent of which are female (Statistics Netherlands (CBS) 2009), while in the UK the self-employment rate is estimated to be 20 per cent for Turks (Basu and Altinay 2002; Altan 2007), 20 per cent of which are estimated to be female (Basu and Altinay 2002; Strüder 2003). In this research, we gathered life-story interviews with Turkish-origin female entrepreneurs.

We spoke with eighteen Turkish female entrepreneurs in the Netherlands, and eight in the UK, to explore how these Turkish migrant entrepreneurs respond to, adjust to, and alter the various political, institutional, and societal opportunity structures. By contrasting the UK and the Netherlands, we were able to show how diverse structures may affect processes of entrepreneurial possibilities and agency.

Comparing Female Turkish Entrepreneurs' Experiences in the Netherlands and the UK

In this pilot study, we observed that the social context or opportunity structure (comprising particularly the networks and social contacts) in the Netherlands is fraught with much more tension than in the UK. The respondents feel their position as (young) females of Turkish origin and entrepreneurs is problematic, as this combination of identities is perceived as incompatible and sometimes even connected with shame.

Familial support may compensate and eventually strengthen the business attitudes and acumen of these female entrepreneurs, and their position as Turkish individuals may become more of an asset than a hindrance, particularly as they become more established and, for example, promote themselves within a culturally specific niche market. Networking was mostly seen as difficult to sustain because of time commitments, and respondents in this research spoke of often feeling excluded due to their gender and ethnicity.

In the UK, Humbert and Essers (2012) conclude that there is a greater usage of business Turkish networks and a greater sense of inclusion within mainstream networks than in the Netherlands. In the study, female Turkish entrepreneurs in the UK mostly do not feel the need to be coached formally, yet some successful female Turkish entrepreneurs seem to coach other minorities to contribute to society. Moreover, entrepreneurialism is picked up 'naturally', respondents in the study commented, and to actively encourage potential entrepreneurs is regarded positively. Regarding finance, the female entrepreneurs are more circumspect, however, as having the right contacts at banks to obtain a loan seems to be essential in both the UK and the Netherlands, just like, in some cases, having the right name or appearance appears an important attribute to attracting backing in both countries.

In the UK, more interviewees indicated a lack of interest in pursuing business loans, as the female entrepreneurs do not see it as desirable to be burdened by repayments. Instead, they choose to be much more reliant on informal sources of funding. Finally, the social opportunity structure appears to be experienced more negatively in the Netherlands, when compared to the experiences of the female Turkish entrepreneurs in the UK. The political climate in the Netherlands has changed over the past two decades, towards becoming more hostile to ethnic minorities, particularly those of Muslim faith. Islam is being used in societal discourses to exclude this group, and the need for these allegedly non-adjusted citizens to integrate is constantly being stressed. This atmosphere makes it difficult for these respondents to come to terms with their sense of identity as entrepreneurs who are also female and also Turkish. In the UK, the female Turkish entrepreneurs feel less different and otherized, and seem to be able to distance themselves more from negative pigeonholing in the media.

The variations in these experiences might be explained by the fact that the political climate towards Turkish Muslims in the UK is less polarized than in the Netherlands. This negative climate apparently, in the view of the female Turkish entrepreneurs interviewed, affects the opinions and sentiments of the various actors of the opportunity structure (not only the societal one) with whom they have to deal. The differences might also be explained from migration, which occurred at different times in the respective countries. Because of migration occurring earlier, the Turkish respondents in the UK might perhaps feel less cultural difference between their community and the British. Moreover, their experiences can also be contextualized within different economies, the UK being a liberal market economy and the Netherlands being a coordinated market economy. Although one might expect that the Dutch coordinated market economy would provide much more institutionalized support, leading to (proportionally) much more entrepreneurship amongst this group than the UK's liberal market economy, alternatively this coordinated market economy might entail too many obstructing rules. Of course, these are only indications, and we cannot, and do not, aim at generalizing the situation of the whole population of female Turkish migrant entrepreneurs, but we may also detect different forms of agency being enacted by these females when connecting with these opportunity structures. They adjust to, deploy, and alter the various opportunity structures in order to enhance their entrepreneurial possibilities in various ways. Some female Turkish entrepreneurs seem to figuratively or literally distance themselves from the negative opinions regarding (Muslim) Turkish people within a Western society, since this atmosphere impedes their entrepreneurial activity. Their way of dealing with the dominant discourse on foreigners and migrant entrepreneurs is to escape negative images. They herewith, if somewhat understandably, sustain this hegemonic discourse on the 'different, Other Muslim'.

However, although seemingly adjusting to the various opportunity structures, the female Turkish entrepreneurs in this study eventually found room to undertake entrepreneurship in their desired way. Some seem to be distancing themselves from the various opportunity structures, as they refuse to engage with any formal institutions. They exploit opportunity structures by conforming to a 'Western' way of doing business, and render their own otherness invisible, both physically, and in entrepreneurial behaviour.

Although the othering by Dutch people in the field of entrepreneurship is bothersome for female Turkish entrepreneurs, they sensibly, patiently, and pragmatically deal with such prejudice in order to be able to perform their entrepreneurship. While building on their growing experience, knowledge, and professionalism, these entrepreneurs subtly try to change the system from within. Some reported being quite pragmatic about not letting their ethnic identity affect their business practices, while at the same time capitalizing on the Turkish community where possible. But there are also female Turkish entrepreneurs who react more aggressively to the negativity they experience in the Netherlands. Some take the opportunity to set up a network for female Turkish entrepreneurs to cooperate.

Moreover, some female entrepreneurs explicitly make use of their gender and ethnic identity as a unique selling point, helping society by, for instance, initiating projects on entrepreneurship at schools. Such female Turkish entrepreneurs actively fight to change the various opportunity structures that surround them, such as their own migrant community. Being energetically involved in several networking and professional organizations, and using them to actively change the way things are done in business in/out of the Turkish community, as well as traditionally gender relations, these female Turkish entrepreneurs can be called active 'change agents'. Of course, these are only some preliminary results, and the number of interviews done in the UK is lower than in the Netherlands. More systematic comparative research regarding the impact of national context on the possibilities and challenges confronting female Turkish entrepreneurs across Europe would provide further insights on the barriers this group experience. For instance, a comparison between the Netherlands, the UK, and Germany, while using both qualitative and quantitative methods to analyse the impact of the social, institutional, and political opportunity structure on this important group of new European professionals, would contribute to a better policy (on a national and European Union (EU) level) to stimulate and support these entrepreneurial change agents. This would not only add to economic development, but also aid the emancipation of these new European female entrepreneurs.

Considering Intersectionality

While doing research on the intertwinement between structure and agency, we noted that identity construction and intersectionality are important theoretical concepts.

Generally, gender and ethnicity seem to be regarded as important identity categories for understanding the identities of female migrants (Buitelaar 1998). Entrepreneurship and Islam are other salient identity categories when studying the multiple identities of female migrant Muslim entrepreneurs. The concept of intersectionality can be used to understand how being a Muslim, for instance, intermeshes with gendered and ethnic practices of exclusion, and how this influences entrepreneurial identities.

Intersectionality provides insights into the complexity of lived multiple identities and into the identity work necessitated by simultaneity of the socially orchestrated identity regulations. This identity work can be regarded as boundary work that people do to react to processes of inclusion and exclusion tied to various identity categories (Lamont and Fournier 1992; Bartkowski and Read 2003). Islam, for instance, connects to how gender is 'done' within a specific religious context, which is 'about how women and men make their femininities and masculinities known to themselves and to each other, through saying and doing things in specific instances' (Torab 1996: 238). Female entrepreneurs of Moroccan and Turkish descent have agency in the construction of their gender identities being a businesswoman, but are also affected by structural constraints provided by gender socialization and patriarchal processes. Moreover, in the dominant academic discourse on entrepreneurship, Islam has been negatively related to successful entrepreneurship. Thomas and Mueller (2000) note that a culture of individualism and achievement has dominated the worldview of entrepreneurship, which is related to Weber's Protestant work ethic. Calvinists were perceived as potentially successful entrepreneurs (Weber and Kalberg 2002) because of skills congruent with the virtues and practices of Calvinism: working hard, using time carefully, innovating, having an internal locus of control, and reinvesting earnings (Anderson, Drakopoulou-Dodd, and Scott 2000; Arslan 2001). According to Weber, Islamic societies were not able to produce 'the spirit of capitalism' because of the warrior ethic, other-worldly Sufism, Oriental despotism, and a lack of individualism (Arslan 2001: 321).

Yet authors such as Shane and Venkataraman (2000: 220) stress that entrepreneurial opportunities come in a variety of forms and do not necessarily equate with capitalism. In the case of immigrant businesspeople who focus on ethnic market niches, entrepreneurship can be a way to retain one's self-esteem, as this economic mobility does not entail cultural assimilation (Porter and Washington 1993).

Different Roles in Different National Contexts

Additionally, postcolonial theorists, such as Said (1978) and Prasad (2003), take note of a typical Orientalist discourse in organization studies which perceive certain non-Western businesses practices to be residues of 'traditional', backward, and primitive cultural practices that are an obstacle to organizational efficiency and effectiveness. In many Orientalist discourses, Islam is pictured as backward, violent, and primitive, which does not tally with honest, ethical, and straightforward ways of doing business (Said 1978). In contrast to the alleged entrepreneurial asset of individualism, the literature on ethnic minority entrepreneurship stresses the advantages of sociability and family relations (Portes 1995). Although a few authors (for example, Sloane 1999) discuss the realities and opportunities of the combination of Islam and entrepreneurship, the standing entrepreneurship literature constructs a hegemonic discourse that suggests the incompatibility of Islamic and entrepreneurial identities. What does this mean for the identities of female Muslim entrepreneurs of Moroccan and Turkish descent? In a research project undertaken in the Netherlands amongst this group of female migrant entrepreneurs (Essers and Benschop 2009), we saw these Muslim female entrepreneurs exhibit complex boundary work (see also Sveningsson and Alvesson 2003), entailing strategies in which Islam is used as a basis for distinction, stratification, and demarcation to facilitate entrepreneurship.

All of the interviewed female entrepreneurs resist traditional, dogmatic approaches of Islam and negotiate their Muslim identity in relation to entrepreneurship. Based on our analysis, we distinguish four kinds of boundary work in relation to gender, ethnicity, entrepreneurship, and Islam. One strategy is to resist the strict sex segregation as advocated by certain sections in Islam. Females may pragmatically relate their job to respectful professions and define their 'limits' by keeping an appropriate distance from male clients. They symbolically create a boundary between themselves and their male clients to conform to gendered norms without jeopardizing their businesses. Another strategy to deal with gender regulations ascribed to Islam is to emphasize the individuality of faith. The female entrepreneurs in this study do this by claiming the right to decide for themselves which religious rules apply to their working lives and which—in their eyes, dogmatic—rules can be disregarded. Thus, they craft an individual Muslim identity and build boundaries within Islam; different Islams are distinguished to create space for religious individualism. They view Muslim identity as an individual matter between Allah and the believer. Therefore, the boundaries of what is (not) allowed are individually set and stretched to accommodate female entrepreneurship. The third form of boundary work involves embracing feminist progressive interpretations of the Qur'an, such as referring to Qur'anic female role models and stressing the morality of work. This provides females with the opportunity to stretch the boundaries of what is acceptable work within gendered and religious regulations. The final form of boundary work involves historicizing and contextualizing the Qur'an, such as stating that the strict gender relations as described in several Qur'anic verses pertain to ancient periods where societies had other gender dynamics. Demarcating earlier societies from contemporary societies helps these entrepreneurs shield themselves from more dogmatic interpretations of the Qur'an. Accordingly, they are able to craft a more individual religious identity to counter more collectivist, universal interpretations within Islam regarding appropriate gender behaviour.

Boundary work closely relates to the notion of identity regulation and identity work, which has been discussed in a recent project (Essers, Doorewaard, and Benschop 2013) in the context of family relations. We studied how female entrepreneurs of Turkish and Moroccan origin in the Netherlands perform their identity work between conflict with, and compliance to, the family regulations, in continuous interplay with their social environment. We found that the patriarchal contexts in the Turkish and Moroccan communities emphasize the 'good woman role' in the private family environment and tend to restrict females from holding public roles. The female entrepreneurs have to manoeuvre strategically between the conflicting roles of the good woman in private contexts and the small business owner in the public. The stories of the interviewed entrepreneurs have demonstrated how these female migrant entrepreneurs are regulated by a set of restrictions and norms regarding gender, ethnicity, as well as small business ownership. These norms and regulations relate to normative discourses, patriarchal norms, and traditional practices, which tell them what to do, and how to behave. Females are expected to behave in a feminine manner and to adhere to female roles, strongly related to the private sphere, such as motherhood and being a housewife (Sadiqi and Ennaji 2006). These norms and practices hinder female migrant entrepreneurs from stepping outside, into the public domain, as business owners. Two important identity regulations can be discerned: the first concerns 'the good woman', the second one the ambiguities regarding 'family support'.

From this research project on family dynamics, a variety of identity work manifestations emerges, all between conflict and compliance. These manifestations of identity work can be placed in four different positions: the two poles of conflict and compliance, and two more hybrid positions of bending and selecting in-between. We also distinguish a fifth manifestation of identity work, which surpasses these poles of conflict and compliance. For the majority of the migrant female business owners we interviewed, only a small and winding path is available in order to become a business owner without bringing shame to the family. Each of them followed their own path, more or less successfully. In so doing, each of them forms, maintains, strengthens, or revises a construction of herself in relation to the claims and demands issued on them. Most identity work manifestations stay within the conflict–compliance dimension. A first category of manifestations can be found on the conflict pole of the strategic manoeuvring continuum.

Conflict-oriented identity work is a visible, active, and sometimes aggressive activity. In order to get what they want, female migrant entrepreneurs need to rebel against the family norms and oppose their family members and acquaintances openly. Another manifestation of conflict-oriented identity work is the activity we describe as blackmail. Blackmail is a form of coercion, through which the blackmailer realizes his or her wishes based on threats. The conflict-oriented responses operate within the set of family norms. The entrepreneurs mostly do not question the family norms; they just want to ignore them. Neither rebelling nor being blackmailed is an easy position, and for both positions female migrant business owners need persistency and a thick skin to convince their relatives that they want to stick to their business owner identity. Such an attitude openly objects to the norm that a female should stay home and should keep a distance from the public sphere. Compared to conflict-orientation, the category 'bending' is characterized by softer and less aggressive interventions. Manipulation, for instance, is a manifestation of identity work which aims at adjusting or bending the environment to someone's wishes. The female entrepreneurs involved in this kind of identity work object to the idea that they ought to perform a subordinate, economically dependent, and reproductive role. Nevertheless, they do not speak their minds freely, but appear to be inclined to use more 'manipulative' tactics to impress their relatives. This strategy contains similarities with Ketner, Buitelaar, and Bosma's (2004) approach, which aims at playing out people or ideas against each other. Telling 'white' lies and other forms of secret behaviour also belong to the bending approach.

We may infer that female migrant entrepreneurs are inclined to display secret behaviour during their childhood in particular, as it is in this period that they live with their parents and are heavily controlled. When they are adults, this secret behaviour is less necessary, as they may physically and emotionally distance themselves from this parental control. This role of secretly opposing family members can be recognized in Ketner, Buitelaar, and Bosma's (2004) secret behaviour approach, regarding the identity strategies among adolescent girls of Moroccan descent in the Netherlands.

Compared with conflicting and bending, this category of identity work does not alter the norms. Instead of openly or secretly trying to fight or adjust the effects of the norms and mores of the family, female migrant entrepreneurs attempt to realize their wishes by taking very small steps. Selectively, they accentuate those norms or suggestions, which, within the limits of the factual situation they are in, will help them on their paths towards small business ownership. We found several examples of this form of identity work. Some female entrepreneurs selectively filter the suggestions that suit their intentions, such as having a good education, and more or less ignore other suggestions stemming from their family. Others apply familiarity to sustain their small business, whereas on other occasions they keep their family away from their company in order to preserve their business ownership autonomy. Sometimes, the female migrant entrepreneurs explain that they had no choice but to accept the rules of the family. Evidently, such female entrepreneurial identity work invokes pragmatism, which entails seeking female autonomy from their families by pragmatically presenting themselves in relation to the family norms on gender and ethnicity. To some extent, this pragmatic approach echoes Bruni, Gherardi, and Poggio's (2005) study on Italian female entrepreneurs, in which females as 'disentrepreneurs' were found to leave the impression (with clients) that they were secretaries instead of the entrepreneur.

Apparently, sometimes it is possible that for a migrant female entrepreneur to succeed in extricating herself from family influence, and thus her identity work surpasses the poles of conflict and compliance. We recognized this in only a few cases, where female entrepreneurs who have a good relationship with their husbands are able to subvert the identity regulation and negotiation process with the rest of their family. Accordingly, such an action does not always result in breaking up the family. The family might not like it, but sometimes the love and respect for their daughter, sister, or wife is stronger than the disappointment that she does not behave completely according to the family norms.

We do not suggest that the overview of identity work we presented is exhaustive, since other narratives may reveal different manifestations. Moreover, dependent on the situation, time, and family relation, each of the presented manifestations of identity work may easily be practised by one and the same female business owner. Overall, our research has shown that, by developing various forms of identity work in response to normative familial standards, the migrant female entrepreneurs in our study are able to maintain—within certain limits—the respect of their relatives, the illusion of female modesty, and their autonomy at the same time.

Reflections

Despite the vast differences in geography covered by the research projects referred to in this chapter and the diversity of contexts and identities, from Indigenous Australian to Turkish Muslim female entrepreneurs for example, we argue that not only are there a range of unique research issues outlined here which run counter to the dominant normative and hegemonic notions of 'the' entrepreneur, there are also threads woven through the experiences of these 'other' entrepreneurs which resonate with similarities despite the diversity of context.

One of the main features which stands out is the way in which these research insights serve to highlight that, for ethnic minority populations and for many female entrepreneurs, the experience of entrepreneur*ing* is one embedded in web-like connectedness to community and family. It is not an individualized or exceptional activity, but rather one which underpins, liberates, or enriches people's sense of identity and cultural context. For many Indigenous entrepreneurs, business activity is a means for supporting family and community; showcasing culture and reinscribing cultural identity in a positive and value-adding way (Foley 2000, 2008; Peredo and Chrisman 2006). Entrepreneurial activity is marked by its intersectionality for the female entrepreneurs highlighted in this chapter also. The disembedding of entrepreneurial activity can be seen in this context to be the 'exceptional' province of the dominant and more mainstream norms which have been established, not around the majority of the world's people with the diversity of contexts which could be represented, but rather positing male 'white' Western experience as if this were the norm against which all other experience should be calibrated.

A further link emerges here between the experiences of Indigenous entrepreneurs and the experiences of female entrepreneurs from diverse contexts and cultural backgrounds—that of postcolonialism. Postcolonial theory (see, for example, Said 1978; Moreton-Robinson 2003; Prasad 2003) takes account of difference and makes visible the oppressive and limiting lens of 'whiteness' and how this tends to normalize Western (Anglo, Christian, and European) experience as the desired norm, and renders invisible the oppressive and colonial nature of the way 'others' are perceived to be lacking, exotic, or primitive. Postcolonial theory highlights how dominant culture interests are served by the continued 'othering' of people with diverse epistemological understandings or from non-Western cultures.

For Indigenous peoples around the world, the pernicious nature of past colonization, with its accompanying violence and systemic dispossession of millions of people worldwide, is not just an historic legacy but a lived experience in the neocolonial present day. Economic engagement through micro, community-based social enterprise, or larger-scale entrepreneurial effort, can be, in this context, not just an act of assimilation, but more often of cultural resilience, continuity, and survival. For female entrepreneurs from diverse cultural backgrounds, engagement in self-actualizing business efforts is a powerful expression of agency and selfhood, and one which is enacted in ways congruent with one's identity and priorities (Essers and Benschop 2009; Essers, Doorewaard, and Benschop 2013). Postcolonial organizational theory enables us to better understand how popular constructions and all-too-frequent insidious, often invisible, taken-for-granted stereotypes and perceptions stigmatize and 'otherize' people from diverse backgrounds. It enables us also to re-evaluate and better appreciate the depth and importance of entrepreneurship as a powerful tool for the expression of agency in diversity.

In this chapter, it has been our aim to extend other critical entrepreneurship contributions to illustrate and analyse diverse entrepreneurs stemming from diverse contexts. By highlighting current research findings on studies which focus, first, on Indigenous entrepreneurs in Australia and, second, on female Muslim Turkish entrepreneurs in the UK and the Netherlands, we have shown how new takes on entrepreneurship in action across different locations and settings can reveal not only new forms of entrepreneurial diversity, but also the increasing diversity of how (and what) entrepreneur*ing* can mean.

References

Ahl, H. (2004). *The Scientific Reproduction of Gender Inequality: A Discourse Analysis of Research Texts on Women's Entrepreneurship*. Malmö: Liber AB.

Altan, C. (2007). Turkish immigrants are among 'biggest benefit claimants'. *Londra Gazete*, 4 October.

Altman, J. (2001). Indigenous communities and business: three perspectives, 1998–2000. Centre for Aboriginal Economic Policy Research ANU Working Paper, no. 9.

Anderson, A., Drakopoulou-Dodd, S., and Scott, M. (2000). Religion as an environmental influence on enterprise culture: the case of Britain in the 1980s. *International Journal of Entrepreneurial Behaviour and Research*, 6(1): 5–20.

Anderson, R. B. (2002). Entrepreneurship and Aboriginal Canadians: a case study in economic development. *Journal of Developmental Entrepreneurship*, 7(1): 45.

Armstrong, P. (2005) *Critique of Entrepreneurship: People and Policy*. Basingstoke: Palgrave Macmillan.

Arslan, M. (2001). The work ethic values of Protestant British, Catholic Irish and Muslim Turkish managers. *Journal of Business Ethics*, 31(4): 321–39.

Banerjee, B. and Tedmanson, D. (2010). Grass burning under our feet: indigenous enterprise development in a political economy of whiteness. *Management Learning*, 41(2): 147–65.

Bartkowski, J. and Read, J. (2003). Veiled submission: gender, power, and identity among evangelical and Muslim women in the United States. *Qualitative Sociology*, 26(1): 71–92.

Basu, A. and Altinay, E. (2002). The interaction between culture and entrepreneurship in London's immigrant businesses. *International Small Business Journal*, 20(4): 371–93.

Bonacich, E. (1973). A theory of middleman minorities. *American Sociological Review*, 38(5): 583–94.

Bruni, A., Gherardi, S. and Poggio, B. (2004). Doing gender, doing entrepreneurship: an ethnographic account of intertwined practices. *Gender, Work and Organization*, 11(4): 406–29.

Bruni, A., Gherardi, S., and Poggio, B. (2005). *Gender and Entrepreneurship: An Ethnographical Approach*. London: Routledge.

Buitelaar, M. (1998). Between ascription and assertion: the representation of social identity by women of Moroccan descent in the Netherlands. *Focaal*, 32: 29–50.

Chakrabarty, D. (2000). *Provincializing Europe: Postcolonial Thought*. Princeton, NJ: Princeton University Press

Chivell, W. (2002). Findings of the South Australian State Coronial Inquest into the deaths of Kunmanara Ken, Kunmanara Hunt and Kunmanara Thompson, 6 September 2002, South Australian Courts Department, Adelaide, SA.

Dana, L. (1995). Entrepreneurship in a remote sub-Arctic community. *Entrepreneurship Theory and Practice*, 20(1): 5772.

Dana, L. (2007). Toward a multidisciplinary definition of indigenous entrepreneurship. In L. Dana and R. Anderson (eds.), *International Handbook of Research on Indigenous Entrepreneurship*. Cheltenham: Edward Elgar, 3–7.

Dana, L. and Anderson, R. (eds.) (2007). *International Handbook of Research on Indigenous Entrepreneurship*. Cheltenham: Edward Elgar.

Escobar, A. (2001) Culture sits in places: reflections on globalism and subaltern strategies of localization. *Political Geography*, 20: 139–74

Essers, C. and Benschop, Y. (2007) Enterprising identities: female entrepreneurs of Moroccan and Turkish origin in the Netherlands. *Organization Studies*, 28(1): 49–69.

Essers, C. and Benschop, Y. (2009). Muslim businesswomen doing boundary work: the negotiation of Islam, gender and ethnicity within entrepreneurial contexts. *Human Relations*, 62(3): 403–23.

Essers, C., Doorewaard, H., and Benschop, Y. (2013). Family ties: migrant businesswomen doing identity work on the public–private divide. *Human Relations*, 16(12): 1645–65.

Foley, D. (2000). *Successful Indigenous Australian Entrepreneurs: A Case Study Analysis*. Brisbane: Merino Lithographics.

Foley, D. (2008). Does culture and social capital impact on the networking attributes of indigenous entrepreneurs? *Journal of Enterprising Communities: People and Places in the Global Economy*, 2(3): 204–24.

Frederick, H. and Foley, D. (2006). Indigenous populations as disadvantaged entrepreneurs in Australia and New Zealand. *The International Indigenous Journal of Entrepreneurship, Advancement, Strategy and Education*, 2(2): 1–16

Fuller, D., Howard, M. and Cummings, E. (2003) Indigenous micro-enterprise development in Northern Australia: implications for economic and social policy. *Journal of Economic and Social Policy*, 2(2): 15–34.

Gross, J., Sheppes, G., and Urry, H. (2011). Emotion generation and emotion regulation: a distinction we should make carefully. *Cognition and Emotion*, 25: 765–81.

Humbert, A. L. and Essers, C. (2012). Connecting with the opportunity structure: Turkish female entrepreneurs in the UK and the Netherlands. In J. Jennings and K. Hughes (eds.), *Women's Entrepreneurship*. Cheltenham: Edward Elgar, 15–36.

Jones, C. and Spicer, A. (2009). *Unmasking the Entrepreneur*. London: Edward Elgar

Ketner, S., Buitelaar, M., and Bosma, H. (2004). Identity strategies among adolescent girls of Moroccan descent in the Netherlands. *Identity: An International Journal of Theory and Research*, 4(2): 145–69.

Lamont, M. and Fournier, M. (eds.) (1992). *Cultivating Differences: Symbolic Boundaries and the Making of Inequality*. Chicago: University of Chicago Press.

Lee-Ross, D. and Mitchell, B. (2007). Doing business in the Torres Straits: a study of the relationship between culture and the nature of indigenous entrepreneurs. *Journal of Developmental Entrepreneurship*, 12(2): 199–216.

Light, I. (2004). The ethnic ownership economy. In C. Stiles and C. Galbraith (eds.), *Ethnic Entrepreneurship: Structure and Process*. Amsterdam: Elsevier Science, 3–44.

Lindsay, N. (2005) Towards a cultural model of indigenous entrepreneurial attitude. *Academy of Marketing Science Review*, 5: 1–17.

McClelland, D. (1987). Characteristics of successful entrepreneurs. *Journal of Creative Behaviour*, 21(3): 219–33.

Macklin, J. (2008). Closing the gap: building an indigenous future. Address to the National Press Club, Canberra, 27 February, <http://jennymacklin.fahcsia.gov.au/node/751>, accessed 22 May 2011.

Moreton-Robinson, A. (2003). I still call Australia home: indigenous belonging and place in a white postcolonizing society. In S. Ahmed, C. Castaneda, and A.-M. Fortier (eds.), *Uprootings/Regroundings: Questions of Home and Migration*. New York: Berg, 23-40.

Nnadozie, E. (2002). African indigenous entrepreneurship: determinants of resurgence and growth of Igbo entrepreneurship during the post-Biafra period. *Journal of African Business*, 3(1): 49.

Ogbor, J. (2000). Mythicizing and reification in entrepreneurial discourse: ideology-critique of entrepreneurial studies. *The Journal of Management Studies*, 37(5): 605–35.

Pearson, C. and Helms, K. (2013). Indigenous social entrepreneurship: the Gumatj clan enterprise. *Journal of Entrepreneurship*, 22: 43.

Pearson, N. (2000). *Our Right to Take Responsibility*. Cairns: Noel Pearson Associates.

Peredo, A., Anderson, R., Galbraith, C., Honig, B., and Dana, L. (2004). Towards a theory of indigenous entrepreneurship. *Entrepreneurship and Small Business*, 1(1–2): 1–20.

Peredo, A. M. and Chrisman, J. J. (2006). Toward a theory of community-based enterprise. *Academy of Management Review*, 31(2): 309–28.

Porter, J. and Washington, R. (1993). Minority identity and self-esteem. *Annual Review of Sociology*, 19: 139–61.

Portes, A. (1995). *The Economic Sociology of Immigration: Essays on Networks, Ethnicity, and Entrepreneurship*. New York: Russell Sage Foundation.

Portes, A., Guarnizo, L. and Haller, W. (2002). Transnational entrepreneurs: an alternative form of immigrant economic adaptation. *American Sociological Review*, 67(2): 278–98.

Prasad, A. (ed.) (2003). *Postcolonial Theory and Organizational Analysis: A Critical Engagement*. New York: Palgrave Macmillan.

Reveley, J. and Down, S. (2009). Stigmatization and self-presentation in Australian entrepreneurial identity formation. In D. Hjorth and C. Steyaert (eds.), *The Politics and Aesthetics of Entrepreneurship*. Cheltenham: Edward Elgar, 162–79.

Sadiqi, F. and Ennaji, M. (2006). The feminization of public space: women's activism, the family law, and social change in Morocco. *Journal of Middle East Women's Studies*, 2(2): 86–115.

Said, E. (1978). *Orientalism*. London: Routledge & Kegan Paul.

Scase, R. and Goffee, R. (1980). *The Real World of the Small Business Owner*. London: Croom Helm.

Shane, S. and Venkataraman, S. (2000). The promise of entrepreneurship as a field of research. *Academy of Management Review*, 25: 217–26.

Shapero, A. (1975). The displaced, uncomfortable entrepreneur. *Psychology Today*, November: 83–8.

Sloane, P. (1999). *Islam, Modernity and Entrepreneurship among the Malays*. New York: St. Martin's Press.
Statistics Netherlands (CBS) (2009). *Allochtonen in Nederland*. Voorburg/Heerlen: CBS.
Steyaert, C. and Katz, J. (2004). Reclaiming the space of entrepreneurship in society: geographical, discursive and social dimensions, *Entrepreneurship & Regional Development*, 16 May, 179–96.
Strüder, I. (2003). Migrant self-employment in a European global city: the importance of gendered power relations and performances of belonging for Turkish women in London. *International Small Business Journal*, 21(4): 485–7.
Sullivan, A. and Margaritis, D. (2000). Public sector reform and indigenous entrepreneurship. *International Journal of Entrepreneurial Behaviour & Research*, 6(5): 265.
Sveningsson, S. and Alvesson, M. (2003). Managing managerial identities: organizational discourse and identity struggle. *Human Relations*, 56(10): 1163–93.
Tedmanson, D. (2008). Isle of exception: sovereign power and Palm Island. *Critical Perspectives on International Business*, 4(2/3), Special Edition: critical reflections on management and organizations, postcolonial perspective: 142–65.
Tedmanson, D. (2014). Indigenous social entrepreneurship: resilience and renewal. In H. Douglas and S. Grant (eds.), *Social Entrepreneurship and Enterprise: Concepts in Context*. Manly, NSW: Tilde University Press, 173–93.
Tedmanson, D. and Guerin, P. (2011). Enterprising social wellbeing: social entrepreneurial and strengths based approaches to mental health and wellbeing in 'remote' indigenous community contexts. *Australasian Psychiatry*, 19(S1): 3–33.
Thomas, A. and Mueller, S. (2000). A case for comparative entrepreneurship: assessing the relevance of culture. *Journal of International Business Studies*, 31(2): 287–301.
Torab, A. (1996). Piety as gendered agency: a study of Jalaseh ritual discourse in an urban neighbourhood in Iran. *Journal of the Royal Anthropological Institute*, 2(2): 235–52.
Weber, M. and Kalberg, S. (2002). *The Protestant Ethic and the Spirit of Capitalism*. Los Angeles, CA: Roxburys.
Weiskopf, R. and Steyaert, C. (2009) 'Metamorphoses in entrepreneurship studies: towards an affirmative politics of entrepreneuring'. In D. Hjorth and C. Steyaert (eds.), *The Politics and Aesthetics of Entrepreneurship: A Fourth Movements in Entrepreneurship Book*. Cheltenham: Edward Elgar, 183–201.
Wekker, G. and Lutz, H. (2001). Een Hoogvlakte met Koude Winden: De Geschiedenis van het Gender – en Etnitciteitsdenken in Nederland. In M. Botman, N. Jouwe, and G. Wekker (eds.), *Caleidoscopische Visies: De Zwarte Migranten en Vluchtelinginvrouwenbweging in Nederland*. Amsterdam: KIT, 25–50.
Westwood, S. and Bhachu, P. (1987). *Enterprising Women; Ethnicity, Economy, and Gender Relations*. London and New York: Routledge.

CHAPTER 20

PRACTICES OF ORGANIZING AND MANAGING DIVERSITY IN EMERGING COUNTRIES

Comparisons between India, Pakistan, and South Africa

ANITA BOSCH, STELLA M. NKOMO, NASIMA M. H. CARRIM, RANA HAQ, JAWAD SYED, AND FAIZA ALI

Introduction

EMERGING countries are those countries which are increasingly industrializing through economic growth and therefore show promise in becoming high-performing economies in the current century. These countries are challenged by newly formed constitutions, fluctuating political power, and deeply entrenched and varied religious and cultural norms. The power differences between minority and marginalized groups and dominant groups are highly varied and structurally entrenched in societal functioning. This chapter compares India, Pakistan, and South Africa, as examples of such emerging countries in terms of organizational diversity practices in relation to each country's definition/s of diversity and equality, as well as major legislative frameworks that protect the rights of diverse groups. The chapter illustrates how organizations within each country (as opposed to across countries) are responding to macro-level legislative practices highlighting the tensions and inconsistencies in applying legislation and its intent, whilst dealing with country-specific realities such as levels of education, economic growth resulting in job opportunities, gender parity, ethnic, language, and cultural parity, sexual and religious acceptance, and other diversity variables. The chapter is concluded by highlighting differences in diversity management (DM) practices in the three countries.

Emerging Countries

The term 'emerging countries', although widely used, is constantly changing. Emerging countries is a term based on a set of evolving criteria and therefore does not refer to a fixed group of countries. Fleury and Houssay-Holzschuch (2012) explain that there are some commonalities to emerging countries, in that they were all previously known as 'underdeveloped' countries, and have only recently become players in the global economic and political power dynamics as a result of implementing financial, economic, social, and political reforms. While this has radically transformed their standard of living, education, income, wealth, and consumption levels, it has also led to deeper inequalities, as the trickle effect has not reached the rural and poor masses. Emerging countries include the much larger economies with lucrative consumer markets such as Brazil, Russia, India, China, and South Africa (BRICS); and the industrial productivity within geographic regions such as in Taiwan, Hong Kong, North Korea, and Singapore, also known as the 'Asian Dragons', or Malaysia, Thailand, Indonesia, and Philippines, known as the 'Baby Dragons'; as well as smaller economic and political powers such as Chile and Turkey, known as the second circle of emerging countries; countries with hazardous and downwards trajectories such as Argentina and Indonesia, known as the third circle of vulnerable countries; and countries like Thailand, Vietnam, Malaysia, Egypt, and the Maghreb, which are on the verge of emergence (Fleury and Houssay-Holzschuch 2012). Pakistan is classified by Goldman Sachs Investment Bank (2013) as one of the 'Next Eleven' most important emerging markets that are set to become the world's largest economies, together with the BRICS countries.

The Link between India, Pakistan, and South Africa

India, originally called Bharat and also known as 'Hindustan' or the land of the Hindus, has evolved into a multicultural society with several major religions, ethnicities, languages, and cultures during its 5000 years of rich and turbulent history of kingdoms, invaders, and conquerors. Independence from the British Empire in 1947 was a landmark crossroad in the recent history of India, with a violent partition, on the basis of religion, displacing over one million people with the creation of the Islamic Republic of Pakistan, which included East Pakistan and West Pakistan. After the first democratic elections in Pakistan in 1970, the country was divided along political lines; the ensuing war was won by East Pakistan, resulting in the formation of the Peoples' Republic of Bangladesh. Both Bangladesh (89.9 per cent) and Pakistan (96.4 per cent) are Muslim-majority countries (Pew Research Centre 2010). Pakistan was created by the British to appease the Muslims of India, who identified themselves on the basis of their religion, as Muslims first, rather than as Indians. However, there were an equally large number of practising Muslims who identified themselves as Indian-Muslims and chose to remain in India, where they account for 13.4 per cent of the population (Census of India 2001). In actual fact, there are more Muslims in India (176,190,000) than in Pakistan (167,410,000) or Bangladesh (133,540,000) (Pew Research Centre 2010), and all three countries are facing serious challenges based on religious diversity issues.

South Africa is host to the world's oldest and largest Indian diaspora; South African Indians recently celebrated their 150th anniversary. The date of 16 November 1860 marks the arrival of the first indentured Indian labourers to the eastern port of Durban, South Africa, to work on the colonial sugar cane plantations (Saha 2010). Today, there are over one million people of Indian origin who have settled in South Africa (Xavier 2010) and 2.5 per cent of South Africans are of Indian descent (Statistics South Africa 2012). Durban is known as the largest Indian city outside of India, with over 800,000 people of Indian descent. The remainder of this chapter contextualizes and describes practices of organizing and managing diversity in the three countries.

India

Country Definition of Equality and Diversity

In the post-independence secular Republic of India, a 'Hindustani' today refers to an Indian, regardless of the religious affiliation to Hinduism (8.6 per cent), Islam (13.4 per cent), Christianity (2.3 per cent), Sikhism (1.9 per cent), Buddhism (0.8 per cent), Jainism (0.4 per cent), or other religions (0.6 per cent) including Zoroastrianism and Judaism, which are all practised widely in the country (Census of India 2001). Although caste has historically been the basis of discrimination in India, there are also other important diversity dimensions, such as the many religions, 22 recognized languages, 398 spoken languages, and 1652 dialects practised in its 28 unique states and 7 union territories, which are evidence of India's rich multilingual, multi-ethnic, and multicultural diversity (Census of India 2001).

In India, unlike other countries, there is no formal definition of diversity encompassing the wider areas of the term, such as race, ethnicity, religion, age, sexual orientation, and so forth. The primary basis of inequality and discrimination stems from the Hindu religious and social traditions, aimed particularly at 'untouchability', arising from the deep-rooted beliefs of purity and impurity of the castes (Haq 2004; Thorat and Attewell 2007). The constitution of India's (1950) Article 15 prohibits discrimination on the grounds of religion, race, caste, sex, or place of birth, 15(3) allows the state to make special provisions for women and children, and 15(4) allows the state to make special provisions for the advancement of any 'socially and educationally backward classes' (other backward classes, OBC) of citizens, for the 'scheduled castes' (SC), and for the 'scheduled tribes' (ST). Article 16 mandates equality of opportunity in matters of public employment, Article 17 abolishes 'untouchability', and Article 29 protects the interests of minorities. Although the term 'affirmative action' (AA) is not used, part XVI of the constitution outlines special provisions relating to certain classes, such as proportional reservation of seats for the SC and ST in the House of the People and also in the Legislative Assemblies of the States. 'Reservation' is defined in the Indian constitution primarily as quotas for the SC/ST/OBC regarding employment in the public sector, higher education, and legislative institutions. In reality, however, various forms of discrimination against the SC, ST, and OBC, especially women and children, are prevalent today.

Legislative and Current History on Diversity and Equality

SC are the outcastes also known as the *achuts* or untouchables. Despite protection in the constitution, they continue to face discrimination in basic day-to-day life (Haq 2004, 2010, 2012, 2013). ST are the indigenous aboriginal peoples or *adivasis*, who belong to tribal communities that are marginalized in the workplace as a result of their limited access to education and employment opportunities due to systemic barriers and widespread discrimination. The SC and the ST are protected under reservation of 15 per cent for the SC, 7.5 per cent for the ST, and 27 per cent for the OBC, based on proportional representation in the total population. The OBC, however, is a work-in-progress, with many contentious issues plaguing the definition, depth, and width of this broad catchment term, since the constitution allows each state to determine its own OBC levels. The Supreme Court of India has capped the total reservations of public sector jobs and seats in public institutions of higher education at 50 per cent on the recommendations of the Mandal Commission. The outcome of the Mandal Commission is currently being challenged by many states where rates of reservation are already exceeding the target for the different reservation groups based on local populations.

In 1995, the central government adopted the Persons with Disabilities (Equal Opportunities, Protection of Rights and Full Participation) Act reserving 3 per cent of jobs for persons with disabilities in central government employment and higher educational institutions, although implementation of these policies is still quite inconsistent (Haq and Ojha 2010).

There are no constitutional reservation quotas for Indian women in the workplace or in higher education. However, Article 243D(1) of the constitution does reserve one third of the seats for women and one third of the SC/ST seats for SC/ST women in the elected panchayats, the rural self-governance system, and the same for the elected municipalities by Article 243T(2) (India 1950). In 2010, the Women's Reservation Bill was passed, requiring reservation of 33 per cent seats for women in Parliament and state legislative bodies. The bill is expected to result in reserving 181 (of 543) seats for women in the Parliament's lower house, Lok Sabha, and 1370 (of 4109) seats in the 28 State Assemblies (*Times of India* 2010).

The World Bank reports that India's women workforce participation rate is one of the lowest in the world, at 13 per cent, compared with 46 per cent in China and 60 per cent in the developed world. In fact, women's workforce participation in India has historically remained unchanged for more than twenty years, despite economic liberalization and double-digit growth rates. Most of the women workers are in the informal unorganized sector, such as rural unwaged agricultural labour, but even after including them the total rate is under 25 per cent, due to barriers to women's participation in the workforce (Nolen 2012).

Socio-Political Dynamics

Workplace opportunities, benefits, and career success in India are attained by those with a good education, where English was the primary language of instruction. Deshpande (2006) argues that the economic forces of liberalization and globalization have generated numerous jobs in the outsourcing industry, but the SC/ST and OBC have been left out of this lucrative job market because of the basic requirement for fluency in English and computer literacy, which undermines their ability to compete due to lack of access to such education.

Private education, where English is the primary language of instruction, is expensive in India. Since it is not regulated by reservations quotas at the primary and secondary schooling levels, private education has resulted in an economic class advantage at the post-secondary levels for the elite, who are educated in English-medium schools. Free public school education, in Hindi, is mandated by the constitution of India, for every child up to the age of 14 years. The public sector higher education institutions, regulated by the obligation to reserve quotas, make accommodations for the SC, ST, and OBC in their admissions processes by relaxing some of the qualification criteria, such as minimum age and minimum cut-off in percentage marks required for admission in public institutions of higher education, as well as targeted training sessions to help SC/ST/OBC students prepare for entrance exams and interviews (Haq 2014).

Tragically, there has been an increasing number of suicides by SC/ST/OBC students over the past few years, as a result of casteism, discrimination, and harassment on the campuses of public higher education institutions that are bound by the reservations policies (Nolen 2012). A new regulation of the University Grants Commission (UGC) has, for the first time, clearly defined harassment and victimization of SC/ST students for colleges and universities, and made harassment and victimization both punishable acts on and off campus. The Prevention of Caste-based Discrimination/Harassment Victimisation and Promotion of Equality in Higher Educational Institutions-Regulation 1012 defines both overt and covert casteism by professors and students, making it mandatory for all institutions to establish an equal opportunity (EO) office and an anti-discrimination officer authorized to address complaints and obliged to resolve them within a two-month timeframe via the ombudsman of the institution (Chopra 2012).

Organizational Diversity Practices

The reservation-regulated public sector focuses exclusively on compliance quotas for the SC and ST, which were first introduced by the British government in India even before independence, and later entrenched in the constitution. A typical organization's reservation profile would be 15 per cent SC, 7.5 per cent ST, 27 per cent OBC, and 3 per cent physically handicapped (PH).

The private sector in India is not bound by reservations and claims to be 'caste-blind' and only 'merit-based' in its human resource (HR) management processes (Haq 2012). It has resisted the need to collect information on the caste of its employees and implement any voluntary AA reservation policies. But increased lobbying efforts by the designated groups, and governmental pressures, have led to some awareness building and voluntary action in the private sector in efforts to escape the threat of the legislated imposition of reservation quotas (Haq 2012).

Currently, the voluntary diversity management efforts by foreign multinational corporations (MNCs) operating in India with corporate Equal Employment Opportunity (EEO) policies focus primarily on women. Economic reforms in India during the early 1990s led to the entry of MNCs, along with their diversity strategies, based on the Western model and primarily targeting gender equality and disability accommodation programmes. Some Indian private sector companies are including diversity as a part of their corporate social responsibility agenda, and acknowledge that there is also a need for the recognition of other salient diversities in the complex Indian context, such as geographic, linguistic, educational, cultural, class, and religious differences, which share equal importance with gender and disability, to increase the socioeconomic participation of the marginalized (Haq 2010).

Srinivas, Haq, and Ojha (2011) explored HR management practices on equality, diversity, and inclusion (EDI) in the private sector within Indian MNCs and foreign MNC operations in India, in order to understand these organizations' underlying philosophies and their efforts at enhancing diversity within their workforce. They examined these diversity practices in comparison with the Indian government's AA policies, applicable to central government-regulated organizations. They report that the local management of the public sector companies does not play a role in setting the reservation quotas, as recruitment is centralized and follows government policies where the selection criteria states the percentage of seats reserved for the SC/ST/OBC/PH categories and applicants are required to present their reservation identity card.

In the private sector, however, the focus of diversity policies was primarily on women, followed by persons with disabilities. For example, a consumer durables Indian subsidiary of a MNC, headquartered in Europe, reported that its employee population consists of 50 per cent women across the organization, while in some areas of its operations, such as HR, the representation of women was higher. Persons with disabilities constituted 3 per cent of their employee population. Their best practices include an annual global employee survey by which, amongst other indicators, the diversity index is measured. Managers are evaluated on their performance in each area, and their bonuses, rewards, and recognitions are tied to their annual achievements. Gender diversity is an aspect of their global operations which, in India, translates into personal safety restrictions on travelling times for women, and an approved list of cab companies and hotels used. Gender diversity is tracked and measured annually.

An Indian subsidiary of a US MNC in agricultural food products with over 1200 employees in India, also reported that their definition of diversity is limited to women only. The MNC measures the progress it makes on gender diversity, since its products are purchased by women, who are the primary purchasing decision makers for many Indian households. It therefore regards the recognition of women as consumers as a strong business case. The Indian operations of an MNC in financial services, headquartered in the United States, also indicated that they have diversity and inclusion policies for women only. The firm does not actively seek women candidates, but once they are recruited into the organization, they are given support to make them 'less disadvantaged'. The organization reported an overall representation of 31 per cent women, except at the higher levels in the organization, which they attributed to the lower percentage of women in the middle to senior levels, explained in terms of attrition of women soon after child birth. India's statutory maternity leave of three months with full pay is respected by the MNC.

Paternity leave, of five days without pay, is also granted, upon request, by this firm. Men primarily use paternity leave in India to accompany their wife to and from her maternal home before and after the delivery. This MNC defines diversity in the United States as including women, African Americans, Hispanics, and people with disabilities, yet, for their Indian subsidiary, it defines diversity in terms of gender only. In their best practices across the globe, this MNC has an active network for women employees. Each chapter for each region or hub is championed by very senior women leaders. This platform provides women with exposure to senior leaders, networking, and career planning. The firm also requires recruitment agencies to provide equal numbers of resumes of eligible men and women when recruiting staff. Data is tracked and reported to the regional and head office on a quarterly and annual basis, detailing the organizational statistics on the number of women hired, promoted, and leaving the organization.

A global staffing services organization in India, with its parent organization in the United States, must comply with the Equal Employment Opportunity Commission's (EEOC) requirements of including the statement 'equal opportunity employer' in all Indian job advertisements, focusing on gender diversity only. This company further provides staffing services to Indian firms and indicated that diversity is not a priority issue in the Indian private sector.

In conclusion, India has complex historical, religious, social, and economic realities which raise numerous barriers and discriminatory outcomes for the SC, the ST, the OBC, persons with disabilities, and women. Despite these barriers, HR management practices that focus on managing diversity and inclusion in India are quite limited in the private sector, where 90 per cent of India's jobs are located. MNCs are focusing on gender issues, recognizing some of the challenges faced by women in the workplace, and implement their voluntary diversity initiatives under the umbrella of their non-Indian parent organization's diversity and corporate social responsibility policies. Meanwhile, public sector organizations, such as the legislature and publicly funded institutions of higher education, are focused on compliance towards reservation quotas for the SC/ST/OBC and the physically handicapped (Haq 2012).

Pakistan

Country Definition of Equality and Diversity

In Urdu, Pakistan's official language, there is no common equivalent for the word 'diversity'. The Urdu word *tanawwo* (literal meaning: difference, diversity) is heavily Arabo-Persian in its origins and is not understood or used by ordinary Pakistanis. The word 'equality' does have a common equivalent in Urdu, that is, *musawat*, a word which is often used to highlight the Islamic principle of equality between people of different genders, races, classes, and so on. However, such definition of equality (*Musawat*) in practice does not include tabooed areas, for example, sexual orientation, or certain tabooed sects or faiths (e.g. Ahmadis, Hindus, Jews, etc.). Another Urdu word which could be used for diversity is *ikhtilaf* (literal: difference), but the word has a generally negative connotation, as it is related to conflict and disagreement. Ironically, diversity remains an uncommon notion in a country which is itself very diverse in religion, sect, ethnicity, and so forth. The lack of a common word for diversity in the Pakistani vernacular also suggests a general lack of attention to DM in societal and organizational contexts. It is, therefore, no surprise that, except for a few provisions for gender equality and mostly rhetorical commitment to religious and ethnic equality, DM has been historically ignored in legal and organizational practice. A few organizations where gender and diversity policies are found generally refer to the word 'diversity' in the English language rather than using a local language substitute.

Legislative and Current History on Diversity and Equality

Pakistan's constitution (Pakistan 1947) guarantees equality to all people irrespective of their gender, religion, race, or creed. However, at the same time, it declares Islam to be the state religion and clearly prohibits any legislation that contravenes the fundamental teachings of Islam. In some respects, the law is quite discriminatory against non-Muslims, who are barred from being elected as the country's president or prime minister. The Ahmadiyya sect (a nineteenth-century offshoot of Sunni Islam) is, in particular, persecuted. The constitution does not allow Ahmadis to declare themselves as Muslims and they are not allowed to freely practise their interpretation and rituals of Islam.

In terms of gender, the Pakistani law is characterized by ambiguity and ambivalence. There are certain Islamic provisions in the law which suggest women's inferiority or subordination to men. However, there is also some evidence of positive action in favour of women, for example, quotas for women in education, employment, and Parliament. Recently, the government has passed anti-sexual harassment legislation to provide better legal protection to working women. The Protection Against Harassment of Women at Workplace Act 2010 was passed by the Pakistan Parliament in January 2010. There is currently a quota reservation system of a minimum of 5 to 10 per cent for women employees in various government departments.

Previous research shows that a very limited legal framework of EO exists in Pakistan (Mullally 1996; Ali 2000, 2006; Goheer 2003; Syed et al. 2009). The national constitution places a ban on discrimination on the basis of gender (Articles 25 and 27) and provides that 'steps shall be taken to ensure full participation of women in all spheres of national life' (Article 34). In order to adopt a gender-neutral approach, Article 263(a) states that 'words importing the masculine gender shall be taken to include female'. Several constitutional provisions undertake a positive obligation on the part of the state for AA to improve the status of women. For instance, Article 25(3) states, 'Nothing in this article shall prevent the State from making any special provision for the protection of women and children.' Within employment contexts, the constitution (Pakistan 1947) requires the state to take special measures for the protection of women workers. According to Article 37(e), 'The state shall make provision for securing just and humane conditions of work, ensuring that children and women are not employed in vocations unsuited to their age or gender, and for maternity benefits for women in employment.'

While Pakistan has ratified several pro-equality conventions, including the Convention on the Elimination of all Forms of Discrimination against Women (CEDAW), the country does not have any autonomous body to oversee cases of discrimination, including gender, ethnic, and religious discrimination in the workplace and wider society.

Socio-Political Dynamics

Pakistan's estimated population in 2012 was over 190 million, making it the world's sixth most-populous country (CIA 2013). The country is diverse not only in terms of religious diversity (Sunni, Shia, Ahmadi, Christian, Hindu, etc.) but also ethnic diversity (Punjabi, Pashtun, Sindhi, Baloch, Saraiki, Hazara, Gilgiti-Balti, etc.). According to the 1973 constitution, Islam is the state religion of Pakistan. With more than 96 per cent of the population adhering to Islam, Pakistan is the second largest Muslim majority country, after Indonesia, in the world (Pew Research Centre 2010). The religious diversity of the Pakistani population is represented in the following statistics: Sunni Muslims 80–85 per cent, Shia Muslims 10–15 per cent, other (includes Christian, Hindu, etc.) 3.6 per cent (Pew Research Centre 2010). The country has more non-Muslims than there are people in either Toronto or Miami.

In terms of ethnicity, there are numerous ethnic groups in Pakistan. These groups not only vary in their local culture and customs but also speak different languages.

The population distribution in terms of ethnic/linguistic diversity is as follows: Punjabi 48 per cent, Sindhi 12 per cent, Saraiki (a Punjabi variant) 10 per cent, Pashtu 8 per cent, Urdu (official) 8 per cent, Balochi 3 per cent, Hindko 2 per cent, Brahui 1 per cent, English (official; lingua franca of Pakistani elite and most government ministries), Burushaski, and other 8 per cent (CIA 2013). The number of Punjabi speakers in Pakistan is greater than the entire population of France; Pushto speakers in Pakistan are greater in number than the population of the whole of Saudi Arabia; Sindhi speakers exceed the population of Australia; Saraiki speakers exceed the population of the Netherlands; Urdu speakers (also known as Muhajris) exceed the population of Cuba; and Balochi speakers are more numerous than the entire population of Singapore.

The case of ethnic and religious diversity in Pakistan is unique because the majority of one ethnicity or Muslim sect in one province may become a minority in another province or area. For example, while Punjabi-speaking people are in majority in the Punjab province, in the rest of the country they constitute a minority. Similarly, while Shia Muslims are a numerical majority in the Gilgit Baltistan province, they remain a minority in almost all other parts of the country. This creates a lot of complexities when it comes to defining, understanding, and implementing EO in the workplace and broader society. For example, a Punjabi-speaking person working in an organization in Balochistan will constitute an ethnic minority in that province, whereas a Baloch working in an organization in Punjab will be considered an ethnic minority in that province. Similarly, a Shia Muslim will usually constitute a Muslim minority employee in organizations in most parts of the country except in Gilgit Baltistan, Parachinar, and certain other parts of Pakistan where Shia Muslims constitute the majority of the local population.

With such a diverse population, there is a dire need for transparent and context-appropriate diversity policies. However, this does not seem to be occurring, as a study on the legislative framework of EEO in Pakistan suggests that the laws and policies of EEO are weakly implemented and lack appropriate administrative bodies (Ali and Knox 2008).

Organizational Diversity Practices

In addition to the socio-political dynamics in Pakistan, adverse stereotypes and prejudices also infiltrate the workplace, causing discrimination and disparities. There is also a lack of implementation of legal and constitutional guarantees of equality in the workplace. For example, it is a legal obligation for employers to provide childcare support facilities in organizations where a specified number of workers are employed (ILO 2004). Enforcement of such requirements, however, is notoriously and openly lax. As a result, many women with small children, particularly those without appropriate family support, cannot continue their employment because there is no one to take care of their children. This lack of legal implementation is particularly problematic in a society where stepping out of the four walls of the home and entering the male order of work may reduce a woman to an object of ridicule (Syed 2008).

Organizations in Pakistan generally pay lip service to EEO and DM (Ali and Knox 2008). In practice, when it comes to equality issues, gender seems to be the focus of attention, while other diversity-related issues such as ethnicity, religion/sect, sexual orientation, disability, and so on, remain ignored. The focus on gender becomes evident through the legislative framework providing for maternity leave, protection of women's rights at work, and the recently introduced sexual harassment law; however, there are no explicit laws protecting the rights of ethnic and religious minorities, disabled persons, or LGBT groups.

In the public sector, there is some evidence of attention to gender equality in the workplace and AA in favour of women. For example, the Small and Medium Enterprises Development Authority (SMEDA), a semi-government organization, includes EEO laws such as maternity benefits and equal remuneration in their staff policies. Due to the fact that Pakistan has ratified the CEDAW convention, all government departments are presumably implementing government directives and laws on gender equality. According to the Pakistan's CEDAW report (2005):

> All public sector agencies have established practices, procedures, and recruitment rules with regard to employment including that of women. Recruitment rules specify the nature of the job, role and responsibility of the position, nomenclature of the post, qualification and experience required, and age according to the job requirements. These do not discriminate on the basis of gender. (p. 69)

Public sector organizations, as well as certain MNCs, are making efforts to implement equality policies in the workplace; however, the focus mainly remains on gender inequality. Issues of ethnic or religious discrimination, are routinely ignored, suppressed, or understated.

MNCs in Pakistan are known to have formal EEO policies, generally under the influence of their head office policies or home country's national laws. For example, Nestlé Pakistan labels itself as a family- and women-friendly organization. The organization has 'set up a day-care centre, and have established a "comprehensive maternity benefits scheme"' for its female employees. According to its 2010 Annual Report, the company believes in the importance of having a dedicated and motivated team to meet the modern challenges. Nestlé is committed to the policy of EO employment (Nestlé Pakistan 2010). Further, the organization has also introduced 'fair remuneration structures' (benchmarking Nestlé employees' pay against other competitive organizations). Another example from MNCs is Citibank Pakistan. The organization celebrated International Women's Day and extended the celebrations over the month of March, to create awareness regarding women's rights at the workplace. Citibank Pakistan has a 'more than favourable female employment rate of 30 per cent versus two per cent nationally within the corporate workforce, with strong female representation on our management committee, and our employee-focused policy framework' (Citibank 2008). Citibank Pakistan has initiated a number of women-friendly programmes, such as maternity, flexible work, and employee assistance schemes. The percentage of women working in Citibank Pakistan is among the highest in the industry (Aurora Ventures 2007).

Diversity and EO is a low priority area in the private sector, where formal commitment to EEO policies is found in large organizations only. In the manufacturing sector (the single major employer of women employees in the private sector), large organizations usually have formal EEO policies. For example, Nishat Chunian Group, a large industry conglomerate, claims to be an EO employer where careers depend on competence, dedication, and leadership potential. The company offers benefits such as flexible office hours, annual and medical leave, maternity leave, and a daycare centre facility for women employees (Nishat 2012). Similarly, Kohinoor Maple Leaf Group (KMLG), a producer of textile and cement, claims to be an EO employer with policies to ensure there is no discrimination on the basis of cast, creed, sex, and religion (KMLG 2008).

A recent study on gender equality in Pakistani organizations highlights how societal, organizational, and individual level factors have a joint effect on EO (or lack thereof) that are available to women employees (Ali 2013). The study, which focused on EO-related issues and challenges facing highly qualified women employees in Pakistani organizations, revealed that the issues and challenges facing women employees can be categorized into three different levels, that is, macro-societal-, meso-organizational-, and micro-individual-level issues. At the macro-societal level, the study highlighted socio-cultural (modesty and inhibition), legal and other structural factors (transport and childcare issues). At the meso-organizational level, workplace-related issues and challenges (such as sexual harassment, income parity, and the glass ceiling effect) and issues of gender stereotyping were outlined. At the micro-individual level, issues related to identity and agency were highlighted. Overall, Ali's (2013) study suggests that focusing exclusively on organizations and holding them solely accountable for the implementation of EO may be inadequate.

Another recent study provides a brief comparison of workforce diversity in public and private sectors in Pakistan (Afzal et al. 2013). The study, conducted in the banking, health, and medical services sectors, reveals that substantial differences exist between employees working in public and private sector organizations due to variances in the conception and application of workforce diversity. The findings of the study show that the middle and operational levels of the workforce are more diverse than the top levels. In general, there is evidence of somewhat better attention to DM in private organizations, while public sector organizations are still lagging behind. Though there are still many hurdles to overcome, the concept of DM is gaining more importance in Pakistani organizations because of diversity's potential benefits for organizational performance (Afzal et al. 2013). DM in Pakistan is still in its infancy, which provides opportunities to both public and private sector employers with regard to the development of context-specific practices and policies.

South Africa

Country Definition of Equality, Diversity, and Legislative History

Defining diversity in South Africa must begin with an understanding of how the African National Congress, which took power in 1994 after decades of institutionalized oppression of the majority of the population, conceptualized the transformation of the country. In its historic Freedom Charter, the African National Congress set forth the principle that 'all national groups shall have equal rights' (African National Congress 1955). The principle of equality was also embedded in preamble of the constitution adopted on 8 May 1996: 'We, the people of South Africa, recognise the injustices of the past; honour those who have worked for justice and freedom in our land; respect those who have worked to build and develop our country, *and believe that South Africa belongs to all who live in it, united in our diversity . . .*' (South Africa 1996; emphasis added). Further, emphasis was placed on the attainment of substantive equality, which requires the removal of structural inequality in all areas of society (Hepple 2009; Maré 2011). Diversity and equality is defined quite broadly in the constitution in chapter 2 section 9, and encompasses 'race, gender, sex, pregnancy, marital status, ethnic or social origin, colour, sexual orientation, age, disability, religion, conscience, belief, culture, language, and birth'. The constitution has been heralded as one of the most progressive in the world (Philip 2012). However, the content of the preamble and subsequent clauses point to one of the major tensions the country has experienced in its transformation since 1994. Balancing the vision of a country united in its diversity but one that also redresses the injustices of the past remains a stubborn challenge at the both societal level and in the workplace (Habib and Bentley 2008; Erasmus 2009).

Subsequent legislation relevant to the workplace reflects the tension between attaining substantive equality for what is referred to as *the previously disadvantaged* and women, without compromising the core principle of a nation where all social groups have equal rights (Hepple 2009). The Employment Equity Act (South Africa 1998a) prohibits discrimination against the categories of diversity specified in the constitution, but also requires AA for designated previously disadvantaged groups: black people (Africans, Indians, and Coloureds), women, and those with disabilities. The latter dimension of the Act has a more narrow definition of diversity than the broad categories contained in the constitution. However, the Promotion of Equality and Prevention of Unfair Discrimination Act (South Africa 2000, 2002), together with other human rights acts (South Africa 2006), were promulgated to strengthen the commitments made in the Bill of Rights of the constitution, and also make explicit reference to family responsibility and status as well as HIV/AIDS.

The Broad Based Black Economic Empowerment Act (South Africa 2003a) further underscores the importance of redress in the government's conception of how equality is to be achieved for black people (Africans, Indians, and Coloureds). The law requires enterprises to establish equity ownership specifically for black people, to accelerate economic equality in the country. Other than the Broad Based Black Economic Empowerment Act, the categories of diversity that organizations in South Africa focus on are the groups designated in the Employment Equity Act (as stated). For instance, gays and lesbians in South Africa do not feature heavily in diversity initiatives, as is the case in many organizations in Western countries where they are included.

Since the passage of the Employment Equity Act, a number of other laws and mandates have been promulgated to achieve equity (see Booysen and Nkomo 2010 for an overview). The Skills Development Act and its amendments (South Africa 1998b, 1999, 2003b, 2008, 2011) require companies to allocate funds to the training and development of the South African labour force, particularly for upskilling the previously disadvantaged. Further, sector or industry charters have been put in place to increase black ownership of businesses and accelerate black representation in management. Dissatisfaction with the progress of women in leadership roles in the private sector in particular has resulted in the Women Empowerment and Gender Equality Draft Bill (South Africa 2012b; Booysen and Nkomo 2014).The goal of the bill is to give real effect to the letter and spirit of the Bill of Rights of the Constitution, to ensure women fully participate in all domains of society. In sum, the definition of diversity in South Africa focuses on what has been referred to in diversity literature as primary (or surface-level) rather than secondary (or deep-level) dimensions (Harrison, Price, and Bell 1998). While current Western-based definitions of diversity stress attention should be paid to both dimensions, the focus on primary dimensions in South Africa is consistent with the need to undo the deep racial and gender inequalities that were entrenched in society and in organizations during apartheid.

Socio-Political Dynamics

Although South Africa has a progressive constitution and labour laws to eradicate all forms of discrimination within organizations, implementing such laws in organizations and within the larger society has been dominated by resistance, non-compliance, and the privileging of racial discrimination over other forms of diversity and exclusion. South African organizations remain deeply racialized and unequal in terms of job opportunities and salaries (Booysen 2007; Seekings 2008; Commission for Employment Equity 2013). Unlike the overt racism of apartheid, racism today is more subtle, but is manifested in business structures and systems (Moloko 2008; Nkomo 2011). In relation to the economically active population, black Africans and Coloureds are the most underrepresented racial groups at senior management levels in South African organizations, with 12.3 per cent and 4.6 per cent management representation respectively during 2012, while whites, whose numbers have declined by 8.9 per cent since 2002, continue to dominate senior and top managerial positions (72.6 per cent), followed by Indians (7.3 per cent) (Commission for Employment Equity 2013). This perceived slow pace of racial transformation among the management cadre has led to a political climate of impatience regarding workplace and societal transformation.

Confusion also exists regarding the status of white women and disabled whites in terms of the Employment Equity and the Broad Based Black Economic Empowerment Acts (Hermann 2012; Booysen and Nkomo 2014). While white women and disabled whites are regarded as previously disadvantaged in terms of the Employment Equity Act, both these groups are excluded under the stipulations of the Broad Based Black Economic Empowerment Act, and, as such, organizations do not earn any points on their Broad Based Black Economic Empowerment scorecards by including white women and disabled whites as part of their workforce (Khuzwayo and Nkabinde 2011; Hermann 2012). White disabled people are therefore excluded from the Broad Based Black Economic Empowerment Act due to their race and not their disability, yet special provisions are made for disabled black Africans (Khuzwayo and Nkabinde 2011; Hermann 2012). Diversity categories are therefore not treated equally, and some are regarded as more important in legislated diversity redress than others.

Since the 1994 democratic elections, there has been a marked increase in the number of foreigners working in corporate South Africa. The 2013 Commission for Employment Equity statistics revealed the following trends for foreign workers employed in corporate South Africa from 2002 to 2012: the number of top and senior management positions for this period increased from 0 per cent to 3.1 per cent (mid period) and 2.5 per cent (end of period), while the percentage of professional and skilled foreign employees increased from 0 per cent to 2.4 per cent (mid period) and 1.5 per cent (end of period) (Commission for Employment Equity 2013). These figures suggest that there is an increase in predominantly foreign black workers in South African organizations which, it is feared, is driven by organizations' need to meet employment equity targets. On 19 October 2012, the first amendment to the Employment Equity Act, namely the Employment Equity Amendment Bill (2012a), was promulgated, which resulted in an adjustment to the term 'designated group'. According to this bill, foreign employees, who became South African citizens after April 1994, are not regarded as previously disadvantaged and they are therefore not recognized in the attainment of employment equity targets.

While some strides have been made to address racial inequalities in the workplace, other forms of discrimination have become largely invisible. One example is South Africa's laws in terms of sexual orientation. South Africa was one of the first countries that prohibited discrimination based on sexual orientation in May 1996 (Belkin and Canaday 2010) and the first country in Africa and the fifth in the world to legalize same-sex marriages (Booysen and Nkomo 2014) through the Civil Union Act (South Africa 2006). However, this constitutional advancement of minority rights was challenged in 2012 by the Congress of Traditional Leaders of South Africa (CONTRALESA), a non-governmental group aiming to preserve black African culture, heritage, and traditions. CONTRALESA demanded that LGBT, and queer rights be removed from the South African constitution. Their proposal was rejected by Parliament, who supported gay rights and marriages (Rousseau 2012). However, the majority of South African workplaces have yet to acknowledge same-sex couples in their benefit policies, resulting in delays in obtaining benefits such as medical and life insurance as well as pensions. Since same-sex couples have to highlight the fact that they are omitted from organizational policy and bring the omission to the attention of managers, the 'coming out' process is expedited, as individuals have to disclose their sexual orientation and face pressure from colleagues and supervisors for which they may not be prepared (Belkin and Canaday 2010).

The use of language has been another muted aspect of diversity in the South African workplace. The 2011 Census reveals that Afrikaans and English are the first languages of approximately 6 million and 4 million of the population respectively, with Afrikaans being the third most used home language in the country (Statistics South Africa 2012). Out of a population of 45 million, the home language of the majority of South Africans is a black African language, with Zulu and Xhosa being the first and second most used home languages in the country (Statistics South Africa 2012). Yet, within South African organizations, the use of English and Afrikaans predominate. A great number of lower-level black African employees have minimal command of these languages, although English is taught in schools as a primary language of communication (Webb 1999). The dominance of English and Afrikaans in workplaces has led to the marginalization of black African languages and has become a barrier for the majority of South Africans in attaining economic prosperity, as only a select few have command of the languages, resulting in their increased access to economic participation and occupational mobility (Webb 2002; Casale and Posel 2011). Until 1994, South African workplaces were dominated by white Afrikaans and English speakers, and therefore very few managers speak a black African language. In addition, perceptions of an employee's proficiency in English and Afrikaans affects appointments and promotions (Grant 2007). Language has therefore become a means of prejudice, although Section 9(3) of the constitution prohibits such discrimination.

Organizational Diversity Practices

DM in South African organizations, when compared to that in other countries globally, has an additional layer of complexity. South Africa is dealing with the relics of legislated discrimination where the racial majority was legally, economically, and culturally disempowered. Organizations are therefore seen as catalysts in giving effect to the moral imperative of broadening participation of this racial majority into positions of leadership and economic power. DM in the South African context therefore differs from the other countries in this chapter in that the majority was previously marginalized; whereas, in India and Pakistan, organizations are attempting to address minority constituents' participation through DM (Booysen et al. 2007). Though the moral imperative should strongly influence organizational strategy and practice, most South African organizations apply mechanistic approaches (Cilliers and May 2002), attempting to meet compliance targets instead of effecting *complex, deep culture change* through *diversity literacy* (Booysen et al. 2007: 13). Since the ethnic imperative is foremost in the mind of the marginalized majority and lawmakers, DM in organizations has been reduced to a racial numbers game (Booysen et al. 2007; Steyn and Kelly 2009), to the detriment of most of the other diversity categories stipulated in the constitution. Some, often smaller, organizations do not place emphasis on DM at all, which leads to dissatisfaction and increased staff turnover (Dombai 1999).

As part of their DM efforts, many South African organizations utilize diversity training into which issues of difference, discrimination, and stereotyping are incorporated. Larger organizations have women's initiatives in an attempt to attract and retain increased numbers of women employees. Due to the legislative imperatives that could result in large fines imposed on organizations that do not comply, diversity training usually includes elucidation of the stipulations of the Employment Equity Act, the Broad Based Black Economic Empowerment Act, and organizational policies that support the implementation of the requirements of the acts. Most South African diversity interventions are based on theories and models derived from international literature, specifically from North America and Europe, with very few derived locally or from other emerging countries. Measuring the impact of diversity training is high on the list of priorities of some companies (Cavaleros, Van Vuuren, and Visser 2002; Fouche, De Jager, and Crafford 2004), in an attempt to verify the hoped-for impact of diversity training. However, organizations soon realize that diversity training is not sufficient as a stand-alone intervention, but should be part of a larger diversity change process (Cavaleros, Van Vuuren, and Visser 2002). A further strategy is the development of diversity competencies for managers, in order to effect implementation of diversity practices that will render positive long-term results. These may include competencies such as tolerance of ambiguity and affiliative leadership styles (Goleman, Boyatzis, and McKee 2002), which correlate highly with treating others with dignity (Visagie, Linde, and Havenga 2011), a key focus of diversity initiatives.

South African organizations invest considerable time and capital in studies on management's and employee's perceptions and experiences regarding DM, in an attempt to gauge how and where organizations could improve these interventions (Cavaleros, Van Vuuren, and Visser 2002; Erasmus 2007). Studies reporting on their perceptions have shown that managers perceive diversity interventions more positively than employees do (Erasmus 2007). Steyn and Kelly (2009) report that racism and white resistance against transformation are prevalent in organizations, and that the biggest resistance to diversity initiatives is found in middle management. Middle managers are those who are tasked with compliance with all the relevant diversity acts. They often have to perform a balancing act between attaining diversity and the demands of performance targets, which is further exacerbated by realities such as skills shortages and lack of experience in managing multicultural teams, poor adjustment behaviour, as well as their own bias and prejudice.

Workforce diversity has resulted in the compilation of DM policies for organizations and institutions. These policies address office and institutional topics such as language mediums, sexual harassment (Gouws 2012), employee benefits, promotion, and staffing. In this regard, childcare is treated from a perspective of cost effectiveness, and not as a vital issue of structural support for diversity. Therefore, if provided, it is usually outsourced. Gouws (2012: 531) eloquently captures this misinformed notion by stating: 'Childcare is seen as a concession for women and not a necessity for working families.'

In a summary of South African organizational DM case studies, Steyn and Kelly (2009) draw attention to difficulties in managing diversity that were evident throughout all the case organizations, namely an inattention to contextual realities, such as the racialized composition of organizations during apartheid and the realities in dealing with complex transformation dynamics where senior management remains predominantly white (Commission for Employment Equity 2013). The neglect of categories other than race in aiming to achieve diversity, coupled with the poor quality of diversity interventions, which are often conducted in a haphazard manner, contributes to the prevailing climate of fear and suspicion, characterized by high levels of anxiety (Pretorius, Cilliers, and May 2012), which entrenches past behaviour.

DM in South African organizations is influenced by the contextual and historical uniqueness of the country. Sadly, efforts in this regard evidence a lack of prioritization of diversity efforts, and are further undermined by an absence of management systems that measure progress on key diversity deliverables. The country's vast array of people underscores the need for dynamic and appropriate DM, instead of the current, rather myopic, goal of meeting compliance demands purely for the sake of meeting those demands.

Comparison of the Countries

As postcolonial societies and emerging economies, India, Pakistan, and South Africa are all struggling with their uniquely nuanced sources of diversity and searching for creative strategies towards achieving the EDI of all citizens in an increasingly globalized economy, workplace, and society. Their perspectives on managing diversity have potentially rich contributions to research and debates on EDI.

On a national level, the equality challenges in India have parallels in Pakistan and South Africa in terms of religion and regional majority/minority conflicts as a result of high numbers of in-migration from other states, in the case of India and Pakistan, and of Africans from other African countries into South Africa. Although these three countries have their equality policies included in their constitution, India and Pakistan do not have an explicit act, similar to the Employment Equity Act in South Africa, which focuses on diversity redress in addition to the protection of workers from discrimination. The three countries also do not deal with immigrant integration in their definition of diversity, despite serious issues of discrimination against interstate labour migration and integration. South Africa has seen an increase in xenophobia (Integrated Regional Information News 2012; Agence France-Presse 2013) yet organizations are employing black African migrants, often to manipulate their AA figures (Commission for Employment Equity 2013), since the skills of African foreign nationals are often perceived as superior to those of their South African counterparts. Pakistan, furthermore, does not have a clear definition of diversity and, as such, the protection of minority rights is not adequately supported through legislation. In contrast to both India and Pakistan, South Africa is addressing the repair of *majority* rights that were previously suppressed to the benefit of a minority.

Within organizations, the three countries show an overall lack of focus on wider diversity categories such as the rights of the LGBT groups, religious minorities, language groups, or different cultures. Indian companies show a predominant focus on castes and the 'reservation' system. South African organizations primarily focus on race. The most important diversity category that Pakistani workplaces concern themselves with is women. The societal culture of Pakistan, which encourages social modesty and inhibition of women, might therefore be the biggest inhibitor of increased participation of women in all levels of organizations when considering diversity initiatives. Women in the workplace are the second biggest category of diversity for both India and South Africa. Throughout organizations in the three countries, DM initiatives seem to be taken seriously when a business case is made. Business cases relate to the importance of aspects such as reflecting customer profiles in employee composition, targeting specific market segments, or understanding the needs of diverse constituents. Slow progress is made in embracing diversity, and each country understands and practises DM differently, depending on its history and socioeconomic imperatives. Ultimately, organizations, not governments, become a catalyst for change and could have great impact on the advancement of the rights of diverse groups if organizational leaders are able to convince themselves of the benefits of DM.

References

African National Congress (1955). African National Congress Freedom Charter. <http://www.anc.org.za/docs.php?t=Freedom%20Charter>, accessed 8 May 2013.

Afzal, F., Mahmood, K., Samreen, F., Asim, M., and Sajid, M. (2013). Comparison of workforce diversity in public and private business organisations. *European Journal of Business and Management*, 5(3): 109–13.

Agence France-Presse (September 2013). 150 Somali owned shops looted in South African rampage. *Capital News*, <http://www.capitalfm.co.ke/news/2013/09/150-somali-owned-shops-looted-south-african-rampage>, accessed 8 October 2013.

Ali, F. (2013). A multi-level perspective on equal employment opportunity for women in Pakistan. *Equality, Diversity and Inclusion: An International Journal*, 28(3): 289–309.

Ali, F. and Knox, A. (2008). Pakistan's commitment to equal employment opportunity for women: a toothless tiger? *International Journal of Employment Studies*, 16(1): 39–68.

Ali, S. S. (2000). *Gender and Human Rights in Islam and International Law: Equal before Allah, Unequal before Man*. The Hague: Kluwer Law International.

Ali, S. S. (2006). Conceptualising Islamic law, CEDAW and women's human rights in plural legal settings: a comparative analysis of application of CEDAW in Bangladesh, India and

Pakistan. In S. S. Ali (ed.), <http://www.unwomensouthasia.org/assets/complete-study.pdf>. Delhi: UNIFEM Regional Office.

Aurora Ventures (2007). Where women want to work, 2007. *Where Women Work*. <http://www.wherewomenwanttowork.com/top50/top50_2007.asp>, accessed 14 April 2013.

Belkin, A. and Canaday, M. (2010). Assessing the integration of gays and lesbians into the South African national defence force. *Scientia Militaria*, 38(2): 1–21.

Booysen, L. (2007). Barriers to employment equity implementation and retention of blacks in management in South Africa. *South African Journal of Labour Relations*, 31(1): 47–71.

Booysen, L. and Nkomo, S. M. (2010). Employment equity and diversity management in South Africa. In A. Klarsfeld (ed.), *International Handbook on Diversity Management at Work: Country Perspectives on Diversity and Equal Treatment*. Cheltenham: Edward Elgar, 118–43.

Booysen, L. and Nkomo, S. M. (2014). New developments in employment equity and diversity management in South Africa. In A. Klarsfeld, L. A. E. Booysen, E. Ng,, I. Roper, and A. Tatli (eds.), *International Handbook on Diversity Management at Work: Country Perspectives on Diversity and Equal Treatment*, 2nd edn. Cheltenham: Edward Elgar, 241–65.

Booysen, L., Kelly, C., Nkomo, S., and Steyn, M. (2007). Rethinking the diversity paradigm: South African practices. *The International Journal of Diversity in Organisations, Communities and Nations*, 7(4): 1–10.

Casale, D. and Posel, D. (2011). English language proficiency and earnings in a developing country: the case of South Africa. *Journal of Socio-Economics*, 40(4): 385–93.

Cavaleros, C., Van Vuuren, L. J., and Visser, D. (2002). The effectiveness of a diversity awareness training programme. *South African Journal of Industrial Psychology*, 28(3): 50–61.

CEDAW (Convention on the Elimination of all Forms of Discrimination against Women) (2005). Combined initial, second and third periodic reports of states parties: Pakistan. *Committee on the Elimination of all Forms of Discrimination against Women*. <http://daccess-dds-ny.un.org/doc/UNDOC/GEN/N05/454/37/PDF/N0545437.pdf?OpenElement>, accessed 15 April 2013.

Census of India (2001). Ministry of Home Affairs, Government of India. New Delhi. <http://censusindia.gov.in/>, accessed 26 April 2013.

Chopra, R. (2012). UGC bars caste bias in campus. *Mail Today*, New Delhi, 4 June, 12.

CIA (Central Intelligence Agency) (2013). The world fact book: Pakistan. *Central Intelligence Agency of the USA*. <https://www.cia.gov/library/publications/resources/the-world-factbook/index.html>, accessed 13 April 2013.

Cilliers, F. and May, M. (2002). South African diversity dynamics: reporting on the 2000 Robben Island diversity experience. A group relations event. *South African Journal of Labour Relations*, 26(3): 42–68.

Citibank Pakistan (2008). Citi Pakistan celebrates international women's month. Citibank website. <http://www.citi.com/pakistan/consumer/aboutus/press/current/18march08.htm>, accessed 13 April 2013.

Commission for Employment Equity (2013). *Commission for Employment Equity Annual Report 2012–2013*. No 97/2013, South African Department of Labour.

Constitution of India (1950). See India (1950).

Constitution of South Africa (1996). See South Africa (1996).

Constitution of Pakistan (1947). See Pakistan (1947).

Deshpande, S. (2006). Exclusive inequalities: merit, caste and discrimination in Indian higher education today. *Economic and Political Weekly*, 41: 2438–44.

Dombai, C. (1999). The influence of organisational culture as a context of meaning on dversity management in multicultural organisations. Unpublished dissertation, Rand Afrikaans University.

Erasmus, L. J. (2007). The management of workforce diversity and the implications for leadership at financial asset services. Masters dissertation, University of Johannesburg, Johannesburg, South Africa.

Erasmus, P. (2009). The unbearable burden of diversity. *Acta Academia*, 41(4): 40–55.

Fleury, A. and Houssay-Holzschuch, M. (2012). For a social geography of emerging countries. *EchoGéo*. <http://echogeo.revues.org/13287>, accessed 20 April 2013.

Fouche, C., De Jager, C., and Crafford, A. (2004). The evaluation of a diversity program. *SA Journal of Human Resource Management*, 2(2): 37–44.

Goheer, N. (2003). *Women Entrepreneurs in Pakistan: How to Improve their Bargaining Power*. Geneva: International Labour Office. <http://www.ilo.org/public/libdoc/ilo/2003/103B09_60_engl.pdf>, accessed 19 November 2013

Goldman Sachs Investment Bank (2013). It's time to redefine emerging markets. Goldman Sachs Asset Management. <http://www.ivci.com.tr/Uploads/GoldmanSachsTurkeyBRIC.pdf>, accessed 19 November 2013.

Goleman, D., Boyatzis, R., and McKee, A. (2002). *Primal Leadership: Unleashing the Power of Emotional Intelligence*. Boston, MA: Harvard Business School Press.

Gouws, A. (2012). Reflections on being a feminist academic/academic feminism in South Africa. *Equality, Diversity and Inclusion: An International Journal*, 31(5/6): 526–41.

Grant, T. (2007). Transformational challenges in the South African workplace: a conversation with Melissa Steyn of Incudisa. *Business Communication Quarterly*, 70(1): 93–8.

Habib, A. and Bentley, K. (2008). *Racial Redress and Citizenship in South Africa*. Pretoria: HRSC Press.

Haq, R. (2004). International perspectives on managing diversity. In P. Stockdale and F. Crosby (eds.), *The Psychology and Management of Workplace Diversity*. New York: Blackwell, 277–98.

Haq, R. (2010). Caste based quotas: India's reservations policy. In M. Özbilgin and J. Syed (eds.), *Diversity Management in Asia: A Research Companion*. Cheltenham: Edward Elgar, 166–91.

Haq, R. (2012). The managing diversity mindset in public versus private organisations in India. *International Journal of Human Resource Management*, 23(5): 892–914.

Haq, R. (2013). Intersectionality of gender and other forms of identity: dilemmas and challenges facing women in India. *Gender in Organisations*, 28(3): 171–84.

Haq, R. (2014). Managing diversity in India: comparing public versus private sector approaches to managing diversity in Indian organisations. In A. Klarsfeld (ed.), *Equality, Diversity and Inclusion*. Cheltenham: Edward Elgar.

Haq, R. and Ojha, A. (2010). Reservations in India. In A. Klarsfeld (ed.), *International Handbook on Diversity Management at Work: Country Perspectives on Diversity and Equal Treatment*. Cheltenham: Edward Elgar Publishing, 139–59.

Harrison, D. A., Price, K. H., and Bell, M. P. (1998). Beyond relational demography: time and the effects of surface and deep-level diversity on work group cohesion. *Academy of Management Journal*, 41(1): 96–107.

Hepple, B. (2009). The aims and limits of equality laws. In O. Dupper and C. Garbers. *Equality in the Workplace: Reflections from South Africa and Beyond*. Cape Town: Juta, 3–13.

Hermann, D. (2012). Disabled whites to be excluded from BBBEE. *Politics Web*. <http://www.politicsweb.co.za/politicsweb/view/politicsweb/en/page71654?oid=279003andsn=Detailandpid=71654>, accessed 26 April 2013.

ILO (International Labour Organisation) (2004). National labour law profile: Islamic republic of Pakistan. *ILO* [specialised labour agency of the United Nations], <http://www.ilo.org/ifpdial/information-resources/national-labour-law-profiles/WCMS_158916/lang--en/index.htm>, accessed 20 April 2013.

India (1950). Constitution of India. <http://indiacode.nic.in/coiweb/welcome.html>, accessed 15 October 2013.

India (1995). Persons with Disabilities (Equal Opportunities, Protection of Rights and Full Participation) Act, 1. <http://socialjustice.nic.in/pwdact1995.php>, accessed 26 April 2013.

Integrated Regional Information News (19 October 2012). South Africa: foreigners still at risk. *IRIN*. <http://www.irinnews.org/report/96589/south-africa-foreigners-still-at-risk>, accessed 26 April 2013.

Khuzwayo, W. and Nkabinde, S. (2011). BEE Act never included white women, says DTI. *IOL Independent Newspapers*. <http://www.iol.co.za/business/news/bee-act-never-included-white-women-says-dti-1.1203584#.UovEOUEaKpo>, accessed 24 April 2013.

KMLG (Kohinoor Maple Leaf Group Pakistan) (2008). Human resources: KMLG cares. KMLG website. <http://www.kmlg.com/kmlg/hrpolicy.php>, accessed 13 April 2013.

Maré, G. (2011). Broken down by race . . . questioning social categories in redress policies. *Transformation*, 77: 62–79.

Moloko, S. M. (2008). Grappling with South Africa's employment equity challenges. Anglogold. <http://www.anglogold.co.za/subwebs/informationforinvestors/reports08/employment-equity.htm>, accessed 24 April 2013.

Mullally, S. (1996). Women, law and employment in Pakistan: from 'protection' to 'equal treatment'? *International Journal of Discrimination and the Law*, 1: 207–32.

Nestlé Pakistan (2010). 'Annual Report 2010'. Nestlé. <http://www.nestle.pk/asset-library/Documents/Financial_Reports/Nestle_Annual_Report_2010_EN.pdf>, accessed 10 April 2013.

Nishat (2012). Nishat Chunian Group: work environment. Nishat website. <http://www.nishat.net/ncg/work-environment-71>, accessed 10 April 2013.

Nkomo, S. M. (2011). The challenge of moving from the letter of the law to the spirit of the law: the challenges of realising the intent of employment equity and affirmative action. *Transformation: Critical Perspectives on Southern Africa*, 77: 132–46.

Nolen, S. (2012). Dying to get ahead. *The Globe and Mail*. Globe Focus. 7 July, F4–F5.

Pakistan (1947). Constitution of Pakistan. <http://www.pakistani.org/pakistan/constitution>, accessed 29 September 2013.

Pakistan (2010). Protection against Harassment of Women at Workplace Act, 4. Government Gazette No F. 9(5)/2009-Legis. <http://www.qau.edu.pk/pdfs/ha.pdf>, accessed 26 April 2013.

Pew Research Centre (2010). The future of the global Muslim population. *Pew Research Religion and Public Life Project*. <http://features.pewforum.org/muslim-population/>, accessed 10 April 2013.

Philip, R. (2012). In love with SA's constitution. *Mail & Guardian*. <http://mg.co.za/article/2012-02-24-in-love-with-sas-constitution>, accessed 27 November 2013.

Pretorius, M., Cilliers, F., and May, M. (2012). The Robben Island diversity experience: an exploration of South African diversity dynamics. *South African Journal of Industrial Psychology*, 38(2): Art. #996.

Rousseau, Y. J. (2012). South Africa: homophobia trending among traditional leaders. *Daily Maverick*. <http://www.dailymaverick.co.za/opinionista/2012-05-09-homophobia-trending-among-traditional-leaders/#.UovIWUEaKpp>, accessed 6 June 2013.

Saha (2010). Indians to celebrate 150 years in South Africa. *South African History Archive.* <http://www.saha.org.za/news/2010/November/the_south_african_indian_community_celebrating_150_years.htm>, accessed 20 November 2013.

Seekings, J. (2008). The continuing salience of race: discrimination and diversity in South Africa. *Journal of Contemporary African Studies,* 26(1): 1–25.

South Africa (1996). Constitution of the Republic of South Africa, 108. *Government Gazette No 17678.* <http://www.info.gov.za/documents/constitution/1996/96cons2.htm>, accessed 26 April 2013.

South Africa (1998a). Employment Equity Act, 55. *Government Gazette No 19370.* <http://www.labour.gov.za/DOL/downloads/legislation/acts/employment-equity/Act%20-%20Employment%20Equity.pdf>, accessed 9 October 2013.

South Africa (1998b). Skills Development Act, 97. *Government Gazette No 29584.* <http://www.gov.za/documents/download.php?f=70755>, accessed 9 October 2013.

South Africa (1999). Skills Development Amendment Act, 53. *Government Gazette No 19984.* <http://bee.b1sa.co.za/docs/The%20Skills%20Development%20Levies%20Act%20No%209%20of%201999.pdf>, accessed 9 October 2013.

South Africa (2000). Promotion of Equality and Prevention of Unfair Discrimination Act, 4. *Government Gazette No 21249.* <http://www.justice.gov.za/legislation/acts/2000-004.pdf>, accessed 9 October 2013.

South Africa (2002). Promotion of Equality and Prevention of Unfair Discrimination Amendment Act, 52. *Government Gazette No 24249.* <http://www.justice.gov.za/legislation/acts/2002-052.pdf>, accessed 9 October 2013.

South Africa (2003a). Broad Based Black Economic Empowerment Act, 53. *Government Gazette No 29617.* <https://www.environment.gov.za/sites/default/files/legislations/bbbee_act.pdf>, accessed 9 October 2013.

South Africa (2003b). Skills Development Amendment Act, 31. *Government Gazette No 25720.* <http://www.info.gov.za/view/DownloadFileAction?id=68008>, accessed 9 October 2013.

South Africa (2006). Civil Union Act, 17. *Government Gazette No. 36552.* <http://www.info.gov.za/view/DownloadFileAction?id=67843>, accessed 9 October 2013.

South Africa (2006). 3 Human Rights Acts: Promotion of Access to Information Act of 2000, Promotion of Administrative Justice Act 3 of 2000, Promotion of Equality and Prevention of Unfair Discrimination Act 4 of 2000. *Cape Town: Siber Ink.*

South Africa (2008). Skills Development Amendment Act, 37. *Government Gazette No 31666.* <http://www.labour.gov.za/DOL/downloads/legislation/acts/skills-development-act/amendments/skilldevact.pdf>, accessed 9 October 2013.

South Africa (2011). Skills Development Amendment Act, 26. *Government Gazette No 35191.* http://www.info.gov.za/view/DownloadFileAction?id=163395 (accessed 9 October 2013).

South Africa (2012a). Employment Equity Amendment Bill, 1112. *Government Gazette No 33873.* <http://www.info.gov.za/view/DownloadFileAction?id=137363>, accessed 9 October 2013.

South Africa (2012b). Women Empowerment and Gender Equality Draft Bill, 701. *Government Gazette No 35637.* <http://www.info.gov.za/view/DownloadFileAction?id=173252>, accessed 10 October 2013.

Srinivas, M., Haq, R., and Ojha, A. (2011). HRM practices in the private sector in India: truly committed to diversity? Managing in a global economy XIV conference proceedings. Eastern Academy of Management—International, Bangalore, India, June.

Statistics South Africa (2012). Census 2011. *Statistics South Africa* [government institution] <http://beta2.statssa.gov.za/>, accessed 26 November 2013.

Steyn, M. and Kelly, C. (2009). Widening circles: case studies in transformation: consolidated report of diversity and equity interventions in Southern Africa project case studies. *Intercultural and Diversity Studies of Southern Africa (iNCUDISA), University of Cape Town*.

Syed, J. (2008). A context-specific perspective of equal employment opportunity in Islamic societies. *Asia Pacific Journal of Management*, 25(1): 135–51.

Syed, J., Özbilgin, M., Torunoglu, D., and Ali, F. (2009). Rescuing gender equality from the false dichotomies of secularism versus shariah in Muslim majority countries. *Women's Studies International Forum*, 32(2): 67–79. .

Thorat, S. and Attewell, P. (2007). The legacy of social exclusion: a correspondence study of job discrimination in India. *Economic and Political Weekly*, 42: 4141–5.

Times of India (2010). Rajya Sabha passes women's reservation bill. *Times of India*, 9 March. <http://articles.timesofindia.indiatimes.com/2010-03-09/india/28137030_1_unruly-scenes-women-s-reservation-bill-constitution-amendment-bill>, accessed 20 November 2013.

Visagie, J., Linde, H., and Havenga, W. (2011). Leadership competencies for managing diversity. *Managing Global Transitions*, 9(3): 225–47.

Webb, V. (1999). Multilingualism in democratic South Africa: the over-estimation of language policy. *International Journal of Educational Development*, 19(4–5): 351–66.

Webb, V. (2002). *Language in South Africa: The Role of Language in National Transformation, Reconstruction and Development*. Amsterdam: John Benjamins.

Xavier, C. (2010). India's strategic advantage over China in Africa. *Institute for Defence Studies and Analyses*.. <http://www.idsa.in/idsacomments/Indiasstrategicadvantageover ChinainAfrica_cxavier_300610>, accessed 15 October 2013.

PART V
INTERSECTIONS OF DIVERSITY

CHAPTER 21

INTERSECTIONALITY AT THE INTERSECTION

Paradigms, Methods, and Application—A Review

DANIELLE MERCER, MARIANA INES PALUDI,
JEAN HELMS MILLS, AND ALBERT J. MILLS

Introduction

OVER twenty years ago, Kimberlé Crenshaw (1989) introduced the idea that civil rights laws lack the ability to address the type of inequality and discrimination faced by people who are oppressed in multiple ways (Crenshaw 1989; Best et al. 2011). Her work has inspired many researchers, of various disciplines, to take on intersectionality in all its complexity. In simple terms, intersectionality is the idea that various forms of oppression interact with one another in multiple, complex ways (Garry 2011).

Although the concept of intersectionality is widely used across a multitude of disciplines, and was rarely criticized for nearly two decades, conflicts are arising. There are issues related to the limitations, implications, and slipperiness of intersectionality as a whole (Garry 2011). Rasky (2011: 239) states: 'it [intersectionality] both explodes into a proliferation of identity categories and implodes into a distillation of such categories into a simplistic model. This tension thoroughly penetrates the concept and is reflected in the way it informs its methodology.' The problems continually arise in an often failing effort to conceptualize and operationalize intersectionality.

This chapter seeks to address the messiness and controversial views of intersectionality. In particular, it explores the various definitions of intersectionality and the challenges involved. We begin with an overview of the history of intersectionality,[1] then comment

---

[1] We do not suggest that this is the history of intersectionality but one version of past developments (see Durepos and Mills 2012, on the problems of historical representation in social sciences research).

on the implications of the link between the paradigmatic approach, conceptualization, and the operationalization of intersectionality.

The (Contested) History of Intersectionality

Simply put, the term intersectionality—which focuses on the idea that various forms of oppression interact in multiple complex ways—has been advancing through feminist studies and critical race studies for over two decades (Garry 2011). The term intersectionality was initially used by legal scholar Kimberlé Crenshaw in her work on violence against women of colour. Initially, she used the concept of intersectionality to denote the various ways in which race and gender interacted to shape multiple dimensions of black women's employment experiences (Crenshaw 1989). Her objective was to demonstrate that many of the experiences black women faced were not confined within the traditional boundaries of race or gender discrimination, and that the intersection of race and gender factors into black women's lives must be captured interdependently with one another (Crenshaw 1991). She later built on this observation by examining the many ways in which race and gender intersect in shaping structural, political, and representational aspects of violence against women of colour (Crenshaw 1991).

Although Crenshaw is credited with being the first, or one of the first, to use the term intersectionality (Garry 2011) the idea of intersecting identities and discrimination has a long history in the social sciences (Collins 2000). In developing her case for intersectionality and interlocking systems of oppression, Patricia Hill Collins (2000: 42) argued that the seeds of the idea can be traced back to the work of W. E. B. Du Bois who 'saw race, class, and nation not primarily as personal identity categories but as social hierarchies that shaped African American access to status, poverty, and power'. She notes, however, that Du Bois omitted gender from his theorizations, reducing it to a personal identity category. In her book *Black Feminist Thought* (1990) Collins sought to define black feminism as including women who theorize the experiences and ideas shared by ordinary black women that provided a unique angle of vision on self, community, and society. More specifically, Collins (1990) conceptualized the structural dimension of intersectionality as a 'matrix of domination' in which sex, race, and other 'axes of oppression' operate together to produce diverse experiences of domination within a structured whole. She found that intersectionality does not engage in an analysis of separate systems of oppression like gender, race, and class as separate entities, but explores how these are mutually constitutive and how they interconnect (Collins 1990; Boogard and Roggeband 2010).

Choo and Ferree (2010: 132) sum up the past work of Crenshaw and Collins thus:

> By emphasizing the differences among women, these scholars not only countered the unwarranted universalizing of white, middle-class, American women's experiences

as women but began a highly productive line of theorizing how lived experiences of oppression cannot be separated into those due to gender, on the one hand, and race, on the other, but rather simultaneously and linked. (Brewer 1993; Glenn 1999; Espiritu 2000)

The last thirty years have seen a growing number of challenges to categorization by race, gender, class, and sexuality from critical feminists (Butler 1990; Reay, David, and Ball 2005; Cole 2009). Many scholars who have taken up intersectionality have generated studies that incorporate data from women of different racial-ethnic and class backgrounds (Naples 1998). Today, feminist scholars believe that race, class, and gender are closely intertwined, and argue that these forms of stratification need to be studied in relation to one another (Choo and Ferree 2010; Rasky 2011). While the concept of intersectionality significantly advanced research on women of colour, it has also led to the realization that all social identity groups can experience multiple forms of oppression in society (McCall 2005).

Defining Intersectionality

Since Crenshaw's work in the early nineties, intersectionality has been emerging in a wide range of disciplines as a framework that more accurately captures the complexities of identities by explicitly linking individual, interpersonal, and social structural domains of experiences (Shields 2008; Dill and Zambrana 2009; Jones, Kim, and Skendall 2012). As stated by Magnusson (2011: 94):

> No single identity category or social category can satisfactorily account for the meanings a person places on his/her social relations, life events and social surroundings, nor for how he or she is responded by those surroundings. Human identity is inherently complex. The meaning content of each of the social categories [sexuality/sexualities, social class, ethnicity and race] I have described here is from the very outset intertwined with each of the other categories; this term is entitled intersectionality.

For example, being a female may mean very different things depending on what other social categories to which a particular female belongs. Similarly, belonging to the social category 'working class' may have different implications for a man than for a woman (Magnusson 2011). According to Rasky (2011), identity can be viewed as experience that is not composed of objective attributes but as a subjective set of dynamics. Identity is therefore multiple and complex, and contingent upon a variety of social, political, and ideological factors (Rasky 2011). Shields (2008) notes that intersectionality should begin with a reflection of the reality of our lives due to the fact that there is no one single identity category that describes how we respond to our social environment or are responded to by others (Shields 2008: 304).

Thus, it has been argued that intersectionality should no longer be approached simplistically in a two- or three-part model. The term has moved well away from the initial analysis of double and triple oppression of race/class/gender identities. From Rasky's (2011) perspective, it is better to conceptualize how the multiple axes of differentiation intersect in specific contexts. In other words, intersectionality must be examined interchangeably at the micro level and the macro level. First, the notion of interlocking oppressions refers to the macro-level connections linking systems of oppression such as race, class, and gender. Second, the notion of intersectionality describes micro-level processes, namely, how each individual and group occupies a social position within the interlocking structures of oppression (Collins 2000; Hurtado and Sinha 2008). These compounded intermeshed systems of oppression in our social structures help to produce:

- Our social relations.
- Our experiences of our own identity.
- The limitations of shared interests among members of the same oppressed group. (Garry 2011: 827)

Choo and Feree (2010) analysed the work of several past scholars (McCall 2005; Prins 2006; Davis 2008) in an effort to highlight dimensions of theorizing that have become part of what intersectionality signifies. They developed three dimensions in total:

(1) The importance of including the perspectives of multiple marginalized people, especially women of colour.
(2) An analytic shift from the addition of multiple independent strands of inequality towards a multiplication, and thus transformation, of their main effects into interactions.
(3) A focus on seeing multiple institutions as overlapping in their co-determination of inequalities to produce complex configurations from the start, rather than extra-interactive processes that are added onto main effects. (Choo and Ferree 2010: 131)

Similarly, Collins (2007) and Dill and Zambrana (2009) have created characteristics used to define intersectionality research. They believed that one must centre the lived experience of individuals; complicate the identity and examine both individual/group identities; explore identity salience as influenced by systems of power and unveil power in interconnected structures of inequality; and, finally, advance intersectionality as part of a larger goal of promoting social justice and social change (Jones, Kim, and Skendall 2012: 702).

As complex and ambiguous intersectionality is, 'with each new intersection, new connections emerge and previously hidden exclusions come to light' (Davis 2008: 77).

Confusing Intersectionalities

Scholars of all disciplines have embraced the call for an intersectional analysis, but its definition is still questioned, leading Kathy Davis (2008) to title intersectionality as a 'buzzword' with as yet unrealized analytic bite (Choo and Ferree 2010). While the concept of intersectionality has advanced significantly since its introduction over two decades ago, there continues to be controversy about what intersectionality is, how it should be conceptualized, whether it concerns individual experiences, theorizing, or identity, or if it is a property of social structures and cultural discourses (Davis 2008: 68). In psychology, for example, intersectionality may be better understood as a framework rather than a theory. Cole (2009: 179) states that intersectionality 'is a paradigm for theory and research offering new ways of understanding the complex causality that characterizes social phenomena'.

It was not until September 2001 that Kimberlé Crenshaw (1989) was invited to introduce the notion of intersectionality before a special session at the World Conference against Racism (WCAR) in Durban, South Africa. According to Yuval-Davis (2006), it was in the expert meeting on Gender and Racial Discrimination that took place in 2000 as part of the preparatory process to the WCAR conference that a more specific analysis and proposal for a specific methodology for intersectionality was attempted. It was discovered that the analytical attempts to explain intersectionality in the reports were very confusing. For example, Crenshaw (2001) stated that intersectionality is 'what occurs when a woman from a minority group ... tries to navigate the main crossing in the city ... the main highway is "racism road". One cross street can be colonialism, then Patriarchy Street ... She has to deal not only with one form of oppression but with all forms ...' (cited in Yuval-Davis 2006: 196). The metaphorical description of intersectionality is very different from the one that appeared in the Australian Human Rights and Equal Opportunities Commission Issue Paper, which stated: 'An intersectional approach asserts that aspects of identity are indivisible and that speaking of race and gender in isolation from each other results in concrete disadvantage' (Yuval-Davis 2006: 197). The nature of these definitions are quite oppositional: Crenshaw seems to focus on structural intersectionality, whereas the Australian Human Rights and Equal Opportunities Commission uses a definition that is strongly linked to the notions of identity.

It is apparent that the concepts of intersectionality continue to remain unstable. However, a number of scholars do not realize that it is not enough to call one's study intersectional. Analysis of intersectionality is both problematic and difficult to operationalize because of the diversity of conceptualization and disciplinary approaches, and thus it is often difficult to identify the most effective intersectional models for one's own research (Naples 2009).

Conflicting Methodological Approaches to Intersectionality

Several kinds of intersectionality theories, concepts, or approaches exist. Many aim at large-scale, structural process, while some focus on social interactions and individual identity processes. The meaning given to terms such as 'intersecting' and 'category' vary among researchers dependent on their approach to intersectionality, and continue to be heatedly debated (Magnusson 2011). Arguably, both old and new approaches continue to be inadequate to the task of studying intersectionality in all its complexity (McCall 2005).

When Crenshaw and other early researchers first introduced the topic of intersectionality, it tended to offer an individualistic approach, emphasizing the ways in which women's social location intersected with race, class, gender, and sexuality, and shaped their lived experiences (Naples 2009). Writings in this regard sought to theorize difference by category and shaped individual experiences and oppression. More specifically, the theory of intersectionality as used by Crenshaw (1989) and Collins (1990) was used as a way of making sense of interlocking societal oppression experienced by subordinate groups. Syed (2010: 61) stated 'for these scholars, intersectionality served as an analytic frame for highlighting the complexities of oppression'. In later studies, Crenshaw (1995) defined the terms structural intersectionality (also known as categorical intersectionality) and political intersectionality. Structural intersectionality represents the ways that the experience of membership in a category varies qualitatively as a function of other group membership one holds (Cole 2008). For example, Crenshaw (1995) stated that the specific convergences of socioeconomic status, race, and gender make it less likely that poor women of colour will receive rape counselling if resources are allocated according to the standards of need of racially and economically privileged women (Shields 2008: 304). In contrast, political intersectionality describes the way that those who occupy multiple subordinate identities may find themselves caught between the sometimes conflicting agendas of two political constituencies to which they belong (Cole 2008). The example Crenshaw (1995) uses here is black women whose political energies are often split between social action agendas based on race and on gender, neither of which may alone adequately address their specific concerns or most pressing needs (Shields 2008: 305). Intersectionality has become strongly linked to the notions of individual identity and identity formation, but it often fails to explore the dimensions of structural intersectionality central to Crenshaw's work (McCall 2005; Verloo 2006; Boogard and Roggeband 2010).

Subsequent work has tended towards a relational approach to intersectionality. The relational approach to intersectionality offers a more historical and regional variation of the earlier themes of difference (Naples 2009). There continues to be controversy towards this approach, dependent upon the researcher. For instance, Weldon (2008) describes the relational approach as the 'intersection-plus' model, focusing on a process-centred understanding where the interaction effects of categories come to play, but only in selected cases. In contrast, McCall (2005) argues that a core element of this approach is comparative analysis: seeing how the interplay among different structures of domination varies we must use a methodology that uses comparisons above the individual; she titles her version of a relational approach 'intercategorical'.

McCall's (2005) contribution is the contention that the notion of intersectionality has introduced new methodological problems and has a limited range of methodological approaches used for studying intersectionality. She uses three intersectionality approaches that are defined in terms of their stance towards categories (i.e. individualistic versus relational models) and, more specifically, in terms of how they understand and use analytical categories to explore the complexity of intersectionality. The approaches are referred to as 'anti-categorical complexity', 'intracategorical complexity', and 'intercategorical complexity', and it must be emphasized that not all research on intersectionality can simply fit within one of the three approaches, as some research belongs partly to one approach and partly to another (McCall 2005). McCall (2005: 1774) concludes:

> The three approaches can be considered broadly representative of current approaches to the study of intersectionality and together illustrate the fact that different methodologies produce different kinds of substantive knowledge and that a wider range of methodologies is needed to fully engage with the set of issues and topics falling broadly under the rubric of intersectionality.

The first approach is called anti-categorical complexity because it is based on a methodology that seeks to deconstruct categorical divisions (McCall 2005). Basically, nothing fits neatly into any single master category due to the fact that categories, including gender and race, are too simplistic to capture the complex social life and lived experiences of individuals (McCall 2005). More generally, the process of categorization itself may lead to exclusion and then, ultimately, inequality. For example, there would be no longer a category of 'gender', no longer two genders but countless genders eliminating the singularity and separateness of social categories (McCall 2005).

The next approach is 'intercategorical complexity' and is quite the opposite of 'anti-categorical complexity' in that it addresses the fact that inequalities exist in society and will continue to be imperfect and ever changing (McCall 2005). Proponents of this methodology focus on using analytical categories to document societal inequalities and the relationships that exist. More specifically, the approach focuses on the complexity of relationships among multiple social groups and not divided into single categories or groups (McCall 2005).

The final approach—'intracategorical complexity'—falls neatly in the middle of the two other approaches. Anti-categorical rejects the use of categories while intercategorical uses categories complexly and strategically. Like the first approach, 'intracategorical complexity' interrogates the boundaries of distinction and recognizes the shortcomings of social analytical categories (McCall 2005). Yet, like the second approach, it acknowledges the stable relationships that social categories represent, but remains critical of them at all times. McCall (2005) calls this 'intracategorical complexity', because 'authors working in this vein tend to focus on particular social groups and neglected points of intersection in order to reveal the complexity of lived experience within such groups' (McCall 2005: 1774).

The association of anti-categorical approach with the complexity introduced by studies on intersectionality may also have resulted from the tendency to combine this approach with 'intracategorical' (McCall 2005). McCall (2005) rejects the 'anti-categorical' and 'intracategorical' approach to intersectionality because she sees them as inadequate, leaving the 'intercategorical complexity' approach as the most realistic option (Naples 2009). Similarly, other critics (i.e. Garry 2011) also state that intersectionality does not abolish identity categories; instead, they become more complex and messy. This is not to say that the use of identity categories in intersectional analysis is not problematic due to the fact that not all situations are intersectional to the same extent; this alone causes researchers confusion because the appropriate intersectionality methodology is not set in stone.

The approaches to intersectionality methodology and analysis continue to conflict. McCall's (2005) three approaches are not the only ones. Many other scholars have developed their own take on studying intersectionality as it is dependent on the way they theorize and analyse research. For example, Naples (2009) developed an approach called the epistemological approach of intersectional analysis, which is rooted in the insights from different theoretical perspectives developed to analyse gender, race, and class inequalities, as well as sexuality and culture. Similarly, an epistemological view is evident in Collins's (2000) work as it centres on the construct of the matrix of domination. The difficulties to operationalize intersectionality stem from the various theories, types, or approaches. Naples (2009: 574) states: 'Each approach to intersectionality... offers a different angle of vision on the complex processes, relationships, and structural conditions that shape everyday life, relations of ruling and the resistance strategies of diverse actors.'

Methodological Design in Intersectionality Analysis

Despite the emergence of intersectionality as a major paradigm of research, there has been little discussion pertaining to intersectionality methodology. Studies of intersectionality are limited in terms of methodology, and the methodological issues are quite complex and inconsistent with past practice (McCall 2005).

Many scholars state that intersectionality is not a methodology, just as it is not a theory of oppression or power (Hurtado and Sinha, 2008; Garry 2011). Intersectionality is more of a framework, and methods or methodologies can be developed that support it. More specifically, intersectionality directs one to the appropriate design and analysis. The problematic part of the design is determining the most appropriate method for 'digging into the details of the ways that the full range of oppression and privileges interact in our societies, life and theories' (Garry 2011: 844).

More often than not, the methodological demands of intersectionality research are quite challenging no matter what research method is chosen. So far, approaches to intersectionality have mostly been used in qualitative field studies. As stated by Shields (2008: 311): 'Intersectionality theory by virtue of its description of multidimensional nature of identity makes investigation through qualitative methods seem both natural and necessary.' The theoretical compatibility and historical links between intersectionality and qualitative methodologies imply that one does not go without the other (Shields 2008; Syed 2010). However, different types and levels of analysis may require different qualitative methods. For example, Dorothy Smith (1987, 1990) uses an institutional ethnographic methodology that is considered one of the most powerful methodologies for intersectional research (Naples 2009). The use of narratives and theoretical interventions essentially created the study of intersectionality, but the use of case studies is considered as well (McCall 2005). However, both can become problematic. In the case of narratives, these can get confusing due to the problems of representation and othering. Questions can lead to personal bias (Butt et al. 1992) and there is the issue of the researcher misinterpreting or construing the stories (Denzin 1989). Cole (2009) explained that this raises the issue of representation and how lives can be represented through text in all their complexity, to quote Phillips (1994: 15) will any old story suffice?' Using case studies as a methodology to study intersectionality can also work, depending on the complexity of the research. Case studies focus on the intensive study of single groups. For example, many feminists who are trained in social science and study intersectionality use the case study method to identify a new or invisible group (McCall 2005).

Although using qualitative methods to study intersectionality is gaining momentum, it is more difficult to use quantitative methods in intersectionality research (Shields 2008). Using quantitative research is very problematic when studying intersectionality because it oversimplifies and separates the very relational and complex intermeshing that intersectionality captures (Shields 2008). Shields (2008) describes the difficulty with using a quantitative method such as analysis of variance (ANOVA). For example, a 2x2 study of sexual orientation and gender allows an analysis of how one variable influences another but it does not allow appreciation of the dependence of one category's definition on the other (Shields 2008). In psychological research, using an ANOVA framework leads to an additive approach of the intersectionality categories, as they are seen as independent from one another. Similarly, McCall's (2005) intersectionality approach, 'intercategorical complexity', uses a quantitative methodology to analyse how categories influence one another.

The question of whether to interpret intersectionality as an additive or as a constitutive process is still a central debate (Yuval-Davis 2006). An additive approach means that social inequality increases with each additional stigmatized identity (Bowleg 2008). One of the problematics of the additive intersectionality model is that it often remains on one level of analysis, the experiential, and does not differentiate between different levels (Yuval-Davis 2006). It conceptualizes people's experience as separate, independent, and summative (Bowleg 2008). For example, Bowleg (2008) used past studies related to black lesbians to determine the intersections of race, sex/gender, and sexual orientation. What she found was that none of the literature review sections of these past studies reference a single intersectionality theorist or mention the word intersectionality. Instead, the 'triple jeopardy approach' to black lesbians' experiences was used, in which all identities were seen as separate entities. Bowleg (2008) realized that every methodological choice made in the past studies represented an additive approach, black+lesbian+women (Bowleg 2008: 314). The point of this discussion is that, in designing the methodology, the wording of the questions shape how participants respond to them. Unfortunately, it can be quite difficult to create the proper questions for intersectionality research. The main issue is how to ask questions about experiences that are intersecting and mutually constitutive without resorting to an additive approach (Bowleg 2008). Often, the way the questions are asked imply that the experience is to be recounted serially and the identities kept separate. Bowleg (2008: 322) sums up the issue at hand quite well:

> While several studies focus on race, age, gender, ethnicity... these studies tend to have limited abilities to answer important questions about intersectionality. First, they often develop meaningful constructs to measure experiences based on intersections of these social identities, relying instead on the erroneous assumption that variables such as race sex... class... are explanatory constructs in and of themselves.

There is obviously no one-size-fits-all methodological solution to incorporating an intersectionality perspective. Not only do the controversial methods and questioning lead to difficulties in operationalizing intersectionality, but the data analysis can cause problems as well. One key issue is how to handle intersectionality data that is implicit rather than explicit. This is especially an issue when the intersectional approach requires a more complex analysis than in more familiar and accessible additive approaches (Bowleg 2008). More specifically, in the case of narratives, there is always the question—what counts as data (Cole 2009)?

In all of the complexity that comes with intersectionality, there are two suggestions to put forth. First, questions about intersectionality should focus on meaningful constructs rather than typical identity categories. For instance, a study with participants who are ethnically diverse and includes demographic measures such as socioeconomic status and sexual orientation is not intersectionality research. A similar study that focuses on the dimensions of participants' experience related to socioeconomic status and sexual orientation would be considered intersectional research (Betancourt and Lopez 1993; Weber and Parra-Medina 2003; Helms, Jernigan, and Mascher 2005; Bowleg 2008). Second, questions should be intersectional in design, that is, the identity categories must be relational and show interdependence, rather than be additive in nature (Bowleg 2008).

Intersectionality and Practice: Paradigms and Applications

Intersectionality has come a long way since its introduction a couple of decades ago. It is now possible to chronicle many approaches to intersectionality that differ by discipline, epistemology, and conceptualization (Naples 2009). Despite this emergence, there has been little development in how to study intersectionality, that is, of its methodology (McCall 2005). The problem lies within the fact that there are such diverse ways of conceptualizing and approaching intersectionality. Attempting to operationalize intersectionality may be a daunting and impossible task because: 'Intersectionality can point us to locations where we need to begin identifying issues and constructing our theories... It does not do the work for us, but tells us where to start and suggests kinds of questions to ask. It sets the stage...' (Garry 2011: 828).

The various ontological, epistemological, and methodological aspects of different paradigmatic positions (Burrell and Morgan 1979) arguably influence the application of intersectionality.

Positivism

From a positivist perspective (Johnson and Duberley 2000), the emphasis on a natural science approach is likely to encourage a focus on more-or-less fixed categories (gender, race, etc.) and an additive approach whereby different categories (often expressed as variables) can be studied and measured to assess their cumulative impact (see, for example, Glauber 2008; Lovell 2000). Here, operationalization requires the codification of a great number of data that will be analysed, with regression analysis showing correlations among categories or variables. To conduct research in this tradition implies being able to see the impact of one type of oppression on another, in a linear and simplifying way. This approach has proven useful in drawing attention to the fact that anti-discriminatory policies may actually miss the mark where a person faces multiple discriminatory factors. The work of Best and colleagues (2011), for example, helped United States court cases on discrimination to support the argument that race and gender disadvantages are interrelated, and that anti-discrimination laws provides less protection where intersected categories are involved.

Nonetheless, some researchers have decried this approach as 'body counting' (Alvesson and Billing 2002), arguing that it serves to reinforce essentialist notions of gender and race (Hearn 2011) as relatively fixed categories (McCall 2005). On the other hand, it has been argued that, regardless of methodological issues, categorization is the basis for discriminatory practices (people do politically categorize others and discriminate based on such categorizations) and that political engagement against discrimination often needs to appeal to people—at least initially—as categories of social actors. Calás and Smircich (1992), for example, contend that feminist poststructuralism needs to take into account the appeal of categorization (e.g. collectives of women) for political action while simultaneously encouraging the deconstruction of the very same 'master' category of gender (see also McCall 2005).

Postpositivism

Beyond positivism, there are a disparate number of 'intellectual traditions' that share a common reaction to positivism in questioning 'social reality and knowledge production from a more problematized vantage point, emphasizing the constructed nature of social reality, the constitutive role of language, and the value of research as critique' (Prasad 2005: 9, cited in Bryman et al. 2011: 57–58). These various approaches focus, to different degrees, on language (e.g. poststructuralism), narrative (e.g. postmodernism), context/history (e.g. postcolonialism), socio-psychological interactions (e.g. critical sensemaking, CSM), and relationships (e.g. actor–network theory, ANT). In the process, we suggest, there are very different implications for the study of intersectionality (or the intersection of different identity formations). We will briefly look at some of the issues involved in selected methodological approaches to the study of the intersections of identity, including critical hermeneutics, critical discourse analysis (CDA), CSM, ANT, and postcolonialism.

Critical hermeneutics focuses largely on textual analysis (Prasad 2002), seeking to derive meaning from such things as the socio-historical context in which selected texts were produced, the situated location of the reader-as-interpreter, and recognition of the role of translation as the researcher attempts to bring both her location and that of the text under review. This approach has been used, among other things, to show how corporate documents have served to shape images of the Arab as Other (Prasad and Mir 2002). It has been less used to understand issues of multiple identity projects.

One immediate problem of this approach is the issue of text itself. In the literal sense of text, the researcher is very much stuck within the boundaries of written documents that may or may not deal with how a person is being viewed, imaged, or employed: any intersecting (discriminatory) identities/structures may be unclear (e.g. a person's name may give little clue as to their ethnic background, gender, age, etc.) and there may be little or no clue as to selected persons' experiences of discriminatory practices (e.g. the intent of the text may serve to reduce the clues to certain experiences). On the positive side, it can be argued that texts can provide important clues to 'naturally occurring' discourses (Phillips and Hardy 2002) that allow the researcher to avoid pre-fixed categories—allowing the character of discriminatory experiences to emerge from the text. This still does not get the researcher past the problem of discriminatory practices that serve to exclude certain people from a given text or set of texts. For example, Mills's (1995, 2006) study of British Airways found that women of colour were largely excluded from corporate texts over much of the first fifty years of the company's operation. Potential ways forward may be to undertake an extensive case study of a single organization over time that has an established archive of materials. Various documents (e.g. newsletters, corporate letters, annual general reports) could then be interrogated and cross-referenced in attempts to understand the way in which discriminatory practices are structured and experienced, as named people are followed in the array of materials. While this may be limited to the people referred to in the various texts (discrimination, for example, is likely to exclude certain people from the texts), it has the advantage of providing clues to the contexts of discrimination and how they may change over time (see Hartt et al. 2012).

CDA involves a focus on the relationship between language and practice that mutually reinforces a sense of the world that is experienced as knowledge (Weedon 1997). Drawing on Foucault (1979), the interrelationships between language, practice, and knowledge are seen as discursive (i.e. the process of producing a discourse). In other words, a discourse can be seen as 'an interrelated set of texts, and the practices of their production, dissemination, and reception, that brings an object into being' (Phillips and Hardy 2002: 3). From this perspective, 'social reality is produced and made real through discourses, and social interactions cannot be fully understood without reference to the discourses that give them meaning' (Phillips and Hardy 2002: 3). This has been used in a number of studies of the production of gender (Thomas and Davies 2002) and avoids the problem of fixed categories. Thomas and Davies (2002), for example, focus not so much on gender as a fixed category, but rather the fluidity of notions of gender and the discursive processes through which they are constructed as seemingly fixed categories.

The contribution of poststructuralism to the study of intersectionality is to move attention away from fixed categories of discrimination to the study of if, how, and where overlapping experiences of discrimination occur and differ over time and across different contexts. The challenges include finding ways to unravel specific discourses of discrimination and show how, at times, they might overlap and, at other times and in different contexts, do not. The size of the challenge is rooted in the various problems of establishing/identifying discourses. For example, in their study of interviews of female executives of multinational companies in Latin America, Paludi and Helms Mills (2015) were able to identify discourses of gender (both notions of masculinity and femininity) and ethnicity (the women's identities as Latin American coupled with issues of race and localized ethnicity). However, these identity clues had to be explored beyond the text to uncover aspects of the context and history of gender relations in Latin America, but also the complex history of the discursive nature of 'Latin America' itself: a vast undertaking in terms of time and the ability to build plausible accounts of emergent discourses.

CSM draws on the work of Weick (1995) by attempting to ground sensemaking in a series of structured (i.e. organizational rules, formative contexts) and discursive contexts. Yet the focus is not only on how people make sense *in* context but how, in the process, they *enact* a sense of context (Helms Mills, Thurlow, and Mills 2010). To date, CSM has been used to understand how the development, maintenance, and change in gendered situations have been rendered plausible (Mills and Helms Mills 2010). More recently, the approach has been used to explore the creation of a sense of race and ethnicity in the development of immigration policies in Canada (Hilde 2013; Hilde and Mills 2015). With a focus on the socio-psychological properties that people bring to bear on creating a sense of a situation, the challenge for CSM is to find ways of studying the same or similar people across a range of situations. Hilde (2013), for example, interviewed Hong Kong Chinese immigrants to Canada to gain an understanding of how they made sense of the experience. Although gender was not a specific aspect of her study, she began to realize as she analysed the data that there appeared to be a difference between respondents in terms of their gendered identity work. The challenge of future work, however, would not be to assume gender differences but rather to track the same group of people across varying situations to see how—in situations not directly linked to immigration status—they feel identified, which identity is prevalent, and to what extent it is experienced negatively.

ANT is, for feminists, arguably one of the more controversial approaches to discrimination (Corrigan and Mills 2012), yet it continues to attract a number of feminist researchers (Singleton and Michael 1993; Haraway 2004; Hunter and Swan 2007). In its focus on actor networks as the site/process of the production of knowledge, ANT (Callon 1999; Law 1999; Latour 2005) refuses to privilege human actors over non-human actors (e.g. computers, texts, laboratory coats) nor to start with a study of knowledge production that sets out to trace a prefixed category of thought. Its focus is on tracing ('reassembling') how an initially disparate assembly of actors comes to produce a particular knowledge. To understand that knowledge is an effect of a particular set of networked relations. For example, the notion of intersectionality would not be seen as a form of universalized or even generally understood knowledge of the world, but rather as something that has various (localized) meanings or even a lack of meaning across different actor networks. Much like we have argued throughout this chapter, the idea of intersectionality differs across paradigmatic networks of scholars.

A central problem levelled at ANT in this regard is the practice of trying to follow the key actors (Latour 2005) in the process of selected network formation, and so on. Thus, for example, many of 'the actors' in studies of mainstream organizations may not include selected people because of their skin colour, assumed ethnicity, age, and so on. Pan American Airways, for example, was dominated by so-called white, American-born men and, to a lesser extent white, middle-class, and American-born women: making the search for intersecting identities very limited and/or restricted to narrowly defined groups (Hartt et al. 2012). Regardless, one way forward is to consider the role of exclusion (or exclusions) as part of the effects of a particular actor network. The challenge would be to extrapolate from the exclusions to assess any intersecting experiences of discrimination.

Postcolonial theory draws on the work of Said (1978) focusing on the role of colonial (and postcolonial) relationships in the construction of images of the Other. In the process, it focuses on issues of power, cultural representation, and geopolitical relationships. As Spivak (1988: 90) argues, 'if you are poor, black and female you get it [discrimination] in three ways. If, however, this formulation is moved from the first-world context into the postcolonial (...) context, the description "black" or "poor" loses persuasive significance.' This statement summarizes the complexity of a postcolonial–intersectionality approach. When intersectionality is approached through postcolonialist lenses, the notions of cultural representation, nation, and First World/Third World countries, emerge as key components to be problematized and contested. Postcolonial theory is linked to the notion of identity in two ways. On the one hand, it problematizes the idea of identity as a fixed construct. On the other hand, identity cannot be seen without culture and how it is represented in each society (Kailo 2001).

Through this focus, postcolonial theory adds a complex series of levels to the debate on intersectionality that ultimately challenges the (Western) culture-bound character of the term itself (Holvino 2010). It draws the focus away from simple categories, individuals, relationships, and structural rules to the broader context of culture and socio-economic practices and histories. Thus, intersecting identity work, it is argued, will vary across socio-political relationships of colonial and colonized positions.

The challenges here include the sheer amount of work it takes to 'uncover' aspects of the various layers involved. For example, understandings of extant identity work in any of a number of Latin American countries would require extensive research on the history of South (and North) America—its people before and after European conquest; the shaping of particular peoples into national identities (Eakin 2007; Ibarra-Colado 2008), and the 'idea' of Latin America itself (Mignolo 2005). Another challenge is to capture the interrelational aspect of intersecting identities. Said (1978), for example, while able to capture the images of Other in the writings of British and French novelists, does not reveal how those images were understood, translated, and/or resisted by those who have been othered. Similarly, the (textual) voice of the oppressed, while revealing reactions to colonial images, does not necessarily capture the interactive character of the process of postcoloniality (Amoko 2006). Finally, postcolonialist approaches also face the challenge of unravelling the construction of different identities across various situations when faced with largely textual traces.

Despite these various challenges in implementing a focus on intersecting discriminatory practices/experiences, postcolonial theory draws attention to the complex and far-reaching problems of reducing intersectionality to categorization and to studying it out of context (in terms of both culture and past events). Possible ways forward include longitudinal case studies, where there is access to various participants across the colonizer/colonized divide, and the possibility of both archival and ethnographic study.

Summary and Conclusion

In this chapter we have discussed the relationship between epistemology, methodology, methods, and application in the study of intersectionality. Our intent was sixfold: first, we wanted to draw attention to the heuristic value of a focus on intersectionality, in so doing we have attempted to reveal the widespread and growing interest in framing discriminatory practices through an intersectionality lens as well as some useful outcomes associated with it. Second, we wanted to reveal the gap between the widespread theorization of intersectionality and the much more limited application (and discussion of the application) of intersectionality. Third, we set out to say something about the discursive—as opposed to universalist—nature of the concept and ensuing debates. We contend that intersectionality cannot be treated as a term that is commonly accepted (or understood) across various research communities, including feminist scholars. Fourth, in focusing on the discursive nature of the idea of intersectionality, we explored the links between the concept and its possible understanding across different epistemological and methodological stances. Our central argument is that the understanding and use of the term intersectionality differs markedly across different paradigms of thought and thus had profoundly different implications for if or how it is applied. Fifth, through an exploration of selected paradigmatic approaches, we attempted to present some of the issues and challenges in studying intersectionality from a specific approach. In the process, we tried to show that issues of ontology, epistemology, and methodology shape the very issues and challenges as starting points of enquiry. For ease of discussion and space we restricted our discussion to selected approaches and also to cases where one particular method or methodology was prevalent. Obviously, a number of researchers employ more than one way of studying a specific problem of discrimination. Our sixth and final point was to reveal the rich but diverse nature of the debates around intersectionality, and to encourage further engagement with issues of implementation.

References

Alvesson, M. and Billing, Y. D. (2002). Beyond body counting: a discussion of the social construction of gender at work. In I. Aaltio and A. J. Mills (eds.), *Gender, Identity and the Culture of Organizations*. London: Routledge, 72–91.

Amoko, A. (2006). Race and postcoloniality. In S. Malpas and P. Wake (eds.), *The Routledge Companion to Critical Theory*. London: Routledge, 127–39.

Best, R. K., Edelman, L. B., Krieger, L. H., and Eliason, S. R. (2011). Multiple disadvantages: an empirical test of intersectionality theory in EEO litigation. *Law and Society Review*, 45(4): 991–1025.

Betancourt, H. and Lopez, S. R. (1993). The study of culture, ethnicity, and race in American psychology. *American Psychologist*, 48: 629–37.

Boogard, B. and Roggeband, C. (2010). Paradoxes of intersectionality: theorizing inequality in the Dutch police force through structure and agency. *Organization*, 17(1): 53–75.

Bowleg, L. (2008). When black + lesbian + woman = black lesbian woman: the methodological challenges of qualitative and quantitative intersectionality research. *Sex Roles*, 59: 312–25.

Brewer, R. M. (1993). Theorizing race, class and gender: the new scholarship of black feminist intellectuals and black women's labor. In S. M. James and A. P. A. Busia (eds.), *Theorizing Black Feminisms: The Visionary Pragmatism of Black Women*. New York: Routledge, 13–30.

Bryman, A., Bell, E., Mills, A. J., and Yue, A. R. (2011). *Business Research Methods*. First Canadian Edition. Toronto: Oxford University Press.

Burrell, G. and Morgan, G. (1979). *Sociological Paradigms and Organisational Analysis*. Burlington, VT: Ashgate Publishing Limited.

Butler, J. (1990). *Gender Trouble: Feminism and the Subversion of Identity*. London: Routledge.

Butt, R., Raymond, D., McCue, G., and Yamagishi, L. (1992). Collaborative autobiography and the teacher's voice. In Ivor Goodson (ed.), *Studying Teachers' Lives*. New York: Teachers College Press, 51–98.

Calás, M. B. and Smircich, L. (1992). Using the 'F' word: feminist theories and the social consequences of organizational research. In A. J. Mills and P. Tancred (eds.), *Gendering Organizational Analysis*. Newbury Park, CA: Sage, 222–34.

Callon, M. (1999). Actor-network theory: the market test. In J. Law and J. Hassard (eds.), *Actor Network Theory and After*. Oxford: Blackwell Publishing, 181–95.

Choo, H. and Ferree, M. (2010). Practicing intersectionality in sociological research: a critical analysis of inclusions, interactions, and institutions in the study of inequalities. *Sociological Theory*, 28(2): 129–49.

Cole, B. (2009), Gender, narratives, and intersectionality: can personal experience approaches to research contribute to 'undoing gender'? *International Review of Education*, 55: 561–78.

Cole, E. (2008). Coalitions as a model for intersectionality: from practice to theory. *Sex Roles*, 59: 443–53.

Collins, P. H. (1990). *Black Feminist Thought: Knowledge, Consciousness, and the Politics of Empowerment*. Boston, MA: Unwin Hyman.

Collins, P. H. (2000). It's all in the family: intersections of gender, race, and nation. In U. Narayan and S. Harding (eds.), *Decentering the Center: Philosophy for a Multicultural, Postcolonial, and Feminist World*. Bloomington, IN: Indiana University Press.

Collins, P. H. (2007). Pushing the boundaries or business as usual? Race, class, and gender studies and sociological inquiry. In C. J. Calhoun (ed.), *Sociology in America: A History*. Chicago: University of Chicago, 572–604.

Corrigan, L. and Mills, A. J. (2012). Men on board: can actor-network theory critique the persistence of gender inequity? *Management & Organizational History*, 7(3): 251–65.

Crenshaw, K. (1989). Demarginalizing the intersection of race and sex: a black feminist critique of antidiscrimination doctrine, feminist theory, and antiracist politics. *University of Chicago Legal Forum*, 140: 139–67

Crenshaw, K. (1991). Mapping the margins: intersectionality, identity politics, and violence against women of color. *Stanford Law Review*, 43: 1241–79.

Crenshaw, K. W. (1995). Mapping the margins: intersectionality, identity politics, and violence against women of color. In K. W. Crenshaw, N. Gotanda, G. Peller, and K. Thomas (eds.), *Critical Race Theory: The Key Writings that Formed the Movement*. New York: New Press, 357–84.

Davis, K. (2008). Intersectionality as buzzword: a sociology of science perspective on what makes a feminist theory successful. *Feminist Theory*, 9: 67–85.

Denzin, N. (1989). *Interpretive Biography*. Newbury Park, CA: Sage.

Dill, B. T. and Zambrana, R. E. (2009). Critical thinking about inequality: an emerging lens. In B. T. Dill and R. E. Zambrana (eds.), *Emerging Intersections: Race, Class, and Gender in Theory, Policy, and Practice*. New Brunswick, NJ: Rutgers, 1–21.

Durepos, G. and Mills, A. J. (2012). *ANTi-History: Theorizing the Past, History, and Historiography in Management and Organizational Studies*. Charlotte, NC: Information Age Publishing.

Eakin, M. C. (2007). *The History of Latin America. Collision of Cultures*. London: Palgrave.

Espiritu, Y. L. (2000). *Asian American Women and Men*. Walnut Creek, CA: Altamira Press.

Foucault, M. (1979). *Discipline and Punish: The Birth of the Prison*. New York: Vintage Books.

Garry, A. (2011). Intersectionality, metaphors, and the multiplicity of gender. *Hypatia*, 26(4): 826–50.

Glauber, R. (2008). Race and gender in families and at work: the fatherhood wage premium. *Gender & Society*, 22(1), 8–30.

Glenn, E. N. (1999). The social construction and institutionalization of gender and race: an integrative framework. In M. M. Ferree, J. Lorber, and B. B. Hess (eds.), *Revisioning Gender*. New York: Sage, 3–43.

Haraway, D. J. (2004). *The Haraway Reader*. New York: Routledge.

Hartt, C. M., Mills, A. J., Helms Mills, J., and Durepos, G. (2012). Markets, organizations, institutions and national identity: Pan American Airways, postcoloniality and Latin America. *Critical Perspectives on International Business*, 8(1): 14–36.

Hearn, J. (2011). Neglected intersectionalities in studying men: age(ing), virtuality, transnationality. In H. Lutz, M. T. Herrera Vivar, and L. Supik (eds.), *Framing Intersectionality: Debates on a Multi-Faceted Concept in Gender Studies. The Feminist Imagination: Europe and Beyond*. Farnham and Burlington, VT: Ashgate, 89–104.

Helms, J. E., Jernigan, M., and Mascher, J. (2005). The meaning of race in psychology and how to change it: a methodological perspective. *American Psychologist*, 60: 27–36.

Helms Mills, J., Thurlow, A., and Mills, A. J. (2010). Making sense of sensemaking: the critical sensemaking approach. *Qualitative Research in Organizations and Management*, 5(2): 182–95.

Hilde, R. K. and Mills, A. J. (2015). Making critical sense of discriminatory practices in the Canadian workplace. *Critical Perspectives on International Business*, 11(2): 173–88. doi: 10.1108/CPOIB-09-2012-0042.

Hilde, R. K. S. (2013). *Workplace (In)Equality: Making Critical Sense of Hong Kong Chinese Immigrant Experience in the Canadian Workplace* (Doctorate of Business Administration), Athabasca University, Athabasca.

Holvino, E. (2010). Intersections: the simultaneity of race, gender and class in organization studies. *Gender, Work and Organization*, 17(3): 248–77.

Hunter, S. and Swan, E. (2007). Oscillating politics and shifting agencies: equalities and diversity work and actor network theory. *Equal Opportunities International*, 26(5): 402–19.

Hurtado, A. and Sinha, M. (2008). More than man: Latino feminist masculinities and intersectionality. *Sex Roles*, 59: 337–49.

Ibarra-Colado, E. (2008). Is there any future for critical management studies in Latin America? Moving from epistemic coloniality to 'trans-discipline'. *Organization*, 15(6): 932–5.

Johnson, P. and Duberley, J. (2000). *Understanding Management Research*. London: Sage.

Jones, S., Kim, Y., and Skendall, K. (2012). Re-framing authenticity: considering multiple social identities using autoethnographic and intersectional approaches. *The Journal of Higher Education*, 83(5): 698–723.

Kailo, K. (2001). Gender and ethnic overlap/p in the Finnish Kalevala. In H. Bannerji, S. Mojab, and J. Whitehead (eds.), *Of Property and Propriety: The Role of Gender and Class in Imperialism and Nationalism*. Toronto and Buffalo, NY: University of Toronto Press, 182–222.

Krieger, N. (1999). Embodying inequality: a review of concepts, measures, and methods for studying health consequences of discrimination. *International Journal of Health Services*, 29: 295–352.

Krieger, N., Rowley, D. L., Herman, A. A., Avery, B., and Phillips, M. T. (1993). Racism, sexism, and social class: implications for studies of health, disease, and well-being. *American Journal of Preventive Medicine*, 9: 82–122.

Latour, B. (2005). *Reassembling the Social*. Oxford: Oxford University Press.

Law, J. (1999). After ANT: topology, naming and complexity. In J. O. Law and J. Hassard (eds.), *Actor Network Theory and After*. Oxford and Keele: Blackwell and the Sociological Review, 1–14.

Lovell, P. A. (2000). Gender, race, and the struggle for social justice in Brazil. *Latin American Perspectives*, 27(6): 85–102.

McCall, L. (2005). The complexity of intersectionality. *Journal of Women in Culture and Society*, 30(31): 1771–800.

Magnusson, E. (2011). Women, men and all the other categories: psychologies for theorizing human diversity. *Nordic Psychology*, 63(2): 88–114.

Mignolo, W. D. (2005). *The Idea of Latin America*. Oxford: Wiley-Blackwell.

Mills, A. J. (1995). Man/aging subjectivity, silencing diversity: organizational imagery in the airline industry—the case of British Airways. *Organization*, 2(2): 243–69.

Mills, A. J. (2006). *Sex, Strategy and the Stratosphere: Airlines and the Gendering of Organizational Culture*. London: Palgrave Macmillan.

Mills, A. J. and Helms Mills, J. (2010). Making sense of gender: self reflections on the creation of plausible accounts. In S. Katila, S. Meriläinen, and J. Tienari (eds.), *Working for Inclusion: Positive Experiences from Academics across the World*. Cheltenham: Edward Elgar, 244–73.

Naples, N. A. (1998). *Grassroots Warriors: Activist Mothering, Community Work, and the War on Poverty*. New York: Routledge.

Naples, N. (2009). Teaching intersectionality intersectionally. *International Feminist Journal of Politics*, 11(4): 566–77.
Paludi, M. I., and Helms Mills, J. (2015). Making sense of gender equality across cultures: applying a global programme in Argentina. In N. Holden, S. Michailova & S. Tietze (eds.), *The Routledge Companion to Cross-Cultural Management*. Abingdon and New York: Routledge, 389–98.
Phillips, D. (1994). Telling it straight: issues in assessing narrative research. *Educational Psychologist*, 29(1): 13–21.
Phillips, N. and Hardy, C. (2002). *Discourse Analysis: Investigating Processes of Social Construction*, vol. 50. Thousand Oaks, CA: Sage.
Prasad, A. (2002). The contest over meaning: hermeneutics as an interpretive methodology for understanding texts. *Organizational Research Methods*, 5(1): 12–33.
Prasad, A. and Mir, R. (2002). Digging deep for meaning: a critical hermeneutic analysis of CEO letters to shareholders in the oil industry. *Journal of Business Communication*, 39(1): 92–116.
Prins, B. (2006). Narrative accounts of origins: a blind spot in the intersectional approach? *European Journal of Women's Studies*, 13: 277–90.
Rasky, C. (2011). Intersectionality theory applied to whiteness and middle-classness. *Social Identities*, 17(2): 239–53.
Reay, D. (1998). *Class Work: Mothers' Involvement in their Children's Primary Schooling*. London: UCL Press.
Reay, D., David, M. E., and Ball, S. (2005). *Degrees of Choice: Class, Race, Gender and Higher Education*. Oakhill: Trentham.
Said, E. W. (1978). *Orientalism*. New York: Vintage Books.
Shields, S. (2008). Gender: an intersectionality perspective. *Sex Roles*, 59: 301–11.
Singleton, V. and Michael, M. (1993). Actor-networks and ambivalence: general practitioners in the UK cervical screening programme. *Social Studies of Science*, 23: 227–64.
Smith, D. E. (1987). *The Everyday World as Problematic: A Feminist Sociology*. Toronto: University of Toronto Press.
Smith, D. E. (1990). *The Conceptual Practices of Power: A Feminist Sociology of Knowledge*. Boston, MA: Northeastern University Press.
Spivak, G. C. (1988). *Can the Subaltern Speak?* Basingstoke: Palgrave Macmillan.
Syed, M. (2010). Disciplinarity and methodology in intersectionality theory and research. *American Psychologist*, 65(1): 61–2.
Thomas, R. and Davies, A. (2002). Gender and the new public management. *Gender, Work and Organization*, 9(4): 372–96.
Verloo, M. (2006). Multiple inequalities, intersectionality and the European Union. *European Journal of Women's Studies*, 13(3): 211–28.
Weber, L. and Parra-Medina, D. (2003). Intersectionality and women's health: charting a path to eliminating health disparities. *Advances in Gender Research*, 7: 181–230.
Weedon, C. (1997). *Feminist Practice and Poststructuralist Theory*, 2nd edn. Oxford: Blackwell Publishers, Inc.
Weick, K. (1995). *Sensemaking in Organizations*. London: Sage Publications Inc.
Weldon, S. L. (2008). Intersectionality. In G. Goertz and A. Mazur (eds.), *Politics, Gender and Concepts: Theory and Methodology*. New York: Cambridge University Press, 193–218.
Yuval-Davis, N. (2006). Intersectionality and feminist politics. *European Journal of Women's Studies*, 13(3): 193–209.

CHAPTER 22

THE INTERSECTIONALITIES OF AGE, ETHNICITY, AND CLASS IN ORGANIZATIONS

EDELTRAUD HANAPPI-EGGER
AND RENATE ORTLIEB

Introduction

In recent decades diversity has gained prominence both in academic debate and in practice as the pressures of internationalization and socioeconomic change have forced societies all over the world to deal constructively with the growing diversity of their workforce, the labour market, and consumer markets. A growing number of organizations, in particular in Western countries, have already implemented policies of diversity management (DM), or have subscribed to a diversity charter in order to explicitly confirm their commitment to diversity and a policy of inclusion. Yet upon closer inspection it becomes clear that in most American or European organizations these policies focus rather narrowly on certain single social categories such as gender, sexual orientation, and age, but do not take several social dimensions or intersectional categories into account (see Hanappi-Egger 2006; Klarsfeld 2010). Hanappi-Egger and Hofmann (2012) point out that, despite this limited purview (e.g. focusing just on women but leaving out the diversity among women), such measures are nonetheless important first steps in reducing complexity by tackling the most pressing issues faced by an organization. Thus, for example, DM programmes in the fields of engineering and science in Austria, which historically suffer from a very low level of participation by women, generally focus on measures to promote women, but do not consider any intra-group heterogeneity of women. This means that these measures address women without taking their background in terms of ethnicity, class, or living contexts—such as motherhood—into account (Hanappi-Egger 2011, 2012).

Scholarly work in the field of DM in Europe has generally concentrated on one of the 'big six' social categories as defined by European anti-discrimination and equal treatment legislation: age, disability, ethnicity, gender, religion, and sexual orientation. This legislation recognizes these categories both separately and as so-called 'multiple' discriminations (European Commission 2007; Schiek and Lawson 2011). While much has already been written by scholars in diversity studies on age and ethnicity, little work has been undertaken on the intersection between these two social categories—and, in particular, their relation with class issues is being understudied.

In this chapter we focus on the intersectionalities of the social categories of age, ethnicity, and class. Following the fundamental contribution of McCall (2005), we define intersectionality as 'the relationships among multiple dimensions and modalities of social relations and subject formations' (McCall 2005: 1771). Rooted in feminist movements and research, proponents of the intersectionality concept proclaimed that being a woman has different meanings, depending on a woman's race and class belongingness. As a reaction to criticisms of feminist research concerning the neglect of such differences, a growing body of literature that explicitly takes the analytical categories of race/ethnicity and class—and their interwovenness—into account evolved. Examples include Adib and Guerrier's (2003) analysis of the multiplicity of gendered identities according to ethnicity/nationality/race and class in the British hotel industry; Bryant and Jaworski's (2011) study on the role of gender, ethnicity, and class with particular respect to skills and job prestige in Australia; Zanoni's (2011) analysis of gender, ethnicity, disability issues, and class in a Belgian manufacturing firm; as well as Lin and Mac an Ghaill's (2013) investigation of the shifting gender identities of men, who, by migrating from rural to urban regions in China, also changed class identity.

These analyses primarily centre on gender and its intersection with two or more other social categories, thereby representing a quite established body of intersectionality literature. In contrast, this chapter refers to much smaller research bodies, since the key social categories under consideration are not gender but age, ethnicity, and class. These three analytical dimensions relate to different aspects of social status: whereas age and ethnicity primarily refer to social categorization and the question of recognition by the social environment in terms of socially accepted identity concepts and corresponding norms, of non-stigmatization and non-marginalization, class refers to the material, economic background of individuals, and therefore is linked to the question of distribution of wealth and social justice. Consequently, the discussion on how to eliminate marginalization and exclusion based on age, ethnicity, and class should, according to Fraser (1995), focus on both of these two factors, namely recognition of various identity concepts and distribution of wealth.

Within diversity studies there is a particular danger of ignoring the question of economic inequality and merely considering the issue of identity building (Zanoni 2011). Hanappi and Hanappi-Egger (2013) argue that the notion of diversity should be investigated in more detail in order to elaborate its interplay with the traditional concept of 'working class'. Fraser (1995) was at the basis of the discussion of social differentiation by highlighting the distinction between the injustice of distribution and the injustice of recognition. As she puts it: 'Here, then, is a difficult dilemma. I shall henceforth call it the redistribution–recognition dilemma. People who are subject to both cultural injustice and economic injustice need both recognition and redistribution. They need both to claim and to deny their specificity. How, if at all, is this possible?' (Fraser 1995: 77; for further discussion see also Fraser 2000; Fraser and Honneth 2003).

Against the background of this dilemma, in the following paragraphs we elaborate on both of its components: issues related to social identity (i.e. the recognition dimension) and issues related to social inequality (i.e. the redistribution dimension). However, corresponding with their prevalence in extant literature, in some paragraphs we put more emphasis on one of the two perspectives, and, on other occasions, we elaborate more on the other. Moreover, we take more functionalist DM perspectives into account (i.e. the business perspective), but also more critically oriented perspectives (as scholarly work on intersectionality historically takes a critical stance). Therewith, we try to capture the large spectrum of approaches within the intersectionality and diversity literature. At the same time, due to the scarcity of research on the intersectionalities of exactly those social categories under consideration in this chapter, restricting the focus to one single perspective would have rested on a very thin literature fundament. The latter is also the reason why the following sections cover only dyadic intersectionalities. A section on the triadic intersectionality of age, ethnicity, and class is lacking since, to the best or our knowledge, no relevant literature on exactly these three social categories (or more) exists.

The remainder of this chapter will proceed in two steps. First, we will introduce the key concepts of age, class, and ethnicity, and present empirical findings concerning the three dyadic relations: age–ethnicity, age–class, and class–ethnicity. Then we will critically reflect on the current academic debate on age, ethnicity, and class, and suggest avenues for future research on the intersectionalities of these categories.

The Age–Ethnicity–Class Dyads

First, we briefly describe the basic concepts of the three analytical categories. With respect to *age* in organizations, the scholarly discourse closely mirrors the long-term demographic trend throughout Europe towards ageing societies. Due to lower birth rates and rising life expectancy, the European population is growing older in terms of a higher ratio of elderly people. For instance, according to European Union (EU) statistics, the share of people aged 65 years and older will rise from 17 per cent to 30 per cent in 2060 (European Commission 2012). In line with this demographic shift, which has provoked recent legislative moves in several European countries towards higher retirement ages, organizational workforces are also ageing (e.g. in Austria, the retirement age of women born from June 1968 was raised from 60 to 65 years, and the law concerning early retirement arrangements was tightened, leading to lower numbers of early retirees). To meet the challenges associated with ageing workforces, many firms implement age management programmes—not only because of the larger numbers of older employees, but also because of the need for intergenerational management in order to exploit the knowledge and expertise of different generations (see e.g. Hanappi-Egger and Schnedlitz 2009).

However, one has to bear in mind that the meaning and connotation of *age* is strongly defined by the particular cultural context. For instance, Hanappi-Egger and Ukur (2011) show that in Kenya—contrary to the majority of Western European countries—age management largely addresses the problem of exclusion faced by younger people. Enjoying high social prestige, 'elderly people' find it is much easier to advance into management positions than younger workers with comparable knowledge, skills, and abilities. Such country differences in attitudes to age have been identified by Hampden-Turner and Trompenaars (1994) between the United States, Japan, Germany, France, Britain, Sweden, and the Netherlands. Similarly, the treatment of older workers can vary considerably across industrial sectors. For example, while employees aged 40 years and over are regarded in the IT (see e.g. Griffiths and Moore 2010) and advertising sectors as rather old, in other industries they may still be characterized as young—see, for example He (2014) for a discussion of the youth-centred image of the creative industries in China.

Ethnicity is related to demographic trends, too, and an issue affecting the daily business of organizations. Today, ethnically diverse workforces are not merely common in international companies but across the board (OECD 2012). Many firms implement programmes such as training in multilingual competence and ethnic networks, as well as measures to promote sensitivity to different religions and beliefs, thereby aiming to eliminate organizational barriers and to exploit the different cultural backgrounds of ethnic minority employees (Ortlieb and Sieben 2013; Ortlieb, Sieben, and Sichtmann 2014).

Even more than in the case of age, ethnicity is a social category that can only be understood within a specific cultural context (Klarsfeld 2010). In Western Europe, with its history of colonialism, bilateral labour agreements in order to combat shortages at domestic labour markets by attracting foreign workers, and diverse immigration policies, the term 'ethnicity' often signifies a mixture of several factors: country of origin, nationality, language, skin colour, religion, and value system. Such a broad meaning of ethnicity is far more complex than the typical US definition of an ethnic group as 'a set of people who share a common cultural background that is often embedded in language and religion' (Proudford and Nkomo 2006: 325).

Similar to age, organizational practices and social connotations related to ethnicity differ according to industrial sector. Prominent examples of industries in which a particular ethnic (or national) background indicates high quality are top restaurants employing a French chef or football teams comprising a Brazilian star player. In addition, there exist large differences between various kinds of ethnic backgrounds, reflecting the social hierarchy of a particular organization and country. For instance, Ortlieb and Sieben (2014), in a case study of a US-headed online trading company in Germany, demonstrate that job holders in higher positions of the formal hierarchy were either native Germans, Americans, or people of a Western European background. Inversely, people of other backgrounds, such as Romanians or those with African roots, worked in the lower rungs. Several organizational practices reinforce this social order, such as recruiting or the assignment of regional responsibilities to certain business units. Consideration of such differences of social status brings us to the third social category covered in this chapter.

Class describes an individual's socioeconomic background, as, for example, by categorizing persons as belonging to the 'upper', 'middle', or 'lower' class according to the amount of their property and the related power in society, politics, and organizations. Class is a general category that can comprise persons of diverse ethnicities, gender, age, sexual orientation, and disability. According to Hanappi and Hanappi-Egger (2013), class refers to the societal position in the productive process and an individual's consciousness of belonging to a certain class—in classical Marxian analysis, the proletariat (working class) versus the bourgeoisie. Class hierarchies are established by education, typically the possession (or lack) of a university degree, while class identity and class symbols provide a 'sense of one's position' in the class division and, consequently, within organizations. In diversity studies class is often ignored, as pointed out by Litvin (1997) and Zanoni and colleagues (2010). In a similar vein, Holvino (2002) stresses that, since class plays a crucial role in organizations in terms of access to promotion and career planning, it should be made visible.

In recent years, the topic of class has gained increasing attention by organization scholars. Examples include the case study by Dacin, Munir, and Tracey (2010) on dining rituals at Cambridge colleges, which demonstrates how this particular organizational practice serves to maintain the British class system, and the conceptual framework by Gray and Kish-Gephart (2013), which explains the mechanisms of 'class work', that is, the institutionalizing processes of creating and maintaining class distinctions in and through organizations. With special regard to diversity, the ethnographic study by Zanoni (2011) in a Belgian car manufacturing firm illustrates how socio-demographic identities are intertwined with the capitalist logic of using labour to maximize profitability.

Such issues are also addressed in the influential work of Bourdieu (e.g. 1986, 1989). According to Bourdieu (1989), class refers to the positioning in a social space ('field'), determined by the individual stock of economic, cultural, social, and symbolic capital. This positioning also depends on the family background—so that there exists a structurally determined package of opportunity for class mobility. Moreover, class (or capital endowment) is closely related to power: generally speaking, the greater an individual's volume of capital, the higher her/his position in the field, lending power, and privileges over other individuals in the same field. In this sense, organizations can be seen as social fields comprising specific mechanisms of inner (class) distinctions and class as referring to special, highly distinctive groups such as management and employees. Thereby, the distinction mechanisms are closely connected to both the external social environment and socio-demographic characteristics such as gender, age, and ethnicity.

Other approaches to class focus less on material and symbolic capital endowment than on an individual's social identity. Skeggs (1997), for instance, identifies a trend of 'disidentification', that is, a reluctance to identify with a particular class (frequently the working class due to negative connotations). Instead, individuals tend to refer to 'people like us' when they are essentially talking about class belonging (Savage, Bagall, and Longhurst 2001). Against the background of the aforementioned recognition–redistribution dilemma brought forward by Fraser (1995), these findings point to a particular problem of DM in organizations: while, on the one hand, diversity scholars and DM practitioners recognize inter-individual differences as to social identities, on the other hand the question is, on what basis should actors deal with redistribution issues if the considered individual's identity does not fit with the pre-set analytical categories?

Before we continue our presentation of age–ethnicity–class intersectionalities, it is important to clarify two issues. First, these analytical categories should be understood in a relational sense. That is, as many intersectionality scholars emphasize (e.g. Anderson 1996; Holvino 2010; Zanoni 2011; Anthias 2013), the categories' meaning and implications only evolve in combination, so that they can only be fully comprehended if considered as interacting forces. Second, it is vital for academics as well as for practitioners not to view individuals who share certain socio-demographic characteristics (e.g. young adults or those belonging to the middle class) as homogeneous groups. Critical diversity scholars have, time and again, pointed out the danger of such essentialism (e.g. Adib and Guerrier 2003; Proudford and Nkomo 2006; Zanoni et al. 2010). Nonetheless, we need to establish some starting point from which to attempt our presentation of the consequences of age–ethnicity–class intersectionalities. Thus, for the sake of clarity and to reduce the inherent complexity, in the rest of this chapter we draw on the three described analytical categories and undertake an analysis of their dyadic intersections.

The Age–Ethnicity Dyad

The intersection of age with ethnicity is related to both social identity and social inequality issues. One example taken from the literature on identity building is Buitelaar's (2006) analysis of the self-descriptions of a woman politician of Moroccan background in the Netherlands. Though the author does not explicitly focus on age, her analysis clearly reveals how aspects of the politician's identity associated with her ethnic background change during the course of her life. This observation, which might easily be replicated within business organizations, underlines the necessity for academics and management practitioners to carefully consider the great diversity within social groups, since an individual's self-understanding is dynamically constructed and dependent upon a variety of aspects such as ethnicity, age, and gender. Regarding inequalities, Barnum, Liden, and Ditomaso (1995) identify a pay gap between ethnic minority/black and ethnic majority/white employees of two US organizations, which increases with age. According to the authors' interpretation, this finding confirms the existence of certain barriers faced by ethnic minorities at the workplace. Since barriers and missed opportunities may accumulate during employment, pay discrepancies will grow by age and tenure.

While these analyses focus on social identity and inequality issues, other research highlights the business case for diversity with special regard to the interplay of the social categories of age and ethnicity. Examples include Balkundi and colleagues (2007), who investigate the role of social networks in organizations for safeguarding tacit knowledge in teams. Based on the theory of homophily, the authors argue that individuals tend to cluster towards others who display 'similarity' in some way or other. Both the age and the ethnic background of co-workers are prevalent characteristics on the basis of which people identify themselves as being similar (see e.g. Ibarra 1992 for a discussion on gender). Age diversity can lead to higher fragmentation of groups due to the formation of age-related subgroups, but also to less rivalry for jobs and promotion between junior and more senior members of organizations. Balkundi and colleagues (2007) conclude from their study of twenty-three production teams within a wood products company in the US: 'Our research spotlights the hitherto neglected structural consequences of older and younger people included in the same work team. The results imply that, irrespective of whether or not a team exhibits high ethnic or gender diversity, the presence of age diversity can protect the team from fragmentation' (Balkundi et al. 2007: 253). In other words, the negative effects of ethnic subgroups may be counterbalanced by age diversity. Thereby, team performance can be increased by processes such as mentoring and decreased rivalry.

Additional insights are provided by Leonard, Levine, and Joshi (2004). These authors have studied the performance impact of diversity within more than 700 US retail stores in which salespersons are demographically matched with customers in terms of age and ethnicity/race. The analyses reveal a robust negative statistical correlation between age diversity and sales, that is, the more diverse in age a store's workforce is, the lower the sales. Regarding ethnic/racial diversity, there are no clear results supporting the assumption of a similarity–attraction effect between employees and customers. While, for stores situated in US communities that have many non-English-speaking people of Asian and Hispanic background, the share of Asian and Hispanic employees is positively correlated with sales, this relationship is influenced by additional, but unknown, factors. Overall, the results of this study point to the dominance of the effect of age diversity on sales over the impact of ethnic diversity. However, causality structures appear much more complex than the simple matching of one or two social categories.

Pelled, Eisenhardt, and Xin (1999) also reveal varying effects of diversity on work team performance within forty-five intra-organizational quality management project teams in three US companies. Considering age diversity and race diversity, the authors show that, although socio-demographic diversity correlates with intra-group emotional conflict, the effect is not the same for age and race: whereas dissimilarity in race (and tenure) increases the frequency of emotional conflict, age diversity decreases such tension.

Alongside this literature, which largely originates from the US, other approaches to the relation of age and ethnicity focus on culturally constructed understandings of age and the management consequences thereof. Hanappi-Egger and Ukur (2011) point to the narrow 'Western' bias of focusing on discrimination against older employees when studying age. Using the case of Kenya as a counterexample against US-based research (as mentioned), they demonstrate how notions of age are culturally shaped, resulting in organizational age management policies that aim for the inclusion of younger employees in prestigious, leading positions. Hence, when considering the impact of ethnicity in age studies, it is necessary to keep different research and management perspectives in mind.

The Age–Class Dyad

Against the background of the Bourdieuian conceptions of the social field and class outlined, the issue of social inequality is closely interconnected with the question of class mobility chances. Accordingly, previous analyses, on the one hand, examine discriminatory practices which are based on the intersection of age and class, while, on the other hand, they study the mechanisms that enable or hinder class mobility at certain life stages.

Regarding recruitment, Ashley and Empson (2013) show that British leading law firms prefer white, privately educated 'elite' young people as trainees. The authors suggest that such a profile satisfies the expectations of clients, in particular 'specific forms of institutional and embodied capital which are arbitrarily legitimized and, compared with relevant credentials and qualifications, relatively scarce' (Ashley and Empson 2013: 237). In Bourdieu's terminology, for people to become a partner—and even trainee—of a leading law firm it is necessary to possess a particular habitus, indicating upper- or at least upper-middle-class membership. In a similar vein, Tatli and Özbilgin (2012a) demonstrate how recruiting practices and the career system of the British arts and cultural sector lead to discrimination against young people from the lower classes. In contrast to law firms, individuals working in arts and cultural organizations do not necessarily need to have a distinctive habitus in order to satisfy the expectations of clients. Instead, these organizations simply offer young interns a very low remuneration. Since professional careers in the arts and cultural sector generally begin with a number of lengthy internships, entry to these professions is effectively blocked to individuals who lack a solid financial backing. In terms of DM, this means that social inequality based on class is reproduced by such recruitment practices—and that class-based inequality could be mitigated through recruitment practices and pay systems that do not favour young professionals of upper-class background.

Focusing on class mobility in terms of career steps, promotion, and higher salaries, the empirical analyses by Featherman, Selbee, and Mayer (1989) reveal that transitions between classes can take place both in early and later phases of the professional career. Thereby, the probability of upward class mobility at an early rather than late stage depends on the societal and structural context. For example, according to Featherman, Selbee, and Mayer (1989), free access to school and other forms of education increases the probability of upward class mobility in earlier career stages. Within organizations, the internal career system also plays an important role, in particular when it comes to the question of the appropriate age (related to professional status) at which individuals are considered 'fit' for the next career rung.

Beyond the question of how organizations foster or hinder class mobility, further research on their potential to create, maintain, or destroy class boundaries at different individual life or career stages is needed. One example is the distinction between 'blue-collar' and 'white-collar' employees that prevails in many organizations, reflecting labour law or collective agreements. This distinction corresponds with disparities in short- and long-term income and career prospects, procedures of socialization in the organization, working time regulations, notice periods, and retirement regulations. However, employers can mitigate these differences by negotiating counteracting company agreements or by setting guidelines for staff contracts that stipulate equal terms for both employee status groups. Research that analyses an employer's motives for harmonizing personnel practices and the mechanisms that support or hinder such practices seems to be particularly promising.

The Class–Ethnicity Dyad

Scholars of intersectionality, such as Anthias (2013), stress the need to integrate ethnicity (and gender) into class studies in order to overcome a monolithic understanding of social groups. However, extant literature is rather fragmented, focusing either on social inequality and discrimination issues associated with the employment of migrant workers and ethnic minorities—hence, members of the lower classes (e.g. Fleischmann and Dronkers 2010; Skuterud and Su 2012) or on the career prospects of highly skilled employees with international roots (e.g. Al Ariss and Syed 2011; van den Bergh and Du Plessis 2012; Tomlinson et al. 2013). This point is also raised by Berry and Bell (2012), who criticize the one-sided focus of mainstream international management research. This literature focuses on highly skilled, well-paid, white Anglo-Saxon (male) 'expatriates' and masks the underprivileged 'migrants', who are less skilled, less paid, and from other countries (and female), though both types of people are employees of multinational corporations.

Although some critics argue that Bourdieu's studies of the society and culture of the Kabyle in Algeria are shaped by ethnocentrism (e.g. Lane 2000; Anthias 2013), we find his approach to class via the different forms of capital helpful when analysing the class–ethnicity intersectionality, because it provides a multidimensional conceptualization of class that relates to economic, educational, and cultural aspects. For instance, Al Ariss and Syed's (2011) qualitative study of thirty-nine highly skilled Lebanese migrants in France highlights the importance of social capital for a successful international career. The immigrants received tremendous support from their friends and family members while they had to apply for visas, study programmes, flats, or job positions. All kinds of capital, if mobilized, helped the immigrants to pursue a professional or even managerial career. This study is an example of research on individuals who are formally members of an ethnic minority, yet who are clearly privileged over less educated immigrants and the native French due to their considerable stock of capital—that is, due to class membership. Similarly, Hernández-León (2004) elaborates the complex mechanisms involved in the various forms of individual capital that enable a group of Mexican immigrants in Texas to maintain their comparatively high (class-related) status by finding an occupational niche in highly skilled jobs linked to the oil industry. The thirty-six immigrants under consideration did not only draw on their social networks to get a well-paid job (in general, companies replaced formal recruitment measures by informal activities within the immigrant network), but they also benefited from their urban–industrial background and the professional skills acquired during their former lives in Mexico.

In a similar vein, Bachan and Sheehan (2010) find that the social networks of Polish immigrants to the UK not only facilitate the search for suitable employment but can also assist in the process of 'occupational upgrading'. Because their social networks worked very well, it took the immigrants on average only one month to find their first job in the UK. Moreover, later on, their social networks helped them to get a subsequent job with even better working conditions. While this kind of job betterment does not automatically entail a shift in class, it is certainly preferable to a downgrade and may indeed open up long-term opportunities. However, Sumption (2009) also highlights the danger that immigrant networks can 'lock-in' ethnic minorities to low-skilled jobs.

While these analyses relate to more material aspects and social inequality, Adib and Guerrier (2003) focus on social identities at work. On the basis of narrative interviews with women hotel employees in the UK, this study shows how the women construct their social identity by differentiating between themselves and 'the others' along varying social categories. For instance, one of the respondents, who, during a management internship, had to do housekeeping tasks, refused to identify as a 'real' chambermaid. By pointing out that, in contrast to her chambermaid colleagues, who all came from Portugal, she was British, this respondent simultaneously distinguished between the (Portuguese) lower-class chambermaids and herself as a (British) middle-class management aspirant.

Other research on the intersection of class and ethnicity critically examines the business case. Rodriguez (2004) shows how US employers actively exploit the social networks of their Mexican employees to recruit and control additional unskilled—that is, lower-class—agricultural workers. The already mentioned ethnographic analysis of blue-collar workers at a Belgian automobile company by Zanoni (2011) is even more sophisticated. The author clearly demonstrates how the discursive construction of ethnicity (and other social categories) by organizational decision makers is intermeshed with business logic. For example, during a process of organizational restructuring at the company, which was accompanied by redundancies, it became obvious that the image communicated by the management of a highly valued workforce diversity is constrained by business needs: while the company, on the one hand, praised workforce diversity as an organizational resource, on the other hand, supervisors interviewed by the study's author relied heavily on the 'usability' of ethnic minority workers within the production process of the company.

All these analyses provide valuable insights into the manifold forms of class–ethnicity intersectionalities and their consequences. Future research that expands this literature, thereby applying different research perspectives and different methodological approaches, would be highly desirable.

Research Challenges Concerning the Intersectionalities of Age, Class, and Ethnicity

The previous discussion in the section 'The Age–Ethnicity–Class Dyads' has shown how the rare attempts at research into the intersectionality of age, ethnicity, and class have generally concentrated on the respective dyads in isolation. Thereby, the three social categories are associated with different aspects of social status. While the analytical categories of age and ethnicity mainly relate to social identity and recognition by others, class is linked to the socioeconomic background of individuals, and therefore refers to social inequality and the different set of materialized living conditions. This divide is mirrored by the related forms of academic research: traditionally, the focus in *diversity studies* tended to lie on social categories such as ethnicity and age rather than class. In contrast, scholars in *class studies* emphasize social inequality and frequently ignore issues of social identity. However, in the meantime there are already contributions that address both aspects. Examples include the study by Zanoni (2011). In addition, Woodhams, Lupton, and Cowling (2015) show that there is a correlation between pay penalty and multiple disadvantages in terms of gender, race, age, and disability. The analysis of pay data from a large UK-based company shows that the pay discrimination of employees increases exponentially with regard to the number of individual disadvantages. In other words, payment of employees differs significantly from the salary of the most privileged group (men, white, non-disabled, mid-career, aged 31–45 years). However, the study still does not integrate a class concept but highlights a correlation between the deviation of the 'ideal worker' and pay discrimination.

We argued that the identification of individual social groups based on age, ethnicity, or class may facilitate understanding of intersectionalities, because this approach reduces complexity. Nevertheless, care must be taken when addressing individual social identity groups not to oversimplify the study of diversity. Management scholars and practitioners should avoid treating social groups as internally homogenous, nor should they neglect the concrete organizational context, because the meaning of social categorization within organizations is strongly shaped by the organizational context and the interplay of a variety of social categories. With respect to this complex and multifaceted issue of intersectionality, Tatli and Özbilgin (2012b) stress the problem that most diversity scholars concentrate on a single diversity category, thereby adopting an *etic* approach. Here, etic means that the social categories under study are pre-set by the researcher and subsequent analyses are based upon unquestioned specifications of social category. Contrary to this, an *emic* approach requires that the meaning of social categories are contextualized, adopting—in the language of McCall (2005)—an anti-categorical approach. Rather than searching for social categories specified *ex ante* and their role in organizational dynamics, an important topic for future research relates to the fundamental question of which social categories are activated in specific organizational contexts and how they are made relevant.

In other words, we suggest that future investigations into the intersectionalities of age, ethnicity, and class (as well as other social categories) should closely examine the mechanisms by which organizational practices (re)inforce or mitigate inequalities associated with the intersections of age, ethnicity, and class.

References

Adib, A. and Guerrier, Y. (2003). The interlocking of gender with nationality, race, ethnicity and class: the narratives of women in hotel work. *Gender, Work and Organization*, 10: 413–32.

Al Ariss, A. and Syed, J. (2011). Capital mobilization of skilled migrants: a relational perspective. *British Journal of Management*, 22: 286–304.

Anderson, C. D. (1996). Understanding the inequality problematic: from scholarly rhetoric to theoretical reconstruction. *Gender and Society*, 10: 729–47.

Anthias, F. (2013). Hierarchies of social location, class and intersectionality: towards a translocational frame. *International Sociology*, 28: 121–38.

Ashley, L. and Empson, L. (2013). Differentiation and discrimination: understanding social class and social exclusion in leading law firms. *Human Relations*, 66: 219–44.

Bachan, R. and Sheehan, M. (2010). On the labour market progress of Polish accession workers in south-east England. *International Migration*, 49: 104–34.

Balkundi, P., Kilduff, M., Barsness, Z. L., and Michael, J. H. (2007). Demographic antecedents and performance consequences of structural holes in work teams. *Journal of Organizational Behavior*, 28: 241–60.

Barnum, P., Liden, R. C., and Ditomaso, N. (1995). Double jeopardy for women and minorities: pay differences with age. *Academy of Management Journal*, 38: 863–80.

Berry, D. P. and Bell, M. P. (2012). Expatriates: gender, race and class distinctions in international management. *Gender, Work and Organization*, 19: 10–28.

Bourdieu, P. (1986). The forms of capital. In J. Richardson (ed.), *Handbook of Theory and Research for the Sociology of Education*. New York: Greenwood, 241–58.

Bourdieu, P. (1989). Social space and symbolic power. *Sociological Theory*, 7: 14–25.

Bryant, L. and Jaworski, K. (2011). Gender, embodiment and place: the gendering of skills shortages in the Australian mining and food and beverage processing industries. *Human Relations*, 64: 1345–67.

Buitelaar, M. (2006). 'I am the ultimate challenge': accounts of intersectionality in the life-story of a well-known daughter of Moroccan migrant workers in the Netherlands. *European Journal of Women's Study*, 13: 259–76.

Dacin, M. T., Munir, K., and Tracey, P. (2010). Formal dining at Cambridge colleges: linking ritual performance and institutional maintenance. *Academy of Management Journal*, 53: 1393–418.

European Commission (2007). *Tackling Multiple Discrimination: Practices, Policies and Laws*. Luxembourg: Office for Official Publications of the European Communities.

European Commission (2012). *Ageing Report: Europe Needs to Prepare for Growing Older*. <http://ec.europa.eu/economy_finance/articles/structural_reforms/2012-05-15_ageing_report_en.htm>, accessed 2 January 2013.

Featherman, D. L., Selbee, L. K., and Mayer, K. U. (1989). Social class and the structuring of the life course in Norway and West Germany. In D. I. Kertzer and W. K. Schaie (eds.), *Age Structuring in Comparative Perspective*. Hillsdale, NJ: Erlbaum, 55–93.

Fleischmann, F. and Dronkers, J. (2010). Unemployment among immigrants in European labour markets: an analysis of origin and destination effects. *Work, Employment and Society*, 24: 337–54.

Fraser, N. (1995). From redistribution to recognition? Dilemmas of justice in a 'post-socialist' age. *New Left Review*, 1: 68–93.

Fraser, N. (2000). Rethinking recognition. *New Left Review*, 3: 107–20.

Fraser, N. and Honneth, A. (2003). *Umverteilung oder Anerkennung? Eine politisch-philisophische Kontroverse*. Frankfurt: Suhrkamp.

Gray, B. and Kish-Gephart, J. J. (2013). Encountering social class differences at work: how 'class work' perpetuates inequality. *Academy of Management Review*, 38: 670–99.

Griffiths, M. and Moore, K. (2010). 'Disappearing women': a study of women who left the UK ICT sector. *Journal of Technology Management & Innovation*, 5: 95–107.

Hampden-Turner, C. and Trompenaars, F. (1994). *The Seven Cultures of Capitalism*. London: Piatkus.

Hanappi, G. and Hanappi-Egger, E. (2013). Gramsci meets Veblen: on the search for a new revolutionary class. *Journal of Economic Issues*, 47: 375–81.

Hanappi-Egger, E. (2006). Gender and diversity from a management perspective: synonyms or complements? *Journal of Organisational Transformation and Social Change*, 3: 121–34.

Hanappi-Egger, E. (2011). *The Triple M of Organizations: Man, Management and Myth*. Vienna and New York: Springer.

Hanappi-Egger, E. (2012). 'Shall I stay or shall I go?' On the role of diversity management for women's retention in SET professions. *Equality, Diversity and Inclusion*, 31: 144–57.

Hanappi-Egger, E. (2013). Backstage: the organizational gendered agenda in science, engineering and technology professions. *European Journal of Women's Studies*, 20: 279–94.

Hanappi-Egger, E. and Hofmann, R. (2012). Diversitätsmanagement unter der Perspektive organisationalen Lernens: Wissens- und Kompetenzentwicklung für inklusive Organisationen. In R. Bendl, E. Hanappi-Egger, and R. Hofmann (eds.), *Diversität und Diversitätsmanagement*. Vienna: Facultas, 327–49.

Hanappi-Egger, E. and Schnedlitz, P. (eds.) (2009). *Ageing Society. Altern in der Stadt: Aktuelle Trends und ihre Bedeutung für die strategische Stadtentwicklung*. Vienna: Facultas.

Hanappi-Egger, E. and Ukur, G. (2011). Challenging diversity management: on the meaning of cultural context: the case of Kenya. Paper presented at the 7th Critical Management Studies Conference, Naples, Italy, 11–13 July.

He, J. (2014). *Creative Industry Districts: An Analysis of Dynamics, Networks and Implications on Creative Clusters in Shanghai. Advances in Asian Human–Environmental Research*. New York: Springer International.

Hernández-León, R. (2004). Restructuring at the source: high-skilled industrial migration from Mexico to the United States. *Work and Occupations*, 31: 424–52.

Holvino, E. (2002). Class: 'a difference that makes a difference' in organizations. *Diversity Factor*, 10: 28–34.

Holvino, E. (2010). Intersections: the simultaneity of race, gender and class in organization studies. *Gender, Work and Organization*, 17: 248–77.

Ibarra, H. (1992). Homophily and differential returns: sex differences in network structure and access in an advertising firm. *Administrative Science Quarterly*, 37: 422–47.

Klarsfeld, A. (ed.) (2010). *International Handbook on Diversity Management at Work: Country Perspectives on Diversity and Equal Treatment*. Cheltenham: Edward Elgar.

Lane, J. F. (2000). *Pierre Bourdieu: A Critical Introduction*. London and Sterling, VA: Pluto Press.

Leonard, J. S., Levine, D. I., and Joshi, A. (2004). Do birds of a feather shop together? The effects on performance of employees' similarity with one another and with customers. *Journal of Organizational Behavior*, 25: 731–54.

Lin, X. and Mac an Ghaill, M. (2013). Chinese male peasant workers and shifting masculine identities in urban workspaces. *Gender, Work and Organization*, 20: 498–511.

Litvin, D. R. (1997). The discourse of diversity: from biology to management. *Organization*, 4: 187–209.

McCall, L. (2005). The complexity of intersectionality. *Journal of Women in Culture and Society*, 30: 1771–80.

OECD (Organisation of Economic Co-operation and Development) (2012). *International Migration Outlook 2012*. Paris: OECD Publishing.

Ortlieb, R. and Sieben, B. (2013). Employment strategies and business logic: why do companies employ ethnic minorities? *Group and Organization Management*, 38: 480–511.

Ortlieb, R. and Sieben, B. (2014). The making of inclusion as structuration: empirical evidence of a multinational company. *Equality, Diversity and Inclusion*, 33: 235–48.

Ortlieb, R., Sieben, B., and Sichtmann, C. (2014). Assigning migrants to customer contact jobs: a context-specific exploration of the business case for diversity. *Review of Managerial Science*, 8: 249–73.

Pelled, L. H., Eisenhardt, K. M., and Xin, K. R. (1999). Exploring the black box: an analysis of work group diversity, conflict, and performance. *Administrative Science Quarterly*, 44: 1–28.

Proudford, K. L. and Nkomo, S. (2006). Race and ethnicity in organizations. In A. M. Konrad, P. Prasad, and J. Pringle (eds.), *Handbook of Workplace Diversity*. London: Sage, 323–44.

Rodriguez, N. (2004). 'Workers wanted': employer recruitment of immigrant labor. *Work and Occupations*, 31: 453–73.

Savage, M., Bagall, G., and Longhurst, B. (2001). Ordinary, ambivalent and defensive: class identities in the north west of England. *Sociology*, 35: 875–92.

Schiek, D. and Lawson, A. (eds.) (2011). *EU Non-Discrimination Law and Intersectionality*. Farnham: Ashgate.

Skeggs, B. (1997). *Formations of Class and Gender*. Cambridge: Polity.

Skuterud, M. and Su, M. (2012). Immigrants and the dynamics of high-wage jobs. *Industrial and Labor Relations Review*, 65: 377–97.

Sumption, M. (2009). *Social Networks and Polish Immigration to the UK*. Economics of Migration Working Paper. London: Institute for Public Policy Research.

Tatli, A. and Özbilgin, M. (2012a). Surprising intersectionalities of inequality and privilege: the case of the arts and cultural sector. *Equality, Diversity and Inclusion*, 31: 249–65.

Tatli, A., and Özbilgin, M. F. (2012b). An emic approach to intersectional study of diversity at work: a Bourdieuan framing. *International Journal of Management Reviews*, 14: 180–200.

Tomlinson, J., Muzio, D., Sommerlad, H., Webley, L., and Duff, L. (2013). Structure, agency and career strategies of white women and black and minority ethnic individuals in the legal profession. *Human Relations*, 66: 245–69.

Van den Bergh, R. and Du Plessis, Y. (2012). Highly skilled migrant women: a career development framework. *Journal of Management Development*, 31: 142–58.

Woodhams, C., Lupton, B., and Cowling, M. (2015). The snowballing penalty effect: multiple disadvantage and pay. *British Journal of Management*, 26: 63–77.

Zanoni, P. (2011). Diversity in the lean automobile factory: doing class through gender, disability and age. *Organization*, 18: 105–27.

Zanoni, P., Janssens, M., Benschop, Y., and Nkomo, S. (2010). Unpacking diversity, grasping inequality: rethinking difference through critical perspectives. *Organization*, 17: 9–29.

CHAPTER 23

PEOPLE WITH DISABILITIES

Identity, Stigmatization, Accommodation, and Intersection with Gender and Ageing in Effects on Employment Outcomes

DAVID C. BALDRIDGE, JOY E. BEATTY, ALISON M. KONRAD, AND MARK E. MOORE

INTRODUCTION

THE prevalence of disability ranges from a reported 3 per cent of the Korean population to 20.6 per cent of the Swedish population aged 20–64, with an average of 14 per cent for nineteen Organisation for Economic Co-operation and Development (OECD) member states (OECD 2003). The 2010 Global Burden of Disease Study funded by the Bill and Melinda Gates Foundation identified the leading causes of disability to be low back pain, major depressive disorder, iron-deficiency anaemia, neck pain, chronic obstructive pulmonary disease, anxiety disorders, migraine, diabetes, and falls (Vos et al. 2012).

Reported disability statistics are contested, however. Even within countries, the term 'disability' is not consistently defined (McLean 2003). For instance, Human Resources and Skills Development Canada (HRSDC) states that 'there is no single, harmonized "operational" definition of disability across federal programs' in Canada (HRSDC n.d.), making counting the prevalence of disability difficult. The most widely accepted definition of disability is provided by the World Health Organization (WHO), 'Disabilities is an umbrella term, covering impairments, activity limitations, and participation restrictions. An impairment is a problem in body function or structure; an activity limitation is a difficulty encountered by an individual in executing a task or action; while a participation restriction is a problem experienced by an individual in involvement in life situations' (WHO 2013). Under such a definition, considerable latitude exists, allowing nations and provinces to include or exclude individuals from disability statistics.

Advocacy groups bemoan the under-counting of members of the disabled community and its downward impact on the perceived need for programmes and supports (Konrad, Leslie, and Peuramaki 2007).

Adults with disabilities are less likely to work for pay than their counterparts without disabilities (Jensen et al. 2005; Bagilhole 2010). The US reports that 61.1 per cent of adults aged 21 to 64 work for pay, compared to 54.8 per cent of adults with non-severe disabilities and only 19.9 per cent of adults with severe disabilities (Brault 2012). Eurostat reports that, in 2002, while 17.8 per cent of adults in fifteen countries of the European Union had a disability, only 14.3 per cent of employed adults were disabled, and 26.0 per cent of working-age adults not in the active labour force were persons with disabilities (Eurostat 2009).

Not all working-age persons with disabilities are able to work, even when provided with workplace accommodations. Some adults with disabilities in the inactive population may be able to work, but may have been discouraged from seeking employment due to perceptions of discrimination or lack of workplace accommodations. Even when such discouraged workers are not considered, however, workers with disabilities experience consistently higher unemployment rates than their non-disabled counterparts. The OECD reported an average unemployment rate of 9.5 per cent among non-disabled workers, compared to 17.2 per cent of workers with disabilities across 17 countries in the late 1990s (OECD 2003).

Disability employment policies are intended to reduce the rate of unemployment and worker discouragement by requiring employers to provide workplace accommodations for workers with disabilities. For example, Title I of the Americans with Disabilities Act of 1990 (ADA) and amended in 2008 (ADAAA) requires employers to provide reasonable accommodations for workers with disabilities, to allow these workers to participate in paid employment in the occupation for which they are qualified. Such accommodations include but are not limited to 'job restructuring, part-time or modified work schedules, reassignment to a vacant position, acquisition or modification of equipment or devices, appropriate adjustment of examinations, training materials or policies, the provision of qualified readers or interpreters, and other similar accommodations' (US Department of Justice 2008). Accommodations are required up to the point of undue hardship to the employer, defined as an action requiring significant difficulty or expense, considering the employer's financial resources and potential impact on the employer's operations (US Department of Justice 2008). The Ontario Human Rights Commission requires similar actions on the part of employers in the province (Ontario Human Rights Commission n.d.). The Dutch Working Conditions Act of January 2007 requires employers to develop a return-to-work plan cooperatively with workers who have become disabled. Return-to-work plans customize the work situation in ways that allow workers with disabilities to continue to contribute value to the organization (Kopnina and Haafkens 2010).

Other policy initiatives require more proactive action on the part of employers, but these policies tend to be limited to the public or publicly regulated sectors of the economy (Bagilhole 2010). For instance, Canada's Employment Equity Act of 1986 required publicly regulated employers (such as banks, broadcasters, telecommunication companies, airlines, railways, and others) to remove barriers as well as implement positive initiatives to increase the employment of people with disabilities (PWD) (as well as women, members of the Aboriginal nations, and visible minority groups). Examples of positive policies include job advertisements on websites providing resources for persons with disabilities, or an apprentice programme directed towards people with disabilities. Covered employers are required to monitor the extent to which their labour force reflects the proportion of workers with disabilities in their industry and set of occupations, and to set goals for improving their statistics (HRSDC 2010). Similarly, the UK's 2005 Disability Discrimination Act requires public sector employers to monitor and report on the extent to which they employ persons with disabilities, and to develop action plans for increasing their statistics (Roulstone and Warren 2006). Research has shown that such proactive policies result in an increase in the employment of women (Leck and Saunders 1992), but less is known about their impact on workers with disabilities.

Disability status intersects with gender and age in its effects on workplace outcomes. Research in multiple countries shows that, as workers age, they are more likely to acquire a disability (Bruyère 2006; Stover et al. 2007; Berecki-Gisolf et al. 2012). For instance, in Canada, 16.6 per cent of the population aged 15 and over has a disability, including 6.1 per cent of adults aged 25 to 34, 9.6 per cent of adults aged 35 to 44, 15.1 per cent of adults aged 45 to 54, 22.8 per cent of adults aged 55 to 64, and 43.4 per cent of adults aged 65 and older (Statistics Canada 2007). In the US, nearly 60 per cent of disability discrimination charges are made by workers age 40 and older (Bjelland et al. 2010). The implication for employers is that ageing workforces will increasingly require accommodations for disability.

Disability status results in systematically different employment outcomes for women and men. Studies from around the world show that women with disabilities are less likely than their male counterparts to be active in the labour force (Eurostat 2001; Karlsson et al. 2006; Oguzoglu 2011; Brault 2012; Lederer, Rivard, and Mechakra-Tahiri 2012). A Swedish study indicates that this gender gap is partly explained by women's lower wages and poorer working conditions (Claussen and Dalgard 2009). Both Finnish and US research indicates particularly negative effects of both workplace and marital conflicts (including experiences of violence) on labour force participation for women with disabilities (Appelberg et al. 1996; Hogan et al. 2011). The implication for employers is that women with disabilities, particularly those in low-quality employment, will be difficult to retain in the labour force.

The purpose of this chapter is to provide an overview of academic research in the field of disability in the workplace. We will summarize and synthesize research results on disability identity development, employment outcomes, stigmatization and stereotyping, and workplace accommodations. Within each of these topics, we highlight research examining the intersection of disability status with other social categorizations, particularly gender and age. We end with a reflection on extant knowledge and directions for future research and practice.

Disability Status and Identity

Diversity scholars have long encouraged us to conceptualize identities as multifaceted and dynamic (Nkomo and Cox 1996). Identities are constructed in response to social interactions, as people come to understand themselves based on information reflected back to them from others. Disability identity is less stable than other social identity markers like race, gender, and sexuality, because we may all experience a disability at some point in our lives. Only 15 per cent of PWD are born with a functional impairment (Siebers 2008), while 85 per cent acquire them later in life. People with disabilities can feel isolated because they do not have peers with disabilities, and they lack role models. In some cases their status is invisible, which makes identification of similar others difficult, and their families of origin are likely to be from the dominant non-disabled culture (Scotch 1988).

The development of an individual's disability identity may begin with trying to act as non-disabled; followed by a period of isolation and conflict; and then finally incorporating disability as part of one's identity (Gilson, Tusler, and Gill 1997). Gilson, Tusler, and Gill (1997) alluded to the component theory of disability identity development which focuses on 'integration', which they define as 'the act of incorporating or combining into a whole' (Gilson, Tusler, and Gill 1997: 39). The integration concept is applied at four levels: integrating into: (1) society; (2) the disability community; as well as (3) integrating one's internal notions of self; and (4) external self-presentation. If all the levels are completed, people with disabilities may claim a 'proud identification' (Gilson, Tusler, and Gill 1997: 45) and freedom to express their authentic selves. Eventually, as people with disabilities come to embrace their disability, they may view their disability as an integral and valued part of their identity, a part they would not eliminate if they had the option (Smart and Smart 2006). As this sense of affiliation grows, a disability culture develops with history, language, and customs (Gilson, Tusler, and Gill 1997). This 'coming out' stage is considered the full fruition of disability identity development (Gilson, Tusler, and Gill 1997), but it is important to note that not all people with disabilities will (or will *want* to) reach this level of collective identity. Living with disability does not automatically translate into claiming a disability identity (Crooks, Chouinard, and Wilton 2008).

Further, disability identity does not develop in isolation. Imrie (2004) notes that people can experience the same disability very differently, depending on their age and gender. Recent empirical work by Riach and Loretto (2009) looks at the relationship between ageing, disability, and unemployment within a sample of unemployed workers in Scotland. Their participants felt that the unemployment and job support systems in place in Scotland imposed disabled identities on them by assuming that their disabilities made them ineligible for work. In their view, employers had conflated the identities of 'incapable', 'older', and 'disabled' to create insurmountable barriers to employment. When they were considered for employment, their age and disability limited the kinds of jobs they were expected to take. Employers assumed that 'disabled' and 'older' workers could only do particular jobs, like sitting at a computer. Some were offered low-level work based on their status as disabled or older, rather than their experience and skill set. This reaction led some of the older workers to lie about their disability on the job applications.

Yet, for these workers, their own experiences of identity were that disability status was more fluid, and that they moved in and out of disability status episodically, depending on their physical condition on any particular day. They had compartmentalized their impairment, instead of incorporating it as a permanent feature of who they are. Riach and Loretto (2009) suggest that this framing of identity by people with disabilities allows them to side-step the disabled/non-disabled dichotomy. The discrimination these older disabled workers experienced was more than just the 'additive' discrimination experienced by either category—it was 'intersectional' discrimination, 'where the components cannot easily be broken down into their constituent parts, and the effect is cumulative rather than additive' (Riach and Loretto 2009: 115).

A recent US study by Ostrander (2008) also focuses on the interplay between disability identity and other identities, highlighting the bracketing of disability identity from other, more valued identities. Ostrander examined the relationship between disability, masculinity, and race, interviewing men who were disabled due to violently acquired spinal cord injuries (often caused by gunshot wounds). He found that a disability identity was inconsistent with their masculine identities, and that the men took steps to assert masculinity in other ways to make up for their perceived physical deficiencies—for example, by carrying a gun. The participants in his study, African American and Latino men, did not believe that their disability affected their racial identities; however, the intersectionality of race and disability was evidenced by the fact that they felt that, due to racial stereotyping, others tended to assume that their disabilities were due to gang violence.

In the disability population, individuals with additional stigmatized identity markers have different experiences of stereotyping and discrimination, and evidence suggests that the effects of multiple categories are cumulative. A recent US empirical study by Shaw, Chan, and McMahon (2012) analysed data from the National Equal Employment Opportunity Commission, which compiled allegations of discrimination under the ADA. Studying the interactive effects of gender, race, disability status, industry, and size of employer on discrimination, their study split disability into the four categories of behavioural, neurological, physical, and sensory impairments. They found clear interactive effects. Women older than 35 years from racial and ethnic minority backgrounds with behavioural disorders represented three of the highest five harassment groups (Shaw, Chan, and McMahon 2012: 88). These women tended to work for very large or very small companies, and frequently represented industries such as manufacturing, health care, public administration, and retail. The researchers suggest that the effects of membership in various stigmatized categories are not merely additive; again, there is an intersectional effect that multiplies the risk of harassment. They note that legal systems should revisit their definitions of discrimination to consider the effects of multiple categories, a consideration scholars have raised regarding the UK as well (Bagilhole 2010).

The problem is that, currently in the legal domain, each kind of discrimination needs to be proven and litigated independently. People may experience discrimination in multiple categories that does not meet the threshold for legal action in any one category, yet, taken as a set, would reach the threshold of discrimination. Current legal options do not allow for the consideration of the effects of multiple stigmatized categories.

Thus far, we have discussed individuals' conceptions of identity, but identity can also be conceptualized at the group level; the contrast between individual and group notions is relevant for the development of a political disability identity. In identity politics, stigmatized groups argue that the categories to which they have been assigned—for example, woman, elderly, disabled—are socially constructed and reinforced. Those groups so labelled challenge their assigned identities and concomitant exclusion: 'They challenge the system of thought that stigmatized them' (Moon 2013: 1340), exposing how dominant and taken-for-granted ideologies can lead to oppression. The concept of intersectionality highlights the way multiple identities intertwine, creating a liminal social space that is 'in-between' the dominant social positions (Holvino 2008: 251). Different identities mutually construct one another, and power relations emerge from people's simultaneously held identities—including race, gender, age, disability status, ethnicity, class, nationality, and sexuality as simultaneous processes of identity (Holvino 2008; Zanoni 2011).

In feminist studies, intersectionality additionally implies the consequences of membership in multiple protected classes, and whether people with these attributes experience more discrimination than those with single membership (Cole 2009). Some work focuses on the additive effects of multiple identity group memberships, highlighting 'double' or 'triple' disadvantages faced by individuals disadvantaged by disability status as well as gender, race/ethnicity, or other devalued identity (Berdahl and Moore 2006). Other research illuminates the distinctive experiences of disadvantage faced by individuals holding different sets of identities (Bagilhole 2010). This inter- and intra-categorical approach implies the need for a programme of research that examines how the experience of ableism differs categorically between persons holding different sets of identities, for instance, younger men with disabilities compared to older women with disabilities.

Historically, disability has been framed as an individual issue to be resolved with individual accommodations. In the traditional biomedical model of disability, disability is defined by medical professionals using medical language—outsiders without direct experience with disability helping passive and compliant patients. Disability is objective and represents an individual's pathology, to be described and categorized in terms of physical functioning and limitations. Internalization of these messages reinforces people with disabilities' alienation and lack of power, leading to a negative self-image. Since disability is an individual affair, the disabled are fragmented, as aspects of collective experience and identity are overlooked (Scotch 1988).

The minority group model of disability identity proposed by Hahn (1994) and developed in reaction to the biomedical model, argues that disability is a social and cultural phenomenon shaped by public policies; disability lives in the relationship between the individual and the environment. This is a political model of identity, arguing for the rights of self-definition and self-determination, elimination of prejudice, and full equality and civil rights under the law (Smart and Smart 2006). Initially, disability advocates focused on the positive social stereotypes, such as overcoming adversity, inner strength, and cheerfulness in the face of adversity (Gilson, Tusler, and Gill 1997). Through legal advocacy, persons with disabilities shaped a minority group identity to support a positive self-image that reflected self-determination and autonomy. As a result of struggle and advocacy based on persons with disabilities identifying themselves as a social group with shared interests, key legislation occurred in multiple countries, for instance, the Rehabilitation Act of 1973 and the ADA of 1990 in the US and the Disability Discrimination Act (1995 amended 2004) and the Disability Discrimination Act (2005) in the UK.

Employment Outcomes of Workers with Disabilities

A review of almost twenty years of research showed that enduring employment status is positively associated with employment outcomes for workers with disabilities (Crisp 2005). Recent Canadian research has shown that, in particular, employment in a permanent full-time job that fully utilizes one's skills and abilities is positively associated with life satisfaction and negatively associated with perceived discrimination among workers with disabilities (Konrad et al. 2012). Unfortunately, workers with disabilities are less likely than their non-disabled counterparts to hold such advantageous positions in the labour market (Bruyère, Erickson, and Ferrentino 2003). Across nations, workers with disabilities are more likely than their counterparts to experience job loss (Magee 2004) and unemployment, including long spells of unemployment (OECD 2003). Temporary work, independent contracting, and part-time employment are almost twice as likely among workers with disabilities as among their non-disabled counterparts (Schur 2002). Research in the UK and the US shows that underemployment, or location in a job where an individual's skills and abilities are not fully utilized, is more prevalent among disabled than among non-disabled workers (Bruyère, Erickson, and VanLooy 2006; Jones 2007; Kaye 2009).

Economists argue that workers with disabilities have poorer employment outcomes than their non-disabled counterparts, due to either differences in productivity, differences in preferences, or discrimination by employers (Jones 2008). Organizational factors affecting the outcomes of workers with disabilities include the development of an inclusive organizational culture, the provision of workplace accommodations, and leadership. The attitudes of organizational members also have a significant influence, including leader and co-workers' attitudes towards working with employees with disabilities. Evidence of the impact of each of these factors on employment outcomes for workers with disabilities is discussed in this section.

Impact of Disability Status on Employment Outcomes

Empirical studies unanimously show that workers with disabilities receive lower pay than their non-disabled counterparts, despite statistical controls for a variety of explanatory factors (Jones 2008). To the extent that disability is associated with reduced productivity, workers with disabilities 'earn' lower wages compared to their non-disabled counterparts, who add more value for the employer (DeLeire 2001; Jones, Latreille, and Sloane 2006). Disability status may result in reduced preferences for participating in paid work due to poor health, fatigue, or pain (Kaye, Jones, and Jans 2010), resulting in increased preferences for leisure over consumption (Jones 2008). Yet many adults with disabilities are willing and able to work for pay (Ali, Schur, and Blanck 2011). However, discriminatory attitudes towards hiring and promoting workers with disabilities documented in North America, Europe, South and East Asia reduce the perceived benefits of working for pay (Bordieri, Drehmer, and Taylor 1997; Harlan and Robert 1998; Bricout and Bentley 2000; Hazer and Bedell 2000; Hunt and Hunt 2000; Kennedy and Olney 2001; Graffam et al. 2002; Geng-Qing Chi and Qu 2003; Wilson et al. 2006; Lengnick-Hall, Gaunt, and Kulkarni 2008; Houtenville and Burkhauser 2012), making reduced preferences for work a rational response to disability status.

A substantial body of research documents that decision makers discriminate against workers with disabilities in workplace staffing decisions. Experimental studies in France and the US show that workers with disabilities are rated lower as potential hires than equivalent workers without a disability (Colella, DeNisi, and Varma 1998; Miceli, Harvey, and Buckley 2001; Louvet 2007), although workers with disabilities receive positive ratings on their personal qualities (Bell and Klein 2001). Particularly valuable have been two field experiments, one in the US and the other in Hong Kong, in which employers were sent job applications by hypothetical candidates, randomly receiving either a candidate with or a candidate without a disability. Both studies found that job applicants with a disability received lower employability ratings than their non-disabled counterparts (Bricout and Bentley 2000; Pearson, Ip, and Hui 2003).

Extending this body of research, Hazer and Bedell (2000) found, in a US experimental study, that workers with disabilities who requested an accommodation were rated as less suitable than others. Leasher, Miller and Gooden (2009) found, in a US study, that people with more positive attitudes towards workers with disabilities, as well as people who were committed to diversity, gave more positive ratings with regard to the likelihood of hiring hypothetical applicants with disabilities. Loo (2004) found that Canadian raters expressing relatively high discomfort around workers with disabilities were more likely to consider such workers to be a burden and to be relatively unproductive. In a Belgian study, Zanoni (2011) found that workers with disabilities, as well as women and older workers, were viewed as unable or unwilling to perform well in an automobile factor lean production system, resulting in the elimination of such workers over time.

US survey studies also show negative attitudes among employers towards workers with disabilities (Lengnick-Hall, Gaunt, and Kulkarni 2008; Dong, MacDonald-Wilson, and Fabian 2010; Houtenville and Burkhauser 2012). Some evidence suggests more negative attitudes towards workers with psychiatric disabilities compared to their counterparts with physical disabilities (Scheid 1998; Hazer and Bedell 2000; Gouvier, Sytsma-Jordan, and Mayville 2003; Dalgin and Bellini 2008). A Dutch study indicated a general lack of awareness of the needs of workers with chronic illness among employers (Kopnina and Haafkens 2010). Knowledge of public policies (Hernandez, Keys, and Balcazar 2004) and prior experience employing workers with disabilities is associated with more positive employer attitudes (Levy et al. 1993; Hernandez, Keys, and Balcazar 2004; McLoughlin 2002; Kontosh et al. 2007; Copeland et al. 2010; Wood and Marshall 2010). Harcourt, Lam, and Harcourt (2005, 2007) found that employers with greater cost concerns over hiring workers with disabilities were more likely to engage in discriminatory behaviour, such as asking disability-related questions on their job application forms.

Workers with disabilities in many countries report several types of discriminatory experiences in the workplace (Bruyère, Erickson, and VanLooy 2004; Piggott, Sapey, and Wilenius 2005; Roulstone and Warren 2006; Lengnick-Hall, Gaunt, and Kulkarni 2008; Shier, Graham, and Jones 2009; Naami, Hayashi, and Liese 2012). US data suggest that about a tenth of workers with disabilities experience some form of discrimination (Kennedy and Olney 2001). These experiences include employers discouraging requests for accommodations (Harlan and Robert 1998), marginalization, fictionalization, and harassment (Robert and Harlan 2006), failure to provide accommodations, unfair rules, denial or delay of promotion, different or harsher standards of performance, assignment to inappropriate job tasks, restriction to a certain type of job, receiving excessive supervision on the job, refusal to hire, unfair compensation, limited access to benefits, and forced retirement (Roessler et al. 2011). Workers who are younger, poorer, and have more severe disabilities are more likely to report experiencing discrimination, and about a third of respondents reporting discrimination leave the workforce permanently (Kennedy and Olney 2001). Hallock, Hendricks, and Broadbent (1998) found that perceptions of discrimination do not neatly coincide with earnings discrepancies attributable to discrimination, but are associated with perceptions of inadequate compensation. The authors concluded that perceptions of discrimination likely arise in many areas and are not limited to compensation issues.

Consistent with this idea, Shaw, Chan, and McMahon (2012) found that a substantial number of US workers with disabilities reported harassing experiences in the workplace. Five sets of workers with disabilities were found to be most at risk of workplace harassment. Consistent with the notion of intersectional effects on discriminatory experiences, four of these groups consisted of women who were members of ethnic minority groups, and the fifth group consisted of men who were members of ethnic minority groups. A Swedish study indicates that gender also interacts with gender-segregated employment, whereby both women and men in the extreme gender minority experience harassment resulting in disability associated with ill-health (Reinholdt and Alexanderson 2009).

Impact of Public Policies on Employment Outcomes

Research has examined the impact on employment outcomes of instituting policy measures. The ADA in the US has received the most research attention to date. Bruyère, Erickson, and VanLooy (2004) found that employers responded to disability non-discrimination legislation by providing needed accommodations to workers with disabilities, indicating positive effects for employment outcomes. Other authors have argued that the ADA in the US reduce the employment and earnings of workers with disabilities due to employers' desires to avoid the costs of workplace accommodations (DeLeire 2000; Acemoglu and Angrist 2001; Beegle and Stock 2003), but research suggests that the observed drop in employment is at least partially attributable to the contemporaneous recession (Bagenstos 2004).

Another factor with the potential to reduce the effectiveness of public policy is poor implementation. For instance, in Canada there is no federal legislation specific to disability status, rather, each province has its own, different set of practices (Kovacs Burns and Gordon 2010). Even though it is a federal-level policy, the ADA has been criticized for poor implementation through case law, which, scholars argue, unduly favours employers (Colker 1999; Hurley 2010), particularly when plaintiffs suffer from psychiatric disabilities (Lee 2001). The overall rate of resolution in favour of the complainant in the US is about 21 per cent (McMahon, Hurley, West et al. 2008). Younger workers are the most likely to prevail, winning their cases about a third of the time (McMahon, Hurley, Chan et al. 2008). Anderson (2006) indicates that a number of courts have required accommodation to be linked to narrowly identified aspects of a disability, rather than reasonableness, and suggests that such narrow interpretation limits the impact of the ADA. A ruling allowing obesity to be covered under the ADA is linked to a 2 to 4 percentage point increase in employment of workers with obesity (Carpenter 2006), suggesting that stronger case law could increase the effectiveness of the Act. Burkhauser (1997) suggests means of strengthening public policies to support paid work among adults with disabilities. The provision of accommodation subsidies and disabled worker tax credits would increase the incentives to employers to hire, train, and retain workers with disabilities.

The separate mobilization of different identity groups (e.g. by gender, race/ethnicity, sexual orientation) has led to the development of a set of public policies that are complex, fragmented, and inconsistent between groups (Bagilhole 2010). For instance, in the UK there are ten separate pieces of anti-discrimination legislation, providing different groups with different levels of protection. Legislation for persons with disabilities covers employment, education, access to goods, facilities and services, and also requires positive action on the part of public sector employers (Bagilhole 2010).

Stigmatization and Stereotyping

Theorists suggest that stigmatization is an important factor explaining the subpar employment outcomes of persons with disabilities (Scheid 2005; Fabian, Ethridge, and

Beveridge 2009). In fact, workplace prejudice based on disabilities can be traced back to the 1960s in the US (Rickard, Triandis, and Patterson 1963). Stigmatization, defined as devaluation or derogation of an individual based upon an attribute viewed as undesirable (Paetzold, Dipboye, and Elsbach 2008), has been identified as obstructing the full inclusion and utilization of those with disabilities in the workforce (Barclay, Markel, and Yugo 2012). Individuals with disabilities have cited stigmas as prominent environmental barriers in their pursuit of gainful employment (Henry and Lucca 2004).

McLaughlin, Bell, and Stringer (2004) purported that employment opportunities have been broadened for persons with disabilities, and advocated for investigations to carefully study the effect of stigmatization on their work experiences. Moreover, their work showed that stigmatization mediated the association between disability type and acceptance. Other researchers accepted the charge of McLaughlin and colleagues to delve into the effect of stigmatization on the employability of those with varying disabilities. Scheid (2005) indicated that employers expressing coercive (concern about being sued) as opposed to normative (concerns about doing the right thing) rationales for compliance were more likely to hold stigmatizing attitudes. In examining the employment potential of individuals with psychiatric disabilities and criminal histories, Tschopp and colleagues (2007) identified stigmatization as a salient impediment to labour force inclusion, and Perkins and colleagues (2009) showed that being gainfully employed diminished as the level of stigmatization encountered by a person with a disability increased. A recent study conducted by Baron, Draine, and Salzer (2013) found stigma to be one of the malicious impediments to the work aspirations of individuals with mental disabilities upon ending their incarnation in the US prison system.

Causes of Stigmatization

Leaders can propagate stigmas of workers with disabilities through hierarchy and organizational culture. Ju, Roberts, and Zhang (2013) concluded, from their review of past research, that employers have reservations about hiring people with disabilities. The competitive values of an organizational culture can also promote the stigmatization of workers with disabilities, and Ruscher and Fiske (1990) found that people are more likely to stigmatize others in a competitive context. Moreover, Rao and colleagues (2010) found that individualistic and competitive values result in the stigmatization of workers with disabilities in an investigation of employers' attitudes in China and the US.

Lack of knowledge leads to greater stigmatization of workers with disabilities. Employers and other stakeholders in the organizational hierarchy may not be knowledgeable regarding the vocational capabilities, as well as the professional aspirations, of applicants and employees with disabilities. For instance, Hall and Parker (2010) emphasized that service providers desire information with regard to employing those with physical and mental afflictions, but do not particularly know how to gain this sought-after intelligence. Knowledge gaps have been underscored in the extant literature when assessing employer attitudes on disability in the workplace. Lengnick-Hall, Gaunt, and Kulkarni (2008) documented that most employers are not very proactive in hiring persons with disabilities, and that most employers hold stereotypical beliefs not supported by the existing literature. According to Houtenville and Burkhauser (2012), individuals with disabilities were perceived as incapable of performing required job duties among surveyed employers in the hospitality industry. The findings of Draper, Reid, and McMahon (2011) for the US indicate substantial discrimination on the basis of being perceived to be disabled among workers without disabilities, demonstrating the stigmatizing effects of a perceived disability status.

Further, the absence of critical facts can distance employers from persons with disabilities; thus fostering stereotyping. In a Dutch study, van't Veer and colleagues (2006) found that stereotypical views about those with mental disabilities were positively correlated with social distance from this population. Social distance seems to be fuelled by overt ableism-related terminology used by employers. In fact, organizational leaders, like most of society, primarily apply the 'ability lexicon' when referring to someone with a physical or mental impairment. Wolbring (2008) maintained that the term ability should not be used solely in relation to persons with disabilities, and highlighted the various forms of abilities displayed in the UK's technological-oriented society.

The stigmatization of people with disabilities demonstrates intersectional effects as well. For instance, the stigmatization of Lebanese women with disabilities is strongly influenced by the role of wife and mother. They tend to be viewed as undesirable marriage partners as well as incapable of learning or adding value in a paid work role. This stigmatization severely curtails their life options and the chances of attaining high-quality employment (Wehbi and Lakkis 2010).

Effects of Stigmatization

Since the extant literature showed that employer attitudes lead to hiring intentions (Fraser et al. 2011) and intention to properly accommodate workers with disabilities (Dong et al. 2013), stigmatization can result in reduced employment opportunities for workers with disabilities. Further, assumptions about capabilities can lead to suboptimal and inequitable job fits for workers with disabilities. Berry and Bell (2012) alleged that stereotyping and discrimination lead to poor outcomes for some job applicants and workers while advantaging others. Colella, DeNisi, and Varma (1998) raised concerns about job-fit stereotypes and stressed the importance of controlling these factors when assessing the contributions of workers with disabilities.

Meta-analysis of 172 studies, primarily from North America but including European, Asian, and African countries, has shown that a poor person–job fit results in dissatisfaction and suboptimal performance in the workplace (Kristof-Brown, Zimmerman, and Johnson 2005). As such, inappropriate job placements may lead workers with disabilities to inadvertently assimilate themselves within an existing organizational culture which condones and heightens stigmatization and stereotyping (Biernat 2003). Moreover, such assimilation can prompt feelings of inferiority, reducing motivation and striving towards career goals (Major and O'Brien 2005), supporting perceptions of being unemployable and poorly skilled (Major 2006). In fact, persons with disabilities may be inclined not to enter the labour market or to withdraw from competitive employment because of threats of being stereotyped as being different or being conscious of the stigmatization that is manifest in the contemporary workplace. Von Hippel, Kalokerinos, and Henry (2013) reported that feelings of stereotype threat were related to more negative job attitudes and poorer work mental health among older workers in Australia. Furthermore, such mindsets were associated with intentions to resign or retire. Additionally, attitudes towards persons with disabilities may vary based on gender. For example, Simkhada and colleagues (2013) found that women in Nepal showed positive views towards the full societal inclusion of people with disabilities.

At an organizational level, stigmatizing categorizations of persons with disabilities can hamper organizational efficacy. Recent Australian research indicated that legitimized discrimination undermines organizational commitment (Jetten, Schmitt, and Branscombe 2013). As such, it is plausible that an organizational climate that tolerates biases on the basis of disability may not be able to sustain staff commitment in the long run.

Remedies for Stigmatization

Previously, knowledge gaps were identified as a relevant reinforcement of stigmas and stereotypes towards people with disabilities. Accordingly, education can be an effective intervention in dispelling these labels. Hunt and Hunt (2004) employed a Solomon four-group quasi-experimental design to evaluate the effect of educational intervention on attitudinal change. They found that educational intervention had a significant positive impact on both participants' knowledge levels and their attitudes, even when the gender of subjects and prior experience with individuals with disabilities were controlled.

The goal of educating employers and organizational leaders can also be attained through having contact with individuals with disabilities. Barr and Bracchitta (2008) indicated that contact was effective in transforming attitudes towards persons with disabilities among baccalaureate educational majors. Prior contact was a factor that positively influenced Japanese employer motivation to hire persons with psychiatric disabilities (Ozawa and Yaeda 2007). Additionally, Novak, Feyes, and Christensen (2011) found that US co-workers were generally more accepting of an employee with a disability if they had the opportunity to get to know the employee as an individual rather than as a stereotype or label; they worked with the employee as an equal peer to accomplish common work goals; and the employer or worksite supervisor unequivocally supported the equality and workplace inclusion of the employee with a disability. Finally, there should be ongoing assessments of how demographic categorizations such as age and gender interact with stigmatization in forming attitudes of individuals with disabilities. Such research should be carried forward through using cross-sectional and longitudinal methods. Moreover, the effect of disability severity on stigmatization is an important question that remains unanswered. For instance, does severity evoke stigmatization in general or is its presence varied across age, gender, and type of disability? Also, do severity and childhood onset of disability interact to stigmatize individuals?

Impact of Workplace Accommodation

In theory, disability accommodation allows people with disabilities to be equals, or at least more equal, in the labour force. In this light, accommodation should decrease both disability stigma and negative stereotypes. Accommodation, however, can also make a disability more visible which, in turn, can lead to increased stigma and negative stereotypes. As noted by Baldridge and Veiga (2001), asking for accommodation can signal new information about one's disability, the need for help, and willingness to assert one's legal rights.

In thinking about workplace disability accommodation, it is important to remember that disability does not mean less able, but rather differently abled. People with disabilities, like their non-disabled counterparts, run the full spectrum from brilliantly able to average to incompetent. People with disabilities, however, lack specific abilities that employees are generally presumed to have, such as the ability to walk, see, hear, stand, and so on. Unfortunately, one area of inability can prevent a person with a disability from contributing his or her abilities. Workplace disability accommodations help mitigate the impact of disability (e.g. a larger computer monitor or text-to-speech software for someone unable to see a standard computer screen) so that people with disabilities can contribute their abilities to their organizations.

Great Britain's Steven Hawking, who is among the most brilliant scientists in the world but who is also almost entirely paralyzed, provides a dramatic example of how an employee can be both extremely disabled and simultaneously enormously able. Without accommodation, Hawkins could contribute little. With accommodation, Hawkins contribution is Herculean. Likewise, many people with disabilities cannot contribute fully, if at all, to organizations unless they receive appropriate accommodation. Lack of accommodation, or under-accommodation, can mean lower performance, underemployment, and often unemployment. Some scholars see accommodation as levelling the playing field. Indeed, this appears to be the intent of those who drafted the ADA. Current research, however, indicates that people with disabilities are lucky to receive even basic accommodation, so, for most persons with disabilities, accommodation is a toehold to gain or maintain employment on an extremely uneven playing field.

Impact on Employment Outcomes

Providing workplace accommodations can reduce productivity differentials and perceptions of discrimination by levelling the playing field in the workplace. US employers report that half of the accommodations provided to workers with disabilities had no cost, and on average, the median dollar amount spent on accommodations that did cost something was $600 (Hendricks et al. 2005). US employers also report several organizational benefits to providing workplace accommodations, including increased worker productivity, employee retention, eliminating the cost of training a new employee, improved interactions with co-workers, and increased company morale, with 61 per cent estimating the average financial benefit of each accommodation at over $1000 (Solovieva, Dowler, and Walls 2011). Research has shown that receiving workplace accommodations improves the outcomes of workers with disabilities in many ways, for instance, increasing job retention (Burkhauser, Butler, and Kim 1995), improving life satisfaction (Konrad et al. 2013), and reducing perceptions of workplace discrimination (Konrad et al. 2013). The provision of accommodations is particularly beneficial to workers who acquired disabilities in childhood (Moore et al. 2011).

Given the benefits to workers with disabilities of receiving accommodations, preferences for working rather than remaining out of the labour force are likely to be affected by the provision of workplace accommodations. The failure of employers to provide reasonable accommodations for workers with disabilities is a form of employment discrimination, and needs to be considered when assessing the impact of disability status on employment outcomes to avoid underestimating the impact of such discrimination.

Research has examined whether employers provide workplace accommodations in a discriminatory way, specifically, by lowering the wages of workers with disabilities to pay for the cost of accommodations. Findings suggest that employers have implemented accommodations in this discriminatory way in both the UK and the US (Charles 2004; Jones and Latreille 2010). Given that half of all accommodations cost nothing and the other half average only $600, discriminating against workers with disabilities by lowering their wages to 'pay for' accommodations is egregious.

Other research indicates intersectional effects on the provision of workplace accommodations. A Canadian study showed that older workers with disabilities were less likely to both request an accommodation and to receive the accommodations they did request. Attributing one's disability to 'natural aging' further reduced the likelihood of both requesting accommodations and receiving requested accommodations, indicating a direct link between perceptual processes and lack of access to workplace accommodations for disability (McMullin and Shuey 2006).

Willingness to Request Disability Accommodation

Research suggests that one important barrier to appropriate workplace accommodation is that people with disabilities often do not request needed accommodation. The reasons are varied, dynamic, and multifaceted. To understand the scope of under-accommodation, it is important to keep in mind that people with disabilities are often unaware of the extent to which disability impacts their work. For instance, an estimated 36 million Americans have hearing impairments, yet only 25 per cent seek help of any kind. Of those who acknowledge their disabilities and seek help, many never request workplace accommodation and most withhold at least some requests for needed accommodation. People with disabilities may be unaware or unwilling to admit to themselves, much less their employer, that they have a disability impacting work performance. On the one hand, this barrier seems easy to overcome. People with disabilities need to step up and ask for the accommodation they need. However, stigma associated with having a disability, needing help, and asserting one's legal rights make this barrier a formidable challenge (Baldridge and Veiga 2001, 2006).

Two recent US studies examine factors that influence the willingness of employees with disabilities to request accommodation. Davison and colleagues (2009) investigated decisions to request accommodation and found that a past accommodation request is the strongest predictor of future accommodation requests. Prior experience also influences perceptions of organizational culture, thus, past accommodation request experiences may directly and indirectly shape the likelihood of future accommodation requests. These authors also find that personal concerns about requesting accommodation mediate the relationship between perceptions of organizational culture and future request likelihood. In another recent study, Baldridge and Swift (2013) looked at the impact of requester age and gender, and found that older employees withheld accommodation requests less frequently. They did not, however, find a significant main effect of gender. Baldridge and Swift also find that the influence of requester age was weaker when disability was more severe and when disability onset was earlier. Moreover, disability severity may influence the strength of the relationship between gender and request-withholding frequency. Together, these studies show the complex interplay between attributes of the person contemplating an accommodation request and the request context. In particular, these studies help explain why people with disabilities are often unwilling to request disability accommodation. Future research is encouraged to continue to explore these dynamics, including the role of individual differences, identity, supervisor, and co-worker attitudes, as well as organizational culture and climate.

Willingness to Provide Accommodation

When people with disabilities do request needed accommodation, many barriers remain. One major barrier is continued employer resistance. Wendt and Slonaker (2007) analysed 10,197 employment discrimination claims in Ohio and found three main patterns in the reasons why employers did not provide appropriate accommodation: (1) some employers sought to avoid inconvenience by not hiring people with disabilities, ignoring employees' disabilities and accommodation requests; (2) other employers transferred, demoted, or reassigned people with disabilities to avoid accommodation; and (3) some employers used absenteeism as an excuse to discipline or discharge employees rather than offer accommodation in the form of schedule flexibility. Williams-Whitt (2007) investigated factors that contributed to accommodation difficulties in the US and found four key contributing elements: (1) managerial reluctance and bias related to added workload and questions about disability credibility; (2) managers frequently excluded the employee with a disability from accommodation planning discussions; (3) managers overinvestigated disability legitimacy and underinvestigated accommodation options; and (4) in some cases union–management tension strained communication and increased distrust.

Mitchell and Kovera (2006) looked at the relationship between disability-onset controllability and accommodation provision in the US and found that fewer accommodations were granted when disability was attributed to the requestors' own behaviour. Moreover, employees with excellent work histories were granted costlier accommodations than those with an average work history. In another study, Shuey and Jovic (2013) investigated whether or not people with disabilities in non-standard employment arrangements (i.e. non-permanent, low-wage, and non-union jobs) are more likely to have unmet accommodation needs. These authors examined data from a large, nationally representative, sample of Canadian workers and found that, despite disability legislation, employees in less secure employment arrangements were more likely to have unmet accommodation needs.

Balser (2007) points out that research on disability accommodation often examines whether or not accommodation was provided but often does not examine the level and appropriateness of accommodation. This is an important consideration because people with disabilities often need very specific accommodations, not just any accommodation. In particular, Balser finds that the capacity of US organizations to make particular accommodations was a more powerful predictor than employees' need for accommodation.

While these findings are perhaps unsurprising, this study offers a reminder of a potential vicious circle in which lack of accommodation leads to underemployment and underemployment increased the likelihood of unmet accommodation needs. Together, these studies shed some light on the conditions in which employers are more likely to under-accommodate or even actively discourage and/or deny accommodation requests. Future research is encouraged to examine training and organizational climates that encourage supervisors to understand and respond to the accommodation needs of employees with disabilities.

Co-Worker Reactions

Once accommodation is granted, people with disabilities may face negative co-worker reactions (Colella 2001). García, Paetzold, and Colella (2005) investigated the relationship between co-workers' personalities (big five personality dimensions) and their judgements of accommodation appropriateness in the US. While the authors did not find evidence of main effect of personality, they did find some evidence of interaction between disability, accommodation, and both agreeableness and openness to new experiences. In another study in the US, Paetzold and colleagues (2008) examined fairness perceptions by manipulating accommodation provision, reward structure, and performance. These authors find that granting an accommodation was seen as less fair than not granting it, but also that accommodation provision was seen as least fair when a person with a disability received accommodation and excelled in performance. Similar to research on employer willingness to provide accommodation, research on co-workers' reactions shows how factors beyond those that are legally permissible under the provisions of the ADA impact co-workers' reactions. Future research is encouraged that examines how co-workers' attitudes towards accommodation can be managed and balanced with privacy needs.

We also note that, to date, much of the research on workplace disability accommodation has investigated individuals and organizations in Canada, the UK, and the US. The United Nations Convention on the Rights of Persons with Disabilities (CRPD), however, has brought increased international attention to disability accommodation by indicating that failure to provide reasonable accommodation to persons with disabilities is a form of discrimination (Petersen 2010). In Europe, the Employment Equality Directive also stresses the importance of accommodation. A recent study by Waddington (2008), however, finds that EC member states interpret the concept of reasonable accommodation differently, with some nations focusing on reasonable cost to employers, while others focus on reasonableness in terms of accommodation effectiveness in allowing persons with disabilities to perform essential employment tasks, and still others stress both reasonable cost and reasonable effectiveness. Future research examining workplace accommodation in other regions is therefore encouraged, because historical, legal, and cultural factors can be expected to play an important role.

Conclusions, Action, and Research Directions

In some countries, public policies require that employers not ask job applicants questions about disability status, but rather focus interview questions on whether the applicant can perform the essential functions of the job, either with or without a reasonable accommodation (Cabot and Slogoff 1995). Once hired, individuals with disabilities can make the choice to request or not request reasonable accommodations that allow them to perform effectively in the workplace. Individuals with invisible disabilities also have the choice of whether or not to disclose their disability status to an employer. US and European research demonstrate that substantial barriers exist that hinder both requests for accommodations and disability disclosure (Baldridge and Veiga 2006; Kopnina and Haafkens 2010; Baldridge and Swift 2013). As such, to be effective, the locus of action for enhancing the employment outcomes of workers with disabilities rests with the employing organizations rather than the individual workers themselves.

Implications for Employers

Research has identified many steps employers can take to improve the employment outcomes of workers with disabilities. Organizational diversity policies that include disability status communicate inclusion (Ball et al. 2005) and are associated with greater compliance with non-discrimination legislation (Scheid 1998), higher wages for workers with disabilities (Jones and Latreille 2010), and greater presence of workers with disabilities in management positions (Moore, Konrad, and Hunt 2010). Being knowledgeable about public policies and workplace accommodations enhances employer intentions to hire workers with disabilities (Chan et al. 2010). Formal retention and integrated disability management practices are associated with hiring workers with disabilities (Habeck et al. 2010). Leadership also makes a difference; specifically, supportive leaders increase the strength of the association between disability diversity practices and the representation of workers with disabilities in management (Moore, Konrad, and Hunt 2010). A culture of fairness that is responsive to the needs of all employees enhances the employment outcomes of workers with disabilities (Schur et al. 2009).

Firms benefit in many ways from accommodating people with disabilities, such as the ability to retain quality employees, an avoidance of costs associated with hiring and training new employees, and an improved sense among employees that the employer values their contributions (Hartnett et al. 2011). Evidence suggests that firms recognize these benefits and act accordingly. For instance, small US firms with interests in accommodating customers with disabilities and workers with disabilities who are already on the job are more compliant with disability non-discrimination legislation (Moore, Moore, and Moore 2007). Firms with greater exposure to disability and benefits costs are more likely to implement diversity management (DM) efforts (Salkever, Shinogle, and Prurshothaman 2000). Corporate social responsibility framing of disability issues in the workplace encourages employers to employ more workers with disabilities in order to enhance their reputations (Dibben et al. 2002), and research suggests that people are more willing to do business with employers who hire workers with disabilities (Siperstein et al. 2006).

Implications for Public Policies

To date, North American public policies take a 'just-in-time' approach to disability accommodation, requiring the employee to make a request and the employer to respond as supportively as possible (e.g. Ontario Human Rights Commission, 2000). The format of this process puts the onus of action on individual employees rather than employers. An alternative developed in the field of architecture and taking a 'just-in-case' approach to disability accommodation is the process of universal design. Universal design means that the building or community is designed to be fully accessible to all individuals regardless of disability status (Steinfeld and Maisel 2012). As such, individuals with disabilities are not required to request changes to the building to accommodate their needs.

Proactive public policies such as the Accessibility for Ontarians with Disabilities Act of 2005 in Canada take such a 'just-in-case' approach by requiring that all providers of goods and services that have at least one employee in Ontario make their customer services processes fully accessible to persons with disabilities (Service Ontario 2007, 11 August). Also in Ontario, educational institutions are moving to a 'just-in-case' approach providing universal instructional design, so that students with disabilities are not required to request accommodations (Ontario Human Rights Commission 2004). In this model, all university classes need to be formatted to be accessible, just in case students with disabilities select the course.

Workplaces are likely to be more complex than university classrooms, and employers may not be able to create all jobs in ways that are fully accessible just in case persons with disabilities apply for them. Yet a university organizational design approach could inspire employers to identify ways to make many jobs fully accessible 'just in case', to limit barriers to employment for workers with disabilities. As workforces age, currently employed persons will acquire disabilities, and planning ahead by becoming creative with job and work-station design is likely benefit employers by reducing uncertainty regarding workforce retention and productivity.

Implications for Research

This review identifies several areas for future research. A number of valuable US survey studies have reported on employer activities (Bruyère, Erickson, and VanLooy 2004; Chan et al. 2010; Hartnett et al. 2011). To deepen knowledge regarding the impact of employer actions, more cross-level studies testing the effects of team factors, such as norms, communication processes, and shared mental models, as well as organizational factors such as culture, climate, policies, and practices on the individual-level employment outcomes experienced by workers with disabilities, are needed to develop both theory and practice. Considerably more work is required to investigate the impact of various team- and organizational-level factors on different categories of persons defined by the intersections across multiple identities, such as gender, age, and race/ethnicity.

A number of useful studies have examined employer perceptions of workers with disabilities and disability non-discrimination policies (Hernandez, Keys, and Balcazar 2000). To build on this knowledge base, studies of the attitudes, perceptions, and actions of leaders who directly supervise workers with disabilities would enhance understanding of what leaders can do to enhance the employment outcomes of workers with disabilities. Such research should attend to intersectional effects of disability, gender, age, and race/ethnicity to accurately describe the different characteristics of ableism experienced by different categories of individuals (e.g. younger visible minority men with disabilities, older white women with disabilities).

Co-workers' attitudes towards working with and accommodating workers with disabilities have been shown to be potentially problematic (Colella, DeNisi, and Varma 1998; Colella 2001; Colella, Paetzold, and Belliveau 2004). To extend this area of research, future work should examine attitudes, perceptions, and actions in teams that include one or more members with a disability, attending to possible intersectional effects of gender, age, and race/ethnicity. Such research would enhance understanding of the experiences of workers with disabilities in team environments as well as actions team members and leaders can take to improve these experiences.

As researchers consider the effects of multiple identities, additional research might explore whether people with multiple stigmatized identities develop an intersectional master status—that is, one that is a cumulative mixture of multiple categories—or if they instead strategically deploy their various individual identities according to the situation. Because identities are socially performed and result from categorization by others as well as personal identification (Bagilhole 2010), it is not easy to turn them on and off at will. It would also be useful to understand more about the dynamics of intersectional identities. Research might investigate if individuals reach the most integrated stages of identity acceptance when they have multiple identities, or if they compartmentalize between their multiple identities. The inter- and intra-categorical approach to research on multiple identities (Bagilhole 2010) implies the need for a programme of research that enhances understanding of the distinct identities defined by the intersections across multiple identities, including disability, gender, age, and other statuses.

Acknowledgements

Alison M. Konrad gratefully acknowledges support from the Corus Entertainment Chair in Women in Management, Ivey Business School, University of Western Ontario.

References

Acemoglu, D. and Angrist, J. (2001). Consequences of employment protection? The case of the Americans with Disabilities Act. *Journal of Political Economy*, 109(5): 915–57.
Ali, M., Schur, L., and Blanck, P. (2011). What types of jobs do people with disabilities want? *Journal of Occupational Rehabilitation*, 21(2): 199–210.
Anderson, C. L. (2006). What is 'because of the disability' under the Americans with Disabilities Act? Reasonable accommodation, causation, and the windfall doctrine. *Berkeley Journal of Employment and Labor Law*, 27(2): 323–82.
Appelberg, K., Romanov, K., Heikkilä, K., Honkasalo, M.-L., and Koskenvuo, M. (1996). Interpersonal conflict as a predictor of work disability: a follow-up study of 15,348 Finnish employees. *Journal of Psychosomatic Research*, 40(2): 157–67.
Bagenstos, S. (2004). Has the Americans with Disabilities Act reduced employment for people with disabilities? *Berkeley Journal of Employment and Labor Law*, 25: 527–63.

Bagilhole, B. (2010). Applying the lens of intersectionality to UK equal opportunities and diversity policies. *Canadian Journal of Administrative Sciences*, 27: 263–71.

Baldridge, D. C. and Swift, M. L. (2013). Withholding requests for disability accommodation: the role of individual differences and disability attributes. *Journal of Management*, 39(3): 743–62.

Baldridge, D. C. and Veiga, J. F. (2001). Toward greater understanding of the willingness to request an accommodation: can requesters' beliefs disable the ADA? *Academy of Management Review*, 26(1): 85–99.

Baldridge, D. C. and Veiga, J. F. (2006). The impact of anticipated social consequences on recurring disability accommodation requests. *Journal of Management*, 32(1): 158–79.

Ball, P., Monaco, G., Schmeling, J., Schartz, H., and Blanck, P. (2005). Disability as diversity in Fortune 100 companies. *Behavioral Sciences & the Law*, 23: 97–121.

Balser, D. B. (2007). Predictors of workplace accommodations for employees with mobility-related impairments. *Administration & Society*, 39(5): 656–83.

Barclay, L. A., Markel, K. S., and Yugo, J. E. (2012). Virtue theory and organizations: considering persons with disabilities. *Journal of Managerial Psychology*, 27(4): 330–46.

Baron, R. C., Draine, J., and Salzer, M. S. (2013). 'I'm not sure that I can figure out how to do that': pursuit of work among people with mental illnesses leaving jail. *American Journal of Psychiatric Rehabilitation*, 16(2): 115–35.

Barr, J. J. and Bracchitta, K. (2008). Effects of contact with individuals with disabilities: positive attitudes and majoring in education. *Journal of Psychology*, 142(3): 225–44.

Beegle, K. and Stock, W. A. (2003). The labor market effects of disability discrimination laws. *Journal of Human Resources*, 38(4): 806–59.

Bell, B. and Klein, K. (2001). Effects of disability, gender, and job level on ratings of job applicants. *Rehabilitation Psychology*, 46(3): 229–46.

Berdahl, J. L. and Moore, C. (2006). Workplace harassment: double jeopardy for minority women. *Journal of Applied Psychology*, 91: 426–36.

Berecki-Gisolf, J., Clay, F. J., Collie, A., and McClure, R. J. (2012). The impact of aging on work disability and return to work: insights from workers' compensation claim records. *Journal of Occupational & Environmental Medicine*, 54(3): 318–27.

Berry, D. and Bell, M. P. (2012). Inequality in organizations: stereotyping, discrimination, and labor law exclusions. *Equality, Diversity & Inclusion: An International Journal*, 31(3): 236–48.

Biernat, M. (2003). Toward a broader view of social stereotyping. *American Psychologist*, 58(12): 1019–27.

Bjelland, M. J., Bruyère, S. M., Von Schrader, S., Houtenville, A. J., Ruiz-Quintanilla, A., and Webber, D. A. (2010). Age and disability employment discrimination: occupational rehabilitation implications. *Journal of Occupational Rehabilitation*, 20(4): 456–71.

Bordieri, J. E., Drehmer, D. E., and Taylor, D. W. (1997). Work life for employees with disabilities: recommendations for promotion. *Rehabilitation Counseling Bulletin*, 40(3): 181–91.

Brault, M. W. (2012). Americans with disabilities: 2010. *Household Economic Studies*, July: 70–131. <http://www.census.gov/prod/2012pubs/p70-131.pdf>.

Bricout, J. C. and Bentley, K. J. (2000). Disability status and perceptions of employability by employers. *Social Work Research*, 24(2): 87–95.

Bruyère, S. M. (2006). Disability management: key concepts and techniques for an aging workforce. *International Journal of Disability Management Research*, 1(1): 149–58.

Bruyère, S. M., Erickson, W. A., and Ferrentino, J. (2003). Identity and disability in the workplace. *William & Mary Law Review*, 44(3): 1173–96.

Bruyère, S. M., Erickson, W. A., and VanLooy, S. A. (2004). Comparative study of workplace policy and practices contributing to disability nondiscrimination. *Rehabilitation Psychology*, 49(1): 28–38.

Bruyère, S. M., Erickson, W. A., and VanLooy, S. A. (2006). The impact of business size on employer ADA response. *Rehabilitation Counseling Bulletin*, 49(4): 194–206.

Burkhauser, R. V. (1997). Post-ADA: are people with disabilities expected to work? *Annals of the American Academy of Political and Social Science*, 549: 71–83.

Burkhauser, R. V., Butler, J. S., and Kim, Y.-W. (1995). The importance of employer accommodation on the job duration of workers with disabilities: a hazard model approach. *Labour Economics*, 2: 109–30.

Cabot, S. J. and Slogoff, R. J. (1995). Interviewing an applicant with a disability. *Supervisory Management*, 40(11): 1, 6.

Carpenter, C. S. (2006). The effects of employment protection for obese people. *Industrial Relations*, 45(3): 393–414.

Chan, F., Strauser, D., Maher, P., Lee, E.-J., Jones, R., and Johnson, E. T. (2010). Demand-side factors related to employment of people with disabilities: a survey of employers in the Midwest region of the United States. *Journal of Occupational Rehabilitation*, 20(4): 412–19.

Charles, K. K. (2004). The extent and effect of employer compliance with the accommodations mandates of the Americans with Disabilities Act. *Journal of Disability Policy Studies*, 15(2): 86–96.

Claussen, B. and Dalgard, O. S. (2009). Disability pensioning: the gender divide can be explained by occupation, income, mental distress and health. *Scandinavian Journal of Public Health*, 37: 590–7.

Cole, E. R. (2009). Intersectionality and research in psychology. *American Psychologist*, 64: 170–80.

Colella, A. (2001). Coworker distributive fairness judgments of the workplace accommodation of employees with disabilities. *Academy of Management Review*, 26(1): 100–16.

Colella, A., DeNisi, A. S., and Varma, A. (1998). The impact of ratee's disability on performance judgments and choice of partner: the role of disability-job fit stereotypes and interdependence of rewards. *Journal of Applied Psychology*, 83: 102–11.

Colella, A., Paetzold, R. L., and Belliveau, M. A. (2004). Factors affecting coworkers' procedural justice inferences of the workplace accommodations of employees with disabilities. *Personnel Psychology*, 57(1): 1–23.

Colker, R. (1999). The Americans with Disabilities Act: a windfall for defendants. *Harvard Civil Rights Civil Liberties Law Review*, 34: 99–162.

Copeland, J., Chan, F., Bezyak, J., and Fraser, R. T. (2010). Assessing cognitive and affective reactions of employers toward people with disabilities in the workplace. *Journal of Occupational Rehabilitation*, 20(4): 427–34.

Crisp, R. (2005). Key factors related to vocational outcome: trends for six disability groups. *Journal of Rehabilitation*, 71(4): 30–7.

Crooks, V. A., Chouinard, V., and Wilton, R. D. (2008). Understanding, embracing, rejecting: women's negotiations of disability constructions and categorizations after becoming chronically ill. *Social Science and Medicine*, 67(11): 1837–46. doi:10.1016/j.socscimed.2008.07.025

Dalgin, R. S. and Bellini, J. (2008). Invisible disability disclosure in an employment interview: impact on employers' hiring decisions and views of employability. *Rehabilitation Counseling Bulletin*, 52(1): 6–15.

Davison, H. K., O'Leary, B. J., Schlosberg, J. A., and Bing, M. N. (2009). Don't ask and you shall not receive: why future American workers with disabilities are reluctant to demand legally required accommodations. *Journal of Workplace Rights*, 14(1): 49–73.

DeLeire, T. (2000). The wage and employment effects of the Americans with Disabilities Act. *Journal of Human Resources*, 35(4): 693–715.

DeLeire, T. (2001). Changes in wage discrimination against people with disabilities: 1948–93. *Journal of Human Resources*, 36(1): 144–58.

Dibben, P., James, P., Cunningham, I., and Smythe, D. (2002). Employers and employees with disabilities in the UK: an economically beneficial relationship? *International Journal of Social Economics*, 29(6): 453–67.

Dong, S., MacDonald-Wilson, K. L., and Fabian, E. S. (2010). Development of the reasonable accommodation factor survey: results and implications. *Rehabilitation Counseling Bulletin*, 53(3): 153–62.

Dong, S., Oire, S. N., MacDonald-Wilson, K. L., and Fabian, E. S. (2013). A comparison of perceptions of factors in the job accommodation process among employees with disabilities, employers, and service providers. *Rehabilitation Counseling Bulletin*, 56(3): 182–9.

Draper, W. R., Reid, C. A., and McMahon, B. T. (2011). Workplace discrimination and the perception of disability. *Rehabilitation Counseling Bulletin*, 55(1): 29–37.

Eurostat (2001). Disability and social participation in Europe. <http://ec.europa.eu/eurostat/en/web/products-pocketbooks/-/KS-AW-01-001>, accessed 1 June 2015.

Eurostat (2009). Prevalence percentages of disability by activity status, sex and age group (26 March). <http://epp.eurostat.ec.europa.eu/portal/page/portal/product_results/search_results?mo=containsall&ms=disability+status&saa=&p_action=SUBMIT&l=us&co=equal&ci=,&po=equal&pi=>, accessed 25 July 2013.

Fabian, E. S., Ethridge, G., and Beveridge, S. (2009). Differences in perceptions of career barriers and supports for people with disabilities by demographic background and case status factors. *Journal of Rehabilitation*, 75(1): 41–9.

Fraser, R. T., Ajzen, I., Johnson, K., Hebert, J., and Chan, F. (2011). Understanding employers' hiring intention in relation to qualified workers with disabilities. *Journal of Vocational Rehabilitation*, 35(1): 1–11.

García, M., Paetzold, R., and Colella, A. (2005). The relationship between personality and peers' judgments of the appropriateness of accommodations for individuals with disabilities. *Journal of Applied Social Psychology*, 35(7): 1418–39.

Geng-Qing Chi, C. and Qu, H. (2003). Integrating persons with disabilities into the work force: a study on employment of people with disabilities in foodservice industry. *International Journal of Hospitality & Tourism Administration*, 4(4): 59–83.

Gilson, S. F., Tusler, A., and Gill, C. (1997). Ethnographic research in disability identity: self-determination and community. *Journal of Vocational Rehabilitation*, 9: 7–17.

Gouvier, W., Sytsma-Jordan, S., and Mayville, S. (2003). Patterns of discrimination in hiring job applicants with disabilities: the role of disability type, job complexity, and public contact. *Rehabilitation Psychology*, 48(3): 175–81.

Graffam, J., Smith, K., Shinkfield, A., and Polzin, U. (2002). Employer benefits and costs of employing a person with a disability. *Journal of Vocational Rehabilitation*, 17(4): 251–63.

Habeck, R. V., Hunt, A., Rachel, C. H., Kregel, J., and Chan, F. (2010). Employee retention and integrated disability management practices as demand side factors. *Journal of Occupational Rehabilitation*, 20(4): 443–55.

Hahn, H. (1994). The minority group model of disability: implications for medical sociology. *Research in the Sociology of Health Care*, 11: 3–24

Hall, J. P. and Parker, K. (2010). Stuck in a loop: individual and system barriers for job seekers with disabilities. *Career Development Quarterly*, 58(3): 246–56.

Hallock, K. F., Hendricks, D. J., and Broadbent, E. (1998). Discrimination by gender and disability status: do worker perceptions match statistical measures? *Southern Economic Journal*, 65(2): 245–63.

Harcourt, M., Lam, H., and Harcourt, S. (2005). Discriminatory practices in hiring: institutional and rational economic perspectives. *International Journal of Human Resource Management*, 16(11): 2113–32.

Harcourt, M., Lam, H., and Harcourt, S. (2007). The impact of workers' compensation experience-rating on discriminatory hiring practices. *Journal of Economic Issues*, 41(3): 681–99.

Harlan, S. L. and Robert, P. M. (1998). The social construction of disability in organizations: why employers resist reasonable accommodation. *Work & Occupations*, 25(4): 397–435.

Hartnett, H. P., Stuart, H., Thurman, H., Loy, B., and Batiste, L. C. (2011). Employers' perceptions of the benefits of workplace accommodations: reasons to hire, retain, and promote people with disabilities. *Journal of Vocational Rehabilitation*, 34(1): 17–23.

Hazer, J. T. and Bedell, K. W. (2000). Effects of seeking accommodation and disability on preemployment evaluations. *Journal of Applied Social Psychology*, 30(6): 1201–21.

Hendricks, D. J., Batiste, L. C., Hirsh, A., Dowler, D., Schartz, H., and Blanck, P. (2005). Cost and effectiveness of accommodations in the workplace: preliminary results of a nationwide study. *Disability Studies Quarterly*, 25(4): 12–12.

Henry, A. D. and Lucca, A. M. (2004). Facilitators and barriers to employment: the perspectives of people with psychiatric disabilities and employment service providers. *Work*, 22(3): 169–82.

Hernandez, B., Keys, C., and Balcazar, F. (2000). Employer attitudes toward workers with disabilities and their ADA employment rights: a literature review. *Journal of Rehabilitation*, 66(4): 4–16.

Hernandez, B., Keys, C., and Balcazar, F. (2004). Disability rights: attitudes of private and public sector representatives. *Journal of Rehabilitation*, 70(1): 28–37.

Hogan, S. R., Unick, G. J., Speiglman, R., and Norris, J. C. (2011). Gender-specific barriers to self-sufficiency among former supplemental security income drug addiction and alcoholism beneficiaries: implications for welfare-to-work programs and services. *Journal of Social Service Research*, 37: 320–37.

Holvino, E. (2008). Intersections: the simultaneity of race, gender and class in organization studies. *Gender, Work and Organization*, 17(3): 248–77. doi:10.1111/j.1468-0432.2008.00400.x.

Houtenville, A. J. and Burkhauser, R. V. (2012). People with disabilities: employers' perspectives on recruitment practices, strategies, and challenges in leisure and hospitality. *Cornell Hospitality Quarterly*, 53(1): 40–52.

HRSDC (Human Resources and Skills Development Canada) (2010). Employment Equity (2 February). <http://www.rhdcc-hrsdc.gc.ca/eng/labour/equality/employment_equity/index.shtml>, accessed 30 August 2010.

HRSDC (Human Resources and Skills Development Canada) (n.d.). Federal disability reference guide. <http://www.hrsdc.gc.ca/eng/disability/arc/reference_guide.shtml>, accessed 1 June 2015

Hunt, B. and Hunt, C. S. (2000). Attitudes toward people with disabilities: a comparison of undergraduate rehabilitation and business majors. *Rehabilitation Education*, 14(3): 267–83.

Hunt, C. S. and Hunt, B. (2004). Changing attitudes toward people with disabilities: experimenting with an educational intervention. *Journal of Managerial Issues*, 16(2): 266–80.

Hurley, J. E. (2010). Merit determinants of ADA Title I allegations involving discharge: implications for human resources management and development. *Advances in Developing Human Resources*, 12(4): 466–83.

Imrie, R. (2004). Disability, embodiment and the meaning of the home. *Housing Studies*, 19(5): 745–63.

Jensen, J., Sathiyandra, S., Rochford, M., Jones, D., Krishnan, V., McLeod, K. et al. Ministry of Social Development (2005). Work participation among people with disabilities: does the type of disability influence the outcome? *Social Policy Journal of New Zealand*, 24 (March): 134–59.

Jetten, J., Schmitt, M. T., and Branscombe, N. R. (2013). Rebels without a cause: discrimination appraised as legitimate harms group commitment. *Group Processes & Intergroup Relations*, 16(2): 159–72.

Jones, M. K. (2007). Does part-time employment provide a way of accommodating a disability? *The Manchester School*, 75(6): 695–716.

Jones, M. K. (2008). Disability and the labour market: a review of the empirical evidence. *Journal of Economic Studies*, 35(5): 405–24.

Jones, M. K. and Latreille, P. L. (2010). Disability and earnings: are employer characteristics important? *Economic Letters*, 106(3): 191–4.

Jones, M. K., Latreille, P. L., and Sloane, P. J. (2006). Disability, gender and the British labour market. *Oxford Economic Papers*, 58(3): 407–59.

Ju, S., Roberts, E., and Zhang, D. (2013). Employer attitudes toward workers with disabilities: a review of research in the past decade. *Journal of Vocational Rehabilitation*, 38(2): 113–23.

Karlsson, N., Borg, K., Carstensen, J., Hensing, G., and Alexanderson, K. (2006). Risk of disability pension in relation to gender and age in a Swedish county; a 12-year population based, prospective cohort study. *Work*, 27: 173–9.

Kaye, H. S. (2009). Stuck at the bottom rung: occupational characteristics of workers with disabilities. *Journal of Occupational Rehabilitation*, 19(2): 115–28.

Kaye, H. S., Jones, E. C., and Jans, L. (2010). Why employers don't hire people with disabilities: research findings and policy implications. *Disability & Health Journal*, 3(2): e6.

Kennedy, J. and Olney, M. (2001). Job discrimination in the post-ADA era: estimates from the 1994 and 1995 national health interview surveys. *Rehabilitation Counseling Bulletin*, 45(1): 24–30.

Konrad, A. M., Leslie, K., and Peuramaki, D. (2007). Full accessibility by 2025: will your business be ready? Ivey Business Journal Online. <http://www.iveybusinessjournal.com/topics/the-organization/full-accessibility-by-2025-will-your-business-be-ready#.UfFk423iETA>, accessed 30 May 2015.

Konrad, A. M., Moore, M. E., Doherty, A. J., Ng, E. S. W., and Breward, K. (2012). Vocational status and perceived well-being of workers with disabilities. *Equality, Diversity & Inclusion: An International Journal*, 31(2): 100–23.

Konrad, A. M., Moore, M. E., Ng, E. S. W., Doherty, A. J., and Breward, K. (2013). Temporary work, underemployment, and workplace accommodations: relationship to well-being for workers with disabilities. *British Journal of Management*, 24(3): 367–82.

Kontosh, L. G., Fletcher, I., Frain, M., and Winland-Brown, J. (2007). Work place issues surrounding healthcare professionals with disabilities in the current labor market. *Work: Journal of Prevention, Assessment & Rehabilitation*, 29(4): 295–302.

Kopnina, H. and Haafkens, J. A. (2010). Disability management: organizational diversity and Dutch employment policy. *Journal of Occupational Rehabilitation*, 20: 247–55.

Kovacs Burns, K. and Gordon, G. L. (2010). Analyzing the impact of disability legislation in Canada and the United States. *Journal of Disability Policy Studies*, 20(4): 205–18.

Kristof-Brown, A. L., Zimmerman, R. D., and Johnson, E. C. (2005). Consequences of individuals' fit at work: a meta-analysis of person-job, person-organization, person-group, and person-supervisor fit. *Personnel Psychology*, 58(2): 281–342.

Leasher, M. K., Miller, C. E., and Gooden, M. (2009). Rater effects and attitudinal barriers affecting people with disabilities in personnel selection. *Journal of Applied Social Psychology*, 39(9): 2236–74.

Leck, J. D. and Saunders, D. M. (1992). Hiring women: the effects of Canada's Employment Equity Act. *Canadian Public Policy*, 18: 203–20.

Lederer, V., Rivard, M., and Mechakra-Tahiri, S. D. (2012). Gender differences in personal and work-related determinants of return-to-work following long-term disability: a 5-year cohort study. *Journal of Occupational Rehabilitation*, 22: 522–31.

Lee, B. A. (2001). The implications of ADA litigation for employers: a review of federal appellate court decisions. *Human Resource Management*, 40(1): 35–50.

Lengnick-Hall, M. L., Gaunt, P. M., and Kulkarni, M. (2008). Overlooked and underutilized: people with disabilities are an untapped human resource. *Human Resource Management*, 47: 255–73.

Levy, J. M., Jessop, D. J., Rimmerman, A., and Levy, P. H. (1993). Attitudes of executives in Fortune 500 corporations toward the employability of persons with severe disabilities: industrial and service corporations. *Journal of Applied Rehabilitation Counseling*, 24(2): 19–31.

Loo, R. (2004). Attitudes toward employing persons with disabilities: a test of HTE sympathy-discomfort categories. *Journal of Applied Social Psychology*, 34(10): 2200–14.

Louvet, E. (2007). Social judgment toward job applicants with disabilities: perception of personal qualities and competencies. *Rehabilitation Psychology*, 52(3): 297–303.

McLaughlin, M. E., Bell, M. P., and Stringer, D. Y. (2004). Stigma and acceptance of coworkers with disabilities: understudied aspects of workforce diversity. *Group & Organization Management*, 29(3): 302–33.

McLean, J. (2003). Employees with long term illnesses or disabilities in the UK social services workforce. *Disability & Society*, 18(1): 51–70.

McLoughlin, C. S. (2002). Barriers to hiring students with disabilities in the workforce. *International Education Journal*, 3(1): 13–23.

McMahon, B. T., Hurley, J. E., Chan, F., Rumrill, P. D., Jr., and Roessler, R. (2008). Drivers of hiring discrimination for individuals with disabilities. *Journal of Occupational Rehabilitation*, 18(2): 133–9.

McMahon, B. T., Hurley, J. E., West, S. L., Chan, F., Roessler, R., and Rumrill Jr, P. D. (2008). A comparison of EEOC closures involving hiring versus other prevalent discrimination issues under the Americans with Disabilities Act. *Journal of Occupational Rehabilitation*, 18(2): 106–11.

McMullin, J. A. and Shuey, K. M. (2006). Ageing, disability and workplace accommodations. *Ageing & Society*, 26(6): 831–47.

Magee, W. (2004). Effects of illness and disability on job separation. *Social Science & Medicine*, 58(6): 1121–35.

Major, B. (2006). New perspectives on stigma and psychological well-being. In S. Levin and C. van Laar (eds.), *Stigma and Group Inequality: Social Psychological Perspectives*. Mahwah, NJ: Erlbaum, 193–212.

Major, B. and O'Brien, L. T. (2005). The social psychology of stigma. *Annual Review of Psychology*, 56: 393–421.

Miceli, N. S., Harvey, M., and Buckley, M. R. (2001). Potential discrimination in structured employment interviews. *Employee Responsibilities & Rights Journal*, 13(1): 15–38.

Mitchell, T. R. and Kovera, M. B. (2006). The effects of attribution of responsibility and work history on perceptions of reasonable accommodations. *Law and Human Behavior*, 30(6): 733–48.

Moon, D. (2013). Who am I and who are we? Conflicting narratives of collective selfhood in stigmatized groups. *American Journal of Sociology*, 117(5): 1336–79.

Moore, D. P., Moore, J. W., and Moore, J. L. (2007). After fifteen years: the response of small businesses to the Americans with Disabilities Act. *Work*, 29(2): 113–26.

Moore, M. E., Konrad, A. M., and Hunt, J. (2010). Creating a vision boosts the impact of top management support on the employment of workers with disabilities: the case of sport management in the USA. *Equality, Diversity & Inclusion: An International Journal*, 29(6): 609–25.

Moore, M. E., Konrad, A. M., Yang, Y., Ng, E. S. W., and Doherty, A. J. (2011). The vocational well-being of workers with childhood onset of disability: life satisfaction and perceived workplace discrimination. *Journal of Vocational Behavior*, 79(3): 681–98.

Naami, A., Hayashi, R., and Liese, H. (2012). The unemployment of women with physical disabilities in Ghana: issues and recommendations. *Disability & Society*, 27(2): 191–204.

Nkomo, S. and Cox, T. (1996). Diverse identities in organizations. In S. Clegg, C. Hardy, and W. Nord (eds.), *Handbook of Organization Studies*. Thousand Oaks, CA: Sage, 338–56.

Novak, J., Feyes, K. J., and Christensen, K. A. (2011). Application of intergroup contact theory to the integrated workplace: setting the stage for inclusion. *Journal of Vocational Rehabilitation*, 35(3): 211–26.

OECD (Organisation for Economic Co-operation and Development) (2003). Transforming disability into ability: policies to promote work and income security. <http://www.oecd.org/els/emp/transformingdisabilityintoability.htm>, accessed 1 June 2015.

Oguzoglu, U. (2011). Severity of work disability and work. *Economic Record*, 87(278): 370–83.

Ontario Human Rights Commission (2000). Policy and guidelines on disability and the duty to accommodate (23 November). <http://www.ohrc.on.ca/sites/default/files/attachments/Policy_and_guidelines_on_disability_and_the_duty_to_accommodate.pdf>, accessed 1 June 2015.

Ontario Human Rights Commission (2004). Guidelines on accessible education (29 September). <http://www.ohrc.on.ca/sites/default/files/attachments/Guidelines_on_accessible_education.pdf>, accessed 1 June 2015.

Ontario Human Rights Commission (n.d.). Disability and human rights. <http://www.ohrc.on.ca/en/disability-and-human-rights-brochure>, accessed 25 July 2013.

Ostrander, R. N. (2008). When identities collide: masculinity, disability and race. *Disability & Society*, 23: 585–97. doi:10.1080/09687590802328451.

Ozawa, A. and Yaeda, J. (2007). Employer attitudes toward employing persons with psychiatric disabilities in Japan. *Journal of Vocational Rehabilitation*, 26(2): 105–13.

Paetzold, R., García, M., Colella, A., Ren, L., Triana, M., and Ziebro, M. (2008). Perceptions of people with disabilities: when is accommodation fair? *Basic & Applied Social Psychology*, 30(1): 27–35.

Paetzold, R. L., Dipboye, R. L., and Elsbach, K. D. (2008). A new look at stigmatization in and of organizations. *Academy of Management Review*, 33(1): 186–93.

Pearson, V., Ip, F., and Hui, H. (2003). To tell or not to tell: disability disclosure and job application outcomes. *Journal of Rehabilitation*, 69(4): 35–8.

Perkins, D. V., Raines, J. A., Tschopp, M. K., and Warner, T. C. (2009). Gainful employment reduces stigma toward people recovering from schizophrenia. *Community Mental Health Journal*, 45: 158–62.

Petersen, C. J. (2010). Population policy and eugenic theory: implications of China's ratification of the United Nations Convention on the Rights of Persons with Disabilities. *China: An International Journal*, 8(1): 85–109.

Piggott, L., Sapey, B., and Wilenius, F. (2005). Out of touch: local government and disabled people's employment needs. *Disability & Society*, 20(6): 599–611.

Rao, D., Horton, R. A., Tsang, H. W. H., Shi, K., and Corrigan, P. W. (2010). Does individualism help explain differences in employers' stigmatizing attitudes toward disability across Chinese and American cities? *Rehabilitation Psychology*, 55(4): 351–9.

Reinholdt, S. and Alexanderson, K. (2009). A narrative insight into disability pensioners' work experiences in highly gender-segregated occupations. *Work*, 34: 251–61.

Riach, K., and Loretto, W. (2009). Identity work and the 'unemployed' worker: age, disability and the lived experience of the older unemployed. *Work, Employment and Society*, 23(1): 102–19. doi:10.1177/0950017008099780

Rickard, T. E., Triandis, H. C., and Patterson, C. H. (1963). Indices of employer prejudice toward disabled applicants. *Journal of Applied Psychology*, 47(1): 52–5.

Robert, P. M. and Harlan, S. L. (2006). Mechanisms of disability discrimination in large bureaucratic organizations: ascriptive inequalities in the workplace. *Sociological Quarterly*, 47(4): 599–630.

Roessler, R., Hennessey, M., Neath, J., Rumrill Jr, P. D., and Nissen, S. (2011). The employment discrimination experiences of adults with multiple sclerosis. *Journal of Rehabilitation*, 77(1): 20–30.

Roulstone, A. and Warren, J. (2006). Applying a barriers approach to monitoring disabled people's employment: implications for the Disability Discrimination Act 2005. *Disability & Society*, 21(2): 115–31.

Ruscher, J. B. and Fiske, S. T. (1990). Interpersonal competition can cause individuating processes. *Journal of Personality & Social Psychology*, 58(5): 832–43.

Salkever, D. S., Shinogle, J., and Prurshothaman, M. (2000). Employers' disability management activities: descriptors and an exploratory test of the financial incentives hypothesis. *Journal of Occupational Rehabilitation*, 10(3): 199–214.

Scheid, T. L. (1998). The Americans with Disabilities Act, mental disability, and employment practices. *Journal of Behavioral Health Services & Research*, 25(3): 312–24.

Scheid, T. L. (2005). Stigma as a barrier to employment: mental disability and the Americans with Disabilities Act. *International Journal of Law & Psychiatry*, 28(6): 670–90.

Schur, L. A. (2002). Dead end jobs or a path to economic well being? The consequences of non-standard work among people with disabilities. *Behavioral Sciences & the Law*, 20: 601–20.

Schur, L. A., Kruse, D., Blasi, J., and Blanck, P. (2009). Is disability disabling in all workplaces? Disability, workplace disparities, and corporate culture. *Industrial Relations*, 48: 381–410.

Service Ontario. Accessibility for Ontarians with Disabilities Act 2005 (2007, August 11).

Scotch, R. K. (1988). Disability as the basis for a social movement: advocacy and the politics of definition. *Journal of Social Issues*, 44(1): 159–72.

Shaw, L. R., Chan, F., and McMahon, B. T. (2012). Intersectionality and disability harassment: the interactive effects of disability, race, age, and gender. *Rehabilitation Counseling Bulletin*, 55(2): 82–91.

Shier, M., Graham, J. R., and Jones, M. E. (2009). Barriers to employment as experienced by disabled people: a qualitative analysis in Calgary and Regina, Canada. *Disability & Society*, 24(1): 63–75.

Shuey, K. M. and Jovic, E. (2013). Disability accommodation in nonstandard and precarious employment arrangements. *Work & Occupations*, 40(2): 174–205.

Siebers, T. (2008). *Disability Theory*. Ann Arbor, MI: University of Michigan Press.

Simkhada, P. P., Shyangdan, D., Van Teijlingen, E. R., Kadel, S., Stephen, J., and Gurung, T. (2013). Women's knowledge of and attitude toward disability in rural Nepal. *Disability & Rehabilitation*, 35(7): 606–13.

Siperstein, G. N., Romano, N., Mohler, A., and Parker, R. (2006). A national survey of consumer attitudes toward companies that hire people with disabilities. *Journal of Vocational Rehabilitation*, 24(1): 3–9.

Smart, J. F., and Smart, D. W. (2006). Models of disability: implications for the counseling profession. *Journal of Counseling & Development*, 84(1): 29–40. doi:10.1002/j.1556-6678.2006.tb00377.x.

Solovieva, T. I., Dowler, D. L., and Walls, R. T. (2011). Employer benefits from making workplace accommodations. *Disability & Health Journal*, 4(1): 39–45.

Statistics Canada (2007). Participation and Activity Limitation Survey 2006: Analytical Report (S. a. A. S. Division, Trans.) *The 2006 Participation and Activities Limitation Survey: Disability in Canada*. Ottawa, Ontario, Canada.

Steinfeld, E. and Maisel, J. (2012). *Universal Design: Creating Inclusive Environments*. Hoboken, NJ: Wiley.

Stover, B., Wickizer, T. M., Zimmerman, F., Fulton-Kehoe, D., and Franklin, G. (2007). Prognostic factors of long-term disability in a workers' compensation system. *Journal of Occupational & Environmental Medicine*, 49(1): 31–40.

Tschopp, M. K., Perkins, D. V., Hart-Katuin, C., Born, D. L., and Holt, S. L. (2007). Employment barriers and strategies for individuals with psychiatric disabilities and criminal histories. *Journal of Vocational Rehabilitation*, 26(3): 175–87.

US Department of Justice (2008). The Americans with Disabilities Act of 1990 as amended. <http://www.ada.gov/2010_regs.htm>, accessed 25 July 2013.

Van't Veer, J. T. B., Kraan, H. F., Drosseart, S. H. C., and Modde, J. M. (2006). Determinants that shape public attitudes towards the mentally ill. *Social Psychiatry & Psychiatric Epidemiology*, 41(4): 310–17.

Von Hippel, C., Kalokerinos, E. K., and Henry, J. D. (2013). Stereotype threat among older employees: relationship with job attitudes and turnover intentions. *Psychology & Aging*, 28(1): 17–27.

Vos, T., Flaxman, A. D., Naghavi, M., Lozano, R., Michaud, C., Ezzati, M. et al. (2012). Years lived with disability (YLDs) for 1160 sequelae of 289 diseases and injuries 1990–2010: a systematic analysis for the global burden of disease study 2010. *Lancet*, 380(9859) (December): 2163–96.

Waddington, L. (2008). When it is reasonable for Europeans to be confused: understanding when a disability accommodation is 'reasonable' from a comparative perspective. *Labor Law & Policy Journal*, 29(3).

Wehbi, S. and Lakkis, S. (2010). Women with disabilities in Lebanon: from marginalization to resistance. *Affilia: Journal of Women & Social Work*, 25(1): 56–67.

Wendt, A. C. and Slonaker Sr, W. M. (2007). ADA's reasonable accommodation: myth or reality. *S.A.M. Advanced Management Journal*, 72(4): 21–31.

WHO (World Health Organization) (2013). Disabilities. <http://www.who.int/topics/disabilities/en/>, accessed 25 July 2013.

Williams-Whitt, K. (2007). Impediments to disability accommodation. *Relations Industrielles/Industrial Relations (RI-IR)*, 62: 405–30.

Wilson, V., Powney, J., Hall, S., and Davidson, J. (2006). Who gets ahead? The effect of age, disability, ethnicity and gender on teachers' careers and implications for school leaders. *Educational Management Administration & Leadership*, 34(2): 239–55.

Wolbring, G. (2008). The politics of ableism. *Development*, 51(2): 252–8.

Wood, D. and Marshall, E. S. (2010). Nurses with disabilities working in hospital settings: attitudes, concerns, and experiences of nurse leaders. *Journal of Professional Nursing*, 26(3): 182–7.

Zanoni, P. (2011). Diversity in the lean automobile factory: doing class through gender, disability and age. *Organization*, 18(1): 105–27.

CHAPTER 24

OF RACE AND RELIGION

Understanding the Roots of Anti-Muslim Prejudice in the United States

ALI MIR, SAADIA TOOR, AND RAZA MIR

Ever since 9/11, Muslims living in the United States (along with those who are perceived to be Muslims, such as non-Muslim Arabs and South Asians) have been subjected to an intensified scrutiny, increasingly viewed with fear and suspicion, and victimized through acts of discrimination and violence at the hands of both state and non-state actors. In much of the discourse about Muslims, whether critical or sympathetic, the organizing logic assumes that there is something called 'Islam', which can explain 'Muslim society', 'Muslim culture', and the 'Muslim mind'. The terms circulating in this discourse are usually in the singular, implying that there is one essential, monolithic 'Islam' which remains consistent across time and space, and that this particular identity accounts for the actions of those who either claim it or are otherwise marked by it through their name, ancestry, national origin, ethnicity, or race.

The discourse and its accompanying policies have had material consequences for the lives of Muslims in the US including surveillance, harassment, intimidation, discrimination, and incarceration. And while there is not yet a significant body of research on this issue, the evidence points to increasing workplace discrimination against those who are perceived to be Muslims (see, for example, Malos 2010; Cavico and Mujtaba 2011; Ghumman and Ryan 2013; see also the annual reports put out by CAIR 2013a). Studies have shown that, in the aftermath of 9/11, Muslim and Arab men working in the US experienced a significant drop in their earnings (Kaushal, Kaestner, and Reimers 2007). In their analysis of the 'discursive character of contemporary hostility towards the *niqab*-wearing Muslim women' in Quebec, Golnaraghi and Mills (2013: 158) outline the links between Islamophobic discourse around the *niqab* (or face veil), state action such as the passing of anti-accommodationist legislation, and Muslim women's ability to access state resources and services from education to health care.

In the US, the spike in the number of complaints filed by those of Middle Eastern and South Asian backgrounds with the Equal Opportunity Employment Commission (EEOC) was so significant that the EEOC created an entirely new category to keep track of these grievances. Responding to a request for data made by the American-Arab Anti-Discrimination Committee (ADC), the EEOC prepared a report indicating that 'Muslim Americans have filed more charges of religious discrimination and retaliation than any other religious group that the EEOC monitors' and that increasingly, a large proportion of these filings include retaliation charges that were brought about against the complainant (ADC 2013). EEOC statistics also show that 'religious-based discrimination claims in the USA have nearly doubled over the last decade and have risen four times more rapidly than any other protected category under the US Civil Rights Act of 1964' (Ghumman and Ryan 2013: 672). Despite being less than 1 per cent of the population (Pew 2011), Muslims accounted for 21 per cent of the filings (EEOC 2011). Hate crimes against Muslims remain high (FBI 2011) as do attacks on Muslim places of worship (ACLU 2011), while anti-Muslim 'hate-groups' continue to spread (Southern Poverty Law Center 2013).

This rise in discrimination directed at Muslims and Arabs by private actors and institutions is, unsurprisingly, accompanied by a rise in anti-Muslim prejudice within US society at large. For instance, polls and surveys show higher feelings of prejudice towards Arab-Americans than any other ethnic group (Bushman and Bonacci 2004), with one nationwide poll finding that 44 per cent of Americans agreed that restricting the civil rights of Muslim Americans was acceptable and even necessary (Sheridan 2006). Such frank and open expression of prejudice against a social group is exceptional in the US today. We argue that the state has itself authorized and legitimized this expression of prejudice and discrimination against Muslims through its own actions.

A particularly important set of examples of such actions are the bills that have been introduced in state legislatures and the US Congress, which are focused on legislating, monitoring, and circumscribing Muslim religious practices. A specifically absurd subset of these are 'red herring bills' passed by six states in the country, which ban *sharia*, a dynamic and varying set of Islamic codes that cannot, under the US Constitution, replace, supersede or displace US law (CAIR 2013b). Sweeps conducted after 9/11 in Muslim neighbourhoods, particularly in the wake of the passage of the 2001 Patriot Act, along with the 2002 National Security Entry-Exit Registration (NSEER) Program (or 'Special Registration')—which demanded that immigrants from a set of Muslim-majority countries (and from North Korea) register with the Justice Department—resulted in the detention and deportation of thousands of Muslims, with thousands of others subjecting themselves to self-deportation (Rana 2011). A 2011 investigative report by *Wired* magazine showed that anti-terrorism FBI training routinely depicted Muslims as violent and the 'Arabic mind' as 'swayed more by words than ideas and more by ideas than facts' (Ackerman 2011, published online). A probe by Associated Press revealed that the New York Police Department (NYPD) had routinely spied on Muslim neighbourhoods, catalogued mosques and restaurants, collected information about congregations, and built up a database on communities that were objects of suspicion purely on the basis of their religious affiliation (Goldman and Apuzzo 2012). Additionally, part of the training of the NYPD officers included the screening of *The Third Jihad*, a documentary filled with images of blood, explosions, and angry mullahs, all of which are then interpreted by 'Islam experts' as proof of a 1400-year-old Muslim conspiracy of world domination coming to a head (Robbins 2011). Further, various news reports have documented the ways in which Muslim communities have been infiltrated by informants (Aaronson 2011), while others have described the conditions of special prisons called 'Communications Management Units'—known colloquially as 'Little Gitmos'—that are mostly designed to quarantine Muslims (Johnson and Williams 2011; Stewart 2011). On 11 March 2011, Representative Peter King, chair of the Homeland Security Committee of the United States House of Representatives, held a hearing entitled 'The Extent of Radicalization in the American Muslim Community and that Community's Response', which was widely denounced by civil rights groups as the reproduction of racism against Muslim Americans (Hakimeh 2012).

These and other related events have clearly established Muslims in America as a particularly stigmatized 'out-group' against which even overt forms of prejudice and discrimination are acceptable and sanctioned. These forms of prejudice have come to be referenced by the term 'Islamophobia'. First formally deployed in a 1997 report by the Runnymede Trust in the United Kingdom to describe the tendency to see Islam as 'a single monolithic block... inferior to the West... barbaric, irrational, primitive, sexist... violent, aggressive [and] threatening', the concept of Islamophobia has gained currency within mainstream, activist, and scholarly circles. It has also become a hotly contested term, with critics arguing that it is too broad and therefore risks silencing valid and appropriate critiques of 'Islam'. Nonetheless, the term and its referents have become the subject of serious scholarly interest (for example, Bunzl 2007; Gottschalk and Greenberg 2008; Fekete 2009; Allen 2010; Esposito and Kalin 2011; Sheehi 2011; Helbling 2012; Kumar 2012), leading a recent review article to declare that the concept 'has come of age' (Klug 2012: 665).

Notwithstanding the examples of the studies on workplace discrimination against Muslims cited in this chapter, the fact of the matter is that there hasn't been sufficient empirical work done yet by management scholars on this issue. This is partly because of the lag between real life and scholarly output—that is, it takes time for discrimination against newly stigmatized groups to be recognized and studied. Additionally, the fact that religion is often an 'invisible' diversity category can make research on discrimination against Muslims difficult. Much of the existing research on workplace discrimination faced by Muslims has focused on the experience of hijabi Muslim women precisely because the hijab is a visible marker of Muslim identity and can be used to index a 'visible stigma' whose effects can be empirically measured (Ghumman and Ryan 2013; Reeves, McKinney, and Azam 2013).

In this chapter, we seek to offer a broad analytical perspective on anti-Muslim prejudice in the United States in order to propose a more complex understanding of the discrimination faced by Arabs and Muslims in society in general and in the workplace in particular. Our intent here is not so much to look at existing modes of workplace discrimination, but to offer a framework for management scholars to engage with the issues surrounding this form of prejudice, and thereby enhance the extant literature in this discipline on diversity and discrimination in the workplace.

We start by locating anti-Muslim prejudice in the US in its historical context in order to demonstrate the lineage which informs and influences the contemporary moment. We then seek to understand the racialization process as it applies to Muslims in the US today by first outlining the history of the idea of race and its evolution over time from its origins (or prehistory) in the religious politics of the *reconquista*, through its transformation into race-as-biology, to its contemporary form via theories of cultural racism. What we attempt to emphasize in this brief history is the fact that religion, specifically the relationship between Islam and Christianity, played a crucial role in the genesis and development of race as an idea, and that this history continues to inform discourses of Islam and Muslims in the US today. We then outline the approach to race offered by critical race theorists who urge that it be understood as 'an unstable and "decentered" complex of social meanings' (Omi and Winant 1994: 55), and as a historically and politically contingent process of racialization or 'racial formation', rather than something with an empirical basis in phenotypic differences. We contend that understanding the ways in which ideas of race, and the forms that racism takes, have changed over time is crucial to grasping what is happening with Muslims in the contemporary period, both within society more generally and thereby, inevitably, within the workplace.

As anti-Muslim discrimination grows as a social and workplace phenomenon, we propose that management scholars, especially those who work on issues of diversity, will have to deploy different frameworks of understanding 'the Muslim question' in the US today in order to think about anti-Muslim prejudice as a form of racism, where race is understood as a technology of power, and racialization (of Muslims, as well as others) as a contingent and political process. It is only by shifting our frame of understanding away from 'religious chauvinism' and towards 'race' and 'racialization' that we can hope to understand and confront anti-Muslim discrimination within organizations and workplaces.

Essentializing Muslims

In 1990, Orientalist scholar Bernard Lewis published *The Roots of Muslim Rage* in which he sought to explain what he called the Muslim world's 'revulsion against America'. He concluded that this 'is no less than a clash of civilizations—the perhaps irrational but surely historic reaction of an ancient rival against our Judeo-Christian heritage, our secular present, and the worldwide expansion of both' (Lewis 1990: 60).

Lewis's theory of the clash of civilizations—which, according to him, 'began with the advent of Islam, in the seventh century, and has continued virtually to the present day' (Lewis 1990: 49)—was catapulted into the mainstream when it was reworked in an influential essay by Samuel Huntington published in *Foreign Affairs*. In this essay,

Huntington (1993) hypothesized that the 'fundamental source of conflict' in the world in the coming years would be neither ideological nor economic, but rather 'cultural'. The 'clash of civilizations', he pronounced, 'will be the battle lines of the future' (Huntington 1993: 22).

It was not a coincidence that Lewis and Huntington made these arguments for civilizational (rather than ideological or economic) clashes in the early 1990s. This was the period in which Cold War ideology had to be reworked in the wake of the break-up of the Soviet Union and the end of the Cold War. As many scholars have argued, this state of affairs required the invention of a new global enemy that the 'free world' could be pitted against, and 'Islam' was a convenient choice, enabled in part by the Western reaction to the Iranian revolution of 1979. Edward Said signalled this coming change both in *Orientalism*, published in 1978, and in *Covering Islam: How the Media and the Experts Determine How We See the Rest of the World*, published in 1981. In a new introduction written for the 1997 edition of *Covering Islam*, Said (1997: lv) laid out the manner in which Islam was being depicted in the media during the 1990s, and its growing status as 'a kind of scapegoat for everything we do not happen to like about the world's new political, social, and economic patterns. For the right, Islam represents barbarism; for the left, medieval theocracy; for the center, a kind of distasteful exoticism'. In Said's view (1997: xi–xii), there was, at this time 'a strange revival of canonical, though previously discredited, Orientalist ideas about Muslim, generally non-white, people—ideas that have achieved a startling prominence at a time when racial and religious mis-representations of every other cultural group are no longer circulated with such impunity'.

Many of these formulaic ideas about Islam form the backbone of anti-Muslim sentiment in the current times. This sentiment relies upon oppositional binaries such as Western liberalism versus Muslim illiberalism, civilization versus barbarism, rationality versus irrationality, and most of all, modern versus traditional. How then are these binaries to be interpreted? Is the purportedly illiberal, barbaric, irrational, and traditional Muslim being interpellated as an inferior race? Does the essentialization of Muslims in the US offer evidence of their racialization?

As Said (1978, 1981) has persuasively argued, Muslims—and Islam—have historically been essentialized in the US, and the West more generally, by reducing their diverse ethnic and national identities to a singular one of 'Muslim'. The common-sense understanding of what it means to be 'Muslim' today is similarly based on an essentialist and reductionist construction of 'Islam', which is understood to be incommensurable with something called 'the West', variously expressed through terms such as 'Western values' and 'Western culture'. Islam, it is argued, is uniquely and exceptionally misogynist (and within certain contexts, homophobic), and this is then presented as proof of Muslims' essentially illiberal nature (Toor 2008; 2012; Selod and Embrick 2013). Islam's essential difference from, and thereby incompatibility with, and/or resistance to 'the West' and its (universalized) liberal values (Lewis 1990; Samman 2012) are offered as the explanation for the 'backwardness' of Muslims and the justification for casting them out of liberal law and politics within the West (Razack 2008). An example of the egregiousness of this discourse can be found in an online piece by Martin Peretz (2010), a Harvard professor and the publisher and editor-in-chief of the *New Republic*, in which he contends that 'Muslim life was cheap, most notably to Muslims' and wonders 'whether I need honor *these people* and pretend that they are worthy of the privileges of the First Amendment which I have in my gut the sense that they will abuse' (emphasis added).

The essentialization of Muslims is tied in the West to their increasing exclusion from the liberal (nation-)state and the rights of citizenship. For the purposes of this chapter, we propose that citizenship can be seen as having two main, interlocking dimensions. The first is membership in the 'nation' (or 'national community'), which is understood as a community of affect, bearing a structural relationship to ideas of kinship—the 'nation' is, after all, often imagined as a *family*, complete with the latter's hetero-patriarchal underpinnings. The second is the way citizenship is usually understood: as membership in the *state*, which is the granter and protector of the rights that this membership accords. Second-class citizenship is, in effect, the result of having formal membership in the state, but not being accorded membership in the community of *affect*, the 'nation'. Being of the wrong race/ethnicity/religion/gender/sexuality can all result in being denied membership in the 'national family', and thereby have one's formal rights of citizenship actually or potentially compromised. The 'casting out' (Razack 2008) of Muslims occurs at both of these mutually reinforcing levels.

Interestingly, the place that the Muslim now occupies vis-à-vis the liberal state bears a striking resemblance to that occupied by 'the Jew' in Europe not very long ago. Several scholars have pointed to the strong similarity between 'the Jewish Question' of the late nineteenth and early twentieth centuries and the 'Muslim Question' today (Mufti 2007; Brown 2008). The strong communal focus of Judaism, it was argued at the time, made it impossible for the Jew to be the fully individuated subject required by liberalism. His strong bonds with co-religionists competed with the normative bonds between individual citizens, thus rendering him inassimilable into the national community. At the same time, his membership in a global (that is, extra-state) community of Jews undermined the primacy accorded to the relationship that the (individual) liberal subject was expected to have to the modern state. The figure of the Jew at that time was thus the figure of 'the stranger', the 'outsider within'. In Mufti's (2007: 38) words, '[t]he figure of the Jew has faced a paradoxical predicament in the culture of the modern West, and has typically been met with a contradictory set of representational demands: on the one hand, as a figure of particularity, it has generated anxieties about the undermining of the universalizing claims and ambitions embedded in the constitutive narratives of modern culture, with the Jews coming to be seen as slavishly bound to external Law and tradition, ritualistic and irrational, and incapable of the modernity and autonomy called for in the development of enlightened, modern subjectivity; on the other, as a figure of transnational range and abilities, it raises questions about deracination, homelessness, abstraction, supra-national identifications, and divided loyalties.' The similarities between anti-Semitism and Islamophobia have been discussed in some detail by a variety of scholars (see, *inter alia*, Kalmar 2009; Meer and Modood 2012). This relationship has a long and complex history, and the silence over it within scholarship on race and anti-Semitism is interesting given its well-documented nature (see Said 2002 and Kalmar 2009; for an explication of its curious effacement in histories of race and racialization, see Rana 2007). The 'Muslim' in the West today is similarly constructed as a 'bad'—in fact, a *dangerous*—immigrant, an outsider who *will not* (indeed, *cannot*) assimilate, and therefore one whose loyalties will always remain in question (Ali 2012; Bazian 2012).

It is notable that the overt and explicit animosity demonstrated in the statements made and circulated about Muslims *within the public sphere* (and this is important) would be impossible to imagine directed against any other social group. Several scholars have argued that the exceptional nature of this animosity requires that anti-Muslim prejudice be understood as a form of racism (see, for instance, Poynting and Mason 2007; Gotanda 2010; Rana 2011; Elver 2012; Meer and Modood 2012). Perhaps unsurprisingly, there is also vehement resistance to any attempt to identify it as such. The standard argument offered for rejecting the framing of anti-Muslim prejudice as racism is that Islam is a religion and therefore Muslims are not a race. Several liberal intellectuals, particularly 'the new atheists' such as Richard Dawkins, Sam Harris, and Christopher Hitchens have been at the forefront of this response, which is encountered so consistently and reflexively that it has attained the status of a meme. On the surface, the argument seems incontrovertible. Islam *is* a religion, and Muslims are not (officially) considered or understood to be a race as race is conventionally understood in the United States today. However, by this token, anti-Semitism cannot be a considered a form of racism since Judaism is also a religion. But just as race and religion were intertwined in the anti-Semitic figure of 'the Jew' in Europe, so, we argue, is the case with 'the Muslim' in the West today.

However, we argue that the 'Muslim question' in the US must be approached through the framework of race and racism for the simple reason that race is the pre-eminent way in which difference has been understood and organized within the US not only from its inception as an independent republic, but from the time of the European conquest of the Americas. Further, as we seek to demonstrate, race and religion have been intricately intertwined throughout the history of the United States, and continue to be so in the most relevant of ways. As several scholars and civil rights organizations have pointed out, this history has had an impact on the structures of discrimination in contemporary workplaces as well (Malos 2010; EEOC 2011; CAIR 2013a; Ghumman and Ryan 2013; Reeves, McKinney, and Azam 2013).

RACE AND RELIGION IN THE US

Scholars of race agree that 'race' as a concept had its genesis in the moment of contact between Europeans and the indigenous people of the Americas in 1492. Richard Omi and Howard Winant (1994: 62), in their highly influential and paradigmatic book *Racial Formation in the United States*, persuasively argue that the conquest 'was the first—and given the dramatic nature of the case, perhaps the greatest—racial formation project'. A new chapter in the US's racial history—a new racial project—began with the arrival of African slaves, and over time, European settlers developed a complex and dynamic racial matrix which all new groups of immigrants (have) had to negotiate and be slotted within (Bonilla-Silva 2001; for a history of race and immigration in the US, see, *inter alia* Takaki 1993).

The most important intervention made by critical race theorists has been to point out the malleability, resilience, and opportunism of the category of 'race' and 'race thinking', and the manner in with the idea of race evolved from its originary moment in religious racism into a biological (scientific, hence secular) racism, and eventually morphed into contemporary cultural ideas of race (Blaut 1992; Omi and Winant 1994; Hartigan 2009).

The concept of race emerged out of the proto-racial concept of 'purity of blood' which was articulated after the *reconquista* as a way to differentiate between 'real' Christians and the Marranos and Mariscos, converted Jews and Muslims respectively (Goldschmidt 2004; Gottschalk and Greenberg 2008). After the European conquest of the Americas in 1492 and the contact with indigenous populations, this concept of 'proto-race' began its evolution into a theory of biological race that we associate with 'classic' racism (Mignolo 2000; Modood 2005; scholars such as Grosfoguel and Mielants 2006 and Samman and al-Zo'by 2008 have gone on to argue anti-Muslim prejudice ought to be seen as *constitutive* of the modern world-system). However, the religious/theological angle did not completely disappear; religion continued to be associated with race, even in the late nineteenth century when a secularized, scientific form of biological racism rose to prominence (Samman 2012).

This biological theory of race remained hegemonic until the horrors of Nazism and the power of the Civil Rights movement combined to render it politically untenable in the mid-twentieth century. As a result, a new, cultural form of racism (often referred to as racism without race) emerged to take its place (Samman 2012). Cultural racism works by replacing the biological case for superior or inferior races with that of superior and inferior *cultures*. The goal and logic remain the same, however: to conclusively establish the innate superiority of the (white, Christian) West. As Blaut (1992: 292) argues, 'cultural racism substitutes the cultural category "European" for the racial category "white"'. This new form of racism has proved to be remarkably resilient and therefore ideologically useful, since it no longer talks about 'race' as we conventionally understand it—that is, race as biology, as phenotype. Cultural racism can therefore circulate unimpeded, and in fact it now saturates and structures the public discourse on inequality in the US, both in the workplace and in the broader society.

Each new instantiation of race and racism did not emerge out of whole cloth to neatly replace the earlier one; instead, even as one form emerged as dominant in any given historical period, the others continued to circulate and reinforce one another in complex ways in response to various political exigencies. In fact, every racial project is legitimated by an articulation (in the Althusserian sense of a mutual imbrication) of different racial discourses. Thus, even while it seemed to have been de-racinated, the discourse of cultural superiority continued to be informed by biological and, indeed, religious ideas of race. The term 'European', for example, carried within it the sense of both whiteness and Christianity. Blaut (1992) cites Weber as the pre-eminent example of the secularization of the older discourse of religious racism and its emergence as cultural racism within the Western intelligentsia (in fact, he refers to Weber the godfather of cultural racism), for behind Weber's famously 'path-breaking' cultural(ist) explanation for social change, lurks religion (Nafissi (1998) argues that, in fact, Weber's cultural racism was not just Orientalist but specifically anti-Muslim). It is, after all the *Protestant* ethic (albeit in a secularized form) which Weber sees as giving rise to and animating modern rational capitalism; his much-celebrated contingent model of sociological explanation has a deep investment in demonstrating that this rational, eminently modern form of capitalism could only have arisen in the (Protestant) West. New theories asserting the cultural superiority of Europeans therefore continued to carry within them the logic of the earlier theories; religious and biological race are embedded in the idea of 'European', which implicitly invokes both whiteness and Christianity (specifically Protestantism).

The new discourse of cultural racism has enabled both domestic and international racial projects. It played a crucial role in both phases of European colonialism, which were justified by the idea of the 'civilizing mission', where 'civilization' indexed a complex mixture of religion and race. In the first phase of the conquest of the Americas, civilization very explicitly meant Christianity. By the nineteenth century, the category of 'European' had itself been racially disaggregated into the 'white' (Northern and Western) and 'non-white' (Southern and Eastern) Europeans, a divide which strongly overlapped with that of Protestant and Catholic. Anti-Catholic Protestant discourses about 'the Black Legend' animated an internal civilizing mission within the US, as the Anglo-Protestant elite sought to manage Catholic Italian, Irish, and Mexican immigrant populations (Haverluk 2002: 48–9). It is easy to forget that the idea that Catholics were not fully American was so mainstream even as recently as the 1960s that the election of (to most people today, the unqualifiedly white) John F. Kennedy to the office of president—an event that took place in the wake of the de-racialization of the Irish and their promotion to the status of white ethnics—was considered a major turning point in US history.

The power of cultural racism has always lain in the fact that it is not recognizable as racism since it is not overtly about 'race-as-biology'. This is also precisely what makes it so pernicious; it can continue to perform the ideological functions of racism without being held open to challenge (see, for example Schiffer and Wagner 2011). The juxtaposition of 'Islam' with 'the West' in the contemporary moment, we contend, illustrates the slipperiness of the discourse of cultural racism, counterposing as it does a religious category ('Islam') with a geographical category ('the West'). Since we have seen that 'the West' carries within it racial and religious connotations, the juxtaposition of the two *forces* us to read race and geography into the category of 'Islam'. Poststructural analysis understands discourse as working precisely through binaries such this ('Islam'/'the West'), whereby one term in the binary is privileged and gains meaning from the other, inferior one. Any statement in which this binary appears is always already a statement about the superiority of the West and its values of rationality, secularism, individualism, and so on. By constructing 'Islam' and 'the West' as hermetically sealed and mutually exclusive categories, this binary ensures that the very idea of a 'Western Islam', and thereby 'Western Muslims', becomes incomprehensible.

The link between race and religion in the US can be further seen through the ways in which Christianity and whiteness are articulated, together with a deeply racialized idea of Christianity legitimating and animating almost every racial project. And so it is not by coincidence that the white supremacist project in the US has always been explicitly Christian in its expression. That it was, and continues to be, a racial project is evidenced by the fact that it was historically aimed not at 'heathen non-Christians' but at Christian African Americans, underlining the ways in which religion in the US was, and still is, deeply raced (in this context, Charles Lincoln (1973) has argued that African Americans turned to Islam as a form of protest against white society). Upstanding white Christian Americans historically looked upon black forms of Christianity either with disdain (towards, for instance, the 'pagan' aspects of black Pentecostal traditions) or fear (of, for instance the 'militant' preachers of the civil rights and specifically Black Power era). The religious right in the US continues to be overwhelmingly white, and almost old-fashioned in its anti-black racism. As a result, despite the profession of religious pluralism and the Establishment Clause, which states that 'Congress shall make no law respecting an establishment of religion' and is commonly read to mean that the US should have no state religion, Christianity (and specifically Protestantism) has always been and continues to be the *de facto* 'national' religion in the country.

Phenotypes and Muslims

We have argued that Muslims are racialized in the US through the discourse of cultural racism. However, as we have also pointed out, cultural racism continues to be articulated with both religious and biological forms of racism. While it is true that Muslims as a whole are not officially designated a singular racial identity in the US, there is nevertheless a common-sense idea of what Muslims 'look like'—a Muslim 'phenotype', as it were. Incidents of discrimination such as removal of (brown, male) passengers presumed to be Muslim from airlines based on the fear of their fellow passengers make this clear. But what does it mean to 'look Muslim'? One aspect of this 'recognizability' has a non-biological basis. Facial hair and clothing, such as the beards sported by certain male Muslims, and the head-coverings of certain Muslim women, have become closely intertwined with Muslim identity (Love 2009). This is testified to by the fact that Muslims (but also 'misrecognized' non-Muslims such as Sikhs) have been profiled and subjected to violence on this basis. The fact that these supposedly identifiable signs of Muslimness are often incorrect—for instance, not all male Muslims sport beards of the sort that have become associated with Muslim male identity and not all Muslim women wear headscarves—is immaterial. What is important is that they have become part of the general public understanding of what Muslims look like, and therefore of how to recognize a Muslim when you see one.

But how is this about *race*? In order to understand this, we must turn to the concept of *racialization* (a process), rather than race understood as a pre-given and stable (biological) identity. One of the ways in which race functions is through 'hypervisibility'. Thus, anything that makes people appear to be 'recognizable' as members of a particular social group, and thereby subject to prejudice and discrimination, must be understood as part of a process of racialization. The fact that Muslim identity in the public consciousness is also associated with a particular skin colour (brown) and certain ethnic, regional, and national identities (such as 'Arab'/'South Asian'/'Middle Eastern') shows that the racialization of Muslims also proceeds through the conventional form of race-as-phenotype.

The proof of the fact that there is there is an image of a Muslim body which exists in the public mind comes from the 'misrecognition' in identifying Muslims, both through false positives and false negatives. The targeting of non-Muslim brown people (such as turbaned Sikhs) is an example of a false positive. The false negative is exemplified by the so-called 'American Taliban' and 'Jihad Jane', two white Muslim 'terrorists', who were white, and recent, converts to Islam. The public discourse with regard to their identity as Muslims was rife with confusion because they were understood to have the 'wrong racial body' (Gotanda 2011: 193). As Gotanda (2011: 193) points out, the use of the qualifier 'American' in the case of the 'American Taliban', 'follows a common practice that distinguishes white Americans from minorities through the use of the term "American"', while the 'notoriety surrounding Jihad Jane and the American Taliban emphasize that they are racial anomalies who have crossed over the racial divide'.

This equation of 'Muslim' with a particular phenotypic identity has been further encouraged by the actions of the US state, which, through its acts of overt profiling, has been instructing the American public that 'looking "Middle Eastern, Arab, or Muslim" equals "potential terrorist"' (Volpp 2002: 19; see also Elver 2012: 124). Perhaps the most explicit proof of the racialization of Muslims is provided by the visual tropes through which they are represented in the mainstream, which, while often featuring turbans and veils, also bear a striking resemblance to older, long-standing anti-Semitic stereotypes, in large part due to the conflation of 'Arab' and 'Muslim' within the US and the long history of racist depictions of Arabs in the US mainstream (Hudson and Wolf 1980; Michalak 1988; Semmerling 2006).

Anti-Muslim Prejudice as a Racial Project

If the argument as so far outlined is persuasive, we need to return to the question of why there is such a huge resistance to seeing anti-Muslim prejudice as a form of racism. What is the investment in the widespread *refusal* to see it as such? We have seen that cultural racism replaced biological racism as the primary modality of race-thinking once the latter became politically untenable, since biology was understood to be about ascription, and culture was not. Thus, there is widespread agreement today that prejudice and discrimination against people on the basis of their biologically ascribed characteristics (race, sex, etc.) is wrong and unjust, since these characteristics are things that people are understood to have no choice over. People's 'culture' (and their religion, as a subset of culture), however, is not understood as an ascribed characteristic, because even though people are born into particular cultural and religious traditions, nothing prevents them from leaving these and accepting new ones, or so the argument goes. In fact, it is claimed that the sign of an enlightened and liberal individual is the willingness to reject the 'culture' (understood as values, norms, etc.) she was born into should it come into conflict with the universal values of 'human rights'. Culture and religion thus become cast within liberal discourse as things amenable to *individual choice*.

And so, ironically, constitutional protections are available in the US, the land of individual freedom and choice, for 'communities of ascription', precisely because ascription implies a *lack* of choice. An example which illustrates how deeply ideas of biological ascription are connected to justifications for legal and constitutional protection in the US is provided by the debate over homosexuality and gay rights. The idea that homosexuality is not a choice, but a form of ascription—that people are born with specific sexual orientations which they carry throughout their lives—has been pivotal to the argument for the equal rights of gays and lesbians, not just in the legal and constitutional arena, but in the court of public opinion. Any other way of understanding sexuality has had to be squashed and marginalized, lest it lend credence to the idea that homosexuality was nothing more than a ('deviant') lifestyle *choice* (see, *inter alia* Goodloe 2012) or a 'controllable stigma'.

And so, according to Ghumman and Ryan (2013), highlighting the fact that not all Muslim women wear the hijab can actually exacerbate negative attitudes towards hijabi women, since they come to be seen as having a 'controllable stigma', one that does not require protection under the EEOC laws. This might explain the pattern of workplace prejudice and discrimination against hijabi women that existing studies, including those by management scholars, have clearly demonstrated (see, for example, Ghumman and Jackson 2010; King and Ahmad 2010; Syed and Pio 2010; Unkelback et al. 2010). Scholars have also noted an ambiguity or confusion within organizations towards the category of religion in general (and Islam in particular) when it comes to operationalizing EEOC rules regarding the prevention of discrimination against its protected categories (see Reeves, McKinney, and Azam 2013).

Once religious affiliation, and thus identity, is constructed as a matter of individual choice, Muslim identity cannot be understood as a form of ascription (see, for example, Meer and Modood 2009: 42). Given the essentialization of Muslims (and their culture) and the construction of 'Islam' as the very negation of liberal values, Muslims who do not openly 'reject' their culture and religion—and particularly those that appear to accept and practise it—become unsympathetic, and even legitimate, targets of criticism in the eyes of many. Thus, the argument that 'Islam is a religion, therefore Muslims are not a race, therefore anti-Muslim prejudice is not racism' serves to neutralize any objections against a wholesale critique of Islam and Muslims, even when that critique deploys arguments and tropes which would be unacceptable when applied to any other social group (Meer and Modood 2009; Khan and Ahmad 2013).

The appearance of new racial groups and the disappearance of old ones in the US has always been deeply connected to political and historical necessities and contingencies, a fact which Omi and Winant (1994) captured in their concept of racial formation. Defining racial formation as 'the sociohistorical process by which racial categories are created, inhabited, transformed, and destroyed', they argue that studying race involves connecting 'the process of historically situated projects in which human bodies and social structures are represented and organized' to 'the evolution of hegemony, the way in which society is organized and ruled' (Omi and Winant 1994: 55). That is, understanding race was, or should be, really about understanding the ideological work done by the concept of race, and by the existence and ordering of racial categories at any given moment in time within a specific society. This ideological work of 'making the links between structure and representation' is done by specific racial projects.

Racial formation within the US has always had both domestic and international aspects, with race being an integral part of both domestic *as well as* foreign policy. The racialization of Filipinos and Mexicans during the Spanish-American War and the internment of Japanese Americans during the Second World War are all examples of racial projects that corresponded to the needs of US foreign policy of that time. During the Cold War, Black radicals (and Black Muslim radicals in particular) from the 1950s to the 1970s were projected as communists.

Wars are always accompanied by a dehumanization of the 'Enemy'. Given the imbrication of race in the US's social, cultural, and political matrix, it is not surprising that US foreign policy, and particularly US wars, have always resulted in this dehumanization being played out through narratives of race, and through the processes of racialization. The 'Enemy' is thus always understood as a *racialized* enemy. It is within this framework that anti-Muslim prejudice and discrimination in the US today must be approached—as the latest in a long line of racial projects.

Conclusion

The evidence is fairly overwhelming that Muslims in the US (and in the West, in general) have been constructed as suspicious bodies by both state and non-state actors, and consequently have been facing a significant, and increasing, amount of discrimination, both in the broader social space and in the workplace. Management scholars, especially those interested in issues of diversity and discrimination, have only recently started paying some attention to this phenomenon, which will only become more important as better empirical data begins to emerge. When management scholarship has approached the topic, it has tended to do so as an instance of religious prejudice. In this chapter, we have sought to demonstrate how race is a far more powerful and useful conceptual framework to apply to this topic. Indeed, we show that the politics of the contemporary moment cannot be understood without coming to terms with the long history of anti-Muslim antagonism in the West, out of which the concept of race was forged.

The constraints of space prevent us from presenting a more complete exposition of the form, content, and extent of anti-Muslim prejudice in the US today, and its relationship to domestic politics (nor have we had the opportunity to talk about the significant, and growing, resistance to this prejudice by Muslims and non-Muslims alike). Islamophobia has literally become an industry in the US today, and, as the report put out by the Center for American Progress (2011) titled *Fear Inc.*, details, a very lucrative one. Other investigative reports (see Cincotta 2011 and Lean 2012) have documented how anti-Muslim prejudice helps to generate and sustain a multi-million-dollar industry in technologies of surveillance, repression, and incarceration.

Scholars have also argued that the antagonism against Muslims should be read as part of the neoliberal project, with the special prisons housing Muslims serving the function of spaces of 'exception', not unlike the Special Economic Zones cropping up in the Third World, where, paradoxically, the law determines that the law does not apply (Agamben 2005). Drawing upon Aihwa Ong's (2006) work, Razack (2008: 11) argues that 'at the heart of neoliberalism is the idea and the practice of the exception, the notion that the government has the right to do anything in the interest of governance'. In the introduction to his magisterial *State of Exception*, Giorgio Agamben (2005: 3) noted that the US action in the post-9/11 period, 'radically erases any legal status of the individual, thus producing a legally unnameable and unclassifiable being'. Along with the creation of 'states of exception', the War on Terror has enabled the increasing designation of Muslims as *homo sacer*—'the sacred or cursed man'—reduced to 'bare life' and stripped of any rights (Agamben 1998). The logic of exception enables the creation of the new gulags where the 'bad' Muslim can be segregated, while his (and this is very much a gendered as well as raced project) increasing relegation to the status of *homo sacer* completes his dehumanization domestically and abroad. It is thus incumbent upon scholars to address the forms which this racialized dehumanization is taking today.

Social scientists studying the issue of diversity have focused on the processes by which Muslims are subjected to routines of organizational exclusion (Torpey 2006; Fortier 2007). Some scholars of organizational diversity have also examined the issue of anti-Muslim prejudice, albeit from the point of view of strategy and policy (Guimond et al. 2013; Reeves, McKinney, and Azam 2013). Our chapter is more likely to find traction with the work of critical diversity studies (see Bendl, Fleischmann, and Walenta 2008; Zanoni et al. 2010), and offers a framework that might be useful to those who approach issues of discrimination from the perspective of social justice, which we strongly believe must underlie, in fact precede, any effective diversity initiative.

REFERENCES

Aaronson, T. (2011). The informants. <http://www.motherjones.com/politics/2011/08/fbi-terrorist-informants>, accessed 30 November 2013.

Ackerman, S. (2011). FBI 'Islam 101' guide depicted Muslims as 7th-century simpletons. <http://www.wired.com/dangerroom/2011/07/fbi-islam-101-guide/>, accessed 30 November 2013.
ACLU [American Civil Liberties Union] (2011). Map: nationwide anti-mosque activity. <https://www.aclu.org/maps/map-nationwide-anti-mosque-activity>, accessed 30 November 2013.
ADC (2013). EEOC statistical data: discrimination and retaliation charges filed by Arab and Muslim Americans. <http://www.adc.org/fileadmin/ADC/ADC_EEOC_Stats_Press_Release_2013.pdf>, accessed 30 November 2013.
Agamben, G. (1998). *Homo Sacer: Sovereign Power and Bare Life*. Stanford, CA: Stanford University Press.
Agamben, G. (2005). *State of Exception*. Chicago: University of Chicago Press.
Ali, Y. (2012). Shariah and citizenship: how Islamophobia is creating a second-class citizenry in America. *California Law Review*, 100(4): 1027–68.
Allen, C. (2010). *Islamophobia*. Farnham: Ashgate Publishing.
Bazian, H. (2012). Muslims—enemies of the state: the new counter-intelligence program (COINTELPRO). *Islamophobia Studies Journal*, 1(1): 163–206.
Bendl, R., Fleischmann, A., and Walenta, C. (2008). Diversity management discourse meets queer theory. *Gender in Management*, 23(6): 382–94.
Blaut, J. M. (1992). The theory of cultural racism. *Antipode*, 24(4): 289–99.
Bonilla-Silva, E. (2001). *White Supremacy and Racism in the Post-Civil Rights Era*. London: Lynne Rienner Publishers.
Brown, W. (2008). *Regulating Aversion: Tolerance in the Age of Identity and Empire*. Princeton, NJ: Princeton University Press.
Bunzl, M. (2007). *Anti-Semitism and Islamophobia: Hatreds Old and New in Europe*. Chicago: Prickly Paradigm Press.
Bushman, B. J. and Bonnaci, A. M. (2004). You've got mail: using e-mail to examine the effect of prejudiced attitudes on discrimination against Arabs. *Journal of Experimental Social Psychology*, 40(6): 753–9.
CAIR (2013a). CAIR Civil Rights Reports. <http://www.cair.com/civil-rights/civil-rights-reports.html>, accessed 30 November 2013.
CAIR (2013b). Legislating fear: Islamophobia and its impact in the United States. <http://www.cair.com/images/islamophobia/Legislating-Fear.pdf>, accessed 30 November 2013.
Cavico, F. J. and Mujtaba, B. G. (2011). Employment discrimination and Muslims in the USA. *Journal for Global Business Advancement*, 4(3): 279–97.
Center for American Progress (2011). *Fear Inc.: The Roots of the Islamophobia Network in America*. <http://www.americanprogress.org/issues/religion/report/2011/08/26/10165/fear-inc/>, accessed 30 November 2013.
Cincotta, T. (2011). *Manufacturing the Muslim Menace: Private Firms, Public Servants and the Threat to Rights and National Security*. Somerville, MA: Political Research Associates.
EEOC (2011). Religion-based charges filed from 10/01/2000 through 9/30/2011 showing percentage filed on the basis of religion-Muslim. U.S. Equal Employment Opportunity Commission. <http://www.eeoc.gov/eeoc/events/9-11-11_religion_charges.cfm>, accessed 30 November 2013.
Elver, H. (2012). Racializing Islam before and after 9/11: from melting pot to Islamophobia. *Transnational Law and Contemporary Problems*, 21(1): 119–74.
Esposito, J. L. and Kalin, I. (eds.) (2011). *Islamophobia: The Challenge of Pluralism in the 21st Century*. Oxford: Oxford University Press.

FBI (2011). Hate crime statistics 2011. <http://www.fbi.gov/about-us/cjis/ucr/hate-crime/2011/narratives/victims>, accessed 30 November 2013.

Fekete, L. (2009). *A Suitable Enemy: Racism, Migration and Islamophobia in Europe.* London: Pluto Press.

Fortier, A. (2007). *Multicultural Horizons: Diversity and the Limits of the Civil Nation.* New York: Routledge.

Ghumman, S. and Jackson, L. (2010). The downside of religious attire: the Muslim headscarf and expectations for obtaining employment. *Journal of Organizational Behavior*, 31(1): 4–23.

Ghumman, S. and Ryan, A. M. (2013). Not welcome here: discrimination towards women who wear the Muslim headscarf. *Human Relations*, 66: 671–98.

Goldman, A. and Apuzzo, M. (2012). NYPD secret police spying on Muslims led to no terrorism leads or cases. *The Guardian*, 21 August. <http://www.theguardian.com/world/2012/aug/21/nypd-secret-muslim-spying-no-leads>, accessed 30 November 2013.

Goldschmidt, H. (2004). Introduction: race, nation, and religion in the Americas. In H. Goldschmidt and E. McAlister (eds.), *Race, Nation, and Religion in the Americas.* New York: Oxford University Press, 3–34.

Golnaraghi G. and Mills, A. J. (2013). Unveiling the myth of the Muslim woman: a postcolonial critique. *Equality, Diversity and Inclusion: An International Journal*, 32(2): 157–72.

Goodloe, A. (2012 [1994]). Choice, biology, and the causes of homosexuality: towards a new theory of queer identity. <http://amygoodloe.com/papers/choice-biology-and-the-causes-of-homosexuality-towards-a-new-theory-of-queer-identity/>, accessed 2 December 2013.

Gotanda, N. (2010). New directions in Asian American jurisprudence. *Asian American Law Journal*, 17(1): 5–61.

Gotanda, N. (2011). The racialization of Islam in American law. *The ANNALS of the American Academy of Political and Social Science*, 637(1): 184–95.

Gottschalk, P. and Greenberg, G. (2008). *Islamophobia: Making Muslims the Enemy.* Lanham, MD: Rowman & Littlefield Publishers.

Grosfoguel, R. and Mielants, E. (2006). The long-durée entanglement between Islamophobia and racism in the modern/colonial capitalist/patriarchal world-system: an introduction. *Human Architecture: Journal of the Sociology of Self-Knowledge*, 5(1): 1–12.

Guimond, S., Crisp, R. J., De Oliveira, P., Kamiejski, R., Kteily, N., Kuepper, B., and Zick, A. (2013). Diversity policy, social dominance, and intergroup relations: predicting prejudice in changing social and political contexts. *Journal of Personality and Social Psychology*, 104(6): 941–63.

Hakimeh, S.-B. (2012) American Muslims as radicals? A critical discourse analysis of the US congressional hearing on 'the extent of radicalization in the American Muslim community and that community's response'. *Discourse & Society*, 23(5): 508–24.

Hartigan, J. (2009). *Race in the 21st Century: Ethnographic Approaches.* New York: Oxford University Press.

Haverluk, T. (2002). Chile peppers and identity construction in Pueblo, Colorado. *Journal for the Study of Food and Society*, 6(1): 45–58.

Helbling, M. (ed.) (2012). *Islamophobia in the West: Measuring and Explaining Individual Attitudes.* London: Routledge.

Hudson, M. J. and Wolfe, R. G. (eds.) (1980). *American Media and the Arabs.* Washington DC: Center for Contemporary Arab Studies, Georgetown University.

Huntington, S. P. (1993). The clash of civilizations? *Foreign Affairs*, 72(3): 22–49.

Johnson, C. and Williams, M. (2011). 'Guantanamo north': inside secretive U.S. prisons. <http://www.npr.org/2011/03/03/134168714/guantanamo-north-inside-u-s-secretive-prisons>, accessed 30 November 2013.

Kalmar, I. D. (2009). Anti-Semitism and Islamophobia: the formation of a secret. *Human Architecture: Journal of the Sociology of Self-Knowledge*, 7(2): 135–44.

Kaushal, N., Kaestner, R., and Reimers, C. (2007). Labor market effects of September 11th on Arab and Muslim residents of the United States. *Journal of Human Resources*, 42(2): 275–308.

Khan, S. A. and Ahmad, A. S. (2013). Sharia law, Islamophobia and the U.S. constitution: new tectonic plates of the culture wars. *University of Maryland Law Journal of Race, Religion, Gender & Class*, 12(1): 123–39.

King, E. B. and Ahmad, A. S. (2010). An experimental field study of interpersonal discrimination toward Muslim job applicants. *Personnel Psychology*, 63: 881–906.

Klug, B. (2012). Islamophobia: a concept comes of age. *Ethnicities*, 12(5): 665–81.

Kumar, D. (2012). *Islamophobia and the Politics of Empire*. Chicago: Haymarket Books.

Lean, N. (2012). *The Islamophobia Industry: How the Right Manufactures Fear of Muslims*. London: Pluto Press.

Lewis, B. (1990). The roots of Muslim rage. *Atlantic Monthly*, 266(3): 47–60.

Lincoln, E. C. (1973). *The Black Muslim in America*. Boston, MA: Beacon Press.

Love, E. (2009). Confronting Islamophobia in the United States: framing civil rights activism among Middle Eastern Americans. *Patterns of Prejudice*, 43(3–4): 401–25.

Malos, S. (2010). Post-9/11 backlash in the workplace: employer liability for discrimination against Arab- and Muslim-Americans based on religion or national origin. *Employee Responsibilities and Rights Journal*, 22(4): 297–310.

Meer, N. and Modood, T. (2009). Refutations of racism in the Muslim question. *Patterns of Prejudice*, 43(3–4): 332–51.

Meer, N. and Modood, T. (2012). For 'Jewish' Read 'Muslim'? Islamophobia as a form of racialisation of ethno-religious groups in Britain today. *Islamophobia Studies Journal*, 1(1): 36–55.

Michalak, L. (1988). *Cruel and Unusual: Negative Images of Arabs in American Popular Culture*. 3rd edn. ADC Issue Paper No. 15. American Arab Anti-Discrimination Committee, Washington, DC.

Mignolo, W. (2000). *Local Histories/Global Designs: Coloniality, Border Thinking and Subaltern Knowledge*. Princeton, NJ: Princeton University Press.

Modood, T. (2005). *Multicultural Politics: Racism, Ethnicity and Muslims in Britain*. Edinburgh: Edinburgh University Press.

Mufti, A. (2007). *Enlightenment in the Colony: The Jewish Question and the Crisis of Postcolonial Culture*. Princeton, NJ: Princeton University Press.

Nafissi, M. R. (1998). Reframing Orientalism: Weber and Islam. *Economy and Society*, 27(1): 97–118.

Omi, M. and Winant, H. (1994). *Racial Formation in the United States from the 1960s to the 1990s*, 2nd edn. New York: Routledge.

Ong, A. (2006). *Neoliberalism as Exception: Mutations in Citizenship and Sovereignty*. Durham, NC: Duke University Press.

Peretz, M. (2010). The New York Times laments 'a sadly wary misunderstanding of Muslim-Americans': but really is it 'sadly wary' or a 'misunderstanding' at all? <http://www.newrepublic.com/blog/77475/the-new-york-times-laments-sadly-wary-misunderstanding-muslim-americans-really-it-sadly-w>, accessed 30 November 2013.

Pew (2011). The future of the global Muslim population. <http://www.pewforum.org/2011/01/27/future-of-the-global-muslim-population-regional-americas/>, accessed 30 November 2013.

Poynting, S. and Mason, V. (2007). The resistible rise of Islamophobia. *Journal of Sociology*, 43(1): 61–86.

Rana, J. (2007). The story of Islamophobia. *Souls: A Critical Journal of Black Politics, Culture, and Society*, 9(2): 148–61.

Rana, J. (2011). *Terrifying Muslims: Race and Labor in the South Asian Diaspora*. Durham, NC: Duke University Press.

Razack, S. (2008). *Casting Out: The Eviction of Muslims from Western Law and Politics*. Toronto: University of Toronto Press.

Reeves, T. C., McKinney, A. P., and Azam, L. (2013). Muslim women's workplace experiences: implications for strategic diversity initiatives. *Equality, Diversity and Inclusion: An International Journal*, 32(1): 49–67.

Robbins, T. (2011). NYPD cops' training included an anti-Muslim horror flick experiments in terror. <http://www.villagevoice.com/news/nypd-cops-training-included-an-anti-muslim-horror-flick-6429945>, accessed 30 November 2013.

Said, E. (1978). *Orientalism*. New York: Vintage Books.

Said, E. (1981). *Covering Islam: How the Media and the Experts Determine How We See the Rest of the World*. New York: Random House.

Said, E. (1997). *Covering Islam: How the Media and the Experts Determine How We See the Rest of the World*. New York: Vintage Books.

Said, E. (2002). *Power, Politics and Culture: Interviews with Edward Said*, ed. G. Viswanathan. New York: Vintage.

Samman, K. (2012). Islamophobia and the time and space of the Muslim other. *Islamophobia Studies Journal*, 1(1): 107–30.

Samman, K. and al-Zo'by, M. (2008). *Islam and the Modern Orientalist World-System*. Boulder, CO: Paradigm Publisher.

Schiffer, S. and Wagner, C. (2011). Anti-Semitism and Islamophobia: new enemies, old patterns. *Race and Class*, 52(3): 77–84.

Selod, S. and Embrick, D. G. (2013). Racialization and Muslims: situating the Muslim experience in race scholarship. *Sociology Compass*, 7/8: 644–55.

Semmerling, T. J. (2006). *'Evil' Arabs in American Popular Film: Orientalist Fear*. Austin, TX: University of Texas Press.

Sheehi, S. (2011). *Islamophobia: The Ideological Campaign against Muslims*. Atlanta, GA: Clarity Press.

Sheridan, L. (2006). Islamophobia pre and post September 11th 2001. *Journal of Interpersonal Violence*, 21(3): 317–36.

Southern Poverty Law Center (2013). Anti-Muslim. <http://www.splcenter.org/get-informed/intelligence-files/ideology/anti-muslim>, accessed 30 November 2013.

Stewart, C. S. (2011). Little gitmo. <http://nymag.com/news/features/yassin-aref-2011-7/>, accessed 30 November 2013.

Syed, J. and Pio, E. (2010). Veiled diversity? Workplace experiences of Muslim women in Australia. *Asia Pacific Journal of Management*, 27(1): 115–37.

Takaki, R. (1993). *A Different Mirror: A History of Multicultural America*. New York: Little, Brown & Co.

Toor, S. (2008). Moral regulation in a postcolonial nation-state: gender and the politics of Islamization in Pakistan. *Interventions: International Journal of Postcolonial Studies*, 9(2): 255–75.
Toor, S. (2012). Imperialist feminism redux. *Dialectical Anthropology*, 36: 147–60.
Torpey, J. (2006). Contested citizenship: immigration and cultural diversity in Europe. *Contemporary Sociology*, 35(6): 609–11.
Unkelback, C., Schneider, H., Gode, K., and Senft, M. (2010). A turban effect, too: selection biases against women wearing Muslim headscarves. *Social Psychological and Personality Science*, 1(4): 378–83.
Volpp, L. (2002). The citizen and the terrorist. *UCLA Law Review*, 49: 1575–1600.
Zanoni, P., Janssens, M., Benschop, Y., and Nkomo, S. (2010). Unpacking diversity, grasping inequality: rethinking difference through critical perspectives. *Organization*, 17(9): 9–29.

CHAPTER 25

INTERSECTIONALITY, SOCIAL IDENTITY THEORY, AND EXPLORATIONS OF HYBRIDITY

A Critical Review of Diverse Approaches to Diversity

GLEN POWELL, LAKNATH JAYASINGHE, AND LUCY TAKSA

THE many pathways available to study diversity and diverse identities present scholars with numerous choices among disciplinary orientations, definitions and conceptualizations, methodologies and focus, particularly on the subject of social identity/ies. Despite the inherently cross-disciplinary nature of the phenomena of diversity and identity, there has been what Shields (2008: 305) described 'as a kind of naive circling of the disciplinary wagons', most notably evident between sociological and psychological approaches, and particularly between those informed by intersectionality and Social Identity Theory. Certainly with feminists in the vanguard, fruitful efforts have been made to break through disciplinary boundaries by psychology scholars (Purdie-Vaughns and Eibach 2008; Shields 2008; Warner 2008; Parent, Deblaere, and Moradi 2013) who have engaged with intersectional perspectives. Initially developed as a metaphor by Crenshaw (1991), intersectionality was soon elaborated 'as a "provisional concept" to demonstrate the inadequacy of approaches which separate systems of oppression, isolating and focusing on one, while occluding the others' (Carastathis 2014: 305). According to Yuval-Davis (2006: 206) intersectional analysis of social divisions came 'to occupy central spaces in both sociological and other analyses of stratification as well as in feminist and other legal, political and policy discourses of international human rights'. Effectively it contributed to the recognition that analysing 'various social divisions, but especially race and gender, as separate, internally homogeneous, social categories' was inadequate.

This perspective, according to Shields (2008: 302), has had more impact on 'academic specializations already concerned with questions of power relations between groups' than psychology which 'has lagged behind' or in which 'intersectionality has had little influence on theory' (Warner 2008: 457). As Shields (2008: 305) pointed out, psychology scholars responded to intersectionality by 'excluding the question; deferring the question; limiting the question'. Hence Parent, Deblaere, and Moradi (2013: 640–1) commented that '[d]espite the noted importance of intersectionality and the growing calls for its integration into psychological research ... challenges remain in the translation of intersectionality frameworks or theories to research questions, methods, and analyses'. Essentially this is because intersectional perspectives stand 'in contrast to the conceptualization of social identities as functioning independently and as added together to form experience' (Warner 2008: 454). For the most part identity research in psychology has continued to be dominated by social identity theory (SIT) which emerged from the work of Tajfel (1982) as a means of interpreting the cognitive dimensions of intergroup relationships. With only rare exceptions (Purdie-Vaughns and Eibach 2008) psychologically trained scholars who have engaged with intersectional perspectives have not attempted to relate the two to each other. The problem here, as Zanoni and colleagues (2010) noted, is that 'the diversity literature has relied on social psychology theories to investigate the effects of a broad variety of differences on group dynamics'.

This chapter considers both intersectional and SIT approaches, recognising their contributions and also identifying issues and gaps. One important issue relates particularly to the conceptualization of emergent identities 'as a uniquely hybrid creation'. An outcome of postcolonial studies (Shields 2008: 305), this notion of hybridity has been developed in studies of 'simultaneous processes of identity, institutional and social practice' (Holvino 2010: 248) and racialized masculine practice and critical masculinities studies which encompass attention to spatial practice and embodiment. As we see it, attention to the identity intersections of gender, race, ethnicity, and sexuality with space and bodily practices can productively extend dialogue across disciplines by highlighting dimensions of multiplicity often overlooked from within disciplinary and even sometimes multi-disciplinary wagon trains. Accordingly, following an overview of intersectional and SIT approaches to identity, the chapter examines how gateways offered by masculinity studies on spatial contexts of racialized masculinity and the bodily experiences of racialized men can enhance understandings of individual identity negotiations and group processes in specific locations, such as Delhi and Sydney, and contribute to more effective operationalizing of intersectional approaches.

A Preliminary Note on Identity

Those who draw on SIT highlight how 'people notice, identify with, and react to the experiences of members of their social identity group regardless of whether they personally share those experiences' (Mollica 2003: 417). SIT provides a useful basis for considering how people categorize themselves and others and also how different identities and different social groups relate to each other. Yet, as Triandafyllidou and Wodak (2003: 205) noted, there has been 'a tendency to take for granted what identity is, or indeed that it IS' in ways that obscure that identity is 'a contested concept and a complex reality', 'context-dependent' and 'dynamic and constantly in evolution' (Triandafyllidou and Wodak 2003: 208; see also Shields 2008: 302). Similarly, some scholars have treated 'collective identity as a stable and cohesive "property" that characterizes a given group at a given point in time' and have thereby neglected to consider 'the internal inconsistencies, tensions and re-elaboration' of various identities. To overcome this neglect, Triandafyllidou and Wodak (2003: 11) suggest that it is important to recognize that '[p]ersonhood is socially constructed through social interaction between individuals and/or between individuals and groups' and that 'collective identities are constantly in a process of negotiation, affirmation or change through the individuals who identify with a given group or social category and act in their name'. Because they see these levels as 'intertwined and mutually constituted', Triandafyllidou and Wodak (2003: 215) argue that 'rather than using identities as "demographic facts"' or 'social categories' in which 'a person may be potentially classifiable by gender, ethnicity, class or age', the focus should be 'on whether, when and how identities are used' (Triandafyllidou and Wodak 2003: 215). Therefore, they propose that attention needs to be given to 'the process of identity formation' (Triandafyllidou and Wodak 2003: 210), so that 'rigid distinctions between individual and collective identities', which take 'identities as an essential quality that people "have" or as something concrete to which they "belong"' (Triandafyllidou and Wodak 2003: 211) can be avoided. This would help to acknowledge the struggles involved in forging and maintaining identities (Bondi 1993: 97) and what Ang (2001: 194) refers to as the 'complicated entanglements' associated with 'the ways in which differences in identity can be negotiated'. According to Shields (2008: 308), 'understanding of the fluidity in and between and within identity categories' can be enhanced by intersectional approaches.

However, investigation of 'different levels of analysis may require radically different strategies' (Shields 2008: 306) and finding the appropriate model for multi-level enquiry can be challenging given the different levels identified by various SIT and intersectional scholars (Collins 1990; Deaux and Martin 2003; Hitt et al. 2007; Syed and Özbilgin 2009). SIT scholarship generally informs analysis of individual cognition and meso-level group dynamics. By contrast, intersectional scholars focus on the interaction of different levels of analysis (McCall 2005; Yuval-Davis 2006), which according to Syed and Özbilgin (2009: 6–7), 'are irreducibly interdependent and interrelated'. As Dill and Zambrana (2009: 11, cited in Carastathis 2014: 307) suggest, 'intersectionality reveals "the workings of power, which is understood as both pervasive and oppressive [...] at all levels of social relations"'. This orientation helps to describe power dynamics generated at the macro societal level but experienced and enacted at both the micro relational level and within the meso organizational level. Potentially, these two perspectives could be used alongside each other to analyse more effectively organizational contexts, but cautiously, with attention paid to clarifying the levels of analysis employed and allowance for categories of analysis to evolve and emerge in the process (Tatli and Özbilgin 2012).

Yet, while multi-level approaches emphasize the importance of context, the role of spatial practices has not figured prominently in either intersectional or SIT scholarship.

Considering Social Identity Theory and Intersectionality

Foundational differences in epistemology, ontology, and methodology exist between SIT and intersectionality (Browne and Misra 2003; Carbin and Edenheim 2013). Yet, both approaches have strengths, weaknesses, and gaps. Neither was intended to be a stand-alone universal theory of identity. SIT's original intention was to explain inter-group relations rather than to 'unravel, conceptually or empirically, the general issues of identity or of the individual's self-concept' (Tajfel 1982: 2). Similarly, the original proposition of intersectionality as a critical tool, explicitly excluded its use as a 'new totalizing theory of identity' (Crenshaw 1991: 1244).

Tajfel's elaboration of SIT set out to explain how cognitive processes shape and function within intergroup relations and to provide a framework for understanding inter-group competition or conflict, in-group/out-group comparison and, when coupled with self categorisation theory, how groups form around shared social categories (Tajfel 1982; Turner et al. 1987). SIT's focus is on collective phenomena generated through individual cognitive processes, such as social comparison, self-enhancement, uncertainty reduction, and internalisation of prototypical group norms (Hogg and Turner 1987). SIT scholarship now recognises that an individual can have as many 'social and personal identities' as they have groups or relationships that matter to them (e.g. Hogg 2006: 115). But for Tajfel, an individual had only one social identity, made up of multiple group memberships. Shortly before his death in 1982, Tajfel settled on a clear definition of social identity, which he suggested should:

> be understood as that *part* of the individuals' self-concept which derives from their knowledge of their membership of a social group (or groups) together with the value and emotional significance attached to that membership... Some of these memberships are more salient than others; and some may vary in salience in time and as a function of a variety of social situations (Tajfel 1981, 255 cited in Tajfel 1982: 2–3, his emphasis).

In other words, for Tajfel and his immediate disciples, an individual's group memberships form his/her social identity, a singular concept, with different memberships or categories within this identity varying in salience.

The conceptualisation of salience has also shifted in the post-Tajfel version of SIT alongside the redefinition of social identity as a collection of multiple identities. First, which identity is salient has become more determined by external circumstances, rather than by the 'value and emotional significance' an actor feels for membership of a group

(Tajfel 1982). As Hogg (2006: 115) describes it, 'in any given situation only one identity is psychologically salient to govern self-construal, social perception, and social conduct. As the situation or context changes, so does the salient identity or the form that the identity takes'. Moreover, salience is thought to involve a social aspect with actors 'strategically competing' with each other to shape the social context, so that subjectively more 'meaningful and self-favoring' identities become salient (Hogg and Terry 2001: 7). There has also been a debate about the possibility of simultaneous salience of multiple identities (Ashforth and Johnson 2001: 46; Hogg 2006: 127).

By contrast, the focus of intersectionality has been on discriminatory processes (Brah and Phoenix 2004; Davis 2008) and informed by the more sociologically and politically oriented concerns of feminist, race and gender scholarship (e.g. Crenshaw 1991; Browne and Misra 2003; Yuval-Davis 2006). From the outset, it has been concerned with the dynamics of identity, power imbalances and multiple sources of oppression that mutually reinforce and exacerbate each other. Feminist scholars are divided on whether to affirm intersectionality as a fully developed theory, or just a concept or reading strategy (Davis 2008: 68) and calls have been made to address the diverse range of methodologies adopted for investigating intersectionality (McCall 2005; Choo and Ferree 2010). There is no doubt that intersectionality provides a means of raising the visibility and audibility of previously invisible and silenced groups. Yet its impact on sociology, according to an assessment undertaken by Jones, Misra, and McCurley (2013: 2) found that only around 17 percent of articles published in the top-ranked 'sociology journals in 2009 were intersectional; the majority were relational, and the fewest use anti-categorical models'. Given that the majority (77%) of the articles were empirical (Jones, Misra, and McCurley 2013: 4) and that numerous scholars who claim to be adopting an intersectional approach take 'an additive approach rather than truly engaging with how social statuses intersect', Jones, Misra, and McCurley (2013: 7) concluded that greater attention needs to be given to theory and methodology in this genre.

Increasingly, efforts have been made to integrate intersectional and SIT approaches (Howard 2000; Azmitia, Syed, and Radmacher 2008; Jones, Kim, and Skendall 2012; Settles and Buchanan 2014). Huddy (2001), for example, accepts the SIT idea that multiple groups are associated with multiple identities, but she rejects the implication that identities are easily manipulated, citing her research into feminist identities (Huddy 2001: 137). Rather than being fluid, flexible, and easily changed in response to circumstances, her findings suggest that some identities are particularly stable within the self-concept. Huddy's research provides evidence that individuals are not simply helpless victims of circumstance, as once they have invested in an identity and integrated it within their self-concept, it remains salient to them in a wide range of situations. Other promising new approaches to intersectionality have included a focus on 'multidimensionality' (Ehrenreich 2002) and 'simultaneity' (Holvino 2010, 2012), where 'differences such as race, gender, class, ethnicity, nationality, and sexuality coexist and are experienced simultaneously, [but] the importance or salience of specific differences at particular moments varies depending on the social context. This makes for identities that are multiple, fluid, and ever-changing, instead of stable and one dimensional' (Holvino 2012: 174). The tension between Huddy and Holvino shows there is room for research that can enhance understanding of the dynamics of power and competition at work as internally salient identities are asserted in the face of externally imposed salience. The critical difference with SIT is that the latter's construal of social identities as 'contextually fluid' (Hogg 2001: 200) seems to suggest that identities are easily and cheaply accumulated and deployed in response to salient external circumstances. In stark contrast to intersectional approaches, this downplays issues of oppression, power, and any sense of struggle.

It is the core purpose of intersectionality to unveil interlocking, overlapping, and contested layers of identity and complex vectors of discrimination, difference, and identity groupings that mutually reinforce and influence each other (Ehrenreich 2002; Yuval-Davis 2006; Nash 2008). An intersectional approach to SIT could arguably ensure the self-concept is understood as more complex than a neat package of atomistic identities waiting to be awakened by the appropriate salience stimulus. Concepts of simultaneous salience and overlapping identities have been proposed to address real world problems where singular social categories are inadequate (Crisp and Hewstone 2000; Ashforth and Johnson 2001: 45), such as in situations where the agent has multiple-salient identities, but the circumstances allow only one such identity to be salient. A good case in point is provided by the distinctiveness of laws focused on race and gender in Australia, which require 'minority ethnic women' to choose whether to present their experiences of simultaneous sexual harassment and racial discrimination 'as being about sex or race'. In effect, the legal regime ignores 'the joint impact of race-and-gender intersectionality' and forces complainants to emphasise the salience of one identity over another (Syed 2007: 1960). Such suppression of potentially salient identities results in what social psychologists Purdie-Vaughns and Eibach (2008) call 'intersectional invisibility'. While intersectionality is not typically described in terms of social identity salience (Crenshaw 1991; Brah and Phoenix 2004), it does facilitate analysis of how people characterised by multiple social categories of identity, difference and disadvantage (Cole 2009), are discriminated against one category at a time (Crenshaw 1991). Hence, some intersectional scholars have addressed the problem of categorisation. For instance, McCall (2005) identified an anti-categorical approach, which avoids stereotyping; an approach that acknowledges the need for categories but stresses their intracategorical complexity, and an approach which may acknowledge the complexity but elects to use categories strategically. Addressing the same problem, Tatli and Özbilgin (2012) propose an emic, rather than etic, approach to social categories. An emic approach allows categories of difference to emerge during research processes, also enabling exploration of power imbalances in identity negotiation, while an etic approach defines categories that remain static throughout. As their systematic literature review reveals, the latter is by far the most common approach to research, but tends to constrain the findings. Similarly, social constructionist perspectives argue for more consideration of the interplay between individual differences and collective identities, as a key insight of intersectionality is that social categories benefit some and disadvantage others who are less prototypical (Huddy 2001; Purdie-Vaughns and Eibach 2008). As Brown (2000) notes, different categories have different social psychological dynamics of occupational groups or political affiliations, versus larger categories like ethnicity, gender, and religion.

Multiple Levels

SIT and intersectionality both conceptualise identity as a pluralist construct that operates on multiple levels. Brewer (2003) makes the point that SIT is a bridge between individual and group levels of analysis. Some scholars note that social categories and interpersonal networks operate as two different levels for identity work (Deaux and Martin 2003). The initial focus on intergroup relations and cognitive processes, along with a growing emphasis on business and organizational contexts and management (Ashforth and Mael 1989; Hogg and Terry 2001) naturally focused SIT on meso and micro level interactions, but rarely on the interplay between differing levels of analysis. And while scholars working from an intersectional perspective, like Choo and Ferree (2010: 134), have called for a multi-level awareness of intersections within and across levels, attention to the groups, networks, organizations and institutions that populate the meso level are often strangely absent from intersectional theorising. The focus tends to be on macro level social structures and norms that impact on individuals who are assumed to be groups because they share a social category or categories.

SIT provides insight into inter-group dynamics, for example analysing the porosity of group boundaries between high and low status groups and the impact of subjective beliefs about legitimacy of group status (Hogg 2006). This offers insight into the complex identity related cognitive processes at work when a minority representative finds themselves accepted inside a dominant in-group. It also suggests a more sympathetic reading of the dynamics at work when the isolated minority representative fails to single-mindedly pursue the interests of their minority group, while negotiating shifting categories, identity entrepreneurship, new in-group expectations and also doing the job they get paid for.

While demonstrating powerful descriptive and explanatory potential, these various conceptions of identity work and the power dynamics that minority representatives experience, are largely concerned with the individual's experience and actions at the micro level of analysis. Intersectional analysis recognises the need for a new multi-categorical group. In contexts that require individuals to conform to single category salience, intersectionality offers a new, hyphenated (Settles and Buchanan 2014) category and asserts its right to recognition. As others identify with the nascent group, through a process of negotiation, struggle, and conflict, it gradually achieves recognition. While intersectionality recognises such entrepreneurial identity work, there is little scholarship on such group creation. Individuals responding to structural pressures by engaging in creative identity work require *collective* identity work, performed at the level of the organization or group. Intersectionality may help to explain the individual's experience, but SIT can contribute insights on group formation (Turner 1982; Ashforth and Mael 1989). On the one hand, SIT struggles with inter-group asymmetry (Brown 2000). On the other, intersectionality provides a framework for mapping the dynamics involved when self-concept and in-group perceptions are out of step, or in conflict with, out-group perceptions or dominant structural perceptions of the identity imposed on a group.

The idea that particular social categories constitute a 'group' is common in the formulation of intersectionality. In her early work Crenshaw (1991) acknowledged the importance of 'groups' consisting of race, gender, sexual orientation and other categories in shifting perceptions from 'isolated and individual' to 'social and systemic'. Indeed she used the term 'group' seventy-seven times in her discussion of identity politics, which she described as a source of 'strength, community, and intellectual development' for these 'groups' (Crenshaw 1991: 1241–2). However, she gave no attention to the processes involved in actual group formation. Crenshaw is not alone in ignoring the potentially difficult and contested process of forming a 'group' as a collective entity once a potentially unifying characteristic has been recognised. McCall (2005: 1778) certainly noted the difference between naming and creating a group, but focused on the complexities raised by the problem that however many new social groups are identified, the complexity of identity resists categorisation into neat groups. While calling for a more detailed and interdisciplinary unveiling of the complexities inherent in intersectional identities, she still tends to assume that 'groups' are pre-existing and available for study.

SIT could supplement the intersectional perspective by facilitating attention to the processes by which individuals 'share a common social identification...or...perceive themselves to be members of the same social category' (Turner 1982: 15). Arguably though both SIT and intersectionality could benefit from consideration of the costs, risks and creative effort involved in the social construction of a group and of the identity factors once the group has emerged, rather than imagining such groups arrive ready formed from the simple discovery of a common social category.

It is important, however, to also acknowledge that identity is fundamentally linked to practices that occur in distinct spaces (Taksa 2000). As Valentine (2007: 19) acknowledged in opening a conversation about intersectionality within feminist geography, an intersectional perspective could contribute to, and benefit from, a focus on the 'dominant spatial orderings that define who is in place/out of place, who belongs and who does not'. Studies in the field of racialised masculinity have made a significant contribution in this regard.

Examining Racialised Masculinities

Attention to the social and cultural intertwining of masculinity and ethnicity in the field of masculinity studies first occurred in the mid-1990s when Cornwall and Lindisfarne produced an edited collection that 'offered a new perspective for viewing gendered identities and subverting dominant chauvinisms on which gender, class, race and other hierarchies depend' (Cornwall and Lindisfarne 1994: 2). This work sought to remedy the anglo-centric orientation of masculinities, which effectively universalised Western perspectives and largely overlooked the intersecting identity experiences of men from non-Western backgrounds. The sentiment within much early scholarship on the intersections of race and masculinity was that masculinities studies was overwhelmingly a discipline organized by Western men, for Western men, and about Western men; resulting in the marginalization of men from 'othered' (racial) contexts. From the late 1990s, then, critical masculinities studies started to engage with the concept of race, especially intersectional ideas about race, and of the place of racialised men within the discipline (Louie and Low 2003). Almost twenty years later, De Neve (2004: 65) noted that few studies of racialised masculine practice had '"localised" the construction of masculinities in specific places or addressed the manner in which they are shaped by particular localities.' Critical masculinities studies has reached out to this literature through the 'postcolonial turn' and expanded upon it.

The most recent substantial addition to this corpus of literature is the edited collection about *Men and Masculinities in Southeast Asia* by Michele Ford and Lenore Lyons (2012b). Apart from this, other noteworthy additions include examinations on: the construction and contestation of racialised masculinities in urban areas (Srivastava 2010); the construction of racialised masculinities in rural areas (Chopra, Osella, and Osella 2004); the masculine experience of second generation migrant males in the developed West (Noble 2007, 2009; Kalra 2009; Thangaraj 2010); racialised masculinities and sexual identity and practice (Boellstorff 2005; Osella and Osella 2006; Caluya 2008); and racialised masculinities and the experience of transnational labour (Datta et al. 2009; Kitiarsa 2012). According to Osella, Osella, and Chopra (2004) much has been written and published on masculine identity and the experience of race since Cornwall and Lindisfarne's influential publication. However, a great deal of this work has been uneven and constrained in scope, particularly when compared with Western masculine formations, their intersections with other identity forms, their spatial patterning, and processes of hegemony and dominance.

Raewyn Connell's theorisations have been enormously useful in the development of an analytical framework examining racialised masculinities. Connell (1987) was arguably the first to cogently conceptualise the existence of plural masculine forms against a backdrop of the material reality of everyday power relations and gender identity. Connell's famous theory of 'hegemonic masculinity' demonstrates that masculinity is heavily defined against femininity, yet is also patterned across competing masculine forms structured through varying levels of dominance: complicit, subordinate, and marginal masculinity conceptualised through intersections of race, class, sexuality, and the like (Connell 1995).

The notion of a suite of masculinities and of the structured relation between hegemonic and subordinate forms has been productively examined in many disciplines, including sociology and critical masculinities studies. But it has also been widely contested and discussed. For example, useful contributions have come from empirical studies demonstrating the socially legitimising role oppositional and negotiated consumption practices may play for men positioned in subordinated social identity categories (Kates 2004). Across many recent ethnographies of racialised masculinity, there are debates over how hegemonic masculinity is conceptualised, and who is represented by it (Coskuner-Balli and Thompson 2013). Beasley's (2008) critique of Connell argued that despite its productive tenor, especially its desire to illuminate the dimensions of multiple masculinities and gendered power relations, Connell's essentialising framework ends up reducing the complexity and specificity of the actual 'doings and sayings' of men. It is noteworthy that, given Connell's structuring framework of masculinity grounded in personality traits and attributes, Connell has acknowledged that some of these criticisms are warranted (Messerschmidt 2008).

Osella, Osella, and Chopra (2004: 1) similarly argue against an over-reliance on approaches to hegemonic masculinity pointing out that much work on racialised masculinity has been 'preoccupied with testing out [Connell's] theory against specific local cases or concerned to argue for or present the specificity of the ethnographic particular.' Ford and Lyons (2012a) make a similar point: that racialised masculinity cannot be reduced to a simple set of abstract meanings, but rather is co-constituted through a matrix of gender processes and meanings calibrated to specific cultural, temporal, spatial, and situational contexts. While Osella, Osella, and Chopra (2004) reject the concept of hegemonic masculinity altogether because of its homogenization and focus on a singular masculine type, Ford and Lyons (2012: 12), following Srivastava (2004), suggest 'it is no longer even possible to conceive of a pristine theoretical and cultural world of "non-Westernness" unmarked by a history of asymmetrical interactions.'

Similar to Ford and Lyons, we understand racialised masculinity as less a psychological than a cultural reality, and focus on questions of subjectivity, the ideological construction of masculinity; and its interaction across other vessels of identity such as sexuality and race. As well as seeing racialised masculinity through a more cultural lens, this chapter—again following Ford and Lyons—also conceptualises masculinity as a strategic interaction and focuses on the construction of identities through local networks of masculine practice, responding to and moulding social situations, and negotiating one's social relations with others (Datta et al. 2009; Thangaraj 2010). Key to this perspective is an emphasis on the vitality of the spaces, places, and situational contexts of the lived experiences of gendered power and practice.

Spatial Contexts of Racialised Masculinity

The sociohistoric and spatial patterning of masculinity and male identity provides evidence that masculinity is a socio-cultural and relational practice. A number of recent works (Osella and Osella 2006; Walsh 2011) catalogue the complex interactions between masculinity, socioeconomic class, ethnicity, transnational labour, and lifestyle in national and immigrant settings, across various geographic locations of, for example, the street and leisure and consumption space, and from within the institutional spaces of the military and the residential slum, and especially the home and work space. A notable feature of this work is its attention to how the physical nature of these spatial contexts shapes and choreographs the very nature of the lived experience of masculinity, and how masculinity is linked to other central categories of social relations. It may well be that some of the most sophisticated theorisations of racialised masculinities practice are themselves influenced by cultural geographies of gender and sexuality (van Hoven and Hörschelmann 2005b; Noble 2009).

Van Hoven and Hörschelmann's (2005a: 5) conclusion that 'space has been shown to be gendered in many ways, while gender itself is seen to be constructed through spatial relations and geographical imaginations' indicates a refined understanding of the negotiated and fluid interplays between space and gender identity. Srivastava's (2010) recent analysis of urban space and commodity politics in Delhi exemplifies this approach. His outline of the way that masculinity unfurls across a number of 'registers', allows us to witness the everyday 'splitting' of masculine identities, the 'crossing' of category 'borders', as identity forms are developed that are more complicated and fragmented in quotidian operation than those presented by traditional portraits of the contemporary man. These ideas are pertinent to a recent Australian case before the New South Wales (NSW) Anti-Discrimination Board in which a Jewish male worker was 'unable to work beyond a certain distance from home on Fridays as he had to get home by sunset for ethno-religious reasons' (Anti-Discrimination Board NSW 2014).[1] Here we see inconsistency and tension between various identities and identity norms, notably between traditional Western masculine breadwinner and employment norms and those associated with ethno-religious identity and practices. These practices challenge our perspectives of how work-based masculinity is constituted and also the ways that work-based spaces can be at once gendered and imbued with 'ethno-religious' implications. Applying Srivastava's insights enables us to discern a multifaceted picture of masculinity and the negotiated manner through which performances of gender practice are enacted in mundane, everyday locales such as the workplace. Significantly, the insights developed through this case study and Srivastava's work stress the spatial and relational dimension undergirding racialised masculinity.

Legitimacy, Spatial Context, and Racialised Masculinity

All identities, including masculine identity, are constructed and operate according to a perceived social fit or difference with broader cultural norms—according to shades of cultural legitimacy (Kates 2004). Noble's (2009: 876) recent work on male identity notes

---

[1] The Anti-Discrimination Board of NSW was set up under the Anti-Discrimination Act 1977 (NSW) to promote anti-discrimination and equal opportunity principles and policies throughout NSW and to administer the Act. It is part of the NSW Department of Justice. It handles complaints of discrimination, investigates and conciliates complaints when appropriate. See <http://www.antidiscrimination.justice.nsw.gov.au/Pages/adb1_aboutus/adb1_aboutus.aspx>.

a growing awareness of the spatial dimensions involved in the process of granting cultural legitimacy to racialised groups of men, including Muslim men. Noble writes of a complex interplay of class, gender, ethnicity, and age 'even within the apparent singularity of Muslim identity.' He argues that the identification of young men as Muslim is only one part of who they see themselves. This approach locates questions of power through a sensitivity towards their deployment in specific places and contexts. Noble emphasises that gender is enmeshed with ethnicity and class. He also hints at its productive potential: that there is a range of masculine legitimacies that can be bestowed on men from racialised backgrounds.

Kenway and Hickey-Moody (2009), for example, take account of the spatialised workings of masculine practice in local geographies, tying male practice to cultural legitimacy within a globalised leisure context. In the process, they develop a more graded conceptualisation of masculinity than Connell's—sacrosanct, subversive, and scorned—that recognises that gender practice can be performed through varying shades of intensity. The overall effect is to develop a more vivid tapestry of the lived masculine experience of the young men in their study. This more nuanced understanding of masculine identification is amply evident in a decision handed down in Australia by the NSW Administrative Decisions Tribunal. Termed the 'bombchucker' case, it involved the loss of an appeal by transport giant Toll Express against a former employee, a Muslim man of Lebanese background who was born in Australia and returned there after attending school in Lebanon and who was subjected to racist slurs by fellow Toll employees. The complainant, Mr Mohamed Abdulrahman, was repeatedly referred to as 'Osama bin Laden' and 'Mokaakaakaahomed' by his manager, who 'asked him to change his name to an Anglo-Saxon name such as "John"' (New South Wales Administrative Decisions Tribunal 2007: 4). Against a backdrop of a culture fractured by panic over the place of young Lebanese Australian men and of Islamic migrant masculinities in a post Sept 11 world (Noble 2007, 2009), the case demonstrates how the work space can be a site where culturally legitimising practices are performed. In this instance, the racial slurs against Abdulrahman served to delegitimate Abdulrahman's cultural background and ignored his Australian origin. A case such as this, involving multiple, simultaneous identity negotiations and in-group and out-group processes could be productively analysed from both intersectional and SIT perspectives.

The Experiences of Racialised Men

The work of Datta (2009) and Caluya (2008) is equally rich in outlining the complex experiences of the intertwinings and intersections of race, ethnicity, masculinity, sexuality, and cultural legitimacy. Here, it is not so much about border crossing and the synching in unison of fundamental social identities as it is about recording both the 'messiness of layered subjectivities and multi-dimensional relations' (Hopkins and Noble 2009: 815) in specific spatial contexts, and the 'circuits of recognition'

(Noble 2009) in racialised men's everyday lives. In Datta's (2009) case, as in the various studies edited by Ford and Lyons (2012b), it is the impact of migration from developing nations to the west—on male identity, conventions, and norms—that is unearthed and examined. Here, the idea of mobility and mobile masculinities arises. Datta (2009: 854) sums up the issue nicely, arguing for the need to 'consider how gendered identities travel and how these identities are remade at each stage of the migration project in relation to a range of different and often contradictory gender regimes encountered in different places.' She argues the need to unpack the category of 'migrant men', acknowledging that a range of vectors enable male migration; and that the impact of migration often confers a 'double masculine consciousness'—subordinate in the host country, yet domineering and hypermasculine in the home country.

Caluya (2008) spins this issue in an interesting direction by incorporating affect and ideas of sexual desire into the mix. His study examines how racialised sexual desire produces precise spatial formations and practices that confine gay Asian men into literal ghettos, or racialised clusters, in gay male cultural space in Sydney. The neatness of Caluya's research is that he challenges us to rethink the nature of racialised and sexually 'liberatory spaces', demonstrating that, often, it is a case of 'smooth' and 'striated' spaces coexisting and shaping each other through choreographed, performative acts involving gender, race, racialism, and desire. In this sense, the discussion shifts from one of categories of social being to the processes and meanings through which racialised masculine experience is formed. From this perspective, masculine identity in the work place is enmeshed within the 'specific particularities of experienced' identities concerning oppression and social inequality (Brown 2012: 542) rather than in essentialist and more singular social constructivist notions of masculine identity. In addition, in his effort to recognise the difficulties of practicing masculinity for those operating from outside of the normative spheres of gender, Muñoz (1999: 6) showed that even 'minority identifications are often neglectful or antagonistic to other minoritarian positionalities' (Muñoz 1999: 8).

In his work on how mainstream understandings of the masculine bodies of racialised gay men articulate questions of felt experience, movement, embodiment, identity ambiguity, fear, and uncertainty, Caluya (2008: 287) alerts us to how power and dominance contain performative elements. An evidence note from the Toll case dramatizes this issue. Let us remember that Mr Abdulrahman was born in Australia. In evidence note 13 (New South Wales Administrative Decisions Tribunal 2006: 21) a choreographed display of masculine power about what constitutes the nature of 'Australian' identity is demonstrated through the way that Mr Abdulrahman's manager, Mr Wallace, routinely repeats the 'Mokaakaakaahomed' slur in face to face encounters and more insidiously—through deliberate calls of this slur over the office loudspeaker system, 'mocking and embarrassing' Mr Abdulrahman over his Lebanese background. Mr Wallace's performative utterance of the racial slurs over the loudspeaker in effect turns the entire Toll work place into a racially striated space of masculine power–one that is affectively experienced by Mr Abdulrahman as mocking, embarrassing, shaming, and humiliating, and reduces his desire to identify with the Australian in-group in his workplace. We see here how analyses attuned to how the male subject experiences discourses of male power have the potential to reshape and deepen our understanding of the interplay between identity, gender, race/ethnicity, space, and bodily movement.

Conclusion

This chapter has considered a number of pathways for the study of diversity and identity. Specifically it has presented an overview of the approaches adopted by scholars under the umbrellas of intersectionality and social identity theory, two of the leading approaches that are rarely considered together. Although fundamentally different in disciplinary origins, epistemology, and ontology as well as political and also ideological orientation, both traverse the same ground exploring identity categories, relations, and multiple levels. Both also seek to make sense of dimensions and categories of individual and group identity. While intersectionality places emphasis on power and oppression, SIT emphasises matters of cognition. Yet both in different ways struggle with multiplicity. Some, generally feminist psychology scholars, have engaged with intersectionality in an effort to extend the boundaries of their discipline. At the same time feminist sociologists have noted that intersectional approaches have been concentrated in specific sub-fields without making great inroads in the majority of highly ranked journals in their field. In the meantime, intersectionality approaches have spread to a range of other fields including geography and masculinity studies. It is particularly in the last named field that great strides have been made to address not only the hybridity of identity/ies but also the everyday negotiations involving practices engaged in by individual and collective bodies operating in space. The bringing together of these diverse approaches to the study of identity/ies, with their diverse and often divergent range of disciplinary and multi-disciplinary orientations, definitions and conceptualizations, methodologies and focus, is intended only as a gateway to further dialogue among scholars concerned to unpack the complexities involved in the analysis of intersections between various categories of identities and relations.

References

Ang, I. (2001). *On Not Speaking Chinese: Living Between Asia and the West*. London: Routledge.
Anti-Discrimination Board NSW (2014) Jewish man's problems with work location (Feb 2014) in Anti-Discrimination Board Conciliations - Race Discrimination -. Employment. <http://www.antidiscrimination.justice.nsw.gov.au/Pages/adb1_resources/adb1_equaltimeconciliation/conciliations_race.aspx>, accessed 10 August 2014.
Ashforth, B. E. and Mael, F. (1989). Social identity theory and the organization'. *Academy of Management Review*, 14: 20–9.
Ashforth, B. E. and Johnson, S. A. (2001). Which hat to wear? The relative salience of multiple identities in organizational contexts. In M. A. Hogg and D. J. Terry (eds.), *Social Identity Processes in Organizational Contexts*. Philadelphia, PA: Psychology Press, 31–48.

Azmitia, M., Syed, M., and Radmacher, K. (2008). On the intersection of personal and social identities: introduction and evidence from a longitudinal study of emerging adults. *New Directions for Child and Adolescent Development*, 120: 1–16.

Beasley, C. (2008). Rethinking hegemonic masculinity in a globalizing world. *Men and Masculinities*, 11(1): 86–103.

Boellstorff, T. (2005). *The Gay Archipelago: Sexuality and Nation in Indonesia*. Princeton, NJ: Princeton University Press.

Bondi, L. (1993). Locating identity politics. In M. Keith and S. Pile (eds.), *Place and The Politics of Identity*. London: Routledge, 84–101.

Brah, A. and Phoenix, A. (2004). Ain't I a woman? Revisiting intersectionality. *Journal of International Women's Studies*, 5: 75–86.

Brewer, M. B. (2003). Optimal distinctiveness, social identity, and the self. In M. R. Leary and J. P. Tangney (eds.), *Handbook of Self and Identity*. New York: Guilford Press, 480–91.

Brown, M. (2012). Gender and sexuality I: intersectional anxieties. *Progress in Human Geography*, 36(4): 541–50.

Brown, R. (2000). Social identity theory: past achievements, current problems and future challenges. *European Journal of Social Psychology*, 30: 745–78.

Browne, I. and Misra, J. (2003). The intersection of gender and race in the labor market. *Annual Review of Sociology*, 29: 487–513.

Caluya, G. (2008). 'The rice steamer': race, desire and affect in Sydney's gay scene. *Australian Geographer*, 39(3): 283–92.

Carastathis, A. (2014) The concept of intersectionality in feminist theory. *Philosophy Compass*, 9(5): 304–14.

Carbin, M. and Edenheim, S. (2013). The intersectional turn in feminist theory: a dream of a common language? *European Journal of Women's Studies*, 20: 233–48.

Choo, H. Y. and Ferree, M. M. (2010). Practicing intersectionality in sociological research: a critical analysis of inclusions, interactions, and institutions in the study of inequalities. *Sociological Theory*, 28: 129–49.

Chopra, R., Osella, C., and Osella, F. (eds.) (2004). *South Asian Masculinities: Context of Change, Sites of Continuity*. New Delhi: Women Unlimited, an associate of Kali for Women.

Cole, E. R. (2009). Intersectionality and research in psychology. *American Psychologist*, 64: 170–80.

Collins, P. H. (1990). *Black Feminist Thought: Knowledge, Consciousness, and the Politics of Empowerment*. Boston, MA: Unwin Hyman.

Connell, R. W. (1987). *Gender and Power: Society, the Person, and Sexual Politics*. Cambridge: Polity Press.

Connell, R. W. (1995). *Masculinities*. Sydney: Allen and Unwin.

Cornwall, A. and Lindisfarne, N. (eds.) (1994). *Dislocating Masculinity: Comparative Ethnologies*. London: Routledge.

Coskuner-Balli, G. and Thompson, C. J. (2013). The status costs of subordinate cultural capital: at-home fathers' collective pursuit of cultural legitimacy through capitalizing consumption practices. *Journal of Consumer Research*, 40(1): 19–41.

Crenshaw, K. (1991). Mapping the margins: intersectionality, identity politics, and violence against women of color. *Stanford Law Review*, 43: 1241–99.

Crisp, R. J. and Hewstone, M. (2000). Multiple categorization of social identity. In D. Capozza and R. Brown (eds.), *Social Identity Processes*. London: SAGE, 149–66.

Datta, K., McIlwaine, C., Herbert, J., Evans, Y., May, J., and Wills, J. (2009). Men on the move: narratives of migration and work among low-paid migrant men in London. *Social and Cultural Geography*, 10(8): 853–73.

Davis, K. (2008). Intersectionality as buzzword: a sociology of science perspective on what makes a feminist theory successful. *Feminist Theory*, 9: 67–85.

De Neve, G. (2004). The workplace and the neighbourhood: locating masculinities in the South Indian textile industry. In R. Chopra, C. Osella, and F. Osella (eds.), *South Asian Masculinities: Contexts of Change, Sites of Continuity*. New Delhi: Women Unlimited (an associate of Kali for Women), 60–95.

Deaux, K. and Martin, D. (2003). Interpersonal networks and social categories: specifying levels of context in identity processes. *Social Psychology Quarterly*, 66: 101–17.

Dill, B. T. and Zambrana, R. E. (2009). Critical thinking about inequality: an emerging lens. In B. T. Dill and R. E. Zambrana (eds.), *Emerging Intersections: Race, Class, and Gender in Theory, Policy and Practice*. New Brunswick, NJ: Rutgers University Press, 1–21.

Ehrenreich, N. (2002). Subordination and symbiosis: mechanisms of mutual support between subordinating systems. *UMKC Law Review*, 71: 251–324.

Ford, M. and Lyons, L. (2012a). Introduction. In M. Ford and L. Lyons (eds.), *Men and Masculinities in Southeast Asia*. Abingdon: Routledge, 1–19.

Ford, M. and Lyons, L. (eds.) (2012b). *Men and Masculinities in Southeast Asia*. Abingdon: Routledge.

Hitt, M. A., Beamish, P. W., Jackson, S. E., and Mathieu, J. E. (2007). Building theoretical and empirical bridges across levels: multilevel research in management. *Academy of Management*, 50: 1385–99.

Hogg, M. A. (2001). Social identification, group prototypicality, and emergent leadership. In M. A. Hogg and D. J. Terry (eds.), *Social Identity Processes in Organizational Contexts*. Philadelphia, PA: Psychology Press, 197–212.

Hogg, M. A. (2006). Social identity theory. In P. J. Burke (ed.), *Contemporary Social Psychological Theories*. Stanford, CA: Stanford University Press, 111–36.

Hogg, M. A. and Terry, D. J. (2001). Social identity theory and organizational processes. In M. A. Hogg, and D. J. Terry (eds.), *Social Identity Processes in Organizational Contexts*. Philadelphia, PA: Psychology Press, 1–12.

Hogg, M. A. and Turner, J. C. (1987). Intergroup behaviour, self-stereotyping and the salience of social categories. *British Journal of Social Psychology*, 26: 325–40.

Holvino, E. (2010). Intersections: the simultaneity of race, gender and class in organization studies. *Gender, Work and Organization*, 17(3): 248–77.

Holvino, E. (2012). The 'simultaneity' of identities: models and skills for the twenty-first century. In C. L. Wijeyesinghe and B. W. Jackson III (eds.), *New Perspectives on Racial Identity Development: Integrating Emerging Frameworks*. New York: New York University Press, 161–91.

Hopkins, P. and Noble, G. (2009). Masculinities in place: situated identities, relations and intersectionality. *Social and Cultural Geography*, 10(8): 811–19.

Howard, J. A. (2000). Social psychology of identities. *Annual Review of Sociology*, 26: 367–93.

Huddy, L. (2001). From social to political identity: a critical examination of social identity theory. *Political Psychology*, 22: 127–56.

Jones, K. C., Misra, J., and McCurley, K. (2013). Factsheet: intersectionality in sociology. *Sociology for women in society*, 1–8. <http://socwomen.org/fact-sheets/Intersectionality>, accessed 30 January 2015.

Jones, S. R., Kim, Y. C., and Skendall, K. C. (2012). (Re-)framing authenticity: considering multiple social identities using autoethnographic and intersectional approaches. *The Journal of Higher Education*, 83: 698–724.

Kalra, V. S. (2009). Between emasculation and hypermasculinity: theorizing British South Asian masculinities. *South Asian Popular Culture*, 7(2): 113–25.

Kates, S. M. (2004). The dynamics of brand legitimacy: an interpretive study in the gay men's community. *Journal of Consumer Research*, 31(2): 455–64.

Kenway, J. and Hickey-Moody, A. (2009). Spatialized leisure-pleasures, global flows and masculine distinctions. *Social and Cultural Geography*, 10(8): 837–52.

Kitiarsa, P. (2012). Masculine intent and migrant manhood: Thai workmen talking sex. In M. Ford and L. Lyons (eds.), *Men and Masculinities in Southeast Asia*. Abingdon: Routledge, 38–55.

Louie, K. and Low, M. (eds.) (2003). *Asian Masculinities: The Meaning and Practice of Manhood in China and Japan*. London: Routledge.

McCall, L. (2005). The complexity of intersectionality. *Signs*, 30: 1771–1800.

Messerschmidt, J. W. (2008). And now, the rest of the story: a commentary on Christine Beasley's 'rethinking hegemonic masculinity in a globalizing world'. *Men and Masculinities*, 11(1): 104–8.

Mollica, Kelly A. (2003). The influence of diversity context on white men's and racial minorities' reactions to disproportionate group harm. *The Journal of Social Psychology*, 143(4): 415–31.

Muñoz, J. E. (1999). *Disidentifications: Queers of Color and the Performance of Politics*. Minneapolis, MN: University of Minnesota Press.

Nash, J. C. (2008). Re-thinking intersectionality. *Feminist Review*, 89: 1–15.

New South Wales Administrative Decisions Tribunal (2006). Abdulrahman v Toll Pty Ltd trading as Toll Express [2006] NSWADT (Administrative Decisions Tribunal) 221. (Last updated 1 August 2006).

New South Wales Administrative Decisions Tribunal (2007). Toll Pty Limited trading as Toll Express v Abdulrahman. [2007] NSWADTAP 70. (Last updated 22 November 2007).

Noble, G. (2007). Respect and respectability amongst second-generation Arab and Muslim Australian men. *Journal of Intercultural Studies*, 28(3): 331–44.

Noble, G. (2009). 'Countless acts of recognition': young men, ethnicity and the messiness of identities in everyday life. *Social and Cultural Geography*, 10(8): 875–91.

Osella, C. and Osella, F. (2006). *Men and Masculinities in South India*. London: Anthem Press.

Osella, C., Osella, F., and Chopra, R. (2004). Introduction: towards a more nuanced approach to masculinity, towards a richer understanding of South Asian men. In R. Chopra, C. Osella, and F. Osella (eds.), *South Asian Masculinities: Context of Change, Sites of Continuity*. New Delhi: Women Unlimited, an associate of Kali for Women, 1–33.

Parent, M. C., Deblaere, C., and Moradi, B. (2013). Approaches to research on intersectionality: perspectives on gender, LGBT, and racial/ethnic identities. *Sex Roles*, 68: 639–45.

Purdie-Vaughns, V. & Eibach, R. P. (2008). Intersectional invisibility: the distinctive advantages and disadvantages of multiple subordinate-group identities. *Sex Roles*, 59: 377–91.

Settles, I. H. and Buchanan, N. T. (2014). Multiple groups, multiple identities, and intersectionality. In V. Benet-Martinez and Y.-Y. Hong (eds.), *The Oxford Handbook of Multicultural Identity*. Oxford: Oxford University Press, 160–80.

Shields, S. A. (2008). Gender: an intersectionality perspective. *Sex Roles*, 59: 301–11.

Srivastava, S. (2004). Introduction: semen, history, desire and theory. In S. Srivastava (ed.), *Sexual Sites, Seminal Attitudes: Sexualities, Masculinities and Culture in South Asia*. New Delhi: Sage, 11–48.

Srivastava, S. (2010). Fragmentary Pleasures: Masculinity, Urban Spaces, and Commodity Politics in Delhi. *Journal of the Royal Anthropological Institute*, 16(4): 835–52.

Syed, J. (2007). 'The other woman' and the question of equal opportunity in Australian organizations. *International Journal of Human Resource Management*, 18(11): 1954–78.

Syed, J. and Özbilgin, M. (2009). A relational framework for international transfer of diversity management practices. *International Journal of Human Resources*, 1(2): 150–67, 2435–6.

Tajfel, H. (1981). *Human Groups and Social Categories: Studies in Social Psychology*. Cambridge: Cambridge University Press.

Tajfel, H. (ed.) (1982). *Social Identity and Intergroup Relations*. Cambridge: Cambridge University Press.

Taksa, L., (2000). Like a bicycle, forever teetering between individualism and collectivism: considering community in relation to labour history. *Labour History*, 78: 7–32.

Tatli, A. and Özbilgin, M. F. (2012). An emic approach to intersectional study of diversity at work: a Bourdieuan framing. *International Journal of Management Reviews*, 14: 180–200.

Thangaraj, S. (2010). Ballin' Indo-Pak style: pleasures, desires, and expressive practices of 'South Asian American' Masculinity. *International Review for the Sociology of Sport*, 45(3): 372–89.

Triandafyllidou, A. and Wodak, R. (2003). Conceptual and methodological questions in the study of collective identities: an introduction. *Journal of Language and Politics*, 2(2): 205–23.

Turner, J. C. (1982). Towards a cognitive redefinition of the social group. In H. Tajfel (ed.), *Social Identity and Intergroup Relations*. Cambridge: Cambridge University Press, 15–40.

Turner, J. C., Hogg, M. A., Oakes, P. J., Reicher, S. D., and Wetherell, M. S. (1987). *Rediscovering the Social Group: A Self-Categorization Theory*. New York: Basil Blackwell.

Valentine, G. (2007). Theorizing and researching intersectionality: a challenge for feminist geography. *The Professional Geographer*, 59: 10–21.

van Hoven, B. and Hörschelmann, K. (2005a). Introduction: from geographies of men to geographies of women and back again? In B. van Hoven and K. Hörschelmann (eds.), *Spaces of Masculinities*. Oxford: Routledge, 1–15.

van Hoven, B. and Hörschelmann, K. (2005b). *Spaces of Masculinities*. Oxford: Routledge.

Walsh, K. (2011). Migrant masculinities and domestic space: British home-making practices in Dubai. *Transactions of the Institute of British Geographers*, 36(4): 516–29.

Warner, L. R. (2008). A best practices guide to intersectional approaches in psychological research. *Sex Roles*, 59: 454–63.

Yuval-Davis, N. (2006). Intersectionality and feminist politics. *European Journal of Women's Studies*, 13(3): 193–209.

Zanoni P., Janssens M., Benschop Y., and Nkomo S. (2010). Unpacking diversity, grasping inequality: rethinking difference through critical perspectives. *Organization*, 17(1): 1–21.

PART VI

WHERE TO GO FROM HERE?

CHAPTER 26

EXAMINING DIVERSITY IN ORGANIZATIONS FROM CRITICAL PERSPECTIVES

The Validity of the Research Process

INGE BLEIJENBERGH AND SANDRA L. FIELDEN

Introduction

RESEARCH on diversity in organizations explores hierarchical organized dichotomies, such as the norm of the ideal worker and its implicit counterpart (Acker 1990; Tienari, Quack, and Theobold 2002). By examining the gender, race, class, age, or sexual orientation dimension of organizations, scholars reveal implicit assumptions about which categories are the norm and which categories deviate. Classical examples are organizations taking men's experiences and masculinity as the norm and women's experiences and femininity as the other (Calás and Smircich 1992; Knights and Kerfoot 2004; Bendl 2005), or the experiences of the white minority as the norm and the black majority as the opposite (Holvino 2008). Feminist and anti-racist scholars have pleaded for critical perspectives on organizations, putting the experiences of people in subordinated categories as central rather than in the margins (Reinharz 1992). They argue that taking the empirical perspective of these subordinate 'others' in the centre of the analysis will positively influence the validity of the research results (Reinharz 1992; Essers and Benschop 2009), where validity is defined as 'whether the claims, implications and conclusions found in a piece of research can be justifiably made' (Mills, Durepos, and Wiebe 2010: 962).

We aim to (further) explore the meaning of validity in research from critical perspectives, by discussing how methodological decisions in different phases of the research process influence the knowledge that is derived. We define a critical perspective as a research approach that aims at revealing organizational norms, in particular hierarchical organized dichotomies, in order to make organizations more inclusive for groups that deviate from the norms. In this sense it differs from mainstream research on diversity in organizations, where gender, race, class, age, or sexual orientation are examined as single variables and organizational norms are taken for granted. In this chapter we illustrate research agendas of scholars who examine diversity in organizations from a variety of critical perspectives, and discuss their methodological decisions and the consequences for the validity of the knowledge they derive in different phases of the research process.

RESEARCH AGENDAS FROM A CRITICAL PERSPECTIVE

Social phenomena in organizations are often explored and explained from the perspective of hegemonic groups, in many cases white, heterosexual, middle-class, able-bodied men (Hearn 1996; Knights and Kerfoot 2004). To attain knowledge that incorporates the perspective of the whole organization, organization studies need to incorporate the empirical perspectives of marginalized groups. To put it bluntly, research from critical perspectives calls for studies that examine organizational phenomena from the perspective of women employees, black employees, lower class, ageing, and disabled workers, among others (Bryant and Jaworski 2011; Zanoni 2011). These studies can reveal how diverse identities in organizations can discursively and materially reproduce unequal power relations and so contribute to changing these power relations.[1]

Organization studies are not only dominated by the perspective of white, middle-class heterosexual men, but also by the perspective of Western organizations (Prasad and Prasad 2002). This suggests that research in organizations with an American or European descent or location is often understood as providing universal knowledge that can be applied in organizations all over the world. To prevent this knowledge from being falsely considered externally valid, organization studies need to involve the perspective of a broader variety of organizations, such as businesses run by immigrants in Western countries (Essers and Benschop 2009) and locally owned organizations in South America (Jabbour et al. 2011), Africa, and South East Asia (Saha 2012). Therefore, using critical perspectives calls for conscious decisions about which persons and organizations in which particular context to examine.

One of the key issues in examining diversity in organizations from critical perspectives is the way in which different strands of diversity are included. Organizations often perceive and treat workplace diversity as a strategic choice (Jonsen, Maznevski, and Schneider 2011), taking diversity initiatives focusing on single identities rather than considering the multiple identities that many diverse groups have to negotiate

---

[1] In line with Chapter 8, this volume, diverse identities are recognized not as matters of 'having', but as discursive processes of 'becoming' (Zanoni et al. 2010).

(Ruwanpura 2008). Previously this has also been true of diversity research, although there is an increasing recognition that research needs to take a more holistic approach towards individuals and their relationships with the organization. For example, Tatli and Özbilgin (2012) argue that diversity research reveals a dominance of an *etic* approach, which takes a single category focus, has static and fixed notions of difference, and therefore limits the inclusion of certain categories. However, to overcome fixed mutually exclusive categories, it is not sufficient just to add elements of diversity together (e.g. gender and race), as the experiences of a black woman are both different and similar to white women and black men (Nash 2008). Tatli and Özbilgin call for an *emic* approach, which starts the analysis of diversity by identifying relations and processes of power that manifest themselves in the struggle for the accumulation of different forms of capital, namely human and social capital. Critical perspectives call for ignoring disciplinary boundaries in empirical research and aim at breaking down universal categories for operationalization: scholars should recognize how all empirical knowledge about diversity is time and space, or in other words, context dependent. This is supported by the work of Özkazanç-Pan (2012), who postulates that the problem is with the very notions of 'inclusive' and 'alternative', which are still theorized based on Western liberal humanist ideas without regard to their metatheoretical assumptions. It is not sufficient for researchers merely to 'contextualize' the participants of diversity research, as diversity cannot be independent of the particular research exercise. They need to investigate the interrelationships between context and power by developing theorizations and practices that turn this modality of power against itself (Ahonen et al. 2013).

There are a number of studies that demonstrate the benefits of analysing the intersection of multiple categories of diversity to understand inequality. For example, Woodhams, Lupton, and Cowling (2013) investigated the impact of multiple categories of disadvantage related to remuneration (i.e. gender, race, disability, and age). They found that those with more than one disadvantaged identity had lower pay than those with a single disadvantage, and introducing more sources of disadvantage results in further remuneration penalties. A less obvious form of discrimination was identified by van Laer and Janssens (2011), who found that it was small exclusionary acts, such as not inviting women to social events, that had the most profound impact on reproducing power differences. These acts potentially endangered the motivation of employees, the way individuals performed, and the way they were consequently evaluated: reproducing gender, racial, and ethnic stereotypes. Disadvantage is socially constructed, thus in order to understand the context within which disadvantage occurs researchers should not only look at the organization, but also at wider society as well. This is clearly demonstrated in the work of Haq (2013) who explores the impact of multiple identities on women in India, including colour, caste, religion, ethnicity, and marital status. Exploring the socio-cultural traditions leading to the intersection of multiple identities offers a paradigm shift from mainstream, Western views of gender as a single dimension of inequality.

Most studies of diversity in organizations typically focus on the organization level, rather than individual or social levels, examining implementation of HR policies and change strategies through organizational practices. This has raised a number of interesting issues, including managers' commitment to diversity (Bell 2011), the level of involvement in implementation (Pitts et al. 2010; Sabharwal 2014), the areas of diversity that need to be addressed (Pless and Maak 2004), and the tendency to focus on specific groups (Roberson 2006). For example, in Brazil Jabbour et al. (2011) found that the beliefs and values held by senior management are crucial to the successful implementation of diversity policies and diversity management requires the strong and continuous support of senior management in order to sustain efforts to implement HR policies. This concurs with work in the UK (Mulholland, Özbilgin, and Worman 2006), US (Kossek, Markel, and McHugh 2003), and Asia (Saha 2012) which showed that if managerial beliefs and values were unfavourable, regardless of the elements of diversity covered by organizational policy, change strategies would be inadequate. For example, recruitment as a change strategy cannot tackle the institutional and structural framework of oppression (Healy et al., 2010) if there is not a positive climate and supportive group norms (Kossek, Markel, and McHugh 2003; Jonsen et al. 2013). HR policies that seek to eliminate discrimination without addressing the underlying unequal power relations tend to lead to unsystematic, uneven, and subjective treatment of different employee groups.

Phases of a Critical Research Process

The methodological decisions in examining diversity from critical perspectives relate to the systematic and theoretical underpinning of the specific methods of data collection and analysis. This has potential consequences for all phases of the research process: it may influence the research questions to ask, the research strategies to apply, the data sources to collect and analyse, and the way to assess both the role of the researcher and the contribution of research. In the following sections we will discuss with examples the consequences of these choices for the validity of the knowledge that is derived.

Research Questions

Using critical perspectives affects the research questions about diversity in organizations that are being asked. Being aware of the interrelatedness of different categories of diversity, scholars may prefer to explore the intersection between them rather than focusing on a single identity. For example, examining class through the lens of gender, disability, and age, in the context of automobile industries (Zanoni 2011), or examining gendered and classed bodies in relation to place, in the context of Australian mining and food industries (Bryant and Jaworski 2011). Nevertheless, we argue that focusing on a particular diversity identity, such as women, migrants, or disabled people, can be a useful step towards empowering marginalized groups, on the condition that scholars recognize the differences within these groups and do not reproduce the differences between marginalized and hegemonic groups. Since the context of knowledge is extremely important in critical diversity research, the research questions will be directed towards explaining a social phenomenon in a particular context rather than making universal claims. This does not disqualify critical research on diversity in organizations from being theory oriented or externally valid, rather it suggests that researchers using this perspective contribute building blocks to theory building via the use of case studies in particular contexts (George and Bennett 2004).

Critical Research Strategies

A critical research agenda influences how researchers attain knowledge about diversity in organizations. Studying diversity in organizations from a critical perspective calls for a research strategy that is suitable for revealing experiences that have not yet been theorized and that nuance or fall outside organizational norms. This will logically lead to a qualitative research strategy that allows for inductive knowledge production and an *emic* perspective (Tatli and Özbilgin 2012). A classical choice would be to conduct comparative or single case studies that allow researchers to examine particular social situations in depth and combine diverse methods of data collection such as open interviews, participant observation, and collecting documents and cultural artifacts. For example, Tomlinson (2010) used comparative case study research to study six organizations in the UK that included refugee women among their volunteers. Another classical research strategy would be the ethnographic study, which allows the researcher to observe an organization from within by performing fieldwork for a longer period. Zanoni (2011) carried out three months of field work in a Belgian car factory, which allowed her to make informal contacts and observe informal communication at the factory gate, in the changing rooms, at the shop floor, and in the cafeteria, in addition to the more formal data collection via semi-structured interviews with employees and the collection of internal and external documents.

Alternative research strategies focus on one particular form of qualitative data collection, mainly open interviews (van Laer and Janssens 2011: Lin and Mac an Ghaill 2013) or collection of documents (van den Brink and Benschop 2012). Van den Brink and Benschop (2012) focused on document analysis to examine the construction of academic excellence in professorial appointments in the Netherlands. They collected 971 appointment reports of application procedures. By comparing the criteria mentioned in the job description to the criteria during the final nomination phase, they were able to reveal what criteria were decisive in distinguishing between the candidates who were nominated and those who were rejected (van den Brink and Benschop 2012: 511).

As mentioned, a particular research strategy that is particularly appropriate in supporting the study of diversity in organizations from critical perspectives is action research (Eikeland 2006). In action research researchers not only study organizations from the perspective of outsiders or minority groups, but also consciously aim to improve the position of these groups by involving them in the research (Reid 2004). For example, Bendl and Schmidt examined diverse strategies of feminist activists at an Austrian university and supported this activism by organizing workshops that allowed discussion and reflection between different generations of women activists (Bendl and Schmidt 2012). As researchers they had been involved in various roles in feminist activism at their own universities and, by presenting their own reconstruction of the changes in national policies and in the managerial structure of their universities to different groups of activists, they were able to identify current needs and potential strategies for further feminist activism in the managerial structures at the university (Bendl and Schmidt 2012: 487). They wanted to give voice to both activists and administrators in order to learn as much as possible from the process of changing organizational reality through human interaction in the implementation of policy and strategy (Eikeland 2006). Räsänen and Mäntylä (2001) and Katila and Meriläinen (1999) also performed action research within their own Finnish university by involving their own colleagues in diversity issues via the use of seminars. Unlike Bendl and Schmidt (2012), they did not address activists but rather tried to support active reflection about diversity among all organization members.

Data Sources, Collection, and Analysis

Organizational research is often based on interviews with or observations of members of hegemonic groups in Western organizations, such as (male) able-bodied managers and (white) professionals, but using such data sources runs the risk of reproducing unequal power relations rather than revealing or criticizing them. As the introduction suggests, critical perspectives on diversity in organizations call for the selection of research participants in empirical categories that fall outside organizational norms, such as migrant workers (Ortlieb and Sieben 2010; van Laer and Janssens 2011; Lin and Mac an Ghaill 2013), (refugee) women employees (Tomlinson 2010), shop-floor workers (Bryant and Jaworski 2011, Zanoni 2011), homosexuals, bisexuals, lesbians (Pringle 2008), or disabled people within organizations (Wilson-Kovacs et al. 2008), businesses run by (women) immigrants (Essers and Benschop 2009), or locally owned small and medium enterprises in non-Western countries (Fielden and Davidson 2005, 2010). The sample can also be taken from mainstream categories (e.g. white professionals), but with the conscious intention to critically analyse the race, gender, sexual, and class identity of the organization rather than take it for granted.

Critical scholars plead for collecting documents and cultural artifacts, such as records, films, objects, and buildings to examine dominant culture (Reinharz 1992: 142). The advantage of examining artifacts is twofold. First, they are naturalistic, since they were not created for the purpose of the study but 'found'. Second, they are 'unobtrusive', since they are not affected by the process of studying them, as in the case when researchers ask interview questions or observe people. As Reinharz (1992) argued, the results of studies based on analysis of documents and artifacts may be potentially more effective in convincing hegemonic groups about the presence of unequal power relations than results of studies based on interviews and observations. For example, Ogbonna and Hassis (2006) collected company documents and cultural artifacts such as promotion videos, company newsletters, and training manuals to analyse the dynamics of employee relationships in an ethnically diverse workforce in the UK. These artifacts helped them to reveal indirect discrimination that was connected to language abilities rather than ethnic background, but which affected groups with diverse ethnic backgrounds disproportionally. Another example is the appointment reports of application procedures of full professors in the Netherlands collected by van den Brink and Benschop (2012), which helped to reveal gender and gendered practices in the construction of academic excellence. On the basis of analysis of documents, combined with interviews with application committee members, they showed that women were disadvantaged and men privileged in the application procedure on the basis of a gendered construction of academic excellence. The fact that documents were produced by the committee members themselves and could be unobtrusively accessed gave the research results credibility.

However, collecting and analysing documents also has potential disadvantages for the validity of knowledge production. Critical scholars have argued that the perspective of marginalized groups is sometimes not represented in official documents, since these documents express the opinions of the majority rather than minorities in organizations (Bleijenbergh 2013). In those cases the personal documents of members of those disadvantaged groups have to be collected to compensate for this bias. Boone Parsons and colleagues (2012) analysed letters from a US-based feminist grass-roots organization from the 1970s, Stewardesses for Women's Rights, to show the internal struggle between the feminist ideals of the founders and the increasing push towards a bureaucratic structure from the leadership of the organization. The organization was set up with the purpose 'to fight sexual and racial discrimination and to ensure that women are given equal employment and promotional opportunities'. However, the development of the feminist grass-roots organization into a corporate business structure, with an executive director who could make autonomous decisions, caused a loss of direct influence of the grass-root members it represented.

Sometimes personal documents are produced for research purposes rather than being 'found' within the organization. Lowson and Arber (2013) engaged twenty women nurses in the UK to produce personal documents such as audio sleep diaries during a three-week period to examine the gender effect of night work on their household responsibilities and childcare. In addition, their partners and children were invited to complete daily audio sleep diaries during a two-week period as well. They analysed seventy-four sleep diaries in total and undertook interviews with all family members, allowing the researchers to show how women night workers undertake complex planning of domestic tasks before their night shifts begin and re-enter established domestic routines after their night shifts end. So, when the perspective of marginalized groups is not represented in official documents, researchers may need to use personal documents such as diaries or letters to incorporate this perspective in empirical research. While collecting official documents may be the most valid choice to examine mainstream perspectives in organizations, the collection of personal documents may be a more valid choice to reflect marginal voices.

Interviewing those who are outsiders to organizations or members of minority groups within organizations is a good alternative for identifying their experiences with and perspectives on organizational phenomena. This has consequences for the sample as outsiders to organizations, or minorities within organizations, may be more difficult to access than members of hegemonic groups, either because of their marginal position or their low number. As a result, researchers often use snowball sampling to identify their research candidates and involve them in the study. For example, van Laer and Janssens (2011) interviewed twenty-six second generation migrant professionals from Turkish or Maghreb backgrounds in Belgium to investigate subtle discrimination at the workplace. Since only a few employees fitted that profile, they started by asking HR managers they were acquainted with and multicultural organizations they knew to identify individuals within this profile and, when contacting these individuals themselves, they asked them to refer them on to other professionals with a migrant background. By interviewing second generation migrant workers in white-collar jobs they selected a group in a token position, potentially vulnerable to subtle rather than blatant discrimination (van Laer and Janssens 2011: 1208). Essers and Benschop (2009) also collected their respondents via snowball sampling when interviewing entrepreneurs with a Moroccan or Turkish background in the Netherlands. This technique was also used by Lin and Mac an Ghaill (2013) who conducted twenty-eight life-history interviews with male peasant workers in China to understand workplace relations of local, non-Western working men. By conducting life-history interviews lasting between one and four hours, they were able to reveal how the men constructed their own identity in the process of moving from a rural context to an urban space. The men's narratives showed how they deployed traditional cultural resources while in the process of constructing modern, urban-located masculine identities in the workplace (Lin and Mac an Ghaill 2013: 501).

Analysis from critical perspectives will often take a reflexive approach, requiring participants to reflect on their knowledge and experiences. For example, Saha (2012) used critical management incidents to explore the impact of values and beliefs on hiring decisions in India. Critical management incidents support the participant to remember critical moments in decision-making and to actively reflect upon them. Saha found that even those managers who were more in favour of hiring minority candidates had mixed attitudes towards those candidates, demonstrating that personal attitudes alone are not sufficient to determine the implementation of recruitment strategies. It is perhaps not surprising that behaviour is not necessarily reflective of attitude, as those involved in the process of transformation towards diversity have complementary and conflicting ways of constructing their own self (Bendl and Schmidt 2012). As a result, the way they construct others is likely to be even more conflicted, inhibiting their ability to understand the different needs and perspectives of those who do not fall within the norm and hence their approaches to diversity management and inclusion (Bell 2011).

Assessing the Role of the Researcher

Another methodological decision to be discussed concerns the position of the researcher in the production of knowledge about diversity. Scholars using critical perspectives argue that the role of the researcher in the research process is not value free (Reinharz 1992). Researchers examining diversity in organizations from critical perspectives are (like researchers in general) expected to reflect upon their own role in the research process (Chapter 16, this volume) to evaluate how they are part of the construction of knowledge (Reinharz 1992; Essers and Benschop 2009). In a reflection upon her life-story interviews with women entrepreneurs of Moroccan or Turkish origin, Essers (2009) argues for the explication of the different social locations of the researcher and the participants examined to show how power structures may be reproduced. She argues that balancing power relations in the data collection, data interpretation, and writing phase of research is difficult to achieve and that researchers should not strive to do so: rather she argues for recognizing the agency of both researcher and participant in accomplishing organizational change (Essers and Benschop 2009). Bleijenbergh, van Engen, and Vinkenburg (2013) reflect upon learning from the way deans in Dutch universities portray women academics as opposite to the ideal academic. The researchers' disciplinary background in arts made them expect publishing in international peer reviewed academic journals to be the requisite for excellence. This was indeed confirmed by interviews with arts deans, but the science deans considered visibility in popular media and valorization of knowledge more important requisites for excellence. The researchers learned that the characteristics of excellence were fluid and changeable, while the deans consistently assumed that women academics deviate from the ideal. The most radical position a researcher can take within the research process is within an action research, aiming at changing organizational reality (e.g. Reid 2004; Bendl and Schmidt 2012). The aim to improve the position of marginalized groups in organizations calls for an involved rather than neutral and distanced position for researchers towards research participants.

Assessing the Research Contribution

As we have argued, studying diversity in organizations from critical perspectives will often lead to context oriented knowledge. How to assess the theoretical contribution of such studies? The overview in this chapter shows that the research contribution, for example, can be found in understanding the interplay between norms and opposite in a specific context, in understanding the way different identity categories intersect, and how inequality, discrimination, and unequal power relations are both reproduced and can be altered. For example, Essers and Benschop (2009) have shown how the theoretical concept of the entrepreneur is based on Western norms and how entrepreneurs with a migrant background switch between identities to meet demands from their ethnic community and the hegemonic Western societal norms. The theoretical contribution is showing how entrepreneurial identities are adapted and negotiated to fit with the specific context. Bleijenbergh, van Engen, and Vinkenburg (2013) showed how the image of the ideal scientist that deans at Dutch universities reproduce is fluid and varies between different academic disciplines, but that the process of 'othering women' is constant. Here the theoretical contribution is that the norm of the ideal worker depends on the specific context, but that its masculine characteristics are continuously reproduced. Further, Bryant and Jaworski (2011) demonstrated how assumptions about gender, embodiment, and place influence how organizations understand and respond to skills shortages in the mining and food and beverage industry in Australia. The ideal of a bodiless, abstract worker dominates the way these industries attract and retain workers in rural and remote areas. The three studies mentioned above reveal how norms are both reproduced and can be altered in very different organizational contexts.

Another contribution of studying diversity from critical perspectives is increasing our theoretical understanding about the relation between agency and structure. Tomlinson (2010) showed the interplay between the agency of refugee women in the UK in negotiating belonging and the structural processes of organizations in perpetuating their status as outsiders. She compared the position of African and Middle East refugee women in the UK with those of Iranian refugee women in the Netherlands (Ghorashi 1997), in that they want to be accepted as equal citizens but were treated as strangers. She argues that refugee women should not be considered as passive victims, but rather as active agents within the limited possibilities available to them (Tomlinson 2010: 292). Consequently, researchers studying diversity in organizations from critical perspectives produce contextual knowledge, but also contribute to larger theories. For example, they contribute to theories about agency and structure by showing the complex interplay between agency and structure for particular diversity identities in particular contexts.

Conclusion

In this chapter we have argued how examining diversity in organizations from critical perspectives influences all phases of the research process, such as how to frame research questions, what research strategies to select, which data sources to collect, and which participants to choose, how to analyse the data, how to assess the role of the researcher, and, finally, what contribution to make with the research in itself. Examining diversity in organizations from critical perspectives calls for research questions that, for example, examine organizational norms, reveal the intersection of different identity categories, or examine the interplay between agency and structure. These questions are often asked for specific places, groups, and time periods, since information about the context is considered very important for understanding social phenomena related to diversity.

We argue that using critical perspectives on examining diversity in organizations calls for an *emic* perspective, that is, the empirical perspective of the marginalized 'other', such as women refugees in labour organizations in their host country, lower class rural workers in an urban context, and entrepreneurs with a migrant background. Sometimes insiders, such as white, male managers in Western organizations, may be research participants as well. Scholars include them in their research with a reflective approach to involve them in organizational change process and to prevent the hegemonic perspective being taken for granted.

We found that scholars studying diversity from critical perspectives often use qualitative research strategies, such as case studies, field studies, or action research, and perform a broad range of methods of data collection, such as participant observation, open interviews, and collecting documents and cultural artifacts, sometimes combined with quantitative research strategies, such as surveys or desk research, analysing existing data. They collect policy documents, but also cultural artifacts, such as records, films, subjects, and buildings, to show how unequal power relations are produced and reproduced. To reveal the perspective of minority groups or outsiders to organizations they may also collect personal documents or ask respondents to produce personal documents for the purpose of the study. Sometimes the use of quantitative research strategies such as surveys is particularly relevant in revealing how particular groups or perspectives have been ignored in theorizing or policymaking.

Examining diversity from critical perspectives calls for an active reflection upon the role of the researchers in producing knowledge, both in performing interviews and observations and in analysing and reporting upon empirical material. With such an approach the agency of both the researcher and the examined is taken into consideration. The knowledge contribution of research is, for example, found in understanding about how organizational norms are reproduced and adapted in specific organizational contexts and what the interplay is between agency and structure for specific groups in specific places at specific times.

This chapter shows a considerable amount of research on diversity in organizations from critical perspectives. Nevertheless, this line of research is of limited size compared with mainstream research on (diversity in) organizations. The future research agenda in this field would be to explore further on an empirical basis areas such as the intersection of different categories of identity in particular contexts and the agency of outsiders in changing organizational structures. In particular, the intersection of (dis)ability, sexual orientation, and class with other identity categories is relatively underexplored (Chapters 9 and 22, this volume). More research would be needed on the position of non-Western organizations in a Western context, or diversity in organizations in the upcoming economies such as those of the BRICS countries (Chapter 20, this volume).

The ultimate aim of this chapter is to contribute to the validity of research about diversity in organizations, by discussing how methodological decisions in different phases of the research process influence the knowledge that is derived and the theoretical contribution that can be made. Scholars in organization studies need to define explicitly what they consider valid knowledge about diversity in organizations and how they think this knowledge should be produced. They should not reproduce hierarchical organized dichotomies in organizations by taking them for granted, but rather reveal the implicit norms that prevail and question them from different perspectives. Using a critical empirical perspective not only potentially influences the whole research process, but ultimately has consequences for the position of the researcher within this process as well. With the discussion and overview in this chapter we hope to support the further development of a critical research practice, in which the researcher recognizes and actively reflects upon her or his role in producing knowledge about diversity in organizations, considering the active role of the ones that are examined in this process as well. Being part of this practice calls for the researcher to reflect upon what the research results mean for making organizations more inclusive.

References

Acker, J. (1990). Hierarchies, jobs, bodies: a theory of gendered organizations. *Gender & Society*, 4(2): 139–58.

Ahonen, P., Tienari, J., Meriläinen, S., and Pullen, A. (2013). Hidden contexts and invisible power relations: a Foucauldian reading of diversity research. *Human Relations*, 66(1): 1–24.

Bell, M. (2011). *Diversity in Organizations*. Mason, OH: Cengage Learning.

Bendl, R. (2005). *Revisiting Organization Theory: Integration and Deconstruction of Gender and Transformation of Organization Theory*. Frankfurt: Peter Lang.

Bendl, R. and Schmidt, A. (2012). Revisiting feminist activism at managerial universities. *Equality, Diversity and Inclusion: An International Journal*, 31(5/6): 484–505.

Bleijenbergh, I. (2013). *Kwalitatief onderzoek in organisaties*. Boom: Meppel.

Bleijenbergh, I., van Engen, M., and Vinkenburg, C. (2013). Othering women: fluid images of the ideal academic. *Equality, Diversity and Inclusion: An International Journal*, 32(1): 22–35.

Boone Parsons, D., Sanderson, K., Helms Mills, J., and Mills, A. (2012). Organizational logic and feminist organizing: stewardesses for women's rights. *Equality, Diversity & Inclusion: An International Journal*, 31(3): 266–77.

Bryant, L. and Jaworski, K. (2011). Gender, embodiment and place: the gendering of skills shortages in the Australian mining and food and beverage processing industries. *Human Relations*, 64(10): 1345–67.

Calás, M. and Smircich (1992) Using the 'F' word: feminist theories and the social consequences of organizational research. In A. Mills and P. Tancred (eds.), *Gendering Organizational Analysis*, Newbury Park, CA: Sage Publications.

Eikeland, O. (2006). The validity of action research: validity in action research. In K. A. Nielsen and L. Svensson (eds.) *Action Research and Interactive Research: Beyond Practice and Theory*. Maastricht: Shaker Publishing, 193–240.

Essers, C. (2009). Reflections on the narrative approach: dilemmas of power, emotions and social location while constructing life-stories. *Organization*, 16(2): 163–81.

Essers, C. and Benschop, Y. (2009). Muslim businesswomen doing boundary work: the negotiation of Islam, gender and ethnicity within entrepreneurial contexts. *Human Relations*, 62(3): 403–23.

Fielden, S. L. and Davidson, M. J. (eds.) (2005). *International Handbook of Women and Small Business Entrepreneurship*. Cheltenham: Edward Elgar.

Fielden, S. L. and Davidson, M. J. (eds.) (2010). *Successful Women Business Owners*. Cheltenham: Edward Elgar.

George, A. and Bennett, A. (2004). *Case Studies and Theory Development in the Social Sciences.* Cambridge, MA: The MIT Press.

Ghorashi, H. (1997). Shifting and conflicting identities, Iranian women political activists in exile. *The European Journal of Women's Studies,* 4(3): 283–303.

Haq, R. (2013). Intersectionality of gender and other form of identity: dilemmas and challenges facing women in India. *Gender in Management: An International Journal,* 28(3): 171–84.

Healy, G., Kirton, G., Özbilgin, M., and Oikelome, F. (2010). Competing rationalities in the diversity project of the UK judiciary: the politics of assessment centres. *Human Relations,* 63(6): 807–34.

Hearn, J. (1996). Deconstructing the dominant: making the one(s) the other(s). *Organization,* 3(4): 611–26.

Holvino, E. (2008) Intersections: the simultaneity of race, gender and class in organization studies. *Gender, Work and Organization,* 17(3): 248–77.

Jabbour, C. J. C., Gordono, F. S., de Oliviera, J. H. C., Martinez, J. C., and Battistelle, R. A. G. (2011). Diversity management; challenges, benefits and the role of human resource management in Brazilian organizations. *Equality, Diversity and Inclusion: An International Journal,* 30(1): 58–74.

Jonsen, K., Maznevski, M. L., and Schneider, S. C. (2011). Diversity and its not so diverse literature: an international perspective. *International Journal of Cross Cultural Management,* 10(1): 35–62

Jonsen, K., Tatli, A., Özbilgin, M. F., and Bell, M. P. (2013). The tragedy of the uncommons: reframing workforce diversity. *Human Relations,* 66(2): 271–94.

Katila, S. and Meriläinen, S. (1999). A serious researcher or just another nice girl?: doing gender in a male-dominated scientific community. *Gender, Work and Organization,* 6(3): 163–73.

Knights, D. and Kerfoot, D. (2004). Between representations and subjectivity: gender binaries and the politics of organizational transformation. *Gender, Work and Organization,* 11(4): 430–54

Kossek, E. E., Markel, K. S., and McHugh, P. P. (2003). Increasing diversity as an HRM change strategy. *Organizational Change Management,* 16(3): 328–52.

Lewis, P. and Simpson, R. (2010). Introduction; theoretical insights into the practices of revealing and concealing gender within organizations. In P. Lewis and R. Simpson (eds.), *Revealing and Concealing Gender: Issues of Visibility in Organizations.* Basingstoke: Palgrave Macmillan, 1–22.

Lewis, P. and Simpson, R. (2012). Kanter revisited: gender, power and (in)visibility. *International Journal of Management Reviews,* 14: 141–58

Lin, X. and Mac an Ghaill, M. (2013). Chinese male peasant workers and shifting masculine identities in urban workspaces. *Gender, Work and Organization,* 20(5): 498–511.

Lowson, E. and Arber, S. (2013). Preparing, working, recovering: gendered experiences of night work among women and their families. *Gender, Work and Organization,* 21(3): 231–43.

Mills, A. J., Durepos, G., and Wiebe, E. (2010). *Encyclopedia of Case Study Research.* Thousand Oaks, CA: Sage.

Mulholland, G., Özbilgin, M., and Worman, D. (2006). *Managing Diversity: Words into Action.* London: Chartered Institutue of Personnel and Development.

Nash, J. C. (2008). Re-thinking intersectionality. *Feminist Review,* 89: 1–15.

Ogbonna, E. and Harris, L. (2006). The dynamic of employee relationships in an ethnically diverse workforce. *Human Relations,* 59(3): 379–407.

Ortlieb, R. and Sieben, B. (2010). Migrant employees in Germany: personnel structures and practices. *Equality, Diversity and Inclusion: An International Journal*, 29(4): 364–79.

Özkazanç-Pan, B. (2012). Postcolonial feminist research: challenges and complexities. *Equality, Diversity and Inclusion: An International Journal*, 31(5/6): 573–91.

Pitts, D. W., Hicklin, A. K., Hawes, D. P., and Melton, E. (2010). What drives the implementation of diversity management programs? Evidence from public organizations. *Journal of Public Administration Research and Theory*, 20(4): 867–86.

Pless, N. and Maak, T. (2004). Building an inclusive diversity culture: principles, processes and practice. *Journal of Business Ethics*, 54(2): 129–47.

Prasad, A. and Prasad, P. (2002). The coming of age of interpretive organizational research. *Organizational Research Methods*, 5: 4–11.

Pringle, J. (2008). Gender in management: theorizing gender as heterogender. *British Journal of Management*, 19: 110–19.

Räsänen, K. and Mäntylä, H. (2001). Preserving academic diversity: promises and uncertainties of PAR as a survival strategy. *Organization*, 8(2): 299–318.

Reid, C. J. (2004). Advancing women's social justice agendas: a feminist action research framework. *International Journal of Qualitative Methods*, 3(3): 1–22.

Reinharz, S. (1992). *Feminist Methods in Social Research*. New York and Oxford: Oxford University Press.

Roberson, Q. M. (2006). Disentangling the meanings of diversity and inclusion in organizations. *Group & Organization Management*, 31(2): 212–36.

Ruwanpura, K. N. (2008). Multiple identities, multiple discrimination: a critical review. *Feminist Economics*, 14(3): 77–105.

Sabharwal, M. (2014) Is diversity management sufficient? Organizational inclusion to further performance. *Public Personnel Management*, 43: 197–217.

Saha, S. K. (2012). Relationship between managerial values and hiring preferences in the context of six decades of affirmative action in India. *Equality, Diversity and Inclusion: An International Journal*, 31(2): 176–97.

Tatli, A. and Özbilgin, M. F. (2012). An emic approach to intersectional study of diversity at work: a Bourdieuan framing. *International Journal of Management Reviews*, 14: 180–200.

Tienari, J., Quack, S., and Theobald, H. (2002). Organizational reforms, 'ideal workers' and gender orders: a cross-societal comparison. *Organization Studies*, 23(2): 249–79.

Tomlinson, F. (2010). Marking difference and negotiating belonging: refugee women, volunteering and employment. *Gender, Work and Organization*, 17(3): 278–95.

van den Brink, M. and Benschop, Y. (2012). Gender practice in the construction of academic excellence: sheep with five legs. *Organization*, 19(4): 507–24.

van Laer, K. and Janssens, M. (2011). Ethnic minority professionals' experiences with subtle discriminiation in the workplace. *Human Relations*, 64(9): 1203–27.

Wilson-Kovacs, D., Ryan, M. K., Haslam, S., and Rabinovich, A. (2008). 'Just because you can get a wheelchair in the building doesn't necessarily mean that you can still participate': barriers to the career advancement of disabled professionals. *Disability & Society*, 23: 705–17

Woodhams, C., Lupton, B., and Cowling, M. (2013). The snowballing penalty effect: multiple disadvantage and pay. *British Journal of Management*, 24(4): 63–77.

Zanoni, P. (2011). Diversity in the lean automobile factory: doing class through gender, disability and age. *Organization*, 18(1): 105–27.

Zanoni, P., Janssens, M., Benschop, Y., and Nkomo, S. (2010). Unpacking diversity, grasping inequality: rethinking difference through critical perspectives. *Organization*, 17(1): 9–29.

CHAPTER 27

FUTURE CHALLENGES FOR PRACTICES OF DIVERSITY MANAGEMENT IN ORGANIZATIONS

YVONNE BENSCHOP, CHARLOTTE HOLGERSSON,
MARIEKE VAN DEN BRINK, AND ANNA WAHL

INTRODUCTION

DIVERSITY in the workforce in terms of social identity categories such as gender, race, ethnicity, age, and class has become a prime concern for organizations in both the public and private sectors, because in today's globalized world organizations need a diverse workforce in terms of knowledge, skills, and abilities (Konrad, Prasad, and Pringle 2006; Zanoni and Janssens 2007; Ortlieb and Sieben 2013). Scholars and practitioners seldom contest the importance of diversity in organizations any more. How to achieve the organizational change that is needed to transform organizations into more inclusive and diverse places to work is, nevertheless, much less obvious.

Organizational processes are complex and difficult to change and we still lack knowledge of which practices have proven to be the most effective in different settings and contexts. Diversity management practices refer to formalized practices developed and implemented by organizations to manage diversity effectively (Yang and Konrad 2011). Different strategies for change have been developed for diversity in general (Jewson and Mason 1986; Kirton and Greene 2010) and gender in particular (Ely and Meyerson 2000b; Benschop and Verloo 2011; Wahl et al. 2011). Overall, the common sense among diversity scholars seems to be that transformative strategies aimed at changing the ways that work is divided, organized, and valued will be most effective to counter inequality. There are different examples of such transformative strategies. First, the post-equity approach that focuses on improving organizational effectiveness by interrupting the processes that produce gender inequalities (Ely and Meyerson 2000b). A second example is diversity/gender mainstreaming that aims to ensure that organizational policies impact evenly on all personnel and eliminate inequalities in organizational routines (Benschop and Verloo 2006; Bacchi and Eveline 2009). Third, strategies to create inclusive organizations use the diversity of knowledge and perspectives that members of different groups bring to the organization to shape the organization's strategy, work, management, and operating systems and its core values and norms for success (Holvino, Ferdman, and Merrill-Sands 2004). However, the transformative diversity interventions that are highly regarded by scholars are still rare in organizational practice. This has to do with their unattractiveness for policymakers and practitioners, because they challenge the core organizational values and practices and there are few practical guidelines on how to achieve transformation (Benschop and Verloo 2011).

In this chapter, we zoom in on a set of diversity practices that prevail in organizations: training, mentoring, and networks. These practices meet scholarly critique for their lack of transformation. They are often seen as targeting 'the Other' employees to get them on a par with the majority employees, leaving the current system intact (Ely and Meyerson 2000b; Zanoni et al. 2010) (see also Chapter 15, this volume). However, it can be questioned whether values, practices, and routines indeed remain intact in the organizations that engage in diversity training, mentoring, and networks.

The aim of this chapter is to assess more effectively the transformative potential of these popular diversity practices. The notion of transformative potential means the potential for diversity practices to diminish inequalities, defined as systematic disparities in power and control over goals, resources, and outcomes (Acker 2006), by changing organizational work practices, norms, routines, and interactions. The chapter is structured as follows. We start with presenting a model that enables a systematic comparison of the transformative potential of diversity training, mentoring, and networks. We then take stock of these three diversity practices and review the literature around them to assess their transformative potential. We end with concluding remarks about the theoretical and practical implications of the model and the future of diversity practices.

The 3D-model

Our starting point for this text is a model originally developed by Wahl (1995) and elaborated by Holgersson and Höök (1997) and Wahl (2003). This model has been expanded further through our joint efforts in discussing and evaluating the different methods for this chapter. The purpose of the model is to structure different key dimensions in management strategies within a gender equality and/or diversity approach. In this comparative analysis, the model will be used to discuss and analyse the transformative potential of the three selected diversity practices. We named this new model *the 3D-model*, which

Table 27.1 The 3D-model: dimensions for the design of diversity practices

Content (C)		Participants (P)		Format (F)	
Focus	Power perspective	Target group	Affiliation	Frequency	Design
Gender equality	Absent or harmonious	Minority	Combination	Single event	Individual
Diversity	Individual	Majority	Internal	Repeated	Interpersonal
Inclusion	Multidimensional	Mixed	External	Programme	Interactive

stands for *Dimensions for the Design of Diversity practices* (see Table 27.1). It is important to note that the model is a matrix that can be read in numerous combinations. All headings represent a question and a choice. Each of the three alternatives of *Focus* can be combined with all alternatives of *Power perspective, Target group, Affiliation, Frequency*, and *Design*. Gender equality programmes can be either power absent, individual, or multidimensional. In addition to this, they can either target a minority group, a majority group, or a mixed group. The same goes for Diversity programmes and Inclusion initiatives. A diversity initiative can, for example, be an internal single event, targeted at a mixed group, with a power absent perspective and interpersonal design. Another diversity initiative can, for example, be a combination of internal and external programme with a multidimensional and interactive approach.

The 3D-model serves three purposes. First, it serves as an analytical framework when comparing the set-ups, consequences, and outcomes of different practices addressing diversity in organizations. Second, it helps when identifying where additional empirical material, that is, case studies of diversity practices in organizations, are needed. Third, the model can serve as an academically informed qualitative assessment tool for practitioners wanting to assess management interventions addressing diversity.

The model helps to systematize knowledge on the different possibilities and combinations that can be chosen when designing diversity practices and work for change and enables a comparative analysis on how different set-ups result in different learning outcomes and implications for transformational change. Previous research has shown that, for example, both the composition of participants as well as the content in terms of underlying theories and concepts has consequences for group processes and learning outcomes (Wahl 1995; Ely and Meyerson 2000b; Lorbiecki and Jack 2000; Höök 2001; De Vries 2010; Kirton and Greene 2010; Wahl et al. 2011).

The 3D-model consists of three dimensions, *Content, Participants*, and *Format*, which in turn are broken down into more detailed sub-dimensions: (C) focus and power perspective, (P) target group and affiliation, (F) frequency and design. Each sub-dimension can be combined in several different ways in the matrix, which allows for an array of different set-ups.

Focus represents the content in terms of problem analysis and knowledge dissemination in the diversity practice. Many strategies are focused on inequalities related to gender and on problems connected to women's subordination in society. Other strategies target diversity issues, and can be specifically linked to one category, for example, ethnicity, sexuality, age, disability, or the intersections of several of these. Diversity practices can either include or exclude gender issues. Some practices are more general in addressing inequalities, aiming at creating a more inclusive culture overall. Whereas diversity is concerned with the numerical representation of diverse employees, inclusion addresses their belongingness and uniqueness in the organization (Shore et al. 2011).

Power perspective refers to if and how the content in the diversity practices addresses power in relation to gender, diversity, or inclusion. The content could be power absent or with a functional and harmonious understanding of power, as is often the case in cross-cultural management and socio-biological views on gender (Romani, Höök, and Holgersson 2011). Power can be addressed as something exercised among and between individuals, or power can be seen as multidimensional in the sense that it simultaneously operates on a societal, organizational, and individual level and that there are inherent conflict of interests (Halford and Leonard 2001; Linghag 2009).

Target group concerns the group composition of participants in the intervention. This is named minority, majority, and mixed in the model. The meaning of these labels varies according to the problem addressed in the intervention. Minority often signifies groups of women, ethnic minorities, LGBT, or young people, but is of course dependent on the local context in the organization. Majority often indicates, for example, men or national majorities. Mixed groups can mean any kind of compositions that represent different categories in relation to the problem addressed in the initiative.

Affiliation is a way to describe where the intervention is located. Many interventions are organized internally, meaning that all participants, sometimes also the course leaders, work in the same organization. Other programmes are organized by external companies or consultants and are composed of participants from many different organizations. Finally, some interventions are a combination of internal and external, for example, mentoring programmes where the mentors are recruited externally and the mentees internally.

Frequency depicts the volume of the intervention. Sometimes it is a single event, for example, one lecture or seminar with an invited speaker. The initiative can also be slightly extended into a series of seminars, lectures or, for example, a three-day course, in the model named as repeated. All initiatives that cover a longer period of time are called programmes, signifying a longer and often more demanding commitment from the participants.

Design refers to the fact that there are several established ways of organizing and setting up interventions addressing diversity. Diversity practices can have a traditional one-way-communication lecturing approach where the individual is addressed or focus on interpersonal activities. There are programmes with more process-oriented and interactive approaches that build on mutual exchange between organizers and participants (Amundsdotter 2010). Sometimes these interactive approaches include initiatives for change or projects aiming at transforming the organizations.

In conclusion, the model will be used here to analyse and discuss the transformative potential of diversity training, mentoring, and networks. Diversity interventions come in many different forms and though there are studies on different specific practices, there is no comparative study providing a more comprehensive picture of the consequences in terms of organizational change. The aim here is to provide such a comprehensive picture building on existing research on diversity practices, in order to understand more fully how knowledge and power relations related to diversity are reproduced or challenged in organizational practices. In the following sections we will discuss diversity training, mentoring programmes, and diversity networks in relation to the different dimensions of the 3D-model.

Diversity Training

Training has been one of the most common responses to anti-discrimination legislation and calls for increased diversity in organizations (Paluck 2006; Anand and Winters 2008). Diversity training is an essential component of diversity programmes in organizations (Roberson, Kulik, and Pepper 2003). According to Bezrukova, Jehn, and Spell (2012: 208), the main objective of diversity training is for people 'to learn how to work effectively with different others which may increase overall success for both organizations and individuals'. The methods employed vary along a continuum from instructional methods to experiential training. Instructional methods are meant to raise awareness of problems associated with lack of diversity or the mismanagement of diversity and of the benefits of diversity. They may convey information on legislation, policies, and/or information about underrepresented groups supposed to replace stereotypes and myths (Ferdman and Brody 1996; Paluck 2006). Experiential methods take a more participatory approach including, for example, practising communication skills, raising awareness of perceptions of diversity, group discussions on 'differences,' and role plays featuring situations with characters with a diverse background (Paluck 2006).

Content

In terms of focus, diversity training comes in many varieties. Sometimes diversity is the label used but the actual content of the training targets a specific issue such as gender equality or inequalities based on ethnicity or race. Also, training builds on different perceptions of diversity, either focusing on social categories such as gender, race, ethnicity, disability, religion, sexuality, or on a broader definition including, for example, differences based on skills, work style, political, or philosophical views (Paluck 2006). Some training programmes focus on inclusion, that is, emphasizing what the categories have in common in order to transform the organizational culture so that everyone feels welcome and can contribute their skills.

Anand and Winters (2008) suggest three approaches to diversity training that roughly correspond to the three diversity paradigms proposed by Thomas and Ely (1996): 'discrimination and fairness' that focuses on numbers and compliance, supports assimilation and colour- and gender-absent conformism; 'access and legitimacy' that promotes acceptance and celebration of difference based on business case arguments; and 'learning and integration' that acknowledges different perspectives and approaches among everyone and focuses on learning and personal development. Scholars have critiqued both the 'discrimination and fairness' and 'access and legitimacy' approach for not addressing power differences and conveying an image of harmonious differences (e.g. Ely and Meyerson 2000a; Lorbiecki and Jack 2000; Höök 2001; Litvin 2002; De Vries 2010). The 'learning and integration' approach, however, rests on the recognition that the power structures in the organization have to change in order for different perspectives to be equally legitimate and for work processes to be changed. In practice, few adopt the 'learning and effectiveness' paradigm (Anand and Winters 2008).

Participants

Diversity training can target a wide variety of groups. According to a review of diversity training literature by Roberson et al. (2003), the composition of the group of trainees is a recurring discussion. According to Roberson et al., some scholars, such as Kirkland and Regan (1997) and Baytos (1995), argue for demographically heterogeneous groups, particularly with respect to visible dimensions of diversity such as gender, ethnicity, and age. The heterogeneity is believed to enhance the quality of discussions since there are many different perspectives to be shared in such a group. However, other scholars highlight the risks involved in heterogeneous groups, for example, of white men feeling attacked (Galen and Palmer 1993) and putting minority participants in awkward positions (Katz 1978), and emphasize the importance of homogeneous groups in order to provide a safer context for discussions about diversity, both for members from dominant groups and disadvantaged groups as, for example, Paige and Martin (1996) and Milliken and Martins (1996).

It is nevertheless common for diversity training to be geared towards all employees in order to raise awareness of prejudice and build skills in order for individuals to monitor their actions and responses to specific incidents in the workplace (Bezrukova, Jehn, and Spell 2012).

Women-only management training has been a popular form of training that can be seen as diversity training, although the aim is not to reduce bias but rather to provide career support. These trainings have been heavily criticized by scholars for failing to adopt a power perspective and thus making women the problem, or making women responsible for the existing gender power relations (Ely and Meyerson 2000a). Moreover, scholars have highlighted that such programmes also reproduce the privileged position of a few white, middle-class women (Eveline 2004; Pini, Brown, and Ryan 2004). Women-only training can nevertheless have a more transformative potential if 'a bifocal approach' is adopted, that is, the training has a power perspective and focuses both on women and on organizational change (De Vries 2010).

In fact, management training, either targeting women and/or men, seldom touches upon issues of power. An exception is Sinclair (2000) who introduced the topic of masculinities in a workshop held for a company executive group and in an MBA class. By addressing masculinities she wanted to avoid focusing on minority groups. However, in order to be able to do this, Sinclair argues that the training needs to foster a discussion among managers about the culture of the dominant group that in turn requires a programme structure that supports reflection and a context where participants can voice vulnerabilities and doubts.

Another example of a diversity training programme that is guided by a power perspective and that has attempted to have an interactive approach targeting male managers is the Walk the Talk-programme, implemented in 1998 at the truck company AB Volvo. The programme included both practical and theoretical modules and aimed to raise the manager's awareness of values, and how they unintentionally include and exclude people. Catalyst, a US-based organization promoting gender equality in the workplace, has published reports describing successful initiatives focusing on male managers such as the Walk the Talk-programme (Prime and Moss-Racusin 2009).

Format

Diversity training is most often carried out on one single occasion, maybe with a refresher session after a certain period of time. There are nevertheless examples of organizations that have more prolonged courses across weeks or months (Paluck 2006). The training can be integrated into a system of diversity related activities within a more comprehensive organizational development effort that would more correspond to the learning and effectiveness paradigm referred to earlier. These integrated programmes, that is, training that is conducted as part of a planned and systemic organizational development effort, are deemed more effective compared to other programmes, in particular the stand-alone training with a 'check-off-the-box' approach (Bezrukova, Jehn, and Spell 2012). There is, nevertheless, still little research into integrated training.

Many organizations have diversity training led by an external consultant, often with one single signature exercise, for example The Story of O or Blue Eye/Brown Eye (Anand and Winters 2008). Training that is carried out over a longer period of time often requires a combination of internal and external consultants to be involved.

Most diversity training follows an intergroup approach, that is, the training is carried out in groups. However, individual managers do receive some form of training when being coached either by an in-house diversity officer or an external diversity consultant. For example, gender equality consultants in Sweden report that there has been an increase in what are called gender coaches who provide support for individuals regarding gender issues (Wahl and Höök 2007). Interactive diversity training is not as common since most training mainly employs instructional methods including lectures, exercises, group activities, and discussions (Bezrukova, Jehn, and Spell 2012). Interactive methods also require more time, which is why it is difficult to apply such methods if the training is not part of a more sustained and integrated effort of organizational change.

In sum, our review of literature on diversity training suggests that these are popular interventions but that they are seldom effective in transforming the structure and culture of an organization if they do not address power, if they are not part of a larger organizational development effort, and if they do not adopt a more experiential approach. According to our review, there are few examples of programmes that adopt a power perspective and an interactive approach to be found in the literature, and possibly also in practice. There are some exceptions like the action research approaches suggested by, for example, Paluck (2006) and Meyerson and Kolb (2000). Such training is part of a larger organizational development effort and has an interactive approach. With the support of knowledge, the participants identify a diversity related issue in their own context, they discuss the problem and possible actions for change, and formulate an action plan. The participants then implement the action plan and monitor the outcomes while continuously reflecting upon the process as a learning activity.

Mentoring Programmes

Mentoring has become a popular diversity practice for advancing the careers of persons from groups that are in a minority on management levels (Blake-Beard 2001; Baugh and Fagenson-Eland 2007). The intervention aims at mimicking the informal relations that exist between senior, more experienced persons and junior, less experienced persons, and that support the junior persons' careers (Ragins and Kram 2007). Formal mentoring refers to relations that are initiated and developed with the assistance of an organization (Ragins and Cotton 1999).

Content

Formal mentoring programmes can have different contents ranging from focusing only on the career development of the mentee to having more transformational ambitions. Scholars question the effectiveness of formal mentoring programmes that do not address power relations in organizations (Pini, Brown, and Ryan 2004). Colley (2001), for example, questions the individual focus that most mentoring programmes adopt, since they seldom address problems on a more structural level. By not addressing power, mentoring programmes send the message to the mentee that it is the mentee who should adapt to the pre-existing conditions (Darwin 2000; McKeen and Bujaki 2007) and thus the status quo in organizations is not challenged (Avotie 2008; De Vries 2010). Women-only programmes that do not address issues of power have been particularly criticized. For example, Meyerson and Kolb (2000) argue that by not addressing structural disadvantage, focus will be on women and not on the organizational culture itself. Mentors need to understand that their contribution does not end with the individual mentee but that they must be active in working for change within the organization (Thomas 2001; Johnson-Bailey and Cervero 2004). Hansman (1998) suggests that training sessions when planning and implementing formal mentoring programmes may be the answer to some of the concerns about cross-race/cross-gender mentoring. She argues that by focusing on issues of gender, race, class, ethnicity, ability, and sexuality, mentors may learn to understand the challenges their mentees face and to critically assess cultural norms at play in organizations.

Indeed, mentoring programmes with the explicit aim of changing the organizational culture often contain some sort of training. The content of this training can vary from a more harmonious view on gender and diversity to a more multidimensional view of power. For example, Höök (2001) describes a women-only management training programme that contained a mentoring module where both the women mentees and the male mentors received training in gender issues. The purpose of the mentoring programme was to involve male managers in gender equality work and to increase their level of awareness and knowledge regarding gender. Höök found that the male mentors did not prioritize the meetings that included training sessions. The meeting that attracted most mentors was the one the CEO attended. On this occasion, the mentoring programme provided an arena for homosocial networking for men, while the women mentees remained in a peripheral position.

Participants

Formal mentoring programmes that are used as an intervention for change most often couple a senior mentor with a more junior person from a group that is in minority within the organization, for example, a senior male executive and a woman in the early stages of a management career (Ragins and Cotton 1999; Ragins 2002).

The basic idea of a mentoring programme is that the mentor should offer the mentee different kinds of support. Kram (1983) suggests that mentors can provide career support, through exposure and visibility, sponsorship, coaching, protection and access to assignments, and psychosocial support, such as acceptance and confirmation, role modelling, friendship, and counselling. Nevertheless, research findings suggest that women receive less coaching, role modelling, friendship, and social interaction than male counterparts in formal mentor programmes (Ragins and Cotton 1999).

Much of the literature on gender and mentoring is focused on the challenges in the mentoring relationships between male mentors and women mentees. In a survey of the literature on formal mentoring programmes, Blake-Beard (2001) identifies issues related to the management of the internal relationship, such as lack of identification between mentor and mentee and negotiating level of intimacy between mentor and mentee, as well as challenges related to the management of the external relationship, for example, handling the relationship with the mentee's supervisor, managing the belief that women participating in formal mentoring programmes are deficient, and dealing with sexual innuendoes. Much of the problems involved in the relationship between a male mentor and a female mentee are indeed related to (hetero)sexuality (Höök 2001).

Similar challenges in cross-race mentoring relations have also been documented. For example, studies have documented that African American mentees experience less psychosocial and career support from European American mentors (Harris and Smith 1999; Thomas 2001). The mentor-mentee relationship is hierarchical in nature and this power relation is magnified in cross-racial and cross-gender mentoring (Ragins 1997; Bowman et al. 1999; Johnson-Bailey and Cervero 2004). This has implications for both the career and the psychosocial support that are essential in successful mentoring relationships (Thomas 2001).

Although less examined, there are formal mentoring programmes where both mentors and mentees are women. Some scholars argue that there are advantages of such mentoring relations since women mentors can be better role models for the women mentees and have greater opportunities of offering emotional support (Gilbert and Rossman 1992). Nevertheless, other studies show that female mentees with women mentors also face dilemmas, such as women mentees having psychosocial unrealistic expectations of their women mentors (Eldridge 1990).

According to our review of the literature, the formal mentoring programmes that are most often discussed in the literature are internal programmes that involve participants that are all employed in the organization. There is, however, little research into external formal mentoring programs that are administered by an organization and where mentors and mentees come from a variety of organizations.

Format

Traditional mentoring programmes assume a one-way relationship, where the mentee learns from the mentor and where the mentor should 'help' the mentee. The focus is thus on the individual mentee and the mentee's needs (Ragins and Kram 2007; De Vries 2010). There are, nevertheless, programmes that view the mentor-mentee relationship as a two-way learning relationship where the mentor is also expected to learn from the mentee (Ragins 2002; Baugh and Fagenson-Eland 2007). There are different approaches to the two-way relationship. Some programmes aim at making individual mentees from underrepresented groups visible to the mentors, assuming that this may alter the mentor's attitudes towards these groups. Although male mentors have, for example, argued that they have learnt something about the organization and women's conditions from meeting with the women mentee (Eliasson, Berggren, and Bondestam 2000; Höök 2001; Avotie 2008), this does not necessarily mean that their perception of why women are not advancing in organizations has changed. In fact, some studies such as Avotie (2008) suggest that mentor's perceptions of women not being willing or being able to pursue a career had been strengthened.

Other programmes have a more explicit two-way relationship approach to mentoring where mentors are also expected to see not only individual mentees but also the barriers that disadvantaged groups meet in organizations (De Vries 2010). One example is the mentoring programme in Höök's study (2001) where the mentees were women and the mentors were (almost) all men but where it was made clear that it was a mutual relationship and the mentors would receive training as well. Giscombe (2007) provides another example of a programme with an explicit two-way relationship where junior women mentored senior managers. In this programme, senior managers learned about the barriers that women faced in the company with the specific goal of changing the career culture within the organization.

More recently, other forms of mentoring have been developed. For example, peer-mentoring programmes seem to be particularly common among faculty members in higher education institutions (Ensher, Thomas, and Murphy 2001). The peer-mentoring model tries to steer away from the traditional hierarchical mentor-mentee relationship and create a network of multiple partners in non-hierarchical, collaborative, and reciprocal partnerships. Interestingly, traditional mentoring programmes can provide an arena for peer-mentoring among mentees. For example, women in women-only mentoring programmes argue that the most important lesson from the programme was not the relationship with the mentor but the network developed among the women mentees (Eliasson, Berggren, and Bondestam 2000; Höök 2001).

Scholars such as Darwin (2000) and Avotie (2008) question the potential of mentoring programmes to contribute to structural change when the focus of the programme is on improving the mentee's individual career opportunities, in particular if the programme lacks a power perspective. Avotie argues, however, that structural change has to start at an individual level and that a potential for change exists when the mentees draw on the opportunities provided by the programme to contribute to change on a structural level.

De Vries, Webb, and Eveline (2006) provide an example of a mentoring programme that has become part of a process of organizational intervention. The programme was part of a larger management development initiative aiming to develop the women and change the culture. Knowledge of the gendered nature of organizations provided the foundation for the women participants when they collectively investigated and discovered underlying assumptions, values, and practices within the organization. The male mentors found that through mentoring they had become more aware of gender issues and had an increased understanding of the situation of women and what issues need to be addressed. Some saw tangible results in an increased numbers of women, others noted a qualitative change in the culture. De Vries, Webb, and Eveline (2006) argue that given that the mentors held senior positions, the significance of their insights from mentoring should not be underestimated.

Diversity Networks

Networks are used in organizations as a diversity tool to provide employees from different backgrounds with information, advice, and social and career support. There are a few different terms for such in-company networks that connect employees from different identity categories.[1] Diversity networks are also called employee groups (Githens and Aragon 2009), employee network groups (Friedman and Holtom 2002), or affinity networks (Foldy 2002). The networks are either created by management or by members of the organization in order to facilitate the inclusion and development of people with different social identities in the organization. There are, for example, women's networks, ethnic minority networks, networks for younger, older, and LGBT employees.

While diversity networks are an often-used intervention in organizations, this popularity is not paralleled by scholarly attention for these networks. In comparison to the many studies on other diversity practices such as training and mentoring, or in comparison to the vast amount of research on organizational networks, there is less attention for these specific types of networks in organizations. Studies that do address this diversity practice focus mostly on in-company women's networks (Bierema 2005; Singh, Vinnicombe, and Kumra 2006; Hersby, Ryan, and Jetten 2009; Coleman 2010; Durbin 2011; Gremmen and Benschop 2011), ethnic minority networks (Friedman, Kane, and Cornfield 1998; Friedman and Holtom 2002; Friedman and Craig 2004), and LGBT networks (Wright et al. 2006; Githens and Aragon 2009; Colgan and McKearney 2012).

Content

Diversity networks are group-level interventions that counter the social isolation of members of social identity groups by providing a place for members to meet each other and develop both strong and weak ties with each other (Friedman and Craig 2004). Diversity networks differ in their focus, with some networks centring on the social and career benefits for their members and other networks also striving for strategic change in the organization (Friedman, Kane, and Cornfield 1998; Gremmen and Benschop 2011).

From our literature review, we observe that diversity networks are formally established to counter the power of informal 'old boys' networks' in organizations. Diversity networks tend to be institutionalized and visible as a formal group that organizes meetings and invites members to those meetings. In contrast, an old boys' network does not have formal members, it does not present itself as a network, and, most importantly, its informality is key to its functioning and power. Old boys' networks function implicitly as the norm for networks because only these networks are perceived as a powerful influence on individual careers and organizational strategy (Cross and Armstrong 2008).

Diversity networks are criticized because they would be easy tools for management to pay lip service to diversity and inclusion (O'Neil, Hopkins, and Sullivan 2011) and increase rather than decrease the isolation of minorities (Pini, Brown, and Ryan 2004). However, some diversity networks have an explicit agenda to change their organizations.

---

[1] In this chapter, we focus on in-company diversity networks only, and do not include cross-organizational networks that exceed the boundaries of the company such as professional or sector level networks.

These networks are more vocal about inequalities, discriminatory practices, and power relations. Other networks tend to focus exclusively on community building and career building for their members, and not so much on changing their organizations. The different aims of networks can be related to the relevance of who initiated the diversity network. Some women's networks in multinationals are initiated by management (Singh, Vinnicombe, and Kumra 2006), whereas other women's networks, ethnic minority, and LGBT networks tend to have a grassroots character and are supported by the company (Friedman and Holtom 2002; Githens and Aragon 2009). A more grassroots origin does not, however, guarantee that the networks take issue with power, inequality, and discrimination, but the networks that do take an activist stance are to be found among these networks. Networks initiated by management as diversity tools are not likely to address structural inequalities, as the benefits for employees and the benefits for the organization tend to be stressed (Singh, Vinnicombe, and Kumra 2006). And even networks that have grassroots origins often legitimize their existence by aligning with organizational effectiveness, appealing to the business case, and stressing the added value of diversity for organizational performance (Githens and Aragon 2009; Gremmen and Benschop 2011).

Participants

Some diversity networks welcome all organizational members who identify or sympathize with an employee group. Other networks restrict access to members of a specific identity category, or even to a subset, as is the case with higher echelon networks (for instance for women in higher management). Diversity networks are predominantly organized around a single social identity. Gender, ethnicity, and sexuality are reported as separate grounds for building networks among women (Bierema 2005; Singh, Vinnicombe, and Kumra 2006; Hersby, Ryan, and Jetten 2009; Coleman 2010; Durbin 2011; Gremmen and Benschop 2011), among ethnic minorities (Friedman, Kane, and Cornfield 1998; Friedman and Holtom 2002; Friedman and Craig 2004), and among LGBT employees (Wright et al. 2006; Githens and Aragon 2009; Colgan and McKearney 2012). There is very little scholarly work on age-related networks for younger or older employees that exist in practice. The available studies focus either on women's networks or on minority networks, without discussing the intersection of those marginalized identity categories. Studies on diversity networks from an intersectionality perspective are missing hitherto. Much remains to be explored about diversity networks, for instance, about additive inequalities such as the positions and experiences of ethnic minority women in networks and other combinations of unprivileged and privileged identities within diversity networks (Verloo 2013). Notably, in the old boys' networks, multiple privileged social identities—white, heterosexual, senior men—come together.

Networks that are meant as a diversity practice in organizations are typically organized internally within a single organization. This does not mean that there can be no communication between similar networks in other organizations, as they sometimes come together in groups or platforms to exchange experiences and strategies (Gremmen and Benschop 2011).

Format

Diversity networks can be seen as programmatic rather than single events. Most networks plan to be present in the organization for a prolonged period of time and have a calendar with multiple activities. Yet, whether members succeed in sustaining the network over a longer period of time depends on the continuous efforts of the people who run the network. Research about the compensation of network board members is lacking, but anecdotal evidence suggests that board members are largely volunteers (Singh, Vinnicombe, and Kumra 2006), who at best receive a small time compensation for their work.

Networks by their design organize different activities. Lectures and training address individuals by traditional one-way communication. Networks also stimulate interpersonal contacts between members, sometimes in the form of informal coaching. But network activities are typically characterized as interactive events; social gatherings, drinks, discussions about company issues and/or career issues, and conferences bring people together around common interests (Friedman and Holtom 2002). The timing of such activities is subject to debate: activities can be planned during work time or can take place after work in employees' spare time. The timing depends on cultural norms about work hours and is certainly a controversial topic in women's networks that are sensitive to work-life balance issues (Gremmen and Benschop 2013).

Overall, we find that diversity networks, as diversity tools, are relatively easy for organizations. The mere presence of the networks can help the organizations parade their diversity. Since these networks are often run voluntarily by employees, many tend to function rather separately from the organization (Donnellon and Langowitz 2009). As such, they render people from minority groups responsible for solving their own isolation and career difficulties. Networks that only focus on community building may meet the needs for social support, but fail to address deeply embedded inequalities in the organization (Gremmen and Benschop 2013). A large part of the diversity networks' activities do not require changes in the work routines and practices.

However, we do see the transformational potential of networks when they address inequalities and engage with daily work practices. Networks that focus on strategic change tend to function as a sparring partner for management and offer strategic advice in several areas. The literature points to several areas for strategic advice: from diversity issues such as creating an inclusive organization, more specific issues such as work-life arrangements or partner benefits, or business issues such as product innovation (Scully 2009; Gremmen and Benschop 2013).

The story of the 'LGBT and Allies Network' in Metropolitan Healthcare reported by Githens and Aragon (2009) is an example of a diversity network striving for organizational change. After fifteen years as an informal network, this network was invited by the diversity manager to become a formally recognized network and take part in the 'Diversity Council'. The group addressed the at times hostile climate towards LGBT workers by increasing awareness of LGBT issues. They collaborated with the women's network to institute domestic partner benefits and to facilitate diversity education sessions to improve the workplace environment.

Discussion and Conclusion

This chapter aimed to come to a better understanding of the transformative potential of three popular diversity management practices. These practices—diversity training, mentoring programmes, and diversity networks—have been critiqued for emphasizing the deficits of diverse employees instead of changing deeply rooted inequalities in organizations. From our review, we found that training, mentoring, and networking can denote many different things. It is as incorrect to dismiss any single of these interventions, as it is to praise them in general. We discussed these three diversity practices using the 3D-model.

Overall, we find that there is not one complete configuration of the 3D-model that generates transformative change. There are, however, specific choices concerning the dimensions of *content* and *format* that show stronger links to transformative potential, in combination with any set of *participants*. These recommended configurations can be found in Table 27.2.

We argue that the key to transformative change is the sub-dimension power perspective. A multidimensional power perspective is needed when choosing content of the diversity practice and when disseminating knowledge. An individual power perspective can help the individual participant to better cope with a problematic situation, but will not necessarily lead to participants challenging organizational inequality structures. Power absent content does not address inequalities in organizations and will hence not aim at organizational transformation. Only with a multidimensional power

Table 27.2 Recommended combinations of the 3D-model for diversity training, mentoring programmes, and diversity networks aiming at transformative change

Content		Participants		Format	
Focus	Power perspective	Target group	Affiliation	Frequency	Design
Gender equality	Absent or harmonious	Minority	Combination	Single event	Individual
Diversity	Individual	Majority	Internal	Repeated	Interpersonal
Inclusion	Multidimensional	Mixed	External	Programme	Interactive

perspective that acknowledges the interplay between structure and agency, can mentoring, networking, and training generate organizational change. For example, networks can address power issues at a strategic level in the organization through their strategic advisory role.

Regarding the subdimension of focus in content, the chosen focus (gender, diversity, or inclusion) will of course both affect and limit the kind of inequalities addressed. But every focus can have transformative potential as long as a multidimensional power perspective is used that can challenge structural discrimination and addresses conflicting interests. Diversity training that fosters awareness among dominant groups about their privileges is an example of the beginning of a transformation of power relations. A focus on gender equality does not necessarily mean that one only focuses on women since a multidimensional power perspective enables discussions on the intersection of gender with other inequalities.

The dimension of participants is the most varying dimension when aiming at organizational change. The choice of participants is often related to a specific targeted inequality, but that is not necessarily so. The target group can be the minority, the majority, or a mix of both. Sometimes it is better to limit the participation to the subordinate or minority groups. This will create a 'room of one's own' when discussing strategies for change and forming a pressure group. In other situations, a mix of participants will be preferred as this opens up dialogue between majority and minority representatives of the organization when discussing transformative actions and goals. This analysis has highlighted the need for more research on majority groups in diversity practices aiming at change, for example, all male participants in diversity training with a multidimensional power perspective aiming at critical reflection and action for change. Majority groups often, but not always, represent the norm of a category. Diversity practices building on reflective and critical perspectives involving participants representing the norm are scarce, and could be developed further. Our review of the literature suggests that the affiliation of the participants can also vary. The combination of internal and external participants is sometimes fruitful in mentoring programmes and management training. The external approach often leads to an exchange of experiences and learning from other organizations' diversity practices.

The format dimension consists of the subdimensions frequency and design. Single events and limited activities in frequency can work as a kick-off or an inspirational start for further discussion and reflection in the organization. Full programmes often offer a longer term commitment and more challenging format in diversity practices. Our analysis suggests that programmes are preferred when choosing frequency, if the intention is to not only put diversity on the agenda but also trigger actions for change. The same goes for design of the format where an interactive approach is preferred over individual or interpersonal approaches, as this will facilitate collective actions being taken involving groups of participants instead of isolated individual agents for change. The interactive design often includes a mix of knowledge input and collective reflections and assignments that helps participants to integrate new insights with awareness of the importance of transformative actions.

Theoretical Implications: Evaluative Remarks about the Model

In this chapter, we have used the 3D-model to take stock of the transformative potential of diversity practices. Most of the studies referred to have been possible to relate to the dimensions and subdimensions in the model. The core contribution of this model is its systematic way of assessing multiple diversity practices. Some of the combinations in the model have proved difficult to find in the academic literature even if they exist in organizational practice. Our use of the model has thus allowed us to uncover gaps in research and in practice. One gap pertains to the need for more research on majority groups in diversity practices aiming at change, for example, all male participants in diversity training with a multidimensional power perspective aiming at critical reflection and action for change. Another gap is research reporting on diversity networks that address power. As for practice, diversity practices building on reflective and critical perspectives involving majority participants representing the norm, for example, training in which majority participants unpack and challenge the implicit norms of the ideal worker, are scarce.

A second contribution is that the model can serve as an academically informed qualitative assessment tool for practitioners. Practitioners can use the model to make more informed choices when designing diversity practices. The model can also enable a better understanding of consequences, limitations, and possibilities when formulating a diversity practice.

A third important contribution is the core attention to power. This has major implications for diversity practice designs since engaging with power is absolutely necessary for transformational change, even though it is seen as high in scary radicalism. The implication is that vested interests in the status quo are at stake and that decision makers in organizations are basically asked to give up their privileges and change their views on organizational practices. In contrast, the legitimacy of diversity practices as contributing to improved performance taps into a managerial discourse and may be an easier way to propagate diversity practices. To address multidimensionality of power requires that structures of privilege and disadvantage are exposed, reflected upon, and changed. This long-term thorny endeavour may, however, not be popular among diversity practitioners and other change agents.

This brings us to some final reflections on the future challenges for research and practice on diversity practices. One such challenge concerns the way that diversity champions can present the need for diversity practices to address multidimensional power to decision makers. Another core challenge is the attention on intersectionality in diversity practices. Most diversity practices tend to focus on single identities, missing the complexities of multiple identities and the simultaneity of disadvantage and privilege (Boogaard and Roggeband 2010). To design diversity practices that can address multiple identities requires a close collaboration between diversity scholars and diversity practitioners. This collaboration helps to combine state-of-the-art theoretical insights with local knowledge to address the simultaneity of disadvantage and privilege at work. The design of diversity practices that do justice to these complexities is a true challenge to the field.

References

Acker, J. (2006). Inequality regimes: Gender, class, and race in organizations. *Gender & Society*, 20: 441.
Amundsdotter, E. (2010). *Att framkalla och förändra ordningen: aktionsorienterad genusforskning för jämställda organisationer*. Stockholm: Gestalthusets Förlag.
Anand, R. and Winters, M.-F. (2008). A retrospective view of corporate diversity training from 1964 to the present. *Academy of Management Learning & Education*, 7: 356–72.
Avotie, L. (2008). *Mentorprogram i jämställdhetens tjänst: att hjälpa eller stjälpa*. Uppsala: Department of Business Studies, Uppsala University.
Bacchi, C. and Eveline, J. (2009). Gender mainstreaming or diversity mainstreaming? The politics of 'doing'. *NORA—Nordic Journal of Feminist and Gender Research*, 17: 2–17.
Baugh, S. G. and Fagenson-Eland, E. A. (2007). Formal mentoring programs. In B. R. Ragins and K. E. Kram (eds.), *The Handbook of Mentoring at Work: Theory, Research, and Practice*. London: Sage, 249–71.
Baytos, L. M. (1995). *Designing & Implementing Successful Diversity Programs*. Englewood Cliffs, NJ: Prentice Hall.
Benschop, Y. and Verloo, M. (2006). 'Sisyphus' sisters: can gender mainstreaming escape the genderedness of organizations? *Journal of Gender Studies*, 15: 19–33.
Benschop, Y. and Verloo, M. (2011). Policy, practice and performance: Gender change in organizations In D. Knights, E. Jeanes, and P. Yancey-Martin (eds.), *The Sage Handbook of Gender, Work and Organization*. London: Sage.
Bezrukova, K., Jehn, K. A., and Spell, C. S. (2012). Reviewing diversity training: where we have been and where we should go. *Academy of Management Learning & Education*, 11: 207–27.
Bierema, L. L. (2005). Women's networks: a career development intervention or impediment? *Human Resource Development International*, 8: 207–24.
Blake-Beard, S. D. (2001). Taking a hard look at formal mentoring programs: a consideration of potential challenges facing women. *Journal of Management Development*, 20: 331–45.
Boogaard, B. and Roggeband, C. (2010). Paradoxes of intersectionality: theorizing inequality in the Dutch police force through structure and agency. *Organization*, 17(1): 53–75.
Bowman, S. R., Kite, M. E., Branscombe, N. R., and Williams, S. (1999). Developmental relationships of Black Americans in the academy. In A. J. Murrell, F. J. Crosby, and R. J. Ely (eds.), *Mentoring Dilemmas: Developmental Relationships within Multicultural Organizations*. Mahwah, NJ: Lawrence Erlbaum, 21–46.
Coleman, M. (2010). Women-only (homophilous) networks supporting women leaders in education. *Journal of Educational Administration*, 48: 769–81.
Colgan, F. and McKearney, A. (2012). Visibility and voice in organisations: lesbian, gay, bisexual and transgendered employee networks. *Equality, Diversity and Inclusion: An International Journal*, 31: 359–78.
Colley, H. (2001). Righting rewritings of the myth of mentor: a critical perspective on career guidance mentoring. *British Journal of Guidance and Counselling*, 29: 177–97.

Cross, C. and Armstrong, C. (2008). Understanding the role of networks in collective learning processes: the experiences of women. *Advances in Developing Human Resources*, 10: 600–13.

Darwin, A. (2000). Critical reflections on mentoring in work settings. *Adult Education Quarterly*, 50: 197–211.

De Vries, J. (2010). *A Realistic Agenda? Women Only Programs as Strategic Interventions for Building Gender Equitable Workplaces*. Perth: University of Western Australia.

De Vries, J., Webb, C., and Eveline, J. (2006). Mentoring for gender equality and organisational change. *Employee Relations*, 28: 573–87.

Donnellon, A. and Langowitz, N. (2009). Leveraging women's networks for strategic value. *Strategy & Leadership*, 37: 29–36.

Durbin, S. (2011). Creating knowledge through networks: a gender perspective. *Gender, Work and Organization*, 18: 90–112.

Eldridge, N. S. (1990). *Mentoring from a Self-in-Relation Perspective*. Paper presented at the Paper presented at the Annual Convention of the American Psychological Association.

Eliasson, M., Berggren, H., and Bondestam, F. (2000). Mentor programmes: a shortcut for women's academic careers? *Higher Education in Europe*, 25: 173–9.

Ely, R. J. and Meyerson, D. E. (2000a). Advancing gender equity in organizations: the challenge and importance of maintaining a gender narrative. *Organization*, 7: 589–608.

Ely, R. J. and Meyerson, D. E. (2000b). Theories of gender in organizations: a new approach to organizational analysis and change. *Research in Organizational Behavior*, 22: 103–52.

Ensher, E. A., Thomas, C., and Murphy, S. E. (2001). Comparison of traditional, step-ahead, and peer mentoring on protégés' support, satisfaction, and perceptions of career success: a social exchange perspective. *Journal of Business and Psychology*, 15: 419–38.

Eveline, J. (2004). *Ivory Basement Leadership: Power and Invisibility in the Changing University*. Perth: University of Western Australia Press.

Ferdman, B. M. and Brody, S. E. (1996). Models of diversity training. *Handbook of Intercultural Training*, 2: 282–303.

Foldy, E. G. (2002). Managing diversity: identity and power in organizations. In I. Aaltio and A. J. Mills (eds.), *Gender, Identity and the Culture of Organizations*. London: Routledge, 99–112.

Friedman, R., Kane, M., and Cornfield, D. B. (1998). Social support and career optimism: examining the effectiveness of network groups among black managers. *Human Relations*, 51: 1155–77.

Friedman, R. A. and Craig, K. M. (2004). Predicting joining and participating in minority employee network groups. *Industrial Relations: A Journal of Economy and Society*, 43: 793–816.

Friedman, R. A. and Holtom, B. (2002). The effects of network groups on minority employee turnover intentions. *Human Resource Management*, 41: 405–21.

Galen, M. and Palmer, A. (1993). White, male, and worried. *Business Week*, 31 January, 50–5.

Gilbert, L. A. and Rossman, K. M. (1992). Gender and the mentoring process for women: implications for professional development. *Professional Psychology: Research and Practice*, 23: 233.

Giscombe, K. (2007). Advancing women through the glass ceiling with formal mentoring. In B. R. Ragins and K. E. Kram (eds.), *The Handbook of Mentoring at Work: Theory, Research, and Practice*. London: Sage, 549–71.

Githens, R. P. and Aragon, S. R. (2009). LGBT employee groups: goals and organizational structures. *Advances in Developing Human Resources*, 11: 121–35.

Gremmen, I. and Benschop, Y. (2011). Negotiating ambivalence: the leadership of professional women's networks. In P. H. Werhane and M. Painter-Morland (eds.), *Leadership, Gender, and Organization*. New York: Springer, 169–83.

Gremmen, I. and Benschop, Y. (2013). Vrouwennetwerken als diversiteitsinstrument in organisaties. *Tijdschrift voor HRM*, 16(3): 32–54.

Halford, S. and Leonard, P. (2001). *Gender, Power and Organisations*. Basingstoke: Palgrave Macmillan.

Hansman, C. A. (1998). Mentoring and women's career development. *New Directions for Adult and Continuing Education*, 1998: 63–71.

Harris, F. and Smith, J. C. (1999). Centrity and the mentoring experience in academia: an Africentric mentoring paradigm. *The Western Journal of Black Studies*, 23: 229–35.

Hersby, M. D., Ryan, M. K., and Jetten, J. (2009). Getting together to get ahead: the impact of social structure on women's networking. *British Journal of Management*, 20: 415–30.

Holgersson, C. and Höök, P. (1997). Chefsrekrytering och ledarutveckling. In E. Sundin and A. Nyberg (eds.), *Ledare, makt och kön* (Vol. 135). Stockholm: SOU.

Holvino, E., Ferdman, B. M., and Merrill-Sands, D. (2004). Creating and sustaining diversity and inclusion in organizations: strategies and approaches. In M. Stockdale and F. J. Crosby (eds.), *The Psychology and Management of Workplace Diversity*. Malden, MA: Blackwell Publishing.

Höök, P. (2001). *Stridspiloter i vida kjolar: om ledarutveckling och jämställdhet*. Stockholm: Stockholm School of Economics.

Jewson, N. and Mason, D. (1986). The theory and practice of equal opportunities policies: liberal and radical approaches. *The Sociological Review*, 34: 307–34.

Johnson-Bailey, J. and Cervero, R. M. (2004). Mentoring in black and white: the intricacies of cross-cultural mentoring. *Mentoring & Tutoring: Partnership in Learning*, 12: 7–21.

Katz, J. H. (1978). *White Awareness: Anti-Racism Training*. Norman: University of Oklahoma Press.

Kirkland, S. and Regan, A. (1997). Organizational racial diversity training. In C. E. Thompson and R. T. Carter (eds.), *Racial Identity Theory: Applications to Individual, Group, and Organizational Interventions*. Mahwah, NJ: Lawrence Erlbaum, 159–75.

Kirton, G. and Greene, A. M. (2010). *The Dynamics of Managing Diversity: A Critical Approach*. Oxford: Elsevier Butterworth-Heinemann.

Konrad, A. M., Prasad, P., and Pringle, J. K. (2006). *Handbook of Workplace Diversity*. London: Sage.

Kram, K. E. (1983). Phases of the mentor relationship. *Academy of Management Journal*, 26: 608–25.

Linghag, S. (2009). *Från medarbetare till chef: Kön och makt i chefsförsörjning och karriär*. Stockholm: KTH.

Litvin, D. R. (2002). The business case for diversity and the 'Iron Cage'. In B. Czarniawska and H. Hopfl (eds.), *Casting the Other: The Production and Maintenance of Inequalities in Work Organizations*. London: Routledge, 180–98..

Lorbiecki, A. and Jack, G. (2000). Critical turns in the evolution of diversity management. *British Journal of Management*, 11: S17-S31.

McKeen, C. and Bujaki, M. (2007). Gender and mentoring. In B. R. Ragins and K. E. Kram (eds.), *The Handbook of Mentoring at Work: Theory, Research, and Practice*. London: Sage, 197–222.

Meyerson, D. E. and Kolb, D. M. (2000). Moving out of the 'armchair': Developing a framework to bridge the gap between feminist theory and practice. *Organization*, 7: 553–71.

Milliken, F. J. and Martins, L. L. (1996). Searching for common threads: understanding the multiple effects of diversity in organizational groups. *Academy of Management Review*, 21(2): 402–33.

O'Neil, D. A., Hopkins, M. M., and Sullivan, S. E. (2011). Do women's networks help advance women's careers? Differences in perceptions of female workers and top leadership. *Career Development International*, 16: 733–54.

Ortlieb, R. and Sieben, B. (2013). Diversity strategies and business logic: why do companies employ ethnic minorities? *Group & Organization Management*, 38: 480–511.

Paige, R. M. and Martin, J. N. (1996). Ethics in intercultural training. In D. Landis, J. Bennett, and M. Bennett (eds.), *Handbook of Intercultural Training*. Thousand Oaks, CA: Sage, 35–59.

Paluck, E. L. (2006). Diversity training and intergroup contact: a call to action research. *Journal of Social Issues*, 62: 577–95.

Pini, B., Brown, K., and Ryan, C. (2004). Women-only networks as a strategy for change? A case study from local government. *Women in Management Review*, 19: 286–92.

Prime, J. and Moss-Racusin, C. A. (2009). *Engaging Men in Gender Initiatives: What Change Agents Need to Know*. New York: Catalyst.

Ragins, B. R. (1997). Diversified mentoring relationships in organizations: a power perspective. *Academy of Management Review*, 22: 482–521.

Ragins, B. R. (2002). Understanding diversified mentoring relationships: definitions, challenges, and strategies. In D. Clutterbuck and B. R. Ragins (eds.), *Mentoring and Diversity: An International Perspective*. Oxford: Butterworth Heinemann, 23–53.

Ragins, B. R. and Cotton, J. L. (1999). Mentor functions and outcomes: a comparison of men and women in formal and informal mentoring relationships. *Journal of Applied Psychology*, 84: 529.

Ragins, B. R. and Kram, K. E. (2007). The roots and meaning of mentoring. In B. R. Ragins and K. E. Kram (eds.), *The Handbook of Mentoring at Work: Theory, Research, and Practice*. Thousand Oaks, CA: Sage, 3–15.

Roberson, L., Kulik, C. T., and Pepper, M. B. (2003). Using needs assessment to resolve controversies in diversity training design. *Group & Organization Management*, 28: 148–74.

Romani, L., Höök, P., and Holgersson, C. (2011). Exploring the diversity management patchwork and its implications for management. paper presented at the European Group for Organizational Studies (EGOS), Gothenburg, Sweden, 6–9 July.

Scully, M. A. (2009). A rainbow coalition or separate wavelengths? Negotiations among employee network groups. *Negotiation and Conflict Management Research*, 2: 74–91.

Shore, L. M., Randel, A. E., Chung, B. G., Dean, M. A., Ehrhart, K. H., and Singh, G. (2011). Inclusion and diversity in work groups: a review and model for future research. *Journal of Management*, 37: 1262–89.

Sinclair, A. (2000). Teaching managers about masculinities: are you kidding? *Management Learning*, 31: 83–101.

Singh, V., Vinnicombe, S., and Kumra, S. (2006). Women in formal corporate networks: an organisational citizenship perspective. *Women in Management Review*, 21: 458–82.

Thomas, D. A. (2001). The truth about mentoring minorities. *Harvard Business Review*, 74: 99–105.

Thomas, D. A. and Ely, R. J. (1996). Making differences matter. *Harvard Business Review*, 74: 79–90.

Verloo, M. (2013). Intersectional and cross-movement politics and policies: reflections on current practices and debates. *Signs*, 38: 893–915.

Wahl, A. (1995). *Men's Perceptions of Women and Management*. Stockholm: Fritzes.
Wahl, A. (2003). 'Sammanfattande kommentarer' (Concluding comments). In *Mansdominans i förändring. Om ledningsgrupper och styrelser*. Statliga Offentliga Utredningar 2003:16. Stockholm: Fritzes, 245–66.
Wahl, A., Holgersson, C., Höök, P., and Linghag, S. (2011). *Det ordnar sig: Teorier om organisation och kön* (2nd edn). Lund: Studentlitteratur.
Wahl, A. and Höök, P. (2007). 'Changes in working with gender equality in management in Sweden. *Equal Opportunities International*, 26: 435–48.
Wright, T., Colgan, F., Creegany, C., and McKearney, A. (2006). Lesbian, gay and bisexual workers: equality, diversity and inclusion in the workplace. *Equal Opportunities International*, 25: 465–70.
Yang, Y. and Konrad, A. M. (2011). Understanding diversity management practices: implications of institutional theory and resource-based theory. *Group & Organization Management*, 36: 6–38.
Zanoni, P. and Janssens, M. (2007). Minority employees engaging with (diversity) management: an analysis of control, agency, and micro emancipation. *Journal of Management Studies*, 44: 1371–97.
Zanoni, P., Janssens, M., Benschop, Y., and Nkomo, S. (2010). Unpacking diversity, grasping inequality: rethinking difference through critical perspectives. *Organization*, 17: 9–29.

CHAPTER 28

FROM HERE TO THERE AND BACK AGAIN

Transnational Perspectives on Diversity in Organizations

BANU ÖZKAZANÇ-PAN AND MARTA B. CALÁS

THE idea of diversity in the workplace and in organizations can be commonly traced back to the *Workforce 2000* report (Johnston and Packer 1987), a research project funded by the US Department of Labor in the mid-1980s. Conventional scholarly citations to this work have focused mostly on demographic changes—race and ethnicity in particular—that were assumed to have taken place in the US workforce by the end of the twentieth century and thereafter, and on addressing how organizations would have to cope with such changes. However, some scholars also noted that this report was produced at a particular moment in US history; a period during which there were debates over existing legal mandates and government policies, such as equal opportunities and affirmative action, aimed at remedying systematic workforce inequalities and discrimination, and to which diversity management might then become a substitute. That is, *diversity* and *diversity management* appeared as concepts and tools that could replace the US's legal rulings to inclusion and equality arising from the women's rights and civil rights movements of the 1960s (e.g. Kelly and Dobbin 1998). Recent literature has noted as well that *diversity management* facilitated the neoliberal political ideologies of US administrations promoting deregulation, privatization, and a concomitant 'flexible' workforce (e.g. Holvino and Kamp 2009).

Altogether, while appearing to be a depoliticized and benign managerial approach, the heritage of US *diversity management* is specific to both the social and political contexts of its time and place, and has not gone without critique (e.g. Litvin 1997, 2006; Lorbiecki and Jack 2000; Prasad, Mills, Elmes, and Prasad 1997). Lately, even the assumption that notions of *diversity in the workplace* originated in this report has been historically reassessed by Nkomo and Hoobler (2014), who note the racist ideologies reinforcing US management practices and writings since the late 1800s.

Despite these critiques, there is still little attention given to the fact that the *Workforce 2000* report was not just about demographic changes but also about the structural economic conditions of the US in relation to other nations at the time (e.g. regarding trade). From the start this report outlined the integration of world economies and suggested other nations would emerge as challengers to US economic dominance, a proposition that was conceived as a potential national threat in the political climate of the late 1980s. In this context, the report, coupled with the prevailing government priorities of the time, could be read as promoting diversity as competitive advantage for the US; that is, the changing demographic trends in the US workforce furthering a form of nationalism through which business and economic competitiveness would meet those global challenges (Calás and Smircich 1993).

Since then much has happened. The notions of *diversity and diversity management* that emerged and took root in the US have travelled, guiding organization and management practitioners and scholars the world over to focus on demographic categorizations when examining relationships between workers' activities and organizational outcomes. Critiques notwithstanding, in principle these ideas have had a successful *global career* by addressing explicitly whether and how *diversity* could differentiate between individuals, differentiate between or within groups, and within or between organizations, and how such differences can enhance organizational performance or somehow limit productive workplace behaviour (e.g. Nishii and Özbilgin 2007). More importantly, however, having left the domestic US setting, these original ideas have also spawned a variety of conceptual modalities beyond simple demographics regarding diversity in organizations (e.g. Boxenbaum 2006; Calás, Holgersson, and Smircich 2009).

Meanwhile, the concurrent expansion of contemporary organizational forms (e.g. multinational and transnational) under conditions of globalization and the acceleration of migratory populations strongly suggests that today the nation-state has gradually lost its privileged position as a dominant form of identification for both organizations and people. Thus, the point of articulation for our observations in this chapter as *transnational perspectives* on diversity in organizations rests on the intersections of these two events: the production and diffusion of diversity and diversity management as scholarly literature beyond the original US perspectives, and the concurrent decentring of the nation-state as identity marker for organizations and many populations the world over (e.g. Jack and Lorbiecki 2007; Calás and Smircich 2011).

Embedded in these dynamics, *the idea of diversity* in the scholarly context of management and organization studies has become an unwieldy subject. The field has developed such a multiplicity of definitions and conceptualizations that 'diversity' has become in some senses *meaningless* (Konrad 2003). Given this plethora of definitions and concepts several scholars have tried to impose some kind of order. For instance, Nkomo and Stewart (2006) suggested a *useful* but very general definition, where diversity is 'a mixture of people with different group identities within the same social system'. Guided by this definition, in their view the field of diversity research comprises various schools of thought including social identity theory, demography, research on racioethnicity and gender, and critical and postmodern contributions. At about the same time, Prasad, Pringle, and Konrad (2006) organized diversity research around four *assumptions* including epistemological stance (i.e. positivist or non-positivist); degree of awareness of power relations between identity groups; level of analysis (i.e. individual, interpersonal, or structural); and concept of identity (i.e. fixed or fluid).

Considering these conceptual and definitional complexities and limits, it may seem that the task here of putting a frame around what constitutes 'the transnational diversity in organizations literature' would resemble Borges's Chinese encyclopedia, as quoted by Foucault (1973) where '"animals are divided into (a) belonging to the Emperor, (b) embalmed,... (e) sirens, (f) fabulous,... (h) included in the present classification, (i) frenzied... (m) having just broken the water pitcher, (n) that from a long way off look like flies"' (Foucault 1973: xv—our abbreviations)[1]. But, as Foucault also observes, 'In the wonderment of this taxonomy [...] the thing that, by means of the fable, is demonstrated as the exotic charm of another system of thought, is the limitation of our own, the stark impossibility of thinking *that*' (Foucault 1973: xv).

Thus, with this caveat in mind, in the following pages we have cautiously drawn some boundaries as a taxonomy defining a very imprecise space—the contours of the contemporary transnational diversity in organizations scholarly literature—with the hope that it will make sense at least within our own current system of thought. As such, this is not intended to be an exhaustive review of what may now have become an incommensurable literature (see, for instance, Özbilgin et al. 2012). Rather, our aim is to delineate a temporary holding space for understanding this shifting territory while exploring a few relevant examples. We also acknowledge that this framing stems from our work and life space—being located in the US—as well as from our membership in communities of critical management scholars inside and outside the US, and from our own experiences as 'naturalized' US citizens, each of us having been born elsewhere in 'the periphery'. It is from this mutable 'here' that we examine the formation and transformation of *the subject of transnational diversity in organizations*, starting from the 'original' as it travelled beyond the US. As we will discuss, this focus on the formation and transformation of *the subject* facilitates understanding the ontological shifts supporting our taxonomical exercise. At the end, we return to Borges's fable to reflect on what are perhaps the most fundamental limitations to exercises of this nature.

---

[1] Foucault cites this example as a heterotopia 'which combine and juxtapose many spaces in one site, creating an intensification of knowledge' (Topinka (2010: 70); that is, making strange the familiar in such a way that one is moved to reflect on the foundations of what has become conventional knowledge—in this case the emphasis on a logic of categorization in Western knowledge.

Framing the Subject of Transnational Diversity in Organizations

We begin by looking at the theoretical background, focusing on identity and demographic categorizations, that is the basis of *the subject* in US scholarly 'diversity in organization' literature. We use this background as a point of reference for better understanding the fundamental transformations of this subject as the diversity literature has spread to other destinations. As we consider these other destinations, the first type of works we examine took their cues directly from the US literature, rooting their arguments within these same notions of identity and demography as if it were a universal subject. While some scholars acknowledged difficulties when applying these ideas to other settings and engaged in culturalist adaptations, most left the original subject unexamined (Adeleye 2011). In our view, these modes of diffusion, which we label *internationalizing diversity*, were and continue to be a transnational event in their own right. In fact, sometimes the original US notions have also become 'others' upon arrival at various destinations. That is, even when following conventional US conceptualizations as a starting point, at times enough epistemological translation and re-assembling have taken place to make the 'original' conceptualizations unrecognizable.

Yet, at present, we can observe at least three additional modes of diffusion within the transnational conceptual space, the first being a mode of *provincializing diversity*. Functioning both as a critique of the subject in conventional US literature and offering an alternative, this mode accounts for the local conditions of its destination. Literatures within this mode make visible the fundamental diversity of the idea of diversity, dislodging the notion of a universal subject from any conceptualization. The next mode, *the simultaneity of diversity*, has acquired a transnational tone while navigating the conceptual space of intersectionality derived from feminist perspectives (e.g. Holvino 2010). In this case, the focus is not on who or what is 'diverse' but on how 'diversity' becomes and on how such becoming functions in any particular place and time. Here, identity categories dissolve by acquiring fluidity and multiplicity, and sometimes become a point of interrogation for all categories of identification. The last mode of diffusion, *the formation of mobile subjectivities*, differs from the other two, however, in that its stance is beyond context. It is first and foremost a request for observing a balancing act, the phenomena of mobility and transnationalism, as a contemporary form of existence and experiences for various populations the world over. The focus of this mode is thus the processes recasting subjectivities as people and organizations become ontologically mobile entities.

At the end we discuss the incommensurability (un)defining the theoretical contours we have traced while we examined these modalities of diffusion. In fact, we present their different contributions independently from each other while also suggesting that there is value in maintaining ontological separation. As we see it, to represent the people in the world in which we all live today we must be able to keep in view a repertoire of very different ontological perspectives on diversity. More importantly, to do justice to this world now we must be able to articulate a post-identitarian transnational understanding (e.g. Calás, Ou, and Smircich 2013).

The Point of Inception in the US: Identity and Demography

The dominant modality from which the study of diversity in organizations emerged and still relies mostly uncritically in the US, social psychology research, is worth considering (see, for instance, Kulik and Bainbridge's 2006 review). This serves as a starting point for understanding its internationalization as well as the ontological limitations it poses for developing transnational perspectives on diversity. In this literature, the concept of identity derives from the 'rational, cognitive individual self' forwarded by Western liberal humanist philosophies and, in particular, by Anglo-American versions of psychology supported by these philosophies. Social psychology expands upon this individualized concept of the self by acknowledging the *social* aspects of identity formation, such that an individual arrives at a notion of her/himself through an exchange with those around her/him (Hogg, Terry, and White 1995; Hogg 2006). The exchange is based on dimensions of difference—for instance, gender, race, ethnicity, class, and so forth—salient for the context and encounter in question but, paradoxically, emphasizes 'identity' as differentiation, separation, and individualization. Less visibly, behind these assumptions there is also a normative 'ideal self', which presupposes an individual associated with the values of Western modernization.

The diversity research literature borrows heavily from various theoretical perspectives in social psychology scholarship, in particular *social identity theory* and *relational demography*. In both of these perspectives, the subject—that is, one's notion of self—is born out of an exchange with another; however, the focus of the research is not on the exchange itself but on the identity differentiation that occurs as a result of it. Concurrently, demographic categories of identification exist a priori and are considered as stable over time and place. This subject of social psychology poses particular limitations for transnational perspectives on diversity when it appears as a complete national identity (e.g. American, Chinese) anywhere in the world without consideration of how social relations may (re)produce different selves and identities across time and space (Triandis, 1995, 2003; Louie 2004). In much of these literatures national identities function as boundaries between a particular 'us' and a generalized 'other' and signal their differentiation.

To illustrate these arguments, below we discuss two examples, one from social identity theory and another from relational demography, which apply these theories to international settings. We believe these two examples from the international management literature clarify in the next subsection how *diversity in organizations* scholarship tends to function under such theories when it crosses national boundaries.

An application of these notions in international management is exemplified by Toh and DeNisi (2007), who developed a theoretical model addressing how the potential success or failure of expatriate managers overseas may be related to whether and how host country national (HCN) employees contribute to the expatriate's socialization in the host country. Drawing on social identity theory, the paper focuses on the role of HCNs extra-role organizational citizenship behaviour in determining the social adjustment of expatriate managers. Since HCNs may display or withhold socializing behaviours that affect the adjustment of the expatriate, it is important that the expatriate manager is not identified as in the out-group. In this case, the salience of different national identities results in group boundaries.

The major points we want to illustrate with this example are the assumptions made about the subject and the unreflective stance of the article regarding the theory it deploys (i.e. social identity theory). This theory may represent the expatriate's behaviour and expectations (probably a Western individual 'self') but may have no resonance with the worldview of the (unidentified) HCNs. Thus, to assume that in their encounters the potential behaviours towards one another can be explained by this one theory is akin to assuming that the notion of humanity—that is, the subject—is universal.

Meanwhile, relational demography draws from social identity theory but the argument about identity formation in relationships is more pointed: demographic similarities evoke attraction between demographically similar individuals, accentuating the positive attributes of each other and leading to positive social identity and self-esteem. Meanwhile, dissimilar individuals tend to view and treat each other less favourably, impacting their identities negatively. As such, demography is a way to understand social relationships between an individual and another as exemplified in dyadic relationships. In these relationships the parties engage in comparing their demographic attributes and social dynamics ensue from there.

In an example of how these notions have travelled to the international management literature, Tsui and Farh (1997) compared and contrasted the Chinese idea of guanxi, defined as the existence of direct particularistic ties between two or more individuals, with the idea of relational demography used by US scholars as discussed above. With these comparisons they aimed to develop an integrative framework comprising guanxi and relational demography. They explicitly based their argument on the presupposition that the idea of demography may be a universal concept with relevance for understanding work behaviour in different cultural settings insofar as individuals in any social cultural context may be characterized by demographic categories. This presupposition extended notions of relational demography to the Chinese context by suggesting that relationships between people based on a common background are also captured by the idea of guanxi. Nonetheless, the authors also presented several culturalist caveats to these presuppositions. They highlighted the possibility of very different social dynamics underlying relational demography and guanxi by recognizing differences in the notion of the subject in each of them: Chinese experiencing themselves as interdependent with the surrounding social context; and this self in relationship to others becoming the focal individual experience, while—in sharp contrast—the Western view, seeing each human being as an independent, self-contained, autonomous entity, who behaves primarily as a consequence of his/her internal attributes.

Not surprisingly, empirical data collected in Chinese contexts showed little overlap between the relational attributes of importance for guanxi and for relational demography suggesting that different processes influenced interpersonal and work outcomes under each of these notions. However, the authors continued to insist in integrating these apparently incommensurable conceptualizations. They argued that modern Chinese tend to assimilate Western values, and individual differences in modernity may fundamentally alter the behavioural pattern of contemporary Chinese. They argued further that an integrative framework may have relevance for cross-cultural research because particularistic ties—such as guanxi—may be a universal phenomenon and also that all individuals in any culture could be described using a set of demographic and background factors.

We have used this article to illustrate how relational demography is internationalized, and also as an example, in contrast to the earlier HCNs example (Toh and DeNisi 2007), of a different way to internationalize the subject in question. While the HCNs article advanced explanations of social identity theory as applicable to anyone, anywhere (i.e. the formation of a universal subject), the Tsui and Farh (1997) article is clear in acknowledging the possible formation of a different kind of subject outside of the premises of relational demography. However, the resolution of the argument continues to maintain the primacy of the Western notion of the subject insofar as it expects the assimilation of 'modern Chinese' into Western values, and, in fact, uses Western culturalist explanations to maintain a range of possibilities within this same system of thought. In this way the argument retrofits relational demography rather than promoting guanxi as a dominant explanation for future Chinese behaviours and contingent work outcomes. At the end, the paper asks for cross-cultural research to ascertain the possibility that both particularistic ties (present in guanxi) and demographics (present in relational demography) are universal processes of identification beyond their cultural contexts. But what the paper reiterates with this gesture is the impossibility of thinking beyond the existence of *universal processes of subject formation*; a mode of thinking dominating the US literature.

In short, the self of this 'identity and demography' literature is a subject position derived by 'casting the Other' through multiple forms of differentiation based on Western social psychology of a positivist persuasion, evidently deemed as a superior form of knowledge (see Tsui et al. 2004) and rooted within the same instrumental organizational aims of managing those deemed different (Czarniawska and Höpfl 2002). As discussed in the examples above, when this self travels to other parts of the world it disguises possible subject formation processes relevant for the context and encounters in question. That is, the self of social psychology becomes the representational gaze for understanding and predicting the behaviours of different people in the world and in organizations as if these processes were essential human universals. In the next section we illustrate how the assumptions behind these theories have travelled under the guise of diversity in organizations.

Internationalizing Diversity

The diffusion of conventional premises (what some address as 'the mainstream') from US diversity in organizations research to other world locations took place during the mid-1990s. Often this literature was developed by authors from the US engaged in international research, sometimes in partnership with local researchers, but also developed as a local or single context research outside the US, and as a comparative literature. These literatures share a common link to the domestic US diversity literature in that more often than not they have adopted uncritically the 'individual' of liberal humanism, its values, and attitudes as its core concept of the subject. Therefore, the categories to examine behaviours whether in single context or comparative modalities tend to be the same. Notwithstanding the Anglo-American modernity from which such notions originated, *diversity* in this literature has been framed as a form of identitarianism whereby people are conceptualized as individuals framed a priori through particular demographic categories regardless of context. As discussed above, this literature is mostly based on socio-psychological constructs and constituted through more or less fixed demographic categories, such as gender, race, class, and so forth, representing an idealized conception of this individual (and its other). Nonetheless, there have also been some innovations in this regard.

Pelled and Xin (2000) offer a relevant example of a conventional comparative study based on relational demography. The issue in question is whether demographic similarities affect relationships between supervisors and subordinates in the same way in two different regions—the US and Mexico—and whether differences and similarities in these two regions may affect the transfer of diversity management programmes across the American–Mexican border. Starting from the premise that demographic similarity between supervisors and subordinates shapes supervisor-subordinate relationship quality in US settings, the study compares these effects between a US and Mexican production facility owned by the same company. Results indicate that demographic similarity influences the quality of relationships between supervisors and subordinates in both locations but with differences in the patterns of these relationships across age and gender (e.g. a reversal in the importance of these demographics in each location). Despite stating that the findings were unexpected, the study holds relational demography intact as capable of demonstrating that the same relational processes occur in both contexts instead of considering the possibility that difference in patterns may also have indicated different processes. Study limitations are reduced mostly to data quality and measurements with the authors reiterating the value of these findings for diversity management.

But there are also some examples in these literatures that question aspects of social-psychological approaches to diversity. Using relational demography, Choi's (2007) single context study in Korea investigated the effect of individual-level dissimilarities as well as of group-level membership heterogeneity (group diversity) on creative behaviour of individual employees. The study emphasizes the need for a multi-level approach to the study of organizational demography, including power relations in diverse groups, something unusual in most other studies of this type. Importantly, at the end the article recognizes the limits of organizational demography in cultures outside the Anglo-American context. Specifically, the author notes that the relational meaning of any demographic characteristic and the social implications of particular demographic categories can be related to national, cultural, and temporal contexts and can differ under these circumstances. Of particular relevance in this example is the emphasis on different meanings for what otherwise would appear, according to these theories, as universal categories in subject formation. Taking recourse to humans as meaning-makers is also conceding to the social construction of subjectivity, which would be anathema to the ontologically essentialist premises supporting the concept of the subject in social psychology.

Fixing the subject of diversity in this manner despite the apparent contradictions of its 'travels'—i.e. promoting diversity in a universalizing mode while obviating that the context and conceptual space from which the notion emerged was very local—has allowed the US-based perspectives to become a practical toolkit for addressing (i.e. managing) differences in organizations and institutions around the world. As noticed by some, the 'management diversity industry' has become global (e.g. Sayers 2008). Pervaded by instrumental rationality as a human resources management (HRM) task, these perspectives have spread pragmatically while conceptually they offer little opportunity for understanding the contradictions of the subject they claim to represent (e.g. D'Netto and Sohal 1999; Scroggins and Benson 2010). In transferring US-based diversity programmes, such as those in multinationals, to various destinations, there is some recognition of local issues and the need to adapt. However, these concerns are associated with organizational practices for 'knowledge transfer' and the desirable management outcomes—i.e. 'the business case'—that should emerge from them, and not with difficulties related to how the subject of diversity is conceptualized (e.g. Süß and Kleiner 2007; Cooke and Saini 2010; Jabbour et al. 2011; Hirt and Bešić 2013). The next section, however, provides different analyses and responses to these issues, as well as new ones that emerge from them.

Provincializing Diversity

The literature in this section, some of which dates from as early as the mid-1990s (e.g. Human (1996) regarding South Africa), represents a fundamental shift in the notions of the subject as represented above. In principle it is a critique of the US diversity scholarly literature and its inability to recognize that context matters, not simply in terms of diversity categories (e.g. Moore 2014), but also that *diversity* is a process of subject formation. That is, 'diversity' is not something that exists a priori because people belong or are ascribed one demographic category or another, no matter how context specific such categories might be. Rather, 'diversity' is a socially constructed label that emerged in a particular place and time to depoliticize for the most part—e.g. transform into an organizational practice—difficult social relations that anteceded such a label in the workplace and elsewhere. The theoretical arguments discussed above were the scholarly side of the same process—that is, a literature that developed in the name of 'diversity' to provide 'neutral scientific' explanations that could be generalized, instead of political and contextual explanations for social relations that already existed (e.g. Cavanaugh 1997; Omanović 2009). And for that purpose, social psychology was ready to hand in a society, that of the US, for which psychological and behavioural explanations for most social processes had become popular culture discourse (e.g. Cushman 1990).

In contrast, the literature examined in this section *provincializes* the US diversity literature by highlighting—explicitly and implicitly—the very local conditions of its appearance, both as a historical event and through its epistemological preferences, *and* by focusing more generally on the social construction of diversity also as a local event. Typically, the theoretical lenses employed to this effect are of interpretive and critical sociological provenance, addressing the notion of the subject as a different ontological entity. Often, but not always, this is *a discursive subject*, constructed in and through the rhetoric and power relations embedded in processes and practices of 'managing diversity' (e.g. Zanoni and Janssens 2004).The examples we review below draw attention to this shift—namely *changing the subject* (Hollway et al. 1984). Later we also address how managerial issues in the earlier literature shifted to other matters of concern under the premises of this one.

In an early and well-known study, Jones, Pringle, and Shepherd (2000) stress that the discourse of 'managing diversity' is based on US-centric assumptions about organizational culture and the politics of difference, and, thus, is ethnocentric and culturally limited in its framing. Their point of departure cautions that asking how universalized notions of 'managing diversity ' from US-derived models can be implemented in Aotearoa/New Zealand is the wrong approach. Instead, it is important *to look at local responses* to the local context. In this context, the relationships between Maori (the Indigenous, original population) and Pakeha (non-Maori settlers mostly of British descent) had been codified in the 1840 Treaty of Waitangi, considered the founding document of New Zealand. From there on, Aotearoa/New Zealand was represented as a bicultural society, generating a discourse of partnership that was seen, at least in the public domain, as requiring the sharing of power, resources, and responsibility between two cultures. This approach was based on a framework of social justice, equity, and eliminating inequality. Thus, the paper calls for a multi-voiced discourse on 'diversity' capable of representing many different contextual modalities. In the authors' view this can only happen if there is tolerance for the ambiguity of notions about difference in organizations. That is, tolerance for the many ways in which the *subject of diversity* can be constituted by the discourse—for instance, as *partners in a bicultural society*—rather than as minorities and majorities through demographic classifications.

Several other studies around the world reiterate these critiques of the US normative discourse and the importance of keeping in mind the historical, contextual, and discursive construction of the subject of diversity more generally. For instance, Nyambegera (2002) explores questions around Human Resources (HR) diversity programmes in multi-ethnic societies in sub-Saharan Africa, noting that understanding of the complex social structure in multi-ethnic societies is missing from contemporary Western models of HRM. Addressing Africa's historical colonial roots, the author highlights how colonizers would play ethnic groups off against one another as a divide-and-rule approach to governance, and stresses that ethnic identity is susceptible to all kinds of political manipulation for establishing control over populations. From this perspective, it is questionable whether the concept of diversity management with its US cultural dominance and emphasis on a priori categorizations can be easily transferred to countries in Africa.

The two studies above point to the fallacy of attempting to universalize practices of 'diversity management' based on contemporary Anglo-American understandings and applications. They emphasize the importance of historical events in defining local contexts and *the notions of the subject* constituted through them. Meanwhile, other studies address the functioning of actual discourses of diversity management in particular locations and also draw attention to their heterogeneity. For example, Point and Singh (2003) examined the websites of over 200 major companies in eight European countries and found that definitions of diversity were often imprecise and idiosyncratic, more likely to suit a company's interests than following uniform and well-understood, consistent notions. These discrepancies attest to the malleability of these ideas as well as to their socially constructed nature, but what are the consequences of this for the construction of the subject? Zanoni and Janssens' (2004) research offers one answer to this question. Using critical discourse and rhetorical analyses of texts from various interviews with Flemish HR managers, they examined how power enters these managers' local discourses of diversity. Focusing on the micro-dynamics of language, the authors show that HR managers generally define diversity on the basis of a few selected diversity axes and as a group phenomenon. These definitions fix diverse employees' representations by constructing them solely as members of reference groups sharing given essences. Through this type of representation, diverse employees are discursively *denied full subjectivity and agency*, which also reaffirms managerial hegemony.

There are other answers as well. Several studies conducted in Northern European countries continue to highlight both the contextual specificity of diversity discourses as well as their ambiguity. For instance, Kamp and Hagedorn-Rasmussen (2004) note that in most European countries diversity management is seen primarily as a way of integrating ethnic minorities, which are also regarded as social problems, into the labour market. In this context, the authors explore whether the introduction of 'diversity management' in Danish organizations might improve this situation. Addressing the dynamic properties of this discourse and the ambiguity in its conception of difference and sameness, their study observed the introduction of discourses emphasizing sameness and integration—even if pointed towards assimilation. That is, diversity in this modality did not focus on individual differences, common in US diversity management discourses. Later on, Risberg and Søderberg (2008) corroborated several points also noted in the latter study, indicating that the discourse of social responsibility seems to be a widespread aspect of managing diversity in European companies. This was also the case in Denmark, as noted by Boxenbaum (2006) with the distinction that a focus on integrating vulnerable groups appears to be unique to Denmark. In this case, *incorporating 'the other'* into the dominant population represents a gesture towards equality, 'Danish style', and therefore its construction of the subject of diversity.

Other studies speak directly about the effectiveness of 'diversity management' discourses to adapt and reproduce pre-existing understandings of local social norms, some of which could further social exclusion. For example, informed by Foucault's notion of discourse, Meriläinen et al. (2009) analysed the websites of the top twenty Finnish companies (in terms of sales) to examine how diversity was represented. Their point was recognition that gender equality is one of Finland's key social discourses, and so it was in these websites. However, the authors argue that by giving priority to *differences between men and women as social groups*—the subject of this discourse—the Finnish diversity discourse highlights power relations of in/equality and dis/advantage between men and women but 'leaves race- and ethnicity-based power relations invisible' (Meriläinen et al. 2009: 234). Similarly, Heres and Benschop's (2010) discourse analysis of ten Netherlands-based multinationals' websites illustrates how adaptations of diversity management may not replace existing local discourses of meritocracy (an individualizing social stance) and equality (a social policy issue) but leave them more or less intact. In that sense, diversity discourses continue to remain stereotypical and applicable only to those subjects constructed as different from the 'norm': *minority and women's issues*.

The formation of the diversity subject becomes more complicated when leaving the purely discursive domain to focus on processes and practices for changing organizations. One study from Switzerland and another one from Sweden illustrate these dynamics. Ostendorp and Steyaert (2009) studied how six major Swiss-based organizations attempted to provide a variety of social interventions for their workers, some of which were explicit as 'diversity interventions' and others that were not. Interviews with providers and participants revealed interpretative repertoires for these interventions that allowed for being different or not. The image of the 'ideal worker' was one norm against which the possibility of difference was articulated, often defeating the intent of 'diversity' programmes. In effect, 'diversity' could become forbidden even by those expected to benefit from it. Differences could only appear and reappear if the image of the 'ideal worker' was challenged by political negotiation.

Moving away from the discursive domain, Omanović's (2013) longitudinal ethnographic case study in a large manufacturing company in Sweden focuses on a programme to establish a diversity initiative. Articulating 'diversity' as a dialectical production process, the issues that unfold over time in the workplace produce contradictions and praxes, and reveal processes of domination over particular sectoral interests attempting to control the direction of diversity production. The dominant interest here was represented by an association already made on the larger Swedish social scale, where ethnicity, gender, and age were related to historically disadvantaged people. Seen in this light, the people to whom 'social diversity' referred were minorities within the organization—regardless of hierarchical or professional position—and their voices were disqualified from the start as 'less than' voices, both in numbers and in value. Doing so, however, did not imply the dominant majority was supporting senior management and the formal hierarchy—who at the start of the case seemed to sympathize with social and economic arguments for diversity. Rather, for most employees it was a way to support their own social (ethnicity, gender, class) 'Swedishness' hierarchy as the legitimate members of the organization and the legitimate members of Swedish society.

These two studies show the other side of the story addressed in the website studies above. While on the websites there are clear signals that the notion of 'diversity' can be institutionalized for reproducing *'the same'*, when observed from the point of view of actual organizational dynamics 'diversity' becomes a contested terrain, suffused with power relations, and given to *flux and transformation of its subject* (e.g. Janssens and Zanoni 2014; see also Katila et al. 2013).

Finally, another area of organizational scholarly work where the subject of diversity has been provincialized comprises a series of studies examining legal domains that include and go beyond organizational practices (Klarsfeld 2009, 2010; Klarsfeld, Ng, and Tatli 2012; Tatli et al. 2012; Klarsfeld et al. 2014). Who is the diversity subject of legal regulations? In an early study, Klarsfeld (2009) starts with the broader French context to contrast how 'diversity' as a voluntary organizational practice in the United States became a way to substitute legal mandates against discrimination, while in France voluntary practices and legal mandates coexist, requiring diversity practices to be understood in their mutual relationships. This argument is formulated through French regulation theory in clear contrast with other varieties of institutional analysis which, unreflectively, seem to position themselves as 'universal' explanations. More generally, the question that most of these studies set out to answer is: What is the local relationship between equality and diversity? This question has formed the basis of two edited collections. The first one (Klarsfeld 2010) had contributions from sixteen countries; and the second one (Klarsfeld et al. 2014) comprises contributions from fourteen countries. In several instances, the information that appeared in the first collection was updated in the second, underlining the dynamic and changing nature of *regulating the diversity subject*. In the words of the editors, '[t]he country cases... demonstrate the three key characteristics of diversity management at work: contextuality, relationality and dynamism' (Klarsfeld et al. 2014: 5).

In short, in provincializing diversity the works in this section illustrate that *the subject of diversity* unfolds historically in a particular location, and it is always subject of/ to change. This includes the very constitution of diversity as a concept in regards to the notion of humanity it represents, *and* in regards to the practices and processes where it takes shape. Here the emphasis on a priori 'identity' categories and categorizations from the US mainstream diversity literature has shifted to a relational understanding of how differences—under the aegis of 'diversity'—become meaningful in situated discourses and practices. That is, differences and differentiation are produced relationally on location, not pre-existent in individuals. These works also underscore that 'diversity' is not a neutral descriptor or qualifier; rather, it is a malleable symbol enacted through power relations when it is applied to people and practices. For instance, difference is invoked and meritocracy serves as an alibi when certain organizational activities, norms, and behaviours, historically associated with some (dominant) people and not others, come into question. In other instances, the notion of diversity is resignified to only apply in very reductive ways, reproducing traditional social understandings of the valuable and the value-less.

More generally, observing its various locations and different understandings, this set of literature highlights the complicated relationships between notions of diversity and notions of inclusion and equality (e.g. Syed and Kramar 2009). In so doing, it serves as additional evidence for challenging the financialization of diversity and its use as an instrumental managerial tool available for managerial control, while offering ways for understanding the multiplicity of the subject of diversity from its inception and observing what it might *become on location*.

The next literature we review can be considered to add an ontological twist insofar as, for the purpose of this review, we are focusing on the formation of *the subject of transnational diversity in organizations*. As we see it, this recent small literature on the *simultaneity of diversity* highlights the complexity of subject formation under the aegis of local 'diversity' discourses and practices, sometimes becoming a point of interrogation for all categories of identification.

The Simultaneity of Diversity

The feminist literature on intersectionality, from which most other literatures claiming an intersectional lens draw, has a complicated history that has become even more intricate over time (Anthias 2013; Carbin and Edenheim 2013). Some recent critiques have reiterated that the origins of intersectionality stem from ideas on US race and black feminism, a literature that emphasized, ontologically, the interaction of power structures and categories of oppression. Later, critical perspectives derived from poststructuralism—including postcolonial and queer theories, as well as diaspora studies—articulated notions of intersectionality for conceptualizing ontologically shifting and multiple identities which also coincided with notions of power in Foucault's works (Davis 2008). However, when the rubric 'intersectionality' became popularized as a 'social constructionist' argument, which paradoxically took for granted the a priori existence and/or stability of 'identity categories', it was also open to being adopted as a liberal feminist discourse free to ignore power relations and oppressive social structures. In short, intersectionality has become, in Carbin and Edenheim's (2013) critique, 'a theory that provides us with an ontology of neither the subject nor power. Intersectionality has foremost become successful precisely because it does not meet the requirements of a theory and hence "everyone" feels that it fits "their way of doing research"' (Carbin and Edenheim 2013: 245).

In light of this, while 'intersectionality' has also become popularized in the organizational literature, we exercise caution in how it is represented in this section. Specifically, below we will highlight works on diversity in organization which, like the original intersectionality literature, keep in view structures of oppression and questions of subject formation within power relations (Collins 1990, 1993; Crenshaw 1991; Yuval-Davis 2006,

2011; Davis 2008; Choo and Ferree 2010). Similar to the literature in the previous section, this literature acknowledges where it originated, and thus admits to a situationally and historically produced diversity subject rather than to a stable set of identifiers for an individual (Werbner 2013). However, one important aim of these works is to focus more incisively on how experiences of the social world, especially in regard to marginalization, inequality, and social hierarchy in organizations (e.g. 'inequality regimes' (Acker 2006)), take place simultaneously through gender, race, class, and so forth, not as identity categories but as material social formations (Holvino 2010; Zanoni et al. 2010).

Among these works, Boogaard and Roggeband (2010) put identity categorization under a critical lens with their examination of the Dutch police force. Their study highlights how organizational inequality is (re)produced and called into question by *ways in which* actors and organizations draw on intersecting gender, ethnic, and organizational identities. Analyses of their findings shed light on two paradoxes: the first paradox shows that by deploying more positive identities to empower themselves, individuals can *de facto* contribute to reproducing inequalities along those same identity axes. However, the second paradox suggests that acknowledging minority officers' specific competences—such as an organizational action—calls into question inequality in terms of gender and ethnicity. In short, by scrutinizing *the subject of diversity* under an intersectional lens, the authors articulate its dynamic and agentic formation. What is at play here is how 'identity categorizations' become materialized and mobilized by the actors themselves. Similarly, Barragan and Mills (2013) argue that in the context of globalization there are a variety of gendered cultural templates that women and men can mobilize. They further contend that due to processes of globalized capitalism, senior women managers in Mexico face local and global discourses offering a repertoire of subjective positions for identity construction. Drawing on feminist poststructuralist conceptualizations of intersectionality and micro-resistance, they observed how these actors adopted, adapted, and rejected available subject positions by concentrating on relational and contextual aspects of identity formation processes.

Meanwhile, several studies focus not on the management side but on the labour side of this story. For instance, Zanoni (2011) examines the intersections of gender, disability, and age in the automobile industry in Belgium with respect to the production and experience of inequality, and shows that the 'diversity subject' is *a classed subject*. Applying intersectionality perspectives informed by black feminist standpoint theories, the study addresses how the meanings of socio-demographic identities such as gender, age, and (dis)ability—namely diversity—are informed by underlying class relations and how such meanings inform class relations between labour and capital. The author counters the identitarian emphasis of less critical intersectionality approaches by arguing that re-conceptualizing diversity through class offers a powerful analytical tool to better understand how unequal power relations play out in contemporary organizations.

In another example pertaining to labour relations, this time in the context of locked-out hotel workers in Canada, Soni-Sinha (2013) goes beyond Marxian analysis and deploys a poststructuralist feminist analysis. The aim of the study is to understand how workers' intersectional subjective identities are constituted and the interrelationships between their investments in and constitution of *collectivities* with regards to industrial action. Further, Alberti, Holgate, and Tapia (2013) use intersectionality insights to examine precarious work from the perspective of trade-union practices regarding equality and diversity. The study explores how unions in the UK organize and recruit low-paid, vulnerable migrant workers and concludes that trade unions tend to consider migrants primarily as *workers*, a universalized labour process subject, rather than as *migrant workers* with particular and overlapping forms of oppression. Insofar as this happens, unions dichotomize workplace and migration issues which exclude marginalized and diverse workers.

In light of globalization, intersectionality can clarify the subject formation of various immigrant groups within different experiences of inequality in organizations. For example, Healy, Bradley, and Forson (2011) demonstrate that Bangladeshi, Caribbean, and Pakistani women in UK public sector organizations experience inequalities differently based on their own historically situated arrival in the UK but that things became more complicated through their everyday organizational life. Informed by what Crenshaw (1991) calls an 'intersectional sensibility', the authors frame their arguments through Acker's (2006) conceptualization of inequality regimes, to demonstrate the complexity and unevenness in the way inequality regimes are produced, reproduced, and rationalized. For instance, at some points women were able to reconcile the work culture with their personal values and exhibited a form of intersectional empowerment, while at another points they experienced intersectional disempowerment resulting from the struggle to reconcile racialized and gendered daily interactions. Similarly, Mirza (2013) outlines how embodied intersectionality allows understanding of the ways in which professional Muslim women who wear the hijab in the UK experience various forms of discrimination both in society and in organizations. This study goes on to address the various discursive and material strategies utilized by such women to challenge dominant narratives of being 'oppressed' in their everyday lives.

Yet there is more to diversity in the context of transnationalism. Note that these last examples of intersectionality pertain to mobile populations—immigrants—but regardless of where they came from we considered them at their point of destination, and available for analysis of subject formation under the aegis of 'intersectionality'. While understanding subjectivities as relationally constituted—the process of subjectification—is a conventional anti-essentialist assumption in current social theory and most conceptualizations of intersectionality, these understandings still anchor the subject in time/space location. This gesture naturalizes located subjects as the norm while ignoring subjects who embody mobile ontological experiences as the common state of affairs. At best, these analyses would show how actors may become 'others' in particular locations at different points in time, but they would miss new articulations of subjectivity and the creation of new social fields produced through the actor's movement as she or he relates to others throughout time/space. As we will explore in the next section, from the transnational perspective that informs this chapter, the mobility and movement of people across borders necessarily changes the very ontology of the subject and calls into question its constitution.

The Formation of Mobile Subjectivities

Some critics of the intersectionality literature, noting the 'identitarian' emphasis it has acquired, often suggest that more attention should be paid to specific sites and locations where new forms of subjectivation may be performed (Staunes 2003; Williams 2005). In principle, they argue for recognizing that race, gender, and class are not properties of individuals or of groups but political relations structuring people's lived experiences while reifying the structural relations of power where they are implicated (e.g. Carastathis 2008).

Puar (2007, 2012) further complicates these critiques when noting the historical and institutional inception of intersectionality in the academic context of women's, gender, and legal studies in the United States during the 1980s, a period of heightened identity politics in the country. The same moment, we should add, when 'diversity' became part of the US management literature. Thus, Puar asks for recognition of the existence of intersectionality as an historical 'event', and its emergence and practice (by whom? and for what?) in the particular context of the changing historical and economic landscapes of neoliberal capitalism. In her argument it is necessary to rethink the notion of 'identity' and its categories as part of such event as well as to note that they are still part of modernist colonial agendas from which the idea of a 'discrete identity' appeared.

Other critics, in particular those involved in transnational feminist and migration research go further in highlighting persistent problems with categorization(s) of identities, including intersectionality, when borders are crossed. For instance, instead of focusing on 'identities', Yuval-Davis (1997, 2006, 2012) recommends taking into account transversal politics, a democratic practice of alliances across boundaries of difference, while Anthias (2006, 2012) suggests the notion of translocational positionality—subject positions tied to situation, meaning, and the interplay of social locations in complex and often contradictory ways. In fact, recent empirical examples reiterate how Western conceptualizations of selves, slotted into categories such as 'gender', 'race', and 'class', are not meaningful everywhere. While Western theories of the subject often 'travel', in the process their meanings change (Nagar 2002; Min 2008; Choo 2012). For instance, Purkayastha (2012) shows how immigrant women from India and Uganda in the US would be racially marginalized differently, consistent with the racist ideologies, interactions, and institutional arrangements of this country. Yet, upon return to their 'home' countries, their situation might again change depending on who is part of the privileged majority versus the marginalized minority *within* a country after having been away. In Purkayastha's words, 'these hierarchies do not always fit the white-yellow/brown-Black hierarchy extant in Western Europe and North America' (Purkayastha 2012: 59).

Thus, how to proceed? In her 1993 book, Kathy Ferguson put forward the notion of 'mobile subjectivities' as a way to reconsider feminist identity claims assumed to be lost under the discursive turn of poststructuralism. This theory allows for maintaining agency without relying on a stable location of either identity (no matter how complex) or of place as a requirement for political engagement and for effecting social change. Through it, the identitarian argument is turned around for '[i]n the shifting temporal and spatial possibilities offered by specific locales, mobile subjectivities find the resources for de-articulating and re-articulating themselves' (Ferguson 1993: 163).

Concrete articulations of the possibility of mobile subjectivities can be found in contemporary mobilities scholarship, developing important insights on interrelations between global hypermobility and subjectivity formation (e.g. D'Andrea 2006). The problem of the subject looms large in these arguments, often inspired by images of nomadism (Deleuze and Guattari 1980; Braidotti 1994) and translocality (Appadurai 1996). Questions emerge about conceptualizations of subjectivity that frame identities in the context of place and time insofar as their possible displacements are not taken into account. Recognizing these limitations, mobility scholars have explored other understandings of subjectivity. For instance, D'Andrea (2006) puts forward the concept of neo-nomad for investigating the cultural effects of hypermobility under conditions of globalization, a contemporary social experience for many, in self, identity, and sociality. In another example, Conradson and Mckay (2007: 168) consider selfhood always as a hybrid relational achievement and advance the idea of translocal subjectivities 'to describe the multiply-located senses of self among those who inhabit transnational social fields'. They follow Appadurai's (1996) notion of translocality which describes how communities in a place become extended through the geographical mobility of their inhabitants. A translocality becomes emplaced *and* recreated through transnational movements and relationships—a transnational social field (see also Levitt and Glick Schiller 2004; Calás and Smircich 2011).

In the process of developing these ideas, scholars have also questioned the assumed relationships between who and what is deemed 'local' versus who and what is deemed 'global', in particular when 'the local' is associated with less affluent places and populations are imagined as fixed in time and space, while 'the global' is associated with affluence, mobility, and positive social change—e.g. modernization. Fortier (2006), among others, draws attention to how certain populations, including immigrants, get lost in these discussions. In her view, this situation requires analysis of the constant interplay between micro and macrophysics of power. These arguments are part of a broader critique of dominant Western social theory and its 'sedentarist' metaphysics (Malkki 1992; Cresswell 2006; Frello 2008), whose traditional analytical premises naturalize and privilege sedentary modes of life and identity such as belonging to a nation and having a home. Along those lines, Wimmer and Glick-Schiller (2002) note that methodological nationalism, the assumption that the nation/state/society is the natural social and political form of the modern world, still informs much Western social theory and methodology. This implies a 'container model of society' (Wimmer and Glick-Schiller 2002: 308) which remains invisible. Transnational mobility, in particular migration movements, is seen as problematic under 'container' theoretical models for '[c]ross border migration... appears as an anomaly, a problematic exception to the rule of people staying where they "belong", that is to "their" nation-state' (Wimmer and Glick-Schiller 2002: 311). Thus, in their view trans-*national* analyses as well as analyses of new spaces constituted through cross-*national* mobilizations of diverse populations—namely transnational social fields—still yield a better understanding of contemporary social and power relations across the world.

In sum, these arguments point out to how difficult it is to imagine subjectivities that could escape the grip of dominant Western social theory and the West's dominant social and political formations. Insofar as the mobile subject is seen as 'the other' of the normally sedentary and nation bound subject, that is, 'the citizen', s/he is theoretically constituted as marginal and exceptional, a 'less than' subject. Understanding mobile subjectivities, their agency, and production processes—for example, being at some time/space dominant, and at others subordinated—would require mobile conceptualizations. This may imply understanding multi-local conceptions of the subject in varying power relationships between those located and those on the move in a continuity of time/space—a translocation. It would also include the transformation of known conceptualizations, which may acquire new but temporary meanings in the process (e.g. Purkayastha 2012), reiterating the importance of rethinking prevailing classificatory schemes, including race, ethnicity, sexuality, and class, through space, time, and actual bodies on the move (Fortier 2006).

We note, as well, that conceptualizations of subjectivity formation from mobilities scholarship and associated critiques of Western epistemologies (e.g. Haverig 2011) converge with current feminist conceptualizations of the subject under globalized capitalism and neoliberalism. At issue here is the emphasis on individualism, choice, and self-empowerment exhibited by the desirable subject of contemporary neoliberal discourses, and potential resistance to it (Gill 2007). What new subjectivities may be 'in formation' under these now apparently *global demands*? Here we suggest that under these circumstances *the subject of diversity* discourses and practices must avoid identity categorizations and be understood, instead, as a *mobile, precarious, and transitory form of subjectivation* (see also, Calás, Ou, and Smircich 2013).

Adib and Guerrier (2003) substantiate our arguments. This is a frequently cited example in the diversity literature referring to intersectionality, however we argue that it is a better example for observing mobile forms of subjectivation. This study addressed how gender, nationality, race, ethnicity, and class intersect and are negotiated to shape the work identities of women management trainees in hotel reception and chambermaid work. All four trainees resided in the UK, but one was British and the other three were immigrants from three different countries. Two, including the UK national, trained in the UK and the other two, in a clear case of transnationalism, trained in the US. While the study articulated the race/ethnicity and nationality of all the trainees, the significance of the immigrant status of three of them is mostly ignored throughout the study until almost the end, in the context of an incident in the US.

While in that country, one trainee, originally from Spain, was sexually harassed by a co-worker from Latin America. In the research interview, the trainee explained that it was mostly immigrant women from several countries who were harassed by this same co-worker, and further noted that this may have been because he lacked a visa and therefore he would not harass American women, who might create trouble for him. In the interview she also reported being able to defuse the advances of the co-worker by drawing on their common language (Spanish) and immigrant status, which helped her claim solidarity with him insofar as they both were subjected to similar difficulties in the workplace. However, while the analyses of this incident note the significance of differentiation among immigrants, in this case from diaspora populations, and the intercrossing of specific ethnicities and genders, for us there is more to the dynamics reported by this trainee. To the extent that the overarching theme is the encounters trainees report in their movements from place to place, they offer excellent examples of subject formation processes that would only be seen, and become meaningful, if studied as occurring in transnational social fields within the phenomenon of mobility itself. What boundaries in time and space are these subjects crossing? What are they becoming as they move on from place to place?

Leonard (2010) is another example of diversity studies worth analysing under mobility premises of subject formation. This study addresses the negotiation and construction of new white subjectivities in the changing global workplace of Hong Kong. It explores how recent changes in the social and political landscape are being accompanied by complex transformations of work and working identities of British expatriates. Here individuals perform as white subjects through discourses of gender and nationality in the interplay between global and local discourses, highlighting how such subjectivities are always unstable. Despite its postcolonial framing, in this article the makings of mobile subjectivities are obvious, precarious, and transitory, except that the subjects are emplaced in the context of Hong Kong with little attention being paid to the fact that *expatriation* is always already a mobile experience of subject formation. What happens up on their return?

As we conclude this chapter, this latter example returns us to the start, where we used an example of the subject of expatriation as understood under premises of social identity theory. The arc we have traced from there to here hopefully underscores that travelling through notions of subject formation, specifically moving after *the subject of transnational diversity in organizations*, is not only a journey through places where the subject forms, but also an expedition to displace ontological assumptions as we moved along. In so doing, we are now arriving at our proclaimed destination—albeit clearly temporary—through which we mark the end of the chapter.

Towards Post-identitarian Transnational Diversity *and* Organization Perspectives

In this last section it is only fitting that we go back to Foucault's (1973) reflections on Borges's Chinese encyclopedia as a basis for our aims in this chapter. The particular argument Foucault was raising in this book was precisely how we have come to know what 'knowledge' '*is*'. Following historical traces of discourses from the sixteenth century on in Europe, he observed how practices such as classification, dividing into classes, creating taxonomies, and so on became associated with science and knowledge as 'human sciences' across what we now take for granted as disciplinary boundaries in linguistics, biology, and economics. What Borges's fable does is to call into question what may be missing for us—in our now conventional system of thought—for understanding such odd classification, which includes a sequence of letters seemingly ordering incongruous elements. What do all the items in that odd list have in common? Having a common ground would allow for things like 'integrating' or 'comparing'; in other words, to develop a common order —a 'table'—for classification of its components, and therefore fostering the possibility of commensurability along any form of classification. That is, to be able to include and exclude, and to discard what doesn't belong to a particular disciplinary discourse.

Needless to say, through the course of this chapter we have tried to challenge established expectations. There are already well-organized classificatory schemes using functionalist approaches for making sense of the literature we have addressed (e.g. Syed and Özbilgin 2009; Tatli and Özbilgin 2012). Yet that is what we have tried to escape (perhaps not very successfully) with each of our taxonomical categories: the assumption that somehow these would be ontologically commensurable as categories in the discourse of 'diversity'. Rather, by fostering possibilities of ontologically incommensurable forms of subject formation between representations in each category, we were opening a door for another possibility: that the transnational subject of diversity *and* organization should not be classified, *as subject formation is an ongoing process with ephemeral duration.*

Thus, what we are asking instead is to keep in mind modalities in our 'taxonomy', from *internationalized* social identity theory, to *provincializing* approaches, to the *simultaneity of diversity* in an intersectionality critical mode, as ontologically incommensurable while coexisting today in the transnational diversity in organization literature. Together they have opened and continue to open spaces for disciplinary discourses of psychology, sociology, and feminism as very different ways of understanding the diversity subject. Yet they are all part of a common problem: their tendency towards keeping alive that dangerous word: 'identity', despite the fact that in most cases they are referring to incompatible metatheoretical notions of subject formation. Maintaining 'identity' as a common lexicon has created a lot of confusion; a particular problem for addressing transnational perspectives if at the same time one wants to address the fact that 'identity' is a ghost of Western individualism at its most fundamental.

Thus, here we put forward the notion of *mobile subjectivities* as another way to think about the subject of diversity *and* organization. As we see it, it is perhaps a more appropriate understanding for contemporary subject formation in a 'post-identitarian' mode. As such, developing this mode of thinking may make it possible to address conditions and experiences of the larger world we all inhabit under globalized neoliberalism. That is, this mode of thinking may highlight our common existence as subjects of a particular kind of power relations, and our common predicaments under such relations, which could easily be concealed by the apparently more benign label of 'diversity in organizations'. Such a 'benign' label does nothing of the kind other than continue to divide us into 'classes', 'races', 'genders' . . . as if it were all that matters.

References

Acker, J. (2006). Inequality regimes gender, class, and race in organizations. *Gender & Society*, 20(4): 441–64.

Adeleye, I. (2011). Theorising human resource management in Africa: beyond cultural relativism. *African Journal of Business Management*, 5(6): 2028–39.

Adib, A. and Guerrier, Y. (2003). The interlocking of gender, nationality, race, ethnicity and class: the narratives of women in hotel work. *Gender, Work and Organization*, 10(4): 413–32.

Alberti, G., Holgate, J., and Tapia, M. (2013). Organising migrants as workers or as migrant workers? Intersectionality, trade unions and precarious work. *International Journal of Human Resource Management*, 24(22): 4132–48.

Anthias, F. (2006). Belonging in a globalizing and unequal world: rethinking translocations. In N. Yuval-Davis, K. Kannabiran, and U. Vieten (eds.), *The Situated Politics of Belonging*. London: Sage, 17–31.

Anthias, F. (2012). Transnational mobilities, migration research and intersectionality. *Nordic Journal of Migration Research*, 2(2): 102–10.

Anthias, F. (2013). Hierarchies of social location, class and intersectionality: towards a translocational frame. *International Sociology*, 28(1): 121–38.

Appadurai, M. (1996). *Modernity at Large: Cultural Dimensions of Globalization*. Minneapolis, MN: University of Minnesota Press.

Barragan, S. and Mills, A. (2013). Top Women Managers Navigating the Hybrid Gender Order in Mexico. Paper presented at 29th EGOS Colloquium, Sub-theme 04: Diversity, Diversity Management and Identity in Organizations. Montréal, Canada.

Boogaard, B. and Roggeband, C. (2010). Paradoxes of intersectionality: theorizing inequality in the Dutch police force through structure and agency. *Organization*, 17(1): 53–75.

Boxenbaum, E. (2006). Lost in translation: the making of Danish diversity management. *American Behavioral Scientist*, 49(7): 939–48.

Braidotti, R. (1994). *Nomadic Subjects: Embodiment and Sexual Difference in Contemporary Feminist Theory*. New York: Columbia University Press.

Calás, M. B. and Smircich, L. (1993). Dangerous liaisons: the 'feminine-in-management' meets 'globalization'. *Business Horizons*, 36(2): 71–81.

Calás, M. B. and Smircich, L. (2011). In the back and forth of transmigration: rethinking organization studies in a transnational key. In E. Jeames, D. Knights, and P. Y. Martin (eds.), *Handbook of Gender, Work, and Organization*. Chichester: John Wiley, 411–28.

Calás. M. B., Holgersson, C., and Smircich, L. (2009). 'Diversity Management'? Translation? Travel? *Scandinavian Journal of Management*, 25: 349–51.

Calás, M. B., Ou, H., and Smircich, L. (2013). 'Woman' on the move: mobile subjectivities after intersectionality. *Equality, Diversity and Inclusion: An International Journal*, 32(8): 708–31.

Carastathis, A. (2008). The invisibility of privilege: a critique of intersectional models of identity. *Les Ateliers de l'éthique*, 3(2): 23–38.

Carbin, M. and Edenheim, S. (2013). The intersectional turn in feminist theory: a dream of a common language? *European Journal of Women's Studies*, 20(3): 233–48.

Cavanaugh, J. M. (1997). (In)corporating the other: managing the politics of workplace difference. In P. Prasad, A. Mills, M. Elmes, and A. Prasad (eds.), *Managing the Organizational Melting Pot: Dilemmas of Workplace Diversity*. Thousand Oaks, CA: Sage, 31–53.

Choi, J. N. (2007). Group composition and employee creative behaviour in a Korean electronics company: distinct effects of relational demography and group diversity. *Journal of Occupational & Organizational Psychology*, 80(2): 213–34.

Choo, H. Y. (2012). The transnational journey of intersectionality. *Gender & Society*, 26(1): 40–5.

Choo, H. Y. and Ferree, M. M. (2010). Practicing intersectionality in sociological research: a critical analysis of inclusions, interactions, and institutions in the study of inequalities. *Sociological Theory*, 28(2): 129–49.

Collins, P. H. (1990). *Black Feminist Thought: Knowledge, Consciousness, and the Politics of Empowerment*. Boston, MA: Unwin Hyman.

Collins, P. H. (1993). Toward a new vision: race, class, and gender as categories of analysis and connection. *Race, Sex & Class*, 1(1): 25–45.

Conradson, D., and Mckay, D. (2007). Translocal subjectivities: mobility, connection, emotion. *Mobilities*, 2(2): 167–74.

Cooke, F. L. and Saini, D. S. (2010). Diversity management in India: a study of organizations in different ownership forms and industrial sectors. *Human Resource Management*, 49(3): 477–500.

Crenshaw, K. (1991). Mapping the margins: intersectionality, identity politics, and violence against women of color. *Stanford Law Review*, 43(6): 1241–99.

Cresswell, T. (2006). *On the Move: Mobility in the Modern Western World*. London: Routledge.

Cushman, P. (1990). Why the self is empty: toward a historically situated psychology. *American Psychologist*, 45(5): 599–611.

Czarniawska, B., and Höpfl, H. (eds.) (2002). *Casting the Other: The Production and Maintenance of Inequalities in Work Organizations* (Vol. 5). New York: Routledge.

D'Andrea, A. (2006). Neo-nomadism: a theory of post-identitarian mobility in the global age. *Mobilities*, 1(1): 95–119.

Davis, K. (2008). Intersectionality as buzzword: a sociology of science perspective on what makes a feminist theory successful. *Feminist Theory*, 9(1): 67–85.

Deleuze, G. and Guattari, F. (1980/1987). *A Thousand Plateaus: Capitalism and Schizophrenia*. Minneapolis, MN: University of Minnesota Press.

D'Netto, B. and Sohal, A. S. (1999). Human resource practices and workforce diversity: an empirical assessment. *International Journal of Manpower*, 20(8): 530–47.

Ferguson, K. E. (1993). *The Man Question: Visions of Subjectivity in Feminist Theory*. Berkeley, CA: University of California Press.

Fortier, A. M. (2006). The politics of scaling, timing and embodying: rethinking the 'new Europe'. *Mobilities*, 1(3): 313–31.

Foucault, M. (1973). *The Order of Things: An Archaeology of the Human Sciences*. New York: Vintage Books.

Frello, B. (2008). Towards a discursive analytics of movement: on the making and unmaking of movement as an object of knowledge. *Mobilities*, 3(1): 25–50.

Gill, R. (2007). Postfeminist media culture: elements of a sensibility. *European Journal of Cultural Studies*, 10(2): 147–66.

Haverig, A. (2011). Constructing global/local subjectivities: the New Zealand OE as governance through freedom. *Mobilities*, 6(1): 103–23.

Healy, G., Bradley, H., and Forson, C. (2011). Intersectional sensibilities in analysing inequality regimes in public sector organizations. *Gender, Work and Organization*, 18(5): 467–87.

Heres, L. and Benschop, Y. (2010). Taming diversity: an exploratory study on the travel of a management fashion. *Equality, Diversity and Inclusion: An International Journal*, 29(5): 436–57.

Hirt, C., and Bešić, A. (2013). Diversity management in different contexts: diverging perspectives from Central and South-Eastern Europe. Paper presented at the Diversity, Diversity Management and Identity in Organizations sub-theme at the European Organization Studies conference, Montréal, Canada.

Hogg, M. A. (2006). Social identity theory. In P. J. Burke (ed.), *Contemporary Social Psychological Theories*. Stanford, CA: Stanford University Press, 111–36.

Hogg, M. A., Terry, D. J., and White, K. M. (1995). A tale of two theories: a critical comparison of identity theory with social identity theory. *Social Psychology Quarterly*, 58(4): 255–69.

Holvino, E. (2010). Intersections: the simultaneity of race, gender and class in organization studies. *Gender, Work and Organization*, 17(3): 248–77.

Holvino, E. and Kamp, A (2009). Diversity management: are we moving in the 'right' direction? Reflections from both sides of the North Atlantic. *Scandinavian Journal of Management*, 25: 395–403.

Hollway, W., Venn, C., Walkerdine, V., Henriques, J., and Urwin, C. (1984). *Changing the Subject: Psychology, Social regulation and Subjectivity*. London: Methuen & Co.

Human, L. (1996). Managing workforce diversity: a critique and example from South Africa. *International Journal of Manpower*, 17(4/5): 46–64.

Jabbour, C. J. C., Gordono, F. S., de Oliveira, J. H. C., Martinez, J. C., and Battistelle, R. A. G. (2011). Diversity management: challenges, benefits, and the role of human resource management in Brazilian organizations. *Equality, Diversity and Inclusion: An International Journal*, 30(1): 58–74.

Jack, G. and Lorbiecki, A. (2007). National identity, globalization and the discursive construction of organizational identity. *British Journal of Management*, 8: 79–94.

Janssens, M. and Zanoni, P. (2015). Alternative diversity management: organizational practices fostering ethnic equality at work. *Scandinavian Journal of Management* (online; in press).

Johnston, W. B. and Packer, A. H. (1987). *Workforce 2000: Work and Workers for the Twenty-first Century*. Indianapolis, IN: Hudson.

Jones, D., Pringle, J., and Shepherd, D. (2000). Managing diversity meets Aotearoa/New Zealand. *Personnel Review*, 29(3): 364–80.

Kamp, A. and Hagedorn-Rasmussen, P. (2004). Diversity management in a Danish context: towards a multicultural or segregated working life? *Economic and Industrial Democracy*, 25(4): 525–54.

Katila, S., Eriksson, P., Gherardi, S., and Murgia, A. (2013). Constructing Diversity in Managerial Ranks in Finland and in Italy. Paper presented at 29th EGOS Colloquium, Sub-theme 04: Diversity, Diversity Management and Identity in Organizations. Montréal, Canada.

Kelly, E. and Dobbin, F. (1998). How affirmative action became diversity management: employer response to antidiscrimination law, 1961–1996. *American Behavioral Scientist*, 41(7): 960–84.

Klarsfeld, A. (2009). The diffusion of diversity management: the case of France. *Scandinavian Journal of Management*, 25(4): 363–73.

Klarsfeld, A. (ed.) (2010). *International Handbook on Diversity Management at Work: Country Perspectives on Diversity and Equal Treatment*. Cheltenham: Edward Elgar Publishing.

Klarsfeld, A., Ng, E., and Tatli, A. (2012). Social regulation and diversity Mmanagement: a Ccomparative study of France, Canada and the UK. *European Journal of Industrial Relations*, 18(4): 309–27.

Klarsfeld, A., Booysen, L.A.E., Ng, E., Roper, I., and Tatli, A. (eds.) (2014). *International Handbook on Diversity Management at Work: Country Perspectives on Diversity and Equal Treatment*. Cheltenham: Edward Elgar Publishing.

Konrad, A. M. (2003). Defining the domain of workplace diversity scholarship. *Group and Organization Management*, 28(1): 4–17.

Konrad, A. M., Prasad, P., and Pringle, J. K. (eds.) (2006). *Handbook of Workplace Diversity*. London: Sage.

Kulik, C. T. and Bainbridge, H. T. J. (2006). Psychological perspectives on workplace diversity. In A. M. Konrad, P. Prasad, and J. K. Pringle (eds.), *Handbook of Workplace Diversity*. London: Sage, 25–52.

Leonard, P. (2010). Organizing whiteness: gender, nationality and subjectivity in postcolonial Hong Kong. *Gender, Work and Organization*, 17(3): 340–58.

Levitt, P. and Glick Schiller, N. (2004). Conceptualizing simultaneity: a transnational social field perspective on society. *International Migration Review*, 38(3): 1002–39.

Litvin, D. (1997). The discourse of diversity: from biology to management. *Organization*, 4(2): 187–209.

Litvin, D. (2006). Diversity: making space for a better case. In A. M. Konrad, P. Prasad, and J. K. Pringle (eds.), *Handbook of Workplace Diversity*. Thousand Oaks, CA: Sage, 75–94.

Lorbiecki, A. and Jack, G. (2000). Critical turns in the evolution of diversity management. *British Journal of Management*, 11: 17–31.

Louie, A. (2004). *Chineseness across Borders: Renegotiating Chinese Identities in China and the United States*. Durham, NC: Duke University Press.

Malkki, L. (1992). National geographic: the rooting of peoples and the territorialization of national identity among scholars and refugees. *Cultural Anthropology*, 7(1): 24–44.

Meriläinen, S., Tienari, J., Katila, S., and Benschop, Y. (2009). Diversity management versus gender equality: the Finnish case. *Canadian Journal of Administrative Sciences/Revue Canadienne des Sciences de l'Administration*, 26(3): 230–43.

Min, D. (2008). What about other translation routes (east-west)? The concept of the term 'gender' traveling into and throughout China. In K. E. Ferguson, and M. Mironesco (eds.), *Gender and Globalization in Asia and the Pacific*. Honolulu, HI: University of Hawaii Press, 79–98.

Mirza, H. S. (2013). 'A second skin': embodied intersectionality, transnationalism and narratives of identity and belonging among Muslim women in Britain. *Women's Studies International Forum*, 36: 5–15.

Moore, F. (2014). An unsuitable job for a woman: a 'native category' approach to gender, diversity and cross-cultural management. *The International Journal of Human Resource Management*, (ahead-of-print), 1–15.

Nagar, R. (2002). Footloose researchers, 'traveling' theories, and the politics of transnational feminist praxis. *Gender, Place, and Culture*, 9(2): 179–86.

Nishii, L. H. and Özbilgin, M. F. (2007). Global diversity management: towards a conceptual framework. *The International Journal of Human Resource Management*, 18(11): 1883–94.

Nkomo, S. M. and Stewart, M. N. (2006). Diverse identities in organizations. In S. R. Clegg, C. Hardy, T. B. Lawrence, and W. R. Nord (eds.), *The Sage Handbook of Organization Studies*. 2nd edn. London: Sage, 520–40.

Nkomo, S. and Hoobler, J. M. (2014). A historical perspective on diversity ideologies in the United States: reflections on human resource management research and practice. *Human Resource Management Review*, 24(3): 245–57.

Nyambegera, S. M. (2002). Ethnicity and human resource management practice in sub-Saharan Africa: the relevance of the managing diversity discourse. *International Journal of Human Resource Management*, 13(7): 1077–90.

Omanović, V. (2009). Diversity and its management as a dialectical process: encountering Sweden and the US. *Scandinavian Journal of Management*, 25: 352–62.

Omanović, V. (2013). Opening and closing the door to diversity: a dialectical analysis of the social production of diversity. *Scandinavian Journal of Management*, 29: 87–103.

Ostendorp, A. and C. Steyaert (2009). How different can differences be(come)? Interpretative repertoires of diversity concepts in Swiss-based organizations. *Scandinavian Journal of Management*, 25: 374–84.

Özbilgin, M., Jonsen, K., Tatli, A., Vassilopoulou, J., and Surgevil, O. (2012). Global diversity management. In Q. E. Roberson (ed.), *The Oxford Handbook of Diversity and Work*. New York: Oxford University Press, 419–41.

Pelled, L. H. and Xin, K. R. (2000). Relational demography and relationship quality in two cultures. *Organization Studies*, 21(6): 1077–94.

Point, S. and Singh, V. (2003). Defining and dimensionalising diversity: evidence from corporate websites across Europe. *European Management Journal*, 21(6): 750–61.

Prasad, P., Mills, A., Elmes, M., and Prasad, A. (eds.) (1997). *Managing the Organizational Melting Pot: Dilemmas of Workplace Diversity*. Thousand Oaks, CA: Sage.

Prasad, P., Pringle, J. K., and Konrad, A. M. (2006). Examining the contours of workplace diversity: concepts, contexts and challenges. In A. M. Konrad, P. Prasad, and J. K. Pringle (eds.), *Handbook of Workplace Diversity*. London: Sage, 1–22.

Puar, J. K. (2007). *Terrorist Assemblages: Homonationalism in Queer Times*. Durham, NC: Duke University Press.

Puar, J. K. (2012). 'I would rather be a cyborg than a goddess': becoming-intersectional in assemblage theory. *philoSOPHIA*, 2(1): 49–66.

Purkayastha, B. (2012). Intersectionality in a transnational world. *Gender & Society*, 26(1): 55–66.

Risberg, A. and Søderberg, A. M. (2008). Translating a management concept: diversity management in Denmark. *Gender in Management: An International Journal*, 23(6): 426–41.

Sayers, J. (2008), Managing diversity. In K. Macky (ed.), *Managing Human Resources: Contemporary Perspectives in New Zealand*. Sydney: Allen and Unwin, 84–107.

Scroggins, W. A. and Benson, P. G. (2010). International human resource management: diversity, issues and challenges. *Personnel Review*, 39(4): 409–13.

Soni-Sinha, U. (2013). Intersectionality, subjectivity, collectivity and the union: a study of the 'locked-out' hotel workers in Toronto. *Organization*, 20(6): 775–93.

Staunes, D. (2003). Where have all the subjects gone? Bringing together the concepts of intersectionality and subjectification. *Nora*, 11(2): 101–10.

Süß, S. and Kleiner, M. (2007). Diversity management in Germany: dissemination and design of the concept. *International Journal of Human Resource Management*, 18(11): 1934–53.

Syed, J. and Kramar, R. (2009). What is the Australian model for managing cultural diversity? *Personnel Review*, 39(1): 96–115.

Syed, J. and Özbilgin, M. (2009). A relational framework for international transfer of diversity management practices. *The International Journal of Human Resource Management*, 20(12): 2435–53.

Tatli, A. and Özbilgin, M. F. (2012). An emic approach to intersectional study of diversity at work: a Bourdieuan framing. *International Journal of Management Reviews*, 14(2): 180–200.

Tatli, A., Vassilopoulou, J., Al Ariss, A., and Özbilgin, M. (2012). The role of regulatory and temporal context in the construction of diversity discourses: the case of the UK, France and Germany. *European Journal of Industrial Relations*, 18(4): 293–308.

Toh, S. M. and DeNisi, A. S. (2007). Host country nationals as socializing agents: a social identity approach. *Journal of Organizational Behavior*, 28(3): 281–301.

Topinka, R. J. (2010) Foucault, Borges, heterotopia: producing knowledge in other spaces. *Foucault Studies*, 9: 54–70

Triandis, H. (1995) The importance of context in studies diversity. In S. Jackson and M. Ruderman (eds.), *Diversity in Work Teams*. Washington D.C.: American Psychological Association, 225–33.

Triandis, H. C. (2003). The future of workforce diversity in international organisations: a commentary. *Applied Psychology*, 52(3): 486–95.

Tsui, A., Egan, T., and O'Reilly, C. (1992). Being different: relational demography and turnover in top-management groups. *Administrative Science Quarterly*, 37(4): 549–79.

Tsui, A. S. and Farh, J. L. L. (1997). Where Guanxi matters relational demography and Guanxi in the Chinese context. *Work and Occupations*, 24(1): 56–79.

Tsui, A. S. and O'Reilly, C. A. (1989). Beyond simple demographic effects: the importance of relational demography in superior-subordinate dyads. *Academy of Management Journal*, 32(2): 402–23.

Tsui, A. S., Porter, L. W., and Egan, T. D. (2002). When both similarities and dissimilarities matter: extending the concept of relational demography. *Human Relations*, 55(8): 899–929.

Tsui, A. S., Schoonhoven, C. B., Meyer, M. W., Lau, C. M., and Milkovich, G. T. (2004). Organization and management in the midst of societal transformation: the People's Republic of China. *Organization Science*, 15(2): 133–44.

Werbner, P. (2013). Everyday multiculturalism: theorising the difference between 'intersectionality' and 'multiple identities'. *Ethnicities*, 13(4): 401–19.

Williams, C. P. (2005). 'Knowing one's place': gender, mobility and shifting subjectivity in eastern Indonesia. *Global Networks*, 5(4): 401–17.

Wimmer, A. and Glick-Schiller, N. (2002). Methodological nationalism and beyond: nation-state building, migration and the social sciences. *Global Networks*, 2(4): 301–34.

Yuval-Davis, N. (1997). *Gender and Nation*. London: Sage.

Yuval-Davis, N. (2006). Intersectionality and feminist politics. *European Journal of Women's Studies*, 13(3): 193–210.

Yuval-Davis, N. (2011). *The Politics of Belonging: Intersectional Contestations*. Thousand Oaks, CA: Sage.

Yuval-Davis, N. (2012). Dialogical epistemology: an intersectional resistance to the 'oppression Olympics'. *Gender & Society*, 26(1): 46–54.

Zanoni, P. (2011). Diversity in the lean automobile factory: doing class through gender, disability and age. *Organization*, 18(1): 105–27.

Zanoni, P. and Janssens, M. (2004). Deconstructing difference: the rhetoric of human resource managers' diversity discourses. *Organization Studies*, 25(1): 55–74.

Zanoni, P., Janssens, M., Benschop, Y., and Nkomo, S. M. (2010). Unpacking diversity, grasping inequality: rethinking difference through critical perspectives. *Organization*, 17(1): 9–29.

Index

Figures, notes, and tables are indicated by "f," "n," and "t" respectively.

AA. *See* Affirmative action
Abdallah, C., 224
Abdulrahman, Mohamed, 529, 530–1
Ableism, 474, 480, 488
Aboriginals. *See* Indigenous communities
Absenteeism, 260, 377
Abuse
  of children, 27, 391*n*2
  of migrant workers, 22
  of power, 332
Academia, 357–69
  accommodation provisions in, 488
  activism in, 33
  ADVANCE initiative for, 111, 112–13
  diversity management in, 359–60, 364–8, 364*f*
  Eurocentrism in, 132–3, 135
  global, 130, 132–4, 136, 138, 141, 143
  institutional level analysis of, 363–6
  methodology for study of, 360–3, 367, 368
  national differences in, 358
  overview, 8, 357–9
  politics of diversity and, 31–3
  practitioner activities and, 45–7
  socialization into, 338, 339–40, 345
  Southern Theory in, 168–9, 170
  translation of qualitative research to, 344–7
  women in, 32
Academy of Management Executive (Cox & Blake), 46
Access and legitimacy paradigm, 237
Accommodation. *See* Workplace accommodation
achuts (untouchables), 411
Acker, Joan, 19, 52, 158, 590

ACT UP (AIDS Coalition to Unleash Power) movement, 196
Action research, 543–4, 547, 549
Activism
  in academia, 33
  feminist, 20–1, 544
  grassroots, 41, 565
  LGBT, 197
Activity limitations, defined, 469. *See also* People with disabilities (PWD)
Actor-network theory (ANT), 448
ADA. *See* Americans with Disabilities Act of 1990
ADC (American-Arab Anti-Discrimination Committee), 500
Additive intersectionality model, 443–4
Adib, A., 455, 463, 593
adivasis (indigenous aboriginals), 411
Adler, N., 375–6, 377
ADVANCE initiative, 111, 112–13
Affinity networks. *See* Diversity networks
Affirmative action (AA)
  assimilation approach of, 84
  criticisms of, 29, 256–7
  defined, 239
  diversity management vs., 44, 237
  geographical differences in, 29–30, 29*n*7, 31
  individual benefits of, 6, 239–41, 246
  legal and moral rationales for, 220
  limitations of, 83
  politicization of, 155
  positive effects of, 29, 31
  quotas and, 42, 84, 240
  in South Africa, 420
Affirmative internationalism, 137

Afigbo, A., 30n8
Africa
    affirmative action programs in, 30
    globalization scholarship in, 139
    human resource diversity programs in, 584–5
African-Americans. *See* Black and minority ethnic (BME) groups
African National Congress, 420
Agamben, Giorgio, 512
Age
    age–ethnicity–class dyads, 454–62, 464–5
    cultural context and, 457
    disability and, 471, 483
    discrimination, 373
    income inequality and, 459
    of workforces, 456–7
Age management programs, 456–7, 461
Agency
    ambiguous diversities and, 222, 230
    in business case for diversity, 264
    in critical sensemaking method, 309, 310
    defined, 309
    of female entrepreneurs, 397–8, 399, 404
    structure and, 548, 549
Ahl, H., 388
Ahmadiyya sect, 415
Ahmed, Sara, 197, 266
Ahonen, P., 159
AIDS Coalition to Unleash Power (ACT UP) movement, 196. *See also* HIV/AIDS
Alberti, G., 22, 590
Ali, Faiza, 8, 408, 419
Allah, 400
Allen, A., 222
Allport, G. W., 114
Altman, J., 392
Alvesson, M., 100, 255, 304
Ambiguous diversities, 218–34
    agency and, 222, 230
    ambivalence and, 228–30, 231
    case study of, 218–19, 224–5, 227–8, 229–30
    contradiction and, 225–8, 230–1
    definitions of, 221
    in diversity management, 219–20, 230
    framework for study of, 221–30
    future research directions, 232
    overview, 5–6, 218–19
    queer theory and, 221–2
    strategic, 222–5, 228, 230–1
Ambivalence
    ambiguous diversities and, 228–30, 231
    of borders and boundary crossings, 184, 185
    in colonialism, 161, 162, 163
    of cultural authority, 185, 186
    in identifications, 188
    in Pakistani law, 415
    as resistance to the dominant cultural imperatives, 164
    of tempered radicals, 20
American-Arab Anti-Discrimination Committee (ADC), 500
Americans with Disabilities Act of 1990 (ADA), 470, 475, 478, 486
Analysis of variance (ANOVA) method, 443
Anand, R., 558
Anangu Pitjantjatjara Yankunytjatjara (APY) Lands, 393, 393n4
Anderson, C. L., 478
Anderson, R., 391, 392
Ang, I., 520
ANOVA (analysis of variance) method, 443
ANT (actor–network theory), 448
Anthias, F., 70n1, 462, 591
Anti-categorical approach, to intersectionality, 70, 441, 442, 465, 523
Anti-Discrimination Board of New South Wales, 528, 528n1
Anti-Discrimination Directives (EU), 70, 206
Anti-Semitism, 504–5
Apartheid, 166, 421, 425
Appadurai, M., 592
APY (Anangu Pitjantjatjara Yankunytjatjara) Lands, 393, 393n4
Aragon, S. R., 566
Arber, S., 545
Arciniega, L. M., 243
Argentina, as vulnerable country, 409
Al Ariss, A., 462
Articulations, 306
Artifacts, cultural, 543, 544–5, 549
Ascribed identity, 117, 510
Ashcroft, B., 186
Ashkanasy, N. M., 376

Ashley, L., 461
Asia, globalization scholarship in, 139
Asian Dragons, 409
Assimilation
  in academia, 350
  in diversity management, 46, 585
  entrepreneurship and, 399, 403
  heteronormative ideals and, 199, 212
  of indigenous research methodologies, 169
  of minorities, 83, 84, 389, 505
  into organizational culture, 480
Association of American Colleges and Universities, 368
Aull Davies, C., 100
Australia
  affirmative action in, 240
  business case for diversity in, 265
  equality-diversity discourse in, 48, 49-51
  feminist activism in, 20-1
  immigrants in workforce in, 235
  Indigenous communities in, 390-5, 390n1
  Anangu Pitjantjatjara Yankunytjatjara Lands of, 393, 393n4
  race and gender laws in, 523
  settler-native relations in, 394
  stereotype threat in, 481
Austria, diversity discourse in, 74, 454
Authenticity, 322-4
Avotie, L., 562
Ayoko, O. B., 245

Baby Dragons, 409
Bachan, R., 463
Bairoh, S., 65
Baldridge, David C., 9-10, 469, 482, 484
Balkundi, P., 460
Balser, D. B., 485
Banerjee, S., 129, 131, 178, 393
Bangladesh, formation of, 409
Barbarism, 503
Barbosa, I., 266
Barley, S. R., 319
Barney, J., 237-8
Barnum, P., 459
Baron, R. C., 479
Barr, J. J., 481
Barragan, S., 589

Barrett, M., 63
Barth, F., 185
Bauman, Z., 331-2
Baumfree, Isabella (Sojourner Truth), 67
Baytos, L. M., 558
Beasley, C., 526-7
Beatty, Joy E., 9-10, 469
Beck, Ulrich, 332
Beckles, H., 24, 24n5
Bedell, K. W., 476
Behavioural disintegration, 244
Belgium
  diversity discourse in, 463
  people with disabilities in, 476
Bell, E., 302
Bell, M. P., 462, 479, 480
Belongingness, in work groups, 115, 284, 376
Bending, in identity work, 401-2
Bendl, Regine, 5, 184, 195, 202-3, 544
Benschop, Yvonne, 10-11, 294, 302, 543, 545, 546, 547, 553, 586
Bensimon, E. M., 359
Benson, J. K., 95
Bergmann, H., 187
Bernstein, Ruth Sessler, 4, 109, 113, 114, 116
Berry, D. P., 462, 480
Best, R. K., 445
Bezrukova, K., 284, 557
Bhabha, Homi K., 135, 161, 162, 163, 164, 166, 167, 175, 176, 185, 186, 187, 306
Bharat. See India
Bias. See also Discrimination; Stereotypes
  common method bias, 290, 292-3
  ethnocentrism, 83, 127, 184, 389, 584
  institutional, 46
  managerial, 240, 424, 485
  unconscious, 18, 112, 118, 120
Biculturalism, 48
Bilimoria, Diana, 4, 109, 111, 113, 117
Bill and Melinda Gates Foundation, 469
Billings-Harris, L., 118
Binary thinking, posthumanist critique of, 98-9
Biological racism, 506, 509
Biomedical model of disability, 474
Bisexuals. See Lesbian, gay, bisexual, transgender, intersex (LGBTI) persons

Biswas, R., 54
Black and minority ethnic (BME) groups. *See also* Ethnicity; Race and racism
   access to power, 17
   affirmative action, impact on, 239–40, 241, 246
   career advancement of, 240
   career satisfaction of, 241, 287–8, 377
   economic restructuring, impact on, 22
   entrepreneurship of, 301–2, 388–9, 403
   equal opportunity initiatives for, 286
   in leadership positions, 376
   pay equity for, 240
   police discrimination and, 26–7
   unemployment among, 17
Black Consciousness movement, 167n4
Black feminism
   critiques of second-wave feminism, 51
   defined, 436
   on intersectionality, 67–9
   sociological imagination and, 18–19
Black Feminist Thought (Hill Collins), 18, 69, 436
Blackmail, 401
Blake, S., 178, 179, 262
Blake-Beard, S. D., 561
Blancero, Donna Maria, 4, 109
Blaut, J. M., 506
Bleijenbergh, Inge, 10, 539, 547, 548
BME groups. *See* Black and minority ethnic groups
Bodenhausen, G. V., 116, 119
Bogaert, S., 91
Böhm, S., 306
Bolivia, *buen vivir* in, 141–2
Boogaard, B., 94, 589
Boon, S. P., 303
Boone Parsons, D., 545
Borchhorst, A., 21
Border control, internal, 164
Borders
   as inclusion/exclusion mechanisms, 182, 184–5, 188
   internal, 390
   liminality of, 184, 186
   between self and others, 184
Bosch, Anita, 8, 408

Bosma, H., 402
Boundary work, 399, 400
Bourdieu, P., 54, 458, 461, 462
Bourgeoisie, 458
Bowleg, L., 443–4
Bowring, M., 200
Boxall, P., 49, 288
Boxenbaum, E., 585–6
Bracchitta, K., 481
Bradley, Harriet, 28, 590
Braidotti, R., 98
Brain drain, 375
Brantlinger, P., 161
Braverman, H., 326
Brazil
   diversity management in, 542
   emergence of, 33, 409, 549
Brewer, J. D., 18
Brewer, M. B., 524
Brewis, J., 200
BRIC (Brazil, Russia, India, and China) countries, 33, 409, 549
Brint, S., 113–14
British Airways, 446
Broadbent, E., 477
Brown, C., 21
Brown, Michael, 26
Brown, R., 523
Bruni, A., 388, 402
Bryant, L., 455, 548
Buckley, T., 116, 118
Buen vivir (living well), 141–2
Buitelaar, M., 402, 459
Burawoy, M., 32, 330
Burgess-Limerick, T., 343
Burke, R. J., 239
Burkhauser, R. V., 478, 480
Burrell, G., 65, 87
Buse, K., 113
Bush, George W., 139
Business case for diversity, 255–77
   agency and subjectivity in, 264
   in codes of conduct, 209
   consumer group representation in, 260–1
   contextual considerations of, 265–6
   critical diversity studies on, 155–8
   critiques of, 6, 262–6, 318

decision-making, creativity and innovation in, 261, 376, 377
defined, 255
as discourse of control, 263–4
dualisms in, 40–5
effectiveness of, 261–2
elements of, 258–61
in emerging countries, 414, 426
employees, attracting and retaining, 259
future research directions, 274
implementation and internationalization of, 155–8
multiculturalism and, 178, 179
organizational, 374–7, 380–1
origins of, 255, 256–7
racism and discrimination in, 264–5
reduced costs and, 259–60
social justice discourses and, 258–9, 266–73, 268–70t, 371
Butler, Judith, 197, 198, 200, 202
Buttner, E. H., 118

Cabral-Cardoso, C., 266
Calás, Marta B., 11, 51, 177, 182, 445, 575
Calori, R., 374
Caluya, G., 529, 530
Calvinism, 399
"Camouflaging power and privilege: a critical race analysis of university diversity policies" (Iverson), 366
Canada
 affirmative action in, 239–40
 business case for diversity in, 265
 diversity discourse of employers in, 267–71, 268–70t
 engineering profession, female representation in, 307
 immigrant workers in, 235, 447
 pay equity in, 240
 people with disabilities in, 470–1, 478, 488
Capitalism
 class and, 76
 colonialism and, 132
 contemporary nature of, 20
 entrepreneurship and, 399
 globalization and, 190, 589, 593
 historical breaks and continuities in, 22
 neoliberalism and, 131, 193, 591
 normalizing power of, 196
 as patriarchal structure, 69
 Protestant work ethic and, 399, 507
Carbin, M., 588
Career advancement, 240
Career satisfaction, 241, 287–8, 294, 377
Caribbean islands, reparation demands of, 24
Carrim, Nasima M. H., 8, 408
Cassell, C., 43, 54, 56
Caste system, 410, 411, 412, 413
Categorization and elaboration model (CEM), 283, 284
Catholicism, 507
CDA (critical discourse analysis), 446–7
CEDAW. See Convention on the Elimination of All Forms of Discrimination against Women
Chadwick, K., 89
Chain referral sampling, 343
Chan, F., 473, 477
Chang, E., 91
Change agents, Turkish female entrepreneurs as, 398
Chapman, D., 202
Charter of Fundamental Rights (EU), 46
Child abuse, 27, 391n2
Childcare facilities, in workplace, 417, 425
Chile, emergence of, 409
Chilisa, Bagele, 169
China
 emergence of, 33, 409, 549
 guanxi in, 580–1
 in management and organization studies, 141
 peaceful rise framework and, 141, 142, 143
 in war on terror, 143
Choi, J. N., 582
Choi, S., 287
Choo, H., 436–7, 438, 524
Chopra, R., 526, 527
Chrisman, J. J., 391, 392
Christensen, Ann-Dorte, 69
Christensen, K. A., 481
Christensen, S., 87
Christianity, 502, 506–7, 508
Chua, R. V. J., 119

Cisgender, 198
Cisnormativity, 196, 197, 199, 210, 211, 213
Citibank Pakistan, 418–19
Citizenship, dimensions of, 504
Civil Rights Act of 1964 (US), 45, 500
Civil Rights movement, 41, 51, 83, 506
Clash of civilizations theory, 129, 137–8, 139, 502–3
Class
  age–ethnicity–class dyads, 454–62, 464–5
  capitalism and, 76
  definitions of, 458
  discrimination based on, 17
  disidentification with, 458–9
  in diversity practice, 19, 589
  institutionalizing processes in creating and maintaining, 458
  middle class, 19*n*1
  power and, 458
Clegg, S., 307
Co-optation mechanisms
  in business case for diversity, 273
  knowledge production and management through, 133–4, 135, 139, 142, 143
  radicalization of, 131
Co-workers, reaction to workplace accommodation, 485–6, 489
Coalition Government (United Kingdom), 29
Cockburn, C., 20
Codes of conduct (CoCs)
  business case for diversity in, 209
  defined, 204
  on harassment, 207–8, 209
  on health and safety, 208
  heteronormativity in, 208, 210, 211, 212, 213
  laws and regulations in, 208–9, 212
  queer theory analysis of, 203, 204–12, 207*t*, 213
  on relationships, 208, 211–12
  sex–gender–sexuality in, 205–8, 207*t*, 210, 211–12
Coding techniques, 92–3, 205, 361–3
Cohen, L., 202
Cole, B., 439, 443
Colella, A., 480, 485
Collective identity, 520, 524
Collectivism
  in equal opportunity approach, 28, 34
  in Islam, 400
  in systemic structures of inequality, 18
Colleges. *See* Academia
Colley, H., 560
Collins, Patricia Hill, 18, 69, 436, 438, 440, 442
Colonial subjectivities, 161, 181
Colonialism and colonization. *See also* Postcolonialism
  capitalism and, 132
  cultural imperialism and, 160
  defined, 160*n*1
  in diversity management, 128, 129–30
  dominant group advantages of, 163
  global, 128, 129–30
  legacies of, 24–5, 162, 167
  in politics of diversity, 23–7, 30, 30*n*8, 33
  slavery and, 24
Coloniality, 128, 130, 131–2, 135–6, 140
Combahee River Collective, 67–8
Coming out process, 423
Commatization, of oppression, 68
Commodity diversity, 94
Common method bias, 290, 292–3
Communications Management Units, 501
Communism, 95
Competency
  of academics, 344
  of employees, 231, 272
  in individual-level diversity, 116–22, 121*t*
  multilingual, 457
  of supervisors, 424
Competitive advantage
  in business case discourse, 255, 257, 265
  diversity management and, 44, 84, 155, 178, 237
  workforce diversity as, 238, 261, 374, 375–6
Competitive individualism, 50
Component theory of disability identity development, 472
Compulsive heterosexuality, 200
The Condition of the Working Class in England (Engels), 319*n*1
Conflict-oriented identity work, 401
Conley, H., 29*n*7
Connell, Raewyn, 168–9, 526, 527, 529
Conradson, D., 592

Constitutive intersectionality model, 443
Construct validity, of research methodology, 290, 291–2, 293
Constructionism, 64, 71
Consumer group representation, in business case for diversity, 260–1
Containment mechanisms
  knowledge production and management through, 133–4, 135, 139, 142, 143
  of military, 137
  in othering processes, 182
  radicalization of, 131
Content mapping approach, 361
Content validity, of research methodology, 291–2
Context model, of global diversity management, 371
Contradiction, 225–8, 230–1
Convention on the Elimination of All Forms of Discrimination against Women (CEDAW), 40, 416, 418
Convention on the Rights of Persons with Disabilities (CRPD), 486
Cooper, J. N., 18
Cornwall, A., 525, 526
Cornwall, J., 53
Corporate Social Responsibility (CSR) Initiatives, 54, 204
Cosmopolitanism, 129, 130, 132, 136, 140
Counter-knowledge, 140
Covering Islam: How the Media and the Experts Determine How We See the Rest of the World (Said), 503
Cowling, M., 464, 541
Cox, Taylor, 46, 178, 179, 237, 262
Crary, Marcy, 4, 109
Creativity
  contradiction and, 228
  in decision-making, 261
  diversity and, 119, 209, 243, 262, 376, 377
  entrepreneurship and, 395
  in qualitative research, 337
  strategic ambiguity and, 223
Creed, D., 200
Crenshaw, Kimberlé Williams, 68–9, 435, 436, 437, 439, 440, 518, 525, 590
Crisp, R. J., 119–20

Critical discourse analysis (CDA), 446–7
Critical diversity studies, 539–52
  assessment of research contributions to, 547–8, 549, 550
  business case for diversity in, 155–8
  critiques of, 75, 101, 177
  data sources, collection, and analysis in, 544–6
  defined, 539–40
  dialectical tradition in, 95–7
  discursive tradition in, 93–5, 96, 180
  in diversity management research, 85, 93–7
  emergence of, 154, 156
  first-wave, 157–8
  future research directions, 549
  on language, 302–3, 446–7
  overview, 5, 10, 153–4, 539–40
  phases of, 542–8
  postcolonialism in, 166–70
  principles of, 85
  qualitative research in, 345, 348, 350–1, 543, 549
  research agendas in, 540–3
  researcher's role in, 547
  second-wave of, 158–9
  strategies for, 543–4, 548–9
  survey of, 154–9
  textual analysis in, 300–1, 302–3
Critical hermeneutics, 446
Critical Management Research (Alvesson & Deetz), 100
A Critical Psychology of the Postcolonial: The Mind of Apartheid (Hook), 166
Critical sensemaking method (CSM), 300, 305, 308–11, 310f, 447
CRPD (Convention on the Rights of Persons with Disabilities), 486
CSR (Corporate Social Responsibility) Initiatives, 54, 204
Cultural artifacts, 543, 544–5, 549
Cultural diversity. *See* Multiculturalism
Cultural globalization, 138
Cultural imperialism, 23, 160, 161, 162
Cultural legitimacy, 528–9
Cultural metacognition, 119
Cultural pluralism, 16, 127, 177, 184
Cultural racism, 179, 506, 507, 508, 509

Dacin, M. T., 458
DAL (diversity-authenticity-leadership) triangle, 323, 324
Dana, L., 391
D'Andrea, A., 592
Danowitz, Mary Ann, 8, 357
Darwin, A., 563
Datta, K., 529, 530
Daus, C. S., 376
Davenport, S., 222
Davidson, D., 113
Davies, A., 447
Davis, Angela, 68
Davis, Kathy, 439
Davison, H. K., 484
Dawkins, Richard, 505
De Beauvoir, S., 23
De Dreu, C. K. W., 283
De Lauretis, Teresa, 196n3
De Neve, G., 526
De Vries, J., 563
De Vries, R. E., 90, 91
Deakin, S., 27
Dean, D., 20
Debebe, G., 116
Deblaere, C., 519
Dechant, K., 258
Decision-making
  bureaucratization of, 42
  creativity and innovation in, 261
  critical moments in, 546
  ethical, 238
  information/decision-making concept, 88
Declaration of Human Rights (UN), 40
Declaration of the Rights of Indigenous Peoples (UN), 390
Decoloniality, 127–8, 130–2, 133–4, 135–6, 140–3, 144
Deem, R., 362
Deep-level diversity, 88, 89, 114, 236
Deetz, S., 100
Defensive internationalism, 137
Dehumanization, of Muslim populations, 511, 512
Deleuze, G., 97, 98
Democracy, organizational, 330
Demographic imperative, 256

Demography, identity and, 579–81
Denis, J.-L., 224
DeNisi, A. S., 480, 580
Denissen, A. M., 303
Denmark
  diversity discourse in, 585–6
  trade unions in, 29
Deshpande, S., 412
Developmentalist fallacy, 133
Diagnostic equality checks, 378–81, 382
Dialectic transformations, 54–6, 55t
Dialectical tradition, in diversity management research, 95–7
Dickens, L., 29
Differences. See Diversity
Dill, B. T., 438, 520
Dimensions for the Design of Diversity practices. See 3D-model of diversity management
Dinsbach, A. A., 90, 91
Disabilities, defined, 469. See also People with disabilities (PWD)
Discourse approach, to equal opportunity, 42
Discourse of control, business case for diversity as, 263–4
Discourse theory (Laclau & Mouffe), 7, 300, 305–8
Discrimination. See also Bias; Oppression; Stereotypes and stigmatization
  age-based, 373
  apartheid, 166, 421, 425
  in business case for diversity, 264–5
  career satisfaction and, 241
  class and, 17
  in employment. See Equal opportunity (EO) initiatives
  at global vs. local levels, 372
  at higher education institutions, 358, 363, 366
  in India, 411, 412
  institutional, 299
  intersectionality and, 86
  language and, 299, 302, 423
  of LGBTI persons, 372
  of Muslim populations, 397, 499–501, 509–12, 590
  in Pakistan, 417

of people with disabilities, 473, 474, 477,
    480, 483, 488
by police, 26–7
positive. *See* Affirmative action (AA)
religious, 500–1
systemic, 44
in UK labour market, 373
of women, 40, 416, 418. *See also* Gender
    differences
Discrimination and fairness paradigm, 237
Discursive closure, 181
Discursive tradition, in diversity management
    research, 93–5, 96, 180
Distancing, in ethnographic research, 320
Ditomaso, N., 459
Diversity
    ambiguous. *See* Ambiguous diversities
    business case for. *See* Business case for
        diversity
    categories and constructions of, 63–5, 71
    commodity, 94
    constructionist perception of, 64, 71
    deep-level, 88, 89, 114, 236
    definitions of, 44, 110, 236, 281, 576–7
    disabled persons. *See* People with
        disabilities (PWD)
    essentialist perception of, 64, 71, 183
    ethnicity. *See* Ethnicity
    gender. *See* Gender differences; Women
    innovation and, 89
    internationalizing, 155–8, 578, 582–3, 595.
        See also Transnational diversity
    intersectionality of, 70–2, 70n1
    linguistic deconstruction of, 71–2
    moral case for, 40, 209, 230, 238. *See also*
        Social justice
    multiculturalism, 175–94. *See also*
        Multiculturalism
    organizational. *See* Organizational diversity
    politics of. *See* Politics of diversity
    provincializing, 578, 583–8, 595
    race. *See* Race and racism
    simultaneity of, 578, 588–90, 595
    surface-level, 236
    workplace. *See* Workplace diversity
Diversity, Ethnicity, Migration at Work (Healy
    & Oikelome), 30

Diversity-authenticity-leadership (DAL)
    triangle, 323, 324
Diversity dividend, 109, 111, 116, 120, 122, 283
Diversity literacy, 424
Diversity management (DM), 127–49. *See
    also* Diversity management outcomes;
    Diversity management research; Global
    diversity management
    affirmative action vs., 44, 237
    ambiguities of, 219–20, 230
    colonialism in, 128, 129–30
    conceptual contradictions of, 226
    critical turn in, 262–6
    critiques of, 156–8, 157t, 180–4, 298–9, 575–6
    definitions of, 358, 359–60, 367, 553
    in emerging countries, 127, 128, 129
    Eurocentrism in, 129, 131, 134, 143
    evolution of, 256–7, 282, 317, 576
    globalization and, 127, 128, 136–43, 144, 576
    heteronormativity in, 195–6
    in higher education institutions, 359–60,
        364–8, 364f
    individual benefits of, 6, 239–41, 239n1, 246
    intersectionality, implications for, 65,
        72–6, 77
    itinerant, 321–6
    knowledge and, 4, 128–36
    as multiculturalist discourse, 178–80
    politics of diversity in, 28–9
    postcolonial critique of, 180–4
    queer theory in discourse of, 202–3
    relational levels of, 358, 361
    rise of, 1, 42–4, 83–4, 127, 128–9, 155
    theoretical frameworks for, 236–8
    3D-model of, 554–7, 555t, 567–9, 567t
    universalization of, 128, 131, 132, 139, 141, 182
Diversity management outcomes, 281–97
    belief in diversity as factor in, 242, 247
    career advancement, 240
    career satisfaction, 241, 287–8, 294, 377
    fault lines and, 243–4, 247
    individual, 239–41, 246
    organizational, 6, 244–6, 247
    overview, 7, 281–2
    pay equity, 240
    strategic orientations and, 245
    survey research on, 7, 282, 284, 285–93

Diversity management outcomes (*Cont.*)
  task types and, 243
  team and group, 6, 241–4, 246–7
  for work groups, 283–4
Diversity management research, 83–108. *See also* Critical diversity studies; Ethnographic research; Qualitative research; Quantitative research; Survey research
  comparative nature of, 182–3
  critical traditions of, 85, 93–7
  future challenges for, 569–70
  interpretative tradition of, 84, 85, 91–3, 93n3
  methodology for, 86–7
  multi-level approaches in, 292, 293–4, 299, 303–5
  multiculturalism in, 187–90
  overview, 4, 83–6
  positivist tradition of, 53, 84, 85, 87–91, 93n3, 183
  postcolonialism in, 188–9
  posthumanist feminism and, 85, 86, 97–100, 101
  queer theory in, 54, 199–203, 201t
  representational nature of, 183
  textual analysis in, 7, 301–5
Diversity networks
  content of, 564–5
  criticisms of, 554, 564, 567
  format for, 566–7
  for LGBT persons, 564, 565, 566–7
  participants of, 565–6
  purpose of, 563–4, 568
Diversity professionals, defined, 20
Diversity Research Network, 262, 287
Diversity scorecards, 359
Diversity toolkits, 8, 47, 372, 373, 378–82, 383
Diversity training programs
  content of, 557–8
  criticisms of, 554, 567
  on disabilities, 481
  format for, 557, 559–60
  participants of, 558–9
  for police, 27
  in South Africa, 424
  for supervisors, 112, 559
  for women, 558–9

DM. *See* Diversity management
Dobbin, F., 155, 246, 286
Doherty, A., 92
Domaining effect, 321–2
Dominquez, C. M., 117–18
Donaldson, L., 45
Dovidio, J. F., 114
Down, S., 319n1
Draine, J., 479
Draper, W. R., 480
Du Bois, W. E. B., 436
Dualisms, 39–61
  in Australian context, 49–51
  dialectic transformation of, 54–6, 55t
  in diversity discourse, 42–5, 43t
  in equal opportunity, 28, 41–2, 43–4, 43t
  gender vs. "other" diversity dimensions, 51–2, 55
  global perspectives vs. local economies, 47–51, 55, 371–2, 382
  mind-body, 97–8
  in New Zealand context, 48–9
  overview, 4, 39–40, 40t
  practitioner activities vs. academic research, 45–7
  in quantitative vs. qualitative methodological approaches, 52–4, 56
  in social justice and business case for diversity, 40–5
Duggan, Lisa, 197, 199
Durkheim, Émile, 67
Dutch Foundation for Psychotechniques (NSvP), 322, 332
Dweck, C. S., 119
Dwyer, S., 89
Dye, Kelly, 6, 255

Economy. *See also* Business case for diversity
  equal opportunity and, 45
  global restructuring of, 22
  of good expectations, 331
  hybrid, 392
  neoliberalism and, 199
Ecuador, *buen vivir* in, 141–2
Edenheim, S., 588
Education. *See* Academia
Edwards, P., 22

EEOC (Equal Opportunity Employment Commission), 500, 510
Ego-bodily relations, 167, 167n4
EGOS (European Group of Organization Studies), 2
Egypt, emergence of, 409
Ehrenreich, B., 319n1
Eibach, R. P., 523
Eisenberg, E. M., 222, 223, 224, 228
Eisenhardt, K. M., 460
Ely, R., 46, 237
Emerging countries, 408–31. *See also* BRIC countries
   business case for diversity in, 414, 426
   characteristics of, 408, 409
   classification of, 409
   comparison of, 425–6
   diversity management in, 127, 128, 129
   India, 409, 410–15
   overview, 8, 408–9
   Pakistan, 409–10, 415–19
   South Africa, 410, 420–5
Emic approaches, 465, 523, 541, 543, 548–9
Employee network groups. *See* Diversity networks
Employees/employment
   affirmative action, impact on, 239–40
   attracting and retaining, 259
   authenticity of, 322, 323
   diversity. *See* Workplace diversity
   host country national, 580, 581
   of people with disabilities, 475–8, 486–7
   public policies, impact on, 478
   survey research on, 286–90, 293
   workplace accommodation and, 482–3
Empowerment
   diversity initiatives and, 163, 382, 542
   intersectional, 590
   psychological safety and, 116
   sociological imagination and, 18
   in South Africa, 420–1, 422, 424
   of women, 19
Empson, L., 461
Empty signifiers, 307
Entrepreneurship, 388–407
   capitalism and, 399
   contextual factors in, 399–403

   of ethnic minorities, 301–2, 388–9, 403
   of female migrants, 302, 388, 395–9, 400–3, 404
   Indigenous, 390, 391–5, 403–4
   individualism and, 388, 392, 395, 399
   intersectionality and, 398–9, 403
   overview, 8, 388–9
   postcolonialism and, 394, 403, 404
   stereotypes in, 388, 389
EO initiatives. *See* Equal opportunity initiatives
Epistemological approach of intersectional analysis, 442
Equal Opportunity Employment Commission (EEOC), 500, 510
Equal opportunity (EO) initiatives. *See also* Workplace diversity
   codes of conduct on, 207
   defined, 239
   discourse approach to, 42
   diversity management critiques of, 156, 157t
   dualisms in, 28, 41–2, 43–4, 43t
   economic rationale for, 45, 220
   for ethnic minorities, 286
   history of, 83
   in India, 412, 413
   individual benefits of, 6, 239–41, 246
   legislative policies on, 40–1, 50
   liberal approach to, 41–2
   in Pakistan, 416, 417, 418–19
   politicization of, 155
   radical approach to, 42
   social justice and, 281
   in South Africa, 420
   survey research on, 286
Equality. *See also* Equal opportunity (EO) initiatives; Social justice
   income, 240, 241
   moral case for, 40
   multinational corporation policies on, 382
   neoliberalism, impact on, 17, 48
Equality toolkits, 378–82
Erkut, S., 243
Escalating indecision, 224
Essed, P., 158

Essentialism
    on difference, 64, 71, 183
    Eurocentrism and, 132
    on language, 71
    Muslim populations and, 502–5, 510
Essers, Caroline, 8, 302, 388, 396, 546, 547
Ethical decision-making, 238
Ethnic groups, defined, 457
Ethnic wars, 137
Ethnicity. *See also* Black and minority ethnic (BME) groups; Indigenous communities
    age-ethnicity-class dyads, 454–62, 464–5
    cultural context and, 457–8
    as negative marker of difference, 26
    in Nigeria, 30–1, 30n8
    in Pakistan, 416–17
Ethnocentrism, 83, 127, 184, 389, 584
Ethnographic research, 317–36
    in critical tradition, 96, 543
    history of, 319, 319m1
    in interpretative tradition, 92
    intersectional analysis in, 443
    on itinerant diversity management, 321–6
    multi-level designs for, 304
    on organizational democracy, 326–30
    overview, 7, 317–19
    subversive potential of, 318, 320, 331, 332
    on workplace diversity, 319–21
Etic approaches, 464–5, 523, 541
Eurocentric liberalism, 130, 139
Eurocentric universalism, 128, 129, 130, 134, 135
Eurocentrism
    in academia, 132–3, 135
    defined, 160
    in diversity management, 129, 131, 134, 143
    in gender and diversity research, 159
    globalization as radicalization of, 130–1, 137
    longue durée of, 130, 130n1, 131, 132, 135
    postcolonialism and, 159, 160–1
Europe/European Union (EU)
    aging workforces in, 456–7
    Anti-Discrimination Directives, 70, 206
    Charter of Fundamental Rights, 46
    management perspectives in, 374
    pay equity in, 240
    people with disabilities in, 470

European Group of Organization Studies (EGOS), 2
Eveline, J., 563
Exclusion
    age and, 457
    by heteronormativity, 203
    historical examples of, 16
    identity categories and, 399
    of Muslim populations, 504
Exclusionary inclusion, 129, 130, 132
Expatriation, 73, 91–2, 462, 580, 594
Exploitative relationships, cultural aspects of, 198–9
Expository textual analysis, 301–2
External intersectionality, 72–4
External validity, of research methodology, 290–1, 294

Fairclough, N., 304, 306
Fanon, Frantz, 136, 161, 166, 167
Farh, J. L. L., 580, 581
Faria, Alex, 4, 127
Fault lines, 243–4, 247
Fear Inc. (Center for American Progress), 512
Featherman, D. L., 461
Federal Human Capital Survey, 287, 291
Feij, J. A., 90, 91
Females. *See* Gender differences; Women
Feminism. *See also* Black feminism; Posthumanist feminism
    activism and, 20–1, 54
    fragmentation of, 51
    on intersectionality, 67–9, 76–7, 474
    postcolonial, 165
    poststructuralism and, 303, 589
    research methodology of, 53
    second-wave, 40, 51, 67
    transnational, 51, 70
Feminism without Borders (Mohanty), 70
Feminist Theory: From Margin to Center (hooks), 68
Ferguson, Kathy, 591
Ferguson (Missouri) race riots (2014), 22, 26
Ferree, M., 436–7, 438, 524
Feyes, K. J., 481
Field of discursivity, 306, 308
Fielden, Sandra L., 10, 539

Fieldwork, in qualitative research, 340–4
Finland
   business case for diversity in, 266
   diversity discourse in, 75, 586
   organizational democracy of software engineers in, 326–30
   term for diversity in, 71–2
Fireplace mentoring sessions, 321, 325, 326, 332
First-wave critical diversity studies, 157–8
Fiske, S. T., 479
Fleischmann, A., 184, 202–3
Fletcher, J. K., 303
Fleury, A., 409
Floating signifiers, 306, 307
Flynn, R. J., 118
Foldy, E., 116, 118, 242
Foley, D., 390
For-profit organizations, diversity discourses of, 269–72, 270t
Ford, Michele, 526, 527, 530
Forson, C., 590
Fortier, A. M., 592
Foster, T., 262
Foucault, Michel, 98, 167, 197, 200, 446, 577, 577n1, 588, 594
France
   diversity discourse in, 75
   higher education institutions in, 358
   people with disabilities in, 476
   term for diversity in, 71
Fraser, N., 455–6, 459
Frederick, H., 390
Freeman, S., 91
F-Secure Corporation, 320, 327–30, 331
Functionalism, 87, 183, 262, 273
Fundamental critiques, of diversity management, 156–8, 157t
Fundamentalist Islam, 138
Furunes, T., 92

Gaertner, S. L., 114
García, M., 485
Gaunt, P. M., 479–80
Gay Rights movement, 52
Gays. *See* Lesbian, gay, bisexual, transgender, intersex (LGBTI) persons
Gebert, D., 284

Gedro, J., 202
Gender coaches, 559
Gender differences. *See also* Men; Women
   in access to power, 17
   in disabilities, 471
   in entrepreneurial stereotypes, 388, 389
   ethical orientation and, 238
   in firm performance, 89
   in income/pay, 40, 240, 241
   in India, 413–14
   institutional practices of, 365
   intersections with sex and sexuality, 197–8, 197f, 205–8, 207t, 210, 211–12
   Islam and, 400
   legislative policies on, 21
   in Pakistan, 418–19
   resistance to normative constructions of, 303
   in UK labour market, 373
Gender performance, 198, 202
Genocide, 391, 391n3
Ghadar, F., 375–6
Gherardi, S., 402
Ghorashi, H., 185, 189
Ghumman, S., 510
Gilbert, J. A., 286–7
Gill, C., 472
Gilroy, P., 23, 24
Gilson, S. F., 472
Ginkel, W. P., 89
Giscombe, K., 563
Githens, R. P., 566
Glick-Schiller, N., 592
Global academia, 130, 132–4, 136, 138, 141, 143
Global Burden of Disease Study (2010), 469
Global colonialism, 129–30
Global coloniality, 128, 130, 131–2, 135, 136, 140
Global Compact (UN), 40–1
Global diversity management, 370–87
   business case for organizational diversity in, 374–7, 380–1
   diagnostic equality checks in, 378–81
   implementation in local economies, 47–51, 55, 371–2, 382
   methodology for study of, 377–8
   models and frameworks for, 370–1
   overview, 8, 370–3

Global diversity management (Cont.)
  toolkits for, 8, 372, 373, 378–82, 383
  in UK labour market, 373–4
Globalization
  capitalism and, 190, 589, 593
  cultural, 138
  diversity management and, 127, 128, 136–43, 144, 576
  hypermobility and, 592
  intersectional effects of, 73, 590
  neoliberalism and, 128–30, 131, 593, 595
  as radicalization of Eurocentrism, 130–1, 137
  workplace diversity and, 32
Goffee, R., 391
Goldman Sachs Investment Bank, 409
Golnaraghi, Golnaz, 6, 255, 499
Gomez-Mejia, L., 179, 183
Gooden, M., 476
Gotanda, N., 509
Gouws, A., 425
Grace, M., 343
Graham, M., 205
Grassroots activism, 41, 565
Gray, B., 458
Greene, A.-M., 20, 28–9
Grewal, I., 70
Grice, S., 273
Griffiths, G., 186
Groeneveld, Sandra, 7, 281, 318
Grosfoguel, R., 133
Grosz, E., 97
Groups
  inclusion practices for, 113–16, 120–2, 121t
  intersectionality and, 524–5
  performance outcomes and diversity, 6, 241–4, 246–7
  social identity theory and, 524, 525
  workplace diversity practices of, 113–16, 120–2, 121t
Groupthink, 243
Growth orientations, 245
Guanxi, 580–1
Guattari, F., 97, 98
Guerrier, Y., 455, 463, 593

Haberstam, Jack, 197
Haberstam, Judith, 197

Hagedorn-Rasmussen, P., 585
Hahn, H., 474
Hakim, C., 240
Hall, J. P., 479
Hall, S., 181
Hallock, K. F., 477
Hampden-Turner, C., 457
Handbook of Workplace Diversity (Prasad), 162–3
Hannappi, G., 455, 458
Hannappi-Egger, Edeltraud, 9, 454, 455, 457, 458, 460–1
Hansman, C. A., 561
Haq, Rana, 8, 408, 413, 541
Harassment
  caste system and, 412
  codes of conduct on, 207–8, 209
  at higher education institutions, 366
  of Muslim populations, 499
  of people with disabilities, 477
  of women, 17
Harcourt, M., 477
Harcourt, S., 477
Hardy, C., 304
Harris, L., 545
Harris, Sam, 505
Harrison, D. A., 115
Härtel, C. E. J., 91, 376
Harter, L. M., 226, 263
Hate crimes, 500
Hausa-Fulani tribe (Nigeria), 30n8
Hawking, Steven, 482
Hazer, J. T., 476
HCN (host country national) employees, 580, 581
He, J., 457
Health, codes of conduct on, 208
Healy, Geraldine, 3, 15, 22, 23–4, 28, 30, 590
Hearn, Jeff, 4, 62, 69
Hegel, Georg, 95
Hegemonic masculinities, 69, 526, 527
HEIs (higher education institutions). *See* Academia
Helms Mills, Jean, 7, 9, 300, 304, 305, 435, 447
Hendricks, D. J., 477
Hendry, C., 376
Henry, J. D., 481

Herbert, J. I., 301
Heres, L., 586
Hernández-León, R., 463
Herring, C., 375
Heteronormativity
  in codes of conduct, 208, 210, 211, 212, 213
  definitions of, 198–9
  in diversity management, 195–6
  exclusion by, 203
  LGBTI performances of, 199
  in organizational culture, 196, 198
  power structure of, 197, 198, 200, 202
Heterosexual matrix, 197–8, 197f, 200, 202, 203
Heterotopia, 577n1
Hewitt, J., 306
Hickey-Moody, A., 529
Hierarchy of oppression, 23, 24
Higher education institutions (HEIs). See Academia
Hijabi Muslims, 501, 510, 590
Hilde, Rosalie, 7, 298, 310, 318, 447
Hindustan. See India
Hitchens, Christopher, 505
HIV/AIDS, 196, 420
Hofhuis J., 118
Hofmann, Roswitha, 5, 195, 203, 454
Hogg, M. A., 522
Holgate, J., 22, 590
Holgersson, Charlotte, 10–11, 177, 553, 554
Holvino, E., 155, 458, 522–3
Holzer, H. J., 239
Homan, A. C., 118, 242, 283
Homo sacer (sacred or cursed man), 512
Homonormativity, 197, 199
Homophily, 460
Homosexuality. See Lesbian, gay, bisexual, transgender, intersex (LGBTI) persons
Hong Kong
  emergence of, 409
  people with disabilities in, 476
Hoobler, J., 179, 576
Hook, Derek, 166–7
Höök, P., 554, 561, 563
hooks, bell, 68
Hornscheidt, A., 72
Hörschelmann, K., 528
Horwitz, I. B., 110
Horwitz, S. K., 110
Host country national (HCN) employees, 580, 581
Houkamau, C., 49, 288
Houlette, M. A., 244
Houssay-Holzschuch, M., 409
Houtenville, A. J., 480
Hubbard, E., 359
Huddy, L., 522–3
Human resource management (HRM)
  actual vs. perceived policies of, 292
  in diversity management, 46, 112, 246, 247, 258, 583
  good practice standards, 22
  performance outcomes and, 284, 292
  positivism and, 89
  survey research on, 285–6
Human rights
  academic discourses of, 136
  in Australia, 391n3, 439
  in Canada, 470
  Declaration of Human Rights (UN), 40
  intersectionality and, 518
  macro framework for, 41
  same-sex relations and, 52
  in South Africa, 420
  universal values of, 510
Humbert, A. L., 396
Humphries, M., 273
Hunt, B., 481
Hunt, C. S., 481
Huntington, Samuel, 502–3
Huntingtonian racialism, 139, 141
Hybrid economies, 392
Hypermobility, 592
Hypervisibility, 509

Identitarianism, 582, 589, 591
Identity. See also Social identity theory (SIT)
  ascribed, 117, 510
  collective, 520, 524
  in critical diversity studies, 180
  definitions of, 437
  demography and, 579–81
  essentialism vs. constructionism on, 64
  of female migrants, 302
  of LGBTI persons, 200, 510

Identity (*Cont.*)
  multiple levels of, 524–5
  othering processes and, 86, 100, 161, 181–2
  of people with disabilities, 472–5
  performances of, 199, 222
  postcolonial theory and, 448
  in qualitative research, 340–4
  shifting nature of, 186, 187
  social confirmation of, 98, 99–100, 116
  social construction of, 53, 117
  stage theory of, 119–20
Identity blindness, 288
Identity politics, 98, 525
Identity work
  of female entrepreneurs, 400–2
  individual-level factors impacting, 118
  intersectionality and, 86, 399
  levels of, 524
  manifestations of, 400–2
  organizational, 164
  of researchers, 350
Igbo tribe (Nigeria), 30*n*8
ILO (International Labour Organization), 40
Immigrants and immigration
  abuse of, 22
  assimilation of, 83
  critical sensemaking method in analysis of, 309–11, 310*f*
  female migrant entrepreneurship, 302, 395–9, 400–3, 404
  politics of diversity and, 21, 22, 25–6
  racialised masculinities and, 530
  social networks of, 462–3
  in workforce, 235, 373, 375, 447, 590
Impairments, defined, 469. *See also* People with disabilities (PWD)
Imperial Leather (McClintock), 70
Imperialism, cultural, 23, 160, 161, 162
Imrie, R., 472
Inclusion
  borders as mechanisms of, 184–5
  defined, 110
  diversity training programs on, 557
  exclusionary mechanisms of, 129, 130, 132
  at group level, 113–16, 120–2, 121*t*
  identity categories and, 399
  leadership and, 284
  organizational climate for, 283–4, 289, 376
  at organizational level, 111–13, 120–2, 121*t*
  principles of, 45
Income. *See also* Class
  gender differences in, 40, 240, 241
  inequality in, 16–17, 40, 240, 241, 373, 459
  of people with disabilities, 476
India, 410–15
  affirmative action in, 240
  caste system in, 410, 411, 412, 413
  comparison with Pakistan and South Africa, 425–6
  education in, 412
  emergence of, 33, 409, 549
  equality and diversity as defined in, 410–11
  independence of, 409
  legislative and current history on diversity and equality, 411–12
  organizational diversity practices in, 413–15
  religion in, 409–10
  socio-political dynamics in, 412
  women in, 411–12, 413–14, 426, 541
Indigenous communities
  in Australia, 390–5, 390*n*1
  entrepreneurship in, 390, 391–5, 403–4
  knowledge systems of, 161, 162, 168, 169–70, 391
  oppression of, 390–1
  unemployment in, 390
Indigenous Research Methodologies (Chilisa), 169
Individualism
  competitive, 50
  entrepreneurship and, 388, 392, 395, 399
  in equal opportunity approach, 28
  neoliberalism and, 593
  religious, 400
  sociological imagination and, 18
  voluntarism and, 27, 28, 34
Individuals
  diversity management benefits for, 6, 239–41, 239*n*1, 246
  workplace diversity competencies of, 116–22, 121*t*
Indonesia
  rise of, 33
  as vulnerable country, 409

Industrial relations, as field of study, 32n9
Inequality. *See also* Discrimination; Exclusion
  in access to power, 17
  defined, 554
  in income/pay, 16–17, 40, 240, 241, 373, 459
  societal effects of, 16–17
Inequality regimes, 52
Information/decision-making concept, 88
Innovation
  in decision-making, 261
  diversity and, 89, 377
Innovative orientations, 245
Institutional bias, 46
Institutional discrimination, 299
Institutional practices of gender, 365
"Institutionalisation of Gender and Diversity Management in Engineering Education" (Leicht-Scholten et al.), 365–6
Institutionalized oppression, 420
Integration and learning paradigm, 237, 283–4
Interaction structuring practices, 114–15
Intercategorical approach, to intersectionality, 70, 441, 442, 443, 474, 489
Interdependence, 72
Interdiscursivity, 322
Internal border control, 164
Internal intersectionality, 72–4, 75
Internal validity, of research methodology, 292–3
International Convention on the Elimination of All Forms of Racial Discrimination (UN), 40
International Labour Organization (ILO), 40
Internationalizing diversity, 155–8, 578, 582–3, 595. *See also* Transnational diversity
Interpretivism, 84, 85, 91–3, 93n3, 300
Intersectional invisibility, 523
Intersectional sensibility, 590
Intersectionality, 62–82, 435–68
  age–ethnicity–class dyads, 454–62, 464–5
  of categories and differences, 63–5, 70–2, 70n1
  challenges of, 76
  criticisms of, 435, 442, 588
  definitions of, 52, 437–9, 455
  discriminatory impact of, 86
  entrepreneurship and, 398–9, 403

  external vs. internal, 72–4, 75
  feminism on, 67–9, 76–7, 474
  globalization and, 73, 590
  history and development of, 66–72, 436–7, 518, 588
  implications for diversity and diversity management, 65, 72–6, 77
  masculinities and, 69
  methodological approaches to analysis of, 440–4
  oppression and, 52, 66, 435, 436–7, 438, 522
  overview, 4, 9, 62–3, 435–6
  paradigms and applications of, 444–9
  in policy development, 69–70
  political, 440
  in politics of diversity, 17, 19–20
  positivism and, 445
  postcolonialism and, 70, 448–9
  postpositivism and, 445–9
  poststructuralism and, 447, 588
  research challenges and, 464–5
  of sex–gender–sexuality, 197–8, 197f, 205–8, 207t, 210, 211–12
  social identity theory and, 521–3, 531
  structural, 440
  transnational diversity and, 73, 74, 588–90
Intersex persons. *See* Lesbian, gay, bisexual, transgender, intersex (LGBTI) persons
Interviews
  protocols/guides for, 92
  in qualitative research, 339, 340, 341–4
  semi-structured, 339, 340, 342, 350, 543
Intracategorical approach, to intersectionality, 70, 441–2, 474, 489, 523
Irish migrants, 25
Islam and Muslims
  in Bangladesh, 409, 410
  clash of civilizations theory and, 502–3
  comparison with Jewish populations, 504–5
  dehumanization of, 511, 512
  discrimination of, 397, 499–501, 509–12, 590
  entrepreneurship and, 399, 400
  essentialization of, 502–5, 510
  of female migrant entrepreneurs, 302, 397, 399, 400
  fundamentalist, 138
  gender segregation in, 400

Islam and Muslims (*Cont.*)
    harassment of, 499
    hate crimes against, 500
    Hijabi Muslims, 501, 510, 590
    in India, 409–10
    Orientalism on, 399, 503
    overview, 10, 499–502
    in Pakistan, 409, 410, 415, 416, 417
    phenotypes of, 508–9
    racialised masculinities of men in, 529
    racialization of, 502, 509
    sharia and, 500
    Shia Muslims, 416, 417
    stigmatization of, 501
    Sunni Muslims, 416
Islamic fundamentalism, 138
Islamophobia, 141, 499, 501, 504–5, 512
Italy
    diversity discourse in, 74
    female entrepreneurs in, 402
Itinerant diversity management, 321–6
Ivancevich, J. M., 286–7
Iverson, S. V., 366

Jabbour, C. J. C., 542
Jack, Gavin, 5, 44, 87, 94, 153, 181, 256, 257, 262, 263
Janssens, M., 94, 188, 263, 264, 302, 541, 546, 585
Jaworski, K., 455, 548
Jay, Alexis, 27
Jayasinghe, Laknath, 10, 518
Jehn, K. A., 284, 557
Jews, comparison with Muslim populations, 504–5
Jewson, N., 41, 42
Joh, J., 119
Johnson, L., 242
Johnston, W. B., 84
Jones, D., 23n4, 42, 584
Jones, K. C., 522
Joshi, A., 460
Jovic, E., 485
Joy, S., 117
Ju, S., 479
Just, Sine Nørholm, 5–6, 218
Just-in-case approach, to workplace accommodation, 487–8

Kaasila-Pakanen, Anna-Liisa, 5, 175
Kalev, A., 246, 286
Kalokerinos, E. K., 481
Kalonaityte, V., 75, 154, 164–5, 167, 175
Kamp, A., 155, 585
Kaplan, C., 70
Kärreman, D., 255, 304
Katila, S., 544
Kauzya, J. M., 30
Kearney, E., 284
Kellough, J. E., 286
Kelly, C., 424, 425
Kelly, E., 155, 246, 286
Kennedy, John F., 507
Kenway, J., 529
Kenya, age management programs in, 457, 461
Ketner, S., 402
Key performance indicators (KPIs), 224, 225
King, Martin Luther, 26
King, Peter, 501
Kirby, E., 226, 263
Kirkland, S., 558
Kirton, G., 16, 20, 28–9
Kish-Gephart, J. J., 458
Klarsfeld, A., 587
Kleiner, M., 91
KMLG (Kohinoor Maple Leaf Group), 419
Knights, David, 4, 83
Knowledge
    categorization of, 72
    counter-knowledge, 140
    dislocation of, 99
    diversity management and, 4, 128–36, 303
    Indigenous systems of, 161, 162, 168, 169–70, 391
    politicization of, 182
    power and, 93–4, 96
    procedural, 365
    of social identities, 119, 521
    sub-knowledges, 128, 133–4, 135–6, 138, 139–42
    subalternization of, 131, 136
    Western construction of, 265
Kochan, T. A., 243
Kohinoor Maple Leaf Group (KMLG), 419
Kolb, D. M., 560–1

Konrad, Alison M., 9–10, 65, 177, 239, 243, 245, 246, 370, 469, 577
Kosofsky Sedgwick, Eve, 197, 202
Kovera, M. B., 485
KPIs (key performance indicators), 224, 225
Kram, K. E., 561
Kramer, V., 243
Kristinsson, K., 88–9
Kulik, C. T., 112, 119
Kulkarni, M., 479–80
Kumar, K., 242, 262
Kunda, G., 319
Kurtulus, F. A., 240
Kwek, D., 183

Labour Government (United Kingdom), 21
Laclau, E., 7, 300, 304, 305, 306
Laclau and Mouffe's discourse theory, 7, 300, 305–8
Lam, H., 477
Langley, A., 224
Language
  critical diversity studies on, 302–3, 446–7
  discrimination and, 299, 302, 423
  essentialist vs. constructionist perspectives on, 71
  interdependence and, 72
  in making of meaning, 255
  in Pakistan, 417
  in qualitative research, 346–7
  in South Africa, 423
Larsen, Jørgen Elm, 69
Latin America
  buen vivir in, 141–2
  decolonial scholarship in, 130–1, 132, 134, 135
  gender relations in, 447
Laws and regulations
  in codes of conduct, 208–9, 212
  on equal opportunity, 40–1, 50
  on gender equality, 21
  intersectionality in, 69–70
  for people with disabilities, 470–1, 475, 478, 487–8
  in politics of diversity, 27–31
  on race relations, 21–2, 45
  on same-sex marriage, 52, 422–3
Lawsuits, 259–60, 377

Layder, D., 15
Leadership. *See also* Supervisors
  authenticity in, 323, 324
  ethnic minorities in positions of, 376
  transformational, 245, 284, 289
  in workplace diversity, 245, 247, 284, 289
Learning frames, 118
Leasher, M. K., 476
Lee, D., 32
Lee, H., 202
Legge, K., 331
Legislation. *See* Laws and regulations
Leicht-Scholten, C., 365
Leitch, S., 222
Lengnick-Hall, M. L., 479–80
Leonard, J. S., 460
Leonard, P., 175, 594
Lesbian, gay, bisexual, transgender, intersex (LGBTI) persons. *See also* Queer theory
  activism among, 197
  coming out process for, 423
  discrimination of, 372
  diversity networks for, 564, 565, 566–7
  exclusion from liberation movements, 196
  heteronormative performances of, 199
  identities of, 200, 510
  legislative rights for, 52
  organizational diversity and, 224
  racialised masculinities and, 530
  in South Africa, 422–3
Levinas, E., 98
Levine, D. I., 460
Lewis, A. P., 200
Lewis, Bernard, 502, 503
Liang, X., 111, 117
Liberal approach, to equal opportunity, 41–2
Liden, R. C., 459
Life-politics, 332
Liff, Sonia, 41
Limerick, B., 343
Lin, X., 455, 546
Lindisfarne, N., 525, 526
Lindsay, N., 391
Lindsay, S., 91
Linnehan, F., 239, 246, 370
Linstead, S., 129, 131, 178
Liquid Modernity (Bauman), 331–2

Little Gitmos, 501
Litvin, D., 42–3, 258, 263, 264, 267, 302, 458
Liversage, A., 302
Lobel, S., 262
Longue durée, of Eurocentric coloniality, 130, 130n1, 131, 132, 135
Loo, R., 476
Lorbiecki, A., 44, 87, 94, 256, 257, 262, 263
Lorde, Audre, 69
Loretto, W., 472, 473
Lorey, I., 72
Louvrier, Jonna, 4, 62, 75
Lowe, K. B., 118
Lowson, E., 545
Luhman, J. T., 330
Lupton, B., 464, 541
Lutz, Helma, 68
Lyons, Lenore, 526, 527, 530

Mac an Ghaill, M., 455, 546
Mackinnon, C., 41
MacNab, B., 114
Macro level research
    critical sensemaking method for, 308
    elements of, 358
    on higher education institutions, 361, 367
    intersectionality in, 438, 520, 524
    politics of diversity and, 20
    on women's employment challenges, 419
Maghreb, emergence of, 409
Magnusson, E., 437
Magoshi, E., 91
Malaysia, emergence of, 409
Males. *See* Gender differences; Men
Malhi, R. L., 303
Management and organization studies (MOS)
    decoloniality and, 141, 142
    globalization and, 127, 128, 129, 130, 139
    pluriversality and, 143, 144
    postcolonialism in analysis of, 175
Managers. *See* Leadership; Supervisors
"Managing a Meritocracy or an Equitable Organization? Senior Managers' and Employees' Views about Equal Opportunities Policies in UK Universities" (Deem), 362
Mandal Commission, 411

Manipulation, in identity work, 401–2
Mäntylä, H., 544
Maori peoples, 48, 51–2, 584
Marcus, George, 320
Marginalized masculinities, 69
Marriage, same-sex, 52, 422–3
Martin, J., 304, 558
Martins, L., 283, 558
Marx, Karl, 67, 95
Marxism, 67, 139, 161, 305, 332, 458
Masculinities. *See also* Racialized masculinities
    entrepreneurship and, 388, 389
    hegemonic, 69, 526, 527
    intersectionality and, 69
    linear rational thinking and, 97–8, 99, 100, 101
    of people with disabilities, 473
Mason, D., 41, 42
Masuch, C., 304
Maternity leave, 414, 416, 418, 419
Mayer, D. M., 284
Mayer, K. U., 461
McCall, L., 70, 71, 441–2, 443, 455, 465, 523, 525
McClintock, A., 70
McCoy, L., 304
McCurley, K., 522
McEnrue, M. P., 377
McKay, D., 592
McLaughlin, M. E., 479
McLeod, P., 262
McMahon, B. T., 473, 477, 480
McMillan-Capehart, A., 243
Meekosha, Helen, 69
Men. *See also* Gender differences; Masculinities
    paternity leave for, 414
    racialized experiences of, 529–31
Men and Masculinities in Southeast Asia (Ford & Lyons), 526
Mental representations, of tasks, 89
Mentoring programs
    content of, 560–1
    criticisms of, 554, 560, 567
    external organization of, 556
    fireplace sessions, 321, 325, 326, 332
    format for, 562–3

participants of, 561–2
for women, 560–1
Mercer, Danielle, 9, 435
Meriläinen, S., 94, 266, 345, 544, 586
Merritt, D., 242
Meso level research
   critical sensemaking method for, 308
   elements of, 358
   on higher education institutions, 361–2, 367
   politics of diversity and, 20
   queer theory as applied to, 202–3
   social identity theory and, 520, 524
   on women's employment challenges, 419
Metacognitive strategies, 119
Metcalfe, B. D., 158, 159, 165
Methodological nationalism, 592
Mexico
   emergence of, 33
   identity construction in, 589
   relational demography in, 582
Meyer, B., 244
Meyerson, D., 20, 228, 229, 560–1
Michaelsen, L. K., 242, 262
Micro level research
   critical sensemaking method for, 308, 311
   elements of, 358
   on higher education institutions, 362
   intersectionality in, 438, 520
   queer theory as applied to, 200, 202
   social identity theory and, 524
   on women's employment challenges, 419
Middle class, 19n1
Migrants. *See* Immigrants and immigration
Millennium Development Goals, 19
Miller, C. E., 476
Miller, J., 53
Milliken, F., 283, 558
Mills, Albert J., 9, 435, 446, 499, 589
Mills, C. Wright, 18, 31
Mind–body dualisms, 97–8
Minorities. *See* Black and minority ethnic (BME) groups; Visible minorities
Minority group model of disability identity, 474–5
MINT (Mexico, Indonesia, Nigeria, and Turkey) countries, 33
Mir, Ali, 10, 32, 33–4, 499

Mir, Raza, 10, 32, 33–4, 499
Mirza, H. S., 590
Misra, J., 522
Mitchell, T. R., 485
MNCs. *See* Multinational corporations
Mobile subjectivities, formation of, 578, 591–4, 595
Mohanty, Chandra Talpade, 70
Molden, D. C., 119
Moore, Mark E., 9–10, 469
Mor, S., 119
Moradi, B., 519
Moral case for diversity, 40, 209, 230, 238. *See also* Social justice
Moral obligation, of Western world, 23, 160
Moreton-Robinson, A., 394
Morgan, G., 65, 87
Moroccan female entrepreneurs, 302, 396, 399, 400–3
Morris, M. W., 119
MOS. *See* Management and organization studies
Moser, Ingunn, 69
Mouffe, C., 7, 300, 304, 305
Muchiri, M. K., 245
Mueller, S., 389, 399
Mufti, A., 160, 504
Multi-level analyses, 292, 293–4, 299, 303–5
Multicultural personality questionnaires, 325, 326
Multiculturalism, 175–94. *See also* Diversity; Ethnicity; Race and racism
   age and, 457
   business case for diversity and, 178, 179
   cultural difference vs., 184–7
   diversity management and, 178–80
   limitations of, 183–4
   overview, 5, 175–7
   paradigms of, 87
   postcolonial critique of, 175, 180–4
   in research methodology, 187–90
   in third space, 184–7, 188, 189–90
Multinational corporations (MNCs)
   business case for diversity and, 265
   codes of conduct, queer theory analysis of, 203, 204–12, 207t, 213
   diversity-related policies and practices of, 246

Multinational corporations (MNCs) (Cont.)
  equality policies and procedures
    for, 382
  global policies of, 371–2, 379, 380, 381
  in India, 413–14
  intersectional transnationalizations
    of, 73, 74
  in Pakistan, 418
  workforce diversity of, 375–7
Munir, K., 458
Muñoz, J. E., 530
Munshi, D., 265
Muslim populations. See Islam and Muslims
Mustapha, A. R., 31
Mutsaers, Paul, 7, 317, 320
Mykletun, R. J., 92

Naff, K. C., 286
Naples, N. A., 442
National Science Foundation (NSF), 111, 113
National Security Entry-Exit Registration
    (NSEER) Program, 500
Nativism, 83
Naturalization, 181
Nemetz, P., 87
Nentwich, J. C., 42
Neocolonialism, 162, 162n2, 188
Neoliberalism
  capitalism and, 131, 193, 591
  diversity management and, 575
  economic, 199
  globalization and, 128–30, 131, 593, 595
  growth of, 18
  impact on equality, 17, 48
  normalizing power of, 196
  principles of, 43, 512
  voluntarism and, 27
Neo-nomads, 592
Nestlé Pakistan, 418
Netherlands
  coordinated market economy of, 397
  diversity discourse in, 74, 585, 586
  ethnic minority representation in
    organizations in, 286
  itinerant diversity management of police
    officers in, 321–6
  people with disabilities in, 470

survey research among public sector
    employees in, 288–90
  Turkish female entrepreneurs in, 302,
    396–8, 400–1
Network groups. See Diversity networks
Neumark, D., 239
New York Police Department (NYPD), 500–1
New Zealand
  affirmative action in, 240
  as bicultural society, 584
  diversity management outcomes in, 288
  equality–diversity discourse in, 47, 48–9, 51
  immigrants in workforce in, 235
  pre-colonial groups in, 23n4
Ng, Eddy S., 6, 235, 239, 242, 245, 246
Nigeria
  emergence of, 33
  ethnic diversity in, 30–1, 30n8
9/11 attacks. See September 11, 2001 attacks
Niqab (face veil), 499
Nishat Chunian Group, 419
Nishii, L. H., 284, 292
Nkomo, Stella M., 8, 65, 179, 408, 576–7
Noble, G., 528–9
Nodal points, 306, 307
Nomadism, 592
Non-fundamental critiques, of diversity
    management, 156, 157t
Non-profit organizations
  diversity discourse of, 269–71, 270t
  social justice discourse of, 271, 272
  workplace diversity practices of, 113, 116
Noon, M., 28, 29, 156, 179, 318, 377
North Korea, emergence of, 409
Norway, women in management positions
    in, 240
Nottingham/Notting Hill race riots
    (1958), 21
Nouri, R., 243
Novak, J., 481
NSEER (National Security Entry-Exit
    Registration) Program, 500
NSF (National Science Foundation), 111, 113
NSvP (Dutch Foundation for
    Psychotechniques), 322, 332
Nyambegera, S. M., 584
NYPD (New York Police Department), 500–1

OBC. *See* Other backward classes
Obesity, as disability, 478
O'Brien, Mary, 68
Occupational upgrading, 463
OECD. *See* Organisation for Economic Co-operation and Development
Ogbonna, E., 545
Oikelome, F., 22, 23–4, 30
Ojha, A., 413
Old boys' networks, 564, 565
Omanović, Vedran, 4, 83, 87, 96, 178, 586
Omi, Richard, 505–6, 511
Ong, Aihwa, 512
Openness to experience, 118
Oppression. *See also* Discrimination; Exclusion
   colonialism and, 162
   commatization of, 68
   hierarchy of, 23, 24
   of Indigenous communities, 390–1
   institutionalized, 420
   intersectionality and, 52, 66, 435, 436–7, 438, 522
Optimal contact practices, 114, 115
O'Reilly, C. A., 262
Organisation for Economic Co-operation and Development (OECD), 204, 235, 469, 470
Organizational democracy, 326–30
Organizational diversity. *See also* Workplace diversity
   business case for, 374–7, 380–1
   critical diversity studies on, 539–50
   in India, 413–15
   LGBTI persons and, 224
   in Pakistan, 417–19
   in South Africa, 423–5
Organizations
   diversity management outcomes for, 6, 244–6, 247
   gendering of, 53
   heteronormative culture of, 196, 198
   inclusion practices for, 111–13, 120–2, 121*t*
   maintenance of group differences in, 163–5, 167
   queer theory in discourse of, 202, 213–14
   survey research on, 285–6, 293
   workplace diversity practices of, 111–13, 120–2, 121*t*
Orientalism, 25, 161, 162, 181–2, 399, 503
Orientalism: Western Conceptions of the Orient (Said), 161, 181, 503
Ortlieb, Renate, 9, 238, 454, 457
Osella, C., 526, 527
Osella, F., 526, 527
Ostendorp, A., 586
Østergaarda, C. R., 88–9
Ostrander, R. N., 473
Oswick, C., 28, 156, 179
Other backward classes (OBC), 410–11, 412, 413, 414–15
Othering processes
   in entrepreneurship, 388, 403
   Orientalism as, 161, 181–2
   postcolonialism and, 403
   in social confirmation of identity, 100
   third space and, 186
Otten, S., 118
Özbilgin, Mustafa F., 8, 29, 358, 361, 370, 461, 464, 520, 523, 541
Ozkazanc-Pan, Banu, 11, 165, 541, 575
Öztürk, Mustafa Bilgehan, 8, 370, 372

Packer, A. H., 84
Paetzold, R., 485
Paige, R. M., 558
Pakeha peoples, 584
Pakistan, 415–19
   comparison with India and South Africa, 425–6
   creation of, 409–10
   equality and diversity as defined in, 415
   ethnic diversity in, 416–17
   legislative and current history on diversity and equality, 415–16
   linguistic diversity in, 417
   organizational diversity practices in, 417–19
   religion in, 415, 416, 417
   socio-political dynamics in, 416–17
   women in, 415–16, 418–19, 426
Palich, L., 179, 183
Paluck, E. L., 560
Paludi, Mariana Ines, 9, 435, 447
Pan American Airways, 448

Parent, M. C., 519
Parker, K, 479
Parker, M., 202, 203, 221
Participant observation, 319, 341, 543, 549. *See also* Ethnographic research
Participation restrictions, defined, 469. *See also* People with disabilities (PWD)
Paternity leave, 414
Patil, V., 70
Patriarchy, 19, 23, 27, 69, 401
Patriot Act of 2001 (US), 500
Pay/pay equality. *See* Income
Peaceful rise framework, 141, 142, 143, 144
Pearson, Noel, 392
Peer-mentoring programs, 563
Pelled, L. H., 460, 582
Peng, P., 240
People with disabilities (PWD), 469–98
　access to power, 17
　discrimination of, 473, 474, 477, 480, 483, 488
　employment outcomes of, 475–8, 486–7
　future research directions, 488–9
　harassment of, 477
　identity of, 472–5
　in India, 411, 413, 414
　legislative policies for, 470–1, 475, 478
　overview, 9–10, 469–71
　prevalence of, 469, 470
　in South Africa, 420, 422
　stigmatization and stereotyping of, 473, 478–82, 484
　unemployment among, 470, 472, 475, 482
　workplace accommodation for, 470, 478, 482–6, 487–8
PepsiCo, 260
Peredo, A., 391, 392
Peretz, Martin, 503–4
Performativity, 197, 198, 202, 203, 222
Perkins, D. V., 479
Pettigrew, A., 376
Phenotypes, of Muslim populations, 508–9
Philippines, emergence of, 409
Phillips, D., 443
Phillips, N., 304
Pieterse, A. N., 89
Pillow, W., 347
Pinar, M., 91
Pio, E., 302
Pitts, D. W., 285, 291
Pluralism. *See also* Multiculturalism
　cultural, 16, 127, 177, 184
　defined, 1
　religious, 508
Pluriversality, 127–8, 130, 131, 134, 143, 144
Poggio, B., 402
Point, S., 265, 266, 585
Police
　discrimination by, 26–7, 500–1
　itinerant diversity management of, 321–6
　multicultural skills initiatives for, 94
Policy development. *See* Laws and regulations
Poling, T. L., 243
Political intersectionality, 440
Politics of diversity, 15–38
　academic careers, influence on, 31–3
　colonial history in, 23–7, 30, 30n8, 33
　in diversity management, 28–9
　history, society, and biography in, 18–22, 33–4
　immigration and, 21, 22, 25–6
　intersectionality in, 17, 19–20
　overview, 3, 15–17
　transversal, 591
　voluntarism and regulation in, 27–31, 34
Porter, Janet, 7, 298, 318
Portugal, diversity initiatives in, 266
Positioning theory, 64
Positive discrimination. *See* Affirmative action (AA)
Positivism
　in diversity management research, 53, 84, 85, 87–91, 93n3, 183
　human resource management and, 89
　intersectionality and, 445
　principles of, 85
　survey research and, 90
　textual analysis and, 300
Postcolonial feminism, 165
Postcolonialism, 159–70
　advantages of utilizing, 175–6
　in critical diversity studies, 166–70
　defined, 159–60
　diversity management and, 180–4

in diversity management research, 188–9
entrepreneurship and, 394, 403, 404
Eurocentrism and, 159, 160–1
identity and, 448
intersectionality and, 70, 448–9
modes of analysis in, 161–2
multiculturalism and, 175, 180–4
prefix debate regarding, 162n2
on workplace diversity, 25, 153–4, 162–6, 265
Posthumanist feminism
  on binary thinking, 98–9
  in diversity management research, 85, 86, 97–100, 101
Postidentitarian transnational diversity, 579, 594–5
Postpositivism, 300, 445–9
Poststructuralism
  on discourse, 64–5, 507
  feminist, 303, 589
  on gendering of organizations, 53
  intersectionality and, 447, 588
  meanings in, 186
  rise of, 42
Powell, Glen, 10, 518
Powell, N. G., 84
Power
  abuse of, 332
  asymmetry of, 181, 190, 299, 303, 306
  class and, 458
  coloniality and, 130, 131, 137
  contextual factors and, 47, 55, 159, 541
  in exploitative relationships, 198–9
  hegemonic masculinities and, 69
  heteronormative, 197, 198, 200, 202
  hierarchical, 185
  inequality in access to, 17
  knowledge and, 93–4, 96
  in managerial relations, 302
  micro and macrophysics of, 592
  performative elements of, 530
  politics of, 394
  of privileged groups, 25, 26
  in qualitative research, 53, 340–4
  race and, 502, 507
  social relations of, 15, 64, 67, 76
  in 3D-model of diversity management, 556, 567–8, 569

Pragmatism, 402
Prakash, G., 161–2
Prasad, Anshuman, 159–60, 162–4, 163n3, 165, 167, 175–6, 265, 399
Prasad, P., 25, 65, 175, 177, 181, 183, 184, 577
Pre-colonial history, 23n4
Prejudice. See Bias; Discrimination; Stereotypes
Pringle, Judith K., 4, 23n4, 39, 65, 177, 577, 584
Process model, of global diversity management, 370, 371
Proletariat, 458
Protestant work ethic, 399, 507
Provincializing diversity, 578, 583–8, 595
Psychological safety, in work groups, 116
Psychopolitical theory of racism, 166–7
Puar, J. K., 591
Public policy. See Laws and regulations
Public-politics, 332
Pullen, A., 303
Purdie-Vaughns, V., 523
Purkayastha, B., 591
PWD. See People with disabilities

Qualitative research, 337–54. See also Ethnographic research
  in critical diversity studies, 345, 348, 350–1, 543, 549
  discipline-specific methodological norms in, 338–40, 350
  on entrepreneurial aspirations in Indigenous communities, 393–5
  fieldwork in, 340–4
  in interpretative tradition, 92
  intersectional analysis in, 443
  interviews in, 339, 340, 341–4
  language issues in, 346–7
  overview, 7, 337–8
  power and identity in, 53, 340–4
  quantitative research vs., 52–4, 56, 339
  reflexivity in, 347–50, 546
  social justice and, 53
  translation to academic writing, 344–7
Quantitative research. See also Survey research
  intersectional analysis in, 443
  qualitative research vs., 52–4, 56, 339

Queer theory, 195–217. *See also* Lesbian, gay, bisexual, transgender, intersex (LGBTI) persons
　ambiguous diversities and, 221–2
　codes of conduct, analysis using, 203, 204–12, 207t, 213
　definitions of, 202
　in diversity management research, 54, 199–203, 201t
　on gendering of organizations, 53
　as multifaceted theoretical concept, 196–9
　in organizational discourse, 202, 213–14
　overview, 5, 195–6
Queerness, defined, 221–2
Quotas, in affirmative action, 42, 84, 240
Qur'an, 400

Race and racism. *See also* Black and minority ethnic (BME) groups; Discrimination
　biological racism, 506, 509
　in business case for diversity, 264–5
　colonialism and, 24
　cultural racism, 179, 506, 507, 508, 509
　legislative policies regarding, 21–2, 45
　in mentoring programs, 562
　origin and evolution of, 505–7
　psychopolitical theory of, 166–7
　race riots, 21, 22, 26
　in UK labour market, 373
　in US, 26, 505–8
Racial formation, 502, 505–6, 511
Racial Formation in the United States (Omi & Winant), 505–6
Racialization process, 502, 509, 511
Racialized masculinities, 525–31
　examination of, 525–7
　legitimacy and, 528–9
　men's experiences with, 529–31
　spatial contexts of, 527–9
Ragins, B., 53
Rainey, H. G., 287
Rancière, Jacques, 330
Rand, E. J., 221–2
Rao, A., 91
Rao, D., 479
Räsänen, K., 544
Rasky, C., 435, 437, 438

Razack, S., 512
Re-categorization practices, 114–15
Reaganomics, 43, 45
Reconquista, 502, 506
Recruitment practices, 46, 73, 377, 461, 542
Red herring bills, 500
Redistribution–recognition dilemma, 456, 459
Reflexive Ethnography (Aull Davies), 100
Reflexive Methodology (Alvesson & Sköldberg), 100
Reflexivity, in research, 53, 99, 100, 347–50, 546
Regan, A., 558
Regulations. *See* Laws and regulations
Reid, C. A., 480
Reinharz, S., 544–5
Relational approach, to intersectionality, 440–1
Relational demography, 579, 580–1, 582
Religion. *See also* Islam and Muslims
　discrimination based on, 500–1
　in India, 409–10
　individualism and, 400
　in Pakistan, 415, 416, 417
　in US, 505–8
Religious pluralism, 508
Renegar, V. R., 225–6, 228
Research methodology. *See also* Diversity management research; Ethnographic research; Qualitative research; Quantitative research; Survey research
　of feminism, 53
　Indigenous, 169–70
　for intersectional analysis, 440–4
　multi-level approaches, 292, 293–4, 299, 303–5
　multiculturalism in, 187–90
　social justice and, 53
　validity of, 290–3, 294, 539, 545–6, 549
Reservation system, in India, 411, 412–13, 415, 426
Resource-based theory, 238, 246
Return-to-work plans, 470
Reverse discrimination, 29, 85, 256. *See also* Affirmative action (AA)
Riach, K., 472, 473
Rich, Adrienne, 197
Richard, O. C., 89, 179, 237–8, 243, 245

Riots, race, 21, 22, 26
Risberg, Annette, 5–6, 218, 585
Rivard, P., 116, 118
Roberson, L., 112, 558
Roberson, Q. M., 111
Roberts, E., 479
Roberts, L. M., 117
Robinson, G., 258
Rodriguez, N., 463
Roggeband, C., 94, 589
The Roots of Muslim Rage (Lewis), 502
Rosen, B., 285
Rosenblatt, V., 114
Rotherham child abuse, 27
Routledge Advances in Feminist Studies and Intersectionality book series, 76–7
Rubin, Gayle S., 197
Ruscher, J. B., 479
Russia, emergence of, 33, 409, 549
Ryan, A. M., 510
Rynes, S., 285

Sabelis, I., 185, 189
Safety, codes of conduct on, 208
Saha, S. K., 546
Said, Edward W., 23, 25, 161, 162, 163, 175, 176, 180–1, 182, 399, 448, 449, 503
Salary. *See* Income
Salipante, P., 114, 116
Salzer, M. S., 479
Same-sex marriage, 52, 422–3
Sampling techniques, 92, 343, 546
Sardy, R., 202
Sartre, Jean-Paul, 161
Sawyer, J. E., 244
Scandinavia
  affirmative action in, 31
  gender equality in, 21
Scase, R., 391
Scattered Hegemonies (Grewal & Kaplan), 70
Scheduled castes (SC), 410–11, 412, 413, 414–15
Scheduled tribes (ST), 411, 412, 413, 414–15
Scheid, T. L., 479
Schermuly, C. C., 244
Schmidt, A., 544
Schwabenland, C., 94–5, 175, 258, 266, 267, 271, 272–3, 371

Scully, M. A., 20, 200, 228, 229
SDSs (strategically deployable shifters), 324
Sears, G. J., 245, 246
Second-class citizenship, 504
Second Sex (de Beauvoir), 23
Second-wave, of critical diversity studies, 158–9
Second-wave feminism, 40, 51, 67
Secret behaviour approach, 402
Selbee, L. K., 461
Self-identity. *See* Identity
Self-techniques, 199
Semi-structured interviews, 339, 340, 342, 350, 543
Sennett, Richard, 328
September 11, 2001 attacks, 139, 140, 499, 500
Sex discrimination. *See* Gender differences; Women
Sex–gender–sexuality, 197–8, 197f, 205–8, 207t, 210, 211–12
Sexuality. *See also* Lesbian, gay, bisexual, transgender, intersex (LGBTI) persons; Queer theory
  intersections with sex and gender, 197–8, 197f, 205–8, 207t, 210, 211–12
  neglect in diversity management discourse, 195–6
  racialization of, 530
  South African protections on, 422–3
Shachaf, P., 91, 92
Shane, S., 399
Shapero, A., 390
Sharia (Islamic law), 500
Sharma, J., 198–9
Shaw, L. R., 473, 477
Sheehan, M., 463
Shepherd, D., 23n4, 584
Shia Muslims, 416, 417
Shields, S., 437–8, 443, 518–19, 520
Shimoni, B., 187
Shore, L. M., 284
Shuey, K. M., 485
Sieben, B., 238, 457
Siim, B., 21
Silverstein, M., 322
Similarity/attraction concept, 88
Simkhada, P. P., 481

Simpson, R., 303
Simultaneity of diversity, 578, 588–90, 595
Sinclair, A., 559
Singapore, emergence of, 409
Singh, P., 240
Singh, V., 265, 266, 585
SIT. *See* Social identity theory
Skeggs, B., 458–9
Sköldberg, K., 100
Slavery, reparations for, 24
Slonaker, W. M., Sr., 484
Small and Medium Enterprises Development Authority (SMEDA), 418
Smircich, L., 51, 177, 445
Smith, Dorothy, 304, 443
Smith, N. J., 32
Snowball sampling technique, 92, 343, 546
Social categorizations, 88
Social change, functionalism vs. radical structuralism on, 87
Social class. *See* Class
Social confirmation, of identity, 98, 99–100, 116
Social constructionism, 523, 588
Social constructivism, 98
Social identity markers, 52
Social identity theory (SIT), 519–25
　emergence of, 519
　on expatriate managers, 580
　on identity differentiation, 579
　intersectionality and, 521–3, 531
　on multiple levels of identity, 524–5
　overview, 10, 519–21
　positivism and, 88
Social integration practices, 114, 115
Social justice. *See also* Affirmative action (AA); Equal opportunity (EO) initiatives
　in business case for diversity, 258–9, 266–73, 268–70t, 371
　dualisms in, 40–5
　equal opportunity and, 281
　in non-profit organizations, 271
　policies for promoting, 16
　research methodology and, 53
Social networks, of immigrants, 462–3
Social psychology
　business-oriented paradigms of, 176, 178
　in critical discursive tradition, 93
　in diversity management research, 155, 157–8, 184, 189–90, 579
　implications of over-focus on, 298–9
　in positivist tradition, 88, 183, 581
Socialism, 95
Socialization
　into academia, 338, 339–40, 345
　of expatriates, 580
　gender, 399
　identity and, 64
　organizational, 90, 462
Socially shared cognition perspective, 89
Socioeconomic status. *See* Class
Sociological imagination, 18–19, 31
Søderberg, A. M., 585
Soni-Sinha, U., 589
Soper, B., 262
South Africa, 420–5
　affirmative action in, 240
　apartheid in, 166, 421, 425
　Black Consciousness movement in, 167n4
　comparison with India and Pakistan, 425–6
　equality and diversity as defined in, 420–1
　Indian populations in, 410
　legislative history on diversity and equality, 420–1
　linguistic diversity in, 423
　organizational diversity practices in, 423–5
　socio-political dynamics in, 421–3
　women in, 421, 422, 426
Southern Theory, 168–9, 170
Southern Theory: The Global Dynamics of Knowledge in Social Science (Connell), 168
Sowards, S. K., 225–6, 228
Spatial contexts, of racialised masculinities, 527–9
Special Economic Zones, 512
Spell, C. S., 557
Spicer, A., 306
Spinoza, Baruch, 98
The Spirit Level: Why Equality is Better for Everyone (Pickett and Wilkinson), 16
Spivak, G. C., 448
Srinivas, M., 413
Srivastava, S., 527, 528

ST. *See* Scheduled tribes
Stafford, Z., 26
Stage theory of identity, 119–20
Stakeholder theory, 238
State of Exception (Agamben), 512
Steele, M., 374
Stephenson, Jacqueline, 6, 235
Stereotype threat, 119, 481
Stereotypes and stigmatization. *See also* Bias; Discrimination; Heteronormativity
   biological basis of, 115
   colonial, 163, 167
   defined, 479
   in diversity discourses, 586
   in entrepreneurship, 388, 389
   of Muslims, 501
   in othering processes, 183
   of people with disabilities, 473, 478–82, 484
   reinforcement of, 184
   uncertainty reduction concept and, 88
Stewart, M. M., 65, 576–7
Steyaert, C., 586
Steyn, M., 424, 425
Stolen Generations, 391*n*3
Stonewall movement, 196
Strachan, Glenda, 4, 39
Strategic ambiguity, 222–5, 228, 230–1
Strategic model of global diversity management, 370, 371
Strategic orientations, 245
Strategically deployable shifters (SDSs), 324
Stringer, D. Y., 479
Structural intersectionality, 440
Structuralism, 87. *See also* Poststructuralism
Sub-knowledges, 128, 133–4, 135–6, 138, 139–42
Subalternization, of knowledge, 131, 136
Subjectivities
   in business case for diversity, 264
   colonial, 161, 181
   mobile, 578, 591–4, 595
Subordinated masculinities, 69
Sufism, 399
Sullivan, Kevin, 257
Sumption, M., 463
Sunni Muslims, 416
Supervisors. *See also* Leadership
   bias of, 240, 424, 485

   competency of, 424
   in diversity management implementation, 542
   expatriate, 91–2, 580
   training programs for, 112, 559
Surface-level diversity, 236
Survey research
   characteristics of, 281
   on diversity management outcomes, 7, 282, 284, 285–93
   on employees, 286–90, 293
   in experimental designs, 283
   in field studies, 283
   future challenges in, 294
   methodological issues in, 290–4
   multi-level designs for, 292, 293–4
   organizational, 285–6, 293
   positivism and, 90
Süß, S., 91
Sustainable development theories, 133, 142
Sustainable livelihoods, 394
Sweden
   diversity discourse and initiatives in, 74, 75, 586–7
   gender coaches in, 559
   racial hierarchies in, 164–5
   social production of diversity ideas in, 96
   term for diversity in, 71–2
Swift, M. L., 484
Switzerland, diversity initiatives in, 586
Syed, Jawad, 8, 358, 361, 408, 462, 520
Syed, M., 440
Systemic discrimination, 44

Taiwan, emergence of, 409
Tajfel, H., 519, 521
Taksa, Lucy, 10, 518
Tapia, M., 22, 590
Tatli, Ahu, 8, 29, 370, 461, 464, 523, 541
Teams. *See* Groups
Tedmanson, Deirdre, 8, 388, 393
Tempered radicals, 20, 228–9, 230, 231, 339
Terrorism, 140, 307, 500. *See also* September 11, 2001 attacks; War on Terror
Textual analysis, 298–316
   applicability of, 299, 311–12
   coding techniques for, 205

Textual analysis (*Cont.*)
  critical hermeneutics and, 446
  critical sensemaking method in, 300, 305, 308–11, 310*f*, 447
  criticisms of, 304–5
  data sources for, 300
  of discourse and rhetoric, 302
  in diversity management research, 7, 301–5
  expository, 301–2
  Laclau & Mouffe's discourse theory for, 7, 300, 305–8
  multi-level approaches to, 299, 303–5
  in theoretical perspectives, 300–1
Thailand, emergence of, 409
The Third Jihad (documentary), 501
Third space, 135, 176, 184–7, 188, 189–90
Thomas, A., 389, 399
Thomas, D., 46, 237, 558
Thomas, P., 306
Thomas, R., 236, 237, 238, 447
3D-model of diversity management, 554–7, 555*t*, 567–9, 567*t*
Tiffin, H., 186
Timmermans, B., 88–9
Toh, S. M., 580
Tomlinson, F., 175, 258, 266, 267, 271, 272–3, 371, 543, 548
Toor, Saadia, 10, 499
Top management teams (TMTs), 244, 247
Tracey, P., 458
Trade unions
  dichotomization of workplace and migration in, 590
  membership declines, 17
  politics of diversity and, 29
Training programs. *See* Diversity training programs
Transformational leadership styles, 245, 284, 289
Transgender persons. *See* Lesbian, gay, bisexual, transgender, intersex (LGBTI) persons
Translocational positionalities, 591, 592
Transnational diversity. *See also* Multiculturalism
  conceptualizations of, 577, 578
  demography and identity in, 579–81
  intersectionality and, 73, 74, 588–90
  mobile subjectivities and, 578, 591–4, 595
  modes of diffusion, 578
  overview, 11, 577
  postidentitarian, 579, 594–5
Transnational feminism, 51, 70
Transnational patriarchies, 69
Transversal politics, 591
Triandafyllidou, A., 520
Trompenaars, F., 457
Truth, Sojourner, 67
Trux, Marja-Liisa, 7, 317, 320
Tschopp, M. K., 479
Tsui, A. S., 580, 581
Tung, R. L., 242
Turkey
  emergence of, 33, 409
  female entrepreneurs from, 396–9, 400–3
Turner, R. N., 119–20
Turnover rates, 260, 284, 377, 424
Tusler, A., 472
Tyler, M., 202

Ukur, G., 457, 460–1
Uncertainty reduction concept, 88
Unconscious bias, 18, 112, 118, 120
Under-accommodation, 482, 483, 485
Unemployment
  of ethnic minorities, 17
  in Indigenous communities, 390
  of people with disabilities, 470, 472, 475, 482
Unions. *See* Trade unions
United Kingdom (UK)
  affirmative action in, 29, 29*n*7
  business case for diversity in, 265, 374–5, 380, 381
  diversity management outcomes in, 294
  feminist activism in, 21
  gender equality in, 21
  immigration in, 235, 373, 590
  income inequality in, 17
  labour market in, 235, 373–4, 375
  liberal market economy of, 397
  migrants in, 21, 25–6
  national self-esteem of, 23–4
  non-profit organizations in, 272
  people with disabilities in, 471, 478, 483

police discrimination in, 26–7
race relations in, 21–2
recruitment practices in, 461
trade unions in, 29
Turkish female entrepreneurs in, 396–8
United Nations (UN)
    Convention on the Elimination of All
        Forms of Discrimination against
        Women, 40, 416, 418
    Convention on the Rights of Persons with
        Disabilities, 486
    Declaration of Human Rights, 40
    Declaration of the Rights of Indigenous
        Peoples, 390
    Global Compact, 40–1
    International Convention on the
        Elimination of All Forms of Racial
        Discrimination, 40
    intersectionality in policy
        development of, 69
United States (US)
    affirmative action in, 29
    business case for diversity in, 265
    Civil Rights movement in, 41, 51, 83, 506
    diversity management discourse in, 42–3
    feminist activism in, 20
    higher education institutions in, 358,
        359, 368
    identity and demography in, 579–81
    immigrants in workforce in, 235
    income inequality in, 17
    Latinization of, 163
    9/11 attacks, 139, 140
    people with disabilities in, 470, 471, 476–7,
        478, 483
    race in, 26, 505–8
    religion in, 505–8
Universal design approach, to workplace
    accommodation, 487–8
Universal diversity, 128, 131, 132, 139, 141, 182
Universities. *See* Academia
Untouchables, 410, 411
Urciuoli, B., 324

Valentine, G., 525
Validity, of research methodology, 290–3, 294,
    539, 545–6, 549

Value-in-diversity hypothesis, 237, 242
Van den Brink, Marieke, 10–11, 543, 545, 553
Van der Zee, Karin, 118, 325
Van Dick, R., 242
Van Engen, M., 547, 548
Van Ginkel, W. P., 242
Van Hoven, B., 528
Van Knippenberg, D., 89, 242, 283
Van Laer, Koen, 7, 337, 339–40, 343–4, 346–7,
    349–50, 541, 546
Van't Veer, J. T. B., 480
Varma, A., 480
Veiga, J. F., 482
Venkataraman, S., 399
Verbeek, Stijn, 286
Verfremdung (distancing), 320
Vertovec, S., 317
Vietnam, emergence of, 409
Vinkenburg, C., 547, 548
Violence. *See also* Abuse
    hate crimes, 500
    race riots, 21, 22, 26
Visible minorities, 256, 265, 328
Vloeberghs, D., 91
Voicing, in ethnographic research, 320–1
Voluntarism, 27–31, 34, 374, 382
Von Bergen, C., 262
Von Hippel, C., 481

Waddington, L., 486
Wages. *See* Income
Wahl, Anna, 10–11, 553, 554
Wajcman, J., 22
Walby, S., 69
Walenta, C., 184, 202–3
Walgenbach, K., 72
Walk the Talk-programme, 559
Wallraff, G., 319n1
War on Terror, 139, 143, 512
Ward, J., 200
Warner, Michael, 197
Warrior ethic, 399
Watson, W. E., 242, 262
WCAR (World Conference against
    Racism), 439
Webb, C., 563
Weber, Max, 20, 67, 399, 507

Weheliye, A., 365
Weick, K. E., 308, 447
Weldon, S. L., 440–1
Wendt, A. C., 484
Westwood, R., 181, 183
Whiteness
　Christianity and, 508
　in normalization of Western experience, 403, 506–7
　political economy of, 394
WHO (World Health Organization), 469
Williams, Fiona, 68
Williams, K. Y., 262
Williams-Whitt, K., 484–5
Wimmer, A., 592
Winant, Howard, 505–6, 511
Winstanley, D., 200
Winters, M.-F., 558
Wodak, R., 520
Woehr, D. J., 243
Wolbring, G., 480
Wolffram, A., 365
Women. *See also* Gender differences
　in academia, 32
　access to power, 17
　affirmative action, impact on, 239–40, 241, 246
　career advancement of, 240
　Convention on the Elimination of All Forms of Discrimination against Women (CEDAW), 40, 416, 418
　disabilities and, 471
　discrimination of, 40, 416, 418
　diversity training programs for, 558–9
　economic restructuring, impact on, 22
　empowerment of, 19
　in engineering profession, 307
　as entrepreneurs, 302, 388, 395–9, 400–3, 404
　firm performance and, 238
　harassment of, 17
　in India, 411–12, 413–14, 426, 541
　maternity leave for, 414, 416, 418, 419
　mentoring programs for, 560–1
　in Pakistan, 415–16, 418–19, 426
　pay equity for, 240
　in South Africa, 421, 422, 426
　on top management teams, 244
Women, Race and Class (Davis), 68
Women of Color movement, 196
Wong, D. J., 32, 33–4
Woodhams, C., 158, 159, 165, 464, 541
Workforce 2000: Work and Workers for the 21st Century (Johnston & Packer), 42–3, 84, 155, 256, 575, 576
Workforce diversification practices, 111, 112, 113
Workplace accommodation
　childcare facilities, 417, 425
　co-worker reactions to, 485–6, 489
　maternity/paternity leave, 414, 416, 418, 419
　for people with disabilities, 470, 478, 482–6, 487–8
　under-accommodation, 482, 483, 485
　willingness to request and provide, 483–5
Workplace diversity, 109–26. *See also* Equal opportunity (EO) initiatives; Organizational diversity
　chronological development of, 39
　definitions of, 50
　disabled workers. *See* People with disabilities (PWD)
　diversity management outcomes for, 283–4
　dualisms in. *See* Dualisms
　ethnographic inquiries into, 319–21
　fault lines in, 243–4, 247
　as field of study, 32
　globalization and, 32
　group-level practices of, 113–16, 120–2, 121*t*
　immigrants and, 235
　individual-level competence in, 116–22, 121*t*
　leadership in, 245, 247, 284, 289
　levels of, 243, 247
　literature review, 110–11
　organization-wide practices of, 111–13, 120–2, 121*t*
　overview, 4, 109–10
　policies and practices for, 246
　postcolonial perspectives on, 25, 153–4, 162–6, 265
　relational dynamics in, 96, 358
World Bank, 19, 412

World Conference against Racism (WCAR), 439
World Health Organization (WHO), 469
Worthley, R., 114
Wrench, J., 156, 272, 274
Wright, P. M., 292

Xenophobia, 425
Xin, K. R., 460, 582

Yap, M., 241

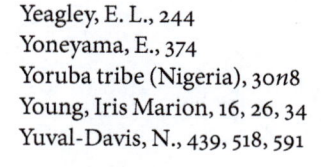

Yeagley, E. L., 244
Yoneyama, E., 374
Yoruba tribe (Nigeria), 30n8
Young, Iris Marion, 16, 26, 34
Yuval-Davis, N., 439, 518, 591

Zambrana, R. E., 438, 520
Zanoni, Patrizia, 7, 94, 153, 154, 157–8, 159, 182, 188, 263, 264, 299, 302, 337, 338–9, 341–3, 345–6, 347–9, 455, 458, 463, 464, 476, 519, 543, 585, 586
Zhang, D., 479